The Philosophy of Susanne Langer

Also available from Bloomsbury

Aesthetic Theory, Abstract Art, and Lawrence Carroll, by David Carrier
Introducing Aesthetics and the Philosophy of Art, by Darren Hudson Hick
The History of Philosophical and Formal Logic, edited by Alex Malpass and
Marianna Antonutti Marfori
The Philosophy and Art of Wang Guangyi, edited by Tiziana Andina and Erica Onnis

The Philosophy of Susanne Langer

Embodied Meaning in Logic, Art and Feeling

Adrienne Dengerink Chaplin

BLOOMSBURY ACADEMIC

LONDON • NEW YORK • OXFORD • NEW DELHI • SYDNEY

BLOOMSBURY ACADEMIC
Bloomsbury Publishing Plc
50 Bedford Square, London, WC1B 3DP, UK
1385 Broadway, New York, NY 10018, USA
29 Earlsfort Terrace, Dublin 2, Ireland

BLOOMSBURY, BLOOMSBURY ACADEMIC and the Diana logo are trademarks of
Bloomsbury Publishing Plc

First published in Great Britain 2020
This paperback edition published in 2021

Copyright © Adrienne Dengerink Chaplin, 2020

Adrienne Dengerink Chaplin has asserted her right under the Copyright, Designs and
Patents Act, 1988, to be identified as Author of this work.

For legal purposes the Acknowledgements on p. vii constitute an
extension of this copyright page.

Cover design: Eleanor Rose
Cover image: Helen Frankenthaler *Blessing of the Fleet* © The Artchives / Alamy

Bloomsbury Publishing Plc does not have any control over, or responsibility for, any
third-party websites referred to or in this book. All internet addresses given in this
book were correct at the time of going to press. The author and publisher regret any
inconvenience caused if addresses have changed or sites have ceased to exist, but can
accept no responsibility for any such changes.

A catalogue record for this book is available from the British Library.

A catalog record for this book is available from the Library of Congress.

ISBN: HB: 978-1-3500-3055-8
PB: 978-1-3502-5403-9
ePDF: 978-1-3500-3057-2
eBook: 978-1-3500-3058-9

Typeset by Newgen KnowledgeWorks Pvt. Ltd., Chennai, India

To find out more about our authors and books visit www.bloomsbury.com
and sign up for our newsletters.

Contents

Acknowledgements

This book has been long in the making. My first introduction to Susanne Langer was in the early 1980s at a graduate school in Toronto while completing my philosophy studies at the Vrije Universiteit Amsterdam. Langer's strikingly insightful writings on the philosophy of art left an immediate and enduring impression on me. After a long interval and a move to England, I returned to Langer with a doctoral thesis on her aesthetics entitled 'Mind, Body and Art: The Problem of Meaning in the Cognitive Aesthetics of Susanne K. Langer'. Much of that research found its way into the chapter on art in this book. By the time of its completion, however, I had become increasingly aware that Langer's aesthetics could not be understood without an awareness of her wider intellectual framework and the specific sources that shaped it. Many misunderstandings and misinterpretations of Langer's conceptual apparatus could be traced back to this lack of historical philosophical understanding. This led me, several decades later, to embark on a more comprehensive study of her work as a whole in the light of its formative influences.

Because of its long gestation I have incurred more debts than I can remember or am able to record. Over the years I presented various papers on Langer at different conferences of the Canadian, British, and Dutch societies of aesthetics as well as those of the International Association for Aesthetics in Rio de Janeiro and Krakow. I am grateful for the feedback received in those settings. Chapters 9 and 10 use material from publications based on those papers: 'Art and Embodiment: Biological and Phenomenological Contributions to Understanding Beauty and the Aesthetic', *Contemporary Aesthetics* 3 (2005) and 'Feeling the Body in Art: Embodied Cognition and Aesthetics in Mark Johnson and Susanne K. Langer', *Sztuka I filozofia/Art and Philosophy* 28 (2016).

Many of my debts go to my various teachers and advisors: the late Johan van der Hoeven, Calvin Seerveld, Sander Griffioen, Paul Crowther and Lambert Zuidervaart. I am very grateful for their careful reading and constructive comments on previous work. I also want to thank Bloomsbury's anonymous readers who made several valuable suggestions. Responsibility for any remaining defects is, of course, entirely my own. Most of all, I owe a deep debt of gratitude to my husband and fellow scholar Jonathan Chaplin, who patiently commented on successive drafts and has been supportive throughout the long journey. I could not have wished for a more congenial and stimulating companion.

Adrienne Dengerink Chaplin
Cambridge, Spring 2019

Note on the Cover Artist

The image on the front cover is a slightly cropped version of Helen Frankenthaler's painting *Blessing of the Fleet* from 1969. Helen Frankenthaler (1928–2011) was an American abstract expressionist painter and major contributor to the history of post-war American painting. She pioneered a soak-stain technique that produces luminous colour washes that merge with the canvas. Between 1958 and 1971 she was married to fellow painter Robert Motherwell.

Photograph of Dr Susanne K. Langer by permission of the Estate of Susanne K. Langer

Introduction

As every person has his mother tongue in terms of which he cannot help thinking his earlier thoughts, so every scholar has his philosophical mother tongue, which colors his natural Weltanschauung.

Susanne K. Langer[1]

This book is a presentation of the philosophy of Susanne K. Langer (1895–1985) against the background of major advances in twentieth-century European and American thought. Langer is one of the most original and fertile American thinkers of the twentieth century, yet her work is still insufficiently recognized and frequently misunderstood. To illuminate the evolution and shape of Langer's thought, this book focuses on her four most formative sources: her mentors Henry Sheffer and Alfred N. Whitehead, and the philosophers Ernst Cassirer and Ludwig Wittgenstein. This reveals how her thinking was not only forged out of a critical engagement with significant intellectual traditions of her time but also anticipated many of the major developments and philosophical 'turns' of ours. The book argues that, apart from a knowledge of these sources and their European roots, interpreters cannot adequately understand the radicality and intellectual breadth of her achievements, nor can they fully recognize her abiding relevance.

Langer's works spanned over fifty years and can be divided into three main periods. The first focused on logic and epistemology: *The Practice of Philosophy* (1930) and *An Introduction to Symbolic Logic* (1937). The second engaged with the philosophy of science, culture and art: *Philosophy in a New Key* (1942), *Feeling and Form* (1953) and *Problems of Art* (1957). The third concentrated on the philosophy of mind, feeling and embodied cognition: *Philosophical Sketches* (1962) and the trilogy *Mind: An Essay on Human Feeling* (1967, 1971 and 1982). Throughout these very diverse works runs one unifying theme: the way humans make sense of the world, or what Langer calls their 'pursuit of meaning', whether in science, language, art, myth, even dreams. The 'new key' in philosophy is the recognition that the basic 'sense-data' and 'facts' that make up human experience and knowledge of the world are inherently symbolic. Facts, on Langer's terms, are formulated events rooted in the perceptions of patterns and forms highlighting particular aspects of the world. The pursuit of meaning and its articulation in communicable forms is, so Langer argues, a deeply embodied fundamental human need.

Despite her impressive output, Langer's work as a whole is still largely unknown. Recurrent refrains among the small numbers of scholars that *do* study her is that she is one of the most 'neglected' (McDermott; Berthoff), 'ignored or disparaged' (Gardner), 'misunderstood' (Reimer), 'unknown' (Johnson), 'undervalued' (Campbell), 'unsung' (Damasio), etc., philosophers of the twentieth century.[2] Campbell provocatively suggests that, were it not impossible to rank unknown figures, it would be tempting to characterize Langer as 'the greatest unknown philosopher in the American tradition'.[3]

While Langer is best known as a philosopher of art, her earlier work on logic and epistemology, and her later work on the embodied mind and feeling deserve equal, if not greater, attention – if only for a better understanding of her philosophy of art itself. Many misinterpretations of her aesthetics could have been avoided if readers had been more aware of her broader intellectual framework as outlined in these earlier and later works. This was, of course, not possible until her later works actually appeared. Yet, as one critic put it, 'Few thinkers of Langer's stature were so criticized, and few continue to be as misunderstood, because misconstruals of her earlier work have not been corrected by that which she was to explain later.'[4] Another significant obstacle to her reception is that her first major first book, *The Practice of Philosophy*, containing most of the guiding principles for her later work, has long been out of print, as has her seminal collection of essays, *Philosophical Sketches*, outlining the central themes of her later trilogy *Mind*. It can only be hoped that a renewed interest in Langer's thought will inspire publishers to produce new editions of these important books.

With a much changed philosophical and disciplinary climate since Langer's time, there are currently signs of a renewed interest in Langer's work, especially in America, Germany, Italy, Poland and the Czech Republic.[5] British interest so far has not been keeping up. Interestingly, in a 1951 review of Langer's best-selling book, *Philosophy in a New Key* (1942), Scottish philosopher of science Lancelot Law Whyte lamented the fact that there had still not been a British edition of the book at the time. As he writes,

> The Harvard edition went out of print, few copies having reached this country. The Mentor edition … appeared in 1948, and over 80.000 copies have been sold. But owing to war conditions, lack of interest by publishers, and the fact that the book does not fall within any one of the dominant 'subjects', such as symbolic logic, philology, philosophy of art, religion, etc., there has as yet been no United Kingdom edition. This has had the unfortunate result that, though known to a handful of specialists, this scholarly, original and delightful work has not yet reached the wider circle of philosophical, scientific and general readers outside the United States.[6]

This, in effect, is still the case. Although, among an older generation, there is still a vague collective memory of her name and the title of her best-selling book, *Philosophy in a New Key* – perhaps some even own a copy of its 35¢ Mentor edition – few British people know much more about Langer than that.

Reasons for neglect

There are several reasons why Langer's work was overlooked and neglected by professional philosophers in Langer's time, not only British but also American. Let me list the major five reasons. First, Langer's philosophy diverted from – and challenged – many of the prevailing paradigms that were informed by the regnant scientistic philosophies. That also meant that the field of study for which Langer had become best known, that is, philosophy of art or 'aesthetics', was not considered a serious topic for rigorous research and was therefore routinely relegated to the margins of the discipline.[7] As W. V. O. Quine summarized the mood at the time, 'Philosophy of science is philosophy enough.'[8]

A second reason for the lack of attention was the fact that Langer's wide-ranging, holistic and boundary-crossing approach did not sit easily with the increasing specialization, technicalization and fragmentation of mainstream professional philosophy. Even though Langer herself, in her early years, actively contributed to the discussion of technical logical problems and to the birth of American analytic philosophy as a whole – she was a co-founder of the Association for Symbolic Logic and review editor for the *Journal of Symbolic Logic* and the *Journal of Philosophy* – she was always more interested in the broader questions of meaning that shaped the way philosophical problems were being formulated.

A third reason for her lack of recognition by fellow philosophers was that her ideas were often ahead of the time, sometimes by several decades.[9] Langer frequently anticipated what were to become major developments or 'turns' in philosophy long before they became widely known and accepted. She was, for instance, one of the first philosophers to emphasize the fundamentally metaphorical nature of language and the importance of social context in its use and understanding; she highlighted the constitutively transformational and hermeneutical character of the human mind and understanding; she drew attention to the pre-theoretical and social aspects of major paradigm shifts in revolutions in science; she emphasized the crucial role of the body and intuition in concept formation and cognition; she was one of the first to recognize and accept a plurality of genuine modes of knowing, including myth and art; she was one of the first to recognize the importance of a better understanding of animal mentality and behaviour for an account of the difference between humans and (other) animals; and she was one of the first philosophers to draw heavily on the results of the empirical sciences, demonstrating how the same 'data' could be interpreted very differently depending on different variables. Her ideas contained radical critiques of modern logocentrism and the traditional subject–object dichotomies of modern thought. Many of these critiques anticipated those developed by such later thinkers as Francois Merleau-Ponty, Thomas Kuhn, Paul Ricoeur, John Searle, Jacques Derrida, Michael Polanyi, Charles Taylor, Antonio Damasio, Mark Johnson, Gilles Deleuze and many others. Donald Dryden calls her 'a prophet and visionary'.[10]

A fourth important reason why Langer's work was not recognized and, indeed, often seriously misunderstood, was a lack of familiarity among her fellow philosophers with the principal European sources that had shaped her thinking. Langer's thought was deeply formed by an engagement with the German neo-Kantian tradition that dominated European philosophy in the early twentieth century. Langer's own German background provided her with the language skills and access to philosophical sources that were largely unknown by her American contemporaries. Frequently, this gave her a much better grasp of the latest developments in European philosophy than that of her fellow philosophers.[11] It also enabled her to draw constructive links between, on the one hand, hermeneutically inclined 'continental' philosophy and, on the other, Anglo-American analytical and pragmatist philosophies.[12]

Last but not least, the fifth reason why Langer's work was often neglected was because of her marginalization as a woman in a predominantly male discipline. Langer developed her philosophy at a time of systemic institutional discrimination against women in the academy in general and deep-rooted cultural prejudice against women in philosophy in particular. Although often referred to as the first female professional philosopher in America, she did not, in fact, have a tenured position until her appointment at the Connecticut College for Women in 1954, at the age of 59. Despite being awarded several honorary degrees and awards, she was not part of the academy's institutional network with its established career paths, privileges and prestige.[13] As a result, she did not exercise the direct influence on students or other scholars that would have been routine for her male colleagues.

Approach

This study is the third comprehensive monograph on Langer's work as a whole. The first, as yet untranslated, is *Susanne K. Langer: die lebendige Form menschlichen Fühlens und Verstehens* (Susanne K. Langer: The Living Form of Human Feeling and Understanding), written by German philosopher Rolf Lachmann in 2000.[14] The second, *Susanne Langer in Focus: The Symbolic Mind*, by American philosopher Robert E. Innis, was published in 2009.[15] Both are excellent expositions of Langer's philosophy as a whole and reveal her as an important twentieth-century philosopher whose radical and innovative thought merits rediscovery and critical development. My book complements these two studies by focusing in detail on her most formative philosophical sources.

In his monograph, Innis locates Langer explicitly in relation to the American semiotic and pragmatist traditions, especially Peirce, James and Dewey.[16] While he admits that American philosophy was 'neither a source nor a resource for Langer', he considers Langer's philosophy to supply 'independent confirmation of some of American philosophy's central theses and focal concerns' and to provide 'an additional resource … for development of its continuing relevance and analytical power.'[17] While I fully agree with Innis's assessment that there are strong overlaps and parallels between Langer's thought and the American tradition, this is nevertheless not the whole story, nor is it the story as told by Langer herself. For good and for bad reasons, Langer often explicitly distances herself from the American semiotic and pragmatists thinkers. Instead, she repeatedly and emphatically points to four thinkers who, she says, have influenced her most, that is, her mentors Sheffer and Whitehead, as well as Cassirer and Wittgenstein. While it is generally known to those with even a cursory knowledge of Langer *that* she was influenced by these four thinkers, there is often a limited understanding of exactly *how* and *to what extent* that influence operated. Moreover, Langer's appropriation of these sources does not always conform to 'standard' readings. Indeed, sometimes it corrects them. Langer's reading of Wittgenstein's *Tractatus*, for instance, challenges the view that it represents a positivist copy theory of language and, instead, interprets it in terms of the same 'symbolic turn' that could be seen in Sheffer, Cassirer and Whitehead. Langer's reading, as I will explain, is much closer to the way the early founders of the Vienna Circle had read the early Wittgenstein. The fact that two its founders, Moritz Schlick and Herbert Feigl, recognized in Langer a kindred spirit based on their reading of her first book, *The Practice of Philosophy*, suggests the need for a more nuanced – and more neo-Kantian – reading of these early Viennese logical positivists than is often the case.

As well as Langer's own readings of her four sources, the sources themselves are currently undergoing revivals and re-readings, generating fresh interpretations and applications. Both Whitehead and Cassirer are attracting a surge of new scholarly interest, and alternative readings of the *Tractatus* by the New Wittgensteinians have drawn renewed attention to the early Wittgenstein. Sheffer, too, is beginning to be rediscovered, partly as a result of the new burgeoning field of history of analytic philosophy. Not only does Langer's early (re-)reading of these four thinkers shed new light on them individually, it also draws out intriguing and previously overlooked parallels *between* their respective philosophies.

In addition to Langer's four main sources, several other thinkers have exercised an influence on and served as an inspiration for Langer. These include Sigmund Freud, Henri Bergson, William James, the *Gestalt* theorists Kurt Koffka, Wolfgang Köhler and Max Wertheimer, and numerous other scholars working in a wide variety of specialist disciplines. Yet, although all these thinkers have in some way found their way into Langer's corpus, none of them had as much formative influence as Sheffer, Cassirer, Whitehead and Wittgenstein. In order to examine their influence more closely, I have taken the unusual step of starting, not with Langer's own texts, but with these sources themselves. Here, my intention has been to bring these sources more alive by placing them in their own historical and philosophical contexts. This approach enables a closer engagement with the thinkers themselves, in the way Langer herself might have encountered them, allowing for a closer comparison between their works and hers.

This approach has the specific advantage of being able to trace the genealogy of several central Langerian terms such as form, feeling, meaning, logic, symbol, act and process, as they arose in their original philosophical contexts. As I hope to make clear, Langer's use of these terms is often idiosyncratic and can be easily misunderstood outside of the context in which they originally germinated. Throughout her work Langer regularly defined and re-defined her foundational key terms to the point of appearing inconsistent or indecisive in her use of them. Langer is fully aware of this risk but considers such ongoing revisions an essential part of the philosophical project. This is evident from some personal correspondence between her and the art critic Herbert Read in 1957. In one his letters Read writes that she has 'no more devoted admirer in the world' than him but that he questions her use of the word 'feeling' in her definition of art ('forms expressive of human feeling') as this suggests 'an all-too-Germanic expressionism.'[18] Langer's reply to Read sheds helpful light on her general approach to philosophical terminology and I will quote it here at some length:

Dear Sir Herbert, …. Your letter caused me considerable distress, for I gather from your criticism that I have completely failed to make my thoughts clear. If, after reading the lecture on Expressiveness [in *Problems of Art*], and also the parallel passages in *Feeling and Form* and even *Philosophy in a New Key*, a competent critic can still insist that 'expression' must mean giving vent to emotion, I can only conclude that I cannot write my native language. You say that *my* use of the word 'feeling' is ambiguous, because to '*most readers*' it connotes emotion rather than sensation. A philosophical writer is always in a quandry, because common words are uncertain coin to most readers. Common words are repositories of old concepts, so in trying to express a new and *ipso facto* unpopular concept we have our choice of giving an unusually broad – or, contrariwise, unusually restricted - meaning to a common word, or inventing technical terms that fill the book with Greek compounds or other neologisms. Since I try to write primarily for the philosophical profession, people trained to use words as they are defined and not as they are commonly bandied out, I usually choose to give familiar words explicit meanings, i.e. meanings to be accepted for the discourse in which I am employing them. One simply cannot be bound, in such difficult discourse, to the viable and vague connotations those words might have for 'most readers.'[19]

In view of Langer's stated explanation of her use of philosophical terms, it becomes all the more important that we examine the original contexts in which they were developed. My close reading of Langer and her sources means that, wherever possible, I have used direct quotations to highlight parallels between them. In the case of Langer, this has the added advantage of putting on display her own eloquent and shining prose.

Considering Langer's explicit acknowledgement of her four main sources, it may seem surprising to find so few direct references to them in Langer's actual texts. I suggest that the principal reason for this is simply that she had so profoundly absorbed their thinking that it had become hard for her to identify exactly what were their thoughts and what were her own. She herself once called it the mark of a great teacher that one was not able to attribute thoughts to them which had become part of the fabric of one's own mentality.[20] Or, as she put it elsewhere, 'As every person has his mother tongue in terms of which he cannot help thinking his earlier thoughts, so every scholar has his philosophical mother tongue, which colors his natural *Weltanschauung.*'[21] Langer's sources had become part of her mother tongue.

Aims and content

The main aim of the book is to illuminate Langer's thought in the light of her formative sources and to rediscover its potential for further critical development. By making the overall architecture of her thought more intelligible, it invites re-readings and re-appraisals of aspects of her philosophy that have often been studied without an understanding of her philosophy as a whole. This applies particularly to her aesthetics which is often discussed in isolation from her earlier and later works.

This book involves close readings and interpretations of the main primary texts and provides extensive quotes. This also enables the book to serve as a first introduction to Langer's works for new readers. For those seeking to follow up critical discussions of detailed aspects of her work, I have supplied ample references in notes.

This book contains ten chapters arranged in three parts. Part One, 'Context' (Chapters 1–3), covers the biographical and cross-Atlantic philosophical context of Langer's philosophy and her status as a woman in philosophy. Part Two, 'Sources' (Chapters 4–7), treats Langer's four main philosophical sources in terms of their different conceptions of *form*: Logical form (Sheffer), Symbolic form (Cassirer), Organic form (Whitehead) and

Expressive form (Wittgenstein). Part Three, 'Contributions' (Chapters 8–10), contains expositions of the three main areas in which Langer made constructive philosophical contributions, treated in chronological order: logic and semiotics in the 1920s and 1930s (Chapter 8); art and aesthetics in the 1940s and 1950s (Chapter 9); philosophy of mind and feeling in the 1960s, 1970s and early 1980s (Chapter 10).

Chapter 1, 'Life and work', presents an overview of Langer's personal and professional life. It describes her education at Radcliffe College under her two mentors Henry Sheffer and Alfred N. Whitehead and points out her role as co-founder of the Association for Symbolic Logic and consulting editor of the *Journal for Symbolic Logic*. It draws attention to the enormous interest in her book *Philosophy in a New Key* – it sold well over a half million copies – but that, despite her growing public profile, she did not gain a permanent position until a late age.

Chapter 2, 'European philosophy in America', locates Langer's thought in the context of important cross-Atlantic developments in philosophy in her time. It describes the many exchanges between American and European philosophers and the rise of logical positivism through the Vienna Circle. It examines the fact that the Circle's founders considered Langer's first book to contain clear resonances with their views. It describes Langer's involvement with the seminal Fifth International Congress for the Unity of Science at Harvard in 1939 which became a gathering point for the refugee philosophers that were to exert an important influence on post-war American philosophy.

Chapter 3, 'Philosophy and women', discusses Langer's status as a women philosopher at a time of large-scale institutional discrimination against women and deep-seated cultural prejudice against women philosophers. The chapter includes a brief history of Langer's *alma mater*, Radcliffe College, a women's college founded to give women access to the education offered to men by Harvard College at a time that Harvard did not accept female students. It concludes by exploring the question whether Langer's philosophy can be said to reflect the fact that she was a woman.

Chapter 4, 'Henry Sheffer: Logical form', outlines the influence of Langer's mentor, the logician Sheffer, on Langer in three important respects. First, his conception of logic as the study of pattern and forms rather than deductive reasoning is shown to have provided the initial basis for Langer's thinking about forms and structures in general, including those in art. Second, his insight that the same reality could be represented by a plurality of (logical) forms, systems and notations is revealed to have influenced Langer's thinking about art as being one form of representation alongside others. Third, his emphasis on the need to focus on understanding the *meaning* of logical concepts and forms, rather than on the refining of their technical notation, is presented as inspiring Langer's lifelong interest in 'the meaning of meaning'.

Chapter 5, 'Ernst Cassirer: Symbolic form', highlights the importance of Cassirer's philosophy of symbolic forms for Langer's concept of art as a non-discursive symbolic form. The chapter provides a brief history of neo-Kantianism and elucidates how Cassirer extended and transformed Kant's fixed and universal forms of intuition and cognition into historically evolving, culturally based symbolic forms of perception and experience. The chapter explains that, although Langer only met Cassirer for the first time in 1941, she had been familiar with his trilogy *Philosophie der symbolischen*

Formen (1923, 1925, 1929) long before it was translated into English in the 1950s. Since Cassirer had always intended a fourth volume on art, Langer's *Feeling and Form* can, in an important sense, be said to have completed that project. The chapter describes how Langer's own English translation of Cassirer's *Sprache und Mythos* (1925) in 1946, provided an early introduction of Cassirer to the English-speaking world prior to the publication of his translated *magnum opus, The Philosophy of Symbolic Forms* (1955–7).

Chapter 6, 'Alfred N. Whitehead: Organic form', focuses on Whitehead's conception of the organism's ongoing fluid and reciprocal engagement with its environment as the model for Langer's biological understanding of human mentality. As part of the first cohort of Whitehead's students after his arrival at Harvard in 1924, Langer witnessed the development of Whitehead's process philosophy first-hand. The chapter discusses the relevance of the three main periods of Whitehead's intellectual development for Langer, including those prior to his arrival in America. It shows how Whitehead's concept of nature as a temporal process with an organic rhythm of birth, growth and decline is reflected in Langer's understanding of art (and music) as a 'living form' and how his notions of feeling and affect as the basic modes of human engagement with the world shaped Langer's notion of art as 'the form of feeling' or as 'the articulation of life *as felt*'. It suggests that Whitehead's conception of philosophy and metaphysics as an 'adventure of ideas' is echoed in Langer's notion of philosophy as 'the pursuit of meaning'. The chapter concludes with a discussion of Whitehead's 'mysticism' and Langer's reservations about what she considered his *too* speculative thinking.

Chapter 7, 'Ludwig Wittgenstein: Expressive form', discusses Langer's reading of the *Tractatus* through the lenses of Sheffer, Cassirer and Whitehead. It provides a brief history of the Vienna Circle and its complex relations to Wittgenstein and argues that, unlike neo-positivist empiricist interpretations of the *Tractatus* by British philosophers Ayer and Russell, Langer's neo-Kantian reading of Wittgenstein has much in common with the readings of Vienna Circle members Schlick and Herbert Feigl. It points out that Langer is one of the first American philosophers to recognize the *Tractatus* as part of a broader linguistic or, on Langer's terms, *symbolic* turn. It is often thought that Wittgenstein's later 'repudiation' of the *Tractatus* was a rejection of a putative copy or correspondence theory of language. Langer's reading reveals a much greater continuity between his earlier and later works than is often assumed. The chapter concludes by highlighting the main point of difference between Wittgenstein and Langer: whereas Wittgenstein urged us to stay silent about matters that lay outside discursive language because they had no adequate form in which they could be expressed, Langer argued that there are non-discursive or 'presentational' forms that can articulate non-verbal lived experience in terms of their structural analogies with human feeling.

Chapter 8, 'The logic of signs and symbols', explains Langer's expanded notion of meaning in terms of three central distinctions: between signs and symbols, between discursive and non-discursive symbolism and between conventional and formulative types of symbolization. It traces Langer's choice of terminology for these distinctions and points out its implications for key questions around indication and representation, reference and denotation, meaning and truth. The chapter focuses on the importance of abstracted patterns or *Gestalten* in Langer's philosophy of perception and cognition and discusses the role of analogy and isomorphism in the process of symbolization.

Chapter 9, 'Art as the form of feeling', discusses Langer's philosophy of art as developed in *Feeling and Form* and *Problems of Art*. For Langer, art and music are not *symptoms* in the sense of self-expression or emotional catharsis, but *symbols* in the Cassirerean sense of vehicles for meaning. The chapter explains the role of intuition and abstraction in Langer's philosophy of art and clarifies her two notions of form in terms of, first, logical structure and analogy and, second, shape, contour or *Gestalt*. The chapter examines the notions of resemblance, representation, semblance and virtuality that undergird her classification of the different arts on the basis of their dominant virtual projection: virtual space (the visual arts); virtual time (music and theatre); virtual power (dance); virtual life (the poetic and narrative arts); virtual memory (architecture). The chapter elucidates Langer's notion of organic or 'living form' as the foundation of her innovative conception of art as the form of feeling. The chapter concludes with an account of Langer's emphasis on the cultural importance of art as the education of feeling.

Chapter 10, 'Mind as embodied meaning', presents Langer's biologically based philosophy of mind and feeling as developed in her trilogy *Mind: An Essay on Human Feeling*. The chapter shows how Langer challenges traditional divisions between mind and body, as well as those between thinking and feeling. On Langer's terms, feeling is not opposed to reason but is a generic term for all human mentality or consciousness, from basic sense awareness to logical reasoning. The chapter describes how, for Langer, symbolization is a fundamental human need alongside biological needs, such as breathing and eating. Unlike other animals, humans *desire to make sense of the world* and do so by means of the production of symbolic forms. The chapter explains Langer's view of the three phases of consciousness as organic, psychical and symbolic; her understanding of the origins of life; and her conception of the difference between humans and (other) animals in terms of their motivations, behaviour and mentality. The chapter elucidates Langer's distinction between feeling as intra-organic bodily processes and feeling as encounters with the external world, and highlights the implications of this model for her understanding of art as the form of internal, organic feeling and of external life as felt. The chapter describes how, for Langer, the most fundamental and primordial encounters with the world, as expressed in art, myth and ritual, are articulations of aesthetic and affective lived experience.

The *Conclusion* draws attention to the numerous ways in which Langer anticipated future developments in philosophy and created possibilities for building bridges between different movements and traditions. It suggests that Langer's main contribution to philosophy lies not primarily in any one contribution to a specific field, but in the way she integrated many diverse fields into a larger philosophical vision rooted in a conception of human beings as symbolic animals. It points out that a key element in this vision was her recognition that the world could be seen through a range of different prisms or 'symbolic forms', each of them highlighting different aspects or dimensions. It further highlights how Langer's emphasis on embodied meaning anticipates postmodern critiques of dichotomies between subject and object, mind and body, reason and feeling, and other logocentrically freighted divides. It shows how Langer draws creatively on her sources and how, in an impressive leap of philosophical imagination, she was able to produce a generative synthesis that opened up new avenues of thought. Finally, the conclusion reflects on the potential for further critical development of Langer's thought.

Part One

Context

Life and work

Public and private

Unlike many twentieth-century philosophers, Langer never wrote her memoirs. She was a private person who, especially in her later years, withdrew from public and social life. What we know about her comes from a small number of letters, interviews and recollections from family, close friends and a few journalists, including music journalist Winthrop Sargeant, who wrote a lengthy profile article on her for the *New Yorker* in 1960, and art critic James Lord, who published an extensive interview with her in the *New York Times Book Review* in 1968.[1] Philosopher Donald Dryden published a comprehensive intellectual biography in 2003 that was subsequently annotated with more details.[2] And Wesley Wehr, a young painter and composer turned palaeontologist, recorded his personal recollections of Langer as a friend, thereby providing a few valuable glimpses into her character and personality.[3] What emerges from these various writings is a portrait of a highly original and independent thinker who combined a fierce logical intellect with an intensely creative and imaginative mind. She was known to impress scholars from diverse disciplines to shed light on seemingly intractable problems in their fields and her formidable skills in logic made her a daunting discussion partner and teacher.[4] Winthrop Sargeant describes her as 'a woman of iron will, impatient of laziness and self-indulgence' while an obituary in the *New York Times* refers to her as 'a maverick'.[5]

Following the successes of *Philosophy in a New Key* and *Feeling and Form* Langer had become an acclaimed author with a high public profile.[6] Yet, she often eschewed public attention and sought peace and solitude in remote places. Matter of fact about her own achievements, she often would play down the originality of her ideas by pointing to the sources that had influenced and inspired her.

Early life and student years

Susanne K. Langer was born in New York in 1895 as the second of five children to Antonio Knauth, a successful corporate lawyer, and his wife Else M. Uhlich Knauth. Having emigrated from Germany to the United States in the 1880s, Langer's parents settled in the Upper West Side of Manhattan in New York's old German émigré 'colony'. Langer grew up in an intellectually and artistically rich milieu with music at its centre. Her maternal grandmother had been a professional pianist who had been close friends with Johannes Brahms, while Langer's father, like Susanne herself later, was an accomplished amateur cellist. She was a gifted child who wrote complex family plays at an early age and read Kant's *Critique of Pure Reason* when she was in her early teens.[7] Long summers were spent at the family's large second home on Lake George where she was free to roam and develop her love for nature. Raised multilingually, Langer spoke German at home and then learned French at a private primary day school. She did not learn English until she was 10 and retained a German accent throughout her life.

After several years of home instruction, Langer enrolled at Radcliffe College in 1916. Radcliffe was a women's college that offered equivalent courses to Harvard University at a time that Harvard did not accept female students. As I will explain in more detail in Chapter 3, although Radcliffe students sat the same Harvard exams as their male counterparts, they did not receive the same Harvard degrees.[8] Langer stayed connected with Radcliffe College until 1942, having become a tutor there in 1926. Langer's undergraduate supervisor was the logician Henry Sheffer who introduced her to the new developments in formal and symbolic logic. Langer recalls having been pleased to discover that this 'traditionally stiff and scholastic pursuit [had] as much scope for originality as … metaphysics'.[9] She had been inspired by Sheffer's ability 'to see logic as a field for invention' and describes 'the growing sense of mental power that came with following his expositions, expecting to understand, even before the end of a discourse, a whole intricate conceptual structure with the same clarity as its simplest initial statements'.[10] Sheffer, in turn, had been clearly impressed with Langer's aptitude for philosophy and logic. As he wrote in a letter of recommendation on her BA graduation in 1920, she had 'a firmer grasp of philosophy problems than many a Harvard Ph.D.'[11]

In September 1921 she married Harvard student William Leonard Langer (1896–1977), who, like Susanne herself, was a second child of a German immigrant family. They spoke German at home. William had just finished his master's degree in modern European history at Harvard and was to become a distinguished scholar in that field. He had been awarded a fellowship at the University of Vienna to study the alliances that had led up to the First World War and they spent their first year of marriage abroad.

During her time in Vienna, Langer attended lectures at the university with, among others, philosopher Karl Bühler. Bühler (1879–1963) was a leading philosopher of language and a *Gestalt* psychologist, who had just been appointed at the philosophy faculty. Bühler's pioneering work on language formation was to prove highly relevant to Langer's thought. He was one of the first to explore how meaning and reference in signs and symbols did not originate in the isolated individual but in the social context of its animal and human ambience.

After returning to Cambridge, William began writing his doctoral dissertation and Susanne commenced her Master's degree at Radcliffe College. On 30 August 1922 their first son, Leonard Charles Rudolph, was born.[12] The birth prompted a return to her childhood love of writing fairy tales and other stories – possibly also inspired by a rekindling of her German roots during her recent visit to Europe – resulting in the publication *The Cruise of Little Dipper and Other Fairy Tales*. It was illustrated by her childhood friend and later professional illustrator Helen Sewell.[13]

After gaining his doctorate in 1923, William was offered a position at the history department at Clark University and the family moved to Worcester. For Langer, this meant a weekly 40-mile train journey from Worcester to Cambridge to continue attending her seminars and lectures. Even so, she completed her Master's degree in 1924 with a thesis entitled 'Eduard von Hartmann's Notion of Unconscious Mind and Its Metaphysical Implications'.

In 1924 Langer started her doctoral studies with British philosopher Alfred North Whitehead who had just arrived in the United States that same year. She completed those studies in two years with a doctoral thesis on Whitehead and Russell's *Principia Mathematica*, entitled 'A Logical Analysis of Meaning'. In May of the same year she gave birth to a second son, Bertrand Walter.

Langer had desired to work with Whitehead because of his co-authorship of the *Principia Mathematica* and his reputation as a philosopher of science. Whitehead's own thinking, however, had moved on to different concerns and topics that were to form the basis of his seminal work *Process and Reality*. Although Whitehead's supervision of her thesis was minimal, his ideas and teaching were to have a major influence on her own thinking. When Langer wrote her first book, *The Practice of Philosophy*, in 1930, Whitehead wrote a short preface for it, commending the book as 'an admirable exposition of the aims, methods, and actual achievements of philosophy'.

From 1924 onwards, Langer had started contributing regular reviews to *The Journal of Philosophy*. Versatile in English, German, French and Italian, she became the journal's main reviewer of foreign publications. This exposed her to insights into the latest developments in philosophy in Europe. In 1926, with Whitehead's recommendation, she published her first article, 'Confusion of Symbols and Confusion of Logical Types' in the British journal *Mind*, then under the editorship of G. E. Moore. The article consisted of a detailed critique of the theory of types as developed by Bertrand Russell in the second edition of *Principia Mathematica* published the year before (1925). Her regular discussions with Whitehead as the co-author of the first edition of *Principia Mathematica* (1910–13) had provided her with valuable insight into the thinking behind this work. Other articles on logic to follow included: 'Form and Content: A Study in Paradox' (1926), 'A Logical Study of Verbs' (1927), 'The Treadmill of Systematic Doubt' (1929) and 'Facts: The Logical Perspectives of the World' (1933), all of which were published in the *Journal of Philosophy*.[14]

Home

When, in 1927, William Langer was offered a tenured position in modern history at Harvard, the family moved back to Cambridge. William Langer's Harvard career included seminal publications such as *The Diplomacy of Imperialism 1890–1902* (1935), on European international relations, and the editorship of *An Encyclopedia of World History* (1940) and the twenty-volume series *The Rise of Modern Europe* (1963).

His academic career was interspersed with periods in government service in the areas of international relations and foreign intelligence, including a year as assistant director of the Central Intelligence Agency in the early 1950s. He received honorary degrees from both Harvard and Yale.[15] His autobiography *In and Out of the Ivory Tower* was completed just before his death in 1977.[16] Dorothy Ross opens her review of it as follows:

> William L. Langer intended this autobiography as an exemplary tale of how a poor boy from an immigrant family made good in America. Distressed by the iconoclasm of the sixties, he offered his life as a testament to the American dream and as a defense of the establishment – its openness to merit, its hard-working patriotism, and its contribution to the American defense since World War II. It is a tribute to Langer's basic good temper and immense intellectual curiosity that the book generally escapes the narrow defensiveness of that purpose.[17]

In his book, William Langer depicts what appears to have been a traditional marriage with little domestic involvement on his part, as can be gleaned from his comment that even the arrival of a second son in 1925 'did not greatly affect the regimen of their lives'. We are told that his 'wife enrolled as a graduate student in philosophy at Radcliffe and usually went to Cambridge by train to attend lectures in modern logica by Henry Sheffer and a seminar by Alfred North Whitehead' and we know from another source that on evening seminars at his home, 'Mrs. Langer [would appear] in the doorway at ten, with beer and coffee'.[18] Yet at no point does he mention that she became an important philosopher and well-known author in her own right.

Teaching and travelling

For Langer, the move back to Cambridge marked the beginning of a long series of part-time tutorships for Langer at her *alma mater* Radcliffe College. Since Radcliffe did not have its own tenured faculty, employment was on a sessional, hourly paid, basis. It was not until 1954, at the age of 59, that Langer secured her first tenured position. Despite her low academic status, however, Langer was highly productive in terms of research and publications. In addition to numerous articles and reviews, she wrote nine books, edited two, and translated one. Her first book, *The Practice of Philosophy* (1930), was well received abroad, attracting praise from leaders of the Vienna Circle.

In 1933 the Langer family had embarked on a European tour which included a visit to the then 74-year-old Edmund Husserl. Langer had discussed Husserl's ideas in her 1926 PhD thesis and she had been keen to meet him. The visit took place at Husserl's home in Schluchsee, Germany, in August 1933, just seven months after Hitler had been appointed chancellor. Since Hitler had imposed a ban on books by Jewish authors, Jewish-born Husserl had been very concerned about the ban's consequences for the planned publication of his vast *Nachlass* and the financing of his editorial assistant Eugene Fink. The Langers even helped him to apply (unsuccessfully) for a grant from the Rockefeller Foundation for the project.[19] Upon his death five years later, Husserl's papers were narrowly rescued from Nazi destruction and transported from Freiburg to Leuven.[20] As will be discussed more fully later, many Jewish European philosophers were to be profoundly affected by the Nazi's racial policies. Many, including Ernst Cassirer, were forced to leave their home country and settle abroad. Post-war American philosophy has been considerably influenced by the influx of émigré philosophers from Europe.

Professional involvements

In 1936 Langer was one of the founders of the Association for Symbolic Logic, alongside significant pioneers in logic such as C. I. Lewis, Alonzo Church and W. V. Quine.[21] The association is still internationally active today. Between 1936 and 1939 Langer served as a consulting editor of the association's new journal, the *Journal of Symbolic Logic*, frequently reviewing new publications in foreign languages as she had done previously for the *Journal of Philosophy*.[22] In 1937 she wrote one of the earliest textbooks on symbolic logic, *An Introduction to Symbolic Logic*, which became a standard text at many universities. It appeared in three editions (1937, 1953 and 1967) and was republished as recently as 2011.[23] Langer was a member of the organizing committee of the Fifth International Congress for the Unity of Science taking place at Harvard University in 1939.[24] Other members of the committee included American philosophers P. W. Bridgman and Quine, as well as European émigrés Herbert Feigl and Rudolf Carnap who had both moved to the United States in previous years. The Congress, which took place during the invasion of Poland, was to become an important international gathering point for major European philosophers who had been forced to flee their countries after Hitler's rise to power. In total, there were two hundred attendees, sixty of whom, including Langer, presented papers.

Publishing success

After the Congress, Langer started to turn her attention to a critical examination of the dominant paradigms that shaped the philosophy of her time. This led to her discovery of the new theme that was emerging in a variety of disciplines and fields of study: the notion of the mind as a symbolic transformer. This 'new key' became the central theme of the book for which she became best known: *Philosophy in a New Key: A Study in the Symbolism of Reason, Rite and Art*.[25] First published by Harvard University Press in 1941, it contained both a synthesis of all her previous thinking as well as the seeds of the works that were to follow. In some ways the book can be considered as an extended research plan for her future work, from *Feeling and Form* in 1953 to the third volume of *Mind: An Essay in Human Feeling* in 1982.

Philosophy in a New Key made publishing history by becoming a major success.[26] When Harvard University published it in hardback in 1941, very few university publishers issued paperbacks. However, in 1945 Penguin Books, a US company with ties to British Penguin, approached Harvard University Press for the rights to publish a cheap 25¢ paperback edition with a larger print run for a $750 advance on royalties.

This new imprint was first published under the name Pelican Books but, following the takeover of Penguin Books Incorporated by the New American Library, issued under the name 'A Mentor Book', with a 35¢ sales price printed on the back. By 1951 over 100,000 copies had been sold. In view of its obvious success, Harvard University Press issued another hardcover edition and, in 1971, published its own paperback edition. It became one of Harvard University Press's best ever sellers. It is estimated that, to date, the total sales of all editions combined, is well over 570,000 copies. As historian and librarian Max Hall tells the story,

> Susanne Langer's book, published in 1942, was *Philosophy in a New Key: A Study in the Symbolism of Reason, Rite, and Art*. She had written two previous books and was known as a logician but, at forty-six, had never held a professorial appointment. Women authors were not new to the Press; indeed the first had appeared on its lists in 1913, the year of its founding. But hardly anyone, woman or man, has ever written a Press book that attained a larger total sale than Susanne Langer's. By 1984 *Philosophy in a New Key* had sold at least 545,000 copies. This figure included about 12,000 in the Press's hardcover; 447,000 as a low-priced commercial paperback; 43,000 as a Harvard Paperback beginning in 1971; at least 32,000 in a Japanese translation; and about 11,000 in nine other translations. The book became required or recommended reading for students of semantics, general philosophy, English, aesthetics, music, and the dance.[27]

Langer's lucid, lively writing had made complex contemporary philosophy accessible not only to philosophers but also to a broad range of readers in fields outside philosophy, including practising artists. Although Langer herself had never pushed for a paperback edition – she had initially been unenthusiastic about the idea – it gave her public recognition and reputation that reached well beyond the narrow confines of the academy and professional philosophy. The book was to give Langer a national profile. She was in growing demand as a public speaker and was sought out for interviews in such publications as the *New Yorker* and the *New York Times Book Review*.[28]

New York

The year of publication of *Philosophy in a New Key* coincided with a difficult period in Langer's personal life. Following strains in their marriage, William left her for another woman and, at his request, the couple divorced in 1942.[29] According to her son Leonard, the break-up affected Langer deeply and contributed to her growing solitary and itinerant life.[30] She ended her long-standing affiliation with Radcliffe College and moved back to her city of birth, New York. She rented an apartment on the East Side in Manhattan from where she embarked on a succession of visiting professorships and temporary appointments at, among others, the University of Delaware (1942–3), the Dalton School (1944–5), New York University (1945–6), Columbia University (1945–50), Northwestern University (1950), the New School of Social Research (1950), University of Washington (1952–3) and the University of Michigan (1954).

Her appointment at Columbia University in 1945 had initially begun as a replacement for Ernst Cassirer who had died very suddenly and unexpectedly from a heart attack in the spring of that year, less than a year after his arrival in New York. Langer had met Cassirer for the first time in 1941 but had already been familiar with his German trilogy *Philosophie der symbolischen Formen* (1923–9) long before it was translated into English. From a letter from Cassirer to Langer one year before his death, it was clear that he had been interested in some form of closer cooperation (*engere Zusammenarbeit*) with her on his research projects, in particular over the book he was working on at the time, *The Myth of the State*.[31] Sadly, this cooperation was never to materialize. She did, however, produce an English translation of his *Sprache und Mythos* which was published in 1946. As is clear from his correspondence, Cassirer had always planned to write a book on art but his premature death prevented that from ever happening. Langer poignantly dedicated her 1953 book *Feeling and Form: A Theory of Art Developed from Philosophy in a New Key* 'to the happy memory of Ernst Cassirer'.

Langer's twelve-year period in New York (1942–54) coincided with New York's eclipsing of Paris as the centre of modern art after the war. Alongside many intellectuals and scholars, there had been an influx of refugee European artists to New York during the war who brought fresh inspiration and ideas to the city. Inspired by the modernist movement in Europe as epitomized by Picasso and Mondrian, New York was beginning to establish itself as a dynamic international centre. The new 'New York School' became associated with such movements as 'abstract expressionism' and 'action painting'.[32]

Some of the students attending Langer's classes at Columbia University were practising artists, some of whom belonging to the (second-generation) abstract expressionist school such as Fay Lansner. Her writings on art had put Langer much in demand as a speaker at art colleges. Her theories based on her notion of art as 'the form of feeling' resonated with the new wave of abstract painters who felt she articulated in philosophical terms what they were grasping for artistically.[33] She also influenced formalist art critic Clement Greenberg as is clear from his many references to her in his 1971 Bennington Lectures.[34] Greenberg is known for his role in promoting the work of painters such as Jackson Pollock and Barnett Newman.[35] Newman himself was highly sceptical about the value of philosophy or theory of art for practising artists. But so, ironically, was Langer herself. She would have been in full agreement with his famous quip which is said to have been directed to her: 'Aesthetics is for artists as ornithology is for the birds', suggesting the irrelevance of academic aesthetics for artistic practice.[36] The comment was first made during a panel discussion in which Langer participated around the theme 'Aesthetics and the Artist' at the fourth annual Woodstock Art Conference in New York in 1952.[37] There is some irony in the fact that it was Greenberg's Langer-inspired criticism that considerably helped to further Newman's career.

Outside America, Langer influenced the Danish abstract painter and art theorist Asger Jorn who adopted many of her concepts for his own theories.[38] Among writers, she was avidly read by Walker Percy, who drew substantially on her ideas in his book *The Message in the Bottle*.[39] English art historian and critic Herbert Read was another admirer, as was the philosopher of art Arthur Danto.[40] Paul Hindemith was one of many musicians who was attracted to her views and is said to have once told a class at Cornell University that Langer's philosophy of music was the only one that made sense to him.[41] Langer may well be the only philosophy of music who had a choreographed dance dedicated to her. A performance of *Batter: A Tribute to Susanne Langer*, choreographed by Kenneth King, took place in the Synod House of the Cathedral of St. John the Divine in New York in 1976.[42]

Connecticut College

It was not until 1954 when, at the age of 59, Langer accepted her first tenured position as professor and chair of the philosophy department at Connecticut College for Women in New London. She moved from her city apartment in downtown Manhattan to a colonial farmhouse in leafy Old Lyme on the coast of Connecticut, where she lived until her death in 1985.[43] Two years after her arrival in Old Lyme, Langer was awarded a substantial annually renewable grant from the Edgar J. Kaufmann Foundation to support her research and writing. Edgar J. Kaufmann was a wealthy Pittsburgh businessman whose son, Edgar Kaufmann Jr (1910–1989), an art collector and philanthropist had become a close friend and admirer of Langer's writing. Kaufmann Jr had studied art and architecture in Europe and had worked as one of Frank Lloyd Wright's apprentices. In 1946 he was appointed the director of New York's Museum of Modern Art's department of industrial design and, from 1963 to 1986, taught architecture and art history at Columbia University.

During her time at Connecticut College, Langer wrote *Feeling and Form* (1953); *Problems of Art* (1957) and *Philosophical Sketches* (1962), the latter consisting mainly of assembled public lectures.[44] In 1962, enabled by the Kaufmann grant, she retired from teaching in order to devote herself entirely to research and writing. While remaining connected to the college as a research scholar and emeritus professor, she embarked on what was to become her final project and *magnum opus*: the trilogy *Mind: An Essay on Human Feeling* (1967, 1971 and 1982).[45] This work attracted the attention of philosophers of mind and consciousness as well as of brain and neuroscientists, receiving positive reviews in specialist science journals.[46]

Langer received several honorary doctorates from various schools and universities, including Columbia University, and was, in 1960, elected to the American Academy of Arts and Sciences. Despite her growing fame and reputation as a writer and a speaker, she avoided public attention and related social duties and formalities. Instead, especially in later life, she increasingly sought solitude, simplicity and stillness. She had bought a wood cabin deep in the woods of Ulster County, New York, where she would spend her summers reading, walking and writing, undisturbed by visitors or telephone.[47] Until a late age, she would venture by canoe into the most remote wilderness she could find. The same pioneering and adventurous spirit that characterized her attitude to nature also characterized her approach to philosophy.

2

European philosophy in America

Langer wrote at a time of major advances in American and European philosophy and was herself an astute and insightful commentator on these developments. This was particularly clear from the panoramic overview and penetrating analysis offered in her article 'The Deepening Mind: A Half-Century of American Philosophy (1950)'.[1] This chapter outlines major developments in European philosophy in the early twentieth century and the important cross-Atlantic exchanges between American and European philosophers that were to lead to the birth of analytic philosophy in America and shape the intellectual climate in which Langer developed her own writings.

The crisis in American philosophy

During Langer's first term of studies at Radcliffe College in the autumn of 1916, Harvard's philosophy department experienced two unexpected losses: idealist philosopher and logician Josiah Royce had died very suddenly at the beginning of the academic term, and this was followed by the death of psychologist Hugo Münsterberg three months later.[2] As Langer recalls,

> It was a hard period for a Department of Philosophy which had boasted of its 'Great Five', James, Royce, Palmer, Santayana and Münsterberg. James had died in 1910; Palmer had retired, Santayana returned to Europe, and a few months after Royce's death, Münsterberg fell dead in a Radcliffe classroom. A few men whose influence was just beginning to reach beyond Harvard were carrying on.[3]

These 'few men' included Henry Sheffer who took over Royce's classes and became Langer's mentor for her undergraduate studies. In addition to this local crisis, however, there was a more far-reaching national one. This crisis concerned the diminished status of philosophy *as such* in the face of the rapid growth and success of the empirical sciences. A growing dissatisfaction and disillusionment with the large metaphysical systems and speculative philosophies, which had dominated the field so far, had led many students to the natural sciences. Philosophy had become dry and unexciting, and irrelevant to a younger generation of American students. As Langer observed,

'Philosophy proper was usually left to persons of tamer temperament – some very learned, some merely earnest, but most of them conservative teachers, rehearsing old arguments, with little heat and equally little light.'[4] Students impressed with the successes of the natural sciences expected philosophy to adopt the same rigorous methods as employed by them. Although this trend was also recognizable in Europe, it was, so Langer argued, more pronounced in America,

> This unreflecting mood of what one can only call 'worldly faith' – blind faith in the conquest of nature through science – was even more marked in America than Europe, partly because our resources were more seductive and the material foundations of our culture more lavish, partly because we had no established philosophical tradition to hold the balance against so much practical activity, as the familiar and respected learning of the European universities did at all times. Philosophy, in that cheerfully intoxicated era, was at best a stepchild everywhere, but in our country it was a waif, and a little immigrant at that. Its ancestors were in England and Germany. In the nineteenth century, only our oldest universities had really had a home for it, and there it had lived in modest seclusion, no trouble to anybody.[5]

As a result, a general disdain for philosophy had been replaced by a growing excitement for the sciences:

> Natural science had not only captured the laurels, but had also lured the best talent of the age into its service. A few excellent men, like Peirce, Royce, and James, do not constitute a profession; and characteristically, even among these three who come immediately to mind, only Royce was primarily a philosopher. Peirce was a logician and mathematician …; James' greatness lay, above all, in psychology.[6]

However, so Langer observes, after the Second World War there had been significant changes in this situation. Two factors, in particular, had contributed to this change. The first was a gradual disillusionment with science, a recognition of its limitation in solving the problems of life and the world. This led to a renewed interest in the wisdom of the great philosophers of the past who wrestled with the big questions about life and the meaning of existence. As she comments,

> The wave of [cultural] optimism has broken in a deluge of fierce disappointment, with war and tyranny, turmoil and want and despair. The blind faith in science has ended in disillusion and no faith at all. For the 'civilized' nations today are destroying their own cultural and economic life faster than they can build it up; however great their scientific achievements, the greatest are always for purposes of destruction. Society has become no more rational, no more humane, and certainly no happier than before the discovery of evolution or the invention of motor vehicles and electronic machines. Splitting the atom has resulted primarily only in splitting mankind.[7]

She continues,

> Thirty-five years of political upheaval and moral collapse have been very sobering. Our country is still the least affected, but by no means unscathed. Every intelligent person feels the inadequacy of popular thought to fathom the cosmos science has revealed, and to guide us in controlling the terrific powers we have harnessed. ... Consequently they will lend an ear to any philosopher, ancient or modern, who is reputed, or even rumored, to understand the laws of nature, life, and mind. Two decades ago Aristotle and Plato were not even names to the majority of college graduates in America. Today the 'basic writings' of these great intellectuals may be bought in the drugstore. ... Whitehead's brilliant but difficult *Science and the Modern World* has a successful career in a pocket edition. In the 1930s such a thing would have been impossible. This is a simple, common-sense index to the new seriousness that besets us.[8]

Even so, Langer writes, disillusionment with science was not the only impetus for a renewed interest in philosophy. A growing awareness of the philosophical dimensions of the scientific enterprise as such led to closer study of its methods and its processes of theory formation. With Einstein's theories of relativity, the question how the natural sciences processed and interpreted data had become even more important. Since science drew increasingly on mathematics for the formulation of its laws, philosophers of science began to realize that laws of physics were ultimately dependent on such non-empirical entities as signs and symbols for their formulation. In Langer's words,

> The second reason for the rebirth of philosophy ... lies in the advance of science instead of the failure of morality. It is the fact that scientific thinking itself, especially in physics, has reached a point where the philosophical foundations implicit in its elaborate structure come into view, and they look entirely different from the metaphysical framework of classical mechanics that philosophers have been aware of heretofore. Space and time, matter and motion, have become problematical again, through the prodigious growth of mathematics and the scientific insight it continues to generate.[9]

This growing interest in the philosophy of science and, specifically, the role of mathematics in philosophy and science attracted many American philosophers to the work of mathematicians Russell and Whitehead in Cambridge and to that of the logical positivists in Vienna. This interest led to the first wave of invitations to European scholars to visit America.

Cross-Atlantic exchanges

One of the first philosophers to receive such an invitation was Bertrand Russell. Since the publication of *Principia Mathematica* in 1910, Russell had gained a growing reputation among young philosophers in America.[10] As George Santayana wrote to Russell in 1912, '[T]here is no one whom the younger school of philosophers in America are more eager to learn of than you.'[11] In 1914 Russell was invited to give Harvard's Lowell Lectures and teach during the Spring Semester.[12] When Royce died in 1916, the philosophy department worked hard to secure Russell as his replacement but President Lowell blocked the appointment due to Russell's political activism and pacifist stance in Britain at the time. Bruce Kuklick writes,

> On the day that Royce died, [department chair] Woods acted: he wrote to Russell that he was the only man who could make good Royce's loss. Russell had consented to come in the spring of 1917, and Woods hoped to have him permanently. But in summer 1916 the British government prosecuted and convicted Russell for his pacifistic activities under the Defense of the Realm Act; he could not leave Britain for the duration of the war. Royce's position, one in the first instance reserved for a logician, was still unfilled after the war, and the department wanted to renew a half-time offer to Russell. But Lowell would now have none of it: great as his abilities were, an iconoclast like Russell would not do at Harvard.[13]

In the event, the post was, initially temporarily, filled by Henry Sheffer, who took over Royce's classes as well as the mentorship of Langer, who had just arrived at Radcliffe to commence her undergraduate studies.

After 1914 Russell continued to lecture at Harvard and other public venues throughout the United States and, in 1940, delivered Harvard's William James Lectures, introduced by his old colleague and co-author of the *Principia Mathematica*, Alfred North Whitehead, who had by then been appointed at Harvard.[14] Based on his reputation as Russell's co-author, Whitehead had been offered a chair at the philosophy department in 1924 but, as we will examine later, his interests had since moved in very different directions.

The Vienna Circle

Another frequent visitor to America was the philosopher Moritz Schlick, founder of the Vienna Circle and the movement that became known as logical positivism.[15] Schlick lectured widely throughout America and was a visiting professor at Stanford University in 1929 and 1932.[16] Schlick is an unexpected but important point of reference when locating Langer in relation to broader philosophical developments in Europe and in America. Schlick was familiar with Langer's first book, *The Practice of Philosophy*, and much in agreement with it. Both Schlick and Langer had a deep admiration for Wittgenstein and drew heavily on the *Tractatus*. Both Schlick and Langer, moreover, had been significantly shaped by the neo-Kantian tradition and this coloured their reading of Wittgenstein in ways that differed significantly from the British empiricist readings of Russell and Ayer. As this is a crucial factor in understanding the affinity between Schlick and Langer, it is necessary to provide a brief history of the Vienna Circle.

As a leading centre of European philosophy in the early twentieth century, Vienna responded to the major revolutionary developments in science – especially Einstein's theories of relativity (1905, 1917) – and in mathematics – especially Russell and Whitehead's *Principia Mathematica* (1910, 1912, 1913). Since 1907 a group of scholars had been meeting regularly as the Ernst Mach Association (*Verein*) named after the distinguished philosopher of science and *Gestalt* psychologist.[17] Ernst Mach (1838–1916) represented the stream of post-Kantian philosophers who opposed the metaphysical idealism of Fichte, Schelling and Hegel, and wanted to re-emphasize the role of sense-impressions in Kant's theory of knowledge. Drawing on Comte's empiricist positivism, Mach's phenomenalist philosophy differed nevertheless from Comte's classic positivism by considering scientific laws as *descriptions* of observable sense-impressions rather than statements about the physical (or, indeed, '*meta*physical') reality behind them. Mach, like the neo-Kantian Cassirer, rejected both physical realism and metaphysical idealism on the grounds of their lingering metaphysical assumptions about ultimate reality.

Mach's ultimate philosophical ideal was to create a 'unified science' around a single method derived from the natural sciences. Philosophy was not merely to include a philosophy of science, it had to become scientific itself. Interestingly, this scientific aspiration for philosophy is described in almost poetic language by Mach in his inaugural lecture in Vienna in 1895:

> As the blood in nourishing the body separates into countless capillaries, only to be collected again and to meet in the heart, so in the science of the future all the rills of knowledge will gather more and more into a common and undivided stream.[18]

It was, as one commentator put it, 'another way of standing Hegel on his head: unification not through metaphysics but through the elimination of metaphysics'.[19]

In 1922 Mach was succeeded by the theoretical physicist Moritz Schlick as professor of *Naturphilosophie*. In the autumn of 1924, Schlick re-kindled Mach's interdisciplinary discussion group, initially known as the Schlick Circle but later to become better known as the 'Vienna Circle'.[20] The core group included the mathematician Hans Hahn, political economist Otto Neurath, mathematician and philosopher Olga Hahn-Neurath, legal theorist Felix Kaufmann, physicist Philipp Frank, Schlick's student Herbert Feigl and assistant Friedrich Waismann, and, from 1926, Rudolf Carnap. Hahn's student, Kurt Gödel, attended intermittently. From 1928, another graduate student, Rose Rand, was an active member who made extensive notes and transcriptions of the discussions between 1930 and 1935.[21] Despite the public appearance of a unified philosophy, however, leading members often pursued very different projects resulting in sharp disagreements and shifting alliances.

In addition to the group in Vienna, a regular gathering of scholars took place in Berlin under the leadership of philosopher of science Hans Reichenbach (1891–1953). Both Reichenbach and Schlick had begun their intellectual careers as neo-Kantians.[22] Neo-Kantians, as we will discuss in more detail in Chapter 5, sought to re-interpret Kant's critical idealism while avoiding any form of Hegelian metaphysical idealism or Comtean scientific positivism. Both Reichenbach and Schlick rejected Mach's phenomenalistic positivist view of knowledge as the passive reception of simple *sense-data* and emphasized instead the active and constructive role of the mind. Drawing on *Gestalt* psychology, they conceived of knowledge as the mind's particular way of ordering the sense-manifold so as to recognize something *as* a thing.[23] Cassirer, Reichenbach and Schlick were in regular contact and lively debate throughout the late 1910s and 1920s and commented on each other's work. All three were leading interpreters of Einstein's theory of relativity and other developments in science and mathematics.[24] In order to pursue their ideal of a science united around a universal method and language, the Vienna Circle had used Whitehead and Russell's *Principia Mathematica* to reduce mathematical formula to symbolic logic. It was, however, Wittgenstein's *Tractatus*, published in 1922, that, even while being differently interpreted, was to become a defining influence on the Circle. For some members at least, the *Tractatus* meant that not only could mathematics be reduced to logic, but *all* philosophical language could be reduced to unequivocal logical propositions, purified from any ambiguities. Meaningful propositions, so they interpreted Wittgenstein, could now be sharply delineated from meaningless pseudo-propositions tainted by metaphysical language.

Wittgenstein's *Tractatus*

Notwithstanding their different interpretations, the *Tractatus* made an overwhelming impression on most members of the Vienna Circle. They read the entire work on several occasions, sometimes reciting it aloud, line by line. Carnap refers to Wittgenstein as 'the philosopher who, besides Russell and Frege, had the greatest influence on [his] thinking'.[25] Schlick, especially, was enthralled. Schlick's wife recalls that he had approached his first meeting with Wittgenstein 'with the reverential attitude of a pilgrim'.[26] As Schlick wrote ecstatically to Cassirer in 1927,

> I have been through the logical school of Russell and Wittgenstein, and now place such heightened demands on philosophical thought that I can read most philosophical productions only with the greatest effort of will. … Even the personality of Wittgenstein (who is likely never to publish anything again) is truly great. The *Tractatus Logico-Philosophicus* I regard as the most brilliant and significant achievement of modern philosophy. … I firmly believe that philosophy has been brought to a critical juncture by the impulse originating from logic, and that we are approaching the Leibnizian ideal of philosophizing. The boundary against empty talk and questioning must be drawn much more sharply than before.[27]

According to fellow Circle members, Schlick's deferential attitude towards Wittgenstein went so deep that it sometimes clouded his critical judgement and made it difficult to distinguish between his own views and those of Wittgenstein. Feigl even suggests that Schlick attributed to Wittgenstein views he had himself developed years earlier:

In his *Allgemeine Erkenntnislehre* (1918) there were … anticipations of some of the central tenets of Wittgenstein's *Tractatus Logico-Philosophicus*. I think it was Schlick's extremely unassuming character, his great modesty and kindliness, and his deep personal devotion to Wittgenstein that made him forget or suppress the great extent to which his views, independently developed and quite differently stated, already contained important arguments and conclusions regarding the nature of logical and analytical validity; the semantic explication of the concept of truth; the difference between pure experience (*Erleben*), acquaintance (*Kennen*), and genuine knowledge (*Erkennen*), etc. Indeed so deeply impressed was Schlick with Wittgenstein's genius that he attributed to him profound philosophical insights which he had formulated much more lucidly long before he succumbed to Wittgenstein's almost hypnotic spell.[28]

In the Preface to the *Tractatus*, Wittgenstein claims that the book 'will perhaps only be understood by those who have themselves already thought the thoughts which are expressed in it – or similar thoughts'.[29] Perhaps, in Schlick's case and, as I will argue, in that of Langer, that was indeed in the case.[30]

Schlick and *The Practice of Philosophy*

In 1930 Schlick was sent *The Practice of Philosophy* by Langer's New York-based publisher Henry Holt. Upon reading the work he wrote an enthusiastic reply with the words, 'Exquisite style, lucid, fluent and brilliant, has been a source of real joy for me'.[31] Schlick's German editors refer to the exuberant language used by Schlick as 'fast überschwenglich' (almost gushing).[32] Schlick's enthusiasm for Langer's book can arguably be explained by their similar conceptions of philosophy – Langer's definition of philosophy as 'the pursuit of meaning' was adopted by Schlick as the title of one of his own lectures – and, significantly, by their very similar readings of Wittgenstein's *Tractatus*.[33] In his 1930 lecture, 'The Future of Philosophy', Schlick states,

> The view which I am advocating has at the present time been most clearly expressed by Ludwig Wittgenstein; he states his points in these sentences: 'The object of philosophy is the logical clarification of thoughts. Philosophy is not a theory but an activity. The result of philosophy is not a number of "philosophical propositions", but to make propositions clear.' This is exactly the view which I have been trying to explain here.[34]

In the same lecture, he refers to Langer's book again as 'very excellent' and states his agreement with her notion of philosophy as the 'pursuit of meaning'. On one point, though, he feels the need to take Langer to task:

> From what I have said so far it might seem that philosophy would simply have to be defined as the science of meaning, as, for example, astronomy is the science of heavenly bodies, or zoology the science of animals, and that philosophy would be a

science just as other sciences, only its subject would be different, namely 'Meaning'. This is the point of view taken in a very excellent book, '*The Practice of Philosophy*', by Susanne K. Langer. The author has seen quite clearly that philosophy has to do with the pursuit of meaning, but she believes the pursuit can lead to a science, to 'a set of true propositions' – for that is the correct interpretation of the term science. Physics is nothing but a system of truths about physical bodies. Astronomy is a set of true propositions about the heavenly bodies, etc. But philosophy is not a science in this case. There can be no science of meaning, because there cannot be any set of true propositions about meaning.[35]

Langer, as it happens, never referred to philosophy as 'a science' in the sense of 'a set of true propositions'.[36] As we will see, she agreed with Schlick – and *pace* Ernst Mach – that philosophy was not a science. Schlick simply misread Langer on this point.[37] Langer agreed with Wittgenstein's view in the *Tractatus* that philosophy is 'not one of the natural sciences' (4.111) and that it is 'not a theory but an activity' (4.112). The word 'practice' in the title of *The Practice of Philosophy* is a direct reference to that. She also agreed with Wittgenstein that 'philosophical work consists essentially of elucidations' and that the 'result of philosophy is not a number of "philosophical propositions", but to make propositions clear' (4.112).[38] However, apart from this minor misreading on Schlick's part, his overall affirmation of her book and his own interpretation of Wittgenstein point to a strong similarity in their respective reading of Wittgenstein. Both understood him not as primarily a philosopher of knowledge, science or logic, but, as was generally recognized only much later, as a philosopher of language. In that context, it is interesting to note that Richard Rorty included Schlick's essay 'The Future of Philosophy' as the first chapter in *The Linguistic Turn: Essays in Philosophical Method* (1967).[39]

Many of Schlick's lecture notes were later reworked for publication and became important documents for the dissemination of logical positivist thought in America. Most important among these were 'The Turning Point in Philosophy' (1930), 'The Future of Philosophy' (1930), 'The Pursuit of Meaning' (seminar 1931/32) and 'Form and Content' (1932).[40]

The Manifesto

When Schlick was abroad on his first visit to Stanford University, Hahn, Neurath and Carnap had, unbeknownst to him, drawn up a manifesto for the Vienna Circle – *Wissenschaftliche Weltauffassung: Der Wiener Kreis* (*The Vienna Circle Manifesto: The Scientific Conception of the World*).[41] It was launched at the First Conference on the Epistemology of the Exact Sciences in Prague in September 1929 and was to become the Vienna Circle's public face. Placing themselves *over against* the (neo-)Kantian tradition and instead within the lineage of empiricists Locke and Hume, positivists Comte and Mach, and logicians Frege and Russell, the authors describe their approach as, on the one hand, 'empiricist and positivist' – knowledge is based on experience which rests on the immediately given – and, on the other, 'logical analytical' – the logical analysis of empirical material enables the unification of all disciplines into one science. Using what they called 'the far-reaching ideas of Wittgenstein', the different approaches taken by Russell's logicism, Hilbert's formalism, and Brouwer's intuitionism could now be united in 'a single solution':

> [L]ogical analysis overcomes not only metaphysics in the proper, classical sense of the word, especially scholastic metaphysics and that of the systems of German idealism, but also the hidden metaphysics of Kantian and modern apriorism. The scientific world-conception knows no unconditionally valid knowledge derived from pure reason, no 'synthetic judgments a priori' of the kind that lie at the basis of Kantian epistemology and even more of all pre- and post-Kantian ontology and metaphysics. ... It is precisely in the rejection of the possibility of synthetic knowledge a priori that the basic thesis of modern empiricism lies. The scientific world-conception knows only empirical statements about things of all kinds, and analytic statements of logic and mathematics.[42]

The overriding message of the Manifesto, however, was the radical erasure of all forms of metaphysics from philosophy – the clearance of 'the metaphysical and theological debris of millennia.'[43] Logical positivism promised a position not only free from metaphysics, but opposed to metaphysics.

Although the movement's anti-metaphysical stance was primarily philosophically based, it was also motivated by social and political developments. Metaphysics was associated with 'irrational' ideas that enabled idealist philosophers such as Hegel, Nietzsche or Heidegger to create mythological notions of nation, race and state that were prone to be misused as instruments of political oppression. One of the aims of positivism was, as Edward Skidelsky described it, '[T]o purge science of the nationalist, imperialist, and racist rhetoric that increasingly accompanied it. Its exorcism of metaphysics was at the same time an exorcism of ideology.'[44] More generally, the Vienna Circle's commitment to a scientific world-conception was based on a socialist desire to improve people's basic living conditions, both through advanced technology and better education. Under the democratic slogan 'knowledge for all', the Ernst Mach Society had produced a range of popular publications and had organized public lectures for general audiences.[45] They supported the Bauhaus's ideals of the New Objectivity (*Neue Sachlichkeit*), with its preference for clean lines and its rejection of ornamentation, which resonated with their philosophical ideals of clarity, transparency and simplicity.[46] As we are told in the Manifesto, 'Neatness and clarity are striven for, and dark distances and unfathomable depths rejected. In science there are no "depths"; there is surface everywhere.'[47] Rejecting obscurity and promoting transparency as much in philosophy as in art, Carnap defends their ideals passionately in the Preface to his book *The Logical Structure of the World* (1928):[48]

> We feel that there is an inner kinship between the attitude on which our philosophical work is founded and the intellectual attitude which presently manifests itself in entirely different walks of life; we feel this orientation in artistic movements, especially in architecture, and in movements which strive

for meaningful forms of personal and collective life, of education, and of external organization in general. ... It is an orientation which demands clarity everywhere, but which realizes that the fabric of life can never quite be comprehended. ... It is an orientation which acknowledges the bonds that tie men together, but at the same time strives for free development of the individual. Our work is carried by the faith that this attitude will win the future.[49]

Despite their missionary zeal for social and political change, Carnap and most other logical positivists aimed to be politically neutral in their philosophical work. The only exception to this neutralism was Neurath. As Carnap recounts it,

All of us in the Circle were strongly interested in social and political progress. Most of us, myself included, were socialists. But we liked to keep our philosophical work separate from our political aims. In our view, logic, including applied logic, the theory of knowledge, the analysis of language, and the methodology of science, are, like science itself, neutral with respect to practical aims, whether they are moral aims for the individual, or political aims for society. Neurath criticized strongly this neutralist attitude, which in his opinion gave aid and comfort to the enemies of social progress. We in turn insisted that the intrusion of practical and especially of political points of view would violate the purity of philosophical methods.[50]

In order to promote the ideals of the Vienna Circle as formulated in the Manifesto, Otto Neurath had founded *The Unity of Science Movement* in 1934. In addition to planning ambitious projects such as the *International Encyclopedia of Unified Science*, edited by Carnap and Morris, and the journal *Erkenntnis* (1930), edited by Carnap and Reichenbach, the movement organized a series of major international congresses in Paris (1935); Copenhagen (1936); Paris (1937); Cambridge, England (1938); Harvard University, Cambridge, Massachusetts (1939) and Chicago (1941). The movement and its congresses were to become a significant focal point for the diaspora of émigré scholars in the 1930s. As we noted earlier, Langer was part of the organizing committee of the 1939 Congress at Harvard.

As became clear later on, however, Schlick had been profoundly unhappy with the Manifesto. In fact, he disliked any manifesto or collective statement. As Feigl records,

Schlick, while appreciative of this token of friendship and admiration, was deeply disturbed by the idea of having originated another 'school of thought'. He was a philosophical individualist; ... The idea of a united front of philosophical attack was abhorrent to Schlick – notwithstanding the fact that he himself promulgated the Viennese point of view in many of his lectures, in Europe and also in the United States.[51]

More importantly, in addition to his aversion to the Manifesto as a collective statement, Schlick also objected to the way its authors used Wittgenstein for their own anti-metaphysical agenda. Wittgenstein himself, in turn, felt protective of Schlick whom he felt was misrepresented in the Manifesto's 'posturing'. As he wrote in a letter to Waismann,

> Just because Schlick is no ordinary man, people owe it to him to take care not to let their 'good intentions' make him and the Vienna school which he leads ridiculous by boastfulness. When I say 'boastfulness' I mean any kind of self-satisfied posturing. 'Renunciation of metaphysics!' As if that were something new! What the Vienna school has achieved, it ought to show not say ... The master should be known by his work.[52]

It was in part in response to Schlick's and Wittgenstein's dissatisfaction with the Manifesto that Schlick's student Herbert Feigl, while spending a year at Harvard on a Rockefeller scholarship, co-authored an extensive article outlining the main tenets of the Vienna Circle's outlook and, in order to forestall what he claimed to be 'unfortunate attempts at labelling this aspect of contemporary European philosophy'. coined the movement's official name 'logical positivism'.[53] As he recalls it in his memoirs,

> I was (after Schlick's brief visits) the first 'propagandist' of our outlook in the United States. ... At Christmas, 1930, Albert Blumberg and I met in New York for a week's vacation, and for work on an article, 'Logical Positivism: A New Movement in European Philosophy', that was published in the spring of 1931 in the *Journal of Philosophy*. It was this article, I believe, that affixed this internationally accepted label to our Viennese outlook.[54]

The fact that the name was internationally acceptable was important because the Vienna Circle's intentional internationalist outlook was a reaction against the growing nationalism of their time. The same desire for internationalization can be seen reflected in the title of the Unity of Science movement's *International Encyclopedia of Unified Science* and in their commitment to international congresses. Although it was acknowledged that the term 'positivism' in the name had the potential disadvantage of negative associations with old-style Comtean positivism – some members of the Vienna Circle had preferred the name 'logical empiricism' – Feigl and Blumberg defended their choice as follows:

> Although it is perhaps the best among many poor ones, the name may suggest a mere rephrasing of traditional positivism. However, this is not the case. Indeed, it is precisely the union of empiricism with a sound theory of logic which differentiates logical positivism from the older positivism, empiricism, and pragmatism. The vigorous empirical tradition of Hume, Mill, Comte, and Mach founded its philosophizing upon the principle that all knowledge is based upon experience. But reacting against the poverty of traditional formal logic, these philosophers fell into the error of carrying their empiricism too far.[55]

Reflecting back on the time of his writing, Feigl notes that he and Blumberg felt they had 'a mission' to further logical positivism in America and that the responses to the movement confirmed a support for it: 'We had, indeed, "started the ball rolling", and for at least twenty years Logical Positivism was one of the major subjects of discussion, dispute, and controversy in United States philosophy.'[56]

Langer and logical positivism

At the beginning of their influential article, Feigl and Blumberg listed three American philosophers whose views they considered to be close to their own. Somewhat unexpectedly, one of those three was Langer:

> [Logical positivism's] foremost philosophical exponents are R. Carnap (Vienna), H. Reichenbach (Berlin), M. Schlick (Vienna), and L. Wittgenstein (Cambridge, England). It is interesting to note that recent American publications by P. W. Bridgman, Suzanne [*sic*] K. Langer, and C. I. Lewis exhibit related tendencies.[57]

The reason for this inclusion was Langer's *The Practice of Philosophy*.[58] In his recollection of his time at Harvard, Feigl confirm that Langer's book had been read with interest in Vienna:[59]

> I was tremendously impressed by many things in the United States. New York was the first overwhelming experience. Soon afterwards there were the scholars at Harvard with whom I was fortunate to become acquainted: in short order, P. W. Bridgman, C. I. Lewis, Henry Sheffer, and of course A. N. Whitehead. In addition there was Susanne K. Langer, of German parents, the wife of Harvard historian William Langer. We had already known in Vienna her fine first book, *The Practice of Philosophy*. At her house a small group of scholars met occasionally for an evening's discussion.[60]

Considering Feigl and Blumberg's claim about 'related tendencies' between Langer and themselves, the question arises what he means by that. What similarities are there between *The Practice of Philosophy* and the main principles of logical positivism as outlined by Feigl and Blumberg? To answer this question we need to take a closer look at the article.

Echoing Schlick and Wittgenstein (and also Langer), the authors restate the claim that philosophy is an activity and that the object of philosophy is 'the logical clarification of thought'.[61] The authors follow the Manifesto's rejection of Kant's synthetic *a priori* propositions and claim that all factual statements are *a posteriori*, based on experience only. Likewise, they hold that logical and mathematical propositions which were previously considered to be synthetic are now cast as being purely analytic or, as Wittgenstein called it, 'tautological'.[62] But the way they account for the way factual statements are based on experience shifts attention from the question of empirical verification to the nature and possibility of logical expression as such. Any system of knowledge, they claim, does not mirror 'the experienced qualitative content as such [but] the formal structure or relations of the given'.[63] Similarly, the propositions of empirical science express the formal structure and point to the content of experience. And what 'knowledge communicates is structure; this it does by means of a symbolism or language'.[64] Language, for Feigl and Blumberg, is 'any medium of communicating knowledge, any set of symbols and their syntax or rules of combination'.[65] All language consists of 'a set of symbols which are to be combined in accordance' with a definite logical syntax' so that 'the relations of words in the proposition represent the relations of elements in the fact'.[66] This is only possible on the basis of a structural similarity between the proposition and the fact. As the authors explain,

> This similarity itself can not be expressed in the same language. To express it we should require a different language in which a proposition would express this similarity in virtue of a similarity between it and the similarity. Russell, in his introduction to Wittgenstein's *Tractatus Logico-Philosophicus,* indicates that the difficulty might be met by an unending hierarchy of languages. Wittgenstein takes the position that the similarity is inexpressible. It shows itself.[67]

The isomorphy between the system of the language and the system of facts enables complex, molecular propositions to be analysed into their constituent, simple atomic propositions. While the meaning or sense (*Sinn*) of an atomic proposition is 'the "being-the-case" or the "not-being-the-case" of the fact which it expresses' the meaning (*Bedeutung*) of a complex word or concept is given 'by explicit definition'.[68] The meaning (*Bedeutung*) of a simple word or name, however, can ultimately only be given 'by pointing to what it stands for in experience'.[69] As Feigl and Blumberg put it,

> Knowledge, though it communicates only the form of the given, none the less is based upon the content, for the words in the atomic propositions are definable only concretely through pointing to the content. *Knowledge expresses the form and points to the content.* [my italics][70]

Accordingly, the truth or falsity of propositions is established under certain conditions, that is, by certain ways of pointing. If it is not possible to provide any conditions, the complex proposition has no meaning.

This view of knowledge, I suggest, lends it a certain provisionality and indeterminacy. This is because one cannot ultimately determine what exactly is being pointed at, that is, what aspect or dimension of the observed phenomenon is meant to be expressed – its size, weight, colour, smell, attractiveness, use, danger and so on. The authors agree that all since all acquisition of knowledge is done inductively, based on incidental observations, the validity of a proposition can never be rigorously established.[71] Moreover, the authors explain, following Heisenberg's indeterminacy principle, '[T]he requisite initial conditions [for any observation] can never be completely measurable and our predictions can accordingly never attain complete certainty'.[72] This means that all sciences 'are essentially applications of pure symbol-patterns to the description of facts'.[73] The movement's method, the authors claim, is phenomenalistic but only in a methodological sense and not in terms of any metaphysical statement about ultimate realities.

What these quotes and passages highlight is that logical positivism, as outlined by Feigl and Blumberg, was not primarily concerned with empirical verifiability as such or with scientifically valid philosophical propositions but with the very nature and of description and expression of observed reality. Put differently, logical positivists are less concerned with scientifically valid knowledge or truth than with the possibility of meaningful expression and language as such, less concerned with epistemology than with semantics. Put differently again, they are concerned with one of Langer's central themes, the question of what kinds of 'facts' can be expressed by what kind of symbolism. Langer's main interest throughout her career was the question of meaning and the expression of meaning. Like Schlick, Langer had been significantly influenced by Cassirer's neo-Kantian conception of symbolic forms and this had also informed her reading of Wittgenstein. That meant that she did not read Wittgenstein as an empiricist philosopher of science or atomistic correspondence theorist but as a philosopher of language and symbolic meaning more generally. This picture both of Wittgenstein and logical positivism differs considerably from the one that Kuhn later refers to as the 'everyday image' of logical positivism.[74]

Everyday image of logical positivism

This 'everyday image' of logical positivists – and, by implication, of the early Wittgenstein – as the gatekeepers of meaningful propositions and scientific knowledge, was in part the result of British philosopher A. J. Ayer's book *Language, Truth and Logic* (1935). In the preface to the first edition, Ayer had claimed that his views 'were derive[d] from the doctrines of Bertrand Russell and Wittgenstein, which *are themselves the logical outcome of the empiricism of Berkeley and David Hume* [my italics]'.[75] Moreover, he claimed, he was 'in the closest agreement [with] those who compose the "Viennese circle", under the leadership of Moritz Schlick, and are commonly known as logical positivists' and of those, so he said, he owed most to Rudolf Carnap.[76] While Ayer's book can be seen to be drawing on some of the language used by Carnap in the Circle's Manifesto, its overall gist is much closer to Hume than to Schlick or to Wittgenstein and does not address the more subtle hermeneutical questions raised by them both. As Friedman comments,

> Extracted from the German intellectual tradition constituting their original philosophical context, the positivists now became identified with a rather simpleminded version of radical empiricism. Indeed, this process had already begun in earnest with the publication of A.J. Ayer's (1936) extraordinary influential popularization of the logical positivist movement, *Language, Truth and Logic.*[77]

It was this image of logical positivism as a naïve sense-based empiricism that became the object of Thomas Kuhn's attack on the movement in his *The Structure of Scientific Revolutions* (1962). Commenting on Ayer's representation of the movement Friedman writes,

It is no wonder, then, that logical positivism, so characterized and identified, provoked an extreme, and one might even say violent, reaction, not only within professional philosophy but also within the humanities more generally. It is no wonder, in particular, that Thomas Kuhn's (1962) eloquent protest against naively empiricist conceptions of the growth of science in *The Structure of Scientific Revolutions* found such a welcome resonance within both professional philosophy and the humanities more generally.[78]

Kuhn later acknowledged in an interview that he had merely relied on Ayer and Russell's versions and had not studied the original sources.[79]

[T]he question as to where I got the picture [of logical positivism] that I was rebelling against in *The Structure of Scientific Revolutions* [is] itself a strange and not altogether good story. Not altogether good in the sense that I realize in retrospect that I was reasonably irresponsible. ... I started reading what I took to be philosophy of science – like Bertrand's Russell's *Knowledge of the External World*, and quite a number of other quasi – popular, quasi philosophical works ... I read a little bit of Carnap, but not the Carnap that people later point to as the stuff that has real parallels to me. ... I have confessed a good deal of embarrassment about the fact that I didn't know it. ... And it was against that sort of everyday image of logical positivism – I didn't even think of it as logical empiricism for a while – it was that that I was reacting to when I saw my first examples of history.[80]

As he found out later upon reading Carnap, he was much closer to some logical positivists than he had initially thought. Ironically, Carnap himself had been very sympathetic to Kuhn's views and had even published the first edition of his book in the series he co-edited.[81] Friedman again:

[A]s scholarly investigations of the past fifteen or twenty years into the origins of logical empiricism have increasingly revealed, such a simpleminded radically empiricist picture of this movement is seriously distorted. Our understanding of logical positivism and its intellectual significance must be fundamentally revised when we reinsert the positivists into their original intellectual context, that of the revolutionary scientific developments, together with the equally revolutionary philosophical developments, of their time. As a result, our understanding of the significance of the rise and fall of logical positivism for our own time also must be fundamentally revised.[82]

Symbolic turn

Since Feigl and Blumberg's account of logical positivism echoes many themes in Langer's *The Practice of Philosophy*, it is possible to see why they included Langer as one of the three American philosophers who displayed similar tendencies. As I will discuss in more detail in Chapter 7, Langer's reading of the *Tractatus* highlights Wittgenstein's preoccupation with the nature and limitations of linguistic expression and this can be seen as part of a broader linguistic or, more generally, '*symbolic* turn' in philosophy at the time.[83] For Langer the new generative idea of the epoch – the 'new key' in philosophy – was the discovery that that our sense-data are primarily symbols and that the 'facts' that make up our knowledge of the world are inherently symbolic. One of Langer's major contributions to this debate is her emphasis on the fact that there is always a plurality of symbolic forms to express the world as it is experienced. When we point to something, there are more than one ways to articulate, describe and refer to what we see (or hear or touch) depending on context and need and interest. Even so, there always remains an element of what Quine later would call 'indeterminacy'. Langer's philosophy of symbolic forms as shaped by Cassirer and Whitehead recognizes that the world has many dimensions, each of which requires a different form of symbolization, whether verbal, visual or aural. 'Empirical verification' does not need to imply physical measurability or quantifiability (although it can also imply that). It means, to borrow Whitehead's language, that the organism *feels* something in its environment that can be identified and pointed at with words or sounds or gestures – 'this', 'that', 'here', 'now', 'I'.

For Schlick even the application of existing words to some experience is a form of knowledge. While rejecting Russell's 'knowledge by acquaintance' understood as 'immediate awareness' as a form of knowledge, Schlick nevertheless holds that the act of naming as such provides real knowledge. As he writes,

> In order to give a name to the colour I am seeing I have to go beyond the immediacy of pure intuition, I have to think, be it ever so little. I have to recognise the colour as that particular one I was taught to call 'blue'. This involves an act of comparison, or association; to call a thing by its proper name is an intellectual act – the very simplest act of the intellect, to be sure – and its result is real knowledge in the proper sense in which we use the word. The sentence 'this is blue' expresses real knowledge, not explanatory but factual knowledge.[84]

In summary, Langer and Schlick agree on the following claims about symbolic naming: first, it goes beyond the immediacy of pure intuition; second, it is a mental act involving an awareness of difference and sameness; third, it presupposes a relatively stable and recurrent moment of consciousness for the application of an existing symbol to an experience; and fourth, whether lingual or non-lingual, it expresses real knowledge. To conclude, Langer had much in common with the original founders of the Vienna Circle and had a very similar reading of the philosopher who influenced them significantly, the early Wittgenstein.

Americans in Europe

In addition to European philosophers visiting America, the traffic also went the other way. Many students benefitting from Frederick Sheldon Traveling Fellowships went to Europe for a year to study with leading philosophers on the other side of the Atlantic. In 1932, Whitehead's doctoral student W. V. O. Quine used his Sheldon Fellowship to study with A. J. Ayer, Kurt Gödel, Alfred Tarski, and Rudolf Carnap. Quine felt attracted to the scientifically minded European logicians and mathematicians as an antidote to what he experienced as the lingering speculative metaphysics at Harvard's philosophy department. While recognizing Whitehead's formidable intellect, he had been disappointed by the fact that he was no longer working on the kind of questions as addressed in his earlier *Principia Mathematica*:

> Whitehead lectured on Science and the Modern World and on Cosmologies Ancient and Modern. I responded little, even after accustoming myself to his accent. ... For a term paper I took refuge in his relatively mathematical material on 'extensive abstraction'. But I retained a vivid sense of being in the presence of the great.[85]

Reflecting on this period in his biography over fifty years later, Quine wrote,

> American philosophers associated Harvard with logic because of Whitehead, Sheffer, Lewis and the shades of Peirce and Royce. Really the action was in Europe. In 1930 and 1931 Gödel's first papers and Herbrand's were just appearing, but there were already other notables to reckon with ... Their work had reached few Americans. ... America's logical awakening was still to come, beginning with Alonzo Church's graduate course in the Princeton mathematics department in the fall of 1931. I was unaware of these lacks. The logic that was offered ran thinner than I had hoped, but I supposed that *Principia* was still substantially the last word.[86]

During his time in Europe, Quine had tried unsuccessfully to organize a meeting with Wittgenstein or, as he referred to it ironically in a letter to his parents, to seek 'an audience with the great prophet', but did receive an invitation from Carnap to stay with him and his wife in Prague.[87] Since Quine deeply admired Carnap's rigorously scientific approach to philosophy, this was a very important visit. Following an intense six-week period of study, Quine returned to Harvard as Carnap's most 'ardent disciple' and most tireless advocate.[88]

In 1936 Columbia University's philosopher Ernest Nagel spent a year in Europe to study what he since referred to as the new movement of 'Analytic Philosophy'. He reports that he had not been allowed to attend Wittgenstein's lectures and that he feels therefore hesitant to comment on his views. As he writes,

> For various reasons Wittgenstein refuses to publish; and even among his students of years' standing there is considerable doubt as to what his beliefs are on crucial issues. My information about Wittgenstein's views depends upon certain notes on his lectures which are in circulation and upon conversations with students and disciples both at Cambridge and Vienna. Mystery and a queerly warped personality lend charm to many a philosophy which otherwise is not very significant.[89]

Despite Nagel suspending judgement on Wittgenstein and retaining an open mind as to his importance – 'in spite of the esoteric atmosphere which surrounds Wittgenstein, I think his views are both interesting and important' – he nevertheless seems to think they are not worth further pursuing. Seemingly ignorant of Langer's 1930 *The Practice of Philosophy* with its clear exposition and account of the importance of Wittgenstein for current philosophy and symbolic logic, Nagel considers the early Wittgenstein obsolete and redundant:

> [A]part from the fact that much of its content is unintelligible to anyone who hasn't had it illuminated by Wittgenstein or his followers, today it represents an *überwundener Standpunkt.* Aside from a few technical matters and the general view that philosophy is an activity rather than a set of theses, I understand he disowns it completely.[90]

'Analytic' philosophy

The title of Nagel's two-part article that records his European experiences, 'Impressions and Appraisals of Analytic Philosophy in Europe', contains one of the earliest uses of the term 'analytic philosophy' before it became current in the 1950s.[91] In the article Nagel specifically refers to the philosophy as he saw it practised in Cambridge under Russell, Moore and Wittgenstein, and in Vienna, Prague, Warsaw and Lwów. Contrasting this philosophy with the philosophical systems built in the traditional grand manner, he describes the main features of the 'analytic philosophy' he encountered as follows. The first is a focus on clarification of the meaning and implications of the knowledge acquired by the special sciences, rather than an attempt to add to it. The second is a concern with method rather than outcome, that is, philosophy conceived as an exercise in clear thinking rather than as body of fixed ideas. Nagel writes that was particularly shocked by the ease with which some philosophers were content to recant previously held positions and published views. The third is a lack of interest in the history of philosophy which is considered to be full of pseudo-questions. The fourth is adherence to some form of common-sense naturalism.

Although Nagel's criteria still capture what we would now broadly consider 'analytic philosophy', key 'analytic' players at the time did not necessarily self-identify as such or identify with others so referred to. Russell, for one, did not refer to himself as an analytic philosopher and wrote in 1940, '[A]s regards method, [he is] more in sympathy with logical positivists than any other existing school.'[92] Interestingly, as Greg Frost-Arnold points out, Langer had coined the term 'analytic' as a type of philosophy even before Nagel. She wrote in her 1930 *The Practice of Philosophy:*

> There is … one type of philosophy based upon a rule of procedure and defining itself thereby – that is the so-called 'logical' or 'analytic' type. It is sometimes called by the misleading name, 'scientific philosophy'.[93]

Langer applies a very different criterion for inclusion than Nagel. For her, the key feature of analytic philosophy is that it never 'applies directly to reality' but to 'the logical expression of it'.[94] This is also the key to understanding her conception of philosophy as 'the pursuit of meaning'. Accordingly, Langer's list of philosophers who fit this description is broader than Nagel's and includes those who would now be considered phenomenologists and pragmatists:

> The methodological broodings of Meinong and Husserl, Dewey and Schiller, Peirce, Russell, and Broad, the formulations of the 'critical' philosophy, have all cleared the way for our recognition of a guiding principle that will define our field, dictate our procedure (of which the analytic method is a perfectly assignable, integral part), and give to philosophy a working basis as well as an ultimate aim: this principle is the pursuit of meaning.[95]

The conception of 'analytic philosophy' as 'the pursuit of meaning' also applies to Langer's own philosophy as the study of the symbolic forms that make up our 'facts' and 'sense-data'. It was this idea that she recognized in the early writings of Wittgenstein and other associates of the Vienna Circle as well as in Cassirer, Sheffer and Whitehead. For all of them, as she had put it in *Philosophy in a New Key*, '[T]he problem of observation is all but eclipsed by the problem of *meaning*'.[96] Although the philosophers in her list may not be considered 'analytic philosophers' in the strict sense, they nevertheless 'cleared the way' for a central preoccupation of what was to become mainstream analytic philosophy: the analysis of the meaning of lingual expression. As Frost-Arnold puts it,

> While her [Langer's] extensional characterization of analytic philosophy (the list of progenitors) does not match our modern extension of 'analytic philosophy circa 1930', her intensional characterization, viz. the 'pursuit of meaning', does foreshadow later justifications for grouping the disparate factions from Moore to Carnap together. ... In picking out the particular paradigmatic (precursors to) analytic philosophy, Langer does not pre-date Nagel. However, her principle for grouping the various philosophers together, which became the standard mid-century, does predate Nagel.[97]

In a special issue of the *Journal for the History of Analytical Philosophy* devoted to women in early analytic philosophy, Langer is one of three women featured alongside British Susan Stebbing (1895–1943) and Polish Maria Kokoszyńska (1905–1981), a member of the influential Lwów-Warsaw school of philosophy.[98] In her article on Langer, Giulia Felappi points out Langer's emphasis on the relevance of logic for other parts of philosophy, including epistemology and metaphysics and her notion of fact as a formulated event.[99] She also draws attention to Langer's early understanding of the relativity of language. Interestingly, the editors claim that the main reason for them to include the 'Harvard School' within analytic philosophy was 'Langer's linguistic variant of Kantianism'.[100]

Pragmatism and logical positivism

In America, philosophers trained in the pragmatist tradition of Dewey and James felt attracted to the new movement of logical positivism not primarily because of its concern with symbolism and the pursuit of meaning but because of its perceived scientific approach to philosophy, its rejection of metaphysics and its concern for philosophy's social impact, especially in the field of education. Chicago semiotician Charles Morris coined a new name for this symbiosis of the two traditions: 'scientific empiricism'.[101] As Morris had been somewhat isolated at Chicago as a scientifically minded empiricist among mainly historians of philosophy and neo-Thomists, he was keen to foster closer links with European logical positivists. With the help of Quine at Harvard, he was able to secure a position for Carnap at his university in 1936 where he was to stay until 1952.[102] Reflecting on the situation of American philosophy on his arrival Carnap writes,

> The contrast to the situation of philosophy in Central Europe, in particular in Germany, was remarkable and for me very heartening. Modern logic, almost unknown among philosophers in Germany, was here regarded by many as an important field of philosophy and was taught at some of the leading universities. The Association for Symbolic Logic and its Journal were founded in 1936. During the past twenty years, while I could observe the development, the recognition of modern logic became more and more widespread. The possibility of its application for the clarification of philosophical problems is by now widely recognized at least in principle, and the majority of philosophers understand at least the elementary parts of symbolic logic.[103]

Carnap goes on to compare the traditional European schools of philosophy – old style Hegelianism, Kantianism and Phenomenology – in Europe with the new 'analytic philosophy' in America. Since Carnap's recollection provide an interesting perspective on the cross-Atlantic context of philosophy in Langer's time, I will quote him at some length:

> In 1936, when I came to this country, the traditional schools of philosophy did not have nearly the same influence as on the European continent. The movement of German idealism, in particular Hegelianism, which had earlier been quite influential in the United States, had by then almost completely disappeared. Neo-Kantian philosophical conceptions were represented here and there, not in an orthodox form but rather influenced by recent developments of scientific thinking, much like the conceptions of Cassirer in Germany. Phenomenology had a number of adherents mostly in a liberalized form, not in Husserl's orthodox form, and even less in Heidegger's version.
>
> Most influential were those philosophical movements which had an empiricist tendency in a wide sense. Pragmatic ways of thinking, mostly in the version derived from John Dewey, were widely represented both among philosophers and in the movement of progressive education, which had won great influence on the methods practically applied in public schools. Many philosophers called themselves realists; their conception came from the movements of Critical Realism and of NeoRealism, which had arisen in the beginning of this century as a reaction against the formerly strong idealism, and which therefore also had an

empiricist tendency. Most of the followers of the movements mentioned rejected metaphysics and emphasized the importance of scientific ways of thinking for the solution of all theoretical problems. In the last twenty years, the ideas of analytic philosophy gained more and more acceptance, partly through the influence of logical empiricism, and also through that of the British movement stemming from G. E. Moore and Wittgenstein.

Thus I found in this country a philosophical atmosphere which, in striking contrast to that in Germany, was very congenial to me.[104]

Refugee philosophers

With growing numbers of European scholars being forced to flee their countries after Hitler's rise to power in 1933, the early exchanges between European and American philosophers were to prove very important. It meant that there was an already well-established international network in the United States that was able to facilitate the integration of these refugee scholars into the American academy.[105] In addition to helping Carnap get a position in Chicago, Morris played an important role in helping other European philosophers to find academic positions at American universities.[106]

Since their first gathering in 1935, the International Congresses for the Unity of Science had been the main meeting point for European and American philosophers.[107] After 1933 this became an even more important gathering place for the many philosophers in exile, including those connected to the Vienna Circle. In 1939 Harvard hosted the Movement's Fifth Congress, which was essentially, as Quine later observed, 'the Vienna Circle, with accretions, in international exile'.[108] Both Langer and Quine served as members of the organizing committee of the Congress, with Quine serving as secretary for the Harvard Committee on Arrangements. Both he and Langer presented papers. The mood is captured by Friedrich Stadler when he writes,

> The *Fifth International Congress for the Unity of Science* took place at Harvard University from September 3 to September 9, 1939 in Cambridge, Massachusetts. It marked the end of the scientific community's great forum dedicated to promoting the *Encyclopedia of Unified Science*, with some two hundred participants and 60 speakers. In spite of the outbreak of World War II, Otto Neurath's International Institute for the Unity of Science had been able to organize the congress with the support of the *American Association for the Advancement of Science*, the *American Philosophical Association*, the *Philosophy and Science Association*, the *History of Science Society* and the *Association for Symbolic Logic*. The congress was opened by James B. Conant, the then president of Harvard University, P. W. Bridgman, Otto Neurath and Charles Morris. Due to the escalation of the war, the abstracts and contributions submitted at the beginning of the conference could not be published, as originally planned, in the ninth volume of *Erkenntnis/Journal of Unified Science*. Only ten of these, already published separately, were included in the reprint of the journal *Erkenntnis*. The remaining preprints mostly languished in Otto Neurath's papers.[109]

Since the opening of the Congress coincided with Britain's declaration of war on Germany on 3 September following Hitler's invasion of Poland two days earlier, several European conference attendees, including Polish philosopher Alfred Tarski, were unable to return to their home countries.[110]

Philosophy in Europe after the war

In Europe, in the meantime, the Vienna Circle and logical positivism had basically disintegrated. The Nazis had banned the meetings of the Ernst Mach Society because of its perceived sympathies with the Social Democrats.[111] Feigl had fled to the United States in 1931 and Hans Hahn had died in 1934. In 1936 Schlick was murdered by a deranged student and Otto Neurath had sought refuge in the Netherlands, even though still active in organizing the movement's international congresses.

When the war had ended, neither logical positivism nor neo-Kantianism played a role of any significance anymore in Europe. German Jewish neo-Kantian philosopher Ernst Cassirer had been forced to flee his country in 1933, ending up, via England and Sweden, in America where he died just before the ending of the war. By that time his books had been banned and burned in Germany and he had left a stack of unpublished papers behind in Sweden. In Germany, at the same time, Heidegger, who had been appointed rector of the University of Freiburg in 1933, was quick to become the new rising star in German philosophy.

Most of the key players of what became known as the Frankfurt School of Critical Theory – Max Horkheimer, Theodor Adorno, Herbert Marcuse, Walter Benjamin and Erich Fromm – had been forced into exile by 1933. Horkheimer had become director of the Institute for Social Research in 1930 and had moved the Institute to Columbia University in 1935. Many members of the school were to write their most seminal articles and books during this period of exile in America. The Institute reopened under Horkheimer in Frankfurt in 1950, followed by the directorship of Adorno from 1958 until his death in 1969. Their student Jürgen Habermas directed the Institute between 1971 and 1983. The school was very influential in Germany after the Second World War. Even so, most philosophical attention in post-war Europe had shifted to France as the centre of the new 'continental' philosophy of existentialism, phenomenology, structuralism and post-structuralism.

Logical empiricism and the Cold War

Since the early 1940s, a new generation of American students was being taught by European philosophers previously associated with the Vienna Circle. The new philosophy's rigorous scientific method with its strict ban on all metaphysical language proved to be an attractive field of research in contrast to the diffuse range of topics that had previously been studied under the name of philosophy. The new philosophy established itself on new terms as a rigorous professional academic discipline with its own clearly defined methods, standards, journals and career paths. Whereas logical positivism in Europe had consisted of a broad-based community of scientists, scholars and artists motivated by shared social and political ideals, in America it became an increasingly specialized class of professional academics, whose philosophical interests became increasingly technical and specialized.

The increasingly apolitical and ahistorical characters of the new philosophy in America was supported by the post-war political climate.[112] Under McCarthy's campaign against communism, all left-leaning intellectuals were treated with considerable suspicion. Because of their political background in Germany, Carnap and several other members of the Vienna Circle were being kept under constant FBI surveillance.[113] Open criticism of the establishment was disapproved of and many universities required faculty members to sign patriotic loyalty oaths.[114] As a result, not only became American university campuses, including Harvard, increasingly depoliticized, so did the curriculum and research. This also applied to logical positivism as it developed in America. As Georg Reisch comments,

> The more we learn about early logical empiricism – its basic values, goals, methods, and the sense of historical mission shared by some of its practitioners – the more foreign and distant it seems when compared with contemporary philosophy of science. ... Knowing as we do now that logical empiricism was originally a philosophical project with cultural and social ambitions, the time is ripe to inquire how the discipline was transformed and how these cultural and social ambitions were lost. The answer defended here is that it was transformed during the 1950s at least partly, if not mainly, by political pressures that were common ... during the Cold War following World War II.[115]

More pointedly, Reisch argues, the whole Unity of Science Movement died because

> its method, values and goals were broadly sympathetic to socialism at a time when the US and its colleges and universities were being scrubbed clean of red or pink elements. The apolitical logical empiricism of the 1950s ... was a new-born child of the cold war.[116]

Langer's place and journey

The years following the 1939 Congress had marked the rapid rise of the new philosophy of science and analytic philosophy in the United States. Harvard became again an important centre for philosophy attracting many prominent visiting scholars including Russell whose 1940 William James Lectures were also attended by Langer.[117] Carnap (and his research associate Carl Hempel) came to Harvard from Chicago on a year-long exchange with Sheffer and formed a weekly discussion group with Quine and Tarski in the academic year 1940–1.[118]

Until the year of the Congress, Langer had been close to many of the new philosophical developments in Europe and America. She was one of the earliest American philosophers to critically engage with Russell and Whitehead's *Principia*

Mathematica and to have her critiques published in the major professional journals. She was also one of the earliest American philosophers to recognize the importance of Frege and the early Wittgenstein. In 1936 she was a co-founder of the Association for Symbolic Logic. In 1937 she wrote one of the earliest textbooks on the new logic, *An Introduction to Symbolic Logic.* In 1939 she was on the planning committee of the seminal International Congress that became the launch pad of the new 'Anglo-American' or 'analytic' philosophy. Because of these various roles and involvements Langer can be said to have played an important role in the birth of analytic philosophy in America. Yet, by the time this new philosophy was beginning to take off in the 1940s and 1950s, she was no longer part of this professional network and had moved on to other philosophical interests as reflected in *Philosophy in a New Key.* After its publication – and her divorce from William – in 1942, she resigned from her teaching at Radcliffe, moved back to New York and began to work seriously on her philosophy of art and aesthetics culminating in *Feeling and Form* and *Problems of Art.* As we will see in Chapter 4, for Langer, as for Sheffer, symbolic logic was never meant to be an end in itself. Like her mentor Sheffer, Langer was primarily interested in the study of logical *meaning* as such rather than the technical refinement of its apparatus, its notational economy. Like Sheffer, and as Royce before him, she conceived of logic as a study of patterns and forms in all realms of life, whether objects, events or processes. So, while professional philosophy was turning increasingly inwards and pre-occupied with piecemeal, detailed analysis of logical problems, Langer began to direct her attention outwards, examining symbolic forms *outside* the realm of symbolic logic.

Against the grain

One of the central themes of *Philosophy in a New Key* was the role of symbolism in the realm of science. Drawing on Cassirer and on Whitehead, Langer rejected any science-based positivist philosophy with a naïve faith in sense-evidence.[119] As she wrote,

> The only philosophy that rose directly out of a contemplation of science is positivism, and it is probably the least interesting of all doctrines, an appeal to common-sense against the difficulties of establishing metaphysical or logical 'first principles'.
>
> Genuine empiricism is above all a reflection on the validity of sense-knowledge, a speculation on the ways our concepts and beliefs are built up out of the fleeting and disconnected reports our eyes and ears actually make to the mind. Positivism, the scientists' metaphysic, entertains no such doubts and raises no epistemological problems; its belief in the veracity of sense is implicit and dogmatic. ... Knowledge from sensory experience was deemed the only knowledge that carried any affidavit of truth; for truth became identified, for all vigorous modern minds, with empirical fact. And so, a scientific culture succeeded to the exhausted philosophical vision. An undisputed and uncritical empiricism – not skeptical, but positivistic – became its official metaphysical creed, experiment its avowed method, a vast hoard of 'data' its capital, and correct prediction of future occurrences its proof.[120]

Langer exposed the empiricists' and positivists' internal contradictions. She pointed out that the phenomena that science studied were not 'sense-data' in the sense of sensed objects but 'readings' on instruments. Highlighting the scientists' unquestioning reliance on mathematics she writes,

> Few mathematicians have really held that numbers were discovered by observation, or even that geometrical relationships are known to us by inductive reasoning from many observed instances. Physicists may think of certain facts in place of constants and variables, but the same constants and variables will serve somewhere else to calculate other facts, and the mathematicians themselves give no set of data their preference. They deal only with items whose sensory qualities are quite irrelevant: their 'data' are arbitrary sounds or marks called *symbols*.[121]

Philosophy in a New Key challenged the major paradox in the philosophy of her time. Her subsequent books on the arts and the mind, in particular *Feeling and Form* and *Mind: A Concept of Human Feeling*, developed these ideas in new directions.

Despite the successes of her books and her growing public reputation, Langer's critique of positivism was largely ignored by the philosophical profession. It was not until two decades later, when Thomas Kuhn launched his attack on positivist philosophy of science in *The Structure of Scientific Revolutions* (1962), that there was a widespread and enthusiastic reception of this kind of critique. Anthropologist Clifford Geertz explains this by observing that, unlike Langer's books, Kuhn's book was 'the right text at the right time':

> Why has *Structure* had such an enormous impact? Why has everyone, from particle physicists and philosophers to sociologists, historians, literary critics, and political theorists, not to speak of publicists, popularizers, and counterculture know-nothings, found in it something either to turn excitedly toward their own ends or to react, equally excitedly, against? It can't just be that the book is bold, innovative, incisive, and marvellously well written. It is all that, and in addition scholarly and deeply felt. But there are other books, within the history of science and outside of it, with such virtues. Excellence and significance, however real, assure neither fame nor consequence. How many people, after all, have attended to Suzanne Langer's *Feeling and Form*? In some mysterious and uncertain way, mysterious and uncertain even to Kuhn, who never ceased to be amazed, puzzled, and seriously troubled about his book's reception, *Structure* was the right text at the right time.[122]

One cannot fail to wonder whether, had Langer been part of the male academic establishment of her time, her ideas might have been taken up earlier.[123] As I discuss in the next chapter, Langer developed her ideas in a time of widespread prejudice against women philosophers. This contributed to her ambiguous status: on the one hand the first female professional philosopher in America, on the other, institutionally homeless and marginalized; on the one hand publicly well-known and admired, on the other, professionally ignored and undervalued.

3

Philosophy and women

Illogical creatures

When Harvard University Press asked philosopher William E. Hocking to review Langer's manuscript for *Philosophy in a New Key*, he wrote back enthusiastically to the editor: 'I am prejudiced against books on philosophy by women; according to this prejudice no woman could write as good a book as she has written.'[1] Although Hocking naturally meant his reply as a compliment and endorsement, his frank admission of his prejudice against women philosophers is indicative of an academic climate in which women were routinely dismissed and excluded. This is confirmed by Arthur Danto. As he writes in his recollections from his time as a philosophy student at Columbia University,

> I studied with Suzanne [*sic*] Langer, the author of *Philosophy in a New Key*. … She was attractive and European, and entered the classroom with a cello. I wrote a paper on Kant's *Third Critique* for her, which she liked a great deal. But the department was not especially supportive of her, since she was a woman. Male professors of no great distinction said that women were just not able to do philosophy.[2]

Langer once commented that 'to be taken seriously by other philosophers during my early years, I had to be at least twice as "logical" as they were. After all, women were usually dismissed as being flighty, illogical creatures.'[3]

Although the mid- to late nineteenth century saw the foundation of several women colleges in America, Ivy League institutions such as Harvard University did not accept women in its degree courses.[4] Indeed, Harvard was one of the last universities to do so and did not become fully co-educational until the late 1970s. Women who wanted to study at Harvard or with Harvard professors enrolled instead at Harvard's neighbouring coordinate institution, Radcliffe College, informally referred to as 'The Harvard Annex'. Harvard professors would repeat the same lectures they had given to Harvard's male students to Radcliffe's female students. Despite receiving identical tuition and passing identical exams to their male counterparts, Radcliffe students were not awarded Harvard degrees.

In 2007, a former dean of Radcliffe College, historian Drew Gilpin Faust, was appointed as the 28th president of Harvard University, its first female president. Gilpin Faust spearheaded a new body of research into the foundation of Radcliffe College and its fraught relation with Harvard.[5] This has provided invaluable insights into the challenges faced by women in Langer's time, and the career disadvantages for those working in then male dominated disciplines such as logic and philosophy. Since Langer's connection with Radcliffe College spanned almost twenty-six years, and since this has been an important factor in her overall career trajectory, I will provide some background history to its foundation.

Radcliffe College

Radcliffe College's roots go back to the Woman's Education Association (WEA), founded in 1872 by a group of Cambridge and Boston women for the main purpose of securing equal access to Harvard College for women as existed for men.[6] Although, prior to 1872, there had been some informal ad hoc arrangements for women to attend selected Harvard lectures, women were not allowed to enrol in degree courses or awarded any degrees. Whereas several other American colleges in the late nineteenth century had gradually started to accept women students, Harvard continued to resist co-education. Charles W. Eliot, Harvard's president from 1869 to 1909, had ruled out accepting women not, so he claimed, on principle but for logistical reasons. As he put it in his inaugural address, '[I]t was not a judgment on the innate capacities of women – only after generations of civil freedom and social equality [would it be possible] to obtain the data necessary for an adequate discussion of woman's natural tendencies, tastes, and capabilities – but as matter of practicality, i.e. the difficult and exceedingly burdensome task [of] necessary police regulations.'[7] Some faculty supported this decision on grounds of Harvard's esteemed tradition and reputation, as they put it, as 'a traditional school of manly character'.[8] As one English professor wrote in Harvard's monthly magazine in 1899, 'Amid all the changes which have occurred since the college was founded in 1636, there has never before been a deviation from the principle that the influences amid which education should be obtained here must remain purely virile.'[9]

Historian Helen Lefkowitz Horowitz writes, 'Harvard as represented by its President and Corporation stood adamantly against bringing women into the university in all roles other than as donors, helpmeets, clerical and library assistants, and servants.'[10] Or, as historian Bruce Kuklick, in his book on Harvard's history, puts it succinctly: 'Harvard was never kind to women.'[11]

The WEA's efforts to secure equal access for women to Harvard proved to be a long journey with endless negotiations and compromises. In order to prepare for the transition, it acquired a building less than half a mile from Harvard College and began to offer classes to female students on the basis of individual contracts with Harvard's instructors. They were required to repeat the same lectures they had given to Harvard's male students to Radcliffe's female students. Starting as a programme of 'Private Collegiate Instruction for Women', it was eventually chartered by the Massachusetts legislature in 1894, allowing the foundation to adopt the name Radcliffe College and to grant its own degrees. While continuing to reject any formal association with Radcliffe College, Harvard nevertheless agreed to take full overall responsibility for the academic supervision of its degrees. Harvard College's president Eliot, in turn, had made use of this arrangement by advertising the teaching opportunities at Radcliffe as extra 'perks' for additional income. This offer had also been made to Whitehead upon his arrival and had been happily accepted.[12]

By the early 1890s, over two hundred Radcliffe women were being taught by seventy male faculty.[13] Although it was widely acknowledged that the standards of admission, instruction and examination at Radcliffe were identical with, if not superior to, those of Harvard, women students were not granted Harvard degrees but Radcliffe degrees countersigned by Harvard's president.[14] Between 1902 and 1930 ten women, including Langer, received degrees in philosophy from Radcliffe College yet none of them appear in the Harvard Archives.[15] With the exception of Langer, most women stopped teaching upon marriage. None of them had a tenured university position. In 1894 the philosopher and psychologist Mary Calkins, who had been a student of William James, Josiah Royce and Hugo Münsterberg, had caused a minor scandal by demanding a degree from Harvard for completing all the degree requirements. Despite Münsterberg's letter to Eliot in which he described Calkins as his 'best pupil', the president had replied that they were 'not prepared to give any Harvard degree to any woman no matter how exceptional the circumstances may be'.[16] As Sally Schwager points out, 'Eliot refused to support *any* plan by which women would earn a Harvard degree because, as he explained, "it would be as much to say that I thought the Harvard course as suitable for young women as for young men – which I do not."'[17]

In the year after Langer left Radcliffe in 1942, Radcliffe undergraduates had, under strict individually approved circumstances, been allowed access to selected courses at Harvard. Even so, by an agreement between the two institutions this number was to stay very limited. By the late 1950s, Harvard accepted a higher percentage of applicants than did Radcliffe. As Drew Gilpin Faust points out,

> This meant that it was in fact much more difficult to get into Radcliffe than into Harvard. In the late 1950s, Harvard was accepting more than 40 percent of its applicants, while Radcliffe took only 18 percent. The deans' lists reflected this differential, with the proportion of Radcliffe students qualifying in the early years of the 1960s nearly half again as large as the proportion of Harvard undergraduates.[18]

In 1963 Harvard agreed to award its degrees to Radcliffe students but still on the condition that, in order to distinguish them from 'proper' Harvard degrees, they were countersigned by Radcliffe College. In the same year women were admitted to the Graduate School of Arts and Sciences.[19] In 1975, that is, well over a hundred years after its foundation, the original aims of the WEA were finally achieved: a merger between the two separate admissions offices of Harvard and Radcliffe. However, it was not until 1999 that the two governing bodies of Harvard and Radcliffe completed the merger of the two institutions and Radcliffe women were able to receive a Harvard degree that was identical to men, that is, without the obligatory signature of the president of Radcliffe.[20]

In 1926 Langer was one of the first doctoral students to complete a dissertation under Whitehead after his arrival at Harvard in 1924. Since the degree was from Radcliffe and not from Harvard it was never registered in the university's archives and has gone largely unnoticed. Paul Weiss, for example, who completed his doctoral studies under Whitehead in 1929, believed that he might 'have been the first, and certainly one of the very few, who wrote their dissertations with [Whitehead]'.[21]

As historian Nancy Weiss Malkiel points out, the eventual acceptance of women at Harvard and other top-ranking universities was often not motived by reasons of gender equality but by self-interest. As she explains in *'Keep the Damned Women Out': Struggling towards Co-education*, the primary drive to co-education in the early 70s for many elite institutions was the need to maintain a first-rate applicant pool.

In Langer's time, Radcliffe women were seriously disadvantaged compared to male students at Harvard. They did not have the same rights and privileges. Their housing was inferior; they had no access to college dining rooms; they were banned from certain parts of the university premises, such as common rooms and libraries – it was only in 1967 that Harvard's Lamont Library was opened to women; they were not part of the collegiate culture that facilitated informal conversations and networking with professors and fellow-students leading to introductions and letters of recommendations to further their careers; they were ineligible for travel grants, junior fellowships and other awards and privileges; they were excluded from decision making roles in academic administration. In short, they were excluded from the academic establishment as a whole with its culture of entitlement and prestige.

Not all Harvard faculty objected to access for women. Langer's supervisor Whitehead, for one, strongly supported equal status for women. While still in Cambridge, UK, Whitehead had been actively involved in campaigning for equal status for women at Cambridge University. In 1907 he even served as the chairman of the Cambridge branch of the Men's League for Women's Suffrage.[22] While teaching at Trinity College he also taught at Girton College, Cambridge's first residential college for women. As with Radcliffe College and Harvard, Girton College's relationship to Cambridge University had been tenuous and fractious since its foundation in 1869. The process of allowing women access to university courses and degrees had been slow and piecemeal, depending to a large extent on the goodwill and discretion of liberal lecturers such as Whitehead. The question of equal access had become a source of bitter controversy. In the year 1897, everyone holding a Cambridge degree – that is, only men – was entitled to vote on a proposal in favour of awarding women university degrees. The day had turned into a near riot and the vote was overwhelmingly defeated. Whitehead recalls the day in his memoirs:

> [D]uring my later years at Cambridge, there was considerable political and academic controversy in which I participated. The great question of the emancipation of women suddenly flared up, after simmering for half a century. I was a member of the University Syndicate which reported in favour of equality

of status in the University. We were defeated, after stormy discussions and riotous behaviour on the part of students.[23]

It was not until fifty years later, in 1948, that Cambridge University officially granted Girton and other women colleges full university status and women students the same degrees as men.[24] There is some irony in the fact that the women's college Whitehead was going to teach at in Cambridge, America, would have to wait even longer, that is, until 1975, to receive its full university status and degrees from Harvard.

Although prior to 1948, Oxford and Cambridge did not allow women, many other universities in Europe were already co-educational. Moreover, the Vienna Circle included several women, such as Olga Hahn-Neurath, Rose Rand and Charlotte Bühler. Scholars like Schlick, Feigl and Carnap were less concerned with the professional status than with the intellectual merit and scholarly quality of their colleagues and interlocutors. Being interested in Langer's work, they were quite likely oblivious of the complex relationship between Harvard and Radcliffe. Indeed, when Carnap applied (unsuccessfully) to the Rockefeller Foundation for a leave of research at Harvard in 1933, he mentioned Langer as one of the philosophers he would have hoped to work with at 'Harvard'.[25] He may well have been surprised to find out that not only did she not teach at the revered institution but that she had not even been allowed to study there. The difference between Harvard and Vienna's attitude to women can also be illustrated by the reception of Langer's first book, *The Practice of Philosophy*. While positively praised by members of the Vienna Circle, it was largely ignored in America. One of the few American philosophers who reviewed it was Charles Baylis. While his review was primarily positive – he wrote, for example, that 'as a cogent argument for the importance of the study of forms and consequently for the vale of mathematical logic, Mrs. Langer's is an excellent book' – his main complaint, oddly, was that the book was 'too difficult for a beginner'.[26] Indeed, apart from a reference in Whitehead's preface to the book as 'an introduction', there is no reason to assume that a book that is being reviewed in the *Journal of Philosophy* would have been written 'for a beginner'.

Invisible

In order to illustrate the disadvantages experienced by Langer in America, a comparison of the career paths of her and W. V. Quine may be instructive. Quine arrived at Harvard for graduate studies in 1930, that is, four years after Langer graduated. Like Langer, Quine was supervised by Whitehead and took classes with Sheffer. Like Langer, he did a doctoral thesis on Whitehead and Russell's *Principia Mathematica*. Upon his graduation in 1932, Quine was offered a four-year appointment as a Harvard Junior Fellow with no teaching commitments. He was also offered a Sheldon Traveling Fellowship enabling him to spend a year in Europe where he was able to meet, among others, Feigl, Tarski and Carnap. In 1936, at age 28, he was appointed to the Harvard Faculty where he stayed until his retirement in 1978. By contrast, despite her BA thesis being praised by Sheffer as having 'a firmer grasp of philosophy problems than many a Harvard Ph.D., and despite having had several articles and two books published by 1936, Langer remained an hourly paid sessional tutor at Radcliffe.[27]

Langer's writings were largely ignored. Quine even spurned her introductory text book *An Introduction to Symbolic Logic*. In 1937 he teaches a basic course in logic but finds it difficult to find a suitable introductory text book. As he writes in his biography,

> I ... gave a basic logic course, required for concentrators in philosophy. No text was available along modern lines. I coped with Eaton's pedestrian *General Logic: An Introductory Survey* [Charles Scriber's Sons, 1931] and Jevon's nineteenth-century *Elementary Lessons in Logic,* [Macmillan and co, 1893] and filled in.[28]

In 1940 he still experiences difficulties in finding a textbook:

> That fall my introductory course in logic resumed, and with it the textbook problem. ... John Cooley was my teaching assistant, and we got by that fall with some mimeograms of his that were to develop two years later into a text of his own.[29]

Quine must have known of Langer's book – and Langer's existence – because their paths would have crossed in a variety of ways. Since 1936, he was one of eight consulting editors with her for the *Journal of Symbolic Logic* and, from 1938, the vice president of the Association for Symbolic Logic which Langer had co-founded in 1936.[30] In 1939 he was, alongside Langer, on the organizing committee of the Congress of the Unity of Science.[31] And he was a colleague of hers at Radcliffe College, a position he referred to as follows in his autobiography:

> In those days undergraduate courses had to be repeated at Radcliffe. It meant preparing additional material, because the girls did not take up time with questions and discussion as Harvard boys did.[32]

Yet, despite his recurring frustrations about the dearth of logic textbooks, he had not bothered to check out Langer's book, as can be gleaned from a letter from him to Carnap in 1938: 'I still have not looked at Mrs. Langer's book; had not been anxious to, for [John J.] Cooley had been impatient with it. Said there was too much metaphorical talk about logic; too little logic.'[33] One wonders whether he was simply too proud – or too embarrassed – to use a logic textbook written by a woman who was teaching at Harvard's 'annex'.[34] Or it may have been a reflection on Quine's own lack of interest in the philosophical dimensions of logic at the time – 'too much metaphorical talk about logic; too little logic'.[35] Quine later admitted that he had not really been interested in the 'speculative' and 'conjectural' nature of philosophy at the beginning of his career:

> My course in the fall of 1937 included one on logical positivism, primarily on Carnap. ... [T]he new course was less satisfying and harder to prepare than the ones in logic that had gone before. The teaching of logic is primarily expository, with an occasional touch of the inspirational. The research that precedes it has

yielded something precise and subtle to explain and something elegant, perhaps, to glory in. The other kind of teaching is shakily speculative. The mood oscillates between the defensive and the conjectural. Exposition on the teacher's part, and effort to grasp on the student's part, cease to be pure and single-minded. I hoped that in time I would take as much satisfaction in characteristically philosophical courses as in logical ones, but this did not come about in forty years.[36]

In the meantime, Langer's book on logic was highly praised by, among others, Herbert Feigl and British logician Susanne Stebbing.[37] It is still in print and used today. It was, as Langer had made clear in her introduction, written both as 'a textbook of symbolic logic and an essay on that logic'.[38] Instead of it being merely an overview of logical systems, the book was to discuss the two main strands of logic – that is, the postulational algebra of Boole and Schroeder, and the mathematical logic of Russell and Whitehead – *with a view to* addressing 'the more foundational questions of how the two relate to each other and are "all of a piece"'.[39] All three philosophers who spurned Langer's book – Quine, Carnap and Cooley – went on to write their own introductions to logic, yet none was to prove as successful in terms of number of editions and prints and to be as highly praised as the one by Langer.[40] As to Quine, it was not until 1951, when his essay 'Two Dogmas of Empiricism' was published – with, as its main merit, its attack on the logical positivists' distinction between analytic and synthetic statements and their supposed reductionism – that Quine became established as a leading analytic philosopher.

Another example of the cultural climate in which Langer's career developed is Ernest Nagel's review of *Philosophy in a New Key*.[41] Having first praised the book for its 'solid grounding in modern logical philosophical analysis', and containing 'an expert knowledge of the materials of the arts, especially music', Nagel spends the best part of his review criticizing Langer's notion of symbol as being the result of a 'simple if natural confusion' between analogy and exemplification. The term 'natural confusion' entirely bypasses the fact that Langer's conception of symbol is a deliberate and radical departure from the standard conception of symbol. In other words, rather than acknowledging that Langer has developed a new conception of symbol that challenged accepted conventional notions, the younger Nagel claims she has made a 'logical mistake'. As philosophers Charles Varela and Lawrence Ferrara comment,

> Is it not odd that the crux of Nagel's critical evaluation is the contention that Langer has made a fundamental mistake in her treatment of the nature of 'symbol'? Odd not because Langer could not have been mistaken, but odd because one masterful specialist in the logic of symbolization is treating another masterful specialist in the same field as a novice who has not mastered the fundamentals. After all, that Langer published a text in symbolic logic four years earlier certainly qualified her for a status at least a cut above a novice. Thus what we have is not a master informing a novice of a mistake but two masterful professionals discovering a difference of opinion on a fundamental issue: one which concerns the established and so conventional view of the logic of 'symbol'.[42]

Career and impact

Despite Langer's growing public reputation as an original, radical and wide-ranging philosopher, she did not have a tenured position until 1954, at age 59. As historian Bruce Kuklick describes it,

> Langer was the token [woman philosopher] of the 1940s and 1950s. Married in 1921 to the luminous Harvard historian, William L. Langer, she spent the first fifteen years after receiving her Ph.D (1927–1942) as a tutor at Radcliffe. This is a lowly position, at the nether end of the academic ladder if on the ladder at all … Upon her divorce in 1942 and the publication of *Philosophy in a New Key*, she left her tutorship, but despite an increasing reputation, she had no permanent employment for twelve years.[43]

Psychologist Howard Gardner writes,

> I think Langer's slender volume [*Philosophy in a New Key*] had a … potent influence on dozens, perhaps hundreds, of other students. And yet the author is not widely cited; she is ignored or disparaged by a significant number of philosophers, and, despite an imposing shelf of books, she never gained a permanent position at a major university.[44]

And philosopher Robert Innis observes,

> Although it would not be correct to say that Susanne Langer has been one of the 'forgotten figures' in American philosophy, it is certainly the case that she has been rather on the margins than in the center of professional philosophical discussions. … Her career was in fact more 'purely' philosophical than 'professionally' philosophical, in the sense that her rather unorthodox academic teaching career was not integral to her ultimate impact.[45]

Although it is true that Langer never had a tenured position at a major university, one should not simply assume that she actively sought or aspired to one. It is by no means clear that she wanted an 'orthodox' career. Until her divorce in 1942 she had been able to combine family (including the raising of two sons), writing and part-time teaching and tutoring at Radcliffe College in ways that seemed to have suited her well. It is clear from a letter from Henry Sheffer in 1943, that she had turned down three offers of full-time 'professorships of philosophy at … women's colleges'.[46] Admittedly, she may not have wanted to teach at a women's college and was waiting and hoping for a permanent position elsewhere. It may also have been difficult for her during that time to leave Cambridge while her husband was teaching at Harvard. But, as Donald Dryden notes, '[T]here is scattered evidence to indicate that she deliberately sought part-time appointments that would allow her to maintain her independence.'[47] She preferred research and writing to teaching.[48] That may explain why, after her divorce and her move to New York in 1942, when her sons were 18 and 20, respectively, she started an itinerary life of temporary positions and visiting professorships at various American universities that enabled her to spend long periods in between at her remote cabin in upstate New York to work on her articles and books.

But her withdrawal into the wilderness was no doubt in part an escape from the hostile environment of professional philosophy. Throughout her life she impressed upon herself and her own female students the need to be 'twice as logical' as men to be taken seriously. But the obstacles to being accepted were just too many. Harvard, as we already heard, 'was never kind to women'.[49] And nor was Columbia University. As philosopher Joseph Margolis recalls,

> I had heard her speak a number of times in one or another of her classes at Columbia. I don't think she was at all at ease at Columbia. For one thing, the men really weren't hospitable to women as philosophers. ... She was definitely not a member of the Department and her own lectures (for courses) were definitely assigned to some general educational program. ... [Langer] presented her own views, chiefly on topics very close to Cassirer's treatment of the human sciences, very knowledgeably on the arts, and sometimes (I seem to remember) on logic.[50]

Another reason for her unease at Columbia was, as Margolis reminds us, the longstanding Langer-Nagel controversy around her notion of symbol. After earning his PhD at Columbia in 1931, Nagel had stayed on to teach there until well in the 1970s. His public rejection of her view of symbols in his 1943 review of *Philosophy in a New Key* would not have helped her reception. Nor did it induce Columbia's philosophy faculty to be more hospitable to her when she took over Cassirer's classes in 1945. Margolis recalls,

> For another [reason for Langer being ill at ease at Columbia], Ernest Nagel had written a review (if I remember correctly) of her treatment of Cassirer's 'symbolic forms'. There was some actual confrontation on the matter, very possibly at Columbia, and Langer was apparently unable to give a satisfactory account of how to assign meaning to symbolic forms (as in music and painting, say) as opposed to giving meaning to words.[51]

Margolis also recalls that, although she was usually 'very composed, professional, a little distant, very modest in her dress, but firm and well informed', she had once broken down at what he remembers was a meeting of the American Society of Aesthetics at Harvard.

> Langer gave a paper. My impression is that someone raised an objection from the floor ... It's quite possible (though I don't remember) that the question at the ASA revived that issue [i.e. the Nagel-Langer controversy]. She broke down in tears at once.[52]

Whether triggered by a sense of philosophical failure or by exasperation with her audience's incapacity and unwillingness to think outside their philosophical boxes, to her male contemporaries Langer's tears will just have confirmed that women were not mentally tough enough to take fair criticism and unable to hold their own. In this misogynistic climate, Langer stood little chance. She was small and soft-spoken, with a German accent. Her pioneering philosophy with its evolving terminology came across as unsystematic and, on their terms, 'illogical'. The men marginalized and ignored her. Langer withdrew, both professionally and socially. Her retreat into the solitude of nature was in part an escape.

Even so, she continued to be much in demand as a public speaker, especially after the publication of *Feeling and Form* (1953). In these public lectures, her unassuming and self-effacing manner came across as a refreshing alternative to the often pompous posturing of many male speakers. As one female scholar, Ann Berthoff, observed,

> [Langer] was a gifted lecturer. I have seen an audience of over two hundred sit enthralled by her presentation of profound and difficult ideas. ... There was absolutely none of the studied showing forth of 'personality' which so often typifies today's performers. She was courteous, formal, witty, without self-indulgence of any sort.[53]

A woman's philosophy?

This raises a final question: can Langer's philosophy itself be considered 'female' or 'feminist'? Does her speaking and writing, whether in content or style, reflect that she was a woman philosopher?[54] To what extent is her way of philosophizing or her approach to philosophy in any way different from that of the men of her time?

Before attempting to answer this question it is important to stress that Langer did not think of herself as a 'woman philosopher' let alone a 'feminist philosopher' and would quite likely have recoiled at the idea. Yet, it could be argued – and some indeed do – that Langer's philosophy displays various features that are also considered central in feminist epistemologies and ontologies.[55] These features include a critique of logocentrism and linear thought; an emphasis on the body, lived experience and cognitive feeling; a rejection of dominant dichotomies such as those between thinking and feeling; reason and intuition; body and mind; fact and interpretation; subject(ivity) and object(ivity). It often involves an inclusive and relational rather than exclusive and oppositional approach to other thinkers. It reflects a desire to synthesize and unite rather than divide and outdo one's interlocutors.

Although most of these features can indeed be found in Langer's work, before concluding that these critiques and approaches are characteristically female or 'feminist', it should be recalled that all these features were also present in the philosophies of the male philosophers, in particular Cassirer and Whitehead, that constituted the formative sources of Langer's own thought. Moreover, several other male philosophers both before and after Langer had made similar critiques or adopted similar approaches, most notably Dewey and James, Bergson, Merleau-Ponty and Deleuze to mention just a few.[56] In other words, if one wants to uphold the idea that there *are* typically gendered features in philosophy, – something that needs a far more detailed discussion than I can offer here –, and that Langer's philosophy displays many so-called female/feminist traits, one surely has to concede that these features are also present in many philosophies written by men – which, of course, may explain why Langer was drawn to them in the first place.[57] In view of the above, I suggest it is not necessarily straightforward to present Langer as a distinctively 'woman philosopher'.

Ironically, despite his self-confessed prejudice against 'books on philosophy by women', Hocking was one of the few Harvard men at the time who recognized the importance and full implications of Langer's work. William Ernest Hocking (1873–1966) was an idealist philosopher who was inspired by his teacher Royce's metaphysics and his emphasis on direct experience. He had also been instrumental in recruiting Whitehead to Harvard's philosophy department, something referred to in his sympathetic memoir 'Whitehead as I knew him'.[58] Hocking wrote this in his reader's report of Langer's manuscript for Harvard University Press:

> The author instructs the public, deluded by those bone-headed positivists, who have deserved well for their industry and hell for their stupidity, that there are meanings in feeling, ritual, myth, music and other art-forms. [Her book] will bring the discussions of 'semantics' into a wider general use than a criticism of word-meanings, bringing it to bear on the interpretation of ritual, myth, and art. [In order to do this] she has brought out a theory of the origin of language in the symbolizing propensities of mankind, and has made a good case for it.[59]

Had it not been for Hocking's positive recommendation, Harvard might never have published *Philosophy in a New Key*.

At a time when a philosopher's influence became increasingly closely connected to their academic status and professional career, Langer had little opportunity of shaping a new generation in the field. Without a tenured university position, she was unable to influence a body of students or establish a school that might be recognized as in some way 'Langerian'. As to her later impact, this may yet have to be seen. Interestingly though, if she *is* yet to have a significant impact, this may well not be *despite* her lack of a professional academic career but *because* of it. Had she become a conventional member of the established profession with its increasingly narrow analytic concerns, she may not have been able or willing to challenge some of its cherished assumptions and entrenched beliefs. Had she gone 'native' in the institution, she might well not have ventured into the uncharted waters she was now brave enough to explore.

Part Two

Sources

4

Henry M. Sheffer: Logical form

Sheffer was best known for his logic teaching and came to specialize in it, but his main concern in logic remained the philosophy of logic. While extolling rigor, he scorned empty formalism and celebrated meaning.

W. V. O. Quine[1]

Philosophy had been gravely damaged, by what the logical positivists, influenced by symbolic logicians like himself, were now doing; the kind of work that 'Carnap and Co.' (as he called them) were engaged upon repelled him — it would ruin real philosophy as he and his master Royce conceived it: 'if any work of mine has done anything to stimulate this development, I had rather not have been born.'

Sheffer as quoted by Isaiah Berlin[2]

Logic as the study of forms

The first and foremost significant influence on Langer's thinking was her undergraduate supervisor, logician Henry M. Sheffer (1883–1964). Langer studied with him between 1921 and 1924 but his philosophy of logic continued to shape her thinking well beyond that. Sheffer's personal and professional life were difficult. Despite his acknowledged brilliance as a logician and a teacher, his fragile mental health, domestic problems and the anti-Jewish sentiments he experienced at Harvard left him in a constant state of vulnerability. Sheffer had emigrated with his Jewish family from the Ukraine to the United States at the age of 10. After attending Boston Latin School, he did his doctoral studies at Harvard University with the leading logician Josiah Royce and, between 1906 and 1910, served as his research assistant at the time that he was developing his new system of formal logic. This new conception did not conceive of logic as a study of principles of inference, as had traditionally been the case, but as a study of relations, patterns and structural forms. As Royce defined it in *The Principles of Logic* (1913), logic is 'the general science of order, the theory of the forms of any orderly realm of objects, real or ideal'.[3] Although Sheffer rejected Royce's metaphysical theories, he did adopt his new and innovative conception of logic. This conception also formed the basis of Langer's symbolic logic and her broader theory of symbolic forms.

Impressed with his student's logical acuity, Royce helped Sheffer obtain a Sheldon Fellowship enabling him to spend a year in Europe visiting its leading logicians.[4] At Royce's introduction, Sheffer attended Russell's lectures in the autumn of 1910 just after Russell had finished the much discussed first edition of the *Principia Mathematica* (1910) which he and A. N. Whitehead had been working on for over ten years. Like Royce, Russell had been impressed with Sheffer's logical insight and dexterity. Fifteen years later he was to adopt his new economizing mathematical operator – the so-called 'Sheffer Stroke' – in the second edition of his *Principia Mathematica* (1925), which he praised as 'the most definite improvement resulting from work in mathematical logic during the past fourteen years'.[5]

Sheffer in Europe

After Cambridge Sheffer travelled throughout Europe while attending lectures with logicians David Hilbert, Ernst Zermelo and Gottlob Frege in Germany and Giuseppe Peano in Italy. He had been able to follow most lectures in their original language since, as Langer informs us, he had 'an extraordinary ear for language'.[6] In addition to a basic knowledge of Hebrew, which his Jewish background had provided him, and a solid training in Greek and Latin, which he had learned at the Boston Latin School, he was fluent in French, German and Italian. As Langer recalls, even his command of his adopted English was remarkable: 'This man without any literary pretensions had a great and accurate command of the tongue he had made his own, so that his lectures and his few brief writings had a rare style and dignity, befitting the nature of his thought.'[7]

The Sheffer stroke

Upon his return to the United States, Sheffer published the article 'A Set of Five Independent Postulates for Boolean Algebras, with Application to Logical Constants' (1913) that included the proposal of the new operator for which he was to become best known, that is, the 'Sheffer stroke'.[8] This stroke ' | ' was meant to replace two operations of a propositional negation and disjunction (-p &-q or 'neither p nor q') with one single operation of non-conjunction (p | q)'.[9] Since Sheffer himself did not consider this notational refinement as of huge importance – indeed, he started to deplore the growing obsession with technicalities like these – it is regrettable that, as Michael Scanlan observes, '[M]ost logicians know nothing more about Sheffer than the Sheffer stroke.'[10]

Sheffer at Harvard

Sheffer arrived at Harvard in the winter of 1916, in the middle of Langer's first year at Radcliffe. He had been called upon at short notice by the philosophy department to take over the classes previously taught by the Royce who, at age 61, had suddenly died at the beginning of the term. This was meant as a temporary arrangement until someone permanent was found. Although not without obstacles and challenges, in the event Sheffer was to remain at the department until his retirement in 1952.[11] With the passing of Royce, Sheffer had now become the leading logician in America although at a time that logic and philosophy were being eclipsed by the natural sciences. As Langer put it, 'Sheffer's powerful mind did much to uphold the intellectual value of a sadly shattered department, and this at a time when the ascendancy of physical science was putting philosophy as such in jeopardy.'[12]

As confirmed by many of his students, Sheffer was not only a great logician but an outstanding teacher and mentor, providing inspiration for a new generation of scholars pioneering in the new fields of philosophy.[13] According to W. V. Quine, who took classes with Sheffer while studying for his PhD under Whitehead, '[H]e kept his classes small and would seldom admit an unenrolled auditor, but if he thought a student was seriously interested in logic, he was generous with his help.'[14] Langer, who attended his lectures given at Radcliffe College, writes,

> As a personage, the young instructor was obscure, indeed all but nameless, but as a person he was the inspirer and intellectual guide of a small group of perceptive, serious students, undergraduates as well as graduates, who looked forward to a new philosophical era, that was to grow from logic and semantics as the old tradition had grown from the value-centered doctrines of the Greek and mediaeval past.[15]

In an unpublished paper, 'Henry Sheffer's Legacy to his Students', Langer pays tribute to Sheffer's 'logical imagination' and his ability 'to see logic as a field for invention' with 'as much scope for originality as in metaphysics'.[16]

While highly successful as a teacher, Sheffer's publication output was deplorably small. His perfectionism in writing, compounded by domestic, financial and recurrent psychiatric hospitalizations, prevented him from a productive publishing career. After a troubled marriage between 1917 and 1928 he lived for most of his life in a small hotel room surrounded by books and piles of papers on which he jotted down his ideas. As Langer recalls it:

> Because this keen and original thinker never committed his thoughts to the printed page, he remained in the position of Instructor or Lecturer until 1927, when a severe nervous breakdown, brought on by professional hopelessness and extreme personal troubles, called general attention not only to his plight but also to his invaluable teaching. At last he received his advancement to Assistant Professor (1927), Associate Professor (1929), and – at very long last – to Professor in 1938. He remained at Harvard until his retirement in 1952.[17]

Bertrand Russell refers to this paucity of publications in his introduction to the second edition of *Principia Mathematica* in 1925:

> It should be stated that a new and very powerful method in mathematical logic has been invented by Dr. H. M. Sheffer. This method, however, would demand a complete re-writing of *Principia Mathematica*. We recommend this task to Dr. Sheffer, since what has so far been published by him is scarcely sufficient to enable others to undertake the necessary reconstruction.[18]

In addition to his fragile mental state and limited publication output, Sheffer was faced with the university's elite White Anglo-Saxon Protestant (WASP) prejudices and anti-Jewish feelings at the time.[19] As early as 1919, British political philosopher Harold Laski who was teaching at Harvard during that time, referred to this cultural climate in a letter to Russell, in the hope to enlist his support for Sheffer's position. Prior to Sheffer's arrival in the spring of 1914, Russell had taught at Harvard and had been highly regarded there. Laski writes,

> I know from your *Introduction to Mathematical Logic* that you think well of Sheffer who is at present at the Philosophy Department here. I don't know if you have any personal acquaintance with him. He is a jew and he has married someone of whom the university does not approve; moreover, he hasn't the social qualities that Harvard so highly prizes. The result is that most of his department is engaged on a determined effort to bring his career here to an end. … Myself I think that the whole thing is a combination of anti-Semitism and that curious university worship of social prestige which plays so large a part over here. Do you know anyone at Harvard well enough to say (if you so think) that Sheffer ought to have a chance? Of course I write this entirely on my own responsibility but I'm very certain that if Lowell could know your opinion of Sheffer it would make a big difference to his future.[20]

Russell is known to have acted decisively upon Laski's request. As he wrote in his autobiography,

> From this time onward I used to send periodical cables to President Lowell, explaining that Sheffer was a man of the highest ability and that Harvard would be eternally disgraced if it dismissed him either because he was a Jew or because it disliked his wife. Fortunately these cables just succeeded in their object.[21]

With Russell's recommendations and, so it seems, additional support of Jewish funding, the department was eventually willing to secure his annual reappointment.[22] Even so, it was not until 1927, after many more letters and further fundraising, that Sheffer got a tenured position. In the end it was Whitehead who, having arrived at Harvard just a few years earlier and having been prompted by Russell, played a decisive role in securing Sheffer's position. The memorandum he wrote on his behalf, while characteristically brief, proved to be compelling:

> Symbolic Logic, as the general theory of structure, has been generalized to its utmost extent by Dr. Sheffer. He has not only enunciated the general principles, but achieved the far more difficult task of making substantial progress in constructing the groundwork of the science.[23]

At this recommendation Sheffer was finally offered a tenured appointment.[24] During those years he was, as Scanlan put it, not only the philosophy department's 'principal teacher of logic at a time when Harvard was viewed as the leading center for the new logic in the United States' but also 'the only capable person in the United States who might be said to have a general theory of logic'.[25] This was to place Langer as a student at the heart of the most important developments in logic at her time.

Having got to know Sheffer well during her student years, Langer undertook to co-edit a Festschrift in his honour with an impressive list of contributions from America's leading philosophers, many of whom were Sheffer's former students.[26] *Structure, Method and Meaning: Essays in Honor of Henry M. Sheffer* was, as Langer poignantly pointed out, 'the only book that ever bore his name'.[27]

Langer's own book on logic *An Introduction of Symbolic Logic* (1937) is heavily indebted to Sheffer and can be considered the main introduction to his overall thinking. As she put it in the preface,

> [A]lthough my text has no predecessor, it has had at least one inspirer: my debt to Professor Sheffer of Harvard is too great to be expressed in any detailed acknowledgements. The underlying ideas of the book – its emphasis upon system, its progress from the specific to the general, from the general to the abstract, its whole treatment of logic as a science of forms – all this is due to his influence. How many lesser ideas also derive from him I am unable to say; it is the mark of a great teacher that one cannot render to him the things that are his. They become part of one's own mentality, and ultimately of the intellectual commonwealth.[28]

The book is written as an introduction to the technical intricacies of the two main strands of logic at the time, that is, the postulational algebra of Boole and Schroeder, and the mathematical logic of Russell and Whitehead. But it also addresses the more foundational questions of how the two relate to each other and are 'all of a piece'.[29] As she writes,

> Symbolic logic is a relatively new subject, and the easiest methods of approach have not yet been determined. In point of arrangement, therefore, this *Introduction* has no predecessor. This is just why it was written: the need of some systematic guide, from the state of perfect innocence to a possible understanding of the classical literature, has become acute and commanding.[30]

In a review of Langer's book, British analytic philosopher L. Susan Stebbing confirms the fact that Langer has provided what she calls 'a glimpse of [Sheffer's] conception of logic' and communicated this to an audience outside his immediate circle:

> There can be no doubt that Dr. Langer has provided an excellent introduction to this subject. She claims that her work has 'no predecessor', from the point of view of arrangement. This claim is just. She professes that it has had 'one inspirer', namely, Prof. Sheffer of Harvard. Since acquaintance with the work of Sheffer is for the most part confined to the circle of his disciples, other students of symbolic logic will be grateful for this glimpse of his conception of logic.[31]

Herbert Feigl, one of the early core members of the Vienna Circle who had moved to the United States in 1931, likewise praised the book for the way it introduced the new field of symbolic logic in the context of important broader philosophical questions about meaning and interpretation:

> [Langer] presents an admirable introduction to this relatively new field [of symbolic logic], written in her lively, lucid manner and replete with well chosen examples and applications. There are enlightening remarks on the nature of logical form, on abstraction and generalization, on language and symbolism. … Throughout the book Mrs. Langer never forgets to explain the meaning and purpose of whatever special technique she may deal with. It is interesting and significant to see that the Aristotelian doctrine of the syllogism – taught for more than two thousand years as the main part of logic – could be taken care of in a brief appendix and as a small part of the class calculus.
>
> … The book serves well as an introduction to *Principia Mathematica* of Whitehead and Russell – the classical treatise of mathematical logic and the logic of mathematics.[32]

In contrast to these positive reviews by leading international logicians, the lacklustre response to the book by Harvard's own logicians was striking. As mentioned earlier, this might be explained by Langer's marginal status or by a general lack of interest in the philosophical foundations of symbolic logic as reflected in Quine's complaint that the book had 'too little logic' and 'too much metaphorical talk'.[33] One wonders whether it was this lack of interest in broader philosophical questions of meaning that Sheffer had in mind when he confided to Isaiah Berlin in 1944:

> [Philosophy] had been gravely damaged, by what the logical positivists, influenced by symbolic logicians like himself, were now doing; the kind of work that 'Carnap and Co.' (as he called them) were engaged upon repelled him – it would ruin real philosophy as he and his master Royce conceived it: '[I]f any work of mine has done anything to stimulate this development, I had rather not have been born.'[34]

It was not until later that Quine was able to recognize the importance of Sheffer's contribution. As he wrote in his obituary of Sheffer in 1964,

> He was best known for his logic teaching and came to specialize in it, but his main concern in logic remained the philosophy of logic. While extolling rigor, he scorned empty formalism and celebrated meaning.[35]

Sheffer's influence on Langer

Sheffer's influence on Langer ranges from her logic and epistemology to her aesthetics and philosophy of mind. First, for Langer, one of Sheffer's main contributions to logic was his attention to the role of notation in logic.[36] As she put it,

Sheffer's chief contribution to logic, and (over his protests) to philosophy, was his demonstration of the influence which notation exercises on the appearance of relational structures, and therewith, of course, on the forms in which problems present themselves.[37]

Sheffer emphasized the fact that difference aspects of reality required different forms of representation, something he referred to as 'notational relativity'. Sheffer, according to Langer, was one of the first to stress its importance:

> This 'notational relativity', as he called it, is familiar matter to semanticists today; but the discovery of its importance for our concepts of objective fact and demonstrable truth was the work of one extraordinary, little-known man, who pointed it out, year after year, to future philosophers, until it went abroad under other names than his and revolutionized theory of knowledge.[38]

For Langer herself, Sheffer's insight in different types of notation became a formative idea in the development of her distinction between discursive and non-discursive types of symbolic forms.

A second feature of Sheffer's logic that significantly influenced Langer was his attention to meaning. For Sheffer, mere logical acuity was never enough. As Quine had put it correctly, Sheffer 'scorned empty formalism'. He considered Russell's *Principia Mathematica* to be overly concerned with the formal and technical aspects of logic at the expense of attention to its meaning. He considered his own celebrated 'Sheffer stroke' as nothing more than a minor technical improvement for the sake of logical economy. In his review of the second edition of *Principia Mathematica*, he even seems to mock Russell for his enthusiasm about the stroke:

> So important, in this treatment of logic, is the matter of *economy* of basic notions, that the authors consider one of the cardinal improvements in the new edition to consist in their substitution, for the two operations of propositional *negation* and *disjunction*, of the single operation of *non-conjunction*.[39]

For Sheffer, that substitution does not solve their major problems. As he explains in a footnote,

> In the old edition the authors do not differentiate sufficiently between the unasserted proposition 'not-p' and the asserted one 'p is false', and between the unasserted proposition 'p or q' and the asserted proposition 'p is true or q is true'. Similarly, in the new edition, they fail to distinguish between the unasserted proposition 'not-p or not-q' and the asserted proposition 'p is false or q is false', i.e., 'p and q are incompatible'.[40]

For Sheffer the extension of logic into pure mathematics distracted attention from the more important matter of the recognition of the changeable and unstable meaning of logic's foundational concepts and terms – class, relation, proposition, function and so on. Sheffer was primarily interested in the question in what way one could establish and determine the initially elusive meanings and interpretations of any newly employed logical concepts: '[One ought] to inquire into the meaning of those very notions – like class, relation, proposition, propositional function – that are presupposed by the symbolic level.'[41] He notes what he calls Russell and Whitehead's ' "logocentric" predicament', that is the problem that, '[I]n order to give an account of logic, we must presuppose and employ logic.'[42] According to Sheffer, it is essential to distinguish between, on the one hand 'the problem of "symbolic analysis" – of notation and interpretation' and, on the other, 'the study of the conditions that make the notational and interpretational phases *significant* and *valid*.'[43] He critiques Russell's 'occasional confusion between the two phases of symbolic analysis – the "notational" and the "interpretational".'[44] For Sheffer, the study of notational form should never overshadow the study of logical meaning. Put differently, the study of the structure of logical form – the question of notation or, in current terminology, its 'syntax' – should always be considered alongside the study and interpretation of its meaning – its 'semantic'. As he once famously said, 'A remark may refer to a mark, ... but a mark cannot.'[45]

It is exactly this concern with meaning, or 'the meaning of meaning', that will also occupy Langer throughout her career. It underlies her distinction between sign and symbol and that between meaning in language, myth, science and art. These themes are already present in her doctoral thesis *A Logical Analysis of Meaning* from 1926 and will be the central concern of her first book *The Practice of Philosophy* from 1930. The theme will subsequently run like a red thread throughout her entire work.[46]

The *third* theme that influenced Langer is Sheffer's notion of form. For Sheffer, as it had been for Royce, logic was not primarily a study of the principles of inference but a study of order and forms, patterns and structures. In *The Principles of Logic* of 1913 Royce had coined his new definition of logic as 'the general science of order, the theory of the forms of any orderly realm of objects, real or ideal'.[47] For Langer, as for Sheffer, logic should never be reduced to the art of correct reasoning. As she was to describe logic's diminished role in *Philosophy in a New Key*: 'The logician, once an investor in the greatest enterprise of human thought, ... found himself reduced to a sort of railroad linesman, charged with the task of keeping the tracks and switches of scientific reasoning clear for sensory reports to make their proper connections.'[48]

Instead, as she already wrote in 1930 in *The Practice of Philosophy*, 'Logic is the science of forms as such, the study of patterns.'[49] And in 1937 she devoted the first two chapters of her *An Introduction to Symbolic Logic* to 'The Study of Forms' and 'The Essentials of Logical Structure'. In 1953 she used the word 'form' in the title of her first book on aesthetics, *Feeling and Form*, and in her contribution to Sheffer's *Festschrift* in 1951 she wrote,

> It was only with the development of mathematics that abstract logical forms became so apparent and, in their appearance, so interesting that some logicians turned their attention to the study of *form as such* and undertook the abstraction of relational patterns from any and every concrete exemplification. ... Russell's leanings toward physical science are so strong that perhaps he does not see the

entire potential range of philosophical studies built on the study of relational logic. Whitehead came nearer to it; Peirce and Royce saw it; but the actual development of systematic abstraction to the point where it can be an eye-opener to philosophers has been the special task of the man to whom these essays are dedicated.[50]

In summary, Sheffer's influence on Langer can be seen to be reflected in three central features of her philosophy: first, his emphasis on the role of notation in the presentation of relational structures and the plurality of forms in which problems can present themselves; second, his stress on the importance of a study of meaning in relation to logical concepts over against a preoccupation with technical refinement and notational economy; and, third, his expanded notion of logic as the study of forms over against a conception of logic as a study of deductive reasoning. Later I will show how Langer's later philosophy of art is not a deviation from her early work on symbolic logic but a direct continuation of it. Meaning, whether in logic or in art, according to Langer, is constituted by the recognition of forms. It is this expanded notion of logic, as a study of meaning in form, which will come to dominate Langer's philosophy of language, science, culture and art.

5

Ernst Cassirer: Symbolic form

The fundamental concepts of each science, the instruments with which it propounds its questions and formulates its solutions, are regarded no longer as passive images of something given but as symbols created by the intellect itself.

Cassirer[1]

Every authentic function of the human spirit has this decisive characteristic in common with cognition: it does not merely copy but rather embodies an original, formative power. … This is as true of art as it is of cognition; it is as true of myth as of religion. … Each of these functions creates its own symbolic forms.

Cassirer[2]

Cassirer's emphasis on the constitutive character of symbolic renderings in the making of 'experience' is the masterstroke that turns the purely speculative 'critical' theory into an anthropological hypothesis, a key to several linguistic problems, a source of psychological understanding, and a guidepost in the maze of Geistesgeschichte.

Langer[3]

This basic need, which certainly is obvious only in man, is the need of symbolization. The symbol-making function is one of man's primary activities, like eating, looking, or moving about. It is the fundamental process of his mind, and goes on all the time.

Langer[4]

Any miscarriage of the symbolic process is an abrogation of our human freedom.

Langer[5]

Language and myth

Langer first met Ernst Cassirer (1874–1945) in the winter of 1941, at a conference of the Eastern Division of the American Philosophical Association. By that time, Cassirer had just moved to America after eight years of exile in Britain and Sweden. Following the rise of Nazism and Hitler's ban on academic positions for Jews, Cassirer had been forced to resign from his post at Hamburg University in 1933.[6] He then taught for two years in Oxford, and five years at the University of Gothenburg. The last appointment had come to an end because he had reached Swedish universities' official retirement age of 67.[7] In 1941 Cassirer had accepted an invitation from Yale University's chair of philosophy Charles Hendel for a visiting professorship at his department, and he had crossed the Atlantic to arrive in time for the autumn term.[8]

When Langer met Cassirer, she had just finished the manuscript of *Philosophy in a New Key* which was about to be published by Harvard University Press. Since the text had drawn significantly on Cassirer and reflected many of his ideas, their meeting was both timely and mutually inspiring. Cassirer's wife, Toni Cassirer, wrote about the meeting in her autobiography:

> Ernst had met Susan [*sic*] Langer, an American philosopher of German origin, already in his first winter here at a congress, and he had been very interested in her work. She was a very serious scholar and her writings had a remarkable affinity with Ernst's ideas.[9]

Toni Cassirer also writes that Cassirer had been interested in working with Langer on further research projects, including his book *The Myth and the State* and, as an initial step, Langer had started to work on a translation of his *Sprache und Mythos* (1925). Sadly, their years of cooperation were not to last long. In the spring of 1944, in his first year of a visiting professorship at Columbia University, Cassirer died unexpectedly from a heart attack on his way home from teaching. Langer, who had only just moved to New York the year before, was called upon to take over his courses at the University, where she was to continue to teach for the next five years. At the time of Cassirer's death on 13 April 1945, Langer had nearly finished her translation of *Sprache und Mythos* which was published posthumously in 1946. She had been able to discuss the material with him at length over the previous years, as is clear from a letter from Cassirer to her dated five days before his sudden death.[10] Langer wrote in the preface *Language and Myth*,

> I offer the translation of this little study (with some slight modifications and abridgments made by the author shortly before his death) both as a statement of a new philosophical insight and as a revelation of the philosopher's work: his material, his technique, and the solution of the problem by a final flash of interpretative genius.[11]

After his move to America in 1941, Cassirer wrote two books in English, *An Essay on Man* and *The Myth of the State*.[12] *An Essay on Man* is often portrayed as an English 'summary' of *The Philosophy of Symbolic Forms* but this is not entirely correct. Following his meeting with Langer and reunions with fellow refugee scholars such as art historians Erwin Panofsky and Edgar Wind, as well as Albert Einstein and Max Wertheimer, it contains much new material that reflects a development in his thinking that had already started during his years of exile in Sweden to which I will return later. It also suggests some influences from Langer, including the book's main structure that reflects that of *Philosophy in a New Key*.[13] Cassirer's second and last book in English, *The Myth of the State*, was also published posthumously in 1946. His major work *Philosophie der symbolischen Formen* (1923, 1925 1929), however, was not to be translated into English until the mid-1950s.[14] As Cassirer's editors Krois and Verene point out, Langer's translation of *Language and Myth* and her own *Philosophy in a New Key* were to play an important role in introducing Cassirer to a North American readership:

> Langer's widely read *Philosophy in a New Key* (1942) and her translation of Cassirer's *Language and Myth* (1946) were a valuable route for many American readers into the philosophy of the symbol prior to the publication of *The Philosophy of Symbolic Forms* in English in the 1950s. Her book on aesthetics, *Feeling and Form*, which is dedicated to Cassirer, appeared in the same year as the first volume of *The Philosophy of Symbolic Forms*, translated in 1953 by Ralph Manheim.[15]

Charles Hendel, likewise, commented that *Philosophy in a New Key* 'presented a view of Cassirer's theory of form and symbol with great freshness and vivacity' and that her translation of *Sprache und Mythos* 'offered an illuminating sidelight upon the development of *The Philosophy of Symbolic Forms*, inasmuch as *Sprache und Mythos* had been published in 1925, between the second part dealing with Myth and the third part on Science'.[16] As a result, Hendel concluded, '[T]he interest in Cassirer was thus being directed toward *The Philosophy of Symbolic Forms*, and readers were prepared for it.'[17]

Philosopher of science

Even before meeting Cassirer in 1941, Langer had been well acquainted with Cassirer's works in German. She may well have been introduced to his writings by her mentor Sheffer and may also have come across them during her year in Vienna in the academic year 1921–2. Cassirer had then just been appointed as professor of philosophy at the newly founded post-war university of Hamburg. Langer frequently refers to him in her 1926 PhD thesis and, before that, in a 1924 review of a *Festschrift* dedicated to Cassirer's teacher Paul Natorp. Interestingly, in that review she singles out Cassirer's contribution as 'the most original' and 'the least neo-Kantian'.[18] In that same year her then supervisor Henry Sheffer had written a review of two translated essays by Cassirer published together under the title *Substance and Function, and Einstein's Theory of Relativity* in 1923.[19] This book was the only English translation of Cassirer's work until Langer's translation of *Sprache und Mythos* in 1946. Considering Sheffer's limited publication record – he had only three known published reviews and five publications in total – his review of this book signals a serious interest in Cassirer on Sheffer's part.

Even well before Langer's and Sheffer's reviews, however, Cassirer's name and reputation had been known at Harvard as is clear from two invitations issued to him in 1913 and 1914. Sadly, on neither occasions had he been able to accept the invitation due to family circumstances. After his forced exile from Germany, so his wife reports, Cassirer had hoped that he would be given another chance but, alas, no further invitation was issued. The fact itself, however, that Cassirer had been invited to Harvard as early as 1913 testifies to his established international reputation. His book *Das Erkenntnisproblem in der Philosophie und Wissenschaft der neueren Zeit* (1906, 1907) had won the Kuno Fischer Gold Medal from the Heidelberg Academy in 1914, and his book *Substanzbegriff und Funktionsbegriff: Untersuchungen über die Grundfragen der Erkenntniskritik* (1910) was considered the best history of all major scientific concepts prior to the twentieth century. Indeed, Cassirer was arguably one of the last systematic philosophers who had a complete grasp of the different sciences and was *au fait* with its latest developments.

Cassirer's life and work

Born in a well-to-do, cultural but not observant Jewish family in Breslau, Cassirer entered his university education in 1892.[20] In time-honoured German tradition he attended several different universities to study with selected well-known professors in their respective fields. In Marburg he studied with Hermann Cohen, the leader of the Marburg School of neo-Kantianism, and became one of his best (and most favoured) students.[21] In addition to philosophy Cassirer studied mathematics, biology and physics, and completed his studies with a dissertation on Descartes in 1899.[22] After his doctorate he moved to Berlin where, three years later, he married his cousin Toni Bondy, née Cassirer, and where, with some interruptions, he lived until 1919.

Cassirer's academic career and intellectual development can be best understood by dividing it into three periods: his time in Berlin (1903–19), his time in Hamburg (1919–33) and his time in exile until his death (1933–45). As we will see in the case of Whitehead, all periods of Cassirer's career prove to be of specific relevance to Langer's thought. Indeed, the order of periods of Langer's thought contains some striking parallels with that of Cassirer: first, philosophy of science and logic; second, philosophy of culture and art; and, third, philosophy of mind and metaphysics. Before discussing each period in more detail, I will provide a brief introduction to the movement of neo-Kantianism in general, as this will be relevant for our later discussions of philosophy of science and logical positivism and their relation to Langer.

Neo-Kantianism

Since the 1860s neo-Kantianism had been the official academic philosophy taught at most German universities.[23] While covering a diverse range of schools, two in particular stand out: the Marburg School, with its leading philosophers Friedrich Lange (1828–1875), Hermann Cohen (1842–1918) and Cohen's student Paul Natorp (1854–1924); and the Baden (or Southwest) School based in Heidelberg, with its leading representatives Wilhelm Windelband (1848–1915) and Heidegger's teacher

Heinrich Rickert (1863–1936). Although a student of both Cohen and Natorp and therefore often considered to belong to the Marburg School, Cassirer does also display many Baden School's features.[24]

In their desire to return to Kantian principles, neo-Kantians generally sought to reinterpret Kant's critical idealism in such a way that it would avoid the extremes of the two main post-Kantian schools, that is, the metaphysical idealism of Fichte, Schelling and Hegel, and the scientific positivism of Comte. In doing so they not only reinterpreted Kant's distinction between *Erscheinung* and *Ding an sich*, but also abolished the latter as a philosophical category altogether. They argued that, since the latter cannot be talked about, it should, *pace* the idealists, not be allowed to function as a metaphysical assumption at all. Thinking and being, according to Natorp, 'exist and have meaning only in their mutual relations to one another'.[25] The mind not only constitutes knowledge and experience, as Kant used to say, it constitutes *being*: being is construed from thinking. Even sense-impressions, by Kant still considered to be the raw material for perception, are themselves products of human thinking: seeing is a mental activity. *Pace* Kant, perception does not begin with the moulding and ordering of passively perceived sense-impressions according to the *Anschauungsformen* of the mind, but in the very constitution of these 'impressions'.

Although this emphasis on the constitutive character of the mind seems to come close to a traditional idealist position, neo-Kantian idealism nevertheless distinguishes itself from metaphysical idealism in two distinct ways: first, as already mentioned, by rejecting the *Ding an sich* as a metaphysical assumption, neo-Kantians turn it into an epistemological category; second, whereas metaphysical idealists conceive the world as the product of an absolute or divine mind, in which (or in whom) the individual mind participates, neo-Kantians conceive it as the product of human consciousness, albeit in accordance with the supra-individual laws of pure reason.

Within neo-Kantianism the Marburg School was primarily interested in mathematics and the natural sciences. This meant that, broadly speaking, Natorp and Cohen favoured Kant's 'theoretical reason' over 'practical reason'. Even though the Marburgers also occupied themselves with ethics and social philosophy, in general, the question 'what can I know?' dominated that of 'what should I do?'

The Baden School, by contrast, is more indebted to Kant's practical reason even though this expressed itself less in an interest in ethics than in a philosophy of culture. Windelband and Rickert realized that the mathematical concepts of the natural sciences could not apply to realms such as history, ethics or social philosophy. Aware of the limitations of rational scientific thought in, for instance, historical research, Windelband sought to demonstrate that the mind could not simply apply universal laws to empirical facts but had to select such 'facts' in the first place. As this could clearly not be done by logical reasoning alone, he argued that the mind must therefore rely on other types of a priori principles.

In order to guarantee the same measure of objectivity for assertions in these areas, they developed a set of a priori norms and principles which were meant to have similar universal validity as scientific principles. Examples of such principles are, for instance, the idea of justice, goodness or beauty. Reminiscent of Plato's doctrine of ideas, all assertions had to be judged by these absolute norms as that which ought to be thought.

Rickert developed this further by dividing reality in three specific realms: first, a realm of 'being'; second, a realm of 'validity' (*Geltung*); and third, an intermediate realm of 'culture' or 'meaning' (*Sinn*). The latter, mediating realm typically is the site of art and religion, seen by Rickert as embodying absolute values.

Like Cassirer, Langer is often most closely associated with the Marburg School. Polish philosopher Stefan Morawski writes,

> Langer's stance, i.e., her reiterated polemics with empiricism, naturalism, and with neo-positivist philosophers of science, her insistent cutting herself off from metaphysics and psychology – all these bear on the Marburg version of neo-Kantianism which characterizes Cassirer's work.[26]

However, as remarked earlier, although indeed widely considered to belong to the Marburg School, Cassirer also reflects distinct *Baden* features in his philosophy. This is evident from his deep interest in culture. His philosophy of symbolic forms in which science, alongside myth, language and art, is understood in terms of specific symbolic forms, is a clear departure from Cohen's strictly scientific model. Moreover, while rejecting the Baden School's conception of universal values, his own hermeneutical conception of symbolic forms as the means by which humans interpret and make sense of the world shows clear affinities with Rickert's realm of meaning or *Sinn*. This also applies to Langer's conception of meaning in myth, a theme that has been explored by theologian Willem van Roo in his comparative study of Cassirer and Langer's notion of symbol in relation to the Christian sacrament.[27]

The Berlin period (1903–19): Theory of knowledge and science

Between 1906 and 1919 Cassirer taught as *Privatdozent* at the University of Berlin.[28] During this period, he focused on philosophy of science, logic and mathematics, resulting in an extensive history of modern philosophy from the Renaissance until Kant. This was published as the first two volumes of *Das Erkenntnisproblem* (1906, 1907). One of the findings of this study was that key stages in the advancement of science are marked by a progressive emancipation from a 'naïve' realism that holds on to the conformity of our knowledge to the world, through the assumption of a world of pre-established things-in-themselves, to the acceptance of a conscious creation of new forms of 'objectification' – or scientific 'objects' – by means of the creation of different kinds of scientific symbols.[29] According to Cassirer,

> The fundamental concepts of each science, the instruments with which it propounds its questions and formulates its solutions, are regarded no longer as passive images of something but as *symbols* created by the intellect itself. Mathematicians and physicists were first to gain a clear awareness of this symbolic character of their basic implements.[30]

It was this early recognition of the symbolic character of scientific and mathematical concepts with which 'the rigid concept of being seems to be thrown into flux' that was to become foundational for the development of the philosophy of symbolic forms, first by Cassirer and later by Langer.[31] As Langer was to formulate it twenty years later:

> Physicists may think of certain facts in place of constants and variables, but the same constants and variables will serve somewhere else to calculate other facts, and the mathematicians themselves give no set of data their preference. They deal only with items whose sensory qualities are quite irrelevant: their 'data' are arbitrary sounds or marks called *symbols*.[32]

Cassirer's first major systematic treatise, *Substanzbegriff und Funktionsbegriff: Untersuchungen über die Grundfragen der Erkenntniskritik* (1910), develops this notion of the fundamental symbolic character of concepts into a major critique of the classical notion of substance – or *ousia* – which was typically modelled on the subject–predicate structure of Aristotelian logic. Since the objects of modern science are not the 'things-in-themselves' but rather ideal relations, a new theory of concepts needs to be rooted in the functional relations of modern mathematics. As Cassirer's teacher Cohen, echoing Kant, had already put it in 1877:

> Not the stars in the heavens are the objects that this [transcendental] method teaches us to contemplate, but the astronomical calculations, those facts of scientific reality are, as it were, the real which is to be accounted for, as that at which the transcendental gaze is directed.[33]

Similar themes were taken up a decade later by Whitehead in *The Concept of Nature* (1920). As we will see later, like Whitehead in England, Cassirer in Germany closely followed Einstein's new theories. For Cassirer these confirmed what he had already begun to explore in *Substanzbegriff und Funktionsbegriff*. Like Whitehead, Cassirer had been able to discuss his theories with Einstein. Although Einstein seemed to have considered Whitehead's applications too speculative, he had found himself in much agreement with Cassirer. He even wrote a sympathetic preface for his essay *Zur Einsteinschen Relativitätstheorie* (1921).[34]

The Hamburg period (1919–33): The philosophy of symbolic forms

Two years before the publication of his book on Einstein's theory of relativity, that is, in 1919, Cassirer had been appointed chair in philosophy at the newly founded University of Hamburg. Hamburg at that time was primarily known as a seaport and city of merchants unlike the cultured university city of Frankfurt.[35] Although Cassirer had also been offered a professorship in Frankfurt, one of the attractions of Hamburg had been an extensive humanities library freshly bequeathed by an affluent local art historian, Aby Warburg.[36] By considerable fortuity, the classification system that Warburg had adopted for his library, was remarkably close to the way Cassirer had begun to conceptualize his own theory of symbolic forms.[37] The books were divided into four categories as pertaining to, first, *Image* as the first stage of human awareness; second, *Word* or the study of language; third, *Orientation* or the study of religion, science and philosophy as products of humanity's search for understanding; and, fourth, *Action* as the patterns of behaviour that form the subject matter of history.[38] As Cassirer wrote,

> The first drafts and other preliminary work for this volume [on myth] were already far advanced when through my call to Hamburg I came into close contact with the Warburg Library. Here I found abundant and almost incomparable material in the field of mythology and general history of religion, and in its arrangement and selection, in the special stamp which Warburg gave it, it revolved around a unitary, central problem closely related to the basic problem of my own work.[39]

Cassirer became close friends with Aby Warburg and the Library's director, art historian Fritz Saxl. Moreover, the library facilitated the exchange of scholars in many other fields than philosophy, such as psychologist William Stern, biologist Jacob von Uexküll and art historian Erwin Panofsky.[40] The latter's seminal essay *Perspective as Symbolic Form* applies – although, as I will show later, also in important aspects misunderstood – Cassirer's notion of symbolic form. As Panofsky saw it,

> [Perspective] may even be characterised as (to extend Ernst Cassirer's felicitous term to the history of art) one of those 'symbolic forms' in which 'spiritual meaning is attached to a concrete, material sign and intrinsically given to this sign.' This is why it is essential to ask of artistic periods and regions not only whether they have perspective, but also which perspective they have. [41]

Cassirer's research at the Warburg found its expression in *The Philosophy of Symbolic Forms* (1923, 1925, 1929).[42] Cassirer always looked back to Kant as the first philosopher to recognize the fundamentally symbolic and constructive nature of the human mind:[43]

> The 'revolution in method' which Kant brought to theoretical philosophy rests on the fundamental idea that the relation between cognition and its object, generally accepted until then, must be radically modified. Instead of starting from the object as the known and given, we must begin with the law of cognition, which alone is truly accessible and certain in a primary sense.[44]

This view was echoed by Langer, as she was to write in *Mind*:

> The door to a wider conception of mind than the impressionable *tabula rasa* of the empiricists … was opened by the Kantian analysis of experience into form and content and the emphasis on the imposition of form by the transcendental Subject.[45]

Yet, and this is an important qualification for both Cassirer and Langer, scientific cognition is 'only one of the many forms in which the mind can apprehend and interpret being'.[46] Cassirer wanted to extend Kant's epistemological 'law of cognition' from the realm of science into other 'forms of knowledge' or realms of culture, including art:

> Every authentic function of the human spirit has this decisive characteristic in common with cognition: it does not merely copy but rather embodies an original, formative power. ... This is as true of art as it is of cognition; it is as true of myth as of religion. All live in particular image-worlds, which do not merely reflect the empirically given, but which rather produce it in accordance with an independent principle. Each of these functions creates its own symbolic forms which, if not similar to the intellectual symbols, enjoy equal rank as products of the human spirit. None of these forms can simply be reduced to, or derived from, the others; each of them designates a particular approach, in which and through which it constitutes its own aspect of 'reality'.[47]

And he concludes,

> [T]he Copernican revolution, with which Kant began, takes on new and amplified meaning. It refers no longer solely to the function of logical judgment, but extends with equal justification and right to every trend and every principle by which the human spirit gives form to reality.[48]

This move implied a rejection of the idea that sense-impressions were merely the raw 'content' or material for the forms of sense perception and categories of the mind. Instead, basic sense-impressions are always already mediated and transformed by mental processing. As Langer was to put it,

> 'Seeing' ... is not a passive process, by which meaningless impressions are stored up for the use of an organizing mind, which construes forms out of these amorphous data to suit its own purposes. 'Seeing' is itself a process of formulation; our understanding of the visible world begins with the eye.[49]

Jürgen Habermas commented on Cassirer's extension of Kant's epistemology in his 1995 Warburg Lecture 'The Liberating Power of Symbols: Ernst Cassirer's Humanistic Legacy and the Warburg Library':

> The Warburg Library also encouraged Cassirer's interests in the sense that it represented the object domains which are especially challenging for an epistemology in the Kantian tradition. *The Critique of Pure Reason* was of course intended to explain how natural-scientific knowledge is possible. The historical sciences of culture only developed later, in the course of the nineteenth century. Cassirer realized that transcendental philosophy could not react to this 'fact of the human sciences' in the same way that Kant, in his time, reacted to the fact of Newtonian physics. From a transcendental standpoint, nature is constituted for

us at the same time as the object domain of the natural sciences. But the human sciences are concerned with cultural structures, which they find already to hand as pre-scientifically constituted objects. The concept of culture itself can no longer be adequately explained in terms of the constitution of a corresponding domain of scientific objects. Rather, the human sciences are themselves cultural constructs, which they are able to turn back and reflect on self-referentially, for example, in the form of the history of science.[50]

The notion that symbols could have a 'liberating power' was first suggested by Langer in 1944 when she wrote,

> A sign is always embedded in reality, in a present that emerges from the actual past and stretches to the future; but a symbol may be divorced from reality altogether. It may refer to what is *not* the case, to a mere idea, a figment, a dream. It serves, therefore, to liberate thought from the immediate stimuli of a physically present world; and that liberation marks the essential difference between human and nonhuman mentality.[51]

Both Langer and Cassirer conceived of sense-perception itself as a form of 'symbolization' or 'ideation'. For Cassirer, symbolic ideation … constitutes vision.'[52] As Langer was to express it later, 'The material furnished by the senses is constantly wrought into *symbols*, which are our elementary ideas.'[53] For both of them, symbolization is the core of the free functioning of the human mind: the mind not only orders and categorizes reality, but also *transforms and constitutes* it. Extending Kant's notion of *Vernunft* to a general concept of 'mind', Cassirer concludes,

> Thus the critique of reason becomes the critique of culture. It seeks to understand and to show how every content of culture, in so far as it is more than a mere isolated content, in so far as it is grounded in a universal principle of form, presupposes an original act of the human spirit. Herein the basic thesis of idealism finds its true and complete confirmation.[54]

Cassirer thus introduces a significant modification of Kant's theory of knowledge: whereas Kant's forms of perception and categories of understanding are fixed and universally available structures of the human mind, Cassirer's symbolic forms are dynamic and historically evolving processes. For Cassirer this was a legitimate extension of Kant that could be justified by an appeal to Kant's notion of the *productive imagination* or *schema*.[55]

Kant and the productive imagination

In Kant's transcendental philosophy, the productive imagination and the *schema* are meant to provide an explanation for the way consciousness is able to establish synthetic relations at a level prior to cognition. Knowledge, for Kant, is constituted on the basis of the a priori conditions of the forms of perception – space and time – and the twelve categories of the understanding. But in his 'Introduction' to the *Critique of Pure Reason*, Kant also hints at a deeper unity: '[T]here are two stems of human knowledge, namely, *sensibility* and *understanding*, which perhaps spring from a common, but to us unknown, root.'[56] This root is later revealed as the spontaneous synthesizing activity of the productive imagination:

> Synthesis in general … is the mere result of the power of imagination, a blind but indispensable function of the soul, without which we should have no knowledge whatsoever, but of which we are scarcely ever conscious.[57]

It is through the mediating role of the productive imagination that one is at all able to apply the right forms and categories to the chaotic influx of sensations as the raw material for these. This synthetic activity takes place at a preconceptual level – it does not as yet produce proper 'knowledge'. This term is reserved for the subsequent conceptualization of the synthesis. To bring this synthesis *to concepts* is a function which belongs to the understanding, and it is through this function of the understanding that proper knowledge is required. What the productive imagination produces is a *schema*. A schema is not a concrete perception, but an image which mediates between the sensuous and the conceptual. In Kant's words,

> Obviously there must be some third thing, which is homogeneous on the one hand with the category, and on the other hand with the appearance, and which thus makes the application of the former to the latter possible. This mediating representation must be pure, that is, void of all empirical content, and yet at the same time, while it must in one respect be *intellectual*, it must in another be *sensible*. Such a representation is the *transcendental schema*.[58]

The adjective 'transcendental' in the last sentence reminds us of the fact that the schema provides the conditions for the possibility in which concepts can be applied to perceptions. Kant illustrates this with the concept 'triangle'. This concept can never correspond with a particular perception, because any particularity undermines the universal character of the abstract concept 'triangle'. There is, however, a general representation of a triangle which is applicable to all concrete instances of triangular phenomena. This representation can only exist in our mind. The same principle applies to, for instance, the concept 'dog'. By means of the productive imagination one can conjure up a representation of a certain four-legged animal, without confining that animal to any particular type or breed.

The schema is *more* than a logical category, since it functions as a synthesis with a perceptual content. It is more 'sensory' than a category because it is a real, even if mental, image (*Phänomenon*). On the other hand, it is not as real as the representation resulting from experience: 'The schema is, properly, only the phenomenon, or sensible concept, of an object in agreement with the category.'[59] Most importantly, however, the schemata are indispensable in the process of the formation of meaning: 'The schemata of the pure concepts of understanding are thus the true and sole conditions under which these concepts obtain relation to objects and so possess *significance*.'[60] According to Charles Hendel, 'The schema's the thing that caught the imagination of Cassirer.'[61] As the unity of and synthesis between concept and intuition, Cassirer used the notion in many and varied forms. In the words of Hendel,

> Had he not been led by various other important considerations to the discovery of a more original theme and title for his work, he might well have presented his own philosophy as an extension of the doctrine of Schema, for it is clearly a stage in his thinking toward the concept of 'symbolic form'.[62]

Verene, likewise, observes, 'Cassirer's [entire] theory of the symbol is essentially a reshaping of Kant's idea of schema.'[63] It is because of the schema that Cassirer can extend Kant's 'critique of reason' to a 'critique of culture' and, ultimately, to a 'metaphysics' of symbolic forms and meaning. As we will see later, this will also apply to Langer's conception of symbol and, in particular, to her notion of abstraction as the 'intuitive' grasping of form.

Cassirer's *The Philosophy of Symbolic Forms*

As was mentioned earlier, although Cassirer's trilogy *Philosophie der Symbolischen Formen* (1923, 1925, 1929) was not translated into English until 1955 and 1957, Langer had read the original German texts long before that. Reflecting back on her own development she wrote in 1956,

> It was in reflecting on the nature of art that I came on a conception of the symbol relation quite distinct from the one I had formed in connection with all my earlier studies, which had centered around symbolic logic. This new view of symbolization and meaning stemmed from the Kantian analysis of experience and had been highly developed in Cassirer's *Philosophie der symbolischen Formen*.[64]

Langer's discovery of Cassirer's quite different notion of symbol from that typically employed in logic or science led her eventually to the notion of symbol as a form of *articulation* rather than *denotation*. As she described it,

> But this symbol concept ... cannot be defined in terms of denotation, signification, formal assignment, or reference. ... Cassirer himself considered the semantic functions that belong to scientific symbols as a special development, which occurred under the influence of language, by virtue of its inherent *generality* together with its *signific* character. But symbolization as such he traced further back. His notion of 'symbol' was more primitive than that of a sign used by common consent to stand for an associated concept; in his sense of the word, a sound, mark, object, or event could be a symbol to a person, without that person's consciously going from it to its meaning. This is the basic concept in his theory of myth.[65]

In order to understand how deeply Cassirer's innovative and evocative conception of symbolic form influenced Langer's mature thought, I will briefly discuss, first, the three volumes as they appeared in his lifetime and, second, the material that Cassirer had meant to be used for a fourth volume but was not published until after his death as part of his *Nachlass*.[66]

Volume 1: *Language* (1923)

One of Cassirer's original insights that captured Langer's imagination was his emphasis on the close connection between language and myth. As he put it in *An Essay on Man*: '[F]or the primitive mind myth and language are, as it were, twin brothers. Both are based on a very general and very early experience of mankind, an experience of a social rather than of a physical nature.'[67] Cassirer points out that 'belief in magic is based upon a deep conviction of the solidarity of life' and that, to the primitive mind, 'the social power of the word, experienced in innumerable cases, becomes a natural and even supernatural force.'[68] Although in language this 'magic function of the word was eclipsed and replaced by its semantic function' and 'is no longer endowed with mysterious powers', he nevertheless believes that 'a word could not "mean" a thing if there were not at least a partial identity between the two' which is not merely conventional.[69] Language is not simply a 'mechanical aggregate of terms' but has a fundamentally cultural and communal character. Crucially, 'The real difference between languages is not a difference of sounds or signs but one of "world-perspectives" (*Weltansichten*).'[70]

For Cassirer, language is the mind's 'eternally repeated endeavour to make the articulated sound an expression of thought'.[71] To fix an object as a permanent focus point is an ongoing, culturally determined practice. Cassirer often refers to the German philosopher of language Wilhelm von Humboldt (1767-1835) to enforce his points, as in the following quote:

> Men do not understand one another by relying on the signs of things, nor by causing one another to produce exactly the same concept, but by touching the same link in each other's sense perceptions and concepts, by striking the same key in each other's spiritual instrument, whereupon corresponding, but not identical concepts arise in each of them. ... When ... the link in the chain, the key of the instrument is touched in this way, the whole organism vibrates and the concept that springs from the soul stands in harmony with everything surrounding the individual link, even at a great distance from it.[72]

Von Humboldt points out that the Greek and the Latin terms for the moon, even though referring to the same object, do not express the same intention or concept. As Cassirer explains: 'The Greek term (*mēn*) denotes the function of the moon to "measure" time; the Latin term (*luna*, *luc-na*) denotes the moon's lucidity or brightness.'[73] This means that, in naming something, one typically focuses on different aspects of one and the same object. Cassirer also mentions nineteenth-century linguist Hammer-Purgstall's observation that the Arabic language has over six thousand terms to describe a camel, all expressing different aspects and details of the animal with respect to shape, colour, age, gait and so on, such that the word for an old, grey camel might be completely different to that for a young, brown one with a limp. As Cassirer observes, 'Such terms bear to each other rather a relation of juxtaposition than of subordination.'[74] Different languages have different ways of classification and can even be indifferent to generic or abstract terms. In Humboldt's words, the diversity of language is 'not a diversity of sounds and signs, but of world outlook.'[75]

Langer, too, will draw heavily on von Humboldt, especially his notion that language is not a work – *ergon* – but an activity – *energeia*. This term indicates that language, like 'meaning', is not a finished product but an ongoing activity. For Humboldt, (as for Langer) '[L]anguages are not really means of representing the truth that has already been ascertained, but far more, means of discovering a truth not previously known.'[76] Jürgen Habermas credits Cassirer for recognizing the significance of Humboldt's ideas for what was to become the linguistic turn in philosophy:

> Cassirer was the first to perceive the paradigmatic significance of Humboldt's philosophy of language; and he thus prepared the way for my generation, the post-war generation, to take up the 'linguistic turn' in analytical philosophy and integrate it with the native tradition of hermeneutic philosophy.[77]

In the sign, the mind can acquire and convey meaning that had previously eluded it. Conversely, meaning, or the 'content of the spirit [is] disclosed only in its manifestations; the ideal form is known only by and in the aggregate of the sensible signs which it uses for its expression.'[78] As Cassirer puts it,

> For consciousness the sign is, as it were, the first stage and the first demonstration of objectivity, because through it the constant flux of the contents of consciousness is for the first time halted, because in it something enduring is determined and emphasized. … Through the sign that is associated with the content, the content itself acquires a new permanence. For the sign, in contrast to the actual flow of the particular contents of consciousness, has a definite ideal *meaning*, which endures as such.[79]

Through the sign or symbol the mind reaches out to the objective nature of things. By giving shape and form to the flux of experience one renders experience available *to oneself*. It should be noted that, in *The Philosophy of Symbolic Forms*, Cassirer used the terms sign and symbol interchangeably and did not, like Langer, make a clear terminological distinction. However, in *An Essay on Man* (1944), he writes, 'For the sake of a clear statement of the problem we must carefully distinguish between *signs* and *symbols*.'[80] Since *An Essay on Man* was written after Cassirer met Langer, it reflects, as Randal Auxier suggests, the 'influence of Susanne Langer on Cassirer's conception of the symbol, and through her, perhaps also Whitehead's influence.'[81]

In her essay 'On Cassirer's Theory of Language and Myth', Langer summarizes Cassirer's view of language in ways that show his influence not only on her view of language but also on her understanding of art:

Language is born of the need for emotional expression. Yet it is not exclamatory. It is essentially hypostatic, seeking to distinguish, emphasize, and hold the object of feeling rather than to communicate the feeling itself. To fix the object as a permanent focus point in experience is the function of the *name*.[82]

More generally, Cassirer's view of the productive rather than re-productive character of language is key to his overall philosophy of symbolic forms. In Langer's words,

[Cassirer's] emphasis on the constitutive character of symbolic renderings in the making of 'experience' is the masterstroke that turns the purely speculative 'critical' theory into an anthropological hypothesis, a key to several linguistic problems, a source of psychological understanding, and a guidepost in the maze of *Geistesgeschichte*.[83]

This also applies to Cassirer's account of myth.

Volume 2: *Mythical Thought* (1925)

Myth and language, for Cassirer, share the same origin.[84] This origin, which it also shares with dreaming, is a consciousness characterized by a conglomerate of shifting and elusive images, pregnant with affective meaning, and often organized along axes such as good and evil, safe and dangerous, holy and unholy, and so on. Langer describes it as follows:

The first dichotomy in the emotive or mythic phase of mentality is not, as for discursive reason, the opposition of 'yes' and 'no', of 'a' and 'non-a', of truth and falsity; the basic dichotomy here is between the sacred and the profane. Human beings actually apprehend *values* and expressions of values *before* they formulate and entertain *facts*.[85]

As Langer points out in her preface to *Language and Myth*, Cassirer was increasingly dissatisfied with traditional theories of knowledge that were only concerned with 'facts' and did not address the 'inveterate belief of all mankind in myth, sometimes crystallized into dogmas, sometimes degraded into vulgar superstition'.[86] Myth was typically dismissed as 'divine revelation, which philosophy could not touch (especially in modern times) [or] as a miscarriage of logical explanation, a product of ignorance'.[87] Cassirer felt strongly, however, that one could not ignore or dismiss myth so easily. As Langer describes Cassirer's position:

Mere ignorance should be agnostic – empty and negative – not exciting and irrepressible. And it dawned on the philosopher that *theory of mind* might well begin not with the analysis of knowledge, but with a search for the reason and spiritual function of this peculiar sort of 'ignorance'. ... Professor Cassirer's great thesis ... is that *philosophy of mind involves much more than a theory of knowledge; it involves a theory of prelogical conception and expression, and their final culmination in reason and factual knowledge.*[88]

Langer's entire philosophy of mind and art is built on that fundamental insight.[89]

On Cassirer's view, both science and myth operate with a notion of causality, but each does so in a different way. Scientific causality starts with the event itself and subsequently aims to identify and isolate specific factors that can serve as explanations for a relation of cause and effect. Science also aims to explain causal relations in terms of universal rules that extend beyond the particular event. In mythical thought, by contrast, a causal relationship is based on association. When two events occur spatially or temporally together, they are *experienced as* causally related. This means, for example, that animals 'which appear in a certain season are … looked upon as the bringers, the cause of this season: for the mythical view, it is the swallow that *makes* the summer'.[90] In mythical thinking, one can take 'every contact in time and space as an immediate relation of cause and effect'.[91] Cassirer refers to this as the principles of '*post hoc, ergo propter hoc*' ('after this, therefore because of this') and '*juxta hoc, ergo propter hoc*' ('next to this, therefore because of this').[92] Whereas science employs the notion of 'accidentals', as that which deviates from a given causal law, in myth, nothing is considered accidental. Likewise, whereas science draws a sharp distinction between the properties of the part and the properties of the whole, myth disregards such a distinction. This explains why, in mythic consciousness, some part or aspect of a person – an item of clothing, someone's name, even someone's shadow or reflection in a mirror – is considered to have the same significance as the person as a whole, and revered or feared for its powers to influence someone's destiny. Likewise, distinctions between the self and the world, subject and object, as well as sign and object, are blurred: 'The name of a thing and the thing itself are inseparably fused'.[93] This gives words and images their power in magic.

Mythical thought thus employs very different categories and schemes of ordering and classifying the world from science, not just at the level of conscious categorization but at the more primitive level of perception, feeling and intuition. Everything can be interpreted in terms of supernatural powers. In the mythical worldview the world is divided between the sacred and the profane, the divine or the demonic. Everything – from spatial and temporal to numerical differentiations – is based on this dichotomy.[94] They constitute, as Langer puts it, 'a world of values, things "holy" against a vague background of commonplaces, or "profane" events, instead of a world of neutral physical facts'.[95] What interests Langer particularly in Cassirer's theory of myth – and what connects it with her later theory of art – is that the symbolic constructions of mythical consciousness are fundamentally rooted in feelings and experiences of *meaning*. Mythical symbols, she says, are 'charged with feeling, and have a way of absorbing into themselves more and more interesting meanings, sometimes even logically conflicting imports'.[96] Moreover, '[T]hey beget a kind of understanding, but not by sorting out concepts and relating them in a distinct pattern' but by bringing together 'great complexes of cognate ideas, in which all distinctive features are merged and swallowed'.[97] Meanings, in mythical thought, are not assigned to things arbitrarily but 'dwell in them as life dwells in a body'.[98] Moreover, what happens in myth also applies to art: there is no clear distinction between form and content, image and meaning. They are fused together.

Volume 3: *The Phenomenology of Knowledge* (1929)

In the third volume of *The Philosophy of Symbolic Forms*, *The Phenomenology of Knowledge*, Cassirer returns to the questions raised in his earlier epistemological studies but now with his much-expanded notion of 'knowledge' as rooted in sense-experience and expressive values. Rejecting both empiricist sensationalism as well as dogmatic realism Cassirer develops a phenomenology of knowledge built on a sophisticated theory of perception that can be said to anticipate Merleau-Ponty's *Phenomenology of Perception* fifteen years later.[99] Indeed, Merleau-Ponty was familiar with Cassirer's work and frequently refers to the third volume of *The Philosophy of Symbolic Forms*. What is also interesting is that, as Samantha Matherne highlights, *both* thinkers draw heavily on Kant's notion of the productive imagination.[100] Echoing insights from *Gestalt* theory, both philosophers hold that an optical experience is always a 'vehicle of meaning' that stands in the service of that meaning.'[101] For both of them, as it was for Whitehead, 'The symbolic process is like a single stream of life which flows through consciousness, and which by this flowing movement produces the diversity and cohesion, the richness, the continuity, and constance, of consciousness.'[102] Cassirer illustrates this with a phenomenological description of how we perceive the expressive meaning of a simple line:

> As we immerse ourselves in the design and construct it for ourselves, we become aware of a distinct physiognomic character in it. A peculiar mood is expressed in the purely spatial determination: the up and down of the lines in space embraces an inner mobility, a dynamic rise and fall, a psychic life and being. And here we do not merely read our inner states subjectively and arbitrarily into the spatial form; rather the form gives itself to us as an animated totality, an independent manifestation of life. It may glide quietly along or break off suddenly; it may be rounded and self-contained or jagged and jerky; it may be hard or soft: all this lies in the line itself as a determination of its own reality, its objective nature.[103]

A far cry from Marburg's supposed scientism, this evocative description of the expressive values of a simple line is as relevant for understanding art as it is myth. If we look at the line as primarily a geometrical or mathematical structure, the expressive qualities recede to the background and vanish from our focus of concentration. It is no longer important whether the line is bright or thick or coloured since our focus is primarily on the relative proportions of the line in relation to other lines thus representing a more universal relational structure. Paying attention to a line's expressive qualities risks being a distraction from putative 'objective' scientific observation. If, on the other hand, we look at the same line in terms of its expressive character, however, a whole different world reveals itself.

The Davos debate

Although the manuscript for the third volume was already completed by 1927, it was not published until 1929. This was the same year that Cassirer was accused by Heidegger for being too tied to Marburg's scientistic conception of knowledge. The accusation was made during a historic debate between them at an international conference in Davos.[104] The debate was set up to discuss their respective interpretations of Kant, but turned into a broader discussion of the role of Kant and neo-Kantianism in philosophy in general. Heidegger criticized Cassirer for what he claimed was his Marburg-inflected overemphasis on Kant's theory of objective knowledge at the expense of his philosophy of the practical reason. According to Heidegger closer attention to the latter would reveal that Kant's metaphysics is not so much a theory of infinite transcendence but of finite existence. For Heidegger real *Dasein* is always historically embodied concrete being. In his words,

> I believe that what I designate with the term *Dasein* cannot be translated by one of Cassirer's concepts. What I call *Dasein* is essentially characterised not only through that which is designated as 'spirit', or as 'life', but rather it is the original unity of the immanent structure of the relatedness of a man who, in his shackledness to the body, stands in a special boundness with 'that-which-is'.[105]

Cassirer, in turn, accused Heidegger of overemphasizing the temporal nature of human existence at the expense of the realm of symbolic forms which function as a mediating middle realm between finite historical bodily being and the world of generality and objectivity that enabled the transcendence of the here and now by means of imaginative thought. As Cassirer put it, 'Everything "general", all giving in to the general is for Heidegger a "fall" – a disregarding of "authentic" *dasein* – a giving in to the inauthenticity of the "they" [*das* "*Man*"].'[106] By contrast, Cassirer maintains, the human spirit always strives towards objectivity and generality by means of symbolic forms and structures. These are the 'roads by which the spirit proceeds towards its objectivization, i.e., its self-revelation'.[107]

Political climate and context

The philosophical debate at Davos cannot be adequately discussed without considering its political context. Whereas Heidegger was known to have close sympathies with National Socialism, Cassirer, like many other Jewish intellectuals, was an advocate of liberal democracy. Indeed, just a year before the debate in Davos, he had defended the Weimar Constitution in a speech at Hamburg University on the occasion of the Republic's tenth anniversary by arguing that

> [T]he idea of a republican constitution is in no sense a stranger, let alone an alien intruder, in the overall context of the history of German thought and culture.

Rather, it grew out of this very ground, and was nourished by its most authentic forces, the forces of idealist philosophy.[108]

One of the issues raised in the press prior to the Davos debate was the question whether Jews such as Cassirer and his teacher Cohen were at all capable of interpreting – or even entitled to interpret –a 'proper' German thinker like Kant. As historian Larry Eugene Jones reports,

> Only weeks before the meeting at Davos Cohen and Cassirer had both been attacked by the extreme nationalist Othmar Spann, a sociology professor at the University of Vienna. In a speech delivered in Hitler's presence in Munich in February 1929, Spann defamed Cohen and Cassirer as 'foreigners' and asserted that it was a pity for Germandom that they should be allowed to take the lead in interpreting Kant.[109]

Jones adds that reports of Spann's speech had appeared in many of the larger German newspapers, so that it is quite likely that the students who attended the Davos conference would have known of it. He suggests that it is even possibly that Cassirer, when accused of being a neo-Kantian in Davos, 'defended Cohen's interpretation of Kant because otherwise it might have looked as if he were not loyal to his teacher in these times of distress'.[110] Despite the fact that Heidegger misrepresented Cassirer's position during the debate or, perhaps, because of it, many younger students felt attracted to the views of Heidegger which were felt to represent the real voice of the German *Volk*.

Four years after the Davos debate, in 1933, Cassirer was forced to resign from his position as rector of Hamburg University, the Warburg Institute's Jewish staff were no longer allowed to lecture at the university and, through the remarkable foresight of its director, the entire Library was moved to London.[111] In the same year Heidegger was appointed rector of the University of Freiburg.

Saying 'yes' or 'no'

Some commentators have suggested that Cassirer should have been more outspoken against the Nazi regime and suggest that *The Philosophy of Symbolic Forms* has no place for social ethics or political philosophy. Helmut Kuhn, for one, complains that 'for Cassirer, life comes into view only as *vita acta*, "life as lived", never as *vita agenda*, "life as it is to be lived"'. For Kuhn this 'accounts for the calm perfection of his thought'.[112] David R. Lipton even suggests that the third volume, written in 1929, the same year as the Davos debate, amounts to a 'regression', to an ahistorical, rationalistic or 'logistic' approach enabling Cassirer to avoid having to deal with the urgent issues of his time.[113] Yet these commentators overlook the fact that, for Cassirer, precisely in order for philosophy itself to function as politically impartial and ethically free, it should refrain from putting itself at the service of any party-political programme or manifesto.[114] Peter Gordon comments that one important reason neo-Kantianism had become 'apolitical' was that it had emerged in reaction to 'the metaphysical indulgences of the mid-nineteenth century' and had tried to 'eschew ideological partisanship in favour of a strictly "professional" ethos'.[115] Moreover, for Cassirer it was not only a commitment to the formal, autonomous character of philosophy as such but especially to his particular version of it as developed in his philosophy of symbolic forms. By understanding – and providing an account of – human culture as 'the process of man's progressive self-liberation' by means of language, art, religion and science, Cassirer implicitly critiqued not only ideologically motivated philosophies but also what he considered Heidegger's fatalistic philosophy of being-in-the-world.[116] For him, the only way one can take a stand in the world – that is, affirming or protesting against it – is by means of symbolic forms, that is, the world of language and culture. As Habermas correctly observes,

> The fact that sensory contact with the world is reworked into something meaningful through the use of symbols is [for Cassirer] the defining feature of human existence, and also constitutes, from a normative standpoint, the basic trait of a properly human order of being. In other words, the objectifying force of a symbolic mediation breaks the animal immediacy of a nature which impacts on the organism from within and without; it thereby creates that distance from the world which makes possible a thoughtful, reflectively controlled reaction to the world on the part of subjects who are able to say 'no'.[117]

In other words, precisely by creating a mediating distance between symbol and the world, philosophy enables humans to move beyond the natural and mythical state – Heidegger's state of *Geworfenheit* – by allowing them to reflect on their conditions and circumstances. This also enables them not just to *re*act but to *act* by means of saying 'yes' or 'no'.

This view of symbols as enabling and empowering human intellectual and moral action in the world is also present in Langer. For her, too, symbol formation enables us to say 'yes' and 'no', which is the basis of freedom of speech. For Langer, freedom of expression is the basis of all personal freedom.'[118] That's why humans should never be constrained in their symbol formations:

> Any miscarriage of the symbolic process is an abrogation of our human freedom. … [T]he most disastrous hindrance is disorientation, the failure or destruction of life-symbols and loss or repression of votive acts. A Life that does not incorporate some degree of ritual, of gesture and attitude, has no mental anchorage. … Freedom of conscience is the basis of all personal freedom. To constrain a man against his principles – make a pacifist bear arms, a patriot insult his flag, a pagan receive baptism – is to endanger his attitude toward the world, his personal strength and single-mindedness. No matter how fantastic may be the dogma he holds sacred, how much his living rites conflict with the will or convenience of society, it is never a light matter to demand their violation. … To be obliged to confess, teach, or acclaim falsehood is always felt as an insult exceeding even ridicule and abuse.[119]

A philosophy of symbolic forms thus conceived has, as it were, an inbuilt ethics. As Habermas observes,

> Cassirer obviously believed that the philosophy of symbolic forms as such had a moral-practical content, which rendered the working out of an independent ethics superfluous. But this philosophy only offers such a content when it is no longer viewed as theory of knowledge applicable to the whole culture, and is seen as a theory of the civilizing process. This process has also to be understood humanistically, as a movement towards increasing civility.[120]

For Langer, as we will see later, such a 'civilizing process' was also an important function of art. Art, for Langer, was one way to express one's freedom, not, as we will see, in terms of human *self*-expression or cultural elevation, but in terms of *the education of feeling*. As she was to put it in *Problems of Art*,

> Art education is the education of feeling, and a society that neglects it gives itself up to formless emotion. Bad art is corruption of feeling. This is a large factor in the irrationalism which dictators and demagogues exploit.[121]

Although Cassirer's writings on Rousseau and the Enlightenment in the early thirties could already be seen to contain an implicit critique of totalitarian conceptions of the state by emphasizing the importance of the individual, near the end of his life Cassirer addresses the German situation explicitly in *The Myth of the State*, the book he had hoped to work on with Langer.[122] In this book he launches his most direct attack on Heidegger's philosophy of *Geworfenheit*:

> I do not mean to say that these philosophical doctrines had a direct bearing on the development of political ideas in Germany. ... But the new philosophy did enfeeble and slowly undermine the forces that could have resisted the modern political myths. A philosophy of history that consists in somber predictions of the decline and the inevitable destruction of our civilization and a theory that sees in the *Geworfenheit* of man one of his principal characters have given up all hopes of an active share in the construction and reconstruction of man's cultural life. Such philosophy renounces its own fundamental theoretical and ethical ideals. It can be used, then, as a pliable instrument in the hands of the political leaders.[123]

This was written in what turned out to be the last year of his life. The manuscript was finished just a few days before his sudden death and published posthumously in 1946. Yet, already before his time in the United States Cassirer had begun to address similar issues. This, as we will show, is clear from the writings he had left behind in Sweden and from his inaugural address at the University of Gothenburg.

After leaving Germany, Cassirer lived an exilic existence on a series of temporary appointments and died never having been able to return to his home country. In Germany, his books, alongside those by other Jewish authors, were burned and banned from libraries and universities for the entire twelve-year period of the Third Reich. This contributed to the fact that, after 1945, Cassirer's works were all but forgotten and remained so until the mid-1980s when the first wave of a Cassirer 'Renaissance' emerged.[124] The general lack of knowledge of Cassirer's work until that time has also played a significant role in the widespread misunderstanding of Langer's work, especially her aesthetics, by analytic philosophers. It is almost impossible to understand Langer's aesthetics outside the neo-Kantian framework as embodied by Cassirer.

Continental divide

The Davos debate is sometimes regarded as the beginning of the 'continental divide' between, on the one hand, the old, scientifically orientated neo-Kantian philosophies as represented by Cassirer, and the new phenomenologically and existentially oriented 'postmodern' or 'continental' philosophies as represented by Heidegger.[125] This impression was enforced by the presence of Carnap who was closely associated with the 'scientistic' Marburg School. Even though Cassirer's view were considerably different from those of Carnap, Carnap's support for Cassirer made them appear as close philosophical allies.[126] This assessment, however, overplays the differences between Heidegger and Cassirer. As Peter Gordon points out, we can only make sense of their disagreement if we understand how much they shared in common.[127] Both Heidegger and Cassirer had been deeply schooled in neo-Kantianism – Heidegger had studied with Rickert at the Baden School – and both embraced a philosophy of cognition that not only sought to transcend scientific knowledge but also was deeply rooted in history. Long before the debate in Davos the two philosophers had been in regular contact and conversation.[128] Heidegger had been interested in Cassirer's views of myth and, in 1928, had published a sympathetic review of the second volume of *The Philosophy of Symbolic Forms*.[129]

Ultimately, the main difference between Cassirer's and Heidegger's philosophies did not lie in their views of science and cognition but in their views of what it meant to be human. For Cassirer, full humanity lies in the freedom and spontaneity to create worlds of meaning as objectified in the different cultural spheres of science, myth language and art. The idea of the creation of forms as a means of human liberation from its animal state was already present in his early books, including *Freedom and Form* (1916).[130] For Heidegger, by contrast, it means a fundamental recognition and acceptance of one's finite, embodied existence as the condition for an authentic way of life and being. In short, whereas Cassirer emphasizes the productive spontaneity and creativity of the human mind, Heidegger stresses its receptiveness in the face of the 'thrownness' of human existence and the basic 'givenness' of the world. As I will show in a later chapter, Langer's biologically based philosophy of mind and embodied meaning can be said to provide a bridge between these two divergent perspectives. But, as I will show, even Cassirer's own later work shows some seeds for a creative convergence.

The period of exile (1933–45): 'Metaphysics'

In his 1935 inaugural address at the University of Gothenburg, Cassirer reveals his growing unease with the failure of philosophy, including that of his own, to 'achieve its intellectual and ethical vocation.'[131] He quotes Albert Schweitzer, whom he had met in Oxford, as saying, 'In the hour of peril, the watchmen slept, whom should have kept watch over us.'[132] In an almost public confession he tells his audience,

> I do not exclude myself and I do not absolve myself. While endeavoring on behalf of the scholastic conception of philosophy … we have all too frequently lost sight of the true connection of philosophy with the world. But today we can no longer keep our eyes closed to the menacing danger. Today the urgency of the time warns us more strongly and more imperatively than ever that there is once again a question for philosophy which involves its ultimate and highest decision. Is there really something like an objective theoretical truth, and is there something like that which earlier generations have understood as the ideal of morality, of *humanity*? … In a time in which such questions can be raised, philosophy cannot stand aside, mute and idle. If ever, now is the time for it again to reflect on itself, on that which it is and what is has been, on its systematic, fundamental purpose, and on its spiritual-historical past.[133]

This statement is not a reversal of his earlier belief that philosophy should not be in the service of (party) politics, but a way of rethinking and developing his thought so that it could lead to a cultural and social critique. Introducing new themes and concepts he ventured into for him as yet unexplored territories such as social philosophy, anthropology and biology. Sadly, because of the upheavals of the war, little of this research was published during his lifetime. When Cassirer moved to America in 1941, he had planned to return to Sweden soon after finishing at Yale. In view of that, he had left all his manuscripts behind hoping to resume work on them upon his return. This was not to happen. Further travel bans by the Nazi regime and his own premature death meant that the Swedish papers were left unattended until the early seventies when they were catalogued and edited by John M. Krois and Donald P. Verene.[134]

As we now know, Cassirer's years in Sweden turned out to be some of his most productive.[135] Of all twenty volumes of Cassirer's *Nachlass*, the majority contains work from this period.[136] Most importantly, these papers show how Cassirer set out to develop an alternative 'metaphysics' in order to provide an underlying source of unity for the multiplicity of symbolic forms. This source or 'ultimate reality' is not, as in traditional metaphysics, a substance, but a dialectical process between 'life' and '*Geist*'.[137]

Although Langer may have had some knowledge of the latest developments in Cassirer's thinking through her conversations with him in America, she will not have had access to his Swedish papers. Even so, it is possible to discern distinct affinities between Cassirer's and her own, albeit somewhat fragmented and unfinished, 'metaphysics' in the third volume of *Mind*. In order to support this suggestion, I will conclude this chapter by highlighting some of the dominant themes in Cassirer's metaphysics.

As for many of his contemporaries, Cassirer's attitude to metaphysics is, to say the least, ambivalent. For the most part his analysis of symbolic forms is an empirical investigation employing empirical methods and, as such, 'independent of any metaphysical theory about the absolute nature of things'.[138] Yet, Cassirer increasingly realizes that any 'analysis' cannot avoid the question of 'synthesis'. As he wrote in 1928, '[A]fter phenomenological analysis has sought to bring out the basic forms of linguistic, mythic, and scientific thoughts, the need for synthesis seems to exert its demand on us all the more urgently and insistently'.[139]

Cassirer's main reflections on metaphysics can be found in the first volume of his *Nachlass* (1995), published as the first chapter of the fourth volume of *The Philosophy of Symbolic Forms* under the title '"*Geist*" and "Life"'.[140] In what follows I draw primarily on this chapter and related material as collected in this volume.

Like Whitehead before him and Langer after him, Cassirer is very clear about what kind of metaphysics he rejects:

> The metaphysics that we combat is twofold, and its claims seem to derive from opposing presuppositions. The worldview of 'Symbolic Idealism' is opposed both to the metaphysics of dogmatic Realism and to the metaphysics of so-called Positivism. It combats something which, despite all their apparent differences, is a common basic feature in both of them: that they see the source of intellectual life and its functions in some kind of 'reproduction' and 'mirroring' of some 'reality' given independently of them. In the older metaphysics this reality is the absolute being of things; in Positivism it is the, no less absolute, givenness of 'simple sensations'.[141]

In line with neo-Kantians' rejection of the *Ding-an-Sich*, Cassirer restates that we cannot isolate some separate, independent reality from the knowing, actively perceiving and form-giving, mind:

> We have access to no 'Being' of any kind – be it metaphysical or psychological in nature – prior to and independently of intelligent action, but only in and through this action. Even the very idea of severing the two from each other, of contrasting in our imagination a purely passive 'givenness' with intellectual [*geistig*] 'activity' is deceptive. There is no form of 'Being' for us outside of these different kinds of action (in language, myth, religion, art, science) because there is no other form of determinacy.[142]

In other words, long before Derrida launched his claim that there is no world 'outside the text', Cassirer argued that, since we have no representation of the world other than the one produced through the prism of our various symbolic forms, we are incapable of making any statements about the world except by means of those very forms.[143]

Yet Cassirer does not reject metaphysics as such. Like Whitehead and Langer, he conceives its role as the pioneering of new frameworks and ideas. As he wrote in his study on the Swedish philosopher Axel Hägerström,

The history of metaphysics is by no means a history of meaningless concepts or empty words ... it establishes a new basis of vision and from it gains a new perspective for knowing the real.[144]

Nor does he deny the existence of a reality independent of a perceiving subject. Like Derrida, Cassirer can be misread on that point.[145] As he makes clear to his students at Yale,

In our former discussions I often had the impression that some of you were thinking that what I defend here is a system of subjective idealism in which the ego, the subjective mind, the thinking self is considered as the center and as the creator of the world, as the sole or ultimate reality. ... [However] The ego, the individual mind, cannot create reality. Man is surrounded by a reality that he did not make, that he has to accept as an ultimate fact.[146]

The main question is what Cassirer means by 'ultimate fact'. For him this is not a particular substance as the result of privileging one aspect of our experience over the other. That was the problem with the traditional metaphysical systems.

In each case a certain aspect of experience has been posited as absolute and then taken in isolation, whereupon this absolute positing is declared to be primordial, being itself. It is always a particular feature of experienced reality that is hypostasized this was as *Ens a se* and *Ens per se*. Now it is being, now becoming, now unity, now plurality, now it is nature, now God, now the soul (the mind), now matter, that are posited in this way as 'absolute', as fundamentally original.[147]

Instead, on Cassirer's view, we should not focus on symbolic forms in their final manifestations – their 'telos' – or abstracted final form. That, he says, is the problem of traditional substance metaphysics: 'Realistic metaphysics agrees with empiricist Positivism in that they both think in terms of substance: they begin with the unitary "simplicity" of the thing, of the existing "world" as present at hand'.[148] By contrast, Cassirer is primarily concerned with 'the dynamics of the giving of meaning'.[149] Like Whitehead, as we will see in the next chapter, he seeks 'to understand and illuminate the riddle of the becoming of form as such – not so much as a finished determination but rather with determination as a process'.[150] Cassirer's metaphysics of symbolic idealism *'begins not with the simple unity of the thing (substance), but with the unity of function'.*[151] As Langer would articulate it later, meaning is not primarily a noun; it is a verb.

The implications of this approach is that 'the unity of geist is to be found only in the plurality of symbolic forms, not as a substantial unity but as a functional plurality'.[152] Most significantly, his metaphysics does not start with 'the primordial fact of so-called Being, but with that of "Life"'.[153] 'Life', for Cassirer, is not the vitalistic power of *Lebensphilosophie*. The problem with *Lebensphilosophie* for Cassirer is that it still operates with the categories of substance metaphysics – it contrasts life with spirit, body with soul, etc. It merely reverses the traditional order of preference. For Cassirer, by contrast, 'geist' and 'life' are not two contrasting poles which are in competition with each other and in need of reconciliation but two *moments* or *aspects* of the same symbolizing process. Whereas 'life' entails the human impulse to make sense of the world by means of expression, 'geist' provides the means to reflect on that understanding and evaluate it with a view to practical orientation. That means that instead of life and geist being opposites they form 'a correlation and cooperation, when regarded from the standpoint of activity, of intelligent creativity'.[154] Life is not left behind in geist but comes to its full potential. They exist in an ongoing reciprocal relation in which each feeds and nurtures the other. This notion of a dialectical process between life and geist brings Cassirer closer to Hegel than to Kant.[155] For him the 'turn to the idea' is not an abdication of life but rather life as 'returning to itself'. Life 'comes to itself' in the medium of the symbolic forms.[156] Referring to Fichte, he holds,

> Consciousness so conceived goes beyond the primordial ground of 'life', but life is thereby neither destroyed nor violated. In the sphere of intellectual consciousness which now arises, life is visible to itself; to use Fichte's expression, it has become pure 'seeing'.[157]

For Cassirer, symbol formation as a process of transformation and 'objectification' is thus not a one-directional process of increasing distancing and alienation from life itself, but a form of homecoming in the sense of Socratic self-understanding. Echoing von Humboldt's notion of *ergeion* or 'work', this Socratic call means for him, '[K]now your *work* and know "yourself" *in* your work; know what you do so you can do what you know.'[158] As Verene summarizes it,

> The key feature of life is its constant transformation into Geist. This transformation into Geist is the continual process of life taking on form, a process that moves from the immediate to the mediate. … The relationship of life and Geist is not one-way. It is bi-directional because the Geist is continually in the process of reemerging from life. Life and Geist are held together as two necessary moments of a dialectic that is parallel to Hegel's in-itself and for-itself.[159]

Even so, Cassirer never develops a Hegelian or, for that matter, Whiteheadian metaphysics of Being beyond his account of the unity of the different symbolic forms. Verene again,

> Cassirer does not engage in speculation after the fashion of Whitehead, namely projecting an account of the various forms of reality and life that are nonhuman developed from an analysis of the human. Instead he relies on Uexküll's biology of the organism and stops within its limits.[160]

Cassirer, in other words, does not probe behind what can be symbolized and recognizes that there are 'necessary and inescapable "limits of conceptualization"'.[161]

For Langer, as for Cassirer, symbolization understood in that way lies at the heart of what it means to be human. It is both an ongoing basic human need for expression and a call for responsible human living:

This basic need which certainly is obvious only in man, is the *need of symbolization.* The symbol-making function is one of man's primary activities, like eating, looking, or moving about. It is the fundamental process of his mind, and goes on all the time.[162]

Even so, for Langer, Cassirer remains too much an idealist. As she wrote in an unpublished note,

> Here is my basic disagreement with Cassirer and consequently a different directedness of interest: the idealist was content to find the animal/human dividing line, and did not seek the natural cause of the division because he did not think of 'Geist' as a natural effect. I do; I want to find the point of specialization where imagination emerges from feeling.[163]

While Langer and Cassirer converged on the idea the symbolic mind as an ongoing process of embodied meaning, they came at it from different directions. For both symbolic forms are the mediators between the subjective and objective world. Yet for Cassirer, they are the roads by which the *spirit* proceeds towards objectivization and self-realisation, whereas for Langer, they are the primary avenues of the organism as a whole. On this front Langer's non-reductionistic naturalism is closer to Whitehead than to Cassirer.

Cassirer and post-war American and European philosophy

One can only guess how much influence Cassirer might have had on the developments of American philosophy had he lived any longer. He arrived in America after the seminal Congress of the Unity of Science at Harvard in 1939 and the 1940–1 discussions between Carnap, Quine and Tarski, but is not known to have played any active role in further debates. Even so, *An Essay on Man* became a popular title on many post-war undergraduate courses and the prestigious *Library of Living Philosophers* had dedicated one of its volumes to him which had to be completed after his death.[164]

In post-war Germany and the rest of Europe Cassirer was soon to be eclipsed by Heidegger and other 'postmodern' schools of philosophy. As Krois and Verene wrote in 1977,

> Although Cassirer's work has been widely read and has had identifiable effects, no school of thought or particular sphere of influence has developed from it and only a limited amount of critical work has, in fact, appeared on it.[165]

As noted, the Cassirer 'renaissance' since the 1990s generated a new surge of interest in Cassirer's life and work, both in America and Europe. Langer can be said to have both anticipated and contributed to this revival with her early recognition of Cassirer as a seminal thinker. In this, as in so many other ways, she was a pioneer. As Krois and Verene pointed out,

> Among contemporary thinkers, Susanne Langer is the one figure who has most developed her thought from the perspective of Cassirer's theory of symbolic forms and whose thought has done the most to extend the spirit of his philosophy.[166]

Langer also extended Cassirer's work in one important area, that is, art. In 1942, Cassirer wrote in a letter to Paul Schilpp, the editor of the volume on Cassirer in *The Library of Living Philosophers*, that 'in the first sketch (*im ersten Entwurf*) of his *Philosophy of Symbolic Forms* he had considered a volume on art, but the "malice" (*Ungunst*) of the times had caused him to put it off again and again.'[167] In the event, apart from one chapter in his *Essay on Man* and three short manuscripts on art in a posthumously published edition, *Symbol, Myth and Culture*, Cassirer never produced any substantial work on art or aesthetics.[168] Langer's much more extensive thinking on philosophy of art was profoundly influenced by Cassirer's philosophy of symbolic forms. As Krois and Verene write,

> Among scholars in the United States who knew Cassirer and his work, the impression grew that an unwritten volume was needed to complete *The Philosophy of Symbolic Forms*, and that this was on art. Cassirer continually mentions the triad of art, myth and religion throughout the three volumes but there is no separate treatment of art. This impression that there should be a volume on art persisted even after Cassirer's death, especially since the one thinker most immediately to carry on from Cassirer's work was Susanne Langer, who, although she was never his student and met him only after he came to the United States, developed a conception of symbolism formulated in terms of aesthetic theory.[169]

Langer can thus rightly be said to have completed Cassirer's intention to write a volume on art. In 1953 she published *Feeling and Form: A Theory of Art Developed from Philosophy in a New Key*. It was dedicated 'to the happy memory of Ernst Cassirer'.

6

Alfred N. Whitehead: Organic form

The disastrous separation of body and mind, characteristic of philosophical systems which are in any important respect derived from Cartesianism, is avoided in the philosophy of organism by the doctrines of hybrid physical feelings and of the transmuted feelings.

Whitehead[1]

The human mind is functioning symbolically when some components of its experience elicit consciousness, beliefs, emotions, and usages, respecting other components of experience. … The organic functioning whereby there is transition from symbol to the meaning will be called 'symbolic reference'.

Whitehead[2]

As soon as feeling is regarded as a phase of a physiological process instead of a product (perhaps a by-product) of it, a new entity metaphysically different from it, the paradox of the physical and psychical disappears; for the thesis I hope to substantiate here is that the entire psychological field – including human conception, responsible action, rationality, knowledge – is a vast and branching development of feeling.

Langer[3]

Principia Mathematica

Whitehead's arrival at Harvard, in 1924, coincided with the start of Langer's doctoral studies. Langer had applied to work with Whitehead (1861–1947) because of his reputation as co-author of the *Principia Mathematica* which she had studied under Sheffer. Although Harvard had appointed Whitehead with a view to consolidating the department's leading status in mathematical logic, by the time he had arrived, however, his thinking had developed into radically new directions. Indeed, to the surprise of faculty and students alike, Whitehead had, in the words of Herbert Feigl, 'turned increasingly metaphysical (or "cosmological") after coming to the United States', while Bertrand Russell commented with characteristic hyperbole: 'In England, Whitehead was regarded only as a mathematician, and it was left to America to discover him as a philosopher.'[4] Like Sheffer, Whitehead was an inspiring teacher, whose lectures, though notoriously difficult, were highly sought after by his students. Often teaching without notes his classes were said to have the character of an event, of seeing ideas develop in the process of teaching. William Hocking recalls, 'He gave the impression of a mind not repeating former results but winning anew the insights he had to convey – it was water from a living spring, not from a faucet.'[5] And Paul Weiss reminisces,

> You would never know from being in his class that he was an author of *Principia Mathematica*. He never referred to it. … His classes were rather strange. If you had a book of pedagogy before you … he would fail miserably on every single count. Nevertheless, I think he was great and exciting. He would be set off by your questions in a direction which was not very clear, but eventually by a process of trial and error would come the answers that were, I thought, exceptionally profound and revealing and would throw the whole discussion in a new light.[6]

British philosopher Dorothy E. Emmet recalls that, in her 1929 classes at Radcliffe College, Whitehead had sometimes asked her to take verbatim notes for him as he felt he could at times express himself better when speaking than in writing.[7] Indeed, for Whitehead, teaching was a way to test out his ideas on students. As part of Whitehead's first cohort of students in 1924, Langer witnessed first-hand the development of Whitehead's thinking before it ended up in print.

Langer completed her doctorate in May 1926. According to Whitehead's biographer Victor Lowe, Whitehead's supervision of her thesis, 'A Logical Analysis of Meaning', had been very minimal: 'He read a few pages of an early draft, to see if she had a good idea. After he saw what she did, she submitted nothing more until the thesis was completed.'[8] The same year, with Whitehead's recommendation to the then editor of *Mind*, G. E. Moore, Langer published her first article, 'Confusion of Symbols and Confusion of Logical Types', in the British journal *Mind*. It contained a detailed critique of the theory of types as developed by Bertrand Russell in the second edition of the *Principia Mathematica* published the year before. Two years later Sheffer also published a review of the work with a very similar critique.[9] In a footnote to her review, Langer reminds the reader that we have 'Prof. Whitehead's authority to state that Mr. Russell is the originator of the type-theory, and sole author of the new Introduction to the second edition of *Principia Mathematica*.'[10] This note refers to a letter written by Whitehead to Moore in 1926 asking him to publish a statement in *Mind* disclaiming his involvement in the second edition.[11] Although Bernard Linsky suggests that this should not necessary be interpreted as a repudiation of Russell's additional work on Whitehead's part but as a courtesy to decline any credit for it, it is far more likely that Whitehead wanted to distance himself from Russell's theory of types and the *Principia Mathematica*'s second edition as a whole.[12]

Despite making very few direct references to Whitehead in her writings, Langer was immensely influenced by Whitehead's thinking. This applies not only to his *Principia Mathematica* but to all his subsequent philosophical work, whether on science, perception, process or education. In 1942, five years after Whitehead's retirement from Harvard and the year of her own departure from Radcliffe, Langer was to dedicate her seminal *Philosophy in a New Key* to Whitehead as 'my great Teacher and Friend'. Since it is not possible to understand Langer's overall philosophy without recognizing its Whiteheadian roots, I will, in this chapter, discuss the main elements of Whitehead's life and writings in terms of their relevance to Langer.

Life and works

According to his biographer Victor Lowe, Whitehead was a private man who had ordered the destruction of all his personal and professional papers after his death with the result that 'no professional biographer in his right mind would touch him'.[13] One of the few people who became close to Whitehead as well as Whitehead's wife Evelyn was Bertrand Russell. He regularly stayed over – with or without his wife Alys – at the Whiteheads' family home, including the Old Mill House in Grantchester which they occupied between 1898 and 1906.[14] Nicholas Griffin claims that most of what is known about Whitehead as a person is known 'because Russell recorded it'.[15]

Whitehead's life and publications can be divided into three periods that broadly correspond to his three different academic positions: first, as a mathematician and logician at Cambridge University from 1884–1910; then, as a philosopher of science at London University from 1910 to 1924 and then, at Harvard from 1924 until 1937 and until his death as a process philosopher and metaphysician. As was the case with Cassirer, since all three periods are relevant to Langer's writing, I will look at each in turn while highlighting some important influences and parallels.[16]

The Cambridge period (1884–1910): Mathematics and symbolic logic

Langer's first interest in Whitehead concerned his *Principia Mathematica* that he co-wrote with Russell in Cambridge. During his time at Trinity College, Cambridge, Whitehead distinguished himself initially more through his teaching – Bertrand Russell describes him as 'extraordinarily perfect as a teacher' – than his writing – during his first twelve years of his teaching he had only published two papers.[17] From the early 1900s, however, he had started to collaborate with his eleven-year-younger former doctoral student Bertrand Russell on what would become *Principia Mathematica* (1910, 1912 and 1913).[18] Based on Gottlob Frege's pioneering work, the work's idea that mathematics could be reduced to formal logic became the foundation of the new field of symbolic logic. In her 1926 doctoral thesis, 'A Logical Analysis of Meaning', Langer was to criticize what she considered *Principia Mathematica*'s too narrowly defined notion of logical meaning. Employing a Shefferian/Roycean notion of logic as a study of forms rather than inferences, she argued that the meaning of propositions was just *one type* of logical meaning among a variety of others. She maintained that logical form and meaning could be found outside propositions, including, as we will see, in the realm of art. As she argued in the thesis, the logical framework for meaning, that is, the four-fold relation between a sign maker, a sign, a 'concept' and an interpreter, is 'similar for all meaning-situations, from the word that "means" a table or a chair, to the Moral Ego that "means" the self-realization of the Absolute'.[19] This early insight laid the foundation for her later distinction between discursive and non-discursive meaning. She realizes the radicality of her broad understanding of meaning and the fact that it may seem idiosyncratic:

> The logical foundation of meaning is a point whereupon there is practically no literature. Kempe, Royce and Sheffer – none of them voluminous writers – are its casual discoverers. But there is a vast literature just beside the point, which sometimes throws valuable lights in our direction. Hence the motley appearance of my bibliography, which takes in such diverse material as Couturat's 'The Algebra of Logic' and Ogden's and Richard's 'The Meaning of Meaning'. For my purpose I have had to avail myself of those works which deal with meaning, in its logical or non-logical aspects, and also of the literature of modern logistic.[20]

This broad range of sources accounts for her capacious concept of logic which she contrasts with the one she encountered in the *Principia Mathematica*. As she wrote in the preface to her thesis,

> The great emphasis which I have given to the question of the *nature of logic* needs, perhaps, some justification. I have had unusual opportunity to discuss the question of *logical systems* with prof. Whitehead, who has taken a very kindly interest in this bit of research, yet to my surprise, I have found the logic of *Principia* inapplicable to the analysis in hand. In view of the fact that our greatest classic in modern logic is his and Mr. Russell's system of 'propositional' logic, I may be pardoned for investigating at such length the reasons why an analysis of meaning could not be based upon it. I have come to the conclusion that the universe of possible meaning-situations *includes* the meaning of propositions, exactly as the universe of possible structures *includes* deductive systems.[21]

This inclusive concept of logical meaning was in large part the product of her research done under Sheffer, whose classes she had continued to attend alongside those of Whitehead. As she explains,

> This analysis of meaning is, essentially, a philosophical application of the purely formal work done in recent years by Dr. Sheffer, which is at present recorded only in a brief unpublished paper. If I have not acknowledged my debt to him in every instance, it is because of the dearth of printed passages for reference.[22]

As is clear from a lecture note by one of Whitehead's students, Whitehead himself is also sympathetic to a Roycean notion of logic as the study of patterns and acknowledged his debt to 'Sheffer's brilliant work'.[23] Many years later, in *Modes of Thought* (1938), he mentions Sheffer again praising him as follows: 'Professor Sheffer … emphasized the notion of pattern, as fundamental to Logic. In this way, one of the great advances in mathematical Logic was accomplished.[24]

It is not known whether Whitehead met Sheffer when the latter visited Cambridge as a student. Sheffer arrived just after Whitehead had left for London in the summer of 1910 to be succeeded by Russell as lecturer in logic and philosophy of mathematics at Trinity College.[25] Sheffer attended Russell's lectures between October and December 1910 and then moved on to visit other logicians in Europe. Sheffer also missed Wittgenstein who was to arrive in October 1911. Wittgenstein spent two years in Cambridge and then moved on to a remote location in Norway where he planned to work on his logic.[26] During his years in Cambridge he attended Russell's lectures and also met Whitehead. Based on his later letters to Russell, Wittgenstein seemed to have had fond memories of Whitehead as, on several occasions, he asks Russell to pass on his greetings.[27] Whitehead and Russell, however, drifted apart both philosophically and politically but remained nevertheless loyal to each other on a personal level.[28] Throughout her work Langer will draw selectively on all four philosophers – Russell, Whitehead, Sheffer and Wittgenstein – and combine their thought in a unique synthesis.

The London period (1910–24): Applied mathematics and philosophy of science

Whitehead's London period marked a move from pure mathematics and logic to applied mathematics and philosophy of science resulting in three major works: *An Enquiry Concerning the Principles of Natural Knowledge* (1919), *The Concept of Nature* (1920) and *The Principle of Relativity with Applications to Physical Science* (1922). Interestingly, when Langer refers to Whitehead in her 1950 article 'The Deepening Mind: A Half-Century of American Philosophy', it is these three books she mentions rather than the books he wrote in America:

> The greatest single achievement in the modern critique of science is that part of A. N. Whitehead's work which is contained in his three most systematic and technical books … , *An Enquiry into the Principles of Natural Knowledge, The Concept of Nature, and The Principle of Relativity*. These books were written in England; but Whitehead, too, afterward (that is, since 1923) elected our country as his home, and has become an integral and noble part of our growing philosophical tradition.[29]

The three works singled out by Langer all engage closely with the latest developments in science, in particular Einstein's theory of relativity.[30] A former student of Whitehead, astrophysicist Arthur Eddington, had led a West African expedition to test out Einstein's calculations on the solar eclipse of 29 May 1919. The expedition's affirmative findings of Einstein's general theory of relativity were presented to the Fellow of the Royal Society and the Royal Astronomical Society and laid the foundations of Einstein's global fame.[31] As a Fellow of the Royal Society and as Eddington's former supervisor, he felt he had a vested interest in the findings. Whitehead recognized that, if true, Einstein's theories would have far-reaching implications not only for science but also for philosophy. In order to prove that, however, the theories needed to be tested beyond their fields of origin, that is, beyond the fields of electromagnetism and light of Einstein's special theory of relativity (1905), and the field of gravity of his general theory of relativity (1915). As Whitehead wrote in *The Principle of Relativity with Applications to Physical Science* (1922),

> The doctrine of relativity affects every branch of natural science, not excluding the biological sciences. … But in testing its truth, if the theory have the width and depth which marks a fundamental reorganisation, we cannot wisely confine ourselves solely to the consideration of a few happy applications. The history of science is strewn with the happy applications of discarded theories.[32]

Above all, Whitehead was interested in the philosophical implications of Einstein's theories:

> To expect to reorganise our ideas of Time, Space, and Measurement without some discussion which must be ranked as philosophical is to neglect the teaching of history and the inherent probabilities of the subject. On the other hand, no reorganisation of these ideas can command confidence unless it supplies science with added power in the analysis of phenomena. The evidence is two-fold, and is fatally weakened if the two parts are disjoined.[33]

As it stood, Whitehead felt that Einstein, as he had put it in *Concept of Nature,* 'cramped the development of his brilliant method in the narrow bounds of a very doubtful philosophy'.[34] For Whitehead, since the most fundamental concepts of science – matter, mind, motion, time and so on – are always shaped within particular philosophical traditions, it is essential to review and interrogate the *meaning* of those concepts when formulating new scientific theories. For him that meant that Einstein's theories could not be accepted merely on the basis of complex mathematical calculations, but that it needed to be reconnected with basic human perception and experience.[35] This is the central theme of Whitehead's *An Enquiry Concerning the Principles of Natural Knowledge* (1919):

> How is space rooted in experience? The modern theory of relativity has opened the possibility of a new answer to this question. The successive labours of Larmor, Lorentz, Einstein, and Minkovski have opened a new world of thought as to the relations of space and time to the ultimate data of perceptual knowledge. The present work is largely concerned with providing a physical basis for the more modern views which have thus emerged. The whole investigation is based on the principle that the scientific concepts of space and time are the first outcome of the simplest generalizations from experience, and that they are not to be looked for at

the tail end of a welter of differential equations. This position does not mean that Einstein's recent theory of general relativity and of gravitation is to be rejected. The divergence is purely a question of interpretation.[36]

Whitehead believed that if Einstein's theories could be applied more broadly, they were to mount a major challenge to Descartes's dualism between, 'on the one hand, *matter* with its simple location in space and time and, on the other, *mind*, perceiving, suffering, reasoning, but not interfering'.[37] That, in turn, would open up the possibility of an active, participating observer, whose position and perspective affected our experience and cognition of the world. Crucially, it would establish an integral connection between the knower and the known that was to reveal the world's radical interconnectedness.[38]

In order to develop his hypothesis, Whitehead challenges the way modern science had separated space and time. For him, time fundamentally affects the way we observe reality: '[W]e do not perceive isolated instantaneous facts, but a continuity of existence. … the ultimate fact for observational knowledge is perception through a duration'.[39] As long as the ultimate facts of science are considered as duration-less instants of time, it is impossible to explain physical phenomena that involve change. While this is most obvious in the phenomena of biology such as growth and decay, it is no less true in physics where phenomena such as velocity, acceleration, momentum and kinetic energy are inexplicable without at least some reference to the past and future.[40] For Whitehead, this dynamic of time and space turns perception into 'an event'.[41] Most importantly, instead of 'passive contemplation' perception is active participation and generation. It is, as Whitehead puts it, 'at the utmost point of creation'.[42] As we will see in the next chapters, exactly the same emphasis on the active role of perception will be found in Langer's later work. Indeed, drawing on Wittgenstein, she takes Whitehead's notion of event even a step further. Not only is perception an event, so is the product of perception – a fact, according to Langer, is 'an intellectually formulated event'.[43] Or, as she puts it in *Philosophy in a New Key*, 'A fact is an event as we see it, or would see it if it occurred for us'.[44]

In *The Concept of Nature* (1920), Whitehead covers very similar ground as in his earlier book, but this time from the angle of the philosophical implications of concrete recent scientific discoveries.[45] In this context, he offers a detailed critique of the traditional notion of substance as rooted in Aristotle's subject–predicate logic.[46] According to Whitehead,

> The unquestioned acceptance of the Aristotelian logic has led to an ingrained tendency to postulate a substratum for whatever is disclosed in sense-awareness, namely, to look below what we are aware of for the substance in the sense of the 'concrete thing'.[47]

This model assumes a split between, on the one hand, 'nature apprehended in awareness' and, on the other, 'nature which is the cause of awareness':

> The nature which is the fact apprehended in awareness holds within it the greenness of the trees, the song of the birds, the warmth of the sun, the hardness

of the chairs, and the feel of velvet. The nature which is the cause of awareness is the conjectured system of molecules and electrons which so affects the mind as to produce the awareness of apparent nature.[48]

This model has led to a schism between, on the one hand, measurable, 'objective', qualities, and, on the other, non-measurable, 'subjective' qualities or, in Lockean language, a division between 'primary' and 'secondary' qualities. For Whitehead, the main problem with this 'bifurcation of nature' is its failure to account for the connection between, on the one hand, the objective, passive and causal aspect of perception and, on the other, the subjective, active and creative side:

> Why – on this theory – should the cause which influences the mind to perception have any characteristics in common with the effluent apparent nature? In particular, why should it be in space? Why should it be in time? And more generally, what do we know about mind which would allow us to infer any particular characteristics of a cause which should influence mind to particular effects?[49]

In order to solve this dilemma, Whitehead turns once more to the notion of 'event'. Understanding 'substance' in terms of an event means that, instead of seeing it in its independence, it is seen in terms of its multiple relationships.[50] A philosophy of nature thus conceived does not distinguish between measurable (size, weight, etc.) and non-measurable (colours, smells, etc.) qualities in terms of objective or subjective but in terms of different type of relations between the observer and the observed – they constitute different kinds of 'abstractions'. As we will see later, the term 'abstraction' will also take centre place in Langer's philosophy. For her, as for Whitehead, all perception is a form of abstraction. Most importantly, there is a plurality of forms of abstractions in which we perceive and conceptualize the world. This is a recurrent theme from the very beginning of her work.

According to Whitehead, not only do we abstract traditional qualities such as size, colour or texture, we also abstract time and space:

> Time is known to me as an abstraction from the passage of events. The fundamental fact which renders this abstraction possible is the passing of nature, its development, its creative advance, [and] the extensive relation between events.[51]

Once fundamental notions such as time, space, matter, relations between subject and object, and mind and body, are being re-conceived, science is no longer confined to the realm of physical and quantifiable things. It can explore objects in their passing of time, their coming and going, growing and decaying: 'A concrete fact of nature always includes temporal passage … what is directly observed is an event.'[52] Whitehead illustrates this with Cleopatra's Needle on London's Victoria Embankment:

> If we define the Needle in a sufficiently abstract manner we can say that it never changes. But a physicist who looks on that part of the life of nature as a dance of

electrons, will tell you that daily it has lost some molecules and gained others, and even the plain man can see that it gets dirtier and is occasionally washed.[53]

Instead of rejecting science for its putative limitations in dealing with the realm of lived experience – a route taken by, among others, Heidegger – Whitehead expands the foundational concepts of science in order to allow it to include so-called 'subjective' experience. The relation between the perceiver and the perceived is to be re-conceived in terms of a plurality of dynamic relationships, not only between subject and object, but also between the senses, in particular between sight and touch. Predating Merleau-Ponty's *Phenomenology of Perception* by over two decades, Whitehead's account of perception is thoroughly phenomenological.[54] Referring to a blue coat he writes,

> What we perceive is an object other than a mere sense-object. It is not a mere patch of colour, but something more; and it is that something more which we judge to be a coat. … [The] concurrence [between different observational modes] in the situations of sense-objects has led to the body – i.e. the percipient event – so adapting itself that the perception of one sense-object in a certain situation leads to a subconscious sense-awareness of other sense-objects in the same situation. This interplay is especially the case between touch and sight.[55]

In order to answer the question how we know what we know, Whitehead turns, in the words of Bruno Latour, not 'backward toward the knowing subject' but '*forward* toward the world in its determination and indeterminacy'.[56] Interpretation, on Whitehead's model, is not something we impose *on* the world but is a response to an invitation *from* the world. It is, in Latour's words, 'the world itself that is "open to interpretation", not because of the weakness of our limited mind but because of the world's own activities'.[57] This profound insight is a central thread in Langer's later work, especially her trilogy *Mind: An Essay on Human Feeling.*

Whitehead develops the idea further in *The Principle of Relativity with Applications to Physical Science* (1922) where he contrasts Einstein's abstracted heterogeneity of time and space with the basic human experience of their fundamental uniformity and unity.[58] Unless we accept such a uniformity between Kant's two forms of perception, it is not possible to develop an inclusive epistemology that embraces both primary and secondary qualities and we risk, so argues Whitehead, falling back into our old dilemmas and dichotomies:

> If we are to avoid this unfortunate bifurcation, we must construe our knowledge of the apparent world as being an individual experience of something which is more than personal. Nature is thus a totality including individual experiences, so that we must reject the distinction between nature as it really is and experiences of it which are purely psychological. Our experiences of the apparent world are nature itself.[59]

Whitehead's extension of Einstein's theories of relativity beyond their original fields of light and gravity thus opens the way to a broader understanding of nature than was previously held: 'Nature is an abstraction from something more concrete than itself which must also include imagination, thought, and emotion.'[60] This attention for imagination and emotion was to play an even more significant role in his later work after his move to Harvard. As we will see, it was also crucial to Langer's notion of mind conceived in terms of human feeling and to her concept of art as the 'form of feeling'.

The Harvard period (1924–47): Metaphysics and process philosophy

Whitehead's move to the United States in 1924 was motivated by a number of factors, one of which was England's mandatory retirement age of 65. At age 63 Whitehead had felt at the peak of his intellectual creativity and energy and was keen to develop the ideas he had started to work on in London. As he had put it in a letter to the philosophy department at Harvard:

> I do not feel inclined to undertake the systematic training of students in the critical study of other philosophers. … If however I should be working with colleagues who would undertake this side of the work, I should greatly value the opportunity of expressing in lectures and in a less formal manner the philosophical ideas which have accumulated in my mind.[61]

Whitehead was offered a five-year position with the department which, delighted to receive a great scholar of such distinction, waved its own American customary retirement age of 65. Historian Kuklick comments,

> [I]n 1924 Lowell appointed the fourth professor, Alfred North Whitehead. He had the intellectual stature of Russell but was as conventional as Russell was unorthodox. Everyone thought Whitehead was perfect: he had all of Russell's talent and none of Russell's handicaps. Woods wrote enthusiastically that Whitehead's presence was sure to revivify philosophy in Cambridge because he was 'a radiating center of benevolence and creative thinking'. He adorned Harvard until 1937.[62]

Even after his retirement in 1937, Whitehead was to remain active with teaching and writing. As it turned out, his life in America was to become the most productive period of his entire career with publications including *Science and the Modern World* (1925), *Religion in the Making* (1926), *Symbolism: Its Meaning and Effect* (1927), *The Function of Reason* (1929), *Process and Reality* (1929), *Adventure of Ideas* (1933) and *Modes of Thought* (1938). According to his son, Whitehead 'fell in love with America' as it realized some of the ideals he had been trying to promote in England.[63] As dean of the Faculty of Science at London University, Whitehead had developed a keen interest in the role and purpose of education. In a famous presidential address in 1916 to the Mathematical Association of England, he stressed the importance of the formation of critical thinking in teaching rather than merely passing on information. As he famously put it in his openings sentences, 'Culture is activity of thought, and receptiveness to beauty and humane feeling. Scraps of information have nothing to do with it. A merely well-informed man is the most useless bore on God's earth.'[64] Whitehead had always been critical of the British education system with its compartmentalization of subjects. Recalling his own undergraduate years at Cambridge, he writes,

> The formal teaching at Cambridge was competently done, by interesting men of first-rate ability. But courses assigned to each undergraduate might cover a narrow range. For example, during my whole undergraduate period at Trinity, all my lectures were on mathematics, pure and applied. I never went inside another lecture room.[65]

Whitehead sees this compartmentalization of subjects and the strict separation between the natural and human sciences or 'humanities' as yet another expression of the same 'bifurcation of nature' that characterized modern philosophy.[66] He valued Harvard's tradition of a natural interplay between the humanities and the natural sciences, as exemplified in William James and Josiah Royce both of whom worked on the interface of philosophy and empirical science. According to Hocking, James 'had opened a psychological laboratory outfitted with calves' brains, scalpels [and] microscopes into the lofty halls of the philosophy department, even though, at the time, also to the shock of some of his colleagues'.[67] Royce, moreover, had encouraged interdisciplinary discussion through informal gatherings at this home, also known as 'The Royce Club'.[68] It had been the members of this club that had lobbied for Whitehead's appointment.[69]

Langer absorbed much of Whitehead's thinking, both from before and during his time in America. Between September 1924 and May 1925, Whitehead gave a course of eighty-five lectures at Harvard, his first ever in general philosophy. In 2017, transcriptions of recently discovered student notes by, among others, William Hocking, have been published as the first volume of the *Edinburgh Critical Edition of the Complete Works of Alfred North Whitehead*.[70] The volume includes hundreds of sketches of Whitehead's blackboard diagrams and shows the development of Whitehead's thinking on the philosophical presuppositions of science in this very formative period. Langer also attended Whitehead's Friday evening seminars in the autumn of 1925 and continued to attend his courses after her graduation.[71] Her detailed notes on Whitehead's course on philosophy of nature from October 1927 to May 1928 have been published in *Process Studies* in 1997.[72]

In order to show the deep and lasting impact of Whitehead's classes on Langer's thought, I will briefly discuss the main works from his time in America and indicate the overlaps with Langer's own writings.

Science and the Modern World: Philosophical *epochs*

In the middle of his first year of lectures, in February 1925, Whitehead gave the Lowell Lectures that were to form the basis of his *Science and the Modern World*. The main theme of the lectures was the relation between philosophical ideas and scientific developments. Whitehead argued that the history of civilization consists of a succession of different 'epochs', each with their own dominant 'generative idea' or 'key'. The latter term is used by Langer in the title of *Philosophy in a New Key*. Such a generative idea or *Weltanschauung* is not usually a set of clear and consciously articulated propositions but, rather, a cluster of tacit assumptions that frame a culture's way and outlook on life.[73] Scientific thought from the sixteenth century through to its most recent expressions has been influenced by what Whitehead calls 'scientific materialism', the belief that ultimate reality consists of 'senseless, valueless, purposeless' brute matter, 'spread throughout space in a flux of configurations'.[74] His time, so Whitehead claims, is in need of a new paradigm. While the mechanistic models of nature may have been successful in explaining certain types of facts, '[W]hen we pass beyond the abstraction, either by more subtle employment of our senses, or by the request for meanings and for coherence of thoughts, the scheme breaks down at once'.[75] If science is to make any strides, a wider field of abstraction was needed, with new models, frameworks and categories.[76] For Whitehead, the concepts of '[t]ime, space, matter, material, ether, electricity, mechanism, organism, configuration, structure, pattern, function, all require reinterpretation'.[77] Any new categories would have 'important consequences in every field of thought', especially in the biological sciences and psychology.[78] Central to Whitehead's new conception of science is the notion of organism instead of matter. Only the notion of organism will allow for a framework that can also accommodate ethical, religious and aesthetic experience.[79]

Science and the Modern World was well received. John Dewey called it 'the most significant restatement for the general reader of the present relations of science, philosophy, and the issues of life'.[80] Art theorist and critic Herbert Read, who was also a great admirer of Langer, likewise writes,

> This is the most important book published in the conjoint realms of science and philosophy since Descartes' *Discourse on Method*. It embodies the material of a revolution in our whole concept of life or being, and seeks to reinterpret not only the categories of science and philosophy, but even those of religion and art.[81]

Langer, too, was impressed by the work and the first chapters of *Philosophy in a New Key* clearly reflect the book's influence. We are told, for example, that every society 'meets a new idea with its own concepts, its own tacit, fundamental way of seeing things; that is to say, *with its own questions*, its particular curiosity'.[82] And she quotes Whitehead with approval in the following passage:

> 'When you criticize the philosophy of an epoch', Professor Whitehead says, 'do not chiefly direct your attention to those intellectual positions which its exponents feel it necessary to explicitly defend. There will be some fundamental assumptions which adherents of all the variant systems within the epoch unconsciously presuppose. Such assumptions appear so obvious that people do not know what they are assuming because no other way of putting things has ever occurred to them. With these assumptions a certain limited number of types of philosophic systems are possible, and this group of systems constitutes the philosophy of the epoch'.[83]

Like Whitehead, she points out that the way questions are being formulated determines and limits the nature and range of answers it can expect, including the answers from science: 'Therefore a philosophy is characterized more by the *formulation* of its problems than by its solution of them.'[84] Echoing Whitehead, she critiques Descartes's division of nature into a *res cogitans* and a *res extensa*, a world of inner experience and an outer world, a mind and a body, subject and object. For a while, she says, this gave rise to a whole range of philosophical schools and systems aiming to explain experience in these terms: empiricism, idealism, rationalism, realism, logical positivism. However, as she argues,

> After a while the confusions and shadows inherent in the new vision became apparent, and subsequent doctrines sought in various ways to escape the horns of the dilemma created by the subject-object dichotomy, which Professor Whitehead has called 'the bifurcation of nature'. ... The springs of philosophical thought have run dry once more. For fifty years at least, we have witnessed all the characteristic symptoms that mark the end of an epoch – the incorporation of thought in more and more variegated 'isms' ... [T]he generative ideas of the seventeenth century ... have served their term.[85]

Langer agrees with Whitehead that their time was in need of a new 'generative idea'. For her, this was the recognition of the fundamentally symbolic nature of human culture and life. As she was to put it in *Philosophy in a New Key*,

> Quotations could be multiplied almost indefinitely, from an imposing list of sources – from John Dewey and Bertrand Russell, from Brunschwicg and Piaget and Head, Köhler and Koffka, Carnap, Delacroix, Ribot, Cassirer, Whitehead – from philosophers, psychologists, neurologists, and anthropologists – to substantiate the claim that symbolism is the recognized key to that mental life which is characteristically human and above the level of sheer animality.[86]

Drawing on Whitehead's later philosophy she will, in her own mature work, deepen this notion to account for the embodied nature of symbolic meaning. Her aim for the trilogy *Mind* is 'to construct a conceptual framework for all biological thinking, from biochemistry to neuro-psychology'.[87] This new conceptual framework is meant to overcome the mind–body dualisms that characterize most modern philosophies and open up new ways of thinking not only about human mentality but also about science, language, religion and, eventually, art.

Whitehead's radical critique of modernism in *Science and the Modern World* predates similar critiques later propounded by post-modern thinkers. As David Ray Griffin writes,

> Having described the scientific and philosophical thought of that period as distinctively modern, Whitehead thereby implied that his own philosophy which sought to unite the philosophical implications of relativity and quantum physics

with the Jamesian rejection of dualism, was distinctively postmodern, although he did not use the term.[88]

Interestingly, Whitehead himself pointed to William James's 1904 essay 'Does Consciousness Exist?' as the end of the modern period. James suggested that consciousness and the physical world are essentially made of the same stuff.[89] Nevertheless, in their critique of Cartesian dualism, scientistic modernism and their emphasis on the philosophical presuppositions of science, both Whitehead and Langer can be considered 'postmodern' thinkers *avant la lettre*.

Religion in the Making: Symbols of orientation

In the preface to *Religion in the Making*, published in 1926, Whitehead explains his approach as follows:

> The train of thought which was applied to science in my Lowell Lectures of the previous year, since published under the title, *Science and the Modern World*, is here applied to religion. The two books are independent, but … they elucidate each other by showing the same way of thought in different applications.[90]

This strategy is not uncommon for Whitehead since he often treats similar topics and themes in different contexts and from different angles. As philosopher Randall Auxier puts it, 'The structure of the inquiry is essentially the same in each book, but the methods vary with the hypotheses under consideration.'[91] This has also led to the unfortunate consequence that he sometimes changes his definitions of concepts depending on the type of enquiry, such as mathematical physics or metaphysics.

Religion, for Whitehead, is both private and personal, as well as public and communicable. On the one hand, he writes, 'Religion is what the individual does with his own solitariness. … [A]nd if you are never solitary, you are never religious. Collective enthusiasms, revivals, institutions, churches, rituals, bibles, codes of behaviour, are the trappings of religion, its passing forms.'[92] Earlier, in *Science and the Modern World*, he had defined religion in almost poetic terms as

> the vision of something which stands beyond, behind, and within, the passing flux of immediate things; something which is real, and yet waiting to be realized; something which is a remote possibility, and yet the greatest of present facts; something that gives meaning to all that passes, and yet eludes apprehension; something whose possession is the final good, and yet is beyond all reach; something which is the ultimate ideal, and the hopeless quest.[93]

For Whitehead, the authority of religion is always 'endangered by the intensity of the emotions which it generates'.[94] Since religion itself cannot provide any direct evidence for a personal transcendent God, it must be founded on 'a rational metaphysics which criticizes meanings, and endeavours to express the most general concepts adequate for the all-inclusive universe.'[95]

Although neither Whitehead nor Langer were known to practice any religion, they do not reject it as such.[96] Instead, they see it as one way of making sense of life, giving it meaning and direction. Religion, for Langer, is one form of symbolization. It is one form of 'abstraction' alongside others, rooted in the world of lived experience. As she puts it, [O]ur most important assets are always the symbols of our general *orientation* in nature, on the earth, in society, and in what we are doing: the symbols of our *Weltanschauung* and *Lebensanschauung*.'[97] As a consequence, religion and science should not be seen as in competition with, but as complementing, each other.

Symbolism: Its Meaning and Effect: Symbolic reference and meaning

Although Langer's notion of symbolism has been predominantly shaped by the neo-Kantian Ernst Cassirer, it is also significantly influenced by Whitehead.[98] Whitehead's short but seminal *Symbolism: Its Meaning and Effect* (1927) is one of the first modern philosophies of perception that takes the body seriously. This is reflected in the two modes or 'components' of perception that make up what Whitehead calls 'symbolic reference', defined as the 'organic functioning whereby there is transition from the symbol to the meaning'.[99] The first mode of perception, called 'presentational immediacy', is rooted in the second, called 'causal efficacy'. The first mode refers to a percipient's conscious direct perception of sense data in the external world – colours, sounds, shapes, and so on – at a particular moment in time. The second mode refers to the felt impact of the external world and events in the environment.

To understand the significance of this new conception of perception it is important to know what Whitehead rejects. First, his notion of 'presentational immediacy' is a critique of Hume's and Kant's – and, we may add, Russell's – notion of sense-data as isolated sense-impressions.[100] According to Whitehead, such 'pure' impressions are the result of an intellectual abstraction after the immediate experience. He illustrates this with the art of painting where it requires years of training to be able to perceive the world primarily in terms of shapes and colours. Sense-date, so Whitehead argues, always form part of a relation between the percipient and the world. More specifically, they are snapshots of a concrete event in a specific location at a particular moment of time. Anticipating Merleau-Ponty, he writes,

> Our perception is not confined to universal characters; we do not perceive disembodied colour or disembodied extensiveness: we perceive *the wall's* colour and extensiveness. The experienced fact is 'colour away on the wall for us'. Thus the colour and the spatial perspective are abstract elements, characterizing the concrete way in which the wall enters into our experience. They are therefore relational elements between the 'percipient at that moment', and that other equally

actual entity, or set of entities, which we call the 'wall at that moment'. ... I call this type of experience 'presentational immediacy'.[101]

Second, Whitehead critiques modern philosophy's rejection of causality as a legitimate object of experience. He refers again to Hume and Kant for whom the observation of causal relations is either the result of habit or an *a priori* category of the understanding contributed by the mind as a condition for human experience. In his words,

> The followers of Hume and the followers of Kant have thus their diverse, but allied, objections to the notion of any direct perception of causal efficacy, in the sense in which direct perception is antecedent to thought about it. Both schools find 'causal efficacy' to be the importation, into the data, of a way of thinking or judging about those data. One school calls it a habit of thought; the other school calls it a category of thought. ... For according to these accounts, causal efficacy is nothing else than a way of thinking about sense-data, given in presentational immediacy.[102]

By contrast, for Whitehead, the experience of causality is not only possible but fundamental to perception. It is a more primitive and primordial mode of perception that also operates in lower organisms. It involves the adaptation or, as Whitehead calls it, the 'conformation' of our bodies to an environment that provides various impulses and pressures. It acknowledges that 'the world discloses itself to be a community of actual things, which are actual in the same sense as we are.'[103] While this may not be obvious with the sense of sight, it is more recognizable in experiences of sounds, textures, smells or tastes. In those instances, we experience the sensations as coming from outside, that is, as the 'cause' of our perceptions. This occurrence is both a physical process and a mode of perception between the organism and its environment. Moreover, we experience this causal relation in time, that is, as the impulse preceding our sensation. Whitehead criticizes what he calls Hume's 'extraordinary naïve assumption of time as pure succession'.[104] In the same way that there are no isolated sense-impressions in space, there are no isolated points of succession in time:

> The notion of pure succession is analogous to the notion of colour. There is no mere colour, but always some particular colour such as red or blue: analogously there is no pure succession, but always some particular ground in respect to which the terms succeed each other.[105]

The notion of causal efficacy, in short, acknowledges the higher and lower organisms' embedded relationship to their environment and the way it impinges on their existence. For Whitehead 'all organisms have experience of causal efficacy whereby their functioning is conditioned by their environment.'[106]

At the end of *Symbolism: Its Meaning and Effects*, Whitehead applies the notion of causal efficacy to the 'symbolic transfer' occurring in art. Exploring the question why art and music can be such powerful conduits for emotions, he suggests that this is the case because of the interaction between the way the body is affected by visual or aural sensations– that is, causal efficacy – and the way it presents those sensations in the form of symbolic forms – that is, presentational immediacy.

Langer's conception of symbolic transformation turns out to display considerable overlaps with Whitehead's notion of symbolic reference. Like Whitehead, but unlike Cassirer, Langer puts great emphasis on the organic character of the relationship between a percipient and their environment. As she had put it in the preface to *Philosophy in a New Key*, 'We need not assume the presence of a transcendental "human spirit", if we recognize ... the function of *symbolic transformation* as a natural activity, a high form of nervous response, characteristic of man among animals.'[107] Langer develops this biologically based account of the mind in her trilogy *Mind: An Essay on Human Feeling*. Echoing Whitehead's two modes of perception, she distinguishes between two types of feeling: feelings that are experienced as autogenic and 'subjective', that is, as produced by the percipient agent, and feelings that are experienced as objective stimuli, that is, as impacted and 'caused' by the external world. For Langer, as for Whitehead, human perception always operates with both modes of feelings *simultaneously*. Only on this conception of perception is it possible to overcome the opposition between the mind and the body, and the bifurcation of the world into what Whitehead called 'the nature apprehended in awareness and the nature which is the cause of awareness.'[108]

Finally, both for Langer and for Whitehead, the status of a symbol and its meaning in a symbolic reference are relative to the context of their use. As Whitehead puts it,

> The human mind is functioning symbolically when some components of its experience elicit consciousness, beliefs, emotions, and usages, respecting other components of its experience. The former set of components are the 'symbols', and the latter set constitute the 'meaning' of the symbols. The organic functioning whereby there is transition from symbol to the meaning will be called 'symbolic reference'.[109]

What this passage highlights is the fact that *both* symbol and its meaning are 'components of experience', that is, mediated aspects of our consciousness. We have no access to a mind-independent reality. Moreover, depending on which component is more readily available or, alternatively, more important to behold, the symbol and its meaning are reversible. This theme will be picked up again in *Process and Reality*.

Process and Reality: The feeling organism

In arguably his best known but also most difficult work, *Process and Reality*, Whitehead presents his comprehensive system of speculative philosophy or, as he refers to it, 'philosophy of organism'.[110] The book is both a synthesis of all his previous thinking and a further development in the light of his key notion of organic process. It is based on the Gifford Lectures that he delivered at the University of Edinburgh during the session 1927–8.[111] As is clear from Langer's detailed lecture notes, many of its seminal ideas were first presented in his courses at Harvard and Radcliffe in the year before.[112]

Actual entities and acts

Central to *Process and Reality* are three concepts: 'process', 'form' and 'actual entities' or 'acts'. Building on his earlier critique of substance metaphysics Whitehead argues that in the philosophy of organism 'it is not "substance" which is permanent, but "form"'.[113] Echoing Heraclites' insight that 'no one crosses the same river twice' an actual entity, on Whitehead's terms, cannot exist without being in process.[114] The process itself is 'the constitution of the actual entity'.[115] Put differently, an actual entity's 'being' is constituted by its 'becoming'.[116] As Whitehead puts it in *Adventure of Ideas*: 'The ultimate realities are the events in their process of origination.'[117] The process of becoming in the actual entity is not mechanically motivated by an external cause or agency but is a self-generating activity. Every entity has a particular rhythm of becoming whereby 'creation produces natural pulsation, each pulsation forming a natural unit of historic fact'.[118] No 'fact' or unit stands on its own. All actual entities are coming out of antecedent actualities and merge with those in their own process of becoming. Whitehead calls this process 'concrescence' – a growing together of things into a novel actuality.

All the above themes and concepts recur in Langer's mature thought. Langer may also have played a role in the development of one of the concepts, that is, 'act' or 'actual entity'. Whitehead's term echoes the notion of *Aktualgenese* coined by *Gestalt* psychologist Friedrich Sander in the early twenties. Sander and developmental *Gestalt* theorist Heinz Werner had done scientific experiments on subliminal forms of perceptual awareness in the earliest stages of image formation.[119] These experiments showed that 'the process of perception developed from an initial stage of a diffuse percept through progressive differentiation and discrimination to a distinct configuration.'[120] Sander had been particularly interested in 'the powerful emotionality associated with early (normally preconscious) stages of perception', as well as 'the powerful pull of something one might want to call "will" toward final consolidation of the image.'[121] In an English paper on aphasia from 1956, Werner was to introduce this phenomenon under the term 'microgenesis'.[122] It refers to the development of a brief direct percept or thought as a dynamic unfolding and differentiation in which the germ of the final experience is already embodied in the early stages of its development. In the words of neuropsychologist Robert Henlon, microgenesis is 'a process model of cognitive formation in which the structural development of mental phenomena is considered to evolve through qualitatively different stages, ultimately emerging in consciousness and behavioural expression'.[123] But the term also came to be used outside psychology and neurophysiology.

Reflecting on the way the term developed, historian of science Anne Harrington draws an explicit link between the notion of microgenesis and Whitehead's later process philosophy:

> [M]icrogenesis may be considered an enduring neurological legacy of a general reorientation in philosophy which began around the turn of the century and that, in various ways, would began to stress the radical historicity of fundamental reality. Keynote contributions in this process of questioning and recasting of problems

have ranged from the concepts of creatively unfolding time (*durée réelle*) in the work of Henri Bergson to the 'process philosophy' of Alfred North Whitehead.[124]

Whitehead had been interested in the *Gestalt* theorists and may himself, in turn, have influenced Werner's ideas when the latter was a visiting professor at Harvard in 1937.[125] Sander's notion of *Aktualgenese* is very similar to Whitehead's notion of 'actual entity'. According to Franz Riffert, it is even possible that Whitehead had first encountered the notion *through* Langer. In the early 1920s Langer had translated Sander's article 'Structure, Totality of Experience, and Gestalt' – the only paper by Sander that was available in English – in which Sander had coined the term.[126] Langer's translation was subsequently published in the edited collection of essays *Psychologies of 1930*.[127] Although this book was published a year after *Process and Reality* it is quite possible, so Riffert suggests, that Whitehead had read Langer's translation before it was published.[128] Equally interesting is Riffert's suggestion that one of the reasons that Whitehead's and Cassirer's thoughts display so many overlaps in their discussions of *Gestalt* is that they *both* drew on Sander and Werner.[129]

Langer herself saw great potential in *Gestalt* theory for art.[130] In her seminal 1964 article on abstraction in art, she refers extensively to the phenomenon of physiognomic perception and points out that this often 'precedes or even replaces perception of physically describable sensory forms'.[131] This turns out to be of considerable relevance for her philosophy of art as a whole. She writes,

> Werner reports that according to Friedrich Sander's finding in *Über Gestaltqualitäten* (1927), 'perception is global first, in contradistinction to a later stage at which the parts become increasingly more articulated and integrated with respect to the whole. Furthermore, much of the initial perceptual quality is dynamic, "physiognomic"; feeling and perceiving are little differentiated, imagining and perceiving not clearly separated.' Klaus Conrad, checking Sander's work in his own researches, found that in peripheral vision, too dim light or too brief tachistoscopic exposure, a figure of bright lines on dark ground 'loses its structure, … but gains a sort of physiognomy (Werner). Certain physiognomical qualities dominate the structural qualities'.[132]

Langer believes that this has direct implications for artistic vision:

> The transformation operating spontaneously and involuntarily at a mental level of sheer perception is precisely the projection of feeling – vital, sensory, and emotive – as the most obvious quality of a perceived gestalt. To take up this sort of emotive import is a natural propensity of percepts in childhood experience. It tends also to persist in some people's mature mentality; and there it becomes the source of artistic vision, the quality to be abstracted by the creation of forms so articulated as to emphasize their import and suppress any practical appeal they would normally make.[133]

She follows this up with an extensive quote on art by Klaus Conrad himself:

One is bound to assume that a creative artist ... conceives at first a kind of bud of the gestalt, ... a process pregnant with possibilities, without structure but with a strong physiognomy, fluctuating and without definite shape, not clearly detached. The subject [i.e., the artist] is then charged with an impulse to elaborate the process ... but without complete freedom, as in front of the finished creation. Only when the work stands fully finished in front of the creator all this has changed, it is fully structured, clear and remote, is experienced with finality and can be perceived at will, with all degrees of freedom. The ... vorgestalt has evolved into the endgestalt.[134]

I return to Langer's views of abstraction in art in Chapter 9, but suffice it to say that the notion of 'act' also plays a central role in her trilogy *Mind*. Indeed, alongside the word 'art' it has by far the most occurrences in the entire book. It is the pivot around which her notions of feeling and form as they relate to art are being developed.[135] As she puts it,

It is with the concept of the act that I am approaching living form in nature, only to find it exemplified there at all levels of simplicity and complexity, in concatenations and in hierarchies, presenting many aspects and relationships that permit analysis and construction and special investigation. The act concept is a fecund and elastic concept.[136]

Act forms can be seen in the living forms of biotic life and in those of art and music:

What gives every act [in art] its indivisible wholeness is that its initial phase is the building up of a tension, a store of energy which has to be spent; all subsequent phases are modes of meting out that charge, and the end of the act is the complete resolution of the tension.[137]

Langer's views of art can thus be seen directly related to Whitehead's notions of actual entity and act.

Feelings and prehensions

With one important exception, to which I return shortly, Langer's larger philosophy of mind and feeling shares many features with Whitehead's process philosophy, most notably: a conception of the reciprocal relation between the feeling organism and its environment; the notion of reversibility of subject and object; a non-dualist anthropology, a non-reductionist naturalism, and an emergentist notion of consciousness.

For Whitehead, the most basic interaction between an organism and its environment is a dynamic he calls 'prehensions' (Langer was to use the term 'pression'). He first coined the term in *Science and the Modern World*:

The word *perceive* is, in our common usage, shot through and through with the notion of cognitive apprehension. So is the word *apprehension*, even with the adjective *cognitive* omitted. I will use the word *prehension* for *uncognitive apprehension*: by this I mean *apprehension* which may or may not be cognitive.[138]

In *Process and Reality*, he develops the term 'prehension' in more detail in the context of a discussion of feeling. In contrast to some of his other works, including his earlier *Adventures of Ideas* and his later *Modes of Thought*, Whitehead's language in *Process and Reality* is very technical and often counter-intuitive, which makes it at times difficult to follow. This is also true of his notion of feeling. Indeed, Whitehead himself refers to it as 'a mere technical term.'[139] This explains why, on Whitehead's terms, feeling is not confined to animate organisms but applies to all organic life and even to non-organic objects. It is often used interchangeably with 'prehension' in the sense of the reciprocal relationship between a thing and its environment. For Whitehead, *all* actual entities are 'prehending' things.[140] The 'philosophy of organism' – this is the term Whitehead employs to refer to his overall philosophy – 'attributes "feeling" throughout the actual world.'[141] Reminiscent of his notion of causal efficacy, a simple feeling is 'the most primitive type of an act of perception, devoid of all consciousness'.[142]

> A simple physical feeling is an act of causation. The actual entity which is the initial datum is the 'cause', the simple physical feeling is the 'effect', and the subject entertaining the simple physical feeling is the actual entity 'conditioned' by the effect. ... All complex causal action can be reduced to a complex of such primary components. Therefore simple physical feelings will also be called 'causal' feelings.[143]

Whitehead's expansive term 'feeling' applies not only to animate and inanimate living organisms but also to inorganic matter and processes. By contrast, Langer's concept of feeling is restricted to the organic realm:

> [T]he phenomenon usually described as 'a feeling' is really that an organism feels something, i.e., something is felt. What is felt is a process, perhaps a large complex of processes, within the organism. Some vital activities of great complexities and high intensity, usually (perhaps always) involving nervous tissue, are felt; being felt is a phase of the process itself.[144]

For Whitehead, prehensions can be either positive or negative. A negative prehension blocks and eliminates stimuli from outside while positive prehensions allow and appropriate them. Only positive prehensions, however, can be called proper feelings: 'A feeling ... is essentially a transition effecting a concrescence.'[145] Put differently: 'A feeling is the appropriation of some element in the universe to be components in the real internal constitution of its subject. The elements are the initial data; they are what the feeling feels.'[146] In higher organisms the most primitive form of experience is 'emotional feeling, felt in its relevance to a world beyond.'[147] Such feeling is 'blind and the relevance is vague'.[148] Yet it is never unmediated: 'emotion in human experience, or even in animal experience, is not bare emotion. It is emotion interpreted, integrated, and transformed into higher categories of feeling.'[149]

Because all things in life are both actors and being acted upon, the terms 'subject' and 'object' are both relative and relational. As Whitehead puts it in *Adventure of Ideas* (1933),

> [S]ubject and object are relative terms. An occasion is a subject in respect to its special activity concerning an object; and anything is an object in respect to its provocation of some special activity within a subject. Such a mode of activity is termed a 'prehension'.[150]

Anticipating Merleau-Ponty's chiastic logic of the intertwining hands as outlined in *The Visible and the Invisible*, Whitehead writes, 'We find ourselves in the double role of agents and patients in a common world, and the conscious recognition of impressions of sensations is the work of sophisticated elaboration'.[151] Whitehead rejects traditional notions of subject–object relations which define the poles in cognitive terms of a knower and a known. While cognition is indeed one mode of prehension in higher organisms, the basis of all human experience is feeling: it is 'the rise of an affective tone originating from things whose relevance is given'.[152] This fundamental insight will be developed in much greater detail by Langer in her trilogy *Mind*.

Emerging consciousness

Feeling, for Whitehead, refers to the myriad types of relationships between actual entities, from causal pulls and pressures in the physical realm, to passive sympathies and sensations in the psychical realm to higher level of social interaction and conceptual judgements in culture. He distinguishes between three successive phases of feelings: first, 'conformal feelings;'; second, 'conceptual feelings' and, third, 'comparative feelings'. In the higher species this includes 'propositional' feelings.[153] Bearing in mind that, for Whitehead, percepts and concepts are not clearly distinguishable, the first phase is characterized by an entity's or, more accurately, an 'event's' relatively passive response and adaptation to its environment, whereas, in the higher phases, the organism is more actively engaged in negotiating the physical impacts of external stimuli. Consciousness happens when 'a synthetic feeling integrates physical and conceptual feelings'.[154] It 'originates in the higher phases of integration and illuminates those phases with greater clarity and distinctness'.[155] As he formulates it in *Process and Reality*,

> The disastrous separation of body and mind, characteristic of philosophical systems, which are in any important respect derived from Cartesianism, is avoided in the philosophy of organism ... [since] conceptual feelings pass into the category of physical feelings ... [and] conversely, physical feelings give rise to conceptual feelings.[156]

As we will discuss in more detail in Chapter 10, this naturalist, non-dualist, emergentist conception of the mind and consciousness anticipates later developments in neurobiology as developed by, among others, philosopher John Searle and neuroscientist Antonio Damasio.

Langer's mature philosophy of mind and feeling shows many debts to Whitehead's process philosophy. First, echoing Whitehead's term 'prehension', Langer coins the term 'pression'. Pression, for Langer, is 'a general designation for a class of relations which obtain between situations and acts'.[157] It is a term that can be preceded by a large variety of prefixes such as 'im-', 'ex-', 'com-', 're-', 'op-' and 'sup-' and is as such a flexible concept which can refer to all kinds of different relations. We return to this later when treating the concept of expression in art. Second, echoing Whitehead's different phases of feeling, Langer distinguishes between feelings that are 'felt as impact' and those that are 'felt as autogenic action' or 'autonomous act'.[158] Third, feeling, for Langer, is the key of human mentality and arises out of lower sensations: 'Feeling, in the broad sense of whatever is felt in any way, as sensory stimulus or inward tension, pain, emotion or intent, is the mark of mentality'.[159] Emphasizing the active dimension of the term 'feeling', Langer treats it as a verbal noun: 'To feel is to do something, not to have something'.[160] As she describes the purpose of her book *Mind: An Essay on Human Feeling*,

> As soon as feeling is regarded as a phase of a physiological process instead of a product (perhaps a by-product) of it, a new entity metaphysically different from it, the paradox of the physical and psychical disappears; for the thesis I hope to substantiate here is that the entire psychological field – including human conception, responsible action, rationality, knowledge – is a vast and branching development of feeling.[161]

We return to all these themes in later chapters.

Abstraction and symbolic form

Although the notion of form does not play as central a role in Whitehead's philosophy as it does in that of Langer and Cassirer, Whitehead also draws a close link between feeling and form. Consciousness, so he writes, 'concerns the subjective form of feeling'.[162] In the philosophy of organism 'it is not "substance" which is permanent, but "*form*"'.[163] Keeping in mind that feelings, or, in Whitehead's terminology, 'positive prehensions', occur both in animate and inanimate entities, they can only appropriate elements in the universe by means of a particular form:

> The doctrine of 'feeling' is the central doctrine respecting the becoming of an actual entity. In a feeling the actual world, selectively appropriated, is the presupposed datum, not formless but with its own realized form selectively germane, in other words 'objectified'.[164]

Following the *Gestalt* psychologists, Whitehead considers 'the selective appropriation' that takes place in feeling, sense-experience and overall perception a particular form of abstraction: 'Sense-perception is the triumph of abstraction in animal experience. Such abstraction arises from the growth of selective emphasis'.[165] They are the result of a particular kind or a particular aspect of a concrete entity depending on interest and relevance. Abstractions include certain elements and exclude others according to the context of the situation and the need of the moment:

> Each perspective for any one qualitative abstraction such as a number, or a colour, involves an infinitude of alternative potentialities. On the other hand, the perspective for a factual occasion involves the elimination of alternatives in respect to the matter-of-fact realization involved in that present occasion, and the reduction of alternatives as to the future.[166]

Whitehead warns against the imposition of one type of abstraction on different kinds of aspects of the world: 'Our danger is to take notions which are valid for one perspective of the universe involved in one group of events and to apply them uncritically to other events involving some discrepancy of perspective.'[167] He also warns against what, in *Science and the Modern World*, he had called 'the fallacy of misplaced concreteness', that is, the error to take one abstraction of the world for the world as a whole or, as one might put it, to reduce the world to one form of abstraction.[168] This, he argues, was the main problem with 'scientific materialism' which fails to acknowledge that the world as described by the physical sciences is not the world as it really or 'concretely' is, but merely an abstraction of certain features while discarding others. As he puts it,

> This fallacy consists in neglecting the degree of abstraction involved when an actual entity is considered merely so far as it exemplifies certain categories of thought. There are aspects of actualities which are simply ignored so long as we restrict thought to these categories. Thus the success of a philosophy is to be measured by its comparative avoidance of this fallacy, when thought is restricted within its categories.[169]

Langer, too, emphasized the importance of recognizing a plurality of forms as the result of different kinds of abstraction. As she wrote in *The Practice of Philosophy*,

> [T]here is no such thing as *the form* of a real thing, or of an event. There is no such thing as pure experience. ... [A]ll experience must have some specific pattern, wherein it may be sensed, though there are many patterns possible within the same reality. All experience, of sense or thought or feeling, is selective; it must formulate its material in some way, and in just one way at a time. All concrete reality has a multiplicity of possible forms, and when it is known to us it has one actual form, with an amorphous 'content'.[170]

Whereas for Whitehead a recognition of form by means of abstraction is a universal feature of all actual entities, for Langer it is confined to organic life as the basis of symbolic human mentality:

> The power of understanding symbols, i.e. of regarding everything about a sense-datum as irrelevant except a certain *form* that is embodies, is the most characteristic mental trait of mankind. It issues in an unconscious, spontaneous

process of *abstraction*, which goes on all the time in the human mind: a process of recognizing the concept in any configuration given to experience, and forming a conception accordingly.[171]

The recognition of the multidimensionality of reality is a powerful tool for unmasking reductionist tendencies in philosophical thought.

Symbolic reference and art

In *Process and Reality* Whitehead returns to notion of symbolic reference first mentioned in *Symbolism: Its Meaning and Effect*. Referring to a mixture of the two 'pure' modes of perception, that is, 'presentational immediacy' and 'causal efficacy', he writes:

> This mixed mode of perception is here named 'symbolic reference'. The failure to lay due emphasis on symbolic reference is one of the reasons for metaphysical difficulties; it has reduced the notion of 'meaning' to a mystery.[172]

As we saw earlier, for Whitehead, the different *percepta* of the two modes of perception are reversible. In principle each can serve either as a 'symbol' or as 'meaning' – '[I]t depends on the constitution of the percipient subject to assign which species is acting as "symbol" and which as "meaning".'[173] It depends on context and the user:

> There is no inherent distinction between the sort of percepta which are symbols and the sort of percepta which are meanings. When two species are correlated by a 'ground' of relatedness, it depends upon the experiential process, constituting the percipient subject, as to which species is the group of symbols, and which is the group of meanings. Also it equally depends upon the percipient as to whether there is any symbolic reference at all.[174]

Langer was to make a similar point later in *Philosophy of a New Key*:

> The difference [between a symbol and its meaning] is, that the subject for which they constitute a pair must *find the one more interesting than the other, and the latter more easily available that the former...* If it were not for the subject, or *interpretant*, sign and object would be interchangeable.[175]

Whitehead illustrates the interchangeability with the following example: 'The word "forest" may suggest memories of forests; but equally the sight of a forest, or memories of forests, may suggest the word "forest".'[176] Whereas in the mode of causal efficacy we perceive something dimly and diffusely, in the mode of presentational immediacy we perceive it clearly and distinctly. Each mode of perception articulates the experience under a different aspect:

> Presentational immediacy is the enhancement of the importance of relationships which were already in the datum, vaguely and with slight relevance. This fact, that

'presentational immediacy' deals with the same datum as does 'causal efficacy', gives the ultimate reason why there is a common 'ground' for 'symbolic reference'. The two modes express the same datum under different proportions of relevance. ... [Different] integrations often involve various types of 'symbolic reference'. This symbolic reference is the interpretative element in human experience. Language almost exclusively refers to presentational immediacy as interpreted by symbolic reference.[177]

It interprets the data of the world in clear and distinct forms. Likewise,

[A]ll scientific observations, such as measurements, ... determinations of sense-data such as colours, sounds, tastes, smells, temperature feelings, touch feelings, etc., are made in the perceptive mode of presentational immediacy; and ... great care is exerted to keep this mode pure, that is to say, devoid of symbolic reference to causal efficacy.[178]

By contrast, the sense-data of causal efficacy are vague and undetermined. They influence an organism's mood and feelings without it having a sense of control over them.

According to Whitehead, the absence of clear perceptions can heighten the 'vague feeling of influences from vague things around us', sometimes pleasant and affirming, other times unpleasant and unsettling.[179] As he describes it,

An inhibition of familiar sensa is very apt to leave us a prey to vague terrors respecting a circumambient world of causal operations. In the dark there are vague presences, doubtfully feared; in the silence, the irresistible causal efficacy of nature presses itself upon us; in the vagueness of the low hum of insects in an August woodland, the inflow into ourselves of feelings from enveloping nature overwhelms us; in the dim consciousness of half-sleep, the presentations of sense fade away, and we are left with the vague feeling of influences from vague things around us.[180]

It is easy to see how Whitehead's description of the organism's vague and indeterminate 'causal' feelings can be compared with the pre-reflective, inchoate feelings experienced by artists. As I discuss in more detail later, Whitehead's two modes of perception show close affinities with Langer's two kinds of symbolic transformation: discursive and presentational. Discursive symbolism, on Langer's terms, formulates human experience in terms of clear and distinct elements, most often words, whereas presentational symbolism, such as myth or art, provides a formulation for the more diffuse, prelingual realm of experience that falls outside language. For Langer, it is the artist's task to articulate as yet 'unnamed' feelings in a non-discursive form in order to render them available for human experience and reflection. Recent interpretations of Whitehead have paid growing attention to Whitehead's potential for philosophy of art and aesthetics. Steven Shaviro, for example, argues that Whitehead's 'affect-based account of human (and not just human) experience [places] aesthetics rather than ontology (Heidegger) or ethics (Levinas) at the centre of philosophical enquiry'. Langer can be said to be one of the first philosophers to recognize and develop this potential in Whitehead.[181]

Philosophy as metaphysics: Scope and limitations

One final major topic is the task and scope of philosophy itself. Whitehead employs the term 'speculative philosophy' or 'metaphysics' to refer to philosophy in its most general sense and the 'Philosophy of Organism' to refer to his own system as developed in *Process and Reality*. As he puts it in the opening paragraphs,

> Speculative Philosophy is the endeavour to frame a coherent, logical, necessary system of general ideas in terms of which every element of our experience can be interpreted. By this notion of 'interpretation' I mean that everything of which we are conscious, as enjoyed, perceived, willed or thought, shall have the character of a particular instance of the general scheme.[182]

On this definition speculative philosophy is an all-embracing theory of the universe – rational, coherent and systematic, yet firmly rooted in embodied human experience in the widest possible sense, that is, including moral, religious and aesthetic experience. As he puts it,

> [The] ideal of speculative philosophy has its rational side and its empirical side. The rational side is expressed by the terms 'coherent' and 'logical'. The empirical side is expressed by the terms 'applicable' and 'adequate'.[183]

Whitehead's term 'necessary' in the phrase 'coherent, logical, necessary system of general ideas' in the first part of his definition should be understood in this context. Every understanding of one aspect of the universe should, in principle, be applicable to other aspects in the sense of 'bearing in itself its own warrant of universality throughout all experience, *provided that we confine ourselves to that which communicates with immediate matter of fact* [my italics]'.[184] His metaphysics, therefore, is not rational in a rationalistic sense, but in a relational or 'coherentist' sense. Reality is conceived as an organic whole in which all parts relate both to each other and the whole. For Whitehead, as it was to be for Langer, speculative philosophy is fundamentally concerned with meaning. This is the central theme of his later works, *Adventure of Ideas* (1933) and *Modes of Thought* (1838)

Adventure of Ideas and *Modes of Thought*

Philosophy, for Whitehead, has two major tasks: analysis and innovation. The first task consists of the analysis of existing language and concepts:

> [The philosopher] takes every word, and every phrase, in the verbal expression of thought, and asks, What does it mean? [He] refuses to be satisfied by the conventional presupposition that every sensible person knows the answer. As soon as you rest satisfied with primitive ideas, and with primitive propositions, you have ceased to be a philosopher.[185]

This philosophically critical attitude also applies to the philosopher's own language: '[T]he philosopher, as he argues from his premises, has already marked down every word and phrase in them as topics for future enquiry.'[186] The philosopher analyses the underlying assumptions of the concepts that the scientist takes for granted:

> In respect to Newtonian Dynamics, the scientist and the philosopher face in opposite directions. The scientist asks for the consequences, and seeks to observe the realization of such consequences in the universe. The philosopher asks for the meaning of these ideas in terms of the welter of characterizations which infest the world.[187]

Whereas science operates on the basis of accepted definitions, philosophy questions the scientist's naïve belief in the transparency and clarity of those definitions. This is what he calls 'The Fallacy of the Perfect Dictionary':[188]

> The Fallacy of the Perfect Dictionary divides philosophers into two schools, namely, the 'Critical School' which repudiates speculative philosophy, and the 'Speculative School' which includes it. The critical school confines itself to verbal analysis within the limits of the dictionary. The speculative school appeals to direct insight, and endeavours to indicate its meanings by further appeal to situations which promote such specific insights. It then enlarges the dictionary. The divergence between the schools is the quarrel between safety and adventure.[189]

This leads to philosophy's second major task, the innovation of concepts by means of the enlargement of the dictionary. Whitehead's description of the 'Critical' and 'Speculative' schools can easily be seen to map onto the emerging distinction between 'analytic' and 'continental' philosophy. And so does his quip when introducing Russell's William James Lectures: 'Bertie thinks I am muddleheaded; but then I think he is simpleminded.'[190] The main point however is, as Michel Weber also observes, that 'the so-called Analytic-Continental divide has *always already* been obsolete for Whitehead.'[191]

Whitehead himself was typically most interested in the enlargement of the dictionary:

> [A]ll men enjoy flashes of insight beyond meanings already stabilized in etymology and grammar. Hence the role of literature, the role of the special sciences, and the role of philosophy [lies] in finding linguistic expressions for meanings as yet unexpressed.[192]

In *Process and Reality*, Whitehead had already argued that, 'under the influence of mathematics, 'deduction has been foisted onto philosophy as its standard method, instead of taking its true place as an essential auxiliary mode of verification whereby to test the scope of generalities.'[193] This has led to the false impression that, in order to build a philosophical system, we need to have clear, distinct and certain premises. In fact, so argues Whitehead, it is the other way around: '[T]he accurate expression of the final generalities is the goal of [philosophical] discussion, not its origin.'[194] The first task of philosophy is to seek expressions that are adequate and can be applied to as broad a field of human experience as possible: the primary task of philosophy is 'descriptive generalisation'.[195] On Whitehead's terms, descriptive generalization is a journey of discovery led by 'the play of a free imagination' while guided by rationality and rooted in empirical observation. In short, it is, 'a method of imaginative rationalization'.[196] He illustrates this with the image of a hermeneutical spiral:

> The true method of discovery is like the flight of an aeroplane. It starts from the ground of particular observation; it makes a flight in the thin air of imaginative generalization; and it again lands for renewed observation rendered acute by rational interpretation.[197]

Descriptive generalizations are never conclusive: '[M]etaphysical categories are not dogmatic statements of the obvious; they are tentative formulations of ultimate generalities.'[198] This calls for appropriate philosophical humility: 'There remains the final reflection, how shallow, puny and imperfect are efforts to sound the depths in the nature of things. In philosophical discussion, the merest hint of dogmatic certainty as to finality of statement is an exhibition of folly.'[199] Similarly,

> Philosophers can never hope finally to formulate these metaphysical first principles. Weakness of insight and deficiencies of language stand in the way inexorably. Words and phrases must be stretched towards a generality foreign to their ordinary usage; and however such elements of language be stabilized as technicalities, they remain metaphors mutely appealing for an imaginative leap.[200]

The metaphoric character of speculative philosophy makes it share a common cause with poetry. As he writes in *Modes of Thought*, 'Philosophy is akin to poetry. Philosophy is the endeavour to find a conventional phraseology for the vivid suggestiveness of the poet.'[201] Again, a comparison with Merleau-Ponty is apt. As Merleau-Ponty was to write in 1945, 'Philosophy is not the reflection of a pre-existing truth, but, like art, the act of bringing truth into being ... True philosophy consists in re-learning to look at the world.'[202] For Whitehead, both philosophy and poetry 'seek to express that ultimate good sense which we term civilization. In each case there is reference to form beyond the direct meanings of words. Poetry allies itself to meter, philosophy to mathematic pattern.'[203]

Philosophy as the pursuit of meaning

Langer's conception of philosophy – or metaphysics – as the pursuit of meaning closely resembles that of Whitehead. For her metaphysics is 'like every philosophical pursuit, a study of meanings'.[204] Langer's interest in meaning goes back to her 1926 PhD thesis 'The Logical Analysis of Meaning'. Four years later, in the book that, according to Auxier, 'more clearly bears the mark of Whitehead's influence than any other [of

Langer's works] with regard to symbols,[205] *The Practice of Philosophy* (1930), she was to write,

> The guiding principle that will define our field, dictate our procedure (of which the analytic method is a perfectly assignable, integral part), and give to philosophy a working basis as well as an ultimate aim: this principle is the pursuit of meaning.[206]

For Langer, as for Whitehead, metaphysics involves both analysis and innovation. First, all philosophy is 'a study of what is *implied* in the fundamental notions which are our natural unconscious formulations of experience ... its immediate task is always the explication of whatever ideas it is dealing with'.[207] In *Mind,* likewise, she writes that metaphysics deals with 'the basic assumptions implicit in our formulation of "facts"'.[208] Second, it involves an expansion of our ideas by means of new formulations and conceptualizations. Since metaphysics is concerned with formulating the most general concepts of all human experience, Langer defends the importance of metaphysics in the face of many criticisms of it at the time. Aware of metaphysics' negative reputation, she writes,

> The ill repute in which metaphysics has fallen is not so much a deserved censure of the pursuit itself as a protest against old doctrines associated with its name. To call a question 'metaphysical' is currently considered, by many scholars, tantamount to calling it 'nonsensical'. But metaphysics, properly speaking, is simply the study of basic assumptions, and a metaphysical question is a question of what, ultimately, we are talking about when we speak of 'the world', or 'fact', or 'experience'.[209]

For Langer there is 'as much metaphysics involved in scientific thinking as in theological, as much in radical empiricism as in idealism, or, for that matter, in mysticism. Every *–ism* bespeaks a metaphysical stand.'[210] Aiming to get this point across to her neo-positivist colleagues, she writes,

> Lord Russell and Mr. Ryle hold with the positivists and most behaviourists that metaphysical issues should be left alone. The general conviction of those schools is that metaphysical ideas are irrelevant to science, since they apply to the universe as a whole, about which nothing can really be known. But ... all scientific analyses when pursued far enough go down to implicit metaphysical propositions, which need not be about the universe as a whole, but about the nature of things in it. Whitehead once defined metaphysics as 'the most general statements we can make about reality'. Whether we make them or not, their content is assumed in less general assertions, because they embody our basic concepts.[211]

Langer was always quite hesitant to refer to her own work as 'metaphysics'. When, in 1967, art critic Herbert Read in his (very positive) review of the first volume of *Mind* had carelessly referred to Langer's work as 'a metaphysical system' she had been incensed and replied, 'I should think that by now Sir Herbert would know the difference between a "metaphysical system" and a scientific line of inquiry'.[212] It was only at the end of her life, at the end of the third volume of *Mind*, that she wrote, very tentatively, of her intentions to construct, if not a metaphysical *system*, than at least a metaphysical *theory*:

> This study of mind should culminate, of course, in a well-constructed epistemological and possibly even metaphysical theory at least as firmly grounded on other people's knowledge and hypotheses as any earlier parts of this essay which have been written in preparation for such a reflective conclusion.[213]

Unfortunately, failing eyesight and old age meant that she was not able to fulfil her intention.

Whitehead's 'mysticism'

Assessing Whitehead's influence on Langer, Donald Dryden correctly observes,

> It is important to distinguish Langer's indirect use of Whitehead's metaphysics from a detailed, systematic *application* of Whitehead's metaphysical categories. … Langer regarded Whitehead's metaphysics as richly suggestive but did not take his categorical scheme as the basis for her work.[214]

We are now in a position to suggest some reasons why Langer did not follow Whitehead all the way. In the preface to *Philosophy in a New Key* Langer acknowledges that 'the writings of the sage to whom this book is dedicated receive but scant explicit mention.'[215] Indeed, considering the many overlaps between Whitehead's and Langer's thought the lack of direct references to Whitehead's work by Langer's may be somewhat puzzling.[216] There may be a variety of reasons for this state of affairs.

First, it may not have been possible to compare her own ideas exactly with those of Whitehead for the simple reason that Whitehead's are exceptionally complex and do not easily lend themselves to clear summaries or straightforward comparisons. As noted earlier, this is partly due to Whitehead's unorthodox methodology and employment of terms which sometimes mean different things in different context and thus cannot always be easily transferred to a different philosophical framework. Second, there were so many overlapping themes in their respective writings that working out their precise agreements and disagreements would simply be too complicated and tedious. She may have felt that the effort of any careful positioning of her standpoint in relation to Whitehead – or any other thinker for that matter – was not worth it. She had her own agenda. Moreover, it may not even have been possible to disentangle which, in the end, were Whitehead's ideas and which her own. What she had once said of Sheffer, might equally apply to Whitehead, that is, that it was 'the mark of a great teacher that one cannot render to him the things that are his' and that his ideas were to become 'part of one's own mentality'.[217]

Third, although Langer found Whitehead's speculative philosophy inspiring and suggestive, she also considered it at times too indeterminate and vague, *too* 'speculative'. On the one hand she agreed with Whitehead that metaphysical categories are 'not dogmatic statements of the obvious; they are tentative formulations of the ultimate generalities'.[218] She also agreed with him that new metaphysical ideas are often vague and 'dimly apprehended', often first formulated in poetry or myth: '[A]new philosophical doctrine which inaugurates a new intellectual era is essentially a myth'.[219] This also applied to the new generative ideas of her own time. As she wrote,

> The springs of European thought have run dry – those deep springs of imagination that furnish the basic concepts for the whole intellectual order, the first discernments, the generative ideas of our *Weltanschauung*. New conceptual forms are crowding them out, but are themselves in the mythical phase, the 'implicit' stage of symbolic formulation.[220]

On the other hand, Langer herself was less 'mythical' or 'mystical' than Whitehead. In an unpublished paper Langer referred to Whitehead's metaphysics as a

> cosmological myth of a divine universe striving for self-realization and enjoying its existence ... [it is] a strange creation by a great scientist [that] goes beyond the inventor's literal conception; it is a genuine philosophical myth – not an allegory or conscious poetic statement, but a living myth, intended as literal truth.[221]

In *Modes of Thought*, Whitehead had even claimed that 'philosophy is mystical. For mysticism is direct insight into depths as yet unspoken'.[222] Dryden suggests that Whitehead's use of the term 'mystical' may well have been inspired by – or, perhaps, derives from – Langer's Cassirerean term for philosophy as 'mythical'.[223] Yet, for Langer there was a lingering sense that Whitehead's philosophy did not sufficiently progress from its mythical or 'mystical' phase to a fully fledged rational and systematic enterprise. Following directly on his comment on philosophy as 'mystical', Whitehead himself had claimed that 'the purpose of philosophy is to rationalize mysticism: not by explaining it away, but by the introduction of novel verbal characterizations, rationally co-ordinated'.[224] As Langer was to put it in her introduction of *Feeling and Form*, 'The business of philosophy is to unravel and organize concepts, to give definite and satisfactory meanings to the terms we use in talking about any subject (in this case art). It is, as Charles Peirce said, "to make our ideas clear"'.[225]

In the end Langer remained non-committal as to Whitehead's philosophical style which was at times, in Hartshorne's words, 'somewhat sparing in argument'.[226] Defending Whitehead against the accusation of unclarity by one reviewer, she generously writes,

> Of course the difficulty of applying criticism to such a philosophy is that its author is obviously trying to break through certain basic, accepted concepts of world-construction, and at times breaks through *those which we still employ to understand his revolution*. Then he becomes unintelligible; but whether forever so, or whether the subtlety of our vocabulary will ever catch up with him, is hard to predict.[227]

Langer's work, even while itself a pioneering project, has the potential to make Whitehead's ideas more intelligible, not least simply because of Langer's greater clarity of expression and formulation of concepts. As Rolf Lachmann suggests,

> Langer's understanding of philosophical work is characterised by a greater methodological discipline and rigor than Whitehead's [and] includes a far more developed conceptualization of the developmental tendencies of elementary processes.[228]

Moreover, even more consistently than Whitehead the scientist, Langer was always concerned that her philosophy was supported by the findings of empirical science. Where Whitehead, in his later work, was inclined to speculation and generalization, Langer often turned to concrete examples from the special disciplines. It could perhaps be argued that, precisely because she was *not* a scientist, she had a more naive faith in the empirical sciences than Whitehead. However, that would be to overlook her nuanced hermeneutical approach to what makes up the world of 'facts'. This will be discussed in the next chapter in the context of Wittgenstein's philosophy.

7

Ludwig Wittgenstein: Expressive form

Every part of a proposition which characterizes its sense I call an expression (a symbol). (The proposition itself is an expression.) Expressions are everything – essential for the sense of the proposition – that propositions can have in common with one another. An expression characterizes a form and a content.

Wittgenstein[1]

A symbol is not a reproduction of its object, but an expression *– an exhibition of certain relevant moments, whose relevance is determined by the purpose in hand.*

Langer[2]

We say that one fact (the arrangement of little black marks) expresses the other (the eruption of the volcano), so the particular relation between them is called Expression. In order to understand language we must investigate the nature of Expression. How can certain facts 'speak of' other facts? That is our problem.

Schlick[3]

Many issues that seemed to concern the sources *of knowledge … now appear to turn partly or wholly on the* forms *of knowledge, or even the forms of expression, of symbolism.*

Langer[4]

My difficulty is only an – enormous – difficulty of expression.

Wittgenstein[5]

Symbolic turn

Although Langer never met Wittgenstein (1889–1951), his *Tractatus* (1921, 1922) influenced her thinking as much as the work of Sheffer, Whitehead and Cassirer.[6] Indeed, she refers to it as 'the extraordinary prophetic gospel of Ludwig Wittgenstein'.[7] In contrast to her minimal citing of those other thinkers, Langer quotes the early Wittgenstein both frequently and extensively.[8] The most extensive discussion of the *Tractatus* can be found in her first book, *The Practice of Philosophy* (1930), where she commends Wittgenstein for his 'excellent account of the logical prerequisites for meaning'.[9] Over ten years later, in *Philosophy in a New Key* (1942), we are told that the 'logical theory on which [her] whole study of symbols is based is essentially that which was set forth by Wittgenstein, some twenty years ago, in his *Tractatus Logico-Philosophicus*.'[10]

In order to appreciate this early recognition, it is worth putting it in context. In America Wittgenstein was for a long time ignored or, if not ignored, dismissed as obscure and impenetrable. Many philosophers shared Brand Blanshard's sentiments when he commented that 'Wittgenstein has the strange distinction of having produced a work on logic beside which the *Logic* of Hegel is luminously intelligible.'[11] Some judged the book to be mere nonsense. Shortly after its publication C. I. Lewis wrote a letter to F. J. Woodbridge, then editor of the *Journal of Philosophy*, saying,

> Have you looked at Wittgenstein's new book yet? I am much discouraged by Russell's foolishness in writing the introduction to such nonsense. I fear it will be looked upon as what symbolic logic leads to. If so, it will be the death of the subject.[12]

Nagel, likewise, initially rejected the work as insignificant, claiming, '[M]uch of its content is unintelligible to anyone who hasn't had it illuminated by Wittgenstein or his followers' and that it represented an *'überwundener Standpunkt'.*[13]

Langer, by contrast, had found the *Tractatus* both exhilarating and illuminating. For her, he shared the 'new key' in philosophy, that is, the discovery that the 'facts' that constitute the world are fundamentally symbolic. The difference between her reading of the early Wittgenstein and that of many of her contemporaries was that Langer's reading was profoundly influenced by Sheffer, Whitehead and Cassirer. For all these thinkers, as she had put it in *Philosophy in a New Key*, the 'problem of observation is all but eclipsed by the problem of *meaning*'.[14] This chapter will demonstrate how Langer was one of the first – if not *the* first – American philosophers to recognize the significance of the *Tractatus* and to read Wittgenstein's work as part of a broader linguistic or, more precisely, *symbolic* turn in philosophy.[15] Langer's reading challenges the standard reading of the *Tractatus* in her time as a positivist copy or correspondence theory about the relation between language and the world. Many such readings also led to major misunderstandings of Langer, in particular her view of isomorphism, as her reliance on Wittgenstein was interpreted as adopting that view. This chapter aims to correct that misunderstanding.

Langer in Vienna

In the year that the *Tractatus* was published, Langer and her husband, William, newly married, lived in Vienna. They had moved there shortly after their wedding in September 1921 for William's research on post First World War European history. Langer had just finished her BA under Henry Sheffer and had started work on her master's thesis – on Eduard Hartmann – which she was to complete two years later.[16]

During her year in Vienna, native German speaker Langer attended the classes of philosopher of language and *Gestalt* psychologist Karl Bühler (1879–1963), who was to influence Langer's thinking on meaning and reference in signs and symbols. Bühler emphasized the fact that meaning does not originate in the isolated individual but in the social context of its animal and human ambiance in an active communicative exchange.[17] As he put it in *Sprachtheorie*, 'If speaking is resolutely determined as action …, I think something like Ariadne's thread will have been found to lead us out of all kinds of complications that are only half understood.'[18] Bühler's early insight in the social 'use' aspect of linguistic meaning and the fact that speech was fundamentally 'action' was to have a major influence on scholars working in developmental psychology and evolutionary semiotics, as well as on philosophers such as Cassirer, Jürgen Habermas, Jan Mukařovský, Roman Ingarden and Michael Polanyi. He also influenced his own students, philosopher Karl Popper and ethologist Konrad Lorenz, as well as Langer from the year she took his classes.[19] Finally, Bühler and his wife, the psychologist Charlotte Bühler, were close friends of the Wittgenstein family and facilitated the first meeting between Wittgenstein and Moritz Schlick at the home of Wittgenstein's sister Margarete Stonborough-Wittgenstein. Although Wittgenstein never mentions Bühler, there are resonances of Bühler's conception of language in Wittgenstein's later notion of meaning as use, which was informed by his study of language development in children while working as an elementary school teacher in Austria.[20]

Wittgenstein's *Tractatus*

The *Tractatus* had a difficult birth and complex history of reception. The first drafts were written by Wittgenstein while studying philosophy with Bertrand Russell in Cambridge between 1911 and 1913, after studying engineering in Manchester. Wittgenstein continued to work on the manuscript during the First World War, both as a soldier and as a prisoner of war. After various rejections the manuscript was eventually published under the title *Logisch-Philosophische Abhandlung* as part of Wilhelm Ostwald's journal *Annalen der Naturphilosophie* in 1921. A year later it was translated in English by C. K. Ogden and published with an introduction by Bertrand Russell under the title *Tractatus Logico-Philosophicus*. Wittgenstein had initially resisted the inclusion of Russell's introduction which he considered to be riddled with misunderstandings, but in the end succumbed since, without Russell's endorsement, no publisher had been willing to publish it.

Since its publication the *Tractatus* has become one of the most enigmatic and elusive texts in the history of analytic philosophy, its dense and minimalist style lending itself to a multiplicity of interpretations. As a result, philosophers working in many different fields – from philosophy of science, language and mind to philosophy of religion, ethics and aesthetics – and with very different agendas, all claim to find something of meaning and value in the work. Depending on where one draws the lines, this highly diverse history of reception can be divided into four or five periods, to which I return later. In terms of its elusive multi-interpretability, however, the work has more in common with a poem than a philosophical treatise. Even so, throughout his life, Wittgenstein felt misunderstood, misrepresented and misappropriated. Shortly after having sent Russell the completed manuscript of the *Tractatus*, Wittgenstein wrote to him,

> The main point [of the Tractatus] is the theory of what can be expressed (gesagt) by prop[osition]s – i.e. by language – (and, which comes to the same, what can be thought) and what cannot be expressed by prop[osition]s, but only shown (gezeigt); which I believe is the cardinal problem of philosophy. ... It is very hard not to be understood by a single soul.[21]

By the time of the *Tractatus'* publication in 1922, a disillusioned Wittgenstein had left the world of academic scholarship and taken up employment as a school teacher in the rural villages surrounding his hometown Vienna. In 1926 he moved back to Vienna in order to work, together with his architect friend Paul Engelmann, on the design and construction of a modernist house for his sister Margarete. In 1929 he returned to Cambridge.

As explained in Chapter 2, the Vienna Circle had been immensely impressed with the *Tractatus* and used it as a significant point of reference for the developments of their own ideas. During Wittgenstein's three-year residence in Vienna, Schlick did all he could to involve him in the Vienna Circle's discussions but, despite his geographical proximity, Wittgenstein refused to attend the Circle's official meetings and only agreed to meet with a small number of people who had been personally invited by Schlick himself. This select core group consisted primarily of Schlick, Feigl, Carnap and Waismann. Waismann took detailed notes of these meetings which were then shared with the larger group. It is clear from these notes that Wittgenstein was often distracted. With his mind on the design of his sister's house, he was not much interested the Circle's discussions and preferred to read poetry instead.[22]

Langer's Wittgenstein

Like Schlick, Langer is most interested in the *Tractatus* for its account of philosophy as 'a pursuit of meaning'. She acknowledges that this account of meaning is 'woven in ... among metaphysical reflections and some excellently subtle logical speculations, which are very interesting but somewhat confusing' and, therefore, proposes to 'render it in extracts'.[23] This leads Langer to single out several theses which are meant to serve as a key to the work as a whole. As it turns out, the extracts constitute the longest set of quotes – four pages in total – she has ever produced in any of her books.[24] Because Langer's interpretation of the *Tractatus* is substantially based on this selection of theses, I will list them here in full:

> 2.1 We make to ourselves pictures [*Bilder*] of facts [*Tatsachen*].
> 2.12 The picture [*Bild*] is a model [*Modell*] of reality.
> 2.13 To the objects correspond in the picture the elements of the picture.
> 2.131 The elements of the picture stand, in the picture, for the objects.

2.14 The picture consists in the fact that its elements are combined with one another in a definite way.

2.141 The picture is a fact [*Tatsache*].

2.15 That the elements of the picture are combined with one another in a definite way, represents that the things are so combined with one another. This connection of the elements of the picture is called its structure, and the possibility of this structure is called the form of representation [*Abbildung*] of the picture.

2.16 In order to be a picture a fact [*Tatsache*] must have something in common with what it pictures.

2.17 What the picture must have in common with reality in order to be able to represent it after its manner – rightly or falsely – is its form of representation.

2.171 The picture can represent every reality whose form it has.

2.181 If the form of representation is the logical form, then the picture is called a logical picture.

2.182 Every picture is *also* a logical picture. (On the other hand, for example, not every picture is spatial.)

2.2 The picture has the logical form of representation in common with what it pictures.

2.221 What the picture represents is its sense.

[4 The thought is the significant proposition.]

4.011 At the first glance the proposition [*Satz*]– say as it stands printed on paper – does not seem to be a picture of the reality of which it treats. But nor does the musical score appear at first sign to be a picture of a musical piece; nor does our phonetic spelling (letters) seem to be a picture of our spoken language. And yet these symbolisms prove to be pictures – even in the ordinary sense of the word – of what they represent.

4.014 The gramophone record, the musical thought, the score, the waves of sound, all stand to each other in that pictorial internal relation, which holds between language and the world. To all of them the logical structure is common.

4.0141 In the fact that there is a general rule by which the musician is able to read the symphony out of the score, and that there is a rule by which one could reconstruct the symphony from the line on a gramophone record and from this again – by means of the first rule – construct the score, herein lies the internal similarity between these things which at first sight seem to be entirely different. And the rule is the law of projection which projects the symphony into the language of the musical score. It is the rule of translation of this language into the language of the gramophone record.

4.015 The possibility of all similes, of all the imagery of our language, rests on the logic of representation.

4.0311 One name stands for one thing, and another for another thing, and they are connected together. And so the whole, like a living picture, presents the atomic fact [*Sachverhalt*].[25]

Taking these theses as her points of entry into Wittgenstein's text, Langer proceeds to develop a position of her own as informed by and in conversation with these theses. In support of Langer's reading of the *Tractatus* I will, where appropriate, draw on other sections of the *Tractatus* or on comments made by Wittgenstein elsewhere.

Facts (*Tatsache* and *Sachverhalte*)

Developing Wittgenstein's assertions that 'we make ourselves pictures of facts [*Tatsachen*]' (*TLP* 2.1) – that is, we construct something – and that '[t]he picture is a fact [*Tatsache*]' – that is, the picture itself becomes the basis for other pictures – (*TLP* 2.141), Langer writes,

> [*A] fact is an intellectually formulated event*, whether the formulation be performed by a process of sheer vision, verbal interpretation, or practical response. A fact is an event as we see it, or would see it if it occurred for us. ... '[For the logician] the *form* of fact is the form of proposition [and for the behaviourist] the form of a fact becomes the form of a specific human response to a specific event.'[26]

A fact, for Langer, is thus both a human product and an act of interpretation – even an observation is a 'fact' in that it provides a form for the conscious mind to reflect on.[27] Crucially, there are not two ontologically different realms – the world of symbols and the world of 'brute facts' – but one world perceived under different aspects and with a view to different needs.

> 'Facts' are the basic formulations of any system of apperception. They are not arbitrary logical constructions, neither are they 'absolute' and stark in their own form – indeed, by pure sense-experience or intuition, if there could be such a thing, facts would not even be apparent.[28]

So when Wittgenstein writes that 'the world is the totality of facts, not of things' (*TLP* 1.1.), Langer reads this in Cassirerean terms, that is, as the world being both mediated and constructed by particular symbolic forms. As Verene puts it,

> In speaking about symbols, we are accustomed to make a distinction between what is symbolic and what is literal. Cassirer's epistemology rejects this distinction. Whatever might be designated as literal is, in fact, on Cassirer's view, simply another formation of experience. The literal is thus itself symbolic. One formation of experience is not more 'symbolic' than the other.[29]

In *An Introduction to Symbolic Logic* she was to argue that even syntax could be a 'fact' in the sense of a picture or form: 'Syntax is simply *the logical form of our language,* which copies as closely as possible the logical form of our thought.'[30] Eli Friedlander, likewise, comments, 'As we read Wittgenstein's account, we realize that pictures *are* facts, and that the question we should ask is ... how certain facts can be used to represent other facts.'[31] This was exactly the way Schlick read Wittgenstein: 'We say that one fact (the arrangement of little black marks) *expresses* the other (the eruption of the volcano), so the particular relation between them is called Expression. In order to understand language we must investigate the nature of Expression. How can certain facts "speak of" other facts? That is our problem.'[32]

Pictures as models

In thesis 2.1 Wittgenstein states that we 'make to ourselves pictures (*Bilder*) of facts' (*TLP* 2.12). This is followed by the sub-thesis that the 'picture (*Bild*) is a "model" (*Modell*) of reality.' (*TLP* 2.12). In order to understand Wittgenstein's meaning and Langer's reading of the word '*Bild*' – Langer most likely will have read the *Tractatus* in German – it is important to know some of its German connotations. While often translated as 'picture', '*Bild*' is equally used to refer to three-dimensional representations and statues – the German word for 'sculptor' is '*Bildhauer*' – and is also used for 'model'. We know from Wittgenstein's 1914 notebooks that the idea of a 'picture theory' had come to him when reading about a Parish court case in which small cars and dolls were being used in order to reconstruct a car accident.[33] In the same way that the relation between the objects in the model corresponded with the relations of the relevant cars, houses and people in the situation of the car accident, so a proposition might serve as a model of a state of affairs by virtue of a comparable correspondence between its parts and those of the world. But Wittgenstein's interest in pictures understood as models goes back much further, that is, to his years of studying engineering in Manchester. One of the text books that influenced him deeply was *Principles of Mechanics* by the German physicist Heinrich Hertz and he twice refers to him in the *Tractatus* (*TLP* 4.04; 6.361).[34] Hertz, who had been a student of Hermann von Helmholtz, used the word *Bild* to refer to models as a way of understanding physical processes. When describing *Bilder* as particular forms of 'representations' Hertz consistently uses the term *Darstellungen* – that is, Kantian cognitive constructs – rather than *Vorstellungen* – that is, passive 'ideas', Humean 'impressions' or Machian 'sensations':

> We form for ourselves models (*Bilder*) or symbols of external objects; and the form which we give them is such that the necessary consequents of the images in thought are always the images of the necessary consequents in nature of the things pictures.[35]

The same phrase used by Hertz to explain the symbolism of physics will be used later by Wittgenstein to explain the symbolism of discursive language as such. Moreover, for Hertz, – as it was to be for Cassirer, Whitehead, Langer and Wittgenstein – the world does not merely allow for one kind of modelling, it opens itself to a plurality of possible *Bilder*. As Hertz wrote,

> Various models [*Bilder*] of the same objects are possible, and these models may differ in various respects. ... Of two models of equal distinctness the more appropriate is the one which contains, in addition to the essential characteristics, the smaller number of superfluous or empty relations; – the simpler of the two.

Empty relations cannot altogether be avoided; they enter into the models because they are simply models, – models produced by our mind are necessarily affected by the characteristics of its mode of modelling them.[36]

In contrast to Mach's positivistic, sensation-based approach to scientific knowledge, Hertz's conception was predominantly neo-Kantian. Both Cassirer and Schlick were great admirers of Hertz and were considerably influenced by him. In *The Phenomenology of Knowledge*, Cassirer refers to Hertz as 'the first modern scientist to have effected a decisive turn from the copy theory of physical knowledge to a purely symbolic theory.'[37] As regards Wittgenstein, Hertz's notion of *Bild* prompted him to think of language and equivalent forms of representation as 'models' that can function like charts, maps, graphs and so on.[38] Crucially, a spatial, visual picture is only one form of modelling reality. As he said, '[E]very picture is *also* a logical picture [but] not every picture is spatial' (*TLP* 2.182). For a piece of music, these 'pictures' can be as different as a gramophone record, a musical thought, a score or the waves of sound. They are like different ways in which the 'logical form' or structure of the music can be represented or translated: 'The picture can represent every reality whose form it has' (*TLP* 2.171). Reading these statements in the light of Hertz will preclude interpretations of Wittgenstein's 'picture theory' in terms of a simplistic correspondence or 'copy theory' of representation. In his biography of Wittgenstein, Ray Monk mentions that as a teenager Wittgenstein had read the *Populäre Schriften* by philosopher of science Ludwig Boltzmann, who presented a Kantian view of science in which 'our models of reality are taken *to* our experience of the world and not (as the empiricist tradition would have it) derived from it' and comments, 'So ingrained in Wittgenstein's philosophical thinking was this view that he found the empiricist view difficult even to conceive.'[39]

The same could be said of Langer. Although there is no evidence that she was directly familiar with Hertz's work, she too accepted that the world could be modelled in many different ways by means of many different structural or logical forms and symbolisms. Conversely, a symbolic pattern 'may be repeated in more than one natural instance … The same formula will fit various meanings.'[40] Moreover, because any object has 'various and variously expressible aspects, all symbolization is necessarily selective.'[41] As we already saw in Chapter 6, Langer holds, following Wittgenstein, that 'there is no such thing as *the form* of a real thing, or of an event.'[42]

For Langer a symbol is therefore 'not a reproduction of its object, but an *expression* – an exhibition of certain relevant moments, whose relevance is determined by the purpose in hand.'[43]

Facts and pictures as perspectives

In her article 'Facts: The Logical Perspectives of the World', Langer writes, 'A fact is that which is expressible in a proposition, and is a *perspective of an event*.'[44] As she points out it this article, many philosophers erroneously assume that 'a *complete analysis* is always exhaustive of the *possibilities of analysis* in its object.'[45] Yet, as she argues, this is not the case because analysis never applies to reality directly but only to the '*conceptual constructions*' or 'forms of realities'.[46] As she explains this,

> [A Werwolf] could appear as wolf or woman or other living creature, and remains the same 'Werwolf,' but there is no form that was its 'real' embodiment; similarly, a proposition expresses a true and sufficient formulation of an actual event, but it is an analysis of form, and therefore of a perspective only.[47]

As Langer will repeat over and over: we cannot conceive of reality other than through *a particular form*. Expressions are different *ways* of conceiving reality. They are not just the sum of different perspectives within one mode of symbolization but different perspectival keys with which we can unlock different aspects or modes of being. In *The Practice of Philosophy* she explains it thus,

> Philosophers generally suppose that an 'absolute' description would be one which included all perspectives. But there we are led astray by a deceptive analogy. The notion of 'perspective' is borrowed from the domain of visual relations; it is perfectly possible to conceive a thing with reference to more than one perspective, because perspectives have points in common, and are parts of one logical system, namely visual space. ... But logical perspectives exclude each other; they cannot be ideally put together. We cannot use the measurements of a map in Mercator projection to draw on the surface of a globe. Yet, when the peculiar functions involved in the former kid of measurement are accepted, the map which resulted from them is exactly as true a replica of the world as the globe.[48]

In sum, on Langer's view, there can be '*several adequate descriptions* of reality'.[49] They are not 'partial in the sense that it leaves out certain portions of the object'.[50] Instead, they are different kinds of abstraction that apply to 'the *whole* of reality' seen through a different form of symbolization. And this is how she read Wittgenstein too.

This 'multi-modal' approach precludes a Kantian dichotomy between the world of observable phenomena and the world of noumena, the world as we know it and the world 'behind' it. It also precludes a dichotomy between a world of science and a world of feeling. When Paul Engelmann wrote that Wittgenstein 'takes immense pain to delimit the unimportant, [which] is not the coastline of that island which he is bent on surveying with such meticulous accuracy but the boundary of the ocean', this should not be read in Kantian terms of safeguarding the integrity of the noumenal world of things-in-themselves.[51] As Friedlander observes, this may impute a false dichotomy to Wittgenstein's thinking – a dualism between land and ocean – a world of logic and science and a world of ethics, art, religion and so on.[52] Instead Wittgenstein was talking primarily about different *logical forms* of the world – those that could be expressed in (logical, discursive) language and those that could not. As Langer was to put it later, 'Many issues that seemed to concern the *sources* of knowledge ... now appear to turn partly or wholly on the *forms* of knowledge, or even the forms of expression, of symbolism.'[53] It is by virtue of the particular logical features that we select for abstraction that there is a certain sameness between a symbol and that what it represents.

Logical structure and analogical form

For Wittgenstein, for something to serve as a model, there has to be an analogy in form: 'To the objects correspond in the picture the elements of the picture' (*TLP* 2.13); 'The elements of the picture stand, in the picture, for the objects' (*TLP* 2.131); 'The picture consists in the fact that its elements are combined with one another in a definite way' (*TLP* 2.14); In a simile or analogy 'one name stands for one thing, and another for another thing and they are together' (*TLP* 4.0311); 'The picture consists in the fact that its elements are combined with one another in a definite way' (*TLP* 2.14); 'That the elements of the picture are combined with one another in a definite way, represents that the things are so combined with one another. This connection of the elements of the picture is called its structure, and the possibility of this structure is called the form of representation of the picture' (*TLP* 2.15); 'In order to be a picture a fact must have something in common with what it pictures' (*TLP* 2.16).[54] Langer, likewise, talks about representation in terms of logical form or analogy:

> A 'logical picture' differs from an ordinary picture in that it need not look the least bit like its object. Its relation to the object is not that of a *copy*, but of *analogy*. We do not try to make an architect's drawing look as much as possible like the house; … All that the plan must do is to copy exactly the *proportions* of length and width, the *arrangement* of rooms, halls and stairs, doors and windows. … The narrow dash that represents the window is not intended to look like one; it resembles the object for which it stands only by its location in the plan, which must be analogous to the location of the window in the room.[55]

One of the key features of any theory of symbolic form is to show 'the importance of configuration for any sort of meaning relation, from the simple denotation of names or suggestiveness of natural signs, to the most intricate symbolic expression, in literal notation or poetic metaphor.'[56] For Langer, as for Wittgenstein, for something to function as a symbolic relationship it has to have a common structure – a logical form. The form of a thing is 'the way its parts are put together. … Differences of form, whether of propositions, geometric figures, musical compositions, or any other matter, depend upon the presence of different sorts of relation within the structure of the thing in question.'[57]

A very similar concept of form and meaning can be found in Schlick. As he wrote in his 1932 article 'Form and Content', 'What you call the "understanding of the true meaning" is an act of interpretation which might be described as the filling in of an empty frame: the communicated structure is filled with content by the understanding individual.'[58] This view echoes Langer's 1926 article of the same title:

> Thus the relation of form and content is not the unqualified, ultimate, two-termed relation which it is generally thought to be. If 'form' always means a form, then

content always means a content, because content is relative to form; content means 'that which is not given as part of this logical structure.'[59]

As we saw, Langer's notion of form was deeply shaped by the Roycean logic of her mentor Sheffer. This logic works on the assumption that all of life displays different patterns that can be represented and captured in various degrees of abstraction:

> Everything, idea, or what not, has a logical pattern; propositions follow such a pattern, and, as Royce has pointed out, … all other things, from dialogues to dinners, have patterns on their own. Moreover, there are certain things whose forms correspond in large degree, as for instance the forms of similar series, such as the series of points in space and of moments in time. This correspondence of configuration may be so close that there may be serious doubt whether we are dealing with two analogous series or with an identical one … we may have various degrees of correspondence.[60]

Wittgenstein was familiar with Sheffer's work as we know from his use of the Sheffer stroke in the *Tractatus* 5.1311. While he does not mention Sheffer's name in any of his writings, it is nevertheless quite possible that he uses the term 'form' in a Shefferian way.[61]

Symbolic reference and meaning

Although an analogical form is essential for something to represent another, it is not enough to form a meaning relation or symbolic reference. It is a necessary but not sufficient condition. An analogical relation is typically symmetrical whereas a symbolic relationship is always asymmetrical. As we will see in more detail in the next chapter, on this point Langer, on account of Whitehead and Peirce's influence, is more explicit and clear than Wittgenstein. Prior to Langer and to Wittgenstein, Whitehead had pointed out that when two different entities or 'facts' share an analogous form, they are capable of *representing each other*: '[T]he thing which is symbol and the thing which is symbolized stand to each other in perfectly definite correlation and anything that may be distinguished, that is a member of any class of entities, may be a term in the relation of symbol and object.'[62] However, it requires a third factor, an interpretant (not necessarily a person) for whom or for which the symbol *means* the object.[63] And this interpretant must be a member of a community of interpreters.

As pointed out by Whitehead in the context of his discussion of causal efficacy and immediate perception in a 'symbolic reference', symbol and symbolized are, depending on context, reversible. While in some context the word 'rose' may conjure up an image of a rose, in other contexts the same word or seeing a rose in nature may conjure up the image of 'love' or 'romance'.[64] This inherent reversibility between symbol and symbolized is particularly effective in the arts. As Whitehead put it in *Symbolism*: 'In the use of language there is a double symbolic reference – from things to words on the part of the speaker, and from words back to things on the part of the listener.'[65] As we saw in the previous chapter, Whitehead had illustrated this idea with the word 'forest' that refers both to the *percepta* of the forest and to the mental picture that is, in a writer's mind, conjured up by the word 'forest'. As he explained: 'A word gathers emotional signification from its emotional history in the past; and this is transferred symbolically to its meaning in the present.'[66] In this context Langer sees a close connection between Whitehead and Wittgenstein:

> Professor A. N. Whitehead, in a little book entitled 'Symbolism: Its Meaning and Effects,' has employed this sort of logical analysis [of symbolic reference] with excellent results. The same approach may be found in a less lucid but perhaps equally interesting philosophical study, the extraordinary prophetic gospel of Ludwig Wittgenstein. Strangely for philosophy, these two writers have reached very similar conclusions by their similar searches; ... from a purely logical point of view, [I] found the formal structure of meaning to be exactly that which they both assume in their respective metaphysics.[67]

These conclusions imply that anything that may be distinguished as a member of any class of entities, may be a term in the relation of symbol and object. And for one to be able to signify the other, one must look for some shared logical pattern.

The fact that Langer sees an affinity between Whitehead's and Wittgenstein's works is perhaps not all too surprising. Wittgenstein had got to know Whitehead through Russell even though Whitehead had already left Cambridge for London by the time Wittgenstein arrived. In his letters to Russell, Whitehead is one of the few people Wittgenstein often refers and sends his greetings to, suggesting a personal fondness of Whitehead on his part.[68] One might assume that he would have read Whitehead's works written after the *Principia Mathematica*, especially *An Enquiry Concerning the Principles of Natural Knowledge* (1919) and *The Concept of Knowledge* (1920), published a few years before the *Tractatus*. Both books and, as Langer points out, his later work on symbolism, display similar views of the logical structure of meaning and the concept of 'fact' as an event.[69] This explains why, when read through the lenses of Whitehead, Wittgenstein's 'picture' theory made perfect sense to her. Wittgenstein, in her view, had provided 'an excellent account of the logical prerequisites for meaning'.[70]

Truth and verification

The fact that there is no single form for representing facts and that one form can represent multiple facts has naturally profound implications for thinking about truth. After all, all 'correspondence' between language and the world is always only *one kind of relation* between a symbolism and what it represents.[71] In the *Tractatus* Wittgenstein describes meaningful propositions as 'truth-functions of elementary propositions'. An elementary proposition, in turn, is 'a truth-function of itself' (*TLP* 5). We are also told that 'the simplest proposition, the elementary proposition, asserts the existence of an atomic fact' (*Sachverhalte* – also translated as 'state of affairs') (*TLP* 4.21). This was often read to mean that elementary propositions are observation statements the truth content of which is to be determined by sense-verification. Sometimes this reading was felt to be supported by Schlick's celebrated phrase 'The meaning of a proposition is the method of its verification'.[72] Yet, neither Wittgenstein nor Schlick considered empirical verification of observable sense-data as either a necessary or a sufficient condition for meaningful sentences or even a privileged criterion for establishing falsity or truth. While Wittgenstein does indeed at times use the word 'verification' (although only after 1926 and not in the *Tractatus*), this should not be interpreted in a *neo*-positivist sense but in the *logical* positivist sense of establishing meaningful propositions which can be said to have *some* basis in immediate experience. Langer agrees that every such meaningful proposition is a truth function. She explains this on the grounds that every simple 'atomic' proposition contains a verb which, by virtue of its function of combining a subject with an object also implicitly asserts something:

> In every proposition there is at least one word – the verb – which has the double function of *combining* the elements named into one propositional form, and *asserting* proposition, i.e. referring to something in reality. It is because of this implicit function of assertion, involved in the very meaning of a true verb, that *every proposition is true or false.*[73]

The view that, as Feigl and Blumberg put it, a 'single atomic proposition is … true when the fact which it asserts is the case, false when it is not the case', does not imply that elementary propositions can be empirically verified.[74] This is because the very elements that make up an elementary proposition do not lend themselves to verification or falsification. As Langer observes, 'A symbol that merely expresses a concept, e.g. an image or a name, is neither true nor false, though it is significant'.[75] Single symbols, therefore, have no truth value, only significance and meaning. As Feigl would say, they can only be pointed at. For Langer, every proposition holds a correspondence between 'certain logical aspects of both entities, so that *both may be known in the same way*, i.e. through the same conceptual schema, and whichever one is more convenient to handle may be taken to represent – not duplicate – the other'.[76]

Even so, this is not a traditional correspondence theory of cognition. As Langer explains: 'This is not the "correspondence" of idea and object, which is supposed to duplicate in experience a thing essentially outside experience'.[77] Put differently, 'A symbol is not a reproduction of its object, but an *expression* – an exhibition of certain relevant moments, whose relevance is determined by the purpose in hand'.[78] Likewise:

> In verbal expression, the mind must correlate words with the artificially separated ingredients of the mathematical idea; in algebra, the constituents that function closely together are rendered by symbols in juxtaposition, and the analogy is traced, almost intuitively, by the eye. Both forms of language are capable of expressing the same thing, but one shares with its object only a very remote and fundamental form, and deviates in many irrelevant particulars, whereas the other shares to a large extent its accidental, particular forms as well; this makes the former mode of symbolization, the verbal, very clumsy, and the latter, the algebraic expression, obvious and convenient.[79]

Langer's understanding of 'truth' as 'true to' in a relation of expression has both a psychological and a pragmatic dimension. It is psychological in that the symbol user has to 'intuit' the logical isomorphism – it cannot be explained from an independent, outside position. Wittgenstein realized this when he introduced the notion of 'showing' rather than 'saying'. It is pragmatic, in that the context determines which is the symbol and what is the symbolized. Although this pragmatic aspect is not foregrounded in the *Tractatus*, it anticipates Wittgenstein's later philosophy of language as defined through use. He once wrote to Russell, in response to being asked how he saw the relation between a thought and a fact:

> I don't know *what* the constituents of thoughts are but I know *that* it must have constituents which correspond to the words of Language. Again the kind of relation of the constituents of thought and of the pictured fact is irrelevant. It would be a matter of psychology to find out.[80]

The most important upshot of this discussion is that for Wittgenstein, as for Langer, a proposition is primarily an expression. As Wittgenstein puts it,

> Every part of a proposition which characterizes its sense I call an expression (a symbol). (The proposition itself is an expression.) Expressions are everything – essential for the sense of the proposition – that propositions can have in common with one another. An expression characterizes a form and a content (*TLP* 3.31):

This also explains why, for Wittgenstein, '*the limits of my language* mean the limits of my world' (*TLP* 5.6).

The fact that a sentence can be 'verified' in many different ways implies that it can have a range of different meanings. Depending on the kind of human experience a method is meant to 'verify', there can be very many different methods. As Wittgenstein told Waismann,

> Sometimes verification is very difficult, for example 'Seitz has been elected mayor [of Vienna].' How should I set about verifying this proposition? Is the correct method to go and make inquiries about it? Or ask the people who were present? But one [witness] was watching from the front and the other one from behind. Or should I read about it in the newspapers?[81]

In other words, neither Wittgenstein nor Schlick considered direct empirical sense-verification as the sole criterion for the meaningfulness of a proposition; it was merely one criterion among others. This also underlines his comment later in the *Philosophical Investigations*, 'Asking whether and how a proposition can be verified is only a particular way of asking "How d'you mean?" The answer is a contribution to the grammar of the proposition.'[82] This comment echoes Schlick's view in the passage immediately preceding his oft-quoted line on verification, which refers not to Wittgenstein's later but to his early work:

Whenever we ask about a sentence, 'What does it mean?', what we expect is instruction as to the circumstances in which the sentence is to be used; we want a description of the conditions under which the sentence will form a *true* proposition, and of those that will make it *false*. The meaning of a word or a combination of words is, in this way, determined by a set of rules which regulate their use and which, following Wittgenstein, we may call the rules of their *grammar*, taking this word in its widest sense. ... Stating the meaning of a sentence amounts to stating the rules according to which the sentence is to be used, and this is the same as stating the way in which it can be verified (or falsified). The meaning of a proposition is the method of its verification.[83]

Schlick's account in 1936 echoes many sentiments expressed earlier by Langer in *The Practice of Philosophy*, most notably the view that a symbol cannot 'duplicate in experience a thing essentially outside experience'.[84] The question of meaning in language is not whether or not it corresponds to something 'in the outside world', but whether its structural form can be *perceived as analogous to something else* – to another symbolization:

Truth is the relation which holds between a symbolic structure and any one of its possible objects. Truth is *always* a relation; it is meaningless to say that a symbol such as a proposition is 'true' without reference to something in the world, *to* which the symbol is true.[85]

Neither Wittgenstein, nor Schlick, nor Langer ever held a correspondence theory of truth – subjects cannot stand outside a symbol–world relation such as to assess the correctness of the correspondence. Wittgenstein's rhetorical question in *Philosophical Remarks* was indirectly already answered in the *Tractatus*: 'Isn't all that I mean: between the proposition and its verification there is no go-between negotiating this verification?'[86] The 'correspondence' or *'adequatio'* is in the configuration of the symbol and its *perceived* analogy in the world. The 'truth' lies in the effectiveness of the logical expression of the symbolic form or 'picture'. In the *Tractatus* Wittgenstein uses evocative language to describe the picture–world relation: a picture works like 'a scale applied to reality' that 'reaches up to it' as 'feelers of its elements with which the picture touches reality' (*TLP* 2.1512; 2.1511; 2.1515). These wordings suggest a deeper continuity between his early and later works than is often assumed. From Waismann's records it is known that, as early as 1931, Wittgenstein had referred to his early work as 'dogmatic'.[87] It is often thought that this meant that he rejected his putative copy-theory of language. However, since he never held such a theory, it is not entirely clear what exactly he considered 'dogmatic'. In the preface to *Philosophical Investigations*, Wittgenstein states that his later work should be read both 'in contrast with and against the background of [his] old way of thinking'.[88] Assuming some form of continuity, Friedlander interprets Wittgenstein's position on truth in the *Tractatus* in Heideggerian terms of disclosure:

This account of truth leads us to appreciate that what is philosophically important is not the question concerning the relation of adequation, but rather the universe of forms that conditions it. One might say there is a deeper notion of truth, which is that of disclosure of *what* things are, or of the form of the world. This distinction reveals yet again Wittgenstein's attempt to separate the perspective of facts from that of objects. The question of disclosing or uncovering the form of objects is a completely different activity from assessing the agreement of sense with reality. Wittgenstein's account distinguishes between a propositional account of truth and falsity, understood as the agreement or disagreement of structures with facts, and the more important idea of the unveiling of form, which is what allows representation at all. ... He refers us to a deeper level of identity between the subject and his world, which is presupposed in the capacity to manipulate language in order to represent the world.[89]

This interpretation of Wittgensteinean truth as a form of 'unveiling' or 'disclosure' – as *a-letheia* – is entirely in line with Langer's approach to language and symbolism in general. This is how she puts it in *Philosophy in a New Key*:

> Sign and symbol are knotted together in the production of those realities that we call 'facts', as I think this whole study of semantics has shown. But *between the facts* run the threads of unrecorded reality, momentarily recognized, wherever they come to the surface, in our tacit adaptation to signs; and the bright, twisted threads of symbolic envisagement, imagination, thought – memory and reconstructed memory, belief beyond experience, dream, make-belief, hypothesis, philosophy – the whole creative process of ideation, metaphor, and abstraction that makes human life an adventure in understanding.[90]

Langer might be seen to be even more consistent on this point than Wittgenstein. In thesis 2.17 Wittgenstein claims, 'What a picture must have in common with reality in order to be able to represent it after its manner – rightly or falsely – is its form of representation' (*TLP* 2.17). But in *The Practice of Philosophy*, Langer criticizes Wittgenstein for suggesting that a picture can ever be a *false* representation. As she writes, 'We cannot really speak of a false picture. If the analogy does not hold there is *no* logical picture. But Mr. Wittgenstein repeatedly uses the term.'[91]

For Langer, Wittgenstein's *Tractatus* formulates the 'new key' that had also been discovered by Sheffer, Whitehead, Cassirer and several other scholars working in different disciplines – that is, the recognition that the 'facts' that make up our knowledge of the world are inherently symbolic in nature and rooted in different laws of projection. As she was to summarize this new discovery in *Philosophy in a New Key*,

> The problem of observation is all but eclipsed by the problem of *meaning*. And the triumph of empiricism in science is jeopardized by the surprising truth that *our sense-data are primarily symbols.*
>
> Here, suddenly, it becomes apparent that the age of science has begotten a new philosophical issue, inestimably more profound than its original empiricism ... the edifice of human knowledge stands before us, not as a vast collection of sense reports, but ... as a structure of *facts that are symbols* and *laws that are their*

meanings. A new philosophical theme has been set forth to a coming age: an epistemological theme, the comprehension of science. The power of symbolism is its cue, as the finality of sense-data was the cue to a former epoch.[92]

According to Langer, the 'new key in philosophy' was the same 'turning point in philosophy' as identified by Schlick in Wittgenstein. Both Langer and Schlick approach Wittgenstein primarily as a philosopher of language, rather than a philosopher of science. Both see him as a philosopher more concerned with meaning than with verification; more interested in the plurality of disciplines understood as different symbolic forms than in one unified science based on the principles of the natural sciences. That Schlick was fundamentally a philosopher of language understood in terms of symbolic forms, rather than philosopher of science understood in terms of as verifiable propositions, was also noted by Schlick's editor, Friedrich Waismann:

> Since knowing, according to Schlick, is not seeing and experiencing, but an operating with concepts, while concepts are represented only by signs and symbols, he recognized at once that the investigation of language was bound to yield profound insights into the problems of philosophy.[93]

As noted before, this point was also recognized by Richard Rorty who included Schlick's essay 'The Future of Philosophy', with its reference to Langer's book, as the first chapter in his anthology *The Linguistic Turn* (1967).[94]

The expressive symbol

For Langer and Wittgenstein, *all* propositions, including scientific ones, are 'expressions'. Wittgenstein does not tire of stressing this in theses 3.31–3.314. Expression, in all these contexts, is not a case of emotional venting, it is symbolic formulation. The difference between symptomatic (self-)expression and symbolic expression – first highlighted by Cassirer – is crucial for understanding both Wittgenstein's and Langer's conceptions of expression. Langer is fully aware that this distinction is often not recognized or acknowledged. As she writes,

> According to our logicians, [pseudo-propositions] are to be treated as 'expressions' in a different sense, namely as 'expressions' of emotions, feelings, desires. They are not symbols for thought, but symptoms of the inner life, like tears and laughter, crooning, or profanity.[95]

Part of Wittgenstein's ongoing struggle with philosophy was his acute awareness that, on his own strict criteria for meaningful language, he could not express anything of importance to him. In the preface of the *Tractatus* he wrote,

> If this work has a value it consists of two things. First that in it thoughts are expressed, and this value will be the greater the better the thoughts are expressed.

The more the nail has been hit on the head. – Here I am conscious that I have fallen far short of the possible. Simply because my powers are insufficient to cope with the task. – May others come and do it better.[96]

Or, as he wrote in his journal during the time of his writing the *Tractatus*, 'My difficulty is only an – enormous – difficulty of expression.'[97] This enormous struggle with the right form of expression was also witnessed by the members of the Vienna Circle during their meetings with Wittgenstein. As Carnap recalls,

When he started to formulate his view on some specific philosophical problem, we often felt the internal struggle that occurred in him at that very moment, a struggle by which he tried to penetrate from darkness to light under an intense and painful strain, which was ever visible on his most expressive face. When finally, sometimes after a prolonged arduous effort, his answer came forth, his statement stood before us like a newly created piece of art and divine revelation.[98]

In *Philosophical Investigations* Wittgenstein was to refer to the limitations of discursive language as follows: 'A picture held us captive. And we could not get outside it, for it lay in our language and language seemed to repeat it to us inexorably.'[99]

Like Wittgenstein, Langer recognized that much what was important in life could not be captured and expressed in scientific or discursive language. Even Russell admitted as much when he wrote,

[O]ur confidence in language is due to the fact that it ... shares the structure of the physical world, and therefore can express that structure. But if there be a world which is not physical, or not in space-time, it may have a structure which we can never hope to express or to know. ... Perhaps that is why we know so much physics and so little of anything else.[100]

Echoing Engelmann's island and ocean metaphor Langer observes,

At best, human thought is but a tiny, grammar-bound island, in the midst of a sea of feeling expressed by 'Oh-oh' and sheer babble. The island has a periphery, perhaps, of mud – factual and hypothetical concepts broken down by the emotional tides into the 'material mode', a mixture of meaning and nonsense. Most of us live the better part of our lives on this mud-flat; but artistic moods we take to the deep, where we flounder about with symptomatic cries that sound like propositions about life and death, good and evil, substance, beauty, and other non-existent topics. So long as we regard only scientific and 'material' (semi-scientific) thought as really cognitive of the world, this peculiar picture of mental life must stand. And *as long as we admit only discursive symbolism as a bearer of ideas, 'thought' in this restricted sense must be regarded as our only intellectual activity.*[101]

However, – and this is an important difference – *pace* Wittgenstein Langer did not believe that one had to remain silent about what one could not speak in scientific terms. She did not share Wittgenstein's defeatist conclusion. The closest Wittgenstein ever came to think about forms outside logic and science was when, inspired by Goethe's morphology of plants, he explored something akin to a 'morphology' of magic rituals and religious ceremonies in 1931. He thought that by presenting such rituals in a particular schema he might, in the words of Monk, 'preserve what was deep about them, without either ridiculing or defending them. It would, in this way, have the "character of magic".[102]

For Langer, by contrast, there was 'an unexplored possibility of genuine semantic beyond the limits of discursive language.[103] Hence, she poses the challenging question,

> Since an inordinate amount of our talk, and therefore (we hope) of our cerebration too, defies the canons of literal meaning, our philosophers of language – Russell, Wittgenstein, Carnap, and others of similar persuasions – are faced with the new question: What is the true function of those verbal combinations and other pseudo-symbolic structure that have no real significance, but are freely used as though they meant something?[104]

Langer's solution to Wittgenstein's problem was not to stay silent but to extend the repertoire of symbolic forms beyond discursive linguistic expressions to include *non*-verbal, *non*-linguistic and *non*-discursive forms of expression. This enabled the articulation of experiences from realms other than the physical world, such as expressed in myth, art and ritual. Langer enters thus the realm that Wittgenstein had wanted to pass over in silence because he believed there was no way of thinking or saying it. As she was to write in 1942, 'The logical "beyond" which Wittgenstein calls the "unspeakable", both Russell and Carnap regard as the sphere of subjective experience, emotion, feeling, and wish, from which only *symptoms* come to us in the form of metaphysical and artistic fancies.' However, so she continued, the field of semantics 'is wider than that of language, as certain philosophers … have discovered.[105] This will become a central theme throughout Langer's work.

Schools of interpretation

At the end of the *Tractatus* Wittgenstein famously writes,

> We feel that even if *all possible* scientific questions be answered, the problems of life have still not been touched at all (*TLP* 6.52). … There is indeed the inexpressible. This *shows* itself; it is mystical (*TLP* 6.522). The right method of philosophy would be this. To say nothing except what can be said, *i.e.* the propositions of natural science, *i.e.* something that has nothing to do with philosophy: and then always, when someone else wished to say something metaphysical, to demonstrate to him that he had given no meaning to certain signs in his propositions. This method would be unsatisfying to the other – he would not have the feeling that we were teaching him philosophy – but it would be the only strictly correct method (*TLP* 6.53). My propositions are elucidatory in this way: he who understands me finally

recognizes them as senseless [*unsinnig*], when he has climbed out through them, on them, over them. (He must so to speak throw away the ladder, after he has climbed up on it.) He must surmount these propositions; then he sees the world rightly (*TLP* 6.54). Whereof one cannot speak, thereof one must be silent (*TLP* 7).

The meaning of these last few clauses of the *Tractatus* has become a key point of debate among Wittgenstein scholars. Controversy hinges on whether to read these as pro- or anti-metaphysical statements and whether Wittgenstein regarded his own philosophy as 'senseless' '*sinnlos*' in the sense of 'without meaning according to his own strict criteria' or in the sense of 'plain nonsense' or 'gibberish'.

More broadly it is possible to identify at least four schools of *Tractatus* interpretations, coinciding with roughly four periods. In order to place Langer's interpretation in relation to these four major schools, I will provide a brief account of each.

In the first group, as represented by Russell from the 1920s onwards, the *Tractatus* was read through British empiricist lenses as a theory of knowledge based on sense-data. As noted in Chapter 2, this view was further popularized through A. J. Ayer's *Language, Truth and Logic* (1936). Wittgenstein had been very unhappy with Russell's introduction to his book which he said misrepresented his views. Ayer later admitted that 'the outlook of the *Tractatus* was misunderstood by the members of the Vienna Circle and the young English philosophers, including myself, who were strongly influenced by it.'[106]

The second group consists of the Vienna Circle's logical positivists in the 1920s and 1930s. This group can be sub-divided into two strands: one emphasizing Wittgenstein's supposed anti-metaphysicalism (mainly Neurath, Hahn and Carnap), the other emphasizing his linguistic turn (mainly Schlick and Feigl). For the first subgroup, Wittgenstein's main contribution to philosophy was his strict delineation between proper philosophical propositions based on the methods of the natural sciences, and metaphysical pseudo-propositions. According to them, Wittgenstein's ban on the latter relegated all theology, ethics and poetry to the realm of irrational emotional expression. For this group, Wittgenstein's own fascination with poetry, the ineffable and mystical had created what Russell described as 'a sense of intellectual discomfort'.[107] Carnap later admitted that his own interpretation of the metaphysical and mystical in the *Tractatus* had been at odds with Wittgenstein's own intentions:

> Early on when we were reading Wittgenstein's book in the Circle, I had erroneously believed that his attitude towards metaphysics was similar to ours. I had not paid sufficient attention to the statements in his book about the mystical, because his feelings and thoughts in this area were too divergent from mine. ... There was a striking difference between Wittgenstein's attitude toward philosophical problems and that of Schlick and myself. Our attitude toward philosophical problems was not very different from that which scientists have toward their problems. ... [Wittgenstein's] point of view and his attitude toward people and problems, even theoretical problems, were much more similar to those of a creative artist than to those of a scientist; one might almost say, similar to those of a religious prophet or a seer.[108]

For Wittgenstein, in turn, Carnap's misunderstanding of his last sentences in the *Tractatus* had been a source of deep frustration. As he wrote to Schlick in 1932, 'I cannot imagine that Carnap should have so completely and utterly misunderstood the last sentences of my book – and therefore the fundamental conception of the whole book.'[109] Although Schlick shared Carnap's attitude towards Wittgenstein's mysticism, his own main interest in the *Tractatus* had been its 'linguistic turn' and its emphasis on logical form. As he wrote in 'The Turning Point in Philosophy', 'The great turning point is … that [all] modes of representation – if they otherwise actually express the same knowledge – must have [a common] logical form.'[110]

The third and arguably most influential body of Wittgenstein interpretations emerged only after his death in 1951, when many of his private notes and letters became available to a wider public.[111] During his life Wittgenstein had been notoriously reticent to comment on his work and its intentions. Much of what we know now about his own views is based on posthumously published notes, letters and memoirs of friends, colleagues and students. These documents became an important new source of information for a third group of readers in the 1950s and 1960s.[112] From within this diverse group of commentators a new 'ethical' or 'metaphysical' reading emerged that that did not read the *Tractatus* as a defence or a celebration of the new and 'improved' language of philosophy but as a lament on its poverty, that is, as a sobering realization of how little scientific propositions could express what was actually meaningful in life. They shared Wittgenstein's view that 'even if *all possible* scientific questions have been answered, the problems of life have still not been touched at all' (*TLP* 6.52). As Wittgenstein's friend, the architect Paul Engelmann, put it in his memoirs,

> Positivism holds – and this is its essence – that what we can speak about is all that *really matters* in life. Whereas Wittgenstein passionately believes that all that really matters in human life is precisely what, in his view, we must be silent about.[113]

Wittgenstein often refers to the fact that the text was less about what was said than about the unsaid, what was left out. In one letter to his friend and prospective publisher of the *Tractatus*, Ludwig von Ficker, he makes this point explicitly:

> The book's point is an ethical one. I once meant to include in the preface a sentence which is not in fact there now but which I will write out for you here because it will perhaps be a key to the work for you. What I meant to write, then, was this: My work consists of two parts: the one presented here plus all that I have not written. And it is precisely this second part that is the important one. … For now, I would recommend you to read the preface and the conclusion, because they contain the most direct expression of the point of the book.[114]

The readers in this third group as represented by, among others, Alice Ambrose, Max Black, Norman Malcolm, G. E. M. Anscombe and Brian F. McGuinness are typically most interested in Wittgenstein's tantalizing hint to what he did *not* write or say – 'Wherof one cannot speak, thereof one must be silent' (*TLP* 7) – and especially in his notion that what cannot be said might still be shown – 'There is indeed the inexpressible. This *shows* itself; it is the mystical' (*TLP* 6.522). The distinction between saying and showing is closely connected to Wittgenstein's other distinction between '*sinnlos*' – that is, failing the criteria for philosophically acceptable or scientific propositions – and '*unsinnig*' – plain nonsense or gibberish. While propositions about justice, love or God might be '*sinnlos*' in not meeting the criteria for valid propositions, that does not mean they are devoid of meaning. Wittgenstein applies this insight to his own text. While the *Tractatus*'s individual propositions fail the criteria for the correct philosophical method – hence Wittgenstein's instruction to dispose of them as serving merely as a ladder – the text as a whole is nevertheless meaningful in that it *shows* what it means to convey, that is, the formal structure of scientific language, *even if* this exposes its limitation.

Wittgenstein's distinction between '*sinnlos*' and '*unsinnig*' also takes a central place, but in reverse importance, in the fourth group of *Tractatus* readers, called the 'New Wittgensteinians' or school of 'resolute reading' originating in the 1980s.[115] This reading rejects the third school's 'standard reading' by claiming that Wittgenstein never intended the *Tractatus* to be read for its philosophical content, however that might be conceived, but for its therapeutic realization that all propositional reasoning was futile. This group focused on the term '*unsinnig*' in the penultimate clause of the *Tractatus*: '[H]e who understands me finally recognizes [these propositions] as senseless [*unsinnig*], when he has climbed over them' (*TLP* 6.54). They argued that, since Wittgenstein had chosen this word deliberately over the term '*sinnlos*', he must be taken seriously, that is, 'resolutely', at his own words.

Logical form as expression

Langer, as will have become clear, cannot be placed very easily in any of the above categories. Her reading of Wittgenstein, shaped and coloured by the thought of Sheffer, Cassirer and Whitehead, combines several elements in a unique synthesis of various elements. Adopting Sheffer's conception of logic as the study of forms, she recognized the importance of Wittgenstein's notion of *logical form* and *structure*. Influenced by Cassirer's and Whitehead's philosophy of symbolic forms, she understood his emphasis on the role of *expression*.[116] And she fully grasped Wittgenstein's deep existential struggle to express 'the problems of life' that fell outside the confines of discursive, scientific language (*TLP* 6.52). Yet, as we will see, she also offers a way out of this dilemma by expanding the range of symbolic forms.

Although Langer rejects Carnap's anti-metaphysical reading, she describes *The Logical Syntax of Language* (1934), as a 'precise and practical corroboration [of] the somewhat diffuse apprehension of our intellectual age, that *symbolism* is the key to epistemology and "natural knowledge"'.[117] Carnap himself writes in his autobiography that the most important insight he gained from Wittgenstein's *Tractatus* was

> that the truth of logical statements is based only on their logical structure and the meaning of the terms. Logical statements are true under all conceivable circumstances; thus their truth is independent of the contingent facts of the world.

On the other hand, it follows that these statements do not say anything about the world and thus have no factual content.[118]

On this point his views are so close to those of Wittgenstein that, in 1932, Wittgenstein even accused Carnap of plagiarizing his ideas.[119] For Langer the affinity between their views had been clear all along. As she wrote in *Philosophy in a new Key,*

> Carnap's admirable book, *The Logical Syntax of Language,* carries out the philosophical program suggested by Wittgenstein. Here an actual, detailed technique is developed for determining the *capacity for expression* of any linguistic system, a technique which predicts the limit of all combinations to be made in that system, shows the equivalence of certain forms and the differences among others which might be mistaken for equivalents, and exhibits the conventions to which any thought or experience must submit in order to become conveyable by the symbolism in question.[120]

She does not object to Carnap's view of scientific language:

> The distinctions between scientific language and everyday speech, which most of us can feel rather than define, are clearly illumined by Carnap's analysis; and it is surprising to find how little of our ordinary communication measures up to the standard of 'meaning' which serious philosophy of language, and hence a logic of discursive thought, set before us.[121]

Keeping in mind Langer's and Wittgenstein's understanding of verification as described above, she does not even object to Carnap's view of verification:

> I can ask whatever language will express; … A proposition which could not, under any (perhaps ideal, impracticable) conditions, be verified or refuted, is a pseudo-proposition, it has no literal meaning. It does not belong to the framework of knowledge that we call logical conception; is it not true or false, but *unthinkable,* for it falls outside the order of symbolism.[122]

It will be clear by now that this conception of verification does not imply a commitment to a radical empiricism or neo-positivist physicalism. For neo-Kantian logical positivists such as Carnap, ultimate reality will always remain an unknown *Ding-an-Sich.* And while scientific language might be the appropriate medium for expressing the physical dimension of reality, there might be other languages to express other dimensions. He merely did not engage in exploring those. This is clear from Carnap's autobiography:

> When speaking to [a scientist] I might talk in a language that could be characterized as realistic or even materialistic; here we looked at the world as consisting of bodies, bodies as consisting of atoms; sensations, thoughts, emotions, and the like were conceived as physiological processes in the nervous system and ultimately physical processes. … In a talk with [someone in a different discipline] I might

adapt myself to his idealistic kind of language. We would consider the question of how things are to be constituted on the basis of the given. ... my way of thinking was neutral with respect to the traditional controversies, e.g., realism vs idealism, nominalism vs. Platonism (realism of universals), materialism vs. Spiritualism, and so on. When I developed the system of the *Aufbau*, it actually did not matter to me which of the various forms of philosophical language I used, because to me they were mere modes of speech, and not formulations of positions. ... The system of concepts was constructed on a phenomenalistic basis ... However, I indicated also the possibility of constructing a total system of concepts on a physicalistic basis. The main motivation for my choice of a phenomenalistic basis was the intention to represent not only the logical relations among the concepts but also the equally important epistemological relations. The system was intended to give, though not a description, still a rational reconstructions of the actual process of the formation of concepts ... The ontological theses of the traditional doctrines of either phenomenalism or materialism remained for me entirely out of considerations.[123]

Like Carnap, Langer did not express statements about ultimate entities, whether physical or non-physical, but was primarily concerned with 'modes or speech' and 'philosophical languages'. However, in contrast to Carnap, she was not mainly interested in scientific language but in *non*-scientific language and *non*-discursive symbolic forms.

Somewhat surprisingly, Langer does not engage with Wittgenstein's later work, published after his death in 1951.[124] It is generally assumed that, in his later life, Wittgenstein denounced the *Tractatus*. In the preface to *Philosophical Investigations* Wittgenstein refers to the work's 'grave mistakes' and, elsewhere, to its 'dogmatism'. Ironically, some readers reject Langer's views because they assume it is based on Wittgenstein's discredited positivist epistemology or, alternatively, deny that the *Tractatus* had any influence on her thought.[125]

Yet, Langer's interpretation helps us discern a sense of strong continuity. It was only in his later life that Wittgenstein explored languages that were not scientific, including everyday language. Many of his observations in *Philosophical Investigations* (1945) would have resonated strongly with Langer. This also applies to his new understanding of linguistic meaning as determined by use rather than reference, something Langer had been interested in since her studies with Karl Bühler, a family friend of the Wittgensteins, in Vienna in the early 1920s. Although it was not always foregrounded, it was, as we will see in the next chapter, an integral part of her definition of symbol. Even so, by the time of publication of *Philosophical Investigations*, Langer's intellectual interest had, once again, moved on and she was to turn her attention to the bodily basis of all symbolic forms, including language. For this she was to draw more on Whitehead than on Wittgenstein.

Part Three

Contributions

8

The logic of signs and symbols

All thinking begins with seeing; *not necessarily through the eye, but with some basic formulations of sense perception, in the particular idiom of sight, hearing, or touch, normally of all the senses together. For all thinking is conceptual, and conception begins with the comprehension of* Gestalt.

Langer[1]

The brain works as naturally as the kidneys and the blood vessels. It is not dormant just because there is no conscious purposes to be served at the moment. ... [I]t is actively translating experiences into symbols in fulfilment of a basic need to do so. It carries on a constant process of ideation.

Langer[2]

Poetry means more than a cry; it has reason for being articulate; and metaphysics is more than the croon with which we might cuddle up to the world in a comfortable attitude. We are dealing with symbolisms here, and what they express is often highly intellectual.

Langer[3]

There is an unexplored possibility of genuine semantic beyond the limits of discursive language.

Langer[4]

Expanded meaning

Langer's logic of signs and symbols is motivated by one overriding concern: to expand the realm of 'meaning' beyond that of discursive, scientific language. Langer rejects Wittgenstein's conclusion to the *Tractatus* that the inexpressible in language is mystical and should remain in silence.[5] She also rejects Carnap's view that the language of metaphysics, ethics and poetry is merely emotional expressions, akin to laughing or crying.[6] If scientific propositions were the only semantic that contained meaning, Langer argues, we could never say anything meaningful about the many things that are important to us. Even Russell admitted as much when he wrote that if language can only express the structure of the physical world, 'perhaps that is why we know so much physics and so little of anything else.'[7]

For Langer, by contrast, there is 'a great deal of experience that is knowable … yet defies discursive formulation, and therefore verbal expression: that is what we sometimes call the *subjective aspect* of experience.'[8] This experience is neither formless nor mystical. It merely requires a different symbolic form for their expression. As she writes,

> The logical 'beyond', which Wittgenstein calls the 'unspeakable', both Russell and Carnap regard as the sphere of subjective experience, emotion, feeling, and wish, from which only *symptoms* come to us in the form of metaphysical and artistic fancies. The study of such products they relegate to psychology, not semantics. And here is the point of my radical divergence from them. Where Carnap speaks of 'cries like 'Oh, Oh', or, on a higher level, lyrical verses', I can see only a complete failure to apprehend a fundamental distinction. Why should we cry our feelings at such high levels that anyone would think we were *talking?* Clearly, poetry means more than a cry; it has reason for being articulate; and metaphysics is more than the croon with which we might cuddle up to the world in a comfortable attitude. We are dealing with symbolisms here, and what they express is often highly intellectual.[9]

Drawing on Sheffer, Cassirer and Whitehead, Langer develops a new, expanded and inclusive concept of meaning that does justice to the rich realm of human experience beyond language and scientific thought.

Langer's suggestion that there could be genuine intellectual meaning in non-scientific propositions was not only a critique of Russell and Carnap but of the kind of logical positivist and analytic philosophy that had come out of the 1939 Fifth International Congress for the Unity of Science. Against that background her *Philosophy in a New Key*, published in 1942, was as radical as it was controversial. As she described the situation,

> The field of semantics is wider than that of language, as certain philosophers – Schopenhauer, Cassirer, Delacroix, Dewey, Whitehead, and some others – have discovered; but it is blocked for us by the two fundamental tenets of current epistemology … (1) That *language is the only means of articulating thought* and (2) That *everything which is not speakable thought, is feeling*.[10]

As Paul Welsh commented,

> Her argument is this: what Carnap, Russell and Wittgenstein say about language is perfectly accurate, but limited. They mistakenly assume, she holds, that what cannot be symbolized in language is meaningless. And this, she says is false. Language can symbolize only certain kinds of ideas, but these are not the only kinds of ideas, and language is not the only kind of symbolism.[11]

Three fundamental distinctions

In this chapter I will show how Langer's new concept of meaning is construed around three seminal distinctions or 'axes': between 'signs' and 'symbols'; between 'discursive' and 'non-discursive' symbolisms; and between 'conventional' and 'formulative' symbolisms. While the first two distinctions are widely recognized and acknowledged, the third distinction is often overlooked and ignored. This has led to a range of misunderstandings of Langer's position as it has failed to take into account two central notions that adhere to her view of signs and symbols, that is, time and process. Drawing on Cassirer and Whitehead, Langer's signs and symbols are not static entities but evolve over time. Not only can symbol and symbolized reverse roles depending on interest and circumstances, symbols can change over time from tentative formulations of inchoate subjective experience into conventional symbols with dictionary meaning. Langer is one of the first philosophers who recognized and foregrounded this aspect of symbols and drew out its many implications.

Signs and symbols

In her Introduction to *Feeling and Form*, in 1953, Langer refers to her symbolic theory as set out in *Philosophy in a New Key* as a 'semantic' theory.[12] Since *Philosophy in a New Key* covers areas as diverse as myth, religion, ritual, science and art, it is clear that, for Langer, the term 'semantic' is not confined to *linguistic* meaning.[13] For Langer, as for Cassirer, 'the field of semantics is wider than that of language' and applies to the hermeneutical project of the pursuit of meaning in anything.[14] For Langer the contrasting term to semantic is not 'non-linguistic' but 'symptomatic' or, as she will refer to it, between symbol-meaning and sign-meaning.

Both signs and symbols are always part of a meaning-pattern involving at least three terms: a sign, a signified and a user or interpreter of the sign.[15] In *The Practice of Philosophy* Langer puts it as follows:

> Failure to realise that all meaning relations are triadic, not dyadic, has given rise to endless confusions and bootless arguments. The relation in such a propositions as: 'A sceptre means royalty' is really not the form 'a R b' but is an incomplete statement involving three terms, thus – 'R (ac.b).' For some term, c, a means b. Thus b, the object, is determined by a, the symbol, and c, the interpretant *for which* (or for whom) *a* means *b*.[16]

In *Philosophy in a New Key* she describes the thought in terms of a 'logical' and 'psychological' aspect in the meaning-pattern:

> Meaning has both a logical and a psychological aspect. Psychologically, any item that is to have meaning must be *employed* as a sign or symbol; that is to say, it must be a sign or symbol *to* someone. Logically, it must be *capable* of conveying a meaning, it must be the sort of item that can thus be employed.[17]

When interpreting a meaning-pattern, one's description of it will differ depending on whether one focuses on the meaning of the symbol or on the intention of the subject:

> We may say that a certain symbol 'means' an object to a person, or that the person 'means' the object by the symbol. The first description treats meaning in the logical sense, the second in the psychological sense. The former takes the symbol as the key, and the latter the subject.[18]

According to Langer, the confusion around this distinction is a result of the inherent ambiguity of the verb 'to mean', which is sometimes used as '*it* means' and sometimes as '*I* mean'.[19] The key to understanding the meaning of a term, she argues, is not to treat it as a quality or property but by viewing it '*as a function, not a property, of terms*'.[20] As she explains,

> There is in fact no quality of meaning; its essence lies in the realm of logic, where one does not deal with qualities, but only with relations. It is not fair to say: 'meaning is a relation', for that suggests too simple a business. ... It is better, perhaps, to say: 'Meaning is not a quality, but a *function* of a term'. A function is a *pattern* viewed with reference to one special term round which it centers; this pattern emerges when we look at the given term *in its total relation to the other terms about it*.[21]

Langer illustrates this with a musical cord. A cord can be interpreted differently depending on which note one takes to be the key: an 'A' with a third, fourth and sixth note above it can be described as a function of 'A' *or* as the second inversion of the seventh-chord on the dominant in the key of 'G' as a function of 'D'. In this example, the main terms of comparison are not notes or words in their relation to their surrounding notes or words, but the relation between the interpreting subject, the sign/symbol and the signified.

Considering Langer's emphasis on the importance of the human interpretant it comes somewhat of a surprise, when she announces that, in her further analysis, she will 'speak of terms (such as words) as "meaning" something', and not 'of people as "meaning" this or that'.[22] However, as we will see, her main interest is in the 'logical' structure of the meaning-relation that determines the relation of terms to their objects. This will also prove to be the key factor in distinguishing between signs and symbols. For Langer, the radical difference between sign-meaning and symbol-meaning can be logically exhibited, for 'it rests on a difference of pattern, it is strictly a different function.'[23]

Signs

On Langer's terms, a sign 'indicates the existence – past, present, or future – of a thing, event, or condition'.[24] In a sign-relation there are three terms: a sign, an object and an interpreter for whom the sign and object stand in a one-to-one causal relation to form a pair. Examples given by Langer are as follows:

Wet streets are a sign that it has rained; A patter on the roof is a sign that it is raining. A fall of the barometer or a ring around the moon is a sign that it is going to rain. In an unirrigated place, abundant verdure is a sign that it often rains there. A smell of smoke signifies the presence of fire. A scar is a sign of a past incident. Dawn is a herald of sunrise. Sleekness is a sign of frequent and plentiful food.[25]

In all these examples signs form part of the same physical situation or condition as the signified. They are, as Langer points out, *symptoms* of states of affairs.[26] The main reason why one term is taken as sign and not as object is that the interpreter 'is interested in the latter and perceives the former' and through the sign 'may apprehend the existence of the term that interests him.'[27] Echoing Whitehead, Langer holds, 'If it were not for the subject, or *interpretant*, sign and object would be interchangeable.'[28]

Signs are typically perceived as indicators that call for action:

Its mechanism may be conceived as an elaboration of the conditioned-reflex arc, with the brain doing switchboard duty, and getting the right or the wrong number for the sense organ that called up the musculature and expects an answer in terms of altered sensations.[29]

Although many signs in sign-relations are 'natural' they do not need to be so. As long as there is an intended or perceived one-to-one, causal relation, natural signs can be man-made: '[J]ust as in nature certain events are correlated, so that the less important may be taken as signs of the more important, so we may also *produce* arbitrary events purposely correlated with important ones that are to be their meanings.'[30] Examples given are as follows: 'A whistle means that the train is about to start. A gunshot means that the sun is just setting. A crepe on the door means someone has just died.'[31]

In other words, even though artificial signs are not part of the physical condition they signify or have a physical causal connection with it, that does not alter the logical relation between sign and object because it does not change the way a subject *receives or responds to* the sign. They are perceived and acted upon *as if* they were causally connected.[32] In both cases, the interpreting subject approaches the sign as an *indicator* of something and it is the latter the subject is primarily interested in. Whether natural or man-made, signs serve to guide our actions by providing pointers to situations of relevance in life. Humans respond instinctively when they

answer bells, watch the clock, obey warning signals, follow arrows, take off the kettle when it whistles, come at the baby's cry, close the windows when [they] hear thunder (17).[33]

Signs can be misinterpreted. The misinterpretation of signs, says Langer, is 'the simplest form of *mistake*.'[34] A bell can be wrongly understood to signal something or be confused with another bell. Likewise, wet streets can be interpreted mistakenly as being the result of rain when, in fact, they have just been cleaned. Responding 'appropriately' to signs is a matter of trial and error and of shared agreement. Future responses are dictated by the success or failure of previous ones in response to a particular sign. Signs function essentially as signals.

Symbols

When we now turn to Langer's notion of symbol, we encounter a different type of meaning-pattern:

> In an ordinary sign-function, there are three essential terms: subject, sign, and object. In denotation, which is the commonest kind of symbol-function, there have to be four: subject, symbol, conception and object.[35]

Unlike signs or signals, symbols do not call for action, but are '*vehicles for the conception of objects*'.[36] According to Langer, this is typically overlooked by genetic and behaviourist psychologists who treat all symbols like signs, that is, in terms of a stimulus-response pattern. Yet, symbols function very differently. Examples given are as follows:

> If I say: 'Napoleon', you do not bow to the conqueror of Europe as though I had introduced him but merely think of him. If I mention a Mr. Smith of our common acquaintance, you may be led to tell me something about him 'behind his back', which is just what you would *not* do in his presence.[37]

In talking *about* things we do not announce things, but we have *conceptions* of them: '*[I]t is the conceptions, not the things, that symbols directly "mean"*'.[38] In summary: the fundamental difference between signs and symbols is their function: signs announce their objects, whereas symbols enable them to be conceived.[39]

Langer's seminal illustration of symbolic conception is the moving story of deaf-blind Helen Keller. Keller used to associate words spelled out on her hands as signals of what was about to happen, such as doing something or going somewhere. However, one day the word 'water' was spelled out to her on her hand while *at the same time* she could feel the water of a cool stream gushing over her hand. At that instance, she writes, the 'mystery of language was revealed to me.'[40]

> I knew then that w-a-t-e-r meant the wonderful cool something that was flowing over my hand. That living word awakened my soul, gave it light, hope, joy, set it free! ... Everything had a name, and each name gave birth to a new thought. As we returned to the house every object which I touched seemed to quiver with life.[41]

Put differently, for Hellen Keller the word 'water' became a name and symbol for something 'by which it could be mentioned, conceived, remembered.'[42] Instead of serving as signals for action or instruments for survival, symbols fulfil a major basic human need to make sense of the world and get a handle on it. In his chapter 'From Animal Reactions to Human Responses' in *An Essay on Man*, Cassirer, too, refers to Keller's story:

The decisive step leading from the use of signs and pantomime to the use of words, that is, of symbols, could scarcely be described in a more striking manner. ... Helen Keller had previously learned to combine a certain thing or event with a certain sign of the manual alphabet. A fixed association had been established between these things and certain tactile impressions. But a series of such associations, even if they are repeated and amplified, still does not imply an understanding of what human speech is and means. In order to arrive at such an understanding the child had to make a new and much more significant discovery. It had to understand that *everything has a name* – that the symbolic function is not restricted to particular cases but is a principle of *universal* applicability which encompasses the whole field of human thought.[43]

Even though a symbol such as a person's name can be *used* as a sign in the sense of indicator, its 'signific' character has to be made clear by means of additional clues, such as one's tone of voice or a gesture such as 'raised eyebrows and a look at the door, interpreted as a *sign* that he is coming.'[44]

Charles Peirce

Langer's emphasis on the triadic rather than dyadic nature of a meaning-relation in signs echoes Charles Peirce's definition of a sign as 'something which stands to somebody for something in some respect or capacity.'[45] Although Peirce's papers were not yet published when she wrote *The Practice of Philosophy*, Langer mentions in a footnote that she had been shown some of his unpublished works by Paul Weiss, another student of Whitehead who, at that time, was editing the papers for publication.[46] By the time of writing *Philosophy in a New Key*, however, the first six volumes of his *Collected Papers* had been published and Langer had been able to take note of his semiotic system with its intricate classifications of signs and symbols. Although she praises Peirce for the pioneering nature of his semiotics and semantics, she also criticizes him for his overcomplex system of categorization:

Charles Peirce, who was probably the first person to concern himself seriously with semantics, began by making an inventory of all 'symbol-situations', in the hope that when all possible meanings of 'meaning' were herded together, ... they would divide the sheep from the goats. But the obstreperous flock, instead of falling neatly into a few classes, each according to its kind, divided and subdivided into the most terrifying order of icons, qualisigns, legisigns, semes, phemes, and delomes, and there is but cold comfort in his assurance that the original 59,049 types can really be boiled down to a mere sixty-six.[47]

This cursory dismissal of Peirce's work is unfortunate although perhaps understandable considering the unsystematic and non-chronological way in which Peirce's manuscripts had been edited and organized in their first editions. Closer inspection of Langer's semantic theory, however, reveals many overlaps with Peirce's semiotics even if they differ in their terminology. For instance, Peirce's definition of sign is very similar to Langer's definition of symbol.[48] Like Peirce's 'formal doctrine of signs', Langer's semantic theory portrays the world as a myriad of signs and symbols that constitute what Langer, following Wittgenstein, calls 'a picture of "facts"' that stands in a plurality of different relations to the world depending on the way the subject views it.[49] Wittgenstein himself had been familiar with Peirce's work through his friend Frank Ramsey and may well have drawn on his ideas.[50] Peirce famously divides the realm of signs in three overarching typological categories: *icons, indices* and *symbols* with each type further subdivided in an intricate system of triadic patterns. Broadly speaking, icons share a common likeness with their object; indices stand in a causal relation with their object, while symbols stand for their object by convention. All three categories re-appear in (though do not exhaust) Langer's divisions but under different names.[51] Her main classification is two-fold, not three-fold: on the one hand *signs* – a category that overlaps with Peirce's index – and, on the other hand, *symbols*, – a category that comprises but exceeds Peirce's categories of icons and symbols.[52] Another point of potential confusion is Langer's use of the term 'interpretant'. Langer uses this in the sense of 'interpreter' whereas, for Peirce, it is what Langer will call 'the conception', that is, the content of the symbolized in someone's mind.[53]

Langer's twofold division of signs and symbols draws primarily on Cassirer but also on Whitehead. Even so, before *An Essay on Man*, Cassirer had not made the sign-symbol as prominent as Langer and may well have been influenced by her account of it in *Philosophy in a New Key*. As he writes in *An Essay on Man*,

> For the sake of a clear statement of the problem we must carefully distinguish between *signs* and *symbols*. … Symbols – in the proper sense of this term – cannot be reduced to mere signals. Signals and symbols belong to two different universes of discourse: a signal is a part of the physical world of being; a symbol is part of the human world of meaning. Signals are 'operators'; symbols are 'designators'.[54]

After the publication of Charles Morris' *Signs, Language and Behavior* (1946), Langer revisited her own terminology and wrote, 'The great advantage of Morris' usage is that is leaves us the word 'sign' to denote any vehicle of meaning, signal or symbol, whereas in my own vocabulary there was no generic term, and the need of it was sometimes obvious.[55] In *Foundations of the Theory of Signs* (1938) Morris had divided Peirce's study of signs into three branches, that is, syntactics as the study of the relation of signs to other signs, semantics as the study of the relation of signs to the things they represent and pragmatics as the study of the use of signs. None of these categories, however, focus exactly on Langer's main interest, that is, the articulation or 'formulation' of meaning. Unlike Langer's philosophy, Morris behaviourist theory is primarily concerned with the *response* to sign stimuli, not with the way they originate. Similarly, despite his interest in the nature of consciousness, Peirce's pragmatist bent leads him to focus primarily on the effects and manifestations of signs on the behaviour of the receiver rather than the way they originate and are being shaped and formed. Langer's main interest is in the way symbolic forms, whether discursive or non-discursive, conventional or formulative, are ultimately rooted in and emerge from embodied human experience. This lends Langer's logic of signs and symbols its unique and original character.

Semiotic and semantic

Langer's theory of symbolic forms is sometimes referred to as a semiotic – rather than her own word 'semantic' – theory.[56] Although both terms are etymologically derived from the Greek word 'semeion' or 'sema' (meaning: 'sign'), the term 'semiotics' has gained a specific philosophical significance since its use by Peirce.[57] Semiotic or 'semiologist' theories such as, for example, proposed by Roland Barthes, look at cultural phenomena, whether images, objects, gestures or music in terms of systems of signification as indicators of cultural trends and social conventions.[58] As is clear from her discussion of art in *Feeling and Form*, this is *not* Langer's primary interest:

> A work of art is often a spontaneous expression of feeling, i.e., a symptom of the artist's state of mind. If it represents human beings it is probably also a rendering of some sort of facial expression which suggests the feeling those beings are supposed to have. Moreover, it may be said to 'express', ... the life of the society from which it stems, namely to *indicate* customs, dress, behavior, and to reflect confusion or decorum, violence or peace. And besides all these things it is sure to express the unconscious wishes and nightmare of its author. All these things may be found in museums and galleries if we choose to note them.[59]

However, so she points out, that kind of expression is not unique to art because anything can always express or 'be a sign of' anything:

> But [these 'expressions'] may also be found in wastebaskets and in the margins of schoolbooks. This does not mean that someone has discarded a work of art, or produced one when he was bored with long division. It merely means that all drawings, utterances, gestures, or personal records of any sort express feelings, beliefs, social conditions, and interesting neuroses; 'expression' in any of these senses is not peculiar to art, and consequently is not what makes for artistic value.[60]

Langer does not consider the world of signs as studied by semioticians 'symbols' but 'symptoms'. Symptoms, on Langer's account, are *unintentional manifestations of certain conditions*. Symbols, by contrast, are *intentional articulations of human experiences* which can turn into conventions. As Langer explains,

> The difference between a symbolic and a symptomatic act may be illustrated by contrasting the intentional genuflexion of a suppliant with the emotional quaver of his voice. There is a convention about the former, but not about the latter. And the *conventional expression* of a feeling, an attitude, etc., is the first, the lowest form of *denotation*.[61]

Discursive and presentational symbolism

With Langer's fundamental distinction between symbols and signs (or 'symptoms', 'signals' or 'indicators') in place, we now turn to two important distinctions *within* her notion of symbol as such. In this section I will discuss the first distinction, that is, discursive and non-discursive or 'presentational' symbolism.

The difference between discursive and non-discursive symbolism is often considered Langer's most significant trademark. As Jerry Gill, for example, comments,

> The axis of Langer's philosophy of art is her absolute dichotomy between the discursive and expressive functions of human symbolic communication. ... This all-encompassing dualism radiates throughout and controls every aspect of Langer's systematic effort to understand and formulate the meaning of aesthetic activity and prehension.[62]

However, this way of putting it is misleading. Not only does Gill mistakenly contrast discursive with 'expressive', – as we have seen, for Langer *all* forms of symbolization are 'expressive' – he downplays the important shared character and unity between the two forms of symbolization. Indeed, one of Langer's main motivations behind the distinction is not to highlight the fact that some symbolic forms – art, ritual, myth – are non-discursive, but that they are genuine *symbolisms*, that is, legitimate carriers of insight and meaning. Discursive and non-discursive symbols, for Langer, are united by a shared *root*, a shared *task* and a shared *logical form*. They share a *common root* in the elementary abstractions of primary perception. All thinking 'begins with *seeing*. ... For all thinking is conceptual, and conception begins with the comprehension of *Gestalt*.'[63] They share a *common task* in that 'the prime office of symbols [is] their power of formulating experience, and presenting it objectively for contemplation, logical intuition, recognition, understanding'.[64] And they share a *common principle of form* in that each operates on the basis of a similarity in structure between symbol and symbolized. They are rooted in an analogy of form and structure. This analogy can ultimately only be grasped by *intuition*. That applies equally to discursive as to non-discursive symbolism. In neither symbolism is there a vantage point outside the symbol–symbolized relation by which one can judge the relation itself.

In summary, while constituted differently in their structural make-up, discursive and non-discursive symbolism have much in common. In Langer's words, 'The parent stock of both conceptual types, of verbal and non-verbal formulation, is the basic human act of symbolic transformation. The root is the same, only the flower is different.'[65] Or as musicologist Wayne Bowman puts it succinctly, 'Behind the striking contrasts between discursive and presentational symbolism lies a shared symbolic mission: the process of symbolic transformation that brings things to our minds and enables us to keep them there.'[66]

Symbols and symbolisms

It is worth noting that in her discussion of discursivity and non-discursivity, Langer no longer primarily speaks of 'symbols' but of 'symbolisms'. This is because, for her, the terms 'discursivity' and 'non-discursivity' do not apply primarily to the symbols as such but to the medium they employ: 'Wherever a symbol operates, there is meaning; and conversely, different classes of experience – say, reason, intuition, appreciation – correspond to different types of symbolic mediation.'[67] So whereas a sentence is a symbol, its medium, language, is a discursive symbolism. This is not always adequately understood by her commentators. Gerry Hagberg, for instance, claims that a 'discursive symbol is simply a word with meaning.'[68] This is not correct. Likewise, whereas a picture is a symbol, its medium, colours and shapes, is a non-discursive symbolism. As Langer explains it in relation to art,

> A work of art is a single, indivisible symbol, although a highly articulate one; it is not, like a discourse (which may also be regarded as a single symbolic form), composite, analyzable into more elementary symbols ... For language, spoken or written, is a *symbolism*, a system of symbols; a work of art is always a prime symbol.[69]

According to Langer, failure to honour this distinction has led to various misunderstandings:

> All the failings of musical hermeneutics ... rest on one cardinal error, the treatment of the art symbol as a symbolism. A work of art is a single symbol, not a system of significant elements which may be variously compounded. Its elements have no symbolic values in isolation.[70]

In summary, symbolic media can be verbal, pictorial, musical, photographical, et cetera and it is the kind of medium that determines the property of the symbolism as 'discursive' or 'non-discursive'. For Langer the 'property of verbal symbolism is known as *discursiveness*.'[71] However, although a word is an element of a composite symbol employing a verbal *symbolism*, a word as such, on Langer's terms, is not 'a discursive symbol'.[72]

Discursive symbolism

Langer's definition of discursive symbolism as a medium rests on two criteria. In its weakest sense discursivity is characterized by linearity and successiveness. On that basis, a discursive symbolism is a symbolism the elements of which can be arranged in a successive order. The paradigm case of this is language in all its variety:

> [A]ll language has a form which requires us to string out our ideas even though their objects rest one within the other; as pieces of clothing that are actually worn one over the other have to be strung side by side on the clothesline. This property of verbal symbolism is known as *discursiveness*; by reason of it, only thoughts which can be arranged in this peculiar order can be spoken at all; any idea which does not lend itself to this 'projection' is ineffable, incommunicable by means of words.[73]

In the sentence 'A killed B', even though A and B were simultaneous with each other in the act of killing, our verbally expressed *ideas* of them take place one after the other: words 'have a linear, discrete, successive order'.[74] They are 'like beads on a rosary'.[75]

In a stronger sense, Langer defines discursive linguistic symbols as a 'composite'. As she explains, 'Its elements are words with fixed meanings. Out of these one can construct, according to the rules of the syntax, composite symbols with resultant new meanings.'[76] Discursive language has a vocabulary and syntax that enables different combinations of the elements according to certain, commonly agreed rules. Langer holds that 'some words are equivalent to whole combinations of other words, so that most meanings can be expressed in several different ways.'[77] This makes it possible 'to *define meanings of the ultimate single words*, i.e. to construct a dictionary'.[78] It also allows for interlingual translation: '[P]ropositions enunciated by one person, in his system, may be *translated* into the conventional system of the other.'[79] In short,

> Language in the strict sense is essentially discursive; it has permanent units of meaning which are combinable into larger units; it has fixed equivalences that make definition and translation possible.[80]

Discursive symbolism does not have to be lingual. Any composite symbol that has elements with conventional meanings and stable designations can be called discursive. As long as its elements have relatively independent meaning discursive symbolism can be found in pictures, maps, graphs, diagrams and so on:

> Just as mnemonic dots and crosses, as soon as they denote objects, can also enter into diagrams or simple pictures, so do sounds, as soon as they are words, enter into word-pictures, or sentences. A sentence is a symbol for a state of affairs, and pictures its character.[81]

Although the elements of a discursive symbols have relatively stable, conventional dictionary meanings, the symbol as a whole is not rooted in convention. When Wayne Bowman, for instance, claims that 'non-discursive symbols differ from their discursive counterparts in that they lack assigned and conventional reference', this is not strictly speaking correct. On Langer's terms this should be rephrased as 'non-discursive symbols differ from their discursive counterparts in that *their elements* such as shapes, colours and lines, lack assigned and conventional reference.[82]

While day-to-day discursive language is sufficient for ordinary communication, it lacks in precision for the purposes of science and requires further formalization to make it as error-free as possible. This was the language aspired to by Carnap and also by Wittgenstein when he wrote,

> In order to avoid these errors [of everyday language], we must employ a symbolism which excludes them, by not applying the same sign in different symbols and by not applying signs in the same way which signify in different ways. A symbolism, that is to say, which obeys the rules of *logical* grammar – of logical syntax.[83]

Discursive language including its 'refinements in mathematical and scientific symbolisms, and its approximation by gesture, hieroglyphics, or graphs', is a perfectly suitable medium to describe the external, physical and empirically observable world.[84]

But, as Langer continuously stresses, it is inadequate to formulate any experiences outside that. This limitation led Langer to seek out the possibility of a *non*-discursive or 'presentational' symbolism.

Presentational symbolism

Non-discursive or presentational symbolism is defined, in the first instance, in contrast to discursive symbolism: that is, it is *non*-linear, *non*-successive and *non*-composite. Non-discursive symbolism is foundational to the development of the mind. It can be found in the most basic forms of human perception and in the highest realms of culture.

> [T]he symbolism furnished by our purely sensory appreciation of forms is a *non-discursive symbolism*, peculiarly well suited to the expression of ideas that defy linguistic 'projection'. Its primary function, that of conceptualizing the flux of sensations, and giving us concrete *things* in place of kaleidoscopic colors and noises, is itself an office that no language-born thought can replace.[85]

Most pictures and visual forms are non-discursive.[86] But unlike discursive forms, their constituting elements – a line, a curve, a dot – are not 'units with independent meanings'.[87]

Unlike discursive symbols which are produced and understood successively, non-discursive symbols are typically grasped as a whole 'in one act of vision'.[88] Their very functioning as symbols depends on the fact that they are involved in a simultaneous, integral presentation. This kind of semantic may be called 'presentational symbolism'.[89]

Resemblance and 'isomorphism'

All symbolization, whether discursive or non-discursive, rests on a 'recognition of a common form in different things'.[90] Langer's conception of a 'common form' contains some echoes of Peirce's 'icon' defined as 'any sign that may represent its object mainly by its similarity'.[91] Even so, similarity is an ambiguous term since, as is often noted, everything is always similar to something else *in some respect*, whether in shape, size, colour, intensity, texture and so on. An 'iconic' symbol always selects and highlights certain features and suppresses others. It should be noted that Langer never uses the term 'isomorphism' despite this often being attributed to her views, arguably because of its misleading connotations with correspondence theories of representation.[92] She recognizes what W. J. T. Mitchell once said about icons: 'One reason why the icon has proved so difficult for semiotics to define is that similarity is such a capacious relationship that almost anything can be assimilated into it.'[93]

As Cassirer observed, because the world is always perceived from one '*angle of refraction*' there can be different kinds of resemblance between a symbol and its object.[94] As we saw in Chapter 5, Cassirer illustrated this with the two different words for moon, either 'refracting' its luminous quality – the Latin term '*luna*' – or its role in measuring time – the Greek term '*mēn*'.[95] Langer likewise observes that one can have several exemplifications of the same logical form which require '*a rule of translation*, whereby one instance of the logical form is shown to correspond formally to the other.'[96] Langer illustrates this with different projections of a world map in which the sizes and shapes of the continents differ from each other. People can read two different projection with relative ease, so she argues, because the geographical relationships 'are not *copied* by either map, but *expressed*, and expressed equally well by both; for the two maps are different *projections* of the same logical form.'[97] Wittgenstein, likewise, was aware of this when he referred to the many different ways in which a piece of music could be represented, that is, in the sounds of a performance, in the score, in the grooves on the record and so on. These different representations have their own mode of projection and are irreducible to each other. Representation is perception *under one aspect*. As Nelson Goodman once put it in *Languages of Art* in 1968,

> [A]n aspect is not just the object-from-a-given-distance-and-angle-and-in-a-given-light; it is the object as we look upon or conceive it, a version or construal of the object. In representing an object, we do not copy such a construal or interpretation – we *achieve* it.[98]

As Plato already observed, an image is not a copy: 'The image must not by any means reproduce all the qualities of that which it imitates, if it is to be an image.'[99] If it were to do so, it would be a *duplicate*, not a representation. Resemblance itself, as we have seen, is not sufficient for representation, that is, for one thing to symbolize another. Unlike analogical relations, a symbol–symbolized relation is not symmetrical: 'The relation of analogy is … different from any actual meaning relation in that it is symmetrical, whereas a symbolic relationship is always asymmetrical.'[100] Symbols not only present but *re*-present.[101] As Whitehead had pointed out, in the symbol–symbolized relation it depends 'on the constitution of the percipient subject to assign which species is acting as "symbol" and which as "meaning".'[102] Langer likewise had argued that if it 'were not for the subject, or *interpretant*, sign and object would be interchangeable.'[103] As mentioned earlier, echoing her Vienna lecturer Karl Bühler, Langer holds that the criteria for symbolic representation are determined by use and by relevance for the interpreting subject:

> The difference [between a sign or symbol and its meaning] is, that the subject for which they constitute a pair must *find one more interesting than the other, and the latter more easily available that the former.* … If it were not for the subject, or *interpretant*, sign and object would be interchangeable.[104]

In short, for Langer, as for Wittgenstein and Whitehead, representation, not resemblance, is the key to a symbolic reference and it is the human interpreter who establishes what constitutes the symbol and what its meaning. This even applies to the identification of what is a discursive or a non-discursive symbolism. For Langer there are no naturally occurring symbols that can be labelled discursive or non-discursive. Beatrice Nelson puts it well,

It would be precisely contrary to Langer's whole analysis to suppose that there might be discursive symbols *simpliciter* and presentational symbols *simpliciter*. Symbols can be seen *as*, analysed *as*, used *as* discursive or presentational, and they will be recognized by their use or in their context.[105]

This important insight also applies to our next distinction between formulative and conventional symbolism.

Formulative and conventional symbolism

In a paper given at Brown University in 1956, 'On a New Definition of Symbol', Langer points out that most studies of language and symbols at her time are only interested in their discursive and instrumental value.[106] As a consequence, she says, two properties of symbols are usually taken as essential characteristics: '[T]he function of *reference*, or direction of the user's interest to something apart from the symbol, and the *conventional* nature of the connection between symbol and the object to which it refers, by virtue of which connection the reference occurs.'[107] She illustrates that with Nagel's definition of symbol as 'any occurrence (or type of occurrence), usually linguistic in status, which is taken to signify something else by way of tacit or explicit conventions or rules of language.'[108] Langer does not deny the importance of reference and convention but claims that that should not lead us to overlook the 'less obvious, but perhaps, at some levels of our mental evolution, equally important [role of symbolism and language]: the *formulation* of experience by the process of symbolization.'[109] This new notion of symbolization, Langer claims, 'stemmed from the Kantian analysis of experience, and had been highly developed in Cassirer's *Philosophie der symbolischen Formen*'.[110] As she explains it,

> [T]his symbol concept ... cannot be defined in terms of denotation, signification, formal assignment, or reference. ... Cassirer himself considered the semantic functions that belong to scientific symbols as a special development, which occurred under the influence of language, by virtue of its inherent *generality* together with its *signific* character. But symbolization as such he traced further back. His notion of 'symbol' was more primitive than that of a sign used by common consent to stand for an associated concept; in his sense of the word, a sound, mark, object, or event could be a symbol to a person, without that person's consciously going from it to its meaning. This is the basic concept in his theory of myth.[111]

In order to do justice to this more primitive notion, Langer proposed a slightly amended version of her symbol definition in *Feeling and Form* (1953):

> I should like to propose a definition of 'symbol' based on this formulative function, by means of which some sort of *conception* is always abstracted from any symbolized experience. In a book published only three years ago, I defined a symbol as 'any device whereby we are enabled to make an abstraction'. I am already doubtful of that definition in its simple, initial form, though it may prove to be tenable. On the

other hand, it may be that some devices whereby we make an abstraction are not complete, bona fide symbols, but that it is safer – at least tentatively – to say: 'Any device whereby we make an abstraction is a symbolic element, and all abstraction involves symbolization.'[112]

This move anticipates Langer's later philosophy of mind and consciousness conceived as a process. As James R. Johnson observes,

> [T]he old symbol as a device does not fit into the organistic processes of Langer's late work. So she postulates a new definition. ... With this new definition, there would be numerous ways of making abstractions, and the processes may demonstrate various degrees of completion and protosymbolic phenomena. ... The formulation of experience through symbolization is a constant process that proceeds below and above the limen of sentience.[113]

This change of definition from symbol as category to symbolization as process is not easy to get across to her contemporaries and at various points Langer seems to struggle with her terminology:

> Works of art, which I am sure have *import,* but not genuine *meaning,* are symbols of a sort, but not of the sort Nagel defined; for neither do they point themselves to something thereafter known apart from the symbol, nor are they established conventions ... they are, I think, quasi symbols.[114]

This tortured language and apparent terminological surrender suggest some of the pressure she felt to make her theories intelligible – and acceptable – to fellow philosophers.[115] One of the very few philosophers who fully understood Langer was the British philosopher Louis Arnaud Reid (1895–1986), a co-founder of the *British Journal of Aesthetics.* Drawing attention to the value of Langer's broader definition of symbol for the understanding meaning in the arts he wrote:

> [I do not] see why she should defer to the self-limited view of meaning held by Nagel and other semanticists, deciding to use the word 'import' instead. ... [K]ow-towing to the logicians doesn't do them, or aesthetics, any good. 'Meaning' is a rich word with a rich variety of content, and should not be used in one logical context only. ... [T]here is a unique thing, *embodied meaning.* [116]

Reid explains the term 'embodied meaning' in terms very similar to Langer: 'I prefer to say that we apprehend patterns of paint and sound, not as "meaning something" or express something, but as *meaningful:* [it is] *embodied meaning.'*[117]

In order to show more clearly how embodied meaning and symbolization are seen as activities and processes rather than nouns and products, it is helpful to take a closer look at the many different ways in which Langer talks about symbolization. Not only will this show the vast variety of instances, it also reveals a certain order of development and progression from formulative symbols to conventional ones.

From formulation to convention

In *Philosophy in a New Key* Langer writes that language is 'a very high form of symbolism; presentational forms are much lower than discursive, and the appreciation of meaning probably earlier than its expression'.[118] This suggests that there are 'lower' and 'higher' forms of symbolism, with some building on others. This is also suggested by Langer's comment that the '*the first indication of symbolic behavior* ... is not likely to be anything as specialized, conscious, or rational as the *use* of semantic'.[119] In other words, formulative and conventional symbols are not binary opposites but lie on a continuum of complexity and specialization.

The following 'inventory' is not meant to be an exhaustive list of all the forms of symbolism as discussed by Langer but to serve as a heuristic device to show the wide variety of entities, activities and processes that are being described by her in those terms.

Symbol as involuntary by-product of brain activity

At the most basic physiological level symbols, for Langer, are by-products of the brain: 'The brain works as naturally as the kidneys and the blood vessels. It is not dormant just because there is no conscious purpose to be served at the moment. ... [I]t is actively translating experiences into symbols, in fulfilment of a basic need to do so. It carries on a constant process of ideation'.[120] Symbolization is a fundamentally embodied activity: 'Mental life begins with our physiological constitution. ... The nervous system is the organ of the mind; its center is the brain, its extremities the sense-organs'.[121] For Langer 'the material furnished by the senses is constantly wrought into *symbols*, which are our elementary ideas'.[122]

In her later work *Mind*, Langer developed these ideas into a comprehensive biologically based philosophy of consciousness. But the basis was already there in her early work. As she wrote in the preface to *Philosophy in a New Key*:

> We need not assume the presence of a transcendental 'human spirit', if we recognize, for instance, the function of *symbolic transformation* as a natural activity, a high form of nervous response, characteristic of man among the animals.[123]

It is important not to interpret Langer's emphasis on the embodied nature of symbolization as a version of philosophical physicalism. As we will show in Chapter 10, Langer does not *reduce* mental activity to physical processes. Mentality permeates every organic level: '[T]he activity of our senses is 'mental' not only when it reaches the brain, but in its very conception, whenever the alien world outside impinges on the furthest and smallest receptor. All sensitivity bears the stamp of mentality'.[124] Both seeing and thinking carry inherent meaning. Drawing on her neo-Kantian roots she rejects the idea of seeing as 'a passive process, by which meaningless impressions are stored up for the use of an organizing mind, which construes forms out of these amorphous data to suit its own purposes'.[125] Instead, seeing itself is 'a process of formulation.' The most important involuntary symbolic by-products of brain activity are dreams. The existence of dreams as ways of processing a wide variety of experiences rather than serving merely biological needs, leads Langer '*to reconsider the entire inventory of human needs*' to include a basic need for symbolization.[126]

Symbol as abstracted form or Gestalt

For Langer 'all thinking is conceptual, and conception begins with the comprehension of *Gestalt*.'[127] *Gestalten* are 'symbols of entities which exceed and outlive our momentary experience.'[128] As she put it elsewhere,

> The symbolic materials given to our senses, the *Gestalten* or fundamental perceptual forms which invite us to construe the pandemonium of sheer impression into a world of things and occasions, belong to the 'presentational' order.[129]

Gestalten are rooted in abstraction – *Gestalt* symbols are the most elementary abstractions of ordinary sense-experience:

> The abstractions made by the ear and the eye – the forms of direct perception – are our most primitive instruments of intelligence. They are genuine symbolic materials, media of understanding, by whose office we apprehend a world of *things*, and of events that are the histories of things.[130]

Without the perception of forms the human mind would not be able to make sense of the world: 'Eyes that did not see forms could never furnish it with *images*; ears that did not hear articulated sounds could never open it to *words*.'[131]

As mentioned before, Langer was very impressed by the work of *Gestalt* psychologists Wertheimer, Köhler and Koffka:

> Unless the *Gestalt*-psychologists are right in their belief that *Gestaltung* is of the very nature of perception, I do not know how the hiatus between perception and conception, sense-organ and mind-organ, chaotic stimulus and logical response, is ever to be closed and welded. A mind that works primarily with meanings must have organs that supply it primarily with forms.[132]

For Langer, the notion of *Gestalt* as an abstraction is not confined to visual perception but applies to all the senses: 'All thinking begins with *seeing*; not necessarily through the eye, but with some basic formulations of sense perception, in the particular idiom of sight, hearing, or touch, normally of all the senses together.'[133] She illustrates this with the example of how a baby conceives new sounds: 'A sound (such as 'da-da' or 'ma-ma', probably) has been *conceived,* and his diffuse awareness of vocalizing gives way to an apparently delightful awareness of a vocable. … A new vocable is an outstanding *Gestalt*.'[134]

Because of the ongoing stream of mental activity, internal images or *Gestalten* are inevitably elusive and transient. This is because their formation is largely subconscious and spontaneous:

The beginnings of symbolic transformation in the cortex must be elusive and disturbing experiences, perhaps thrilling, but very useless, and hard on the whole nervous system. It is absurd to suppose that the earliest symbols could be *invented*; they are merely *Gestalten* furnished to the senses of a creature ready to give them some diffuse meaning.[135]

Symbol as significant 'metaphoric' form

For Langer 'meaning ... accrues essentially to forms.'[136]

The earliest manifestation of any symbol making tendency, therefore, is likely to be a mere *sense of significance* attached to certain objects, certain forms or sounds, a vague emotional arrest of the mind by something that is neither dangerous nor useful in reality.[137]

As such, all *Gestalten* inherently carry what Cassirer called 'symbolic pregnance'.[138] Instead of perceiving meaningless sense-date on which meaning is super-imposed, all perception involves some kind of interpretation of the significant features and characteristics of the perceived *Gestalt*. This interpretation is typically based on the physiognomic characteristics of a perceived form – a rising line, a balanced shape, a smooth curve, a sharp edge and so one. According to Langer, unlike other primates, humans project 'bodily feeling into forms presented to the eye'.[139] Kinesthetic, thermal, tactual, and other such corporeal feelings are ' "seen" in the shapes that meet our eyes [and] confront us as possible implements, obstacles, more or less permanent carriers of their own qualities.'[140] As we will discuss in more detail in Chapter 10 in relation to the work of Georg Lakoff and Mark Johnson, such features are 'felt qualities' based on the human's 'body-schema'. As Langer writes, 'The objectification of the subjective sense of balance – and, perhaps, of physical tensions generally – has a natural counterpart, the subjectification of the protosymbolic object as an image.'[141] All these forms of projection constitute early forms of symbolization:

The mental act of 'projecting' ... lets the subjective element ... be perceived as an external datum, i.e., as a quality belonging to an independently existing object; and that object, which thus presents our own sensory feeling to us, is a primitive symbol.[142]

Many early symbols of projection originate in dreams and operate in a dream-like manner: 'Objects that could function as dream-symbols have a mysterious significance for the waking mind, too, ... the imaginative process is carried over from dream to reality; fantasy is externalized in the veneration of "sacra".'[143] For a receptive consciousness, fire, water, starry skies and similar phenomena, can stand for a wide range of meanings. Snakes and bulls embodying basic feelings of fear and strength can serve as sacred symbols: 'The symbols that embody basic ideas of life and death, of man and the world, are naturally sacred.'[144] Dreams thus give shape and articulate subconscious feelings:

[Dreams] do not denote [ideas] for the dreamer as words denote their objects. Yet the relation of dream figments to their meanings is one of *formulation* of the supposed unconscious 'dream thought' and in fact a rather complex abstraction of the emotional aspects of experiences; and the element common to symbol and 'meaning' is a formal one – an abstract element.[145]

Like dreaming, mythical consciousness is characterized by a conglomerate of shifting and elusive images, pregnant with affective meaning, and often organized along the axis of good and evil, safe and dangerous, holy and unholy and so on.

The first dichotomy in the emotive or mythic phase of mentality is not, as for discursive reason, the opposition of 'yes' and 'no', of 'a' and 'non-a', or truth and falsity; the basic dichotomy here is between the sacred and the profane. Human beings actually apprehend *values* and expressions of values *before* they formulate and entertain *facts*.[146]

In dreams and myth, there is, so Langer argues, 'no ... duality of form and content.'[147] Symbol and idea are one:

In our most primitive presentations – the metaphorical imagery of dreams – it is the symbol, not its meaning, that seems to command our emotions. In dream-experience we very often find some fairly commonplace object – a tree, a fish, a pointed hat, a staircase – fraught with intense value or inspiring the greatest terror. ... We cannot distinguish [its meaning] from its symbolic incarnation which, to literal-minded common sense, seems trivial.[148]

Symbols carry meanings that can be transferred to other realms. This is the origin of metaphoric thinking.

The best guarantee of [the] symbolic function [of images] is their tendency to become metaphorical. ... The image of a rose symbolizes feminine beauty so readily that it is actually harder to associate roses with vegetables than with girls. Fire is a natural symbol of life and passion, though it is the one element in which nothing can actually live. Its mobility and flare, its heat and color, make it an irresistible symbol of all that is living, feeling, and active.[149]

An interest in symbols and forms irrespective of their practical meaning facilitates the formulation of otherwise ineffable thoughts or feelings:

A mind that is very sensitive to forms as such and is aware of them beyond the common-sense requirements for recognition, memory, and classification of things, is apt to use its images metaphorically, to exploit their possible significance for the conception of remote or intangible ideas.[150]

Even though metaphor is 'the law of growth of every semantic', the principle of metaphor extends beyond linguistic expressions:[151]

A metaphor is not language, it is an idea expressed by language, an idea that in its turn functions as a symbol to express something. It is not discursive and therefore does not really make a statement of the idea it conveys; but it formulates a new conception for our direct imaginative grasp.[152]

Metaphoric uses of images predominate in fantasy, dreams and sacrament: 'The symbolic status of fantasies ... is further attested by the regularity with which they follow certain basic laws of symbols. Like words and images, they have not only literal reference to concepts, but tend to convey metaphorical meanings.'[153] Human mentality is exemplified by the 'madly metaphorical fantasies' of the 'riotous symbolism of dreams'.[154] The key principle underlying all metaphor is analogy and isomorphism, that is, a recognition of some shared structure and form. This principle, as we will see, underlies not only fantasy, myth and dreams, but also logic and language.

Symbol as 'sign' for practical intelligence.

A *Gestalt* is not only a form with transferrable metaphorical meaning but a form *of* something. This is essential for day-to-day survival or what Langer calls 'practical intelligence' or 'practical vision'.[155] As she describes it,

> It is fortunate that our first understanding of forms is normally a literal comprehension of them as *typical things* or *such-and-such events;* for this interpretation is the basis of intelligent behavior, of daily, hourly, and momentary adjustment to our nearest surroundings. It is non-discursive, spontaneous abstraction from the stream of sense-experience, elementary sense-knowledge, which may be called *practical vision.*[156]

Practical vision lies on the limen of signs and symbols. Indeed, in practical vision images 'function both as symbols of thought and as signs for behavior'.[157] In sign-mode practical vision calls for immediate actions. Depending on user and context, one and the same item can serve both as a sign and as a symbol:

> This [practical vision] is the meeting-point of thought, which is symbolic, with animal behavior, which rests on sign-perception; for the edifice which we build out of literal conceptions, the products of practical vision, is our systematic spatio-temporal world. The same items that are *signs* to our animal reflexes are contents for certain *symbols* of this conceptual system.[158]

For Langer, this 'dual operation of a datum as sign and symbol together is the key to realistic thinking: the envisagement of *fact*.'[159] It is important here to keep in mind Langer's Wittgensteinean notion of 'fact' as an '*intellectually formulated event*, whether the formulation be performed by a process of sheer vision, verbal interpretation, or practical response'.[160] That means that symbols can be both instruments of conceptual reflection and of practical intelligence to negotiate its environment with a view to meeting a human's basic needs.

Symbol as vocable: Origins of language

According to Langer, speech is 'the readiest active termination of that basic process in the human brain which may be called *symbolic transformation of experiences*.'[161] Moreover, a vocable is 'the readiest thing in the world to become a symbol when a symbol is wanted'[162] As she explains,

> A new vocable is an outstanding *Gestalt*. It is a possession too, because it may be had at will, and this itself makes it very interesting. … Moreover an articulate sound is an entirely *unattached* item, a purely phenomenal experience without externally fixed relations; it lies wide open to imaginative and emotional uses, syn-aesthetic identifications, chance associations.[163]

As Cassirer and von Humboldt had already suggested, the first vocalizations will quite likely have had a purely expressive character. Langer, likewise, suggests that speech and poetic song might originally have been one, and that speech was originally a formalization of voiceplay. It was only at a later stage that humans begin to associate sounds with entities, words with the world. Associations are stimulated, affirmed and consolidated by the social environment. This already happens in early childhood as Langer suggests in her chapter on language:

> The next sharp and emotional arrest of consciousness, the next deeply interesting experience that coincides with hearing or uttering the vocable, becomes fixed by association with that one already distinct item; it may be the personality of the mother, the concrete character of the bottle, or what not.[164]

Langer is well aware that any theory of the origins of language is by necessity speculative but she argues that a new understanding of symbolization gives it a new legitimacy: 'The notion that the essence of language is the formulation and expression of conceptions rather than the communications of natural wants … opens a new vista upon the mysterious problem of origins.'[165] According to her, the first symbolic value of words was likely to have been purely connotative. A string of syllables such as the word 'hallelujah' used in the context of a ritual, is not a name of anything but an expressive noun with an associated meaning.[166] However, the habitual association of a purely fanciful sound with a particular ritual would eventually lead one to connect the two together:

> The utterance of conception-laden sounds, at the sight of things that exemplify one or another of the conceptions which those sounds carry, is first a purely expressive reaction; only long habit can fix an association so securely that the world and the object are felt to belong together, so that one is always a reminder of the other. But when this point is reached, the humanoid creature will undoubtedly utter the sound in sport … until he may be said to *grasp* a conception of it by means of the sound: and *now the sound is a word*.'[167]

From expressions of private feelings vocables have now turned into public expressions of 'conceptions'. This is most evident in the learning of proper names. For Langer, a name is a prime symbol: 'The simplest kind of symbolistic meaning is probably that which belongs to proper names. A personal name evokes a conception of something given as a unit in the subject's experience, something concrete and therefore easy to recall in imagination.'[168] But, in principle, any word can gradually serve as a vehicle for conception. It all depends on the kind of association and on their use by the subject. As we saw earlier: '[S]igns *announce* their objects to him, whereas symbols *lead him to conceive* their objects.'[169] Speech and language, then, are 'the gradual accumulation and elaboration of verbal symbols':[170]

> Most of our words are not signs in the sense of signals. They are used to talk *about* things, not to direct our eyes and ears and noses toward them. Instead of announcers of things, they are reminders. ... They serve ... to let us develop a characteristic attitude toward objects in absentia, which is called 'thinking of' or 'referring to' what is not here. 'Signs' used in this capacity are not *symptoms* of things, but *symbols*. ... The development of language is the history of the gradual accumulation and elaboration of verbal symbols.[171]

A symbol is a vocal sound that represents a class of private *conceptions*. A conception mediates between subjective perception and public concept – that is, between a particular experience of something such as a chair, and the universal class of chairs falling under the concept 'chair'. Once a sound is recognized and accepted as representing certain conceptions, these conceptions can become public *concepts*. Any word or mark can connote a conception and, once it has become a public concept, can 'denote the thing itself'.[172] That's why, at one point, Langer says that 'a concept is all that a symbol really conveys.'[173]

Symbol as vehicle for reference and denotation

As outlined earlier, Langer locates the main difference between the logical pattern of a sign structure and that of a symbol in the fact that the first announces and the second (re)presents its object. In the case of names this implies an act of denotation:

> Since a name, the simplest type of symbol, is directly associated with a conception ... one is easily led to treat a name as a 'conceptual sign', an artificial sign which announces the presence of a certain idea. ... [Yet, this] misses *the relation of conceptions to the concrete world*, which is so close and so important that it enters into the very structure of 'names'. A name, above all, *denotes* something.[174]

In this moment or stage of symbolization there is no longer a mythical identification between symbol and object. Symbols are no longer linked to specific contexts which evoke private conceptions but, instead, stand for general concepts which are applicable to classes of external phenomena. This freeing of language from its original context, so argues Langer, is essential for the formation of language as a form of communication:

> [D]enotation is the essence of language, because it frees the symbol from its original instinctive utterance and marks its deliberate *use*, outside of the total situation that gave it birth. A denotative word is related at once to a conception, which may be ever so vague, and to a *thing* (or event, quality, person, etc.) which is realistic and public; so it weans the conception away from the purely momentary and personal experience and fastens it on a permanent element which may enter into all sorts of situations.[175]

That means that, for Langer, a word like 'hallelujah', while still functioning symbolically, 'cannot fairly be called language; for although it has connotation it has no denotation.'[176]

For a proper name such as 'James' to denote someone it should be 'associated with a conception that "fits" the actual person.'[177] Recalling the difference in number of terms between a sign and a symbol Langer holds that in a relation of denotation there have to be four terms: subject, symbol, concept(ion) and object. General concepts are rooted in private and embodied conceptions:

> Concepts are abstract forms embodied in conceptions; their bare presentation may be approximated by so-called 'abstract thought', but in ordinary mental life they no more figure as naked factors than skeletons are seen walking the street. Concepts, like decent living skeletons, are always embodied – sometimes rather too much.[178]

Talking about the word 'house' she writes,

> It is by virtue of … a fundamental *pattern*, which all correct conceptions of the house have in common, that we can talk together about the 'same' house despite our private differences of sense-experience, feeling, and purely personal associations. *That which all adequate conceptions of an object must have in common, is the concept of the object.* The same concept is embodied in a multitude of conceptions. It is a *form* that appears in all versions of thought or imagery that can connote the object in question.[179]

Denotation encompasses connotation:

> The connotation of a word is the conception it conveys. Because the connotation remains with the symbol when the object of denotation is neither present nor looked for, we are able to think about the object without reacting to it overtly at all.[180]

Whereas the term 'denotation' refers to the four-term relation as a whole, *connotation* refers to the immediate relation between a name and its conception. This places connotation at the heart of symbolization since it allows humans to articulate their understanding of something without regard to the question whether or not the entity does in fact exist. Indeed, it is only in the realm of denotation that error can take place, that is, a *mis*-application of a word in its conventional use. As she explains,

There is a psychological act involved in every case of denotation, which might be called the *application* of a term to an object. The word 'water', for instance, denotes a certain substance because people conventionally *apply* it to that substance. Such application has fixed its connotation. We may ask, quite reasonably, whether a certain colorless liquid is or is not water, but hardly whether water 'really' means that substance which is found in ponds, falls from clouds, has the chemical constitution H_2O etc.[181]

It is on the basis of longstanding general use that applications of a term increase people's knowledge of the attributes of what is being referred to. When examining a liquid substance, for instance, one can, based on one's previous experiences of specific applications, determine whether or not one can apply the word 'water' to the particular substance under observation. This means that we can have a symbol with a very strong connotative sense but a weak denotative one:

> The connotation of the word, though derived from an age-long application, is more definite now than some cases of the word's applicability. When we have *misapplied* a term, i.e. applied it to an object that does not satisfy its connotation, we do not say that the term 'denoted' that object; one feature in the tetradic meaning-relation is missing, so there is no real denotation – only a psychological act of application, and that was a mistake.[182]

Even so, mistakes are also possible in connotative acts: in the same way as one might be clear about the connotation of a specific word, but be confused about whether or not it applies to a certain substance, one can also have a clear conception of what or whom a word denotes but be much less certain about its connotation: 'We may know that the symbol "James" applies to our next-door neighbor, and quite mistakenly suppose it connotes a man with all sorts of virtues and frailties. This time we are not mistaking James for someone else, but we are *mistaken about James*.'[183] For Langer the relation between connotation and denotation is 'the most obvious seat of *truth and falsity*':

> If [a word] already has a connotation, then it cannot be given an arbitrary denotation, nor vice versa. I cannot use the word 'kitten' *with its accepted connotation* to denote an elephant. … To call an elephant 'kitten', not as a proper name but as a common noun, is a mistake, because he does not exemplify the connoted concept. Similarly a word with a fixed denotation cannot be given an arbitrary connotation, for once the word is a name (common or proper), to give it a certain connotation is to *predicate* the connoted concept of whatever bears the name. If 'Jumbo' denotes an elephant, it cannot be given the connotation 'something furry', because Jumbo is presumably not furry.[184]

In summary, over time, so Langer argues, frequently used images and expressions become gradually consolidated in the day-to-day language of a particular speech community where by means of what Nagel calls the implicit or 'tacit conventions of language'. They become part and parcel of day-to-day language. Implicit conventions become explicit by means of some form of 'social contract'. This is the case in the seventh moment of symbolization.

Symbol as product of agreement and convention.

When symbol formation takes place by some form of agreement, the symbols take on an arbitrary and associative character. As we observed earlier, Langer had been struck by the fact that mathematicians dealt with 'data' that were 'arbitrary sounds or marks called symbols' and that, when scientists make use of mathematics it is entirely 'at their discretion to say, "let x mean this, let y mean that"'[185] As such decisions are made by agreement in order to reduce the possibility of multiple meanings, they are essential in the realm of formal logic: 'Logical symbolism is the extreme of literal expression, and a logician's (or mathematician's) intention is to allow no leeway at all for alternative or additional meanings.'[186] In *Feeling and Form* Langer holds that the main principle underlying conventional symbols is that of association: 'A word or mark used arbitrarily to denote or connote something may be called an associative symbol for its meaning depends entirely on association.'[187] In these instances of symbol use, there is no real need for a resemblance or isomorphism between the symbol and what it represents. In the case of a conventional symbol agreed by fiat, there is, in contrast to, for instance, the art symbol, no longer an interest in the symbol itself. In *Problems of Art* Langer refers to such conventional symbols as mere instruments akin to signs: '[I]n appreciating its meaning our interest reaches beyond it to the concept. The word is just an instrument. Its meaning lies elsewhere, and once we have … identified something as its denotation we do not need the word anymore.'[188] Instead of there being an integral link between symbol and symbolized based on a perceived shared form or structure, there is now a purely arbitrary connection: 'Since any single sense-datum can, logically, be a symbol for any single item, any arbitrary mark or counter may connote the conception, or publicly speaking: the concept, of any single thing, and thus denote the thing itself.'[189] Put more strongly, for a conventional symbol to be practically effective in its use, it should have *as little as possible* in common with its object:

> Another recommendation for words is that they have no value except as symbols (or signs); in themselves they are completely trivial … A symbol which interests us *also* as an object is distracting [such as if] for instance, … the word 'plenty' were replaced by a succulent, ripe, real peach … The more barren and indifferent the symbol, the greater is its semantic power.[190]

The conventional symbol lies at the opposite end of the earliest formulative symbols in which form and meaning were inseparable. Once a conventional symbol has been established upon agreement, it can be used effectively for practical and other purposes. The more effective as tool and instrument, the less significant it becomes as a symbolic form.

Objections and responses

As will be clear from this inventory, apart from the last two notions, most of the instances of symbolization mentioned above, do not conform to the generally accepted criteria for symbols by her fellow philosophers. Langer is well aware of that. She acknowledges that her semantic theory 'points to the existence of forms, i.e. of *possible symbolic material*, at a level where symbolic activity has certainly never been looked for by any epistemologist.'[191] This is reflected in the responses to her work. As Nagel, for instance, writes,

> [W]hat is not clear from Mrs. Langer's account is the precise sense in which 'presentational symbols' *are* symbols ... Mrs. Langer is quite definite on the point that in any situation of symbol-meaning, there must be a subject, a symbol, a conception and an *object* (p. 64) [of *Philosophy in a New Key*]. What *object* is symbolized? ... What, other than itself, does the sensory form 'represent'? ... [T]he perplexed reader, remembering that symbols must have objects in order to be symbols, must conclude either that sensory forms are not symbols at all, or that they are 'symbols' in a radically new and hitherto unspecified sense.[192]

John Hospers, similarly, asks,

> [W]hat can be meant by a presentational symbol? I should have thought that the very essence of anything's being a symbol is that it is used to stand for (represent) something else. Is not a symbol that merely presents, not represents, a contradiction in terms? I can see no way out of this difficulty unless a presentational symbol is defined in a way which is quite at variance with the obvious implications of the term.'[193]

Hospers problem with Langer's presentational symbol is not only that it lacks an identifiable object, but that one cannot demonstrate that it symbolizes anything at all. As he puts it,

> [T]he objection arises here: no matter what the things symbolized may be, be they emotional states or images or what have you, and no matter how varying-with-context and difficult of access they may be, still, as long as it is claimed that there *are* things symbolized, what basis is there for the claim and how could such a claim be defended in the face of conflicting ones?[194]

Another objection to Langer's use of the word 'symbol' is that it becomes too polysemic, general and vague. In a review of *Mind* Harold Osborne, for one, complains that Langer's uses of the term 'symbolism' across the fields of art and biology have 'no more than a verbal identity in the two spheres' and concludes: '[T]here is a tendency throughout to ascribe excessive interpretative value to concepts which are so widely articulated that they can mean anything at all – or nothing – in any context at all.'[195]

What is clear from these objections is that none of these philosophers have fully understood – or been willing to accept –, first, that Langer's symbols are not to be taken as entities but as *processes* and *functions* of meaning relations and, second, that they are not static but evolve over time. Symbolic activity, as Langer perceives it, permeates all levels of human consciousness and existence, from the most basic human feelings and engagements with its environment to its highest level of intellectual activity. Seen as symbolic *processes* rather than products, and as activities rather than achievements, symbols capture the ever-evolving nature of meaning formation as rooted in lived human experience. As Cassirer once put it,

> The symbolic process is like a single stream of life and thought which flows through consciousness, and which by this flowing movement produces the diversity and cohesion, the richness, the continuity, and constancy, of consciousness.[196]

At all these levels the embodied mind aims to make sense of its experience by creating symbolic forms that reach out to the world or, as Wittgenstein put it in relation to a picture or model, serve as 'feelers of its elements with which the picture touches reality'.[197] In this pursuit of meaning formulation is not a means to achieve something else, but an adventure of discovery and disclosure. Symbolization is not an instrument, it is a 'primary interest'.[198]

In later life Langer became increasingly interested in the formulative function of symbolic activity. In the world of human consciousness and culture, formulative symbolic meaning is part of the organism's process of exploration, interpretation and orientation. Langer's notions of symbol and symbolization are thus not only logical but also *anthropo*-logical categories. As she repeatedly points out, symbolization is rooted in an embodied encounter with the world. All formulation of experience is at root *embodied* meaning, where the term 'meaning' is not a noun but a verb. As Innis puts it with reference to the American pragmatist tradition,

> Langer has shown how to combine in a nuanced way the 'experiential' and the 'semiotic', pushing meaning 'up' and pushing it 'down' in clearly defined ways. Her philosophy, like much of the American philosophical tradition, is both a *philosophy of experience* and a *philosophy of meaning*. Her 'new key' shows how these two central philosophical foci can be related to one another and integrated, just as Peirce's theory of signs and Dewey's pragmatist analysis. Philosophy, on Langer's terms, is not bare conceptual analysis nor the rearrangement of facts, but a broadly conceived analysis of essentially *embodied* meanings, in the broadest sense of that term.[199]

All cultural activities, including art and science, are the result of exploration and of 'naming' discovered meaning.[200] Both presentational and formulative symbols can articulate experiences as yet not encountered or expressed or, indeed, can *imagine* possible worlds. This is a central element of the process of imaginative disclosure as it takes form in art. This will be the topic of the next chapter.

9

Art as the form of feeling

Art is the objectification of feeling, and the subjectification of nature.

Langer[1]

If music has any significance it is semantic, not symptomatic. … Music is not the cause or the cure of feelings, but their logical expression.

Langer[2]

Cultures begin with the development of personal and social and religious feeling. The great instrument of this development is art.

Langer[3]

Art education is the education of feeling, and a society that neglects it gives itself up to formless emotion. Bad art is corruption of feeling. This is a large factor in the irrationalism which dictators and demagogues exploit.

Langer[4]

Philosophy of art should begin in the studio, not the gallery, auditorium, or library.

S. K. Langer[5]

Philosophy of art and aesthetics

Langer has always been best known as a philosopher of art or aesthetician, and until the publication of *Mind*, almost all scholarly interest focused on this aspect of her work.[6] Between 1950 and 2000, roughly one hundred articles discussed some aspect of her aesthetics, many of them published in the main aesthetics journals – the *Journal of Aesthetics and Art Criticism* and the *British Journal for Aesthetics* – or in general philosophy journals such as the *Journal of Philosophy*, *The Review of Metaphysics* and *Mind*.[7] Although I will refer to many of these articles in the notes, the aim of this chapter is not to engage with these detailed discussions, valuable as they are in drawing out both strengths and weaknesses, but to place Langer's aesthetics in the context of her broader philosophy of logic and symbols and her later work on the embodied mind. In the introduction to her main book on art, *Feeling and Form: A Theory of Art Developed from Philosophy in a New Key*, Langer writes that she 'must beg the reader to regard *Feeling and Form* as, in effect, Volume II of the study in symbolism that began with *Philosophy in a New Key*.'[8] As we will see, Langer's philosophy of art is as much steeped in the thought of Sheffer, Whitehead, Wittgenstein and Cassirer as the rest of her philosophy. Cassirer had always hoped to write a fourth volume on art, and Langer's work can be seen as fulfilling that task after his untimely death in 1944. Indeed, *Feeling and Form*, her main book on art from 1953, is dedicated to 'the happy memory of Ernst Cassirer'.

Langer wrote *Feeling and Form* at a time of relative quiet in aesthetics. Aesthetics was not considered a serious field in philosophy on account of what John Passmore called its perceived 'woolliness' and 'dreariness'.[9] As a result, it was routinely relegated to the margins of philosophy. As Quine had put it, 'philosophy of science is philosophy enough'.[10]

Langer's aesthetics stretches beyond traditional questions of beauty, aesthetic judgement and taste. By addressing more fundamental questions such as sense perception, affective experience and human understanding, Langer returns aesthetics to its pre-Kantian origins in Alexander Baumgarten and Giambattista Vico.[11] In so doing, she relocates aesthetics from the margins of philosophy to its very centre.

Langer's attempt to develop an integrated systematic account of art and music as part of a larger aesthetic or 'metaphysical theory' did not sit easily with the piecemeal agendas of philosophical debates still weary of the old idealist grand stories. As the founder of *The British Journal of Aesthetics*, Harold Osborne, observed in 1972,

> In aesthetics, as in some other branches of philosophy, the trend of fashion has been on the whole unfavourable even to the relatively unpretentious theory construction which was attempted in the previous half century such as Santayana or Croce, Dewey or Collingwood. Perhaps the closest approximations to this sort of unified systematization in aesthetics are to be found in the works of Susanne Langer in America (*Mind: an Essay on Human Feeling*, Vol. 1, 1967; and earlier writings), Louis Arnaud Reid in England (*Meaning in the Arts*, 1969) and Luigi Pareyson in Italy.[12]

As highlighted in previous chapters, one of the guiding themes underlying *Philosophy in a New Key*, as well as Cassirer's philosophy of symbolic forms, was a desire to expand the realm of meaning and semantics beyond discursive language. Countering Russell's pessimism – 'Perhaps that is why we know so much physics and so little of anything else' – and Wittgenstein's existential despair about our inability to express anything of meaning about the non-physical world, Langer writes,

> I do believe that in this physical, space-time world of our experience there are things which do not fit the grammatical scheme of expression. ... But they are not necessarily blind, inconceivable, mystical affairs; they are simply matters which require to be conceived through some symbolistic schema other than discursive language.[13]

In *Problems of Art*, this non-discursive realm is described in phenomenological terms as the nameless dimension of subjective lived experience:

> [T]hat is what we sometimes call the *subjective aspect* of experience, the direct feeling of it – what it is like to be waking and moving, to be drowsy, slowing down, or to be sociable, or to feel self-sufficient but alone; what it feels like to pursue an elusive thought or to have a big idea. All such directly felt experiences usually have no names – they are named, if at all, for the outward conditions that normally accompany their occurrence. Only the most striking ones have names like 'anger', 'hate', 'love', 'fear', and are collectively called 'emotion'. But we feel many things that never develop into any designable emotion.[14]

Art, so argues Langer, is a non-discursive symbolic form that can capture subtle nuances of human feelings that fall outside the standard garden-variety named emotions such as joy, sadness, anger or fear.

Langer first addressed the question of the nature of art in the appendix of her 1926 PhD thesis, 'An Analysis of Meaning'. The leading theme there was the question whether art and music can convey any meaning and, if so, what kind. This question would remain a central concern in all her writings on art, from *Feeling and Form* (1953) and *Problems of Art* (1957) to her essays in *Philosophical Sketches* (1962) and the first volume of her trilogy *Mind: An Essay on Human Feeling* (1971). Seminal articles on art include 'Abstraction in Art' in the *Journal of Aesthetics and Art Criticism* (1964) and two articles in *The Hudson Review* (1950), 'The Principles of Creation in Art' and 'The Primary Illusions and the Great Orders of Art'.[15]

Philosophy of art, so Langer argues, should begin 'in the studio, not the gallery, auditorium or library'.[16] Throughout her life she had always taken a keen interest in the way artists worked and *talked about* their work – their ideas, their materials, their motivations, their challenges, their techniques and so on. She sought to translate the often metaphorical language used by artists into a language that could illuminate and deepen a philosophical understanding of the nature of art.

While teaching as a visiting professor at the University of Washington, her composer and painter friend Wesley Wehr had introduced her to a large network of artists and musicians in the Seattle area. These included poets Elizabeth Bishop and Richard Selig and musician Eva Heinitz, as well as leading figures of the Northwest School of abstract expressionism: Guy Anderson, Mark Tobey and Morris Graves.[17] According to Wehr, even though artists often 'used words vague and loosely', Langer was very adept at grasping what they were saying, but when philosophers did the same, 'she had no patience with imprecise language or quasi-mystical mumbo jumbo'.[18]

Langer herself neither expected nor encouraged artists to read philosophy of art or aesthetics. Wehr even notes Langer's reservations about artists reading her own books in case it made them 'self-conscious and overly theoretical'.[19] Although she may have been the target of Barnett Newman's quip that 'aesthetics is for artists as ornithology is for the birds', she entirely agreed with its sentiment.[20]

Langer's philosophy of art does not focus primarily on the finished product, the 'work of art', but on the creative processes that produce it. Her main interest is the question: how and what does the artist 'create'? To explore that question, Langer draws on the three major distinctions as outlined in her logic of signs and symbols: between sign and symbol, between discursive and non-discursive symbolism and, most importantly although least recognized, between conventional and formulative symbolism.

Langer's philosophy of art has been much criticized for the same reasons that her notion of presentational symbol was criticized by Nagel and others. These critics assume that, when something is called a symbol, a subject has access to both the symbol and the object in order to make the connection. For Langer, by contrast, a symbol is a form *through which the object is being perceived*. On that principle, a presentational symbol is rooted in the projection of perceived resemblances onto a perceptual entity. It is not an 'objective' correspondence between symbol and symbolized but a way to present an elusive, diffuse and transient experience in a relatively stable and enduring tangible form. It provides the experience an integrated unity which it lacks in the mind's stream of consciousness. It is this understanding of a presentational symbol that lies at the base of Langer's philosophy of art.

Music as presentational symbol

In Langer's logic of signs and symbols, art is a symbol, not a signal or symptom. Art is not self-expression or emotional catharsis but *a vehicle for meaning*. It is a *presentational* symbol capable of formulating elusive affective experience. It *shows* what cannot be said.[21] Langer's first serious treatment of an art form is her chapter on music in *Philosophy in a New Key*. Because of its non-representational character, Langer considers sound 'the *easiest* medium to use in a purely artistic way'.[22] As a result, so she argues, music is less caught up with questions around truth, morality, imitation or utility than painting, literature or architecture.

Langer rejects expression theories of music that assume a transmission of the emotional state of the composer via a performer to an audience. To illustrate the point, she refers to two contrasting theories of musical meaning held by, respectively, composers C. P. E. Bach and Ferrucio Busoni. Bach claims that 'a musician cannot otherwise move people, but he be moved himself', and must be able to induce in himself all those affects which he would want to arouse in his auditors.[23] Busoni, by contrast, holds that 'just as an artist, if he is to move his audience, must never be moved himself – lest he lose, at that moment, his mastery over the material – so the auditor who wants to get the full operatic effect must never regard it as real, if his artistic appreciation is not to be degraded to mere human sympathy'.[24] Agreeing with Busoni, Langer claims that while musicians can indeed convey musical feelings or moods, they do not express their internal emotional state at the time or, indeed, switch their emotions on and off at the tip of a baton.[25] Even if the acoustic effects of music can cause certain physical changes in a listener – such as tapping, increased heartbeat or a sense of calm – these somatic effects only last as long as the stimulus is effective.[26] For Langer, these somatic effects are *side* effects of the main musical experience. They occur irrespective of whether the listener is musical or not. In other words, while music *can* work therapeutically as a means of cathartic expression, that is not its primary function. A person in emotional turmoil does not resort to a song or dance but to crying, wailing or shouting: 'the laws of emotional catharsis are natural laws, not artistic'.[27] As she puts it succinctly, '*sheer self-expression requires no artistic form*'.[28]

Langer's critique of expression theories of art and music is also directed at fellow philosophers.[29] Carnap, for one, believed that 'the aim of a lyrical poem [is] to express certain feelings of the poet and to excite similar feelings in us'.[30] It is on those very grounds that Carnap denies art any meaning. Just like speculative metaphysical proposition, the arts do not have any proper representational value but are akin to laughing and crying. They have no meaning or truth value. Langer challenges this by arguing that the arts can be true carriers of meaning and are 'a source of insight, not a plea for sympathy'.[31] Thus she claims,

> If music has any significance it is semantic, not symptomatic. Its 'meaning' is evidently not that of a stimulus to evoke emotions, nor that of a signal to announce them; if it has an emotional content, it 'has' it in the same sense that language 'has' its conceptual content – *symbolically*. It is not usually derived *from* affects nor intended *for* them ... it is *about* them. Music is not the cause or the cure of feelings, but their *logical expression*.[32]

One precedent of Langer's position is R. G. Collingwood's *The Principles of Art* (1938), in which we are told,

> The expression of emotion must not be confused with what may be called the betraying of it, that is, exhibiting symptoms of it. When it is said that the artist in the proper sense of that word is a person who expresses his emotions, this does not mean that if he is afraid he turns pale and stammers; ... The characteristic mark of expression proper is lucidity and intelligibility; ... A person who writes or paints or the like in order to blow off steam, ... may deserve praise as an exhibitionist, but loses for the moment all claim to the title of artist.[33]

Langer finds much to agree with Collingwood in *Feeling and Form* but disagrees strongly with his exclusion of the crafts from the category of art and his too narrow conception of symbol, which he conceives of as an artificial sign.[34]

An important philosopher of music *after* Langer whose position on expression is almost identical to hers is Peter Kivy. Kivy argued that music is not an 'expression of' but '*expressive of*' certain emotions.[35] In the same way that the sad expression of a Saint Bernard dog should not be interpreted as a sign of the dog's inner state of mind, so the 'sad feel' of some music should not be interpreted as the expression of the inner state of mind of the performer or composer.[36] For Kivy, as for Langer, the music is 'expressive of' sadness; it *conveys* it. As philosopher of music Albert van der Schoot observes, 'in spite of [Kivy's] recognition of [Langer's] pioneering role in the question of music's relation to the emotions, he finds it hard to accept that Langer preceded his Saint Bernard by almost half a century'.[37]

Panofsky's symbolic forms

Recalling our discussion of the difference between 'semiotics' and 'semantics' in the previous chapter, the sign–symbol distinction as conceived by Langer and Cassirer is often not adequately understood by theorists of art. This can be illustrated by Erwin Panofsky's theory of art. Panofsky was a close colleague of Cassirer at Hamburg University and the Warburg Institute and attributes several of his insights to Cassirer. In an important early essay on perspective, Panofsky draws on Cassirer as follows:

> [Perspective] may even be characterised as (to extend Ernst Cassirer's felicitous term to the history of art) one of those 'symbolic forms' in which 'spiritual meaning is attached to a concrete, material sign and intrinsically given to this sign.' This is why it is essential to ask of artistic periods and regions not only whether they have perspective, but also which perspective they have.[38]

A decade later, in his essay 'Iconography and Iconology: An Introduction to the Study of Renaissance Art' (1939), Panofsky refers again to Cassirer. This essay outlines three levels of meaning in art: The first is the primary or natural subject matter (this entails the recognition of certain configurations as representing objects or people). The second is the 'iconographical' or conventional subject matter (this refers to the identification of objects and people as standing for particular individuals or ideas – a male figure with a knife as St Bartholomew, a skull symbolizing death, etc.). In a footnote, Panofsky correctly points out that, at this level, symbolic meaning operates 'not in the Cassirerian, but in the ordinary sense, e.g., the Cross, or the Tower of Chastity.'[39] The third level is the 'iconological' or intrinsic meaning (this consists of the apprehension of the 'underlying principles which reveal the basic attitude of a nation, a period, a class, a religious or philosophical persuasion – *unconsciously* qualified by one personality and condensed into one work [my italics].[40] In order to explain this third level of meaning, Panofsky refers explicitly to Cassirer: 'In thus conceiving of pure forms, motifs, images, stories and allegories as manifestations of underlying principles, we interpret all these elements as what Ernst Cassirer has called 'symbolical' values.'[41] Unfortunately, this is not Cassirer's concept of symbolic forms. Panofsky failed to grasp Cassirer's distinction between symbols as intentional vehicles for meaning and unintentional signals or symptoms of a society's values or 'worldview'. This is clear from the following passage:

> [O]ur synthetic intuition [must] be corrected by an insight into the manner in which, under varying historical conditions, the general and essential tendencies of the human mind were expressed by specific themes and concepts. This means what may be called a history of *cultural symptoms* – or '*symbols*' in Ernst Cassirer's sense – in general. [my italics][42]

Although Cassirer made his distinction between signs and symbols only clearer later, in *An Essay on Man*, contrary to Panofsky's claim, Cassirer's 'symbols' are not primarily 'cultural symptoms'. As Christopher Wood correctly observes, 'Panofsky departed essentially from Cassirer when he accepted the totalizing metaphor of the *Weltanschauung*.'[43] By assuming a shared worldview (*Weltanschauung*) underlying all cultural expressions, Panofsky is more Hegelian than Cassirerean or neo-Kantian.[44] On that model, art is studied primarily as an expression of a *Zeitgeist*, 'a point of departure for unravelling the *Weltanschauung* of a particular period in time'.[45] That's why some art historians, including his friend Paul Oskar Kristeller, regard Panofsky more as a historian of culture than as an art historian. Based on Panofsky's interest in discovering the deep structures of cultural products, some read Panofsky as a 'proto-semiotician'.[46] Giulio Argan calls him 'the Saussure of art history'.[47] Panofsky's (mis-)use of Cassirer exposes some of the misunderstandings of Cassirer's notion of symbolic forms as exemplified in art and, by implication, Langer's.

Symbols in art and the art symbol

Langer distinguishes clearly between, on the one hand, symbols that appear as *elements* in art and, on the other, symbols that constitute the work as a whole.[48] Whereas symbols *in* a work of art have historically developed or assigned conventional meanings 'in the full sense that any semanticist would accept', the art symbol *as a whole* is literally ineffable.[49] As she puts it,

> Symbols used in art lie on a different semantic level from the work that contains them. Their meanings are not part of its import, but elements in the form that has import, the expressive form. The meanings of incorporated symbols may lend richness, intensity, repetition or reflection or a transcendent unrealism, perhaps an entirely new balance to the work itself. But they function in the normal manner of symbols: they mean something beyond what they present in themselves.[50]

In summary, art works, for Langer, are neither merely cultural symptoms of the time nor conventional pictorial or poetic illustrations of pre-existing ideas or themes.[51] Instead, they are symbolic forms that serve the formulation of elusive and ineffable human experience.

Symbol and symbolism

While an art work is a 'symbol', it is not a 'symbolism'. A symbolism, as we have seen, is a system of symbols the elements of which have conventional meanings and are governed by specific rules of combination and use. The elements of a work of art or music, by contrast, do not have independent meaning and cannot be understood outside the context of the work as a whole. As Langer writes,

> All the failings of musical hermeneutics … rest on one cardinal error, the treatment of the art symbol as a symbolism. A work of art is a single symbol, not a system of

significant elements which may be variously compounded. Its elements have no symbolic values in isolation.[52]

Likewise,

> A work of art is a single, indivisible symbol, although a highly articulate one; it is not, like a discourse (which may also be regarded as a single symbolic form), composite, analyzable into more elementary symbols.[53]

The elements in art or music are always 'newly created' for the purposes of the whole.[54] Likewise, when apprehending a work of art, 'the complex whole is seen or anticipated first' before the viewer pays attention to the individual elements.[55]

> The import of an art symbol cannot be built up like the meaning of a discourse, but must be seen *in toto* first; that is, the 'understanding' of a work of art begins with an intuition of the whole presented feeling. Contemplation then gradually reveals the complexities of the piece, and of its import.[56]

As non-discursive, presentational symbols do not 'say' but 'show', revealing and disclosing as yet unformulated meanings, their import cannot be explained by means of another symbolism:

> [A]rtistic import, unlike verbal meaning, can only be exhibited, not demonstrated to any one to whom the art symbol is not lucid. Since there are no semantic units with assigned meanings which, by paraphrase or translation, could be conveyed by equivalent symbols, as words may be defined or translated, there is no way of further identifying the import of a work.[57]

The function of art echoes what Langer said of perception in general: 'Its primary function, that of conceptualizing the flux of sensations, and giving us concrete *things* in place of kaleidoscopic colors and noises, is itself an office that no language-born thought can replace.'[58]

Art and intuition

Intuition, for Langer, whether artistic or otherwise, is not a mystical or metaphysical irrational vision but a 'fundamental intellectual activity', which produces logical or semantic understanding'.[59] It is the basic capacity to see forms and configurations:

> There are certain relational factors in experience which are either intuitively recognised or not at all, for example, distinctness, similarity, congruence, relevance. These are formal characteristics which are protological in that they 'must be seen to be appreciated'.[60]

In this context she draws, yet again, on the importance of *Gestalt* perception:

> This power which is called insight or intuition, is based upon our perception of patterns, which some enlightened psychologists have recognized as the principle of 'Gestalt', and which is 'form' in a really general sense.[61]

Intuition is not only needed to apprehend the meaning of non-discursive (or presentational) symbolic forms but also discursive forms. Both logic and art depend on 'protological' intuition for insight into the 'nature of relations whereby we recognize distinctions and identities, contradictions and entailments, and *use*'.[62] Interestingly, Langer considers her view of intuition as akin to John Locke's 'natural light'. In his preface to *Process and Reality*, Whitehead had referred to Locke as the writer who 'most fully anticipated the main positions of the philosophy of organism', especially in *Essay on Human Understanding*.[63] Langer quotes Locke as saying that by natural light 'the mind perceives, that white is not black, that a circle is not a triangle, that three are more than two, and equal to one and two'.[64] The mind perceives such truths 'by bare intuition, without the intervention of any other idea'.[65] *Artistic* intuition, for Langer, is not more mysterious or irrational than *logical* intuition. *Both* are 'incommunicable, yet rational'.[66] The difference between them lies in the kind of form each aims to intuit or 'abstract'. Already in *The Practice of Philosophy* Langer had referred to the role of intuition in logic and science:

> A scientist of genius is a person who can apprehend a new concept through some natural medium, for whom there are unprobed patterns in nature, which catch his mind's eye so that he can *see* the general form of a system which becomes lucid for others (and even for him) only as he gives it literal expression. This is the logical process which in popular parlance is called 'having a hunch'.[67]

As she explains, this is not fundamentally different from artistic intuition:

> The artist also, if he can lay claim to genius, must find symbolisms in nature; but his expression is intensive, and only clarifies the material to the point of making the hunch vaguely contagious. … [T]he scientist must have insight to convey intellectual knowledge, and the artists must have insight to inspire insight. This power which is called insight or intuition, is based upon our perception of patterns [and forms].[68]

It is this fundamental intuition of Langer herself, that enables her to move effortlessly from the realm of symbolic logic in the 1920s and 1930s to the realm of art and aesthetics in the 1940s and 1950s and the biology of mind in the 1970s and 1980s. As Cornelia Richter puts it, 'No matter what subject she dealt with, be it psychological or artistic phenomena, be it music or poetry, animal life or human society, naturalistic principles or ethics and morality – she always searched for the inner laws and structures that characterize its form and structure. In this regard Susanne Langer was always a philosopher of logic.'[69]

Art and abstraction

As we saw in the previous chapter, for Langer, every intuited form is always an abstraction. This is because all symbolization is rooted in a 'formulative function, by means of which some sort of *conception* is always abstracted from any symbolized experience'.[70] Echoing Kant, she writes,

> Our merest sense-experience is a process of *formulation* ... A tendency to organize the sensory field into groups and patterns of sense-data, to perceive forms rather than a flux of light-impressions, seems to be inherent in our receptor apparatus ... [T]his unconscious appreciation of forms is the primitive root of all abstraction, which in turn is the keynote of all rationality.[71]

For Langer, perceptual abstractions are the foundation of perception and intelligence and the power of abstraction is as important in the arts as it is in science. As she argues in *Problems of Art*, 'All genuine art is abstract':[72]

> The schematized shapes usually called 'abstractions' in painting and sculpture present a very striking technical device for achieving artistic abstraction, but the result is neither more nor less abstract than any successful work in the 'great tradition', or for that matter in Egyptian, Peruvian, or Chinese art – that is, in any tradition whatever.[73]

Discussions of abstraction in art and in science feature throughout Langer's entire work, from sections in *The Practice of Philosophy* (1930) to 'A Chapter on Abstraction' in the first volume of *Mind* (1967).[74] In all cases, as she already wrote in *An Introduction to Symbolic Logic*, abstraction entails an abstraction of *form*: it is 'the consideration of logical form apart from content'.[75] And as she writes in *Problems of Art*,

> Both in art and in logic (which carries scientific abstraction to its highest development), 'abstraction' is the recognition of a relational structure, or *form*, apart from the specific thing (or event, fact, image, etc.) in which it is exemplified.[76]

Likewise,

> The power of understanding symbols, i.e. of regarding everything about a sense-datum as irrelevant except a certain *form* that it embodies, is the most characteristic trait of mankind. It issues in an unconscious, spontaneous process of *abstraction*, which goes on all the time in the human mind: a process of recognizing the concept in any configuration given to experience, and forming a conception accordingly.[77]

This understanding of abstraction as the gradual foregrounding of a form goes ultimately back, via Cassirer, to Kant's 'forms of intuition' as the universal, transcendental conditions for perception.

Two notions of form

As will have become clear from previous chapters, the notion of form can be conceived in many different ways: symbolic form of perception (Cassirer), logical or structural form (Sheffer), organic or living form (Whitehead) and expressive form (Wittgenstein). More generally, it is possible to distinguish between two main types of forms, those which are defined primarily in terms of their relational structure and those that are defined primarily by their shape or *Gestalt*. In Langer's aesthetics, the first conception of form enables the articulation of the dynamic structure of internal emotional life; the second highlights the charged feeling accompanying an external form.[78] In Langer's work there is a gradual shift in attention from the first to the latter.

Form as structure: Analogy

Langer's earliest reflections on form focus primarily on a form's configuration of the internal elements, its relational structure. She refers to this type of form typically as 'logical form'. or, following Wittgenstein, 'logical picture'.[79] As she wrote in *An Introduction to Symbolic Logic*,

> Whenever we draw a diagram, say a ground plan of a house, or a street-plan to show the location of its site, or a map, or an isographic chart, or a 'curve' representing the fluctuations of the stock-market, we are drawing a 'logical picture' of something.[80]

As we saw earlier in the chapter on Wittgenstein, a 'logical picture' differs from an ordinary picture in that it does not need to look like its object. Its relation to its object is not that of a *copy* but of *analogy*, and, as Langer points out, 'it is only by analogy that one thing can *represent* another which does not resemble it'.[81] Maps, scores and diagrams can represent countries, songs and market fluctuations because the relational configuration of relevant elements remains stable despite changes in material, size, colour or appearance:

> [In a diagram] any attempt at *imitating* the parts of an object has been given up. The parts are merely indicated by *conventional* symbols, such as dots, circles, crosses, or what-not. The only thing that is 'pictured' is the relation of the parts to each other. *A diagram is a 'picture' only of a form.*[82]

A logical form operates on the basis of analogy. Langer often uses domestic examples to illustrate this: lampshades, jelly moulds, clothing patterns and so on. Two suits of the same pattern may be 'cut of different cloths' but still keep their 'logical form'.[83] They show how something is put together or constructed. A logical symbolic form is not 'a reproduction of its object, but an *expression* – an exhibition of certain relevant moments, whose relevance is determined by the purpose in hand'.[84] Neither Langer's nor Wittgenstein's picture theory should therefore be read as a 'copy', 'imitation' or 'correspondence' theory, as unfortunately several critics of Langer's philosophy of art have done. [85]

Both Langer and Wittgenstein emphasize the multiplicity of 'world-projections'.[86] Wittgenstein follows Hertz's view that one can have various models (*Bilder*) of the same object and that 'these models may differ in various respects'.[87] Langer, likewise, claims that there 'can be *several adequate descriptions* of reality'.[88] Just one of these is language, and 'to *understand* language is to appreciate the analogy between the syntactical construct and the complex of ideas, letting the former function as a representative, or "logical picture" of the latter'.[89] The main role of forms understood in terms of their relational structure is representation, clarification and instruction.[90] This also applies to ordinary visual pictures:

> The only characteristic that a picture must have in order to be a picture of a certain thing is an arrangement of elements analogous to the arrangement of salient visual elements in the object. A representation of a rabbit must have long ears; a man must feature arms and legs.[91]

The main difference between a picture and a diagram is that the first is non-discursive and the second discursive. That is, in the first case, the lines of an 'ear' or the curves of a 'nose' do not have an independent meaning outside the context of the picture. [92] As Langer says, [T]he 'areas of light and shade that constitute a portrait, a photograph for instance, have no significance by themselves. In isolation we would consider them simply blotches'.[93] This also applies to the elements that constitute logical form in music.

Like language, music, for Langer, is a logical picture.[94] However, while the logical form of language lends itself to analogies with discursive and scientific thought, the logical form of music enables other analogies. The structure of music is analogical to 'sentient, responsive life'.[95] It exhibits the logical expression of feelings.[96] As she puts it in *Feeling and Form*,

> The tonal structures we call 'music' bear a close logical similarity to the forms of human feeling – forms of growth and of attenuation, flowing and stowing, conflict and resolution, speed, arrest, terrific excitement, calm, or subtle activation and dreamy lapses – not joy and sorrow perhaps, but the poignancy of either and both –the greatness and brevity and eternal passing of everything vitally felt. Such is the pattern, or logical form, of sentience.[97]

Instead of expressing joy or sadness as such, music can reflect '*only the morphology of feeling*'.[98] Interestingly, Langer suggests that it is 'quite plausible that some sad and some happy conditions may have a very similar morphology'.[99] Langer is not unaware of a precedent of her views of music. Referring to musicologist Eduard Hanslick's formalist definition of music as *tönend bewegte Formen* (dynamic sound patterns), she even claims it is 'a well-established fact [that] musical structures logically resemble certain dynamic patterns of human experience'.[100]

Nevertheless, she argues – and this is her main point – that 'the analogy between music and scientific language breaks down if we carry it beyond the mere semantic function in general which they are supposed to share'.[101] This is because. unlike science, music is meant to show not how feelings *work*, but how they *appear*. For Langer, 'the art symbol is an image, not a model'.[102] Models illustrate 'a principle of construction apart from any semblance'.[103] They are the key instruments of science. An image, by contrast, is 'a rendering of the appearance of its object in one perspective out of many possible ones'.[104] An image 'abstracts the semblance of its object, and makes one aware of what is there for direct perception'.[105] As Langer explains,

> An image does not exemplify the same principles of construction as the object it symbolizes but abstracts its phenomenal character, its immediate effect on our sensibility or the way it presents itself as something of importance, magnitude, strength or fragility, permanence or transience, etc. It organizes and enhances the impressions directly received.[106]

An art image creates a 'significant form' based on the phenomenal aspects of an object. Whereas models operate on the basis of structural relations, images operate on the basis of shape or *Gestalt*.[107]

Form as shape: *Gestalt*

It was not until the late 1950s that Langer pays serious attention to the notion of form based on contour and shape. As she writes,

> There seem, indeed, to be two meanings of the word 'form' involved in the two fields, respectively. A logician, mathematician, or careful epistemologist … [consider form as] the logical form of discourse, the structure of propositions expressed either in ordinary language or in the refined symbolism of the rational sciences. … Why, then, call anything 'form' that is not capable of such presentation? Yet artists do speak of 'form' and know what they mean; and, moreover, their meaning is closer than that of the logicians to what the word originally meant, namely, 'visible and tangible shape'.[108]

The artistic form, for Langer, 'is a perceptual unity of something seen, heard, or imagined – that is, the configuration, or *Gestalt*, of an experience'.[109] A *Gestalt* operates with a particular principle of abstraction that is also inherent to perception itself when it spontaneously organizes impinging sensations into larger units. This is 'the tendency to closure of form, to simplification'.[110] A *Gestalt* form is based on the contour of a shape as it emerges from an undefined background. Philosopher of cybernetics Norbert Wiener argues that one of the reasons for being able to interpret line drawings is that 'the eye receives its most intense impression at boundaries, and … every visual image in fact has something of the nature of a line drawing'.[111] The perception of a *Gestalt* is the result of a scanning process whereby salient features are emphasized, especially the outline, and others suppressed. This pattern recognition is essential for human and non-human animal survival as it enables instant recognition of prey or danger. It also plays an important role in peripheral vision. Different animals scan differently according to context, challenges and needs. In the human environment, social and cultural differences inform the way salient features are noted and abstracted from the welter of experience while countless other stimuli are ignored. Despite their shared optical physiology, humans do not scan identically. As the history of art testifies, artists see the world differently – they scan and select different visual stimuli. This, among other things, accounts for different developments of style.

What makes 'optical scanning' important for art is that, by eliminating all but the essential features, the emotive side of perception is emphasized and enhanced by the intensification of a form's outlines. This provides forms with an emotional charge and 'lends them a different sort of emphasis from that which the perceptual apparatus itself provided'.[112] All perceptual abstraction inherently carries an emotive aspect: 'the centrally based emotion seems to be carried along with the perception that started it, and is shaped in its progress by the forms which automatic sensory abstraction has already prepared'.[113] In art this emotive aspect is reinforced to the point that it can serve to articulate feelings in other contexts.

> In art forms are abstracted only to be made clearly apparent, and are freed from their common uses only to be put to new uses: to act as symbols, to become expressive of human feeling.[114]

In the aesthetic imagination a form can untie itself from its original source. It can ban 'all irrelevancies that might obscure its logic, and [divest] it of all its usual meanings so it may be open to new ones'.[115] The artist lifts its appearance out of its day-to-day functioning: 'To present things to sight which are known to be illusion is a ready … way to *abstract* visible forms from their usual context.'[116] Abstraction in art, on Langer's terms, does not mean absence of representation but emphasis of form.[117] For her, the 'abstraction of gestalt from an actually given object by seeing it as an image of some entirely different thing – a plant, a roof, a boat, a human or animal figure – is a very ancient source of representational art'.[118] Or as she put it in *Mind*,

> Representation, far from being a non-artistic competing interest, is an orienting, unifying, motivating force wherever it occurs at all in the early stages of an art; it is the normal means of 'isolating abstraction', or abstraction by emphasis.[119]

One of Langer's examples is a Palaeolithic sculpture of a horse's head in a cavern in the Dordogne where the shape of the head is suggested by the shape of the rock wall. In that case the creation of the horse's head is not based on observation of a real horse but on the imaginative 'seeing' of a horse as suggested by shapes and lines on the cave wall.

Leonardo da Vinci, likewise, encouraged his students to look for images of battlefields in the lines and cracks on old walls in the same way that one can 'see' ghosts and elephants in cloud formations in the sky. The walls and clouds invite the artistic eye to see things in them and, in turn, stimulate the aesthetic imagination to create 'significant forms':

> In the realm of plastic art, quite apart from symbolic intent, the intuitive seeing of one thing in another is an invaluable means of abstracting not only shapes, but nameless characteristics ... the resulting gestalt 'is and is not' its avowed object. ... the artist sees the gestalt emerge as something in its own right.[120]

This description of the 'seeing-in' process explains how artists do not typically have a preconceived idea of what they want to express but 'play around' with the marks on their canvas, sounds on their keyboard or words on their paper until they feel 'just right' for the expression of something that was not previously known even to the artists themselves, having not been articulated before then. Langer concludes:

> In European art the imitation of nature became an obsession, beginning with the Renaissance and culminating in the present popular standard of so-called 'photographic truth to nature'. But the great masters ... always knew that the abstractive power of representations lay not so much in giving virtual forms the semblance of being objects, as in seeing and using their resemblance to objects.[121]

Five notions of form: Tatarkiewicz

In his book *A History of Six Ideas: An Essay in Aesthetics* (1980), Polish philosopher of art Władysław Tatarkiewicz notes that there are at least five senses in which the word 'form' is being used: first, as 'the *arrangement of parts*'; second, as 'what *is directly given to the senses*'; third, as 'the boundary or *contour* of an object'; fourth, as 'the *conceptual essence* of an object' (as in Aristotle's notion of *entelechy*); and fifth, as 'the *contribution of the mind*' (as in Kant's forms of perception).[122] Tatarkiewicz points out that some of the confusion surrounding the term can be traced back to the single Latin translation of what were originally two words in Greek:

> From the outset the Latin *forma* replaced two Greek words: *morphe* and *eidos*; the first applied primarily to visible forms, the second to conceptual forms. This double heritage contributed considerably to the diversity of meanings of 'form'.[123]

Interestingly, referring to Cassirer's notion of symbolic forms, he comments,

> We recall the words of the contemporary philosopher Ernst Cassirer who wrote that to see the forms of things (*rerum videre formas*) is no less important a task for man than to know the causes of things (*rerum cognoscere causas*) (*Essay on Man*, 1944, chap. 9). Though beautiful, this formula is not quite precise because it is unclear which of the ... concepts of form discussed above Cassirer intends.[124]

Tatarkiewicz's observation may helps us to see how Langer's two different notions of form – relational structure and overall shape – can be seen as an advance on Cassirer. While her notion of form as relational structure is chiefly conceptual and derived from symbolic logic, her notion of form as shape is predominantly perceptual and derived from *Gestalt* theory. What we will see is that *both* notions of form play a central role in her theory of music and art, although not always entirely clearly distinguished. The first, structure-based notion typically applies to the internal configuration of a symbolic form, the second, shape-based notion applies to the overall contours of its external appearance. This difference maps onto different kinds of artistic expressions. Music, for instance, can be seen as the logical expression of feeling in terms of its internal structural analogy with sentient life, visual art is often experienced as logical expression of feeling in terms of its overall spatial analogy with a perceived object.

Confronted with a flood of criticisms and misunderstandings of her notion of 'the art symbol' in *Philosophy in a New Key* and *Feeling and Form*, Langer continued to look for better terms to describe what she had in mind.[125] In *Problems of Art* she rejects the then popular term 'significant form' as used by Clive Bell and other formalists for its connotation with signals and signification and writes, 'I prefer Professor Melvin Rader's phrase, which he proposed in a review of *Feeling and Form*: "expressive form". … I have used it ever since.'[126] Even so, Langer's underlying conception remains the same: art and music are not models but *images* of feeling.[127] They show the way feelings 'feel' or *appear*. The artist shows 'the appearance of a feeling, in a perceptible symbolic projection.'[128] They create what Langer calls 'a semblance' or 'virtual image'. We will return to Langer's notion of feeling in our next chapter on the mind. But first we will need to take a closer look at her notions of semblance and virtual image.

Semblance and virtual image

Semblance, on Langer's terms, is not mistaken perception or wilful deception. Nor is it mirroring or mere fantasy. Semblance is the presentation of sheer form to the eye or ear.[129] Even 'a building, a pot, [or] a patterned textile' can present semblance or what she calls 'a virtual image'. Semblance in art creates a 'virtual' image. Even while made out of things that are 'out there' and 'real', such as paint, sounds or stone, the virtual image presents itself to the senses only. When one approaches an object purely on the basis of its appearance, it transforms into a semblance or virtual object:

> It becomes an image when it presents itself purely to our vision, i.e., as a sheer visual form instead of a locally and practically related object. If we receive it as a completely visual thing, we abstract its appearance from its material existence. What we see in this way becomes simply a thing of vision – a form, an image. It detaches itself from its actual setting and acquires a different context.[130]

To apprehend an object in that way requires aesthetic imagination. As Arthur Berndtson correctly points out,

Though the aesthetic object may have the material and solid foundation that a building may have, it is only through the imagination that the material of the object is transformed into a semblance.[131]

At the most basic level, simple decorative devices, such as zigzag lines, scrolls, circles or triangles, have the power to transform physical realities (spots of paint, etc.) into a virtual world with a life of its own:

> [T]he forms in a design – no matter how abstract – have a *life* that does not belong to mere spots. Something arises from the process of arranging colors on a surface, something that is created, not just gathered and set in a new order: that is the image. It emerges suddenly from the disposition of the pigments, and with its advent the very existence of the canvas and of the paint 'arranged' on it seems to be abrogated.[132]

All arts, whether visual, musical, gestural or poetic, create virtual worlds by means of an abstraction of the semblance of lived, subjective experience. It organizes our sensed and felt engagement with the world and presents it in a unified objectification of experienced reality. Although semblance is a central feature that occurs in all arts, different art forms operate with different primary and secondary illusions to create different virtual images such as virtual space, virtual time, virtual power, virtual life and virtual memory. In *Feeling and Form* Langer discusses four major types of virtuality as exemplified in four major forms of art: visual art, music, dance and the poetic or narrative arts.

Virtual space: Visual art

The dominant illusion in all visual art, Langer says, following art theorist Adolf Hildebrand, is *virtual space*.[133] As soon as a plain surface is broken up, either through cracks, stains or other natural occurrences, or by means of the deliberate application of marks, spots or lines, the surface comes 'alive' as a virtual space.[134] Even the simplest decorative devices can establish that. While often denigrated as a low form of artistic expression, Langer refers to decorative design as 'the most natural and potent source of *styles*'.[135] This is because '*form is first*, and the representational function accrues to it'.[136] Decorative devices do not copy something but enable things being seen in them. Once a surface has thus been brought 'to life', the forms and shapes can be adjusted and modified to highlight their perceived resemblance with familiar objects, transforming them into flowers, animals and human scenes. Colours which, in first instance, would have been purely ornamental are subsequently associated with particular hues in nature – blue with sky, green with grass and so on – or be applied symbolically – blue for spiritual, red for passion and so on. Decorative shapes and colours are experienced as suggestive of the dynamic rhythms and forms of emotional life. This basic principle underlies all visual arts: 'The purpose of all plastic art is to articulate visual form, and to present that form – so immediately expressive of human feeling that it seems to be charged with feeling – as the sole, or at least paramount, object of perception'.[137] Echoing Hildebrand, Langer holds that the artist not only shapes *in* space but also engages in the shaping *of* space: a virtual visual field or picture plane.[138] Colours, textures, lines and shapes all contribute to this: they make space 'visible'. The primary illusion of virtual space comes with the first marks on a surface:

> Just establish one line in virtual space, and at once we are in the realm of symbolic forms. The mental shift is as definite as that which we make from hearing a sound of tapping, squeaking, or buzzing to hearing speech, when suddenly in midst of the little noises surrounding us we make out a single word. The whole character of our hearing is transformed. … Exactly the same sort of reorientation is effected for sight by the creation of any purely visual space. The image, be it a representation or a mere design, stands before us in its expressiveness: significant form.[139]

Whereas paint and canvas are 'materials', colours and lines are 'virtual elements'. Hence, we do not speak of 'warm paints' but of 'warm colours'. Their 'meaning' is determined by their role in relation to the whole. Langer distinguishes virtual space from physical space in three ways. First, virtual space is primarily visual. Its illusion can be shattered if approached by means of another sense such as touch.[140] This explains the often complex sensory reactions which sculpture elicits, evoking the desire to handle and touch, even though the tactile experience may potentially confuse the visual one, such as when a soft-skinned animal is sculpted in hard stone. Second, it is created, rather than given, by virtue of a specific form of perception and attention on the part of the artists, sometimes called 'the aesthetic attitude'. Third, virtual space is self-contained and independent from physical space. The picture frame (or cave wall) sets virtual space apart from its surroundings, with which it, unlike other objects in that space, has no ontological continuity.

In his 1960 *Art and Illusion*, art historian Ernst Gombrich famously argues that it is not possible for a viewer to pay simultaneous attention to a painting's material make-up, the canvas and paints, and to its virtual image or 'illusion'.[141] It is as with looking at a combined image of a duck and a rabbit: you can see only one or the other at any one time. Twenty years later, in *Art and Its Objects*, Richard Wollheim critiqued Gombrich's view by arguing that if one looks at a painting one always sees a representation *in* the medium. This requires the spectator to attend simultaneously to representation and medium.[142] Langer's distinction between materials (the canvas, the paint) and medium (tints, colours, brushstrokes, etc.) can be said to provide a way out of this dilemma. Unlike blobs of paints, a medium consists of symbolic marks inviting interpretation. Hence, whereas Gombrich speaks about the material surface, Wollheim talks about the virtual medium. Langer's more sophisticated *three*-fold distinction bridges the gap: the materials (e.g. canvas, paper, paint, bronze, wood), the medium (e.g. warm colours, spontaneous brush strokes, sharp edges) and the virtual image – the 'illusion' or 'semblance' (e.g. a landscape, a sunrise, a figure or a significant non-representational form or shape as in abstract art).

Within the basic primary illusion of virtual space, Langer identifies three further sub-modes, corresponding to the way in which each of the three main plastic art forms – painting, sculpture and architecture – establish their illusion of space. Painting, according to Langer, creates a 'virtual scene', defined as *'a space opposite the eye and related directly and essentially to the eye'*.[143] Sculpture creates *'virtual kinetic volume'* and makes 'tactile space visible'.[144] Architecture, finally, creates what Langer calls 'an ethnic domain'.[145] It sets apart a space and turns it into a virtual realm that expresses the human imprint of life. It shows the way humans inhabit their world, their fears, their hopes, their desires. As she puts it,

> [Architecture's] symbolic expression … embodies the feeling, the rhythm, the passion or sobriety, frivolity or fear with which any things at all are done. That is the image of life which is created in buildings; it is the visible semblance of an 'ethnic domain', the symbol of humanity to be found in the strength and interplay of forms.[146]

Drawing on le Corbusier, and reminiscent of Hegel, Langer refers to architecture as 'the semblance of that World which is the counterpart of a Self. It is a total environment made visible'.[147] This is particularly evident in religious or sacred spaces, from Stonehenge and temples to medieval cathedrals and contemporary mosques or, in some cases, financial banks and art galleries. This explains why most great architecture consists of public buildings rather than private dwellings catering for domestic needs.

Virtual time: Music

Langer's analysis of the primary illusion of music is rooted in the notion of 'musical duration' as an image of subjective time. Music is the abstracted form of lived time.

> The semblance of this vital, experiential time is the primary illusion of music. All music creates an order of virtual time, in which its sonorous forms move in relation to each other – always and only to each other, for nothing else exists there. Virtual time is as separate from the sequence of actual happenings as virtual space from actual space.[148]

Musical time differs from physical time in two ways. First, as a composed image music has a unity that is intuitively and aurally perceived as a *Gestalt*: music *'makes time audible, and its form and continuity sensible'*.[149] Second, in contrast to physical time which is linear and one-dimensional succession of momentary 'states', virtual time has a virtual depth and volume: this is music's *secondary* illusion.[150] Langer holds that the fact that the primary illusion of one art may appear, like an echo, as a secondary illusion in another suggests the underlying unity of the arts. Hence there can be illusions of time in visual art:

> As space may suddenly appear in music, time may be involved in visual works. A building, for instance, is the incarnation of a vital space; in symbolizing the feeling of life that belongs to its precincts, it inevitably shows us time, and in

some buildings this element becomes impressively strong. Yet architecture does not create a perceptible totality of time, as it does of space; time is a secondary illusion.[151]

The spatial illusions created in music are enforced by harmonic structures that allow the listener to experience sounds not only in terms of spatial qualities such as higher and lower but also in terms of development and *movement*. Development in music is heard differently every time a piece is being played since every new occasion contains the memory and anticipation of the previous one.

Langer's notion of musical and 'subjective time' is not dissimilar to Henri Bergson's idea of 'real time' (*la durée réelle*) or 'duration'. Langer credits Bergson for his insight that

> every conceptual form which is supposed to portray time oversimplifies it to the point of leaving out the most interesting aspects of it, namely the characteristic appearances of passage, so that we have a scientific equivalent rather than a conceptual symbol of duration.[152]

But she critiques him for not recognizing that there can be a symbolism that can capture this experience of the passage of time and resorting to a view of music as 'a completely formless flow'.[153] For Langer, by contrast, music creates symbolic forms that can articulate lived, virtual time 'by the movement of audible forms'.[154]

Virtual power: Dance

Langer was one of the first philosophers to undertake a philosophy of dance.[155] Dance, for her, is not merely a bodily accompaniment to music or a 'moving picture' but a highly developed art form in its own right with its primary illusion being '*gesture*'.[156] Dance's virtual gestures are *symbols*, not symptoms or signals of someone's inner state. Like music or painting, they render *ideas* about feelings available for perception and reflection. Because dance's gestures create the image of an inner vital force, Langer defines dance's primary illusion as 'virtual power': 'The primary illusion of dance is a virtual realm of Power – not actual, physically exerted power, but appearances of influence and agency created by virtual gesture.'[157] Dance articulates the subjective experience of free will and agency. It projects an image of being alive and about being aware of being alive with all that entails. Dance is, Langer says, '*actual movement, but virtual self-expression*.'[158] The feeling of inner power, according to Langer, is 'our most immediate self-consciousness', a very basic primary sensation.[159] Its portrayal underlies all kinds of dance, from the magic and ecstatic to the waltz and classical ballet, tap and clog, funeral and social dance. Because they are meant to create a virtual image, dances are designed to be performed for an audience, even if the audience is imaginary or the dancer himself. They are meant 'to break the beholder's sense of actuality and set up the virtual image of a different world; to create a play of forces that *confronts* the percipient, instead of engulfing him.'[160] It is the presence of a (real or imagined) audience that 'transforms dance into an artistic discipline'.[161]

Virtual life: The poetic or narrative arts

In addition to literature, drama or poetry, Langer's 'poetic arts' include non-lingual narrative arts such as miming or silent puppetry or marionettes, which Langer considers variants of drama. All of them have as their primary illusion the creation of 'virtual life' or 'virtual history'. The primary illusion created by *poesis* is 'a history entirely "experienced"'.[162] Like all other arts, the literary work is an illusion, a pure appearance, 'as complete and immediate as the illusion of space created by a few strokes on paper, the time dimension in a melody, the play of powers set up by a dancer's first gesture'.[163] It is evoked immediately after reading or hearing opening lines which can be imagined to be preceded by the words 'Once upon a time … '. For Langer, the poet's task is 'to create the appearance of "experiences", the semblance of events lived and felt, and to organize them so they constitute a purely and completely experienced reality, a piece of *virtual life*'.[164] In this context Langer uses the term 'life' in two distinct though related senses: first, in the biological sense as the organic functioning of a vital organism and, second, in an existential or what she calls 'social' sense. In the second sense it refers to everything that *happens to* an organism, that is, what it encounters in life and how it responds to it. In addition to being virtual and abstracted, the form of life in the poetic arts is also organic. I will briefly deal with each feature in turn – that is, virtuality, abstracted form and organicity – before raising the question of Langer's exact view of the relation between art and life.

First, in line with Langer's central theme that the world can be presented by a plurality of symbolic forms, the virtual form or illusion of life appears under the aspect it is given in the telling. The story, joke, poem or the like transforms actual life into a virtual form with its own accents and values, thus giving it both an intensity and a unity which is lacking in actual life. Since the main form of life is abstracted from the directly experienced personal life events, the narrative gives to the reader an ordered structure that enables it to make sense of the poem's 'world'.

> To be imaginatively coherent, the 'world' of a poem must be made out of events that are in the imaginative mode – the mode of naive experience in which action and feeling, sensory value and moral value, causal connection and symbolic connection are still undivorced.[165]

This experienced interconnectedness of 'fact' and 'value' is typical for poetic discourse:

> [V]irtual events are qualitative in their very constitution – the 'facts' have no existence apart from values; their emotional import is part of their appearance; they cannot, therefore, be stated and then 'reacted to'. They occur only as they seem – they are *poetic facts*, not neutral facts toward which we are invited to take a poetic attitude.[166]

Poetic facts or virtual events can be activities, sights or thoughts. As long as an idea is used for poetic purposes, any kind of subject matter can be used, even moral, didactic or philosophical topics. A good poet, says Langer, 'can handle even the most treacherous material' and turn it into an illusion of virtual experience.[167] In the same way that all visual art is 'abstract', all verbal poetry is 'pure'. It creates a 'virtual history'.[168] The purpose of the creation of such a virtual history is

> to construct that history in an exact and significant form. The 'formal parts' do not reinforce the statement; they are reinforced by it. The items are 'chosen' (which means, they occurred to the poet) because they serve the formal whole.[169]

This is established by means of the sensuous qualities of language, rhythm, diction and so on. For Langer, the 'fullest exploitation of language, sound and rhythm, assonance and sensuous associations, is made in lyric poetry'.[170] The creation of a semblance typically develops from confused beginnings, via a growing sense of clarity to its mature conception.

This formal aspect is achieved by means of the second characteristic: abstraction. The semblance of life events is abstracted from immediate personal life events in the same way as the primary illusions are abstracted in the other arts:

> For the primary illusion of literature, the semblance of life, is abstracted from immediate, personal life, as the primary illusions of the other arts – virtual space, time, and power – are images of perceived space, vital time, felt power. Virtual events are the basic abstraction of literature, by means of which the illusion of life is made and sustained and given specific, articulate forms.[171]

Langer's subsequent subdivision of the literary arts into poetry, prose and drama is based on their main mode of abstraction.[172] Whereas all literary arts create a 'semblance of life' or 'virtual history', lyric poetry does so in the tense of the 'timeless present', narrative poetry and prose in the mode of 'memory' and drama in the mode of 'destiny'.[173] To this she adds in an appendix the major mode of film as that of 'dream'. Even if these different categories of the poetic arts are not always immediately obvious or, for that matter, entirely convincing, they nevertheless draw attention to the way different art forms entail different projections. It could be argued that, for Langer, the poetic arts do not, as suggested by, for instance, Kendal Walton, create a world of 'make-belief' but one of 'dis-belief' – a suspension from the practical world of action.[174] Instead, they all contain an element of 'once upon a time' or, perhaps equally important, of 'suppose that'. They create an infinite plurality of possible worlds that may have happened in the past or that may happen in the future. As such, they nurture the artistic imagination and, in turn, may nurture empathy as the ability to envisage not only other states of affairs but also other states of mind. This is an important factor in the case for the importance of art education. Art, Langer says, educates feeling.

Art and life

Reviewing Langer's four main virtual modes – virtual 'space', 'time', 'inner power' and 'life's history' – the question arises how each relates to concrete life. To what extent can the abstracted semblances, as captured in artistic forms, tell us something about the concrete world from which they are being lifted? Put differently, what aspect or dimension of the world is being 'abstracted'?

On the one hand, Langer's formalism seems to suggest that actual life events have no bearing upon the meaning of the work. It is not the meanings and associations of the represented life events which make art a symbol of feeling but the meanings and associations conveyed by the visual or other forms employed to represent them:

> A poem always creates the symbol of a feeling, not by recalling objects which would elicit feeling itself, but by weaving a pattern of words – charged with meaning, and colored by literary associations – akin to the dynamic pattern of the feeling.[175]

On the other hand, aware of the difficulties associated with this position, Langer herself raises the question,

> If poetry [and, by implication, all art] is never a statement about actuality, has it then nothing to do with life, beyond the ultimate reference of its composed forms to vitality itself, i.e. through their artistic function of expressing the morphology of real human feeling? Has nothing of the artist's own biography gone into the illusion, except by accident …?[176]

In answering this question Langer intriguingly combines an expressionist with a formalist position. As this not only illuminates her position on art itself but also locates it in relation to her broader philosophy, I will quote it at some length:

> Every good work of art has … something that may be said to come from the worlds, and that bespeaks the artist's own feeling about life. This accords with the intellectual and, indeed, the biological importance of art: we are driven to the symbolization and articulation of feeling when we *must* understand it to keep ourselves oriented in society and nature. So the first emotional phenomena a person wants to formulate are his own disconcerted passions. It is natural to look for expressive materials among the events or objects that begot those passions, that is, to use images associated with them, and under the stress of real emotion, events and objects perceived are prone to appear in a *Gestalt* congruent with the emotion they elicited. So reality quite normally furnishes the images; but they are no longer anything in reality, they are forms to be used by an excited imagination.[177]

In other words, aesthetic perception *itself* consists of a symbolic form expressive of the artist's feeling.[178] It is the artist's task to highlight, modify and refine that form into an artistic whole. This, according to Langer, is 'the work of composition, the struggle for complete expressiveness, for that understanding of the form which finally makes sense out of the emotional chaos'.[179] This can also explain why great art is capable of evoking universally shared feelings that transcend the particular event or experience that inspired the work in the first place.

Poetry and language

As discussed in the previous chapter, Langer often uses language as the paradigm of discursive symbolism, that is, a symbolism in which the elements have independent and conventionally agreed-upon meanings and in which 'the meanings [of the elements] are successively understood'.[180] This view of language has attracted various criticisms. Paul Welsh, for one, rejects the idea that words are always heard as independent units:

> Grammar can 'tie' words together but it cannot tie image-conceptions together … image conceptions of words do not appear in the sentence in the form they possess as separate words.[181]

A large number of elements in language, including articles, prepositions, auxiliary verbs and so on, do not have independent meaning. They modify and qualify words. Casual conversational language, even if following proper rules of grammar and syntax, does not convey its meaning in a linear manner, nor is it received that way. If one could grasp the meaning of a sentence only by first grasping individual words, day-to-day communication would soon grind to a halt. *Pace* Russell, Carnap and Wittgenstein, word order in a day-to-day sentence does not mirror order of entities referred to. It does not apply in informal communication nor does it always apply in languages that do not have the same syntax as English, such as classical Latin.

Conversely, sequentiality is not confined to language. Paintings can be read in a sequential way and can be said to have some kind of a vocabulary or syntax.[182] As Mary Reichling, for instance, observes,

> In stressing the holistic nature of the music symbol, Langer seems to lose sight of the importance of the various elements as syntactical considerations. For example, timbre can function syntactically as form defining in such works as Charles Ives' *Unanswered Questions*, or in a fugue where subject and answer might be assigned to different instruments.[183]

Langer would not disagree in principle with some of these counterexamples. When referring to day-to-day discourse she acknowledges the holistic nature of its production and reception:

> [T]he greatest virtue of verbal symbols is … their tremendous readiness to enter into *combinations*. … This makes it possible for us to grasp whole groups of meanings at a time, and make a new, total, complex concept out of the separate connotations of rapidly passing words.
>
> Herein lies the power of language to embody concepts not only of things, but of things in combination, or *situations*.[184]

Rather, when contrasting language with art, or verbal with visual symbolisms, Langer takes one kind of language as her point of departure, that is, the highly formalized and ideal language of science and symbolic logic. However, she is well aware that language can be used both for discursive *and* for non-discursive ends.[185] Poetic language, for instance, is not 'discourse' in the sense of 'discursive language'.[186] As she puts it,

> Language is the material of poetry, but what is done with this material is not what we do with language in actual life; for *poetry is not a kind of discourse at all*. What the poet creates out of words is an *appearance* of events, persons, emotional reaction, experiences, places, conditions of life; these created things are the elements of poetry; they constitute what Cecil Day Lewis has called 'the poetic image'.[187]

In other words, this passage shows that the classification of language does not depend on its syntactic structure – whether linear or non-linear – but on what it 'creates out of' it: its semantic meaning. While discursive language is a *symbolism*, that is, a system of symbols, a work of poetic art, such as a poem or a play, is always a prime symbol.[188]

Languages of art: Nelson Goodman

It could be argued that a more fine-grained system, such as that developed later by, for instance, Nelson Goodman, might have pre-empted some of the confusion around Langer's theory of language in relation to art. A brief comparison with Goodman's categorizations in *Languages of Art* (1976) will prove instructive in this respect. Goodman mentions Langer's work alongside that of Peirce, Cassirer and Morris, but, as he informs us in the introduction, he does not discuss their respective positions since 'this would give a purely historical matter disproportionate and distracting prominence'.[189]

Instead of Langer's two types of symbolisms, Goodman identifies three categories: digital, analogue and discursive symbolisms, or what he calls 'symbols systems'. Each symbol system operates in combination with any of four further features that are classified in two pairs of distinctions: dense versus articulate, and syntactical versus semantic.

Articulate symbolisms, on Goodman's terms, contain differentiated elements which are distinct and discrete. Dense symbolisms, by contrast, contain elements which operate on a continuum. In a dense symbolism, one can always allow for a third character between any two and a difference in one element will immediately affect another.[190] This distinction maps fairly comfortably on Langer's distinction between discursive and non-discursive symbolism.

Syntactical features, in turn, concern the rules for combination of symbols within a symbol scheme while semantic features concern the relation between a symbol scheme and its referent or what Goodman calls a 'compliance class'.[191] Different combinations of the above distinctions allow for a greater variety of characterizations of symbolisms/symbol systems than Langer is able to allow for with her discursive/non-discursive or presentational distinction.

Digital symbolic systems, such as musical scores, for instance, are both syntactically and semantically articulate. Such systems contain differentiated syntactic characters which, in turn, have a clear and unambiguous semantic reference. Analogue systems, by contrast, are both syntactically and semantically dense.[192] Goodman illustrates this by comparing an analogue clock with a digital one. Whereas a digital clock reports the time unequivocally – that is, it is, for instance, *either* 7.00 am *or* 7.01 am with nothing in between – an analogue clock registers time on a continuum, the exact points of which cannot be specified. Discursive systems, finally, are syntactically articulate but semantically dense. This characterization would have given Langer a more suitable vocabulary in relation to the poetic and literary arts. Indeed, even though a poem makes use of a symbolism containing clearly differentiated characters, poetic *meaning* does not mirror this differentiated syntactic structure.

It should be emphasized, however, that, in the broader contexts of their respective philosophies, Goodman's nominalist framework prevents a straightforward comparison with Langer. Unlike Langer's symbols, which operate on a continuum of mental processes, Goodman's symbols are always the products of agreement and convention. Goodman rejects any isomorphic or analogous connection between symbol and symbolized:

> Resemblance disappears as a criterion of representation, and structural similarity as a requirement upon notational or any other languages. The often stressed distinction between iconic and other signs becomes transient and trivial.[193]

Whereas for Langer symbol and symbolized must have 'some common logical form', for Goodman *all* symbols are conventional:

> Descriptions are distinguished from depictions not through being more arbitrary but through belonging to articulate rather than to dense schemes; and words are more conventional than pictures only if conventionality is construed in terms of differentiation rather than of artificiality.[194]

Although Goodman shows some interest in 'Cassirerean' symbols as 'ways of worldmaking' in his later work, his primary focus is always on a symbolism's notation – whether diagrams, measuring instruments or musical scores – rather than its role as a vehicle for meaning.[195]

The main and arguably *only* advantage of Goodman over Langer in this context is his more sophisticated fourfold system of categories – that is, articulate/dense and syntactic/semantic – instead of Langer's two – discursive and non-discursive – as it allows for more accurate descriptions of different symbol systems. Even so, Langer anticipated many of Goodman's major ideas by well over forty years, including his notions that visual and non-visual objects and events 'can be represented by either visual or non-visual symbols' and that 'a picture in one system may be a description in another'.[196] This also applies to his views of meaning in art. Even while rooted in convention, artistic meaning, for Goodman, is not confined to denotative reference. This is clear from his insightful article 'How Buildings Mean'.[197]

Art as living form

As noted earlier, artists create, construct and compose forms that are suggestive of human feeling. They create images and *Gestalten* that can be *perceived as* resembling the flow, structure and texture of feelings that express life as felt. For art to serve as 'the objectification of feeling', its forms have to be recognized as analogical to the dynamic tensions of sentient life.[198] It is this perceived resemblance between 'actual organic tensions and virtual perceptually created tensions' that leads Langer to the idea of 'organic form' in art.[199] In order to serve as a symbol of feeling, the artistic form should be organic; it should have the appearance and semblance of a 'living form'.

As Langer points out, 'life' and 'organic form' are widely used metaphors in talk about art. Works are often described in terms of their 'vitality', 'spirit', 'animation', 'heartbeat', 'pulse', 'organic unity' and so on. When we say that a work contains 'feeling' we mean that it has artistic 'vitality' and exhibits 'living form'.[200] These metaphors are so strong that they are no longer recognized as biotic metaphors. Yet, as Langer says, 'works of art are not really organisms with biological functions'.[201] So 'Why must every form symbolic of feeling appear to be "living"? ... What justifies the employment of that metaphor ... to such lengths as the whole literature of art exhibits?'[202]

In order to answer this question Langer examines, first, the particular features of actual organisms; second, the general features of artistic creation by virtue of which the semblance of life is produced; and, third, the way this semblance empowers the artist to imagine and articulate the life of feeling and human experience.

A key characteristic of living organisms is their lack of constancy: the 'whole vast system is in unceasing flux'.[203] Every cell 'is perpetually breaking down, and perpetually being replaced. ... It actually has no sameness of material substance from second to second'.[204] As a result, so Langer argues, echoing Whitehead, an organism is not a static, physical substance. It is a process or an event that contains dynamic patterns of changes. Its unity is primarily functional. Even so, 'the self-identity of the higher organisms ... is more convincing than the self-identity of the most permanent material concretion, such as a lump of lead or a stone'.[205] This is why human identity is not seen to lie in bodily permanence but in personality, that is, a continuum of behaviour and activity.

Organic theories of art have a long tradition going back to Aristotle. In that tradition, organic form often means the following: interdependent relatedness of the part–whole relation, unity in diversity, dialectical rhythm, dynamism, the time-cycle of growth and decay, complexity, individuation and proliferation, internal purposiveness and so on. Langer draws on these various characteristics when she explains what she means by 'living form'. As she writes, for instance, about dynamic rhythm, 'The essence of all composition ... is the semblance of *organic* movement, the illusion of an indivisible whole. ... The most characteristic principle of vital activity is rhythm'.[206] Rhythm is primarily a relation between tensions rather than a matter of equal divisions of time: 'harmonic progressions, resolution of dissonances, directions of "running" passages, and "tendency tones" in melody all serve as rhythmic agents'.[207] Drawing on the notion of organic form in terms of its part–whole relation, she argues,

In a work of art, however modest, the peculiar character of life is always reflected in the fact that it has no parts which keep their qualitative identity in isolation. In the simplest design, the virtual constituents are indivisible, and inalienable from the whole. ... The unity of a work of art stems primarily from the interdependence of its elements and is further secured by this dialectical pattern of their relations.[208]

The same applies for decorative design:

Pure decorative design is a direct projection of vital feeling into visible shape and color. Decoration may be highly diversified, or it may be very simple; but it always has what geometric form, for instance a specimen illustration in Euclid, does not have – motion and rest, rhythmic unity, wholeness. Instead of mathematical form, the design has – or rather, it *is* – 'living' form, though it need not represent anything living. ... Decorative lines and areas express vitality in what they themselves 'do'.[209]

Langer draws on Whitehead's notion of acts when comparing organic acts in nature with organic forms in art. Acts, as we discussed before, are the smallest biological units, equivalent to molecules or atoms in physics. They typically consist of a phase of acceleration or intensification, triggered off by an initial charge of energy which needs to be spent, and a subsequent subsiding of a distinguishable pattern, followed by a cadence. Large acts can subsume smaller acts, be reinforced, inhibited or interrupted. All this is part of living form.[210] The logical form of acts is projected in the art symbol irrespective of whether or not the work represents a living creature: '[T]here is no need of 'imitating' anything literally alive in order to convey the appearance of life. Vital forms may be reflected in any elements of a work, with or without representation of living things.'[211] Likewise,

All artistic elements ... have formal properties which, in nature, characterize acts. ... Every element seems to emanate from the context in which it exists. This appearance shifts from one created element – tension, gestalt, contrast, accent, rhythm or any that one may select – to another.[212]

Even the growth development of an organism can be reflected in its living form: 'What makes an organism look individual is not the possession of unique features, ... but the fact that the ontogenetic processes of its individuation ... are encoded in its bodily form. This is the basis of "living form" in nature.'[213] Langer illustrates this with an example provided by morphologist D'Arcy Thompson, whose book *On Growth and Form* she often refers to:

In the marble columns and architraves of a Greek temple we still trace the timbers of its wooden prototype, and see beyond these the tree-trunks of a primeval sacred grove; roof and eaves of a pagoda recall the sagging mats which roofed an earlier edifice ... So we see enduring traces of the past in the living organism – landmarks which have lasted on through altered functions and altered needs; and yet at every stage new needs are met and new functions effectively performed.[214]

Langer sees organic forms not only in the biotic realm but also outside it. She points, for example, to genuine rhythmical cycles in inorganic nature: 'rhythm is the basis of life, but not limited to life.'[215] These can be seen in, for instance, the kinetic swing of a pendulum or the breaking of waves in the sea. Likewise, the part–whole relation or the phenomenon of a permanent shape underneath changing circumstances can be seen in the shape of a waterfall. One could also think of the rhythmic occurrence of seasons, chemical reactions or geological variations caused by climate change. Langer points out the potential of these forms for rhythm in art and music:

> Such phenomena in the inanimate world are powerful *symbols* of living form, just because they are not life processes themselves. The contrast between the apparently vital behavior and the obviously inorganic structure of ocean waves, for instance, emphasizes the pure semblance of life, and makes the first abstractions of its rhythm for our intellectual intuition.[216]

In cultures dominated by magical thinking, Langer argues, the semblance of life in some cases of inanimate natural phenomena is so strong that one takes them to *be* alive.

Langer's conception of artistic forms as alive and organic recalls Kant's conception of beauty as the free and harmonious interplay of forms in nature and art. For Kant, any object of beauty, whether man-made or natural, embodies aesthetic ideas: 'We may in general call beauty (whether natural or artistic) the *expression* of aesthetic ideas.'[217] What is particularly interesting in relation to Langer is that, for Kant, man-made objects are meant to look *as if* they are natural, alive and spontaneous, whereas beautiful forms found in nature happen to look *as if* they were purposefully designed. In man-made art this applies as much to so-called high or fine art as to beautiful ornaments, crockery or wallpaper. Both Langer and Kant therefore recognize a strong analogy between the forms of nature and those of art.[218] For Langer, organic form 'appears in nature as it appears in art, and no matter how much scientific analysis may fragment it, every part still reflects and represents the whole; the image of life is restored.'[219] Art has the task to create forms that evoke the *semblance* of a 'purposeful' organism. For art to articulate forms of feeling, it has to *feel* 'alive'.

Langer's view of art as the structure and form of feeling resonates strongly with the abstract expressionist movement as it emerged in America in the 1950s and 1960s. Langer was influenced by a number of abstract artists and, in turn, influenced various artists and critics, including the art critic Clement Greenberg.[220] Although the philosophically trained painter Robert Motherwell was primarily influenced by Dewey's *Art as Experience*, there are strong Langerian resonances when he writes,

> The function of the artist is to express reality as felt. In saying this, we must remember that ideas modify feelings. The anti-intellectualism of English and American artists has led them to the error of not perceiving the connection between the feeling of modern forms and modern ideas. By feeling is meant the response of the 'body-and-mind' as a whole to the events of reality. ... It is because reality has a historical character that we feel the need for new art. ... The medium of painting is color and space: drawing is essentially a division of space. Painting

is therefore the mind realizing itself in color and space. The greatest adventures, especially in a brutal and policed period, take place in the mind. Painting is a reality, among realities, which has been felt and formed. It is the pattern of choices made, from the realm of possible choices, which gives a painting its form. The content of painting is our response to the painting's qualitative character, as made apprehendable by its form. This content is the feeling 'body-and-mind'. The 'body-and-mind', in turn, is an event in reality, the interplay of a sentient being and the external world. The 'body-and-mind' being the interaction of the animal self and the external world, is just reality itself. It is for this reason that the 'mind', in realizing itself in one of its mediums, expresses the nature of reality as felt.[221]

Motherwell's reflections on the nature of art can be read as an artist's statement of Langer's views. For him, as for her, abstract expressionism was not an empty formalism unrelated to the world; it was about the world *as felt*. Form was never an end in itself, but a way to express 'body-and-mind' feeling and meaning.

Form and meaning

As mentioned earlier, the fact that meaning can be found not only in discursive propositions but also in art was already recognized by Langer as early as 1926. As she wrote in the appendix to her PhD thesis,

> Meaning as it is found in art and religion has ever been the stumbling-block of any precise definition. It is probably this 'unexplored' field, with its suggestion of vast complexity and ineffability, that has given rise to such 'dynamic' concepts as Schiller's 'energetically projected' activity or Strong's 'unfathomed beyond which we cannot contemplate but can only intend'. But a logical analysis of meaning should reveal the formal aspect of even such 'higher' meanings as those of poetry and music, religion and mythology.[222]

As we now know, for Langer, this symbolism is not an irrational, instinctive outpouring of emotions but has its own distinctive forms of representation, its own 'logic'. This logical form can be shown *and* analysed, as Whitehead and Cassirer had already begun to do. For Langer the stakes were high:

> A theory of meaning which either must ignore such phenomena as the significance of Art ... or else must refer these to an indescribable 'higher' sense, commits exactly the sins of narrowness which logical philosophy is supposed to avert: it explains all the indisputable phenomena, but cannot throw any light upon those which are problematic and therefore interesting.[223]

For her, the ability to deal with 'higher' forms of meaning was a crucial test case for *any* theory of meaning and epistemology. Much of what Wittgenstein had relegated to the realm of 'showing' or the 'inexpressible' can, so she argues, be articulated in a non-discursive or 'presentational' symbol or symbolism. Art is a prime example of non-discursive symbolism and artists are the formative creators and appreciators *par excellence* of this distinctive symbolic form. As she wrote in *The Practice of Philosophy*, '[Artists], living through the eye, the musical hearing, the bodily senses, see more *meaning* in artistic wholes, i.e. in things, situations, feelings etc. than they can ever find in propositions'.[224] They feel, so she wrote, echoing Wittgenstein, 'the peculiar poverty of the conventional language. The things they appreciate are simply *non-discursive symbols*'.[225] For Langer, art provides understanding of feelings and insight into lived experience.[226] This phenomenological understanding gives art a *cognitive* value: 'Self-knowledge, insight into all phases of life and mind, springs from artistic imagination. That is the cognitive value of the arts'.[227]

Art and cognition

For Langer, artists not only convey meaning through art, but they also provide knowledge and cognition:

> Their knowledge, being intensive, is much harder to communicate than propositional knowledge, especially where it is humanly impossible to express it in words; but it is knowledge none the less, and the process of apperceiving such meanings is the same as that of understanding a sentence.[228]

The answer to the question of whether or not art is cognitive often depends less on one's view of art than on one's definition of 'cognition' or 'knowledge'. Broadly speaking, there are two types of knowledge. On the one hand, there is knowledge that has been variously described as 'knowing that', 'factual knowledge' or 'knowledge by description' (Russell). On the other hand, there is so-called 'direct' or 'intuitive' knowledge (Bergson), 'tacit knowledge' (Polanyi) or 'knowledge by acquaintance' (Russell).[229] Examples of direct, intuitive knowledge are 'knowing' the taste of mango, the smell of wood, one's own child, danger or love. For those holding a propositionalist view of knowledge, cases like that do not constitute 'proper' knowing. But Schlick, too, had his reservations:

> [U]nfortunately there is ... a very common use of the word 'knowledge' which ... has given rise ... to the most fundamental mistake of the philosophy of all times. The misuse I am speaking of occurs when the word 'knowledge' is applied to what is often called 'immediate awareness' or ... 'intuition'. ... When we look at a leaf, we get an immediate acquaintance with a particular quality of 'green'. Is there any reason or justification to speak of this acquaintance as a kind of ... 'knowledge'? ... Mr. Bertrand Russell distinguishes between 'knowledge by acquaintance' and 'knowledge by description' but why should the first be called 'knowledge' at all? The word 'acquaintance' alone seems to me sufficient, and then we can emphasize the distinction between *acquaintance* and *knowledge*. There is no similarity of meaning between the two.[230]

Likewise,

> When we have *knowledge* of something (whatever it is – let us call it *x*), we always
> know something *about x*. What we know consists of propositions – we know *that*
> *x* is white and granular, we know *that* it reacts chemically with *y*, etc. These are all
> facts *about x*, and constitute *knowledge* of *x*. ... [Knowledge] is more than mere
> awareness. Through mere awareness of the blue sky do we come to know what
> 'blue' really is?[231]

For Langer, by contrast, following Russell, direct, intimate knowledge of something is
a proper form of knowledge. Distinguishing 'knowledge *of* things' from 'knowledge
about them', she refers to the first type of knowledge as 'that direct intimacy which our
senses give us, the look and smell and feel of a thing – the sort of knowledge a baby
has of its own bed, its mother's breast, ... what Bertrand Russell has called "knowledge
by acquaintance".[232] By contrast, the second type of knowledge requires some kind
of insight into its nature: 'To know something *about* an object is to know how it is
related to its surroundings, how it is made up, how it functions, etc., in short, to know
what *sort* of thing it is.'[233] As she puts it, 'A child may know the taste and feeling of a
scrambled egg, without knowing that it is an egg which has been scrambled.'[234]

In Langer's conception of art, however, we encounter a *third* type of knowledge,
lying somewhere between the two kinds mentioned above:

> Art ... gives form to something that is simply there, as the intuitive organizing
> functions of sense give form to objects and spaces, color and sound. It gives what
> Bertrand Russell calls 'knowledge by acquaintance' of affective experience, below
> the level of belief, on the deeper level of insight and attitude.[235]

Art, on this view, gives 'knowledge by acquaintance' but transcends direct experience
as it *articulates* this experience in a symbolic *form*. This symbolic form is not
propositional: to 'understand the "idea" in a work of art is therefore more like *having
a new experience* than like entertaining a new proposition'.[236] Instead, art is a non-
discursive symbolic form that can nevertheless provide knowledge and insight.
However, its meaning or 'import' cannot be explained in words but can only be *shown*.
Langer is fully aware that this is a controversial view. As she writes,

> This creates a real epistemological impasse: artistic import, unlike verbal meaning,
> can only be exhibited, not demonstrated to any to whom the art symbol is not lucid.
> Since there are no semantic units with assigned meanings which, by paraphrase or
> translation, could be conveyed by equivalent symbols, as words may be defined or
> translated, there is no way of further identifying the import of a work.[237]

Not surprisingly, this novel idea of artistic meaning and knowledge invited critique
from fellow philosophers. Unable to distinguish between Langer's *three* types of
knowledge, Hospers, for instance, asks,

But are tasting the mango and hearing music really cases of knowing? If so, they are surely quite different from knowing *that* something is the case? Are not the two, indeed, completely and irrevocably different?[238]

On Langer's account, there is a difference between tasting a mango and hearing music since only music is a symbolic form conveying meaning.[239] Put differently, the difference between, on the one hand, tasting a mango, sensing a mood or feeling in love and, on the other, hearing music, looking at paintings or listening to a poem is that the latter phenomena serve as a vehicle for the *conception* of direct experiences. It goes beyond the directly felt sensations by naming and objectifying them. Art, music and poetry give a *form* to 'knowledge by acquaintance'. There is, as we have seen in Chapter 8, no difference in principle between a perceptual *Gestalt*, an artistic form and discursive knowledge. All three are products of the transformative power of the human mind rooted in bodily intuition. Art is merely one kind of knowledge among others. As the Hungarian philosopher of science and erstwhile pianist Ervin László put it,

> Knowledge, Langer affirms, is considerably wider than our discourse. ... The residue, left over when everything that can be grasped by common-sense cognition and by theory construction has been deducted, is still very large. It is the ineffable sphere of intimate human experience, unique but no less meaningful. Artists seek to give it meaning by creating works of art and preserving for all eternity, as it were, the fleeting impressions of the moment. The creation of such work helps clarify meaning. ... Art can *express* vague meanings and render them conscious. This is the function of artistic creativity which makes it one of the many kind of human *cognitive* activities.[240]

For Langer, art is 'the objectification of feeling, and the subjectification of nature'.[241] This gives art a central role in the formation of culture.[242]

Misunderstandings and misrepresentations

Langer's philosophy of art has been the most debated of her entire philosophy, and within that, her notion of art as symbol has attracted most critical attention. Some early critiques were based on misunderstandings because readers did not have the advantage of reading Langer's later work. Other misunderstandings were due to a lack of familiarity with her earlier books or her sources that had laid out some important principles for her later philosophy. Most criticism was due to a refusal to accept – or failure to grasp – Langer's novel notion of the fundamentally formulative and metaphorical nature of presentational symbols that rely on the producer's act of 'projection' and the perceiver's act of 'seeing-in'.[243] We already referred to John Hospers's critique of Langer's position in line with Nagel's objections. Various other influential philosophers misrepresented her position. One of her earliest critics, Morris Weitz, dismisses Langer's aesthetics as being rooted in a Wittgensteinian correspondence theory that holds 'that language is some sort of mirror of the world', a view which, Weitz claims, has been 'refuted, and by no other more certainly than by the later Wittgenstein himself'.[244] Kingsley Price, likewise, dismisses Langer on the grounds that she follows the early Wittgenstein, who, so he claims, 'along with the positivists, believes that one thing cannot symbolize another ... unless the names in the symbol stand for the parts of the other'.[245] Not only do Weitz and Price misrepresent Langer, they misunderstand Wittgenstein. Joseph Margolis, in turn, wrongly attributes to Langer 'the untenable thesis that all art is language'.[246] George Dickie, likewise, mistakenly characterizes Langer's philosophy as an 'imitation theory'.[247] Roger Scruton misrepresents Langer's 'Crocean' theory of representation in art as an imitation theory and her philosophy of mind as containing 'a Cartesian conception of inner life'.[248] His dismissal is categorical:

> The impact of these two writers [i.e. Nelson Goodman and Langer] on the philosophy of music has been such, that it may seem remarkable that I devote so little space to discussing them. However, I am convinced that recent criticisms have so effectively undermined their arguments, that it is no longer necessary (as once perhaps it was) to make a long and tedious detour in order to rebut them.[249]

Another strong dismissal and misrepresentation of Langer's work can be found in a review of *Feeling and Form* by a young Richard Wollheim for *The Burlington Magazine*. Having misunderstood and misrepresented Langer on almost every front, he concludes his review as follows:

> This book has been widely acclaimed in America as initiating a new phase in aesthetic thought: and even in England there have been found critics to attest to its philosophical importance. It is because I believe these claims to be quite unjustified and this book to mark a retrogressive step in the understanding of art, that I have presumed to review it at such length.[250]

Based on their own flawed understanding of the early Wittgenstein, many early critics mistook Langer's idea of a congruence of perceived *form* – of an *isomorphy* – between art and feeling as a direct *correspondence* between them.[251] Fortunately, some later critics were no longer under that impression. Roger A. Shiner, for example, in his entry for the *Dictionary of Modern American Philosophers*, is one of the few philosophers who recognizes that Langer's notion of the art symbol draws on Wittgenstein's 'picture theory' understood in terms of 'projections' rather than copies of the world.[252]

The cultural importance of art

In 1957, Langer published a collection of her public lectures on art under the title *Problems of Art*. Following *Philosophy in a New Key* and *Feeling and Form*, Langer had become a much sought-after speaker on the lecture circuit and many invitations came from art or music colleges, societies or professionals in the arts, including dancers. The lectures are lucid statements of her key philosophical themes without the complex technical philosophical underpinnings and can still serve as an excellent introduction to her philosophy of art today. In one of the lectures she addresses the topic of the cultural importance of art.

All cultures, Langer claims, 'begin with the development of personal and social and religious feeling [and the] great instrument of this development is art'.[253] Productive artistic periods formulate 'new ways of feeling' and often announce or initiate some major cultural shift or renewal.[254] Precisely because feelings have forms, so argues Langer, they can be educated:

> Most people are so imbued with the idea that feeling is a formless total organic excitement in human beings as in animals, that the idea of educating feeling, developing its scope and quality, seems odd to them, if not absurd. It is really, I think, at the very heart of personal education.[255]

This, in turn, has important implications for art education and art's role in culture:

> Art education is the education of feeling, and a society that neglects it gives itself up to formless emotion. Bad art is corruption of feeling. This is a large factor in the irrationalism which dictators and demagogues exploit.[256]

Langer identifies three reasons why art education is important. First, art 'makes feeling apparent, objectively given so we may reflect on it and understand it'.[257] Second, existing forms as expressed by art may be used as expressions for actual feelings in the same way that 'language provides forms for sensory experience and factual observation'.[258] And third, art is a way to educate the senses to 'see nature in expressive form'.[259] It teaches how the actual world can be seen as symbolic of feelings and become 'personally significant':[260]

> [T]he artist's eye ... lends expressiveness and emotional import to the world. Wherever art takes a motif from actuality ... it transforms it into a piece of imagination, and imbues its image with artistic vitality. The result is an impregnation of ordinary reality with the significance of created form. This is the *subjectification of nature,* that makes reality itself a symbol of life and feeling.[261]

Langer will return to this idea in her essay 'The Cultural Importance of Art' in 1962 in *Philosophical Sketches*, where she writes that it is the primary function of art 'to objectify feeling so that we can contemplate and understand it'.[262] To make felt reality conceivable and memorable is a product of the 'process of imagination'.[263] In times of cultural change, art formulates new ways of feeling. This makes art education so important, to nurture and train imaginative artists with the skills to create new forms that are capable of formulating new experiences. Feelings, in short, are not formless expressions but structured patterns. It was the striking discovery that art, as the form of feeling, reflected organic form that made Langer turn to study the organic nature of feeling and of mind itself. The fruits of this innovative and far-reaching research resulted in her trilogy *Mind: An Essay on Human Feeling*, the topic of our final chapter.

10

Mind as embodied meaning

It was the discovery that works of art are images of the forms of feeling, and that their expressiveness can rise to the presentation of all aspects of mind and human personality, which led me to [construct] a biological theory of feeling that should logically lead to an adequate concept of mind. ... The fact that expressive form is always organic or 'living' form made the biological foundation of feeling probable.

Langer[1]

Instead of accepting 'mind' as a metaphysically ultimate reality, distinct from the physical reality which subsumes the brain, and asking how the two can 'make liaison', one may hope to describe 'mind' as a phenomenon in terms of the highest physiological processes, especially those which have psychical phases.

Langer[2]

Disconnected data

After two decades of work in logic and semiotics, and another two in philosophy of art and culture, Langer, in her late 60s, embarked on what was to become her final major project: an enquiry into the nature of human mentality, culminating in her trilogy *Mind: An Essay on Human Feeling* (1967, 1971 and 1982). Building on Sheffer's and Wittgenstein's logics of form and the organic symbolic theories of Whitehead and Cassirer, she developed a biologically based, non-dualist theory of mind and consciousness that straddled the sciences and the arts. Drawing on the most recent developments in biology, zoology, ethology, psychology, cognitive studies and neuroscience, Langer's conception of mind entails a radical revision of the then dominant mind–body approaches.

Since Langer's death in 1985, major developments in genetics have transformed the biological sciences. Likewise, new scanning and imaging technology has led to dramatic new research in the neurosciences. Yet, even without the benefit of this advanced research and technology, Langer's insightful philosophical hunches anticipated many developments in the field.[3] As one neuroscientist put it in 2018, 'Langer anticipated where we were going long before many of us knew it, and did so with lucid style, philosophical insight, and amazing grace.'[4]

Langer's main contribution to the neurosciences was not the discovery of more data or facts but a new hermeneutical framework. As Cassirer had put it once in relation to understanding human culture,

> Our technical instruments for observation and experimentation have been immensely improved, and our analyses have become sharper and more penetrating. We appear, nevertheless, not yet to have found a method for the mastery and organization of this material. When compared with our own abundance the past may seem very poor. But our wealth of facts is not necessarily a wealth of thoughts. Unless we succeed in finding a clue of Ariadne to lead us out this labyrinth, we can have no real insight into the general character of human culture; we shall remain lost in *a mass of disconnected and disintegrated data* which seem to lack all conceptual unity. [my italics][5]

For Langer, the special sciences do not arise from putative objective facts rooted in neutral observation but are always already rooted in a particular way of seeing the world:

> The sciences are really born of philosophy; they do not simply arise from controlled observation when philosophy is finally slain and cleared away to permit their growth. They are born under quite special conditions – when their key concepts reach a degree of abstraction and precision which make them adequate to the demands of exact, powerful, and microscopically analytic thinking. Philosophy is the formulation and logical exploration of concepts.[6]

While always tentative and modest, philosophy endeavours, in the words of Whitehead, 'to frame a coherent, logical, necessary system of general ideas in terms of which every element of our experience can be interpreted'.[7] Or as Langer wrote in the introduction to *Mind*,

> The serious philosophical need of our day is a conceptual structure that may be expanded simply by modification (not metaphorical extension) of definitions in literally meant scientific terms. ... To construct such concepts is, I believe, the task of professional philosophers; it is too large to be done by other intellectual workers on a basis of incidental insights reflected on in leisure hours. It requires familiarity with philosophical ideas, both general and technical readings in many fields, and logical training to the point of a *liberated logical imagination*; competences which may be demanded of philosophers, but hardly of anyone else. [my italics][8]

Moreover, these 'elements of our experience' are not isolated sense-data merely in need of a different ordering. In Whitehead's words,

> The notion of the complete self-sufficiency of any item of finite knowledge is the fundamental error of dogmatism. Every such item derives its truth, and its

very meaning, from its unanalysed relevance to the background which is the unbounded Universe. Not even the simplest notion of arithmetic escapes this inescapable condition for existence. Every scrap of our knowledge derives its meaning from the fact that we are factors in the universe, and are dependent on the universe for every detail of our experience. ... There is no entity which enjoys an isolated self-sufficiency of existence.[9]

Whitehead's acceptance of the contextual and relative nature of sense-data contrasted sharply with Russell's desire for clarity and certainty reflected in his atomistic view. It had also led to their growing apart following the first edition of the *Principia Mathematica*. A disappointed Russell wrote in his memoirs,

It was Whitehead who was the serpent in this [mathematical] paradise of Mediterranean clarity. He said to me once: 'You think the world is what it looks like in fine weather at noon day; I think it is what it seems like in the early morning when one first wakes from deep sleep.' I thought this remark horrid, but could not see how to prove that my bias was any better than his.[10]

Russell had tried to enlist Wittgenstein, who he thought shared his atomistic view, to replace Whitehead as co-author for the second edition, but Wittgenstein was much closer to Whitehead's view than to Russell's and wrote the *Tractatus* instead. Whitehead's – and Langer's – view of knowledge is that of a gradual process in which forms and patterns emerge, *Gestalt*-like, out of an undefined background. Starting with vague feelings and hunches the world gradually gains a clearer – or different – focus depending on interest and need. This process is not only an account of the way we gain scientific knowledge; it is an account of the process of perception and consciousness itself. In a striking comment on the way her own mind works, expressed in an interview for the *New York Times*, Langer reflects,

I have always had ... a great freedom with abstractions. I find logic and mathematics easy – but not visual mathematics. For instance, I always have to translate in my mind all geometry or visual constructions into algebra. What really was decisive for me, though, was 10 years' study of symbolic logic. That taught me how to hold many ideas simultaneously in my mind. I can entertain a proposition without having to say that I do or don't believe it. One plays with many possible forms at once. It's the gestalt principle, as for example, when one looks at a wallpaper that has a particular geometric pattern and sees alternative configurations, triangles, that is, jumping suddenly to form larger triangles, stars or parallelograms. The ideas with which I work are analogous to such an ambiguous pattern. To be able to deal in this manner with abstract ideas is essential when one is trying to break through the historical limitations of theory.[11]

When reading her later work, it is important to keep these reflections in mind as the wealth of empirical details sometimes make it difficult to keep sight of the larger picture. As Arthur Danto put it in the foreword of the abridged version of *Mind*,

> Her sense of philosophical responsibility required Susanne Langer, as she undertook to chart the entire domain bounded by the human body and by human culture, to master all the relevant sciences over this immense territory. … [This] supporting material obscures the philosophical architecture, like a dense scaffolding, and renders inaccessible to philosophical scrutiny one of the most audacious philosophical visions of recent times.[12]

It is the aim of this final chapter to illuminate the philosophical architecture.

Reasoning and feeling

A key element in Langer's philosophy of mind and consciousness was her early recognition of the importance of the role of feeling and affect. Rather than opposing feeling and reason, Langer sees them as integrally connected and interdependent. More radically even, Langer locates feeling at the very centre of human mentality out of which reason evolves. As she describes the purpose of *Mind: An Essay on Human Feeling*,

> As soon as feeling is regarded as a phase of a physiological process instead of a product (perhaps a by-product) of it, a new entity metaphysically different from it, the paradox of the physical and psychical disappears: for the thesis I hope to substantiate here is that the entire psychological field – including human conception, responsible action, rationality, knowledge – is a vast and branching development of feeling.[13]

Anticipating scholars such as neuroscientist Antonio Damasio, biologist Gerald Edelman and cognitive linguists George Lakoff and Mark Johnson, Langer locates reason in the organism's affective engagement with the world.[14] Feeling, in turn, is a form of embodied cognition.[15]

Or, to put that more accurately, embodied cognition, as well as language, is ultimately rooted in feeling. As Margaret Browning described Langer's contribution to, for instance, psychoanalysis,

> [Langer's] conceptualization of the human mind can provide psychoanalysts with a unique framework with which to theoretically combine interpretive and biological approaches to their work. Langer's earlier work in the philosophy of symbols directs her investigation into the biological sciences along the lines of sentience and imagination, which in turn become the cornerstones of her theory of mind. Langer's understanding of the continuing transformation of affect into language is a decisive contribution yet to be built upon by others.[16]

Or as Arthur Danto put it in a review of *Mind*, 'Merely to have recognized [the mind's] character, let alone carried its analysis so systematically far, has been to make as immense and transformative a contribution to philosophy as I can imagine.'[17]

Langer has a particular interest in the implications of the idea of the embodied mind for philosophical anthropology. As explained earlier, Langer distinguishes humans from other animals by the human mind's capacity for symbolic transformation. This capacity is rooted in a uniquely human need. This need is not, as is most commonly thought, a need for shelter, food and sex in the ongoing struggle for survival but the need for meaning – that is, the need to make sense of the world. As Browning puts it,

> Neither Damasio nor Edelman appreciates the radical shift in consciousness that accompanies the advent of symbolic thinking. They do not understand that the project of symbolic thinking is to make the world *explicitly meaningful*, beyond whatever advantages we gain for survival by conceptualizing the world and our place in it.[18]

Langer's study of the mind as a study of embodied meaning emerged from her studies of art.[19] Works of art as living forms can illuminate the workings of the mind as an organic process. Since art creates a form, or image, of the mind, it can serve as a map for representing the elusive flow of feeling and consciousness that cannot be articulated in discursive language. For philosopher of music education Bennett Reimer, this attempt to 'extrapolate a science of psychology from the facts of artistic/aesthetic functioning was, and remains, unprecedented in the history of thought'.[20]

Throughout her work, Langer sought to explain the mind with a focus on 'the meaning of meaning'. In her early work she focused her attention on the semantic and semiotic aspects of signs and symbols, while in her middle period she explored the non-discursive character of meaning as exemplified in art. In her latest work she turns to the biological and neurological basis of meaning in a wide-ranging study of mind and feeling. Throughout these periods there is a strong continuity of enquiry as she herself makes clear in various prefaces to her books. Her trilogy *Mind* thus builds on her previous writings, and she introduces it with an important question:

> [O]ne fundamental question was not answered – indeed, scarcely raised – in *Feeling and Form*: Why must artistic form, to be expressive of feeling, always be so-called 'living form'? That it must be was noted and discussed there in an early chapter; also that such 'organic' or 'living' form is a semblance, since works of art are not actually vital organisms. By why is that semblance necessary? Aristotle already declared that organic form was the most important feature of any composition ... He also observed that it need only seem, not actually be, life-like. But why?[21]

And her answer is this:

> It was the discovery that works of art are images of the forms of feeling, and that their expressiveness can rise to the presentation of all aspects of mind and human personality, which led me to the present undertaking of constructing a biological theory of feeling that should logically lead to an adequate concept of mind, with all that the possession of mind implies.[22]

More specifically,

> The fact that expressive form is always organic or 'living' form made the biological foundation of feeling probable. In the artist's projection, feeling is a heightened form of life; so any work expressing felt tensions, rhythms and activities expresses their unfelt substructure of vital processes, which is the whole of life. If vitality and feeling are conceived in this way there is no sharp break, let alone metaphysical gap, between physical and mental realities, yet there are thresholds where mentality begins, and especially where human mentality transcends the animal level, and mind, *sensu stricto*, emerges.[23]

Langer's argument that the living *form* of art makes 'the biological *foundation* of feeling probable' may, at first, seem problematic. As we saw in the previous chapter, she had initially argued that, if feeling is organic, and if art is the form of feeling, then art has organic form. In her own words,

> If feeling is a culmination of vital process, any articulated image of it must have the semblance of that vital process, rising from deep, general organic activities to intense and concerted acts, such as we perceive directly in their psychical phases as impacts or felt actions.[24]

But in the passage quoted earlier she turns this around and now argues that, if art has organic form, and if feeling is 'imaged' in art, then feeling *itself* is organic. In other words, apart from the argument seeming circular, she no longer seems to make a distinction between entities that have organic *form* and entities that *are* organic. She may even appear to be guilty of what Whitehead had called the 'fallacy of misplaced concreteness', that is, to mistake the abstract – the living form – for the concrete – organic life.[25] But that is to misunderstand her notion of image in art. An image is different from a model. An image shows how something appears; a model shows how something works. As she explains,

> The art symbol … sets forth in symbolic projection how vital and emotional and intellectual tensions appear, i.e. how they feel. It is this image that gets lost in our psychological laboratories, where models from non-biological sciences and especially from intriguing machinery have taken the field, and permit us to analyse and understand many processes, yet lead us to lose sight of what phenomena we are trying to analyse and understand.
>
> Here the image of feeling created by artists … serves to hold the reality itself for our labile and volatile memory, as a touchstone to test the scope of our intellectual constructions. And once a measure of adequacy is set up for theories, models of biological processes may be taken from anywhere – billiard balls, crystal formations, hydraulics, or small-current engineering. A philosophy of life guided by the vital image created by artists (all true artists, not only the great and celebrated ones) does not lead one to deprecate physical mechanisms, but to seek more and more of them as the subtlety of the phenomenon increases. The better

one knows the forms of feeling the more there is to account for in the literal, sober terms of biological thinking, and the bolder such thinking tends to become.[26]

In the artist's *projection*, Langer says, 'feeling is a heightened form of life'.[27] Because living form in art is expressed as a continuum between *unfelt* vital processes and *felt* emotional tensions, it suggested to her the *idea* that feelings themselves may be composed of a similar continuum. Yet, this would still need to be argued separately and independently – as she ventured to do in *Mind*.

This interpretation can be supported by the fact that, long before her 'discovery that works of art are images of the forms of feeling', she already had a hunch that mental activity was biologically based. As we pointed out in an earlier chapter, this is clear from a comment in the 1941 preface to the *first* edition of *Philosophy in a New Key*:

> We need not assume the presence of a transcendental 'human spirit', if we recognize … the function of *symbolic transformation* as a natural activity, a high form of nervous response, characteristic of man among the animals.[28]

Her 'discovery' merely confirmed that initial hunch and gave her the impetus to find an independent route to establish the biological basis of human mentality. Her exploration of art may well have planted a seed for the idea, but it did not provide the empirical evidence.

Although Langer's preface to *Philosophy in a New Key* shows that she assumed a biological basis of the symbolic mind, this was not foregrounded until much later. As Bennett Reimer observes,

> It is obvious in hindsight that she glimpsed from the start the [biological] theory of mind she was later able to propound, in that evidence abounds that she was entertaining later ideas at earlier stages. But those who were reading Langer were able to do so only in light of what she was then saying – not with the foresight (such as was indwelling in her) that her understanding of art was based on something reaching to the roots of human mentality.[29]

Philosophy and psychology

One of the pressing philosophical questions in Langer's time was, and still now is, whether the study of the mind or 'psyche', 'soul', 'consciousness' or 'feeling' – the terminology itself being part of the debate – should be studied by the natural sciences or by the 'human sciences' or 'humanities'. Philosopher and neurobiologist Owen Flanagan points out that, in the late 1880s and 1890s, 'William James had switched his Harvard appointment several times between medicine, psychology, and philosophy before settling in the philosophy department for the remainder of his career'.[30] Moreover, James, as well as Mary Calkins and John Dewey, held simultaneous presidencies of both the American Philosophical Association and the American Psychological Association.[31] Langer's lack of references to either James or Dewey remains a source of puzzlement since, as Innis has also pointed out in his monograph, there are numerous overlaps between Langer and the pragmatist tradition, not least in the way they combine philosophical studies with empirical enquiry. Felicia Kruse shows how Langer often misrepresents Dewey's views by suggesting that he reduces human experience, including aesthetic experience, to animal drives and needs. The only reason to explain her cursory dismissal of Dewey's philosophy is that she did not recognize in him – and, for that matter, James – a version of the 'symbolic turn'.[32]

By the time Langer wrote *Mind*, the separation between philosophy and psychology had been firmly established.[33] Psychology had been keen to prove itself as a reputable empirical science by banning all speculative theories about the soul, the inner life or subjective feeling. As Langer describes it,

> The consensus of social scientists, especially in America, is that such a metaphysical problem as the existence of something called 'feeling', 'consciousness', or 'subjective experience' lies outside the realm of factual description which is the realm of science, and that consequently one may hold any philosophical opinion on such matters without the least effect on one's scientific investigations and findings.[34]

The only respectable method in psychology in Langer's time was scientific behaviourism. This method either ignored the existence of internal experience or relegated it to metaphysics by which, as Langer puts it, 'they understand (or rather, misunderstand) some kind of fanciful natural history deduced from the postulates of traditional ethics and religion'.[35] Because of behaviourism's dominant role in psychology, sociology and other related fields of study, these studies were often referred to as 'the behavioural sciences'.[36] Yet, as she points out, the term is not simply descriptive but directive: it expresses a methodology that implies 'an accepted belief about the relation of metaphysics to those sciences, if not about metaphysics itself'.[37]

Langer rejected the central working concepts of behaviourism for human mentality based on 'stimulus' and 'response'. These concepts, so she argued, were derived from experiments on laboratory animals on the mistaken assumption that they could be stretched and generalized to cover the psychological dimension of human experience. For her, these terms quickly decline in usefulness beyond their artificial laboratory context.[38] Moreover, although stimuli and responses can be observed and recorded, they do not furnish any principles of analysis for the relations between different observed events. Psychology, according to Langer, does not have a sufficiently strong conceptual apparatus to deal with 'its own essential subject matter – mental phenomena'.[39]

> Among all the facts with which psychologists deal, the one they seem least able to handle is the fact that we feel our own activity and the impingements of the world around us. The metaphysical status of 'feelings', 'contents of consciousness', 'subjectivity', or of the private aspects of experience generally, has been an asses' bridge to philosophers ever since Descartes treated *res extensa* and *res cogitans* as irreducible and incommensurable substances.[40]

It is this ingrained Cartesian dichotomy that Langer's bio-symbolic philosophy of mind sets out to challenge.

Meaning as process

Langer's trilogy *Mind: An Essay on Human Feeling* (1967, 1971 and 1982) was written over a period of two decades and is divided into six parts of unequal length. Volume I has three parts: Part One, 'Problems and Principles', sets out the problem by means of exposing the impotence of contemporary science to explain feeling; Part Two, 'The Import of Art', returns to themes dealt with in *Feeling and Form* and argues that the form of feeling as projected and objectified in works of art can, as a virtual image, serve as a basis for the study of human feeling; Part Three, 'Natura Naturans', deals with the origins of life as the beginning of the evolutionary process which will eventually lead to the emergence of feeling and mind. Volume II contains just Part Four, 'The Great Shift', exploring the differences between human and animal behaviour and mentality. Volume III contains the final two parts: Part Five, 'The Moral Structure', considers the many different cultural forms of symbolic functioning as manifested in myth, art and religion, as well as ethics, societal structures and politics; Part Six, finally, entitled 'The Open Ambient', consists of only twenty pages containing some loose reflections on the growing role of mathematics in physics, physico-chemistry and electro-biochemistry. Since the topic of art in Parts One and Two has been largely addressed in the previous chapter and since Parts Five and Six can be considered as 'applications' of her central theory, I will, in this chapter, focus particularly on Parts Three and Four dealing, respectively, with the origins of life and the difference between humans and other animals.[41] Langer discusses these topics in terms of three phases: 'the organic phase', 'the psychical phase' and 'the symbolic phase'.

What is clear from all these chapters is that feeling and meaning are not nouns but verbs, not substances but processes. This is Langer's paradigm-shifting contribution to the philosophy of mind as embodied meaning.

Phases of life

The organic phase

One of the central questions raised in *Mind* is how to account for the mind's emergence within the larger evolution of life from inorganic to organic, plants to animals and animals to humans. Langer observes that, although there is no disagreement about 'life' being the main object of biology, there is much disagreement about what that concept means. For Langer herself, there is no absolute dividing line between living and non-living entities. Drawing on Austrian biologist Ludwig von Bertalanffy's studies, she points out that some viruses or physiochemical element can only live in other organisms but not on their own, and that some non-living matter such as hair, nails or egg shells are part of an organism as a living whole.[42] In view of that, Langer argues, any definition of the difference between a non-organic and an organic phase in the course of evolution is ultimately pragmatic, a question of what does and doesn't fit within an overall theory.[43] Most attempts to understand living entities so far have been either in terms of chemical processes or mechanistic physics. Since these have failed, so Langer claims, a new framework is called for. For her, this framework is rooted in the biological notion of 'act'.

Acts

Definitions of life, Langer says, are based on certain 'peaks of activity which are centres of recognizable phases'.[44] Following Whitehead, in the context of life, Langer refers to these phases as 'acts'. Acts are the smallest biological units, the equivalent of molecules and atoms in physics. It can be used for natural life at all levels of simplicity and complexity. The act form consists of a distinguishable pattern described by Langer in terms of the following: an inception, a development containing a rise, an acceleration and an intensification, a consummation, a slowing down, a termination and a cadence.[45] Although this form is typical for living entities, it can also be found in other phenomena including, as we have seen, the phenomenon of music. Acts typically subsume other acts, or span other acts which continue after their own consummation.[46] The higher the organism, the more complex the act relations. To make 'act' a proper working concept, it should be freed from its tacit value connotations with intentional, rational or conscious human acts. Genuine biological acts are any movements that are characterized by an initial charge of energy which needs to be spent, whether voluntary or involuntary. Once the energy is spent, any course of action can be modified in numerous directions, by inhibition, interruption, re-enforcement and so on.

The main advantage of the act concept for Langer is that it allows for an empirically based scientific description of biological phenomena without recourse to causal terminology as used in physics. The 'causality' of living entities, whether in cell division or animal behaviour, cannot be interpreted in physical terms of transposition of matter in space or transmission of motion and heat from one body to another. While an external event or 'stimulus' can initiate a behavioural act in an organism, the action that is 'triggered' by the stimulus does not draw its energy directly from the stimulus but from intra-organic chemical processes. Hence, the understanding of the complex relation between the external stimulus and the subsequent response or behaviour in the organism cannot be determined causally but needs to be understood in terms of *process*, from its build-up of tension and energy through to its consummation and cadence.

Origins of life

The first phase, or 'impulse', is an integral part of the act itself. Langer defines it as a 'discharge of energy' which emerges from a fluid situation containing an indeterminable combination of 'effective' and 'ineffective' variables.[47] For Langer, this process may also shed new interpretative light on biogenesis. The origin of life, so she argues, cannot be explained merely in terms of a series of heightened chemical reactions, as was suggested by biochemists Alexander Oparin and Stanley Miller, but is the result of very particular patterns of interchanges between the evolving organism and its environment.[48] They consist of repetitive natural patterns, such as the beat of the waves on a rock, or the flow of a waterfall, which over time carves out a cavity or shape or what Langer calls a 'matrix'. A matrix gradually takes on a permanent shape regulating the movements of the ongoing flux.[49] Over time this can turn into a self-contained ecosystem that can sustain itself and even propagate:

> The beginning of the life process ... certainly appears to all scientific inquirers as a formation of patterned activities ... until they constitute a matrix in which their own form becomes modified or even entirely blurred, so it can only be found again by analytic abstraction. Such living matrixes may have various degrees of coherence and persistence; but they are systems, self-sustaining and ... self-propagating, wherein every event is prepared by progressively changing conditions of the integral whole. Every distinguishable change, therefore, arises out of the matrix, and emerges as an act of an agent; for such a vital matrix is an agent.[50]

These 'proto-acts', Langer suggests, belong to both chemistry and biology and are the first foreshadowing of genuine life. They exhibit 'a *form of motion*, or a *dynamic form*'.[51] The transition from chemical activity to life is the result of the new impact of the environment – the matrix – on the chemical activity, thereby germinating *qualitative* differences in the proto-organic patterns. The origin and advance of life, so Langer suggests, is 'a fabric of burgeoning acts, in literally billions of pressive relations which automatically adjust the elements of that incredibly complex mechanism to each other, so that it exhibits itself as an inscrutable matrix of "living matter"'.[52] A key element in this account of the evolution of life is the assumption that changes in scale or degree can become changes of kind and of character. For instance, properties of large molecules as described in terms of classical mechanics are qualitatively different from the properties of their chemical subgroups, which are described in terms of quantum mechanics. Similarly, the movement of small water waves can be best explained by means of the principle of surface tension, whereas the movement of large waves is best understood with the help of the principle of gravity.[53] This shows that a change in quantitative scale and complexity can lead to a change in qualitative properties. There is thus no '*saltus naturae*' from inorganic to organic nature, but a gradual, evolutionary 'emergence'.

Motivation and ambient

Although there are many mechanical or causal relations in the realm of life, the more important relation to understand life's dynamic is that called 'motivation'. Motivation, for Langer, is not 'moral intention' or 'inner drive'. It is the neurogenic impulse which leads an organism, whether human or animal, to do seemingly undirected activities for the sake of exploring its environment. This exploratory, ostensibly playful behaviour cannot be explained merely in terms of a stimulus response or as an instinctive drive geared towards preservation or food. Instead, so argues Langer, it is the natural outcome of an intra-organic explorative motivation which is not aimed at anything in particular and does not have any particular goal in mind. Even so, this 'aimless' behaviour has an effect on its environment and on itself. The organism's locomotion and body movements leave traces and trails in their environment which, in turn, can effect other changes. When an organism reacts to an external stimulus, it can itself cause new stimuli as a result of its own actions and reactions.[54]

Although an organism is constantly affected by its ever-changing physical environment, whether climate or tidal fluctuations, it is never entirely determined by it. Drawing on Jacob von Uexküll's notion of 'Umwelt', Langer holds that different organisms in the same environment have very different environmental situations or 'ambient worlds'. The world of extra-organic events is not the same for a mosquito, a snake and a cat.[55] The same external conditions and influences have different values for different organisms. Their peripheral organs receive or block different stimuli. Whereas some external events remain the same and stop at peripheral contact, others, such as oxygen, food, warmth or light, or social and cultural influences, enter the organism itself and become part of it. External stimuli effect changes to the organism that influence its reaction and response and can, over time, change the organism itself. As Langer describes it,

> A response ... is an act , arising from a situation that reflects a general, accumulated condition of the organism. The condition stems from acts long past that still affect all emerging situations through their (now completely integrated) traces in the matrix of activities, the organism itself. They have continued themselves in its special form, its disposition.[56]

This applies to physical influences – Langer quotes many examples from chemistry and micro-biology – but also to psychological, social or cultural influences, such as when long-term, gradually building up abuse can result in sudden aggression. Such responses cannot easily be explained in terms of a simple stimulus-response model. For Langer, an organism's actions and behaviour are the result of both 'nature' and 'nurture', of genetic make-up and environmental and cultural influences. Because coded cells have native impulses which can develop in numerous different ways, some seeds can lay waiting for a hundred years till the conditions are right for them to develop their own potential, whereas others never will. In such a waiting state, 'some microscopic lives appear to have remained unbroken for millions of years, and have resumed their rhythms and vial impulses when a new ambient, fit to implement their actualization, was given again'.[57]

In higher nervous systems, a complete act can be represented in genetically coded form, merely awaiting an adequate trigger, either internal or external. The motivated organism and its ambient are thus in a constant reciprocal and interdependent relation.

It is in the course of explaining this dynamic, reciprocal relation that Langer coins the new term 'pression'. Pression is 'the class of relations which obtain between situations and acts'.[58] As the term can be preceded by a large variety of prefixes such as 'im-', 'ex-', 'com-', 're-', 'op-', 'sup-' and so on, it is a flexible concept which can refer to all kinds of different relations between situations and acts. On Langer's view, an organism defines its own ambient in distinction from the environment it shares with other creatures. This ambient is the result of a unique blend of 'pressive' forces that interact with this particular organism. The most essential kind of pression is 'self-expression', which is an organism's impulse to actualization and individuation.[59]

Individuation and involvement

Individuation is the result of a long process of evolutionary differentiation beginning with simple acts such as cytological differentiation and parturition to the development of the mind and individual personality. The most primitive one, Langer suggests, was 'the isolation of a protoplasmic unit by a completely surrounding membrane, selectively penetrable under osmotic pressure'.[60] Individuation is a condition for the emergence of living creatures, even though these might not even have been as complex as the simplest living cell today.

In most vital phenomena, individuation operates in conjunction with its reverse: 'involvement'. Examples of the latter are mutual control of cells in a tissue and of tissues in a body, bisexual reproduction and, on a larger scale, herds, communal nests and hives, processes of human communication and human society.[61] Because most cells cannot live on their own, they need to integrate their functions into self-contained, stable and vitally active systems. This increased involvement leads to rhythmic cycles, which in turn result in the formation of a self-sustaining metabolism characteristic of any biological mechanism. For Langer, rhythmic concatenation 'is what really holds an organism together from moment to moment'.[62] This is particularly evident in the dynamic equilibrium of the bodies of human and non-human animals where 'the larger rhythms that rise and fall with our sleeping and waking, moving and eating, are superimposed on the myriad microscopic activities and unconscious repetitive pulses that compose the organic matrix'.[63] Individuation and involvement are the conditions for sensibility and feeling.

The psychical phase

Sensibility and feeling are dependent on the development of sensory cells in the peripheral surface of an organism. The peripheral surface, a membrane or skin, enables sensory acts to be felt. The skin is the most adaptable sense organ. It enables an organism's first behavioural acts that impact on its surroundings. This applies especially for mobile creatures who can enter new environments. The specialized sense organs of eyes and ears, by contrast, enable events in the world outside the skin to influence events inside it without touching or penetrating its barriers or surroundings. Whereas most sensations occur without the organism's awareness, repeated sensory neuron patterns may enter what Langer calls a 'psychical phase'. This happens when 'a creature's behavioral actions fall under the influence of its felt encounters and become organized to anticipate repetitions of such episodes'.[64] At that stage, behaviour 'comes to be guided and developed by feeling, which at this level had best be termed "awareness"'.[65] Such an awareness or 'presentation' may be very momentary and disappear as soon as the stimulation goes. As she explains,

> Between stimulations there may be no feeling at all; even the response may not be a felt act, but a disappearance of feeling, as the concerted excitation subsides and falls below the threshold of psychical presentation. Such considerations [suggest] that the first felt acts were sensory.[66]

Feeling, for Langer, is not the same as 'feelings' or 'emotions' such as joy, anger or sadness. It is both more subtle and more expansive:

> I am using the word 'feeling' not in the arbitrarily limited sense of 'pleasure or displeasure' to which psychologists have often restricted it, but on the contrary in its widest possible sense, i.e., to designate *anything that may be felt*. In this sense it includes both sensation and emotion – the felt responses of our sense organs to the environment, … and of the organism as a whole to its situation as a whole, the so-called 'emotive feelings.'[67]

It is important to remember that feeling, for Langer, is not a noun but a verb. What she tries to convey in the above passage is that the intentional objects of feeling are not merely the garden variety of emotions but the often much subtler feelings as well as 'bodily' feelings such as a headache, temperature, balance, a desire, a fleeting thought – in short, '*anything that may be felt*'. That explains why, for Langer, the entire psychological field is 'a vast and branching development of feeling.'[68]

Impact and action

Feeling, for Langer, can be divided into two modes of feeling corresponding to the two main sets of fibres in the central nervous system, the sensor and the motor neurons. The first modes are *felt as impact* while the second are *felt as autogenic action*.[69] The first mode is experienced as 'objective', as coming from outside: 'Sensations arise from within the body, too, but more typically the sources of sensation are peripheral; and they always carry, however vaguely, some indication of an impingement met and dealt with.'[70] The second mode of feeling is experienced as 'subjective', as coming from within. Although this mode of feeling encompasses 'emotions', they are less intense, more foundational and more elusive:

> They are felt to arise without the attack of a sensory impact, and to proceed from within us toward their termination in expression, which may be muscular motion, or the forming of an image apparent in the space between our eyes and their focus point, or an act of tonal imagination proceeding still more vaguely toward the outside world.[71]

While 'objective' feeling is often felt as acute, 'subjective' feeling is felt as emerging gradually. The interplay of feelings felt as coming 'from outside' and those felt as coming 'from within' forms the foundation of all human thinking and behaviour.

Feeling as intra-organic

Feeling, for Langer, is thus not a disembodied state of mind but a phase in the organism's sensuous and embodied engagement with its environment. It is the phase where sensations are being felt.

> We feel warmth, pinprick, ache, effort, and relaxation; vision is the way the optic apparatus feels the impingements of light, and hearing is the way the auditory structures feel sound waves; we feel bodily weakness or high tonus, and we feel expectation, frustration, yearning, fear, satisfaction.[72]

Langer compares this dynamic with the physical changes undergone by physical objects under different physical circumstances, such as when iron is being heated:

> Ordinarily we know things in different phases as 'the same' – ice, water and steam, for instance – but sometimes a very distinctive phase seems like a product. When iron is heated to a critical degree it becomes red; yet its redness is not a new entity which must have gone somewhere else when it is no longer in the iron. It was a phase of the iron itself, at high temperature. Heat is not a thing, but an agitation, measurable in degrees, not amounts, and when the iron is no longer hot there will be comparable degrees of heat, or of some equivalent process or sum total of processes, outside the iron. But the redness simply disappears; it was a phase of the heated iron.[73]

In the same way that heat and redness can increase and fade in terms of degrees, so can feeling. It may be sharp and acute or vague and fleeting:

> It may develop suddenly, with great distinctness of quality, location and value-character, for instance, in response to a painful stimulus; or similarly, only with less precise location in the organism, like a shock of terror; or a deeply engendered process may go gradually, perhaps barely, into a psychical phase of vague awareness – come and gone – a sense of weariness or a fleeting emotive moment.[74]

Many organic processes such as the dynamic rounds of metabolism, digestion, circulation and endocrine action are normally not felt. Only those organic activities that rise at times above a certain limen of nervous intensity enter into a psychical phase. This is the 'phase of being felt'.[75] Whatever their intensity or length of duration, feeling forms part of the intra-organic process as *a mode of appearance*. It is, however, 'an appearance which organic functions have only for the organism in which they occur, if they have it at all'.[76] Likewise,

> The phenomenon usually described as 'a feeling' is really that an organism feels something, i.e., something is felt. What is felt is a process, perhaps a large complex of processes, within the organism. ... A phase is a mode of appearance, and not an added factor.[77]

Langer's conception of intra-organic feeling is arguably one of her most original insights but also one of the most difficult to fully grasp. Philosopher Peter Bertocci, for one, raises the following questions: 'Why can we unify such different processes as emotion, sensing, responsibility, and reason by reference to "being felt"?'[78] Moreover,

> If there are no feelings without intra-organic processes of a certain kind, and if these processes, as felt, are in a certain phase, does the 'being felt' 'appear' and 'go' without modifying the processes? ... What difference does 'being felt' (or mentality) make to the intra-organic processes to which it is phasal or from which it 'emerges' as phasal?[79]

Some of the ambiguities attached to Langer's formulations are semantic. As mentioned already, Langer does not use the term 'feeling' as a noun but as a verb or, more precisely, a 'verbal noun'. For her, 'to feel is to do something, not to have something'.[80] It is a transitive verb where the object 'something' can, on Langer's view, designate *anything that can be felt*', whether inside or outside the body. Even so, 'what is felt is always action in an organism' even if some of it is felt as an encounter.[81] One way to explain Langer's position is by comparison with a more recent view as developed by neuroscientist Antonio Damasio.

Antonio Damasio and emotions

Like Langer, Damasio stresses the central role of feeling for human mentality and consciousness.[82] Drawing on his own clinical experience and laboratory research, Damasio's book *Descartes' Error: Emotion, Reason, and the Human Brain* (1994) comes to very similar conclusions as Langer about the mind. He stresses, for example, the significance of the outer membrane as the sensor of external signals, an understanding of mental images in terms of neural firing patterns, the idea that mental images are maps or representations of sensations, and the idea that felt experience is the basis of consciousness as such. In his subsequent book *The Feeling of What Happens: Body and Emotion in the Making of Consciousness* (1999), Damasio identifies three stages of feeling that lead to consciousness as it unfolds as a biological process: first, *a state of emotion* which consists of the organism's *first-order* sensorimotor mapping of its own body as triggered by the outside world (this can be compared with Langer's feeling as impact); second, a *state of feeling*, which involves the emergence of repeated *neural patterns* creating unconscious *second-order* mental images as representations of these first-order encounters (this can be compared with Langer's feelings as autogenic action); third, *a state of feeling made conscious*, also referred to as 'a feeling of feeling', where the organism becomes aware of the first- and second-order modes of feeling and the connection between them (this can be compared with Langer's interplay of the two modes of feeling as the basis for human action and behaviour, as well as, in her case, symbolization).[83] Like Langer, Damasio struggles to find the right terminology for what he is trying to explain. Referring to the first two stages of feeling that are not conscious, he writes, 'Someone may suggest that perhaps we should have another word for "feelings that are not conscious", but there isn't one. The closest alternative is to explain what we mean."[84] Langer would have concurred.

Before either Langer or Damasio, it was William James who had sought to formulate the relation between feeling and consciousness as rooted in the body. As he wrote in 1884,

> Our natural way of thinking about ... standard emotions is that the mental perception of some fact excites the mental affection called the emotion, and that this latter state of mind gives rise to the bodily expression. My thesis on the contrary is that *the bodily changes follow directly the perception of the exciting fact, and that our feeling of the same changes as they occur is the emotion.*[85]

When James searched for a generic term to refer to all mental states, he rejected the term 'feeling' on account of the negative connotations it had in his time and settled instead on 'thinking'.[86] Langer, by contrast, chose 'feeling' over both 'thinking' and 'consciousness' as the first was too close to discursive reason and the second too close to the term 'realm of consciousness' understood in terms of a 'mental substance'. For that same reason she rejects Freud's term 'the unconscious'. Both are, for her, deceptive figures of speech since 'there is no "realm" or "system" of consciousness [or the unconscious] which contains "ideas" in the sense of Locke and his successors'.[87] These problems, according to her, could all be avoided if feeling was seen not as a substance but as a phase in a process:

> If one conceives the phenomenon of being felt as a phase of vital processes, in which the living tissue (probably the nerve or a neuronal assembly) feels its activity, the problem ... of how the nerve impulse can be 'converted' into thought and thought into nerve impulse ... becomes a different sort of problem. The question is not one of how a physical process can be transformed into something non-physical in a physical system, but how the phase of being felt is attained, and how the process may pass into unfelt phases again, and furthermore how an organic process in 'psychical phases' may induce others which are unfelt.[88]

Yet, as we have seen, the main influence on Langer's notion of feeling was not James but Whitehead.

Whitehead and feelings

As we saw earlier, in response to Descartes's 'disastrous separation of body and mind', Whitehead developed a philosophy of organism around different forms of feeling ranging from 'physical' and 'imaginative' to 'conceptual' and 'propositional'.[89] Physical feeling, on Whitehead's terms, is called 'causal' feeling as it is the effect of an external 'cause' or datum.[90] More broadly, a feeling is 'the appropriation of some element in the universe to be components in the real internal constitution of its subject. The elements are the initial data; they are what the feeling feels'.[91] Sense-data, for Whitehead, are not isolated sense-impressions but elements in a relation between a percipient and the world. As he had put it in *Symbolism*, 'We do not perceive disembodied colour or disembodied extensiveness: we perceive *the wall's* colour and extensiveness. ... I call this type of experience "presentational immediacy".'[92] Whitehead's two basic modes of perception, that is, 'causal efficacy' and 'presentational immediacy', can be seen reflected in Langer's two modes of feeling, that is, felt as causal impact or felt as autogenic action.[93] Most importantly, though, and unlike Damasio's neuroscience, Whitehead's organic philosophy involves a concept of the mind as a symbolic transformer. His two modes of perception create a dynamic and organic 'symbolic reference', in which there is a 'transition from the symbol to the meaning'.[94] This is the basis for human mentality and consciousness. Indeed, for Whitehead, consciousness arises when 'a synthetic feeling integrates physical and conceptual feelings'.[95] For Langer, too, symbolic consciousness is an integral component of her biological philosophy of mind. Significantly, symbolic functioning marks the difference between human and animal mentality.

The symbolic phase

If feeling is the mark of all (human and non-human) animal mentality, symbolization is the mark of all *human* mentality. As we have seen in our discussion of Langer's logic of signs and symbols, symbolization is the key to human expression and freedom. It enables humans to reflect on their conditions and circumstances and to *act upon* rather than merely *react* to them. This is the ground of and condition for human responsibility. Whereas animals react to the world in terms of signs and symptoms, humans interpret the world by means of symbols. Unlike involuntary signs and symptoms, symbols are intentional articulations of human experiences. As Langer puts it in *Philosophy in a New Key*, 'Between the clearest animal call of love or warning or anger, and a man's least, trivial *word* [or symbol in general], there lies a whole day of Creation – or in modern phrase, a whole chapter of evolution'.[96] In the world of human culture, symbolic meaning is an essential part of a person's life of exploration, interpretation and orientation in the world.

Animal behaviour and mentality

In order to understand the human mind, we need, so says Langer, a far better understanding of the mind of animals: 'To form any hypothesis of the evolution of human mind from its presumable animal origins, we need first of all a much clearer idea of animal mentality than we are employing in zoology or psychology today.'[97] In view of that, most of the second volume of *Mind* is devoted to a study of the interpretation of animal behaviour. Drawing on numerous studies on animal instinct and repertoire, acts and ambients, language and communication, values and feelings, Langer provides multiple case studies involving some radically new interpretations of these phenomena.[98] One recurring critique of the ethologists of her time, including Jacob von Uexküll, Nikolaas Tinbergen and Konrad Lorenz, is that they assign motivations to animals on the basis of superficial similarities with humans.[99] This anthropomorphizing attitude leads to terms such as 'courting ritual', 'distraction behaviour', 'communication', 'social hierarchy', 'ceremonial dance' and so on. For

Langer, these terms imply the kind of purposeful, intentional behaviour that can only be found in humans since it depends on the ability to imagine possible outcomes which, in turn, requires symbolic '*Vorstellungen*' or representations.[100]

According to Langer, this terminology reflects the ethologists' 'desire to find the evolutionary continuum of animal life, and especially mental life, from fish (if not from protozoon) to man.'[101] For semiotician Charles Morris, for one, there is no sharp line in the 'evolution of intelligence from the animal world to man.'[102] For Langer, by contrast, 'all animal behaviour is instinctive, arising from organic sources as impulse seeking expression in motor action, and guided to direct or indirect consummation by acts of perception.'[103] Animals are not less perceptive or less intelligent. In fact, they perform many tasks far more efficiently and well beyond human capacities, while their sense organs and sensibility often outshine those of humans, such as, for example, 'the distance vision of hawks, the night vision of owls and other nocturnal beasts [and] the feats of migration and homing which are quite unaccountable in terms of human means of pathfinding.'[104] However, animal space is always 'action space'; it is known primarily practically and functionally.[105] Once a specific course of behaviour is triggered, the animal is driven to bring it to its consummation. In animal acts, 'the over-all tension is preformed in the impulse, and the act is apparently not controlled by an image of external conditions to be achieved, but by a constant internal pressure toward its consummation.'[106] Significantly, the 'beginning and the end of the act are its essential elements – impulse and consummation – spanned by a single arc of nervous tension.'[107] This also applies to behavioural acts which seem to involve long-term foresight or planning, such as nest building, food hoarding or the building of large bower structures. Langer explains this in terms of very large 'instinctive acts' in which the tension holds over a long period of time.[108] The reason that symbol-less animals can operate so effectively is that their major instinctive acts are highly articulated units that are not sidetracked by doubt or confused by awareness of alternative options. Their acts are imprinted in their bodies. Animals do not envisage alternative possible worlds, nor are they able to envisage themselves as perceived by other animals. Animal actions, on Langer's view, are not guided by perception or choice but by 'suggestion' and 'empathy'. Empathy is 'a direct physical reaction inherent in the perception of other beings, especially of the perceiver's own kind.'[109] When animals notice the slightest movement of other animals in their own kind, they experience it as if they were feeling the movement themselves. Human sympathy, by contrast, depends on the ability to imagine someone else's experience and 'have a reaction of our own to the imagined feeling we attribute to him.'[110] It requires a symbolic act of imagination. Even a torturer depends on a sense of 'sympathy' understood thus. Unlike sympathy, empathy works instinctively – infectiously and contagiously. It is an 'involuntary breach of individual separateness.'[111] Subjective and objective feeling are fused into one, making animals highly attuned to each other. This can explain the behaviour of 'care' between one member of a species and another. By seeing another animal in pain or fear, the animal suffers the feeling itself, as if seeing itself in a mirror. Suggestion, likewise, triggers a need for immediate action to follow some animal's example, even if it is not pure imitation but some different kind of expression.[112] This can, for example, be seen in the highly synchronized movements of animals moving in herds or in flocks. The take-off of a flock of birds or change in direction in a school of fish requires only a minute bodily twitch of one member in order to cause all the others to follow. Animals do not 'communicate' with each other, they 'commune'. Again, their behaviour displays involuntary breaches of individual separateness. Some of these kinds of behaviours and feelings can also be found in, and are introspectively known by, humans.

Ironically, for some behaviourists, Langer's method of interpreting animal behaviour is itself too anthropomorphic in that it extrapolates non-observable animal mentality from observations based on human introspection. According to Marja Zuidgeest, for instance, ethological terminology such as 'survival action' or 'distraction behaviour' does not imply intentional behaviour but merely indicates that certain observable behaviours have observable consequences.[113] But this is missing Langer's point. Langer seeks to study animal behaviour precisely with a view to understanding animal mentality yet without falling back on what she considers the misleading anthropomorphic language of traditional behaviourist descriptions. Langer wants to study animal mentality, or what she calls the 'psychical phase' in animals, precisely in order to distinguish it from the psychical phase in humans. As she put it in the second volume of *Mind*,

> We have so far found no biological concepts on which to base any indirect methods for the study of psychical phases in animal life. This leaves us with the direct, natural method of imputing an essentially human mentality to non-human agents, and two attitudes toward that practice: simple acceptance of its naïve anthropomorphism, or a really equally simple summary declaration that there is no way of finding out anything about animal feeling, so the best policy is to deny or at least ignore its existence. The first is a misguided approach, the second an acceptance of failure at the mere sight of the task.[114]

While avoiding 'naïve anthropomorphism', Langer (re-)interprets animal behaviour with a view to gaining insight into their 'psychical phase'. For her, that means that animal behaviour should be studied not merely on the basis of observable behaviour and causal patterns but in terms of organic acts. And because 'the psychical moments of animal acts are different from ours, it means that the [organic] acts are different, perhaps from their very impulses to their consummations'.[115] In order to understand this difference, Langer turns to an examination of the human brain.

Adaptation and specialization: The human brain

To understand what constitutes human mentality in distinction from that of (other) animals, Langer draws on the German philosophical anthropologist Arnold Gehlen's insight that the more specialized the organism, the less adaptable it is to different environments. Following Nietzsche's description of the human species as '*das noch nicht festgestellte Tier*' ('the not yet determined animal'), Gehlen pictures humans as helpless '*Mängelwesen*' ('deficient beings') whose physical inadequacies need to be complemented with a brain that can adapt to various environments.[116] He refers to this as man's '*Weltoffenheit*' ('openness to the world'). While not disagreeing with

Gehlen, Langer nevertheless points out that 'no organism can be unadapted *ab initio* to its surroundings, or it could not have evolved there'.[117] According to her, the brain itself is 'both anatomically and functionally as genuine a specialized organ as the elephant's trunk or the bee's honeysack'.[118] Moreover, both humans and (other) animals choose and adapt to their habitats on the basis of their particular proclivities and abilities.[119]

Different specializations lead to different kinds of adaptions in physiology or behaviour.[120] Sometimes behaviour compensates for inadequate physique. Some animals with eyes placed laterally on their heads may need to move their heads continuously to focus on an object.[121] Many specializations progressively refine a particular organ so that it can exploit its ambient more effectively.[122] A snake's temperature organ, a beaver's dentition and a hawk's vision are all examples of this. Liewise the human brain, so Langer argues, is also a specialization of a particular organ that facilitates adaptation.[123] Langer rejects the idea that all specialization leads to 'fixation in a narrow ambient or to over-growth of special features – horns, tusks, scales – [thus] making the species unviable'.[124]

Langer also challenges the popular palaeoanthropological conception that the main distinction between humans and their ancestors lies in the increased size of the human brain. Instead, she claims, it was the seemingly insignificant change in the shape of feet which proved crucial in the evolutionary development. This change enabled humans to walk upright, thereby freeing the hands from their supportive role in moving from one place to another, be it walking, climbing or swinging. The upright position, in turn, changed the balancing position of the head, which led to a reorganization of the brain's substructures and functions. The main change took place in the cortex, which gradually adopted a leading role in the development of the entire central nervous system. This development led to a raised intensity in the electrical and chemical processes of the nervous tissues, resulting in a greater refinement of peripheral and central sensitivity and feeling.[125] Moreover, Langer suggests, the most important value of the freeing of the hands does not just lie in their increased manipulative powers, but in their gradual specialization as a sense organ. As she writes evocatively,

[T]he human hand is a complex organ in which the distribution of sensory nerves and the extremely refined musculature coincide, as they do in our eyes and ears, to implement perception of form, location, size, weight, penetrability, mobility and many consequent values. Its measured movements and the coordinate orientation of its parts, which permit fingering of objects, make it capable of judging qualities of surfaces – rough, smooth, varied, patterned – and their characteristic ways of absorbing or reflecting heat, which give us information of temperature contrasts and gradients. The two hands working together can negotiate a single complex impression [and] the sensory reactions of the skin and underlying structures are engaged together in the tactual perception of substances: feelings of pressure and release of pressure, of warm and cold impingements, pin-pointed encounters with resistance, oiliness, wetness, and mixtures like sliminess, hairiness, stickiness. The result is that we have not only a report of surfaces and edges, but of volume imbued with multimodal, often nameless qualities.[126]

Langer's observations on the role of the hands are particularly interesting in relation to aesthetic theories that acknowledge the importance of the body and the tactile aspects of art. For Langer, the tactile sensitivity of the hand evokes 'aesthetic' sensations such as 'furry', 'smooth', 'soft', 'slimy', 'prickly' and so on. Most of these have strong implicit associations with pleasure or displeasure, attraction or disgust. Langer suggests that, in the earliest signs of speech, these expressions would have lent themselves easily to metaphorical uses beyond the realm of tactile qualities. This is because, like all aesthetic perceptions, they 'meet and merge with emotional elements which are not current sexual, maternal or hostile feelings toward other beings, but modes of consciousness, felt attitudes, which motivate the earliest artistic expressions, dance and vocalization'.[127] In other words, they lend themselves to symbolic expressions.

Rethinking human needs

Following Gehlen, Langer holds that changes in the tactile senses and the brain led to an intensified receptiveness of the human mind to outside stimuli which resulted in an overstimulation. To unburden this load, impulses no longer result in direct instinctive responses but in mental images, a process referred to by Gehlen as '*Entlastung*'.[128] Langer suggests that sleep psychologists and neurologists have arrived at largely similar conclusions by apparently independent approaches, when suggesting that dreaming is a cerebral completion of acts which could not be overtly consummated.[129] However, this storage of excess impressions leads to a radically new ability, which is to 'observe' and 'imagine' things that play no direct role in the current activities of the observer. This means, Langer suggests, that a cerebrally started neural activity involving external stimuli can produce an internal retinal image. In other words, the 'common optic structures of primate brains [entail] a neural mechanism of visual imagination' that forms the biological underpinning of the human capacity to symbolize.[130] As she puts it,

> The underlying unity of the central nervous organ, the brain, could be expected to carry the function of imagination into other sensory systems, too, and finally establish it apart from any special sense as a cortical faculty in its own right. Here it becomes the groundwork of symbolization, conception, and all other peculiarly human forms of cerebration; the evolution of mind is on its way.[131]

The cerebral activity that results in symbolic activity has no obvious survival value. Langer challenges those genetic and behavioural psychologists who claim that, compared to the minds of other animals, the human mind is merely a more complex and more efficient switchboard to process man's needs for survival. As Langer points out, mental phenomena such as dreams, mythical thinking or aesthetic imaginings make the mind in fact a very *in*effective organ for survival. Indeed, these mental musings with no zoological aims are more likely to interfere with life's practical tasks. More often than not, their disregard for empirical evidence seems to result in 'mistakes'.

So why do most people nevertheless attach so much value to dreams, myth and art to the point of these overriding more elementary needs, such as food, sex or shelter? What is the point of this storehouse of cerebral acts which could not be overtly consummated?

These questions led Langer to a radical reconsideration of the inventory of human needs. One primary human need which is not present in animals is the need for reflection on life as a means of exploration and orientation. For Langer, echoing Socrates, the unexamined life is not worth living. The readiest termination of such reflection can be found in the forms of language and speech. But there are many other forms of expression that aim to make sense of the world.[132] These include art, rite and religion.[133]

The meaning of the body: Mark Johnson

In recognizing art as part of a larger complex of human needs for the making of meaning and orientation, Langer anticipates by over forty years Mark Johnson's *The Meaning of the Body: Aesthetics of Human Understanding* (2007).[134] Johnson refers to Langer on a couple of occasions but does not cite her as a major influence.[135] Johnson claims that 'art is an exemplary form of human meaning-making [and that] understanding the nature of the arts could give us profound insight into how humans experience and construct meaning in their lives'.[136] For Johnson, as for Langer, an 'aesthetics of human understanding' is not confined to the study of art, beauty or aesthetic experience in the traditional sense but entails an exploration of the whole spectrum of 'qualities, feelings, emotions, and bodily processes that make meaning possible'.[137] It concerns our primordial, embodied, visceral connection with the world.

Johnson is one of a growing group of 'second-generation' cognitive scientists who, over the last two decades, have focused on the reciprocal relationship or 'coupling' between an organism and its environment and, in particular, on the role of the organism's sensorimotor processes in the formation of cognition.[138] Whereas 'first-generation' cognitive scientists typically worked with neo-Cartesian computational models and artificial intelligence, 'second-generation' scientists emphasize the crucial role of the sensing body for cognition in language and other forms.[139] Like Langer, Johnson points out that different organisms have different 'body schemas' and, consequently, different interactions with their environments. A body schema, for Johnson, is, in the words of Sean Gallagher, 'a system of sensory-motor capacities that function without awareness or the necessity of perceptual monitoring'.[140] Different body schemas lead to different 'Umwelts' or ambients. Like Langer, Johnson identifies location and movement in space as the foundational feature of an organism's engagement with its surroundings.[141] Through spatial movement, an organism gains direct experience of trajectories, direction, obstacles, weight, pressure, balance, gravity and so on. Depending on their shape, different organisms move about differently. The *Umwelt* of an eyeless tick that negotiates its environment on the basis of smell and temperature is different from that of a multisensory organism such as a human being. The human body schema provides a different pattern of perception based on the body's vertical relationship to the ground. This provides humans with a particular sense of up and down, front and back, near and far, balanced and unbalanced, curved and straight and so on. These foundational experiences shape the way humans view the world.

Like Langer, Johnson holds that in human conceptualization basic image schemas are extended into other realms. Drawing on his early work on metaphor done with Georg Lakoff, he argues, 'One of the chief ways that humans are different [from non-human animals] is that we have neural mechanisms for metaphorically extending image schemas as we perform abstract conceptualisation and reasoning.'[142] Such metaphorical extensions do not imply any rupture or gap between lower and higher levels within an organism: ' "Higher" cognitive processes have to emerge from complex interactions among "lower"-level capacities.'[143]

Echoing *Philosophy in a New Key*'s central theme that 'there is an unexplored possibility of genuine semantic beyond the limits of discursive language', Johnson writes, 'One of the greatest impediments to an appreciation of the full scope of embodied meaning is the way philosophers of language focus almost exclusively on *language* (i.e., spoken and written words and sentences) as the bearer of meaning.'[144] Instead, he claims, we need to recover 'the deep processes of meaning, by looking beyond and beneath the formal, structural, conceptual, propositional, representational dimensions of meaning.'[145] Moreover, in order to appreciate the pre-reflective and subconscious realms of qualitative feeling and sensorimotor experience, we have to look 'beyond linguistic meaning and into the processes of meaning in the arts, where immanent bodily meaning is paramount.'[146] Like Langer, Johnson believes that the study of the form of art can help illuminate aspects of the mind which otherwise remain obscure and elusive. Langer, as we have seen, wrote that art is the 'logical form' of sentient life and vital experience and that artistic form 'is congruent with the dynamic forms of our direct sensuous, mental, and emotional life; works of art are projections of "felt life" ... into spatial, temporal, and poetic structures.'[147] Referring to Langer, Johnson, likewise, emphasizes the structural analogies and shared patterns of process between art or music and the life of feeling:

> Music is meaningful because it can present the flow of human experience, feeling, and thinking in concrete, embodied forms – and this is meaning in its deepest sense. ... [I]t appeals to our felt sense of life.[148]

Likewise,

> In any musical work ... there is a structure and pattern of temporal flow, pitch contours, and intensity (loudness/softness) that is analogous to felt patterns of the flow of human experience.[149]

Indeed, there is not much in Johnson's book that had not already been said before by Langer.[150] There is nevertheless one important point on which their views diverge. This is the nature and the role of internal mental representation. Johnson rejects internal representations as an unhelpful legacy of first-generation cognitive science:

> What I am denying is that we have mental *entities* called 'concepts' or 'representations' in our 'minds' and that thinking is a matter of manipulating these

entities by surveying their properties, discerning their relations to each other and to mind-external objects, and arranging them in internal acts of judgment.[151]

To support his view Johnson refers to brain scans that show that conceptualization in the brain does not take place in 'highly specialised brain regions that are physically and functionally' separate from areas responsible for perception and motor movement'.[152] Instead, so he claims, drawing on research by neurologist Marc Jeannerod, '*imagining* certain motor actions activates some of the same parts of the brain that are involved in actually performing that action'.[153] Thinking and doing are not of an ontologically different order: 'concrete concepts are realised neurally as sensorimotor schemas that organize functional neural clusters into meaningful, integrated gestalts.'[154]

Even if these imaging results had been available to Langer, she would not likely have considered them conclusive for rejecting the existence of internal images. Again, it is a question of the interpretation of these 'facts'. For her, the same findings might even have supported the existence of 'mental entities' such as concepts and representations. Drawing on *Gestalt* theorists and Cassirer's philosophy of symbolic forms, Langer sees no tension between mental representations and their biological foundation as 'stable patterns of neural activation'. On the contrary, it is precisely *because* internal representations display a biologically 'stable pattern' or *Gestalt* in the ongoing flow of stimuli and neural activity that they can adopt a symbolic representational function. That is precisely what enables humans to recall and imagine things in their absence, 'off-line' from their immediate experience. This representational understanding of symbol does not commit Langer to a dualistic conception of mind. Instead, it gives mental representations a proper biological footing, planted in humans' first embodied encounters with the world.

Animal symbolicum

Aiming to challenge substantialist dualist anthropologies, Cassirer wrote in 1944,

> The philosophy of symbolic forms starts from the presupposition that, if there is any definition of the nature or 'essence' of man, this definition can only be understood as a functional one, not a substantial one. ... Man's outstanding characteristic, his distinguishing mark, is not his metaphysical or physical nature – but his work. ... it is the system of human activities which defines and determines the circle of 'humanity'.[155]

It was in that context that he coined the term *animal symbolicum*:

> Reason is a very inadequate term with which to comprehend the forms of man's cultural life in all their richness and variety. But all these forms are symbolic forms. Hence, instead of defining man as an animal rationale, we should define him as an *animal symbolicum*.[156]

Without symbolism, Cassirer claimed, 'man's life would be confined within the limits of his biological needs and his practical interests; it could find no access to the "ideal world" which is opened to him from different sides by religion, art, philosophy, science'.[157]

For Langer, too, symbolic activity is the defining mark of humanity.[158] Symbols, for her, cover a wide range of phenomena from simple perceptual *Gestalten* and words to works of art and scientific theories. Even so, symbolization is not primarily about products but about *processes*. It is an activity done by an agent: the human organism with all its diverse needs and responsibilities. She rejects Darwin-based teleological terminology that suggests hidden mythical agents such as 'nature' or 'the environment' as reflected in popular phrases such as 'Mother Nature designed it this way' or 'evolution solved this problem so-and-so'. Even the notion of natural selection itself inclines to the assumption that there is something like a 'selector' even though, as she points out, 'the factory manager is discretely left nameless'.[159] But she also critiques genetic theories that place the body's genes at the sole centre. Humans are not, as Richard Dawkins was to put it later, 'survival machines – robot vehicles blindly programmed to preserve the selfish molecules known as genes'.[160] Finally, Langer also rejects computer-based cybernetic models of personhood such as that proposed by Norbert Wiener, in which the central nervous system serves as the main coordinating centre. That, for her, reduces the human nervous system to a mechanically modelled communication system more suited to a computer than to humans.[161]

Langer's anti-dualist stance discards, on the one hand, any theory that explains personhood in terms of a separate entity or agency. But she also rejects any monist solutions, whether materialist or idealist, that select a physical or metaphysical principle as the sole origin of personhood. For Langer, agents 'cannot figure as ultimate unanalysable entities, like the "metaphysical Subject", the Mover of "his" arms and legs, completely self-identical, "implied" by the occurrence of acts, but not accessible to empirical or historical study'.[162] For her, the only agent of life is the organism or embodied human being itself. Such an agent is chiefly determined by its biological 'individuation'. More specifically, it is the pattern of the smallest biological unit, that is, the biological 'act', with its enfolded precoded potential which determines the outcome as a whole. This applies from the earliest signs of life, in the isolation of protoplasmic units by a surrounding membrane, to the highest forms of individuation, the evolution of human beings. The way such an organism develops is the result of the chance interactions between its genetically coded impulses and the impacts of its ambient. Even so, every stock contains countless unexpressed genes which will only actualize their potential when external conditions enable them to do so.[163] According to Langer, 'man is probably as full of unrealized potentialities as the lower creatures'.[164]

In view of the developments in neuroscience since Langer, it is no longer controversial – indeed it has become commonplace – to accept that mental phenomena are part of the brain's embodied natural history. Langer, however, was one of the first philosophers to develop a comprehensive account of the mind's biological roots and to recognize its importance for understanding human perception and cognition.[165] Not long after Langer, it was John Searle who drew attention to the neurobiological processes of human mentality. Seemingly unaware of Langer's work, he writes,

> All mental states, from the profoundest philosophical thoughts to the most trivial itches and tickles are caused by neurobiological processes in the brain. … Neuronal processes cause mental states and events. … Mental phenomena, such as my present state of conscious awareness of the table in front of me, are higher-level features of the brain. … Mental phenomena are above all biological phenomena and they are as real as any other biological phenomena, such as growth, digestion, photosynthesis or the secretions of bile. They cannot be reduced to something else, such as behaviour or computer programs.[166]

For Searle, this view is the only solution to the apparent paradox of dualism and materialism. He refers to his position as 'biological naturalism', which he defines in terms of two short propositions: 'Brains cause minds' and 'Minds are higher-level features of brains'.[167] Moreover, Searle, like Langer, holds that higher-level complex physical structures may adopt new, emergent properties, which are not reducible to, and are inexplicable in terms of, their physical constitution. This position is generally referred to as 'emergentism', another term that could well apply to Langer's view.[168] Even so, neither label sufficiently acknowledges that, for Langer, humans are *symbolic* animals. Andreas Weber's reference to Langer as a 'proto-biosemiotic' thinker captures her position more adequately as it shows how the origins of human meaning-making are located in the symbolizing capacities of the self-organizing organism.[169] Whatever the labels given to her position – non-reductionist naturalism, evolutionist emergentism, biosemiotic organicism – Langer holds that humans are 'by nature' creatures in pursuit of meaning. This she illustrates by a wealth of examples in Parts Five and Six that make up Volume III of *Mind*.

Philosophical anthropology

In the third and last volume of her trilogy, Langer sets out what can best be described as a holistic, biologically based, philosophical anthropology.[170] The volume draws on a wealth of ethno-anthropological studies as well as wider research ranging from mathematics and physics to ethology and linguistics.[171] Many anthropological studies focus on non-Western cultures in which the relation between self and world is not described in terms of the modern categories of subject and object. This interest can be seen reflected in some her chapter titles, such as 'The Spirit-World', 'The Dream of Power', 'Dreams' Ending: The Tragic Vision', 'The Ethnic Balance', 'The Breaking' and 'The Open Ambient'. Often, Langer provides highly original, sometimes idiosyncratic, interpretations of phenomena and practices, such as dreams, magic, sorcery, taboos, the rise of cities and the roots of mathematics in the visual and physical experience of dancing and drumming.[172] But the central theme around which these discussions circle remains the 'great shift' from animal instinct to human symbolization, not only in the individual but in tribal communities and modern societies. The key motivation for the initial gradual process of individuation of the organism out of its natural ambient and instinctive behaviour is an intensification of feeling in which organisms become conscious agents of their actions and activities. This emerging self-awareness is the basis for humans' sense of morality in the light of their own mortality. It also involves a 'breaking' of myth out of its original setting to new forms of expression in art and religion.[173]

It is important not to read Langer's account of increased individuation and liberation from the instinctive and impulsive need to act on stimuli as a story of progression or evolutionary advance. Although the growth of the brain has created unprecedented potentialities for the human mind to develop the sciences and civilizations, it has come with a price. That price is a disturbance of what Langer calls 'the ethnic balance'.[174] With the growth of the brain, humans lost many valuable instincts. These include the loss of certain physical capacities, such as a natural sense of balance (or 'righting reflex') or spatial awareness, but also a natural sense of 'communion' as can be found in the natural bond between mother and child in distinction from a social 'community'.[175] In order for the individual not to outgrow its connection to its natural ambient, the group or society creates measures, from religious rituals and rites to laws and punishments, to counter the excesses of individuation in which the connection with nature and with fellow human beings gets lost.

> The higher the cultural expression of a society rises, the more tenuous becomes the balance between the physical security and strength of the stock and the autonomy of its members. Every behavioural act carries the possibility of upsetting the equilibrium of the social order in which successive generations are born, mature, and age, think, command, negotiate their conflicts and develop their separate minds, each unique, unlike any that was before. The primal and perennial work of social organization is not to fix the bounds of behavior as permanent lines, which would make all evolutionary process impossible, but to retrieve the vital balance every time some act, public or private, has upset it.[176]

For Langer, religion has always played a key role in maintaining the 'ethnic balance', by limiting extreme individuation and enabling individuals to feel themselves part of a larger social and natural ambient. This is vital for any individual's sense of belonging and orientation in life: 'Even as the power of symbolic thought creates the danger of letting the mind run wild, it also furnishes the saving counterbalance of cultural restraint, the orientating dictates of religion.'[177] Religion is both a product of the symbolic power of the mind and a means to curb its excessive power.

Although Langer always talks positively about religion, she rarely refers to her own 'beliefs' – with one exception. This is a passage at the beginning of *Philosophy in a New Key* which is rarely discussed. She writes,

> That man is an animal I certainly believe; and also, that he has no supernatural essence, 'soul' or 'entelechy' or 'mind-stuff', enclosed in his skin. He is an organism, his substance is chemical, and what he does, suffers, or knows, is just what this sort of chemical structure may do, suffer, or know. When the structure goes to pieces, it never does, suffers, or knows anything again. … Now this is a mere declaration of faith, preliminary to a heresy. The heresy is this: that I believe there is a primary need in many, which other creatures probably do not have, and which actuates all

his apparently unzoölogical aims, his wistful fancies, his consciousness of value, his utterly impractical enthusiasms, and his awareness of a 'Beyond' filled with holiness. Despite the fact that this need gives rise to almost everything that we commonly assign to the 'higher' life, it is not itself a 'higher' form of some 'lower' need; it is quite essential, imperious, and general, and may be called 'high' only in the sense that it belongs exclusively (I think) to a very complex and perhaps recent genus. ... This basic need, which certainly is obvious only in man, is the *need of symbolization.*[178]

In other words, although Langer herself does not believe in a divine being or afterlife, she holds that an 'awareness of a Beyond filled with holiness' is part of the human condition and provides life with a larger frame of reference and social structure as expressed in various rituals. Ritual, according to Langer, is even older than religion and is 'the scaffolding in which all religious thought has taken shape'.[179] Rituals are symbolic practices that enable humans to enact their commitments in life. As she explained it in *Philosophy in a New Key,*

[I]n primitive society, a daily ritual is incorporated in common activities, in eating, washing, firemaking, etc., as well as in pure ceremonial; because the need of reasserting the tribal morale and recognizing its cosmic conditions is constantly felt. In Christian Europe the Church brought men daily (in some orders even hourly) to their knees, to enact if not to contemplate their assent to the ultimate concepts.[180]

The most important symbols, therefore, are those that can serve as vehicles for the articulation of ultimate values and principles: the 'symbols of our *Weltanschauung* and *Lebensanschauung*'.[181] Lamenting the loss of meaningful, communal symbols that can provide structure and orientation in life, she writes,

Human life in our age is so changed and diversified that people cannot share a few, historic, 'charged' symbols that have about the same wealth of meaning for everybody. The loss of old universal symbols endangers our safe unconscious orientation. The new forms of our new order have not yet required that rich, confused, historic accretion of meanings that makes many familiar things 'charged' symbols to which we respond instinctively. For some future generation, an aeroplane may be a more powerful symbol than a ship; its poetic possibilities are perhaps even more obvious.[182]

Religious symbols do not primarily articulate a discursive world *view* but a non-discursive world *feeling*. Langer highlights the need for new symbolic forms to capture the feeling and lived experience of modern life. Such symbols are to serve as vehicles for conception and reflection as a condition for orientation: 'we are driven to the symbolization and articulation of feeling when we *must* understand it to keep ourselves oriented in society and nature.'[183]

Final years

In the final chapter of *Mind*, 'The Open Ambient', Langer was hoping to show how the natural sciences and mathematics are ultimately rooted in physical embodied experience. But the hindrances of old age prevented her from doing so in the way she had planned. In a poignant passage in the foreword to Part Six of her trilogy, called 'Mathematics and the Reign of Science', she writes,

> This study of mind should culminate, of course, in a well-constructed epistemological and possibly even metaphysical theory, at least as firmly founded on other people's knowledge and hypotheses as any earlier parts of this essay which have been written in preparation for such a reflective conclusion. But the hindrances of age – especially increasing blindness – make it necessary to curtail the work at what should be its height and contract the end into no more than a sketch of its presumptive final section. Further research is impossible when the footnote print, photostat, or typewriting are unreadable, and normal fonts not much easier.[184]

This is one of the very few times that Langer makes a reference to herself and that to her own fragile body. The passage evokes a sad sense of loss that her still fertile mind is no longer able to put its rich insights and thoughts to typewriter and paper. In the end, the final chapter contains no more than fifteen pages of somewhat rambling anthropological observations, even while ending with a characteristically insightful commentary on the relation between drumming, dancing and mathematics.

As mentioned at the beginning of this chapter, it would be wrong to suggest that, because Langer turns to the empirical sciences at the end of her life, she regressed from a critical hermeneutical approach to a positivist empiricist one.[185] On the contrary, Langer's detailed attention to empirical data is meant to demonstrate not only that these can be interpreted in a plurality of ways but that they themselves are a form of interpretation or 'symbolic transformation' of the experience as encountered by the embodied self. As she had put it as early as 1930, 'facts themselves might be differently formulated, according to the notions through which they are apprehended'.[186] Nor does Langer's biological naturalism imply a reduction*ist* view of human life. For humans, as symbolic animals, 'nature' is always an 'open ambient' in which they live in an ecological, reciprocally transformative, relation.[187]

Langer seeks to open up new ways of seeing and interpreting the data of the natural and the life sciences with a view to generating new ways of theorizing about them. As is clear from the many appreciative comments from contemporary scientists, the potential of her philosophy for understanding human mentality and consciousness is only just beginning to be recognized.[188] Langer realized from early on that facts are relative to the subject's perception and that different ways of seeing and interpreting data could lead to important advances in science, something also famously shown later by Thomas Kuhn, another student of Henry Sheffer, in *The Structure of Scientific Revolutions*.[189] As Langer wrote in the introduction to *Mind*,

The foundations of a theory cannot be factually proven right or wrong; they are the terms in which facts are expressed, essentially ways of saying things, that make for special ways of seeing things. The value of a philosophical outlook does not rest on its sole possibility, but on its serviceability, which can only prove itself in the long run … . [A]ll I am seeking to do is to explain why I hold the views presented … and to contribute to the work of more or less likeminded thinkers, dealing with the paradoxes of experience that always harbour the seeds of new conceptions.[190]

Her own philosophical outlook remains, as Danto once put it, 'one of the most audacious visions of recent times'.[191]

Conclusion

Looking back over Langer's impressive oeuvre, one cannot fail to be astonished at the sheer breadth of her intellectual interests. Few philosophers can be said to have mastered so many fields of philosophy – logic, semiotics, aesthetics, philosophy of science, philosophy of mind, philosophy of culture and several more – as well as so many specialist disciplines – mathematics, biochemistry, biology, ethology, neuroscience and many others.

Even in her close engagement with the empirical sciences Langer always remained an 'analytical philosopher' in a Cassirerean sense, concerned more with the meaning of data rather than the expansion of them. Data and facts, for Langer as for Wittgenstein and Whitehead, are formulated events *seen under some aspect*. She also always remained a logician in a Shefferian sense, looking for meaningful patterns and configurations in objects, events and ideas. Langer's ability to see *new* forms and *Gestalten* in familiar things enabled her to make the dramatic 'paradigm shifts' that brought fresh understandings to long-standing philosophical problems, including the relation between body and mind, brain and human consciousness. Her 'Copernican' revolution, as inspired by Whitehead, was the recognition that human mentality was an ongoing bodily and biological process that was nevertheless not causally determined by, or reduced to, its biological substratum. This process expressed itself in a need that was unique to human animals: the need to make sense of the world and to express that understanding freely. Her view of human mentality as symbolic transformation shows how meaning-formation takes place 'all the way down' – at the level of sense perception and simple observation – and 'all the way up' – at the level of scientific inquiry and human quest for the meaning of life. As Innis correctly observes, by combining a philosophy of *experience* with a semiotic philosophy of *meaning*, it shares much with the American pragmatist tradition.[1]

With her liberated logical imagination, Langer re-discovered and re-habilitated the rich worlds of meaning that lay outside science – myth, ritual and, especially, art – against the restrictive conventions of her age. By devoting her life to the recognition of meaning-formation in these deprecated fields, she marked out a pioneering path that many later thinkers were to follow in diverse and fascinating ways.

Holistic vision

Langer's main contribution to philosophy, I suggest, lies not only, or even primarily, in any one contribution to any one specific field, but in the way she was able to connect diverse fields with each other by means of a recognition of their shared roots and sources, whether in the sciences or in philosophy. As few other philosophers, Langer saw the world and human life both in its intricate interconnectedness and in its dynamic openness to multiple meaningful interpretations, each of them disclosing a different aspect of the world. Her large-scale philosophical symphony of interweaving themes was held together by one central 'new key': the recognition of the mind's transformative power and the basic human need to pursue meaning.

Langer's intellectual intuition enabled her to discern previously unnoticed connections not only between disparate phenomena but between diverse sources. She found inspiration for her ideas partly in the conception of form developed by the *Gestalt* theorists but, more significantly, in the philosophies of Sheffer, Cassirer, Whitehead and Wittgenstein. Having read Kant in her early teens, Langer took from him the idea of the forms of perception and the mind's transformational role in understanding the physical world. From Cassirer she learned how Kant's principle could be extended from the formation of scientific knowledge to all processes by which the human mind gives form to reality. Unlike Kant's forms of perceptions and categories of thought, however, Cassirer's symbolic forms are not fixed and universally valid structures of the human mind but dynamically and historically evolving processes of transformation which allow reality to be experienced and represented in a plurality of ways, whether through science, language, myth, ritual or art. Inspired by Whitehead, Langer developed this insight further: in addition to recognizing the mental and symbolic nature of all sense perception and understanding, she asserts the biological nature of all mental activity. The knowing mind itself is always already part of the world that it is trying to understand. Thinking does not so much constitute being, as some neo-Kantians had suggested; as a living dynamic process thinking is always already *part* of being. Langer adopted – and adapted – Whitehead's view of nature as a temporal process with an organic rhythm of growth and decline, as well as his notion of the intrinsic reversibility of the symbolic reference. She also found inspiration for her ideas on form in Sheffer's emphasis on the role of patterns in logic and his idea of 'notational relativity' as referring to different possible descriptions of one and the same entity. And she recognized the importance of Wittgenstein's conception of 'fact' conceived as an expression or formulation of an event rather than as a mirror-copy of the world 'as it is.' Langer, in a major leap of philosophical imagination, recognized similar patterns of ideas in these highly diverse thinkers and produced a new and original synthesis from her deep engagement with the most fruitful philosophies of her time. As Polish philosopher Stefan Morawski puts it, 'Langer assimilates from her predecessors everything that seems worthy to her of revalued continuation and further cultivation. … [They] are treated as members of the same intellectual family, seeking the same distilled philosophical truth.'[2] In doing so, she refused to draw the commonly accepted but often misleading distinction between, on the one hand, 'studying the history of philosophy' and, on the other, '*doing* philosophy'.

Plurality of aspects

A key element of Langer's vision was her recognition that the world could be seen through a range of different prisms or 'symbolic forms', each highlighting different aspects or dimensions of reality. Different disciplines, in turn, focus on different aspects by means of abstracting different patterns and forms. This process of abstracting already starts at the level of perception. Perception, for Langer, is always perception of *a* symbolic form with an amorphous content. One of her decisive recurring claims is that there is no such thing as *the* form of *the* real world. Everything is always perceived under some aspect. Any one entity can be presented by a plurality of possible forms, each highlighting a different – and mutually irreducible – dimension. This should prevent all forms of reductionism, or what Whitehead had called the 'fallacy of misplaced concreteness', that is, the error of taking one abstraction or description of the world for the world as a whole.

The hugely important implication of this approach is that science is not the only way reality can be described as 'it really is.' The world is not only known in its quantifiable, physical aspects but also in its many significant other dimensions - historic, psychological, environmental, economic, aesthetic, ethical, political and so on. All these different aspects call for a different – yet equally valid – form of understanding. Langer's philosophy thus allows for a fruitfully pluralistic epistemology that seeks to do justice to the full depth and breadth of human experience and knowing of the world.

Embodied meaning

Symbolic forms, for Langer, are the result of conscious or subconscious abstractions of certain salient features of the world. Such abstractions are not merely mental constructions but are rooted in the reciprocal engagement between the body-subject and its environment. Unlike animals, humans engage with the world through myriad bodily based, symbolically processed perceptions and conceptions that transcend and liberate them from their direct survival needs for food and shelter. This points to a more fundamental human need: the need for meaning and understanding. This need is expressed in the mind's unceasing production of symbolic forms – from dreams and simple sensations to complex calculations and conceptual constructions – that make up the human universe of meaning.

Langer's conception of human mentality as embodied meaning – conceived of as a verb – challenges the deep-seated dichotomies that have plagued modern philosophy since Descartes. For Langer, human mentality is biologically based, defined first of all in terms of sensing and feeling rather than reasoning or calculating. This enabled her to break radically with Descartes's dichotomy between *res cogitans* and *res extensa* and comparable oppositions between mind and body, subject and object, feeling and thinking, faith and reason, and so on. By taking feeling as the overarching category for human mentality and consciousness, with rational thinking as a subcategory, Langer placed embodied meaning and experience at the heart of human understanding and existence.

Langer's emphasis on the body-subject's lived experience is contemporary with and anticipates much phenomenological philosophy. Likewise, her critique of logocentrism anticipates *post*modern philosophers' critiques of modern ways of thinking. Langer does not confine herself to a critical deconstruction of these ways, but builds a constructive, visionary response to – and correction of – modern philosophy's many bifurcations and deficiencies.

Bridging divides

Not only is Langer's constructive philosophy an important achievement in itself, it is also a model for any philosophy aiming to build bridges, both within its own edifice and with other fields of experience and enquiry. I will identify five areas where Langer's inclusive philosophy either exemplifies or facilitates the overcoming of unhelpful divides.

The *first* divide Langer bridged was that between the humanities and the natural sciences. In his 1959 Rede lecture 'The Two Cultures and the Scientific Revolution', British scientist/novelist C. P. Snow lamented the schism and mutual disdain between natural scientists and literary intellectuals. In contrast to today, Snow felt that, in his time, an education in the sciences was not respected as much as one in literature or the classics and that this was a hindrance to scientific progress. His analysis was heavily criticized by, among others, literary critic F. R. Leavis, who argued that, to the contrary, there was a serious lack of an 'educated public' in England and this had led to a serious intellectual and moral decline. Over sixty years later, the 'two cultures debate' still lingers. Although, nowadays, 'interdisciplinarity' is much championed, it cannot be ignored that there is still much incomprehension, indifference and ignorance about the workings of each other's fields. This is largely due to the large schism in style, method and culture between the humanities and the natural sciences. Almost a hundred years ago, in *Science and the Modern World* (1925), Whitehead had considered the main task of philosophy 'to end the divorce of science from the affirmations of our aesthetic and ethical experiences'.[3] Langer's philosophy not only facilitates productive interdisciplinary dialogue between the sciences and the humanities, but it helps them to discover their shared origin in symbolic consciousness. Langer's emphasis on the common root of discursive and non-discursive symbolic expressions as vehicles for conveying meaning, rather than as signs calling for action, highlights how the humanities and natural sciences are both instances of a larger human enterprise: the symbolic projection as a way of disclosing meaning and making sense of the world. To the extent that the natural sciences and the humanities can see their own endeavours as part of this larger, deeply human, cultural project, mutual curiosity, respect and fruitful collaboration can emerge.

The *second* divide overcome by Langer was the divide between philosophy and the special sciences. Langer's philosophy draws on a wide range of special sciences such as linguistics, theories of art, biochemistry, physiology, biology, psychology, ethology, anthropology, neurology, and social and cultural history. Many philosophers steer away from drawing on empirical sciences for fear that this might contaminate the 'purity' of their philosophy. Although the newly emerging field of 'experimental philosophy' does make use of empirical data, often based on surveys, it does not critically probe the nature of data as such. Langer's hermeneutically sophisticated philosophy operates on the assumption that all data are abstractions of certain aspects of experience and thus 'relative' to the perceiver's focus of interest. This recognition of the 'relativity' of data does not imply 'relativism' in the sense of data being arbitrary, unreliable or untrue. Instead it recognizes that data are 'relational', that is, abstractions from a whole to which they are related, and in relation to an embodied, perceiving subject. Rather than contaminating philosophy's putative purity, Langer's self-critical, perceptive use of empirical data exposes the myth of 'pure' rational thinking and allows for a closer connection between philosophy and the empirical world.

The *third* divide that Langer transcends is that between analytic and continental philosophy. When Whitehead quipped in his introduction to Russell's 1940 William James Lecture that 'Bertie thinks I am muddleheaded; but then I think he is simpleminded', he articulated mutual sentiments that are often attributed to representatives of the analytic and continental tradition. The exchanges between John Searle and Jacques Derrida in the early 1970s – Searle accusing Derrida of 'obscurantism' and Derrida attacking Searle's 'superficiality' – are merely another variation on the theme. The wording of the distinction between 'continental' and 'analytic' is itself confusing in that it compares a geographical distinction with a methodological one. This can be illustrated by the fact that several founders of analytic philosophy, such as Carnap and Tarski, were geographically 'continental'. Methodologically, analytic philosophy can be best characterized by its aim of clarifying key philosophical concepts and propositions, as well as common sense language and terms, with a view to resolving – or dissolving – philosophical problems. Continental philosophers, broadly speaking, also seek clarity but not mainly about linguistic terms and propositions, but in describing the elusive world of pre-reflective lived experience (especially phenomenologists) or analyzing fundamental questions about human existence (especially existentialists). Similarly, continental philosophers such as Derrida and Deleuze seek to articulate the incongruous, *a*-logical experiences beneath and beyond the meanings of existing concepts with a view to gaining access to an as yet ineffable or 'symbolized' world. Based on the above characterizations, Langer straddles both traditions effortlessly.[4]

For Langer, following Whitehead, philosophy has two major tasks: analysis and innovation. In 1938, Whitehead had described the difference between two schools of thought – the 'Critical School' and the 'Speculative School' – in ways that can be compared with the difference between analytic and continental philosophy. Whitehead claimed that the Critical School 'confines itself to verbal analysis within the limits of the dictionary', while the Speculative School 'enlarges the dictionary' by appealing to direct insight.[5] According to him, the Critical School *repudiates* speculative philosophy, while the Speculative School *includes* critical philosophy. His own verdict on the divergence between the schools is that it is 'a quarrel between safety and adventure'.[6] Needless to say, Whitehead himself, like Langer, felt more attracted to adventure. For both of them the role of philosophy, in dialogue with the humanities and the sciences, was to find linguistic expression for meanings as yet unexpressed. What Michael Weber said about Whitehead applies equally to Langer: the so-called Analytic–Continental divide had always been obsolete to him. Langer's philosophy, in short, offers a constructive model for bridging the divide between the analytic and continental traditions by uniting careful analysis with creative innovation, safety and adventure, *in one project*.

The *fourth* divide that Langer tries to overcome is that between Western and non-Western philosophy. Although Langer did not actively study or engage with non-Western philosophies as such, her lifelong interest in mythology, anthropology and non-Western forms of thinking enabled her to move beyond the traditional poles of empiricist positivism and rationalist logocentrism that mark much modern Western philosophy. Like Wittgenstein, Langer often felt misunderstood by her contemporaries. Wittgenstein often withdrew from the world of Western philosophy and turned to poetry for inspiration, especially the Indian poet Rabindranath Tagore. Langer, in turn, was fascinated by Cassirer's insights in *pre*-modern, mythical thought and ended up translating his *Language and Myth*. In one striking letter to an Indian philosopher she wrote that she felt that her own philosophy was sometimes better understood by non-Western readers than by Western. When a leading Indian philosopher and musicologist, Sushil Kumar Saxena, took a serious interest in Langer's aesthetics and published a book in which he compared it with a Hindustani aesthetics of rhythm and dance, she replied,

> Among all the reactions to my own ideas which I have received, yours has been one of the most gratifying. Unlike most of the others who have put their previous ideas into my words, I feel that you have understood what I have actually said. Perhaps your Indian background is more conducive to understanding than our Western habits of thought.[7]

While this, in itself, is not enough evidence to assert confidently that Langer's philosophy can bridge Western and non-Western modes of thinking, it provides a hint of its potential in this direction that is worthy of further exploration.

A *fifth* and final example of a divide that Langer's thought has the potential to bridge comes from the field for which she was best known, her philosophy of art. This divide concerns the pervasive hierarchical rift between, on the one hand, 'high art' as the world of the 'art institution' with its art galleries, art market, art colleges, art fairs, art prizes, critics, curators, collectors and investors and, on the other, 'low art', that is, all other forms of art such as folk art, liturgical art, popular art, public art, street art, community art, and so on. This distinction has its roots in the modern period, when the rise of separate institutions for viewing art, or listening to music, contributed to the idea that 'fine' or 'high' art is primarily an object of aesthetic contemplation and is meant to be attended to 'for its own sake.' This view of art overlooks the fact that, for much of human history, art has been a social practice that was embedded in religious, commemorative, political or other practices.[8] Today, due to various factors, the 'art world' has become ever more disconnected from these embedded artistic practices, either routinely ignoring these forms or, alternatively, inflating them and annexing them into its own market economy. Although a philosophy cannot itself directly change social practices, it can expose and challenge the theories implicitly sustaining them. Langer's philosophy of art implicitly challenges the institutional theory of art, as proposed by George Dickie and Arthur Danto in the 1980s, in which the institution becomes the main validator of art. Langer, by contrast, holds that, whether high or low, pure or applied, public or private, Western or non-Western, any form of artistic expression that imaginatively articulates pre-reflective, affective experience, properly falls within the single category of 'art'. For her, this is not an evaluative or aspirational term but a term of description of a particular, non-discursive way of symbolizing that results in the art form.

Ahead of her time

Although Langer *anticipated* many major turns in philosophy, she cannot be said to have *influenced* them – at least not in any demonstrable way. While several well-known philosophers with ideas not dissimilar to Langer are known to have read her works – Thomas Kuhn, Nelson Goodman, Paul Ricoeur, Michael Polanyi, Peter Kivy, Richard Wollheim, Arthur Danto and Mark Johnson, among others – there is no evidence that they have been directly influenced by her. At least they make very few references to her in their work. This suggests either that they have developed their ideas quite independently from her and happened to have come to very similar conclusions, or they may have been reluctant to acknowledge her because of her marginalized status in the profession.[9] Whatever the case, Langer's substantial intellectual legacy invites rediscovery and critical development in a much changed philosophical and cultural climate.

Critical development

There is something poignant about the fact that Langer's own capacious philosophical symphony was cut short at the end. Following her announcement that she could no longer continue due to failing eyesight, she writes,

> But even in its curtailed form, I hope my little concluding essay to end an Essay may serve what I consider the true purpose of the whole book: to suggest some ideas which other people may be able to use for their own work, anywhere and everywhere in the great domain of philosophical thought. Whatever may be wrong with it, all the dross that needs elimination notwithstanding, my fondest wish for it is that what is true or new in it may eventuate in a parade of projects for young thinkers with long ways to go.[10]

This modest description of the 'true purpose' of her life's work characterizes Langer's passion for philosophy and her selfless approach to her ambitious project. She is acutely aware of the loose threads and incomplete trains of thoughts in her corpus, and looks to a new generation of scholars to continue her project with fresh energy and creativity.

Let me suggest, by way of conclusion, just one major area that deserves much further attention. This is Langer's intriguing work on animal mentality and behaviour.

In a century in which humanoid robots and transhumanism are quickly becoming some of the most pressing topics in philosophy, it is surprising to observe how little rigorous philosophical work has so far been done on the difference between humans and (other) animals. In such a context, Langer's animal philosophy becomes particularly relevant and important. Langer is one of the very few twentieth-century philosophers who engaged in an extensive, empirically based, philosophical study of animal behaviour, repertoire, motivations, instincts, acts, ambients, values and so forth, with a view to establishing the 'great shift' from animal to human mentality. This she located in symbolic consciousness: unlike animals who react to signs, humans use symbols as vehicles for meaning that can refer to the past and to possible future events. At the same time, so she acknowledges, some chimpanzees display what could be called 'proto-symbolic' behaviour. This, in turn, invites further questions about the 'great shift' from instinct-driven animal to *animal symbolicum*, and about the implications of this shift for the enduring question of what it means to be human.

Langer herself invited young thinkers 'anywhere and everywhere' to take up the questions she was no longer able to pursue. She did much of the groundwork and planted many seeds. Her creative, critical thinking was always in flux and dynamic. Philosophy, for Langer, was above all 'an adventure of ideas'.[11] If this book has created curiosity among younger thinkers to continue that adventure, as she had done with the thinkers that inspired her, it will have achieved its purpose.

Notes

Introduction

1 Susanne K. Langer, 'On Cassirer's Theory of Language and Myth', in Paul Arthur Schilpp, ed., *The Philosophy of Ernst Cassirer*, The Library of Living Philosophers, Vol. 6 (La Salle, IL: Open Court, 1949), p. 381.

2 John J. McDermott, 'Symposium on Susanne K. Langer: A Foreword', *Transactions of the Charles S. Peirce Society* 33.1 (1997), p. 132; Ann E. Berthoff, 'Susanne K. Langer and "The Odyssey of the Mind"', *Semiotica* 128.1-2 (2000), p. 1; Howard Gardner, *Art, Mind, and the Brain: A Cognitive Approach to Creativity* (New York: Basic Books, 1982), p. 49. Bennett Reimer, 'Langer on the Arts as Cognitive', *Philosophy of Music Education Review* 1.1 (Spring 1993), p. 49; Robert Innis, 'Symposium on Susanne K. Langer: Introduction', *Journal of Speculative Philosophy* 21.1 (2007), p. 1; James R. Johnson, 'The Unknown Langer: Philosophy from the New Key to the Trilogy of Mind', *Journal of Aesthetic Education* 27.1 (1993), p. 63; James Campbell, 'Langer's Understanding of Philosophy', *Transactions of the Charles S. Peirce Society* 33.1 (1997), p. 143; Antonio Damasio, *The Feeling of What Happens: Body and Emotion in the Making of Consciousness* (San Diego, CA: Harcourt, 1999), p. 287.

3 Campbell, 'Langer's Understanding of Philosophy', p.133.

4 Reimer, 'Langer on the Arts as Cognitive'.

5 Recent books on Langer include: Barbara Kösters, *Gefühl, Abstraktion, symbolische Transformation: zu Susanne Langers Philosophie des Lebendigen* (Frankfurt am Main: Peter Lang, 1993); Krzysztof Guczalski, *Znaczenie muzyki: znaczenia w muzyce: próba ogólnej teorii na tle estetyki Susanne Langer* (Krakow: Musica Iagellonica, 1999); Rolf Lachmann, *Susanne K. Langer: die lebendige Form menschlichen Fühlens und Verstehens* (München: W. Fink, 2000); Sushil Saxena, *Hindustani Sangeet and a Philosopher of Art: Music, Rhythm, and Kathak Dance vis-à-vis Aesthetics of Susanne K. Langer* (New Delhi: D.K. Printworld, 2001); Lucia Demartis, *L'estetica Simbolica di Susanne Katherina Langer* (Italy: Centro internazionale studi di estetica, 2004); Carlo Brentari, *La Nascita della Coscienza Simbolica: L'antropologia Filosofica di Susanne Langer* (Trento: Università degli studi di Trento, 2007); Cornelia Richter, *Naturalisierung des Geistes und Symbolisierung des Fühlens: Susanne K. Langer im Gespräch der Forschung* (Marburg: Tectum-Verlag, 2008); Agnes Neumayr, *Politik Der Gefühle: Susanne K. Langer und Hannah Arendt*, 1. Aufl. (Innsbruck: Innsbruck University Press, 2009); Robert E. Innis, *Susanne Langer in Focus: The Symbolic Mind* (Bloomington: Indiana University Press, 2009); Symposia and special focus journal issues on Langer include: 'Langer Symposium', *The Journal of Philosophy* 81.11 (November 1984), pp. 641–63 (with contributions from: Arthur C. Danto, 'Mind as Feeling; Form as Presence; Langer as Philosopher', pp. 641–7; Ronald De Sousa, 'Teleology and the Great Shift', pp. 647–53; Stefan Morawski, 'Art as Semblance', pp. 654–63); 'Special Focus Issue', *Process Studies* 26.1-2 (April 1997), pp. 57–150 (with contributions from: Rolf Lachmann, 'Special Focus Introduction', pp. 57–61;

Donald Dryden, 'Whitehead's Influence on Susanne Langer's Conception of Living Form', pp. 62–85; Randall Auxier, 'Susanne Langer on Symbols and Analogy: A Case of Misplaced Concreteness?', pp. 86–106; Rolf Lachmann, 'From Metaphysics to Art and Back: The Relevance of Susanne K. Langer's Philosophy for Process Metaphysics', pp. 107–25; Rolf Lachmann, 'Susanne K. Langer's Notes on Whitehead's Course on Philosophy of Nature', pp. 126–150); 'Symposium on Susanne K. Langer', *Transactions of the Charles S. Peirce Society* 33.1 (1997), pp. 133–200 (with contributions from: John J. McDermott, 'Symposium on Susanne K. Langer: A Foreword', pp. 131–2; James Campbell, 'Langer's Understanding of Philosophy', pp. 133–47; Richard M. Liddy, 'Susanne K. Langer's Philosophy of Mind', pp. 149–60; Vincent Colapietro, 'Reading as Experience', pp. 861–8; Donald Dryden, 'Susanne K. Langer and American Philosophic Naturalism in the Twentieth Century', pp. 161–82; Richard E. Hart, 'Langer's Aesthetics of Poetry', pp. 183–200); 'Symposium on Susanne K. Langer', *Journal of Speculative Philosophy* 21.1 (2007), pp. 1–43 (with contributions from: Robert E. Innis, 'Symposium on Susanne K. Langer: Introduction', pp. 1–3 and 'Placing Langer's Philosophical Project', pp. 4–15; Felicia Kruse, 'Vital Rhythm and Temporal Form in Langer and Dewey', pp. 16–26; Donald Dryden, 'The Philosopher as Prophet and Visionary: Susanne Langer's Essay on Human Feeling in the Light of Subsequent Developments in the Sciences', pp. 27–43); 'Polanyi and Langer', *Tradition and Discovery: The Polanyi Society Periodical* 36.1 (2010), pp. 6–41 (with contributions from: Walter B. Gulick, 'Polanyi and Some Philosophical Neighbors: Introduction to this Issue', pp. 6–7; Robert E. Innis, 'Between Articulation and Symbolization: Framing Polanyi and Langer', pp. 8–20; Walter B. Gulick, 'Polanyi and Langer: Toward a Reconfigured Theory of Knowing and Meaning', pp. 21–37; Vincent Colapietro, 'Acknowledgment, Responsibility, and Innovation: A Response to Robert Innis and Walter Gulick', pp. 38–41); Special Issue on Langer, *Sztuka I filozofia/Art and Philosophy* 48 (2016), pp. 5–79 (with contributions from: Adrienne Dengerink Chaplin, 'Feeling the Body in Art: Embodied Cognition and Aesthetics in Mark Johnson and Susanne K. Langer', pp. 5–11; Martina Sauer, 'Ikonologie und formale Ästhetik: eine neue Einheit. Ein Beitrag zur aktuellen Debatte in Kunstwissenschaft und Kunstphilosophie im Anschluss an die (Bild-)Akt-Theorien Susanne K. Langers und John M. Krois', pp. 12–29; Agnė Kulbytė, 'Susanne K. Langer as a Romantic Thinker', pp. 30–8; Albert van der Schoot, 'Kivy I Langer o ekspresyjnoś, pp. 39–45; Maria Kominek-Karolak, 'Hermeneutyka muzyki Susanne K. Langer', pp. 46–55; James R. Johnson, 'Langer nieznana: od Nowego sensu filozofii do trylogii o umyśle', pp. 70–9).

6   Lancelot Law Whyte, 'Review of: *Philosophy in a New Key*', *British Journal for the Philosophy of Science* 2.5 (1951), p. 68. Whyte adds, 'Mrs Langer appears to understand better than another writer known to him the essential character of the symbolic transformation of experience … and more precisely the universal human and psychological factors underlying the origins and growth of all cultural activities, as against the special forms characteristic of particular cultures.' p. 69.

7   Although there is no consensus about the terminology, aesthetics, as a study of the nature of beauty, art and sense perception, is generally considered to be a sub-discipline of philosophy. If the topics falling under aesthetics are studied primarily empirically, it can also fall under psychology, sociology, art history, cultural theory, evolutionary biology or any other related field.

8   W. V. Quine, 'Mr. Strawson on Logical Theory', *Mind* 62.248 (October 1953), p. 446. Ironically, her direct engagements with biology and other empirical sciences in her

later work was sometimes seen to undermine the putative 'purity' of professional philosophy.

9   Mary Reichling, 'A Woman Ahead of Her Time: The Langer Legacy', *Philosophy of Music Education Review* 6.1 (1998), pp. 12–21.

10 Donald Dryden, 'The Philosopher as Prophet and as Visionary: Susanne Langer's Essay on Human Feeling in the Light of Subsequent Developments in the Sciences', *Journal of Speculative Philosophy* 21.1 (2007), pp. 27–43.

11 Langer read works by philosophers such as Gottlob Frege, Edmund Husserl, Cassirer and *Gestalt* theorists Friedrich Sander and Heinz Werner long before they were translated into English.

12 Her own writings were always in dialogue with the most recent scholarly publications on both sides of the Atlantic; and her ability to survey and distil the main trends of the philosophy of her time can be seen reflected in her magisterial 1950 article, co-authored with her research assistant Eugene T. Gadol, 'The Deepening Mind: A Half-Century of American Philosophy', *American Quarterly* 2.2 (Summer 1950), pp. 118–32.

13 Howard Gardner put it thus, 'Langer has never broken into the charmed circles of mainstream philosophers'. Gardner, *Art, Mind and the Brain*, p. 54.

14 Rolf Lachmann, *Susanne K. Langer: die lebendige Form menschlichen Fühlens und Verstehens* (München: W. Fink, 2000).

15 Robert E. Innis, *Susanne Langer in Focus: The Symbolic Mind* (Bloomington: Indiana University Press, 2009).

16 See also Robert E. Innis, 'Placing Langer's Philosophical Project', *Journal of Speculative Philosophy* 21.1 (2007), pp. 4–15.

17 The whole passage reads as follows:

> While … American philosophy in any traditional sense was neither a source nor a resource for Langer, her philosophical project can be an additional resource for it and for development of its continuing relevance and analytical power. It supplies independent confirmation of some of American philosophy's central theses and focal concerns and supplies new sets of conceptual tools for broadening its appeal and exemplifying its essentially open character. (Innis, *Susanne Langer in Focus*, p. 3)

18 Letter from Sir Herbert Read to Susanne K. Langer, 28 June 1957. Susanne Langer papers, Houghton Library, Box 3.

19 Letter from Langer to Sir Herbert Read, 29 August 1957. Susanne Langer papers, Houghton Library, Box 3.

20 Susanne K. Langer, *Introduction to Symbolic Logic* (First edition, London: George Allen & Unwin, 1937), p. 11.

21 Susanne Langer, 'On Cassirer's Theory of Language and Myth', in Paul Arthur Schilpp, ed., *The Philosophy of Ernst Cassirer*, The Library of Living Philosophers, Vol. 6 (Evanston, IL: Library of Living Philosophers, 1949), p. 381.

1 Life and work

1   Winthrop Sargeant, 'Philosopher in a New Key', Profiles, *New Yorker* 36 (3 December 1960), pp. 67–100. Sargeant (1903–1986) was a violinist turned classical music and jazz journalist, who had been the music editor for *Time Magazine* from 1937 to 1945

and was a regular music columnist for *The New Yorker* from 1949 to 1972; James Lord, 'A Lady Seeking Answers', *The New York Times Book Review* (26 May 1968), pp. 4, 5, 35. Lord (1922–2009) was well known for his memoirs and biographies of artists, especially Giacometti and Picasso whom he had known personally after befriending them in the cafes and salons of post-war Paris.

2 Donald Dryden, 'Susanne K. Langer 1895–1985', in P. B. Dematteis and L. B. McHenry, eds, *American Philosophers Before 1950*, Dictionary of Literary Biography, Vol. 270 (Farmington Hills, MI: Gale, 2003), pp. 189–99. Subsequent annotated version unpublished. The biography is based on one meeting with Langer and various interviews with family and friends. In 1995 Dryden was involved with the inventory of Langer's papers housed at the Houghton Library at Harvard. The papers were donated by Susanne Langer's eldest son Leonard C. R. Langer between 1985 and 1995, with two further instalments in 2003 prior to his death in 2009.

3 Wesley Wehr, 'Susanne K. Langer: Philosopher of Art and Science', in Wesley Wehr, ed., *The Accidental Collector: Art, Fossils, and Friendships* (Washington, DC: University of Washington Press, 2004), pp. 106–43.

4 According to one story, in a heated debate among scientists, she had identified and clarified the key issue with such lucidity that the physicist Robert J. Oppenheimer had sent her a letter afterwards thanking her for her intervention. Wehr, *Accidental Collector*, pp. 124, 125.

5 Sargeant, 'Philosopher in a New Key', pp. 90, 91. William R. Greer, 'Susanne K. Langer, Philosopher, Is Dead at 89', *New York Times*, 19 July 1985, p. A12. In a recorded conversation between Langer and the poet Elizabeth Bishop, Langer admits her impatience with lazy thinking. The conversation was first published in the *Harvard Review* (Winter 1993), pp. 128–30. Reprinted in Wesley Wehr, *The Eighth Lively Art: Conversations with Painters, Poets, Musicians & the Wicked Witch of the West* (Washington, DC: University of Washington Press, 2000), pp. 185–90.

6 Susanne K. Langer, *Philosophy in a New Key: A Study in the Symbolism of Reason, Rite, and Art* (Third edition, Cambridge, MA: Harvard University Press, 1980); *Feeling and Form: A Theory of Art Developed from Philosophy in a New Key* (New York: Charles Scribner's Sons, 1953).

7 Sargeant, 'Philosopher in a New Key', pp. 90, 91.

8 The fact that Langer entered her undergraduate studies at the relatively late age of 21 may have been related to her fragile health. Langer suffered chronic health problems stemming from a cocaine poisoning she suffered as a child when a pharmacist made an error in filling in a prescription. This had required frequent periods of home instruction. Dryden, 'Susanne K. Langer 1895–1985', p. 190. There is no evidence for Winthrop Sargeant's suggestion that she would have delayed her studies because of her father disapproval of women's education since her older sister had already gone to college before Langer. Sargeant, 'Philosopher in a New Key', p. 67ff.

9 Quoted in Dryden, 'Susanne K. Langer', p. 191.

10 Ibid.

11 Ibid.

12 In the 1941 Preface to *Philosophy in a New Key*, she expresses her thanks to her son Leonard for his 'help with the indexes', p. xv.

13 Susanne K. Langer, *The Cruise of Little Dipper and Other Fairy Tales* (New York: New York Graphic Society, 1923). Helen Sewell was also the illustrator of the early editions of the well-known series of children books by Laura Ingalls Wilder.

Langer dedicated her book *Problems of Art* to Sewell with the inscription 'To my lifelong Socratic teacher in the Arts, Helen Sewell'.

14 Susanne K. Langer, 'Confusion of Symbols and Confusion of Logical Types', *Mind* 35 (April 1926), pp. 222–9; 'Form and Content: A Study in Paradox', *Journal of Philosophy* 23 (5 August 1926), pp. 435–8; 'A Logical Study of Verbs', *Journal of Philosophy* 24 (3 March 1927), pp. 120–9; 'Facts: The Logical Perspectives of the World', *Journal of Philosophy* 30 (30 March 1933), pp. 178–87.

15 'William L. Langer: Historian of Diplomacy (1896–1977). Memorial Minute adopted by the Faculty of Arts and Sciences, Harvard University', in Herbert F. Vetter, ed., *Notable American Unitarians 1936–1961: Concise, Personal Biographies of over 100 American Unitarians Who Changed the World* (Cambridge, MA: Harvard Square Library, 2007), pp. 133–5. See also: Langer, William L. (1896–1977), Harvard University Faculty Memorial Minute, http://www.harvardsquarelibrary.org/ biographies/william-l-langer/. (accessed 15 April 2019).

16 William Langer, *In and Out of the Ivory Tower: The Autobiography of William L. Langer* (First edition, Sagamore Beach, MA: Watson Publishers International, 1978; Reprint: New York: Walter de Gruyter, 1991).

17 Dorothy Ross, 'William Langer. *In and Out of the Ivory Tower: The Autobiography of William L. Langer*', *American Historical Review* 84.1 (February 1979), p. 123.

18 Robert Lee Wolff, 'William Leonard Langer', *Proceedings of the Massachusetts Historical Society*, Third Series, 89 (1977), p. 190.

19 When Husserl retired from his Freiburg professorship in 1928, he was succeeded by his pupil Heidegger who, in 1933, became rector of the university.

20 Since 1938 Husserl's *Nachlass* has been looked after and edited by the Husserl-Archives in Leuven. Sebastian Luft, 'Die Archivierung des Husserlschen Nachlasses 1933–1935', *Husserl Studies* 20 (Dordrecht: Kluwer Academic, 2014), pp. 4–5.

21 C. J. Ducasse and Haskell B. Curry, 'Early History of the Association for Symbolic Logic', *Journal of Symbolic Logic* 27.3 (September 1962), p. 257.

22 Langer did not mince her words in her reviews. Concluding her review of an article by a French logician she writes, 'There are only two possible explanations for an article so obsolete at the time of its appearance: either, that it was written as a review of Goblot's book at the time when that work was new (1918), and has lain dormant like Rip Van Winkle all these years, or else, that a logician whose reading is limited to the French language (as M. [*sic*] Picard's footnotes suggest) can actually miss a whole movement of thought that happens to have grown mainly in other countries. In either event, the *Revue* [*de Metaphysique et de Morale* (18.4): 478–490] gives a surprising amount of space to so little that is new.' 'Jacques Picard, "Syllogisme catégorique et syllogisme hypothétique" (premier article)', *Journal of Symbolic Logic* 1.2 (June 1936), p. 64. In 1945 she criticizes an author for his poor literary skills as follows: 'It is truly a pity that this author's literary style is so far below his professional competence that a very interesting essay is completely ruined by clumsy rhetorical affectations'. Review of *The Enjoyment of the Arts* by Max Schoen', *Philosophy and Phenomenological Research*, 5.4 (June 1945), p. 609. And in a review of Gilbert Ryle's *The Concept of Mind* (1949), she comments, 'One can never even tell whether the nameless intellectualist whom Professor Ryle is demolishing is the Man in the Street, or is a real philosopher, someone of the calibre of Russell, Carnap, and Lewis. ... The result of the author's cavalier treatment of all and sundry colleagues is that he often fights a straw man, so his victory, though complete, is too easy.' 'In Praise of Common Sense: A Review of "*The Concept of Mind* by Gilbert Ryle"', *Hudson Review* 4.1 (Spring 1951), p. 147.

23   Susanne K. Langer, *An Introduction to Symbolic Logic* (First edition,
     New York: Houghton Mifflin; London: George Allen & Unwin, 1937); Second
     revised edition and third edition (New York: Dover Publications, 1953 and 1967);
     Republication of the second edition (New York: Dover Publications, 2011).

24   Joel Isaac,*Working Knowledge: Making the Human Sciences from Parsons to Kuhn*
     (Cambridge, MA: Harvard University Press, 2012), p. 155.

25   Susanne K Langer, *The Practice of Philosophy* (New York: Henry Holt, 1930); *An
     Introduction to Symbolic Logic* (New York: Houghton Mifflin; London: George Allen &
     Unwin, 1937).

26   Max Hall, *Harvard University Press: A History* (Cambridge, MA: Harvard University
     Press, 1986), pp. 80 and 117.

27   Ibid., p. 80.

28   Sargeant, 'Philosopher in a New Key', pp. 67–100.

29   William remarried a year after his divorce to Rowena Morse Nelson. He died in 1977,
     a few months after completing his autobiography. Obituary 'William Langer Dies at
     81', *New York Times*, 27 December 1977.

30   The comments by Langer's son Leonard were passed on to Rolf Lachmann in a
     conversation in 1992. Rolf Lachmann, *Susanne K. Langer: die lebendige Form
     menschlichen Fühlens und Verstehens* (München: W. Fink, 2000), p. 23, footnote 25.
     Her friend Wesley Wehr records that she once told him, 'I know what divorce can
     be like, having been through it myself. At first, it tears you to pieces. But then you
     just want to get through it, and be done with it, and get on with your own life.' Wehr,
     Accidental Collector, p. 135.

31   Letter from Cassirer to Langer dated 8 April 1944. Quoted in Rolf Lachmann, *Susanne
     K. Langer*, p. 25.

32   Artists associated with the modern movement in New York included Hans Hofmann,
     Milton Avery, John D. Graham, Mark Rothko, Willem de Kooning, Arshile Gorky,
     Clyfford Still, Jackson Pollock, Robert Motherwell, Helen Frankenthaler, Lee Krasner,
     Ad Reinhardt, Herbert Ferber and Barnett Newman. The image on the front cover is a
     painting by Helen Frankenthaler, called *Blessing of the Fleet*, 1969.

33   For a later Langerian reading of Barnett Newman, see Renée van de Vall, *Een Subliem
     Gevoel van Plaats: Een Filosofische Interpretatie van het werk van Barnett Newman*
     (Groningen: Historische Uitgeverij, 1994), pp. 121–34.

34   The lectures were recorded and published in Clement Greenberg, *Homemade
     Aesthetics* (Oxford: Oxford University Press, 2000). The material in Part II is excerpted
     from *Clement Greenberg: The Bennington Seminars,* edited by Peggy Schiffer Noland.

35   Significantly, Greenberg endorses Newman in his essay, 'Feeling Is All' in the *Partisan
     Review* 19.1 (January/February 1952) as 'a very important and original artist'.

36   The quip is quoted in the chapter, 'Barnett Newman: The Living Rectangle', in Harold
     Rosenberg, *The Anxious Object: Art Today and Its Audience* (New York: Horizon
     Press, 1964), p. 172. For a more extensive statement see: 'I consider the artist and
     the aesthetician to be mutually exclusive terms. The possibility that they could
     meet together to discuss either art or aesthetics on some equal footing was to me
     so absurd that I have come [instead] as an ordinary citizen to witness the event. ...
     I have insisted on coming here as a citizen because I feel that even if aesthetics is
     established as a science, it doesn't affect me as an artist. I've done quite a bit of work
     in ornithology; I have never met an ornithologist who ever thought that ornithology
     was for the birds.' Barnett Newman, 'Remarks at the Fourth Annual Woodstock Art

Conference', in John P. O'Neill, ed., *Barnett Newman, Selected Writings and Interviews* (New York: Alfred A. Knopf, 1990), pp. 242, 247.

37 The conference was co-sponsored by the American Society for Aesthetics and the Woodstock Artists Association. Other speakers at the conference included David Smith, Franz Boaz and painters Mark Rothko and Robert Motherwell. Motherwell (1915–1991) studied philosophy and aesthetics at Stanford (BA, 1937) and Harvard and art history at Columbia University with art historian Meyer Shapiro. Although his periods at Harvard and Columbia co-incided with those of Langer, he makes no reference to her writings in his essays or interviews. Even so, his conception of art as organized feeling that permeates all his art critical writings, is deeply Langerian. Dore Ashton, ed., *The Writings of Robert Motherwell* (Berkeley: University of California Press, 2007). See, for instance: 'We feel through the senses, and everyone knows that the content of art is feeling' and 'Feelings must have a medium in order to function at all; in the same way, thought must have symbols. It is the medium, or the specific configuration of the medium that we call a work of art that brings feeling into being.' 'Beyond the Aesthetic', *Design* (April 1946), pp. 14, 15. Reprinted in *The Writings of Robert Motherwell*, pp. 54, 55..

38 For an account of Langer's influence on Jorn, see Graham Birtwistle, *Living Art: Asger Jorn's Comprehensive Theory of Art between Helhesten and Cobra (1946–1949)* (Utrecht: Reflex, 1986), pp. 109, 122.

39 Walker Percy, *The Message in the Bottle* (1954) (New York: Farrar, Strauss and Giroux, 1981).

40 In a private letter to Langer, Herbert Read writes, 'You have no more devoted admirer in the world, and I have been reading your new book *Problems of Art,* with unfailing enthusiasm.' 23 June 1957. Houghton Library archive, Box 3. In his foreword to the abridged version of *Mind*, Danto refers to the content as '[o]ne of the most audacious philosophical visions of recent times'. Susanne K. Langer, *Mind: An Essay on Human Feeling*, ed. Gary van der Heuvel (Baltimore, MD: Johns Hopkins University Press, 1988), p. vi.

41 Wehr, *Accidental Collector*, p. 123.

42 http://archive.danceheritage.org/assets/42ce0ec8-8d40-4f71-bc24-6b12ef54c6a6 (accessed 15 April 2019).

43 Sargeant puts it thus, 'She managed to live an appropriately solitary life of contemplation in a community whose addiction to cocktail parties and weekend sociability [was] pursued with a determination that frightened even hardened visitors from Manhattan.' Sargeant, 'Philosopher in a New Key', p. 67.

44 According to semioticist Ann Berthoff, Langer was a gifted lecturer who could keep large audiences captivated with her ideas and comments, '[A]nyone reading *Philosophical Sketches* can join such an audience, since almost all of these ideas were first lectures.' Ann E. Berthoff, 'Susanne K. Langer and "the odyssey of the mind"', *Semiotica* 128.1-2 (2000), p. 29.

45 Susanne K. Langer, *Problems of Art* (New York: Charles Scribner's Sons, 1957); *Philosophical Sketches* (Baltimore, MD: Johns Hopkins University Press, 1962); *Mind: An Essay on Human Feeling*, Vols I, II and III (Baltimore, MD: Johns Hopkins University Press, 1967, 1971 and 1982).

46 A reviewer for the journal *Science* referred to her trilogy *Mind* as 'a radically revised conception of the nature of the reality which all sciences are trying to describe'. Robert B. MacLeod, 'Review of *Mind I*', *Science* (29 September 1967), quoted by Donald Dryden, 'Susanne K. Langer 1895–1985', in P. B. Dematteis

and L.B. McHenry, eds, *Dictionary of Literary Biography: American Philosophers before 1950*, Vol. 270 (Farmington Hills, MI: Gale, 2003), p. 198. Another reviewer wrote: 'No contemporary philosopher has combed the literature of the sciences more painstakingly and interpreted it with greater insight.' Dryden also mentions that Langer 'was invited by the biologist C. H. Waddington to join fifteen other biologists, physicists, and mathematicians in an interdisciplinary symposium on the theoretical foundations of biology held in 1968 in Bellagio, Italy' (ibid., p. 198).

47 Sargeant, 'Philosopher in a New Key', p. 67.

2 European philosophy in America

1   Susanne Langer and Eugene T. Gadol, 'The Deepening Mind: A Half-Century of American Philosophy', *American Quarterly* 2.2 (Summer 1950), pp. 118–32.

2   Münsterberg had been recruited by William James to oversee his experimental psychology laboratory.

3   Susanne K. Langer, 'Henry M. Sheffer, 1883–1964', *Philosophy and Phenomenological Research* 25.2 (December 1964), p. 306. Dates of the five philosophers are: William James: 1842–1910; George Santayana: 1963–1952; George Herbert Palmer: 1842–1933; Josiah Royce: 1855–September 1916; Hugo Münsterberg: 1863–December 1916.

4   Langer and Gadol, 'The Deepening Mind', p. 119.

5   Ibid., pp. 118, 119.

6   Ibid., p. 119.

7   Ibid.

8   Ibid., pp. 119, 120.

9   Ibid., p. 120.

10 Because of his marriage to the American-born Quaker Alys Pearsall Smith, a graduate of Bryn Mawr College and a women's rights campaigner, Russell was a regular visitor to America. Russell was married Alys from 1894 to 1922.

11 Quoted in Barry Feinberg and Ronald Kasrils, eds, *Bertrand Russell's America: His Transatlantic Travels and Writings, Volume One, 1896–1945* (London: Allen & Unwin, 1973; Routledge, 2014), p. 12. Russell first lectured in America in 1896 and last in 1951. Like Whitehead later, Russell had initially an idealistic picture of America as an example of democracy and freedom.

12 The lectures were subsequently published as *Our Knowledge of the External World as a Field for Scientific Method in Philosophy* (1914). One of Russell's students in that class was the poet T[homas] S[tearns] Eliot, who was writing a dissertation on the British Philosopher Francis H. Bradley. He refers to Russell's class in his poem 'Mr Appolinax.' Bernard Linsky, 'Notes on Bertrand Russell', *Blog Entry*, Friday, 30 May 2014. https://commons.trincoll.edu/rring/2014/05/30/notes-on-bertrand-russell (accessed 18 May 2019).

13 Bruce Kuklick, *The Rise of American Philosophy: Cambridge, Massachusetts 1860–1930* (New Haven, CT: Yale University Press, 1977), pp. 410, 411. Although Russell was attracted to what he initially conceived as America's free spirit, his own experiences of the country did not always match up to his idealized picture. In one letter home he refers to what he experienced as the stifling and pompous atmosphere at Harvard as 'hell'. In addition to his strong ties to Britain this may

also explain why, despite repeated invitations and requests from Harvard and other American universities, Russell never accepted a permanent position. Kirk Wills, "'This Place is Hell": Bertrand Russell at Harvard, 1914', *The New England Quarterly* 62.1 (March 1989), pp. 3–26.

14 In the same year that he delivered the William James lectures at Harvard, in 1940, Russell was offered an appointment at the City College of New York. The offer was subsequently withdrawn after protests about his liberal views on sexual morality.

15 Like Russell, Moritz Schlick was married to an American.

16 During his 1929 visit to Stanford University, the American philosopher and future editor of the Library of Living Philosophers, Paul Arthur Schilpp served as the assistant of Schlick and arranged for more invitations to European philosophers to come to America. For details of Schlick's lecture schedules see 'Editorisher Bericht', in Johannes Friedl and Heiner Rutte, eds, *Moritz Schlick Erkenntnistheoretische Schriften* 1926–1936, Kritische Gesamtausgabe Abteilung II, Band 1.2 (Wien: Springer, 2013), pp. 365–70.

17 Mach occupied the chair for 'the history and philosophy of the inductive sciences' at the University of Vienna from 1895 to 1901.

18 Quoted in Gerald James Holton, *Science and Anti-Science* (Cambridge, MA: Harvard University Press, 1993), p. 32.

19 Holton, *Science and Anti-Science*, p. 2.

20 The name '*Wienerkreiss*' (Vienna Circle) was originally suggested by Otto Neurath, with the intention of evoking pleasant local associations such as the Vienna woods or Viennese waltz. See Friedrich Stadler, 'The Vienna Circle: Context, Profile and Development', in Alan Richardson and Thomas Uebel, eds, *The Cambridge Companion to Logical Empiricism* (Cambridge: Cambridge University Press, 2007), p. 13.

21 Rose Rand, *Minutes and Transcriptions from the Vienna Circle*, 1931, undated Box 10, Folder 9. Rose Rand Papers, 1903–1981, ASP.1990.01, Archives of Scientific Philosophy, Special Collections Department, University of Pittsburgh; http://digital. library.pitt.edu/u/ulsmanuscripts/pdf/31735061817833.pdf (accessed 16 April 2019).

22 Edward Skidelsky, *Ernst Cassirer: The Last Philosopher of Culture* (Princeton, NJ: Princeton University Press, 2008), p. 255.

23 Moritz Schlick, *General Theory of Knowledge (1918)*. Quoted in Skidelsky, *Ernst Cassirer*, p. 134.

24 Moritz Schlick, *Raum und Zeit in der gegenwärtigen Physik: Zur Einführung in das Verständnis der Relativitäts- und Gravitationstheorie* (Berlin: Springer, 1922). Translated as *Space and Time in Contemporary Physics: An Introduction to the Theory of Relativity and Gravitation* (New York: Oxford University Press, 1920); Hans Reichenbach, *Relativitätstheorie und Erkenntnis Apriori* (Berlin: Springer, 1920). Translated as *The Theory of Relativity and A Priori Knowledge* by Maria Reichenbach (Berkeley: University of California Press, 1965); Ernst Cassirer, *Zur Einsteinschen Relativitätstheorie. Erkenntnistheoretische Betrachtungen* (Berlin: Bruno Cassirer, 1921). Translated as *Einstein's Theory of Relativity* (Chicago, IL: Open Court, 1923). Einstein, in turn, wrote responses to these works. Schlick wrote an influential review of Cassirer's views: 'Kritizistische oder empiristische Deutung der neuen Physik?' *Kant-Studien* 26 (1921), pp. 96–111.

25 Rudolf Carnap, 'Intellectual Autobiography', in Paul Arthur Schilpp, ed., *The Philosophy of Rudolf Carnap, The Library of Living Philosophers*, Vol. 11 (La Salle, IL: Open Court, 1963), p. 24.

26 Ray Monk, *Ludwig Wittgenstein: The Duty of Genius* (London: Vintage Books, 1991), p. 242.

27 Moritz Schlick, letter to Ernst Cassirer, 30 March 1927. Schlick–Cassirer
    Correspondence, Archive of the Vienna Circle, University of Amsterdam. Quoted in
    Skidelsky, *Ernst Cassirer*, p. 138. Wittgenstein's 'hypnotic spell' is also hinted at in John
    Maynard Keynes' quip to his wife upon Wittgenstein's return to Cambridge: 'Well,
    God has arrived. I met him on the 5.15 train.' Quoted in Monk, *Ludwig Wittgenstein*,
    p. 255.

28 Herbert Feigl, *Inquiries and Provocations: Selected Writings 1929–1974*, in Robert
    S. Cohen, ed., Vienna Circle Collection, Vol. 14 (Dordrecht: D. Reidel, 1982), p. 21.
    Schlick was the only person who was trusted by Wittgenstein to organize any
    meetings of the Circle with him. The meetings were small gatherings of trusted
    philosophers that included Schlick's student Herbert Feigl, and, for a short period,
    Rudolf Carnap.

29 Ludwig Wittgenstein, *Tractatus Logico-Philosophicus* (1922), Trans. C. K. Ogden
    (London: Routledge, 1996), p. 27.

30 For an account of the similarities between Schlick's and Wittgenstein's views of
    language see Aldo Gargani, 'Schlick and Wittgenstein: Language and Experience', in
    Stuart Shanker, ed., *Ludwig Wittgenstein: Critical Assessments: From the Notebooks
    to Philosophical Grammar: The Construction and Dismantling of the Tractatus*, Vol. 1
    (Abingdon: Routledge, 2000), pp. 275–86.

31 'Letter from Moritz Schlick to Henry Holt & Co, 22 March, 1931', Johannes Friedl and
    Heiner Rutte, eds, *Moritz Schlick: Die Wiener Zeit: Aufsätze, Beitrage, Rezensionen
    1926–1936* (Wien: Springer Verlag, 2008), p. 383, footnote 7.

32 The full footnote reads: 'Schlick bekam das Buch im Sommer 1930 vom New Yorker
    Verlag zugeschickt, im Antwortschreiben lobt er das Werk fast überschwenglich
    [exquisite style, lucid, fluent and brilliant, has been a source of real joy for me] mit
    der Einschränkung, dass der zweite Teil des Buches genüber dem im ersten Teil
    dargestellten wahren Methode der Philosophie, der Methode der logischen Analyse,
    wieder in eine traditionelle Haltung zurückfällt, also nach der oben eingeführten
    Terminologie philosophische und wissenschaftliche Einstellung vermengt.' Friedl and
    Rutte, *Moritz Schlick: Die Wiener Zeit*, p. 383, footnote 7. The footnote only appears in
    the German edition and not in Moritz Schlick, 'The Future of Philosophy', in Richard
    Rorty, ed., *The Linguistic Turn: Essays in Philosophical Method* (1967) (Chicago,
    IL: University of Chicago Press, 1992), pp. 43–53.

33 Johannes Friedl and Heiner Rutte comment: 'Den Ausdruck "Pursuit of Meaning"
    übernimmt Schlick von Langer'. Johannes Friedl and Heiner Rutte, eds, *Moritz Schlick
    Erkenntnistheoretische Schriften 1926–1936*, Kritische Gesamtausgabe Abteilung II,
    Band 1.2 (Wien: Springer Verlag, 2013), p. 297, footnote 3.

34 Moritz Schlick, 'The Future of Philosophy', in Johannes Friedl and Heiner Rutte,
    eds, *Moritz Schlick: Die Wiener Zeit: Aufsätze, Beitrage, Rezensionen 1926–1936*
    (Vienna: Springer-Verlag, 2008), p. 387. The first record of a lecture under this title is
    in the *Proceedings of the Seventh International Congress of Philosophy*, held in Oxford
    in 1930, Gilbert Ryle ed. (Oxford: Oxford University Press, 1931), pp. 112–16. An
    extended version of the lecture was presented at the University of California in 1932
    and published in *College of the Pacific Publications in Philosophy*, Vol. 1 (Stockton,
    CA, 1932), pp. 45–62, and *University of California Publications in Philosophy*
    15 (Berkeley: University of California, 1932), pp. 99–125. It was subsequently
    published in Henk L. Mulder and Barbara F. B. Van de Velde-Schlick, eds, *Moritz
    Schlick: Philosophical Papers*, Vol. 2 (1925–1936) (Dordrecht: D. Reidel, 1979),
    pp. 171–6. Other reprints include Yuri Balashov and Alexander Rosenberg, eds,

Philosophy of Science: Contemporary Readings (London: Routledge, 2002), pp. 8–21. And, more recently, Friedl and Rutte, *Moritz Schlick: Die Wiener Zeit*, pp. 371–92. My references are taken from Friedl and Rutte's 2008 edition.

35 Moritz Schlick, *Moritz Schlick: Die Wiener Zeit*, p. 383.

36 Schlick's supposed critique likely draws on the following two theses by Wittgenstein: 'Philosophy is not one of the natural sciences. (The word "philosophy" must mean something which stands above or below, but not beside the natural sciences) (4111)' and 'The result of philosophy is not a number of "philosophical propositions", but to make propositions clear' (4.112). Ludwig Wittgenstein, *Tractatus Logico-Philosophicus* (1922), trans. C. K. Ogden (London: Routledge, 1996).

37 In *The Practice of Philosophy* Langer wrote, '*Philosophy, which is the systematic study of meaning, comprises all the rational sciences* [i.e. mathematics and logic]'. S. K. Langer, *The Practice of Philosophy* (New York: Holt, 1930), pp. 35, 36. She also wrote that all 'sciences not only are, but must be, *born of* philosophy' and that 'a natural science is philosophical until, and only until, it is scientifically respectable.' Langer, *The Practice of Philosophy*, p. 41.

38 The Vienna Circle Manifesto states, '*[T]here is no such thing as philosophy as a basic or universal science alongside or above the various fields of the one empirical science;* there is no way to genuine knowledge other than the way of experience; there is no realm of ideas that stands over or beyond experience.' Hans Hahn, Otto Neurath and Rudolf Carnap, 'The Scientific Conception of the World: The Vienna Circle (Manifesto)', in Marie Neurath and Robert S. Cohen, eds, *Empiricism and Sociology*, Vienna Circle Collection, Vol. 1 (Dordrecht: D. Reidel, 1973), p. 316.

39 Moritz Schlick, 'The Future of Philosophy', in Richard Rorty, ed., *The Linguistic Turn: Essays in Philosophical Method* (1967) (Chicago, IL: University of Chicago Press, 2002), pp. 43–53.

40 Reprints of 'The Future of Philosophy' and 'Philosophy as a Pursuit of Meaning' can be found in Johannes Friedl and Heiner Rutte, eds, *Moritz Schlick Erkenntnistheoretische Schriften* 1926–1936, *Kritische Gesamtausgabe Abteilung II*, Band 1.2 (Wien: Springer Verlag, 2013), pp. 125–145. Schlick's lecture 'Form and Content, An Introduction to Philosophical Thinking' (1932) is printed in Moritz Schlick, *Gesammelte Aufsätze*, 1926–1936 (Vienna: Gerold, 1938; Olms, Hildesheim, 1969), pp. 151–249. Reprinted in Henk L. Mulder and Barbara F. B. Van de Velde-Schlick, eds, *Moritz Schlick: Philosophical Papers*, Vol. 2 (1925–1936) (Dordrecht: Reidel, 1979), pp. 285–369.

41 Hahn, Neurath, and Carnap, 'The Scientific Conception of the World', pp. 299–318.

42 Ibid., p. 308.

43 Ibid., p. 317.

44 Skidelsky, *Ernst Cassirer*, p. 17. Cassirer was to address the problem of ideology in his book *The Myth of the State* (New Haven, CT: Yale University Press, 1946). Ideological factors had also played a significant role in the notorious debate between Cassirer and Heidegger in Davos, just four months before the publication of the Vienna Circle's Manifesto. The presence and support of Carnap for Cassirer at that debate had re-enforced the impression of a stronger contrast between Cassirer and Heidegger than might have been the case otherwise. Carnap's socialist and scientistic worldview stood in stark contrast with Heidegger's anti-technology sentiments and his ideological Nazi sympathies.

45 Several members of the Vienna Circle were engaged in community projects. Neurath was general secretary of the 'Austrian association for estate-housing and

allotments', a collection of self-help groups aiming to secure housing and allotments for its members. For Neurath's work, see Christopher Burke and Matthew Eve, eds, *Otto Neurath: From Hieroglyphics to Isotype: A Visual Autobiography* (1945) (London: Hyphen Press, 2010).

46 Some members of the Vienna Circle gave lectures at the *Bauhaus* and the house built by Wittgenstein for his sister between 1926 and 1928 was also built on the *Bauhaus* principles.

47 Neurath, 'The Scientific Conception of the World', p. 306.

48 Rudolf Carnap, *Der logische Aufbau der Welt* (1928), subsequently translated as *The Logical Structure of the World*, trans., Rolf A. George (Berkeley: University of California Press, 1969).

49 Rudolf Carnap, Preface to first edition, *The Logical Structure of the World*, p. xviii. In their Manifesto, written a year after *Der logische Aufbau der Welt,* they write, 'Of course not every single adherent of the scientific world-conception will be a fighter. Some, glad of solitude, will lead a withdrawn existence on the icy slopes of logic; some may even disdain mingling with the masses and regret the "trivialized" form that these matters inevitably take on spreading. However, their achievements too will take place among the historic developments. ... *The scientific world-conception serves life, and life receives it.*' Neurath, 'The Scientific Conception of the World', pp. 317, 318. For a movement committed to the erasure of 'emotive' metaphysical and theological language, Carnap uses surprisingly emotive and poetic language, such as 'we feel', 'carried by the faith' and '*serves life, and life receives it.*'

50 Carnap, 'Intellectual Autobiography', p. 23. For a critique of recent voices claiming that the early logical positivists developed a political philosophy of science see Sarah S. Richardson, 'The Left Vienna Circle, Part 1: Carnap, Neurath, and the Left Vienna Circle Thesis', *Studies in History and Philosophy of Science* 40 (2009), pp. 14–24.

51 Feigl, *Inquiries and Provocations*, p. 22.

52 Monk, *Ludwig Wittgenstein*, p. 283. Wittgenstein's phrase 'The master should be known by his work' echoes Matthew 7:16 'Ye shall know them by their fruits' (King James Translation). The meaning of both phrases is very similar: showing is a form of doing. Like Cassirer and Wittgenstein, Schlick had a broad interest beyond the natural sciences. He was interested in poetry and the arts and had even written a work on evolutionary aesthetics in his early life. See, for instance, Moritz Schlick, 'Das Grundproblem des Ästhetik in entwicklungsgeschichtlicher Beleuchtung', *Archiv für die gesamte Psychologie* 14 (1909), pp. 102–32; trans. 'The Fundamental Problem of Aesthetics Seen in an Evolutionary Light,' *Moritz Schlick Philosophical Papers: Volume 1: (1909–1922)*, pp. 1–24. For a comparison of Schlick with the Chinese philosopher Li Zehou, see Jim Shelton, 'Li Zehou and Moritz Schlick on the Roots of Beauty', *Frontiers of Philosophy in China*, 9.4 (2014), pp. 602–14.

53 The article referred to is A. E. Blumberg and Herbert Feigl, 'Logical Positivism: A new Movement in European Philosophy', *Journal of Philosophy* 28.11 (1931), pp. 281–96.

54 Feigl, 'The Wiener Kreis in America' (1969), in *Inquiries and Provocations*, pp. 57, 70.

55 Blumberg and Feigl, 'Logical Positivism', pp. 281, 282.

56 Feigl, 'The Wiener Kreis in America' (1969), in *Inquiries and Provocations*, p. 71.

57 Blumberg and Feigl, 'Logical Positivism', p. 281.

58 In a footnote, the authors mention the specific publications associated with the thinkers listed: P. W. Bridgman's *The Logic of Modern Physics* (New York: Macmillan, 1927); S. K. Langer's *Practice of Philosophy*, and C. I. Lewis' *Mind and the World-Order*

(New York: Charles Scribner's Sons, 1929). Blumberg and Feigl, 'Logical Positivism', p. 281.

59 The only scholar I have come across who mentions that Langer's work was known by members of the Vienna Circle is philosopher Kris McDaniel. See his 'Ontology and Philosophical Methodology in the Early Susanne Langer', in Sandra Lapointe and Christopher Pinnock, eds, *Innovations in the History of Analytical Philosophy* (London: Palgrave Macmillan, 2017), pp. 265–98.

60 Feigl, 'The Wiener Kreis in America' (1969), p. 69. Feigl goes on to say that 'there were the "soirées" at Whitehead's house; most of them were long, rambling, but thoroughly captivating soliloquies – on all sort of subjects – by the amiable, thoroughly British, philosopher. Whitehead had turned increasingly metaphysical (or "cosmological") after coming to the United States a few years earlier. His lectures were rather poetic, … though when his students handed him term papers, he was dismayed with their imitations of his flowery style.' pp. 69, 70.

61 Blumberg and Feigl, 'Logical Positivism', p. 292. Compare with Wittgenstein: 'Philosophy is not a theory but an activity. … The result of philosophy is not a number of "philosophical propositions", but to make propositions clear.' (4.112).

62 Blumberg and Feigl, 'Logical Positivism', p. 292. Compare with Wittgenstein: 'No part of our experience is also a priori. Everything we see could also be otherwise. Everything we can describe at all could also be otherwise. There is no order of things a priori (5.634).'

63 Blumberg and Feigl, 'Logical Positivism', p. 286.

64 Ibid., p. 286.

65 Ibid., p. 283.

66 Ibid., p. 287.

67 Ibid.

68 Ibid.

69 Ibid.

70 Ibid., p. 288.

71 Ibid., p. 291.

72 Ibid.

73 Ibid., pp. 291, 292.

74 Thomas Kuhn, 'A Discussion with Thomas Kuhn', in J. Conant and J. Haugeland, eds, *The Road since Structure* (Chicago, IL: University of Chicago Press, 2000), pp. 305–6. Quoted in Alan Richardson, '"That Sort of Everyday Image of Logical Positivism": Thomas Kuhn and the Decline of Logical Empiricist Philosophy of Science', in Alan Richardson and Thomas Uebel, eds, *The Cambridge Companion to Logical Empiricism* (Cambridge: Cambridge University Press, 2007), p. 361.

75 A. J. Ayer, *Language, Truth and Logic* (1936) (New York: Dover Publications, 1946), p. 31.

76 Ibid., p. 32.

77 M. Friedman, *Reconsidering Logical Positivism* (Cambridge: Cambridge University Press, 2007), p. xiv.

78 Friedman, *Reconsidering Logical Positivism*, p. xiv–xv.

79 Kuhn, 'A Discussion with Thomas Kuhn' (1995), pp. 305–6.

80 Quoted in Alan Richardson, '"That Sort of Everyday Image of Logical Positivism,"' p. 361.

81 Thomas Kuhn's *The Structure of Scientific Revolutions* (Chicago, IL: University of Chicago Press, 1962). First published in *International Encyclopedia of Unified Science*, volume II, number 2 (1962).

82 Friedman, *Reconsidering Logical Positivism*, p. xv.

83 For a discussion of Wittgenstein's 'symbolic turn' prior to the *Tractatus*, see chapter 6 of Michael Potter, *Wittgenstein's Notes on Logic* (Oxford: Oxford University Press, 2009), pp. 63–9.

84 Moritz Schlick. 'Form and Content', *Gesammelte Aufsatze*, p. 195. It must be noted that, in Schlick's example, the sentence 'This is blue' can be understood as a response to two independent questions, namely, 'what *colour* is this?' and 'what does the colour "blue" look like?' However, although the emphasis in both cases is slightly different, – that is, in the first case the answer would read 'this is *blue*', whereas in the second '*this* is blue' – in both cases the questioner would already have some preconceived idea of the category 'colour'. Hence, *pace* Langer, Schlick holds that the act of naming consists primarily in the correct application of the pre-existing concept 'blue' to the colour at hand. Wittgenstein refers to a similar point in a footnote in *Philosophical Investigations*, Rush Rhees and G. E. Anscombe, eds, trans. G. E. Anscombe (Oxford: Blackwell, 1967), p. 18e.

85 W. V. Quine, *The Time of My Life: An Autobiography* (Cambridge, MI: MIT Press, 1985), p. 140, p. 83.

86 Ibid.

87 Ibid., p. 88.

88 Dagfinn Føllesdal and Douglas B. Quine, eds, W. V. Quine, *Quine in Dialogue* (Cambridge, MA: Harvard University Press, 2008), p. 42. For an account of Quine's role in the development of American analytic philosophy, see Joel Isaac, 'W. V. Quine and the Origins of the Analytic Philosophy in the United States', *Modern Intellectual History* 2.2 (2005), pp. 205–34.

89 Ernest Nagel, 'Impressions and Appraisals of Analytic Philosophy in Europe I', *Journal of Philosophy*, 33.1 (1936a), pp. 16, 17. Preceding this passage he writes, '[A] letter from a friend in Vienna assured me that in certain circles the existence of Wittgenstein is debated with as much ingenuity as the historicity of Christ has been disputed in others. I have seen Wittgenstein, though only casually, and therefore feel competent to decide that question.'

90 Nagel, 'Impressions and Appraisals', p. 17.

91 Ibid., pp. 5–24; 'Impressions and Appraisals of Analytic Philosophy in Europe II', *Journal of Philosophy*, 33.2 (1936b), pp. 29–53.

92 Quoted in Greg Frost-Arnold, 'The Rise of "Analytic Philosophy": When and How Did People Begin Calling Themselves "Analytic Philosophers"?', in Sandra Lapointe and Christopher Pincock, eds, *Innovations in the History of Analytic Philosophy*, p. 31.

93 Langer, *Practice of Philosophy*, p. 17

94 Ibid., p. 67.

95 Ibid., p. 21

96 Langer, *Philosophy in a New Key*, p. 21.

97 Greg Frost-Arnold, 'The Rise of "Analytic Philosophy"', p. 40.

98 Maria van der Schaar and Eric Schliesser, eds, 'Women in Early Analytic Philosophy', Volume Introduction, *Journal for the History of Analytical Philosophy* 5.2 (2017), pp. 1–5. The authors make a couple of factual mistakes. They say that all three women belong to the first group of women who became recognized philosophers by 'obtaining a permanent university position in philosophy'. p. 1. Langer only gained a 'permanent' position at Connecticut College in later life and this was not a university. They also suggest that women colleges in America made it easier for women to

graduate at a university, but, as they themselves point out, Vienna University accepted women students already in 1895, whereas Harvard did not award any degrees to women until 1963.

99 Giulia Felappi, 'Susanne Langer and the Woeful World of Facts', *Journal for the History of Analytical Philosophy* 5.2 (2017), pp. 38–50.

100 Schaar and Schliesser, 'Women in Early Analytic Philosophy', p. 4.

101 Rudolf Carnap, 'Replies and Systematic Expositions', in Paul A. Schilpp, ed., *The Philosophy of Rudolf Carnap*, The Library of Living Philosophers, Vol. 11 (La Salle, IL: Open Court, 1963), p. 860. For an account of the two-way relationship between pragmatism and logical positivism, see *Journal for the History of Analytical Philosophy* 3.3 (2015).

102 Quine's helpful welcome of Carnap in the United States reciprocated the warm reception he had received from the Carnaps during his and his wife's six-week stay in Prague in 1932.

103 Carnap, 'Intellectual Autobiography', pp. 38, 39

104 Ibid., p. 39.

105 Jewish European philosophers who found positions at different universities across America include: Feigl (University of Iowa), Rudolf Carnap (Chicago; University of California), Carl Hempel (Chicago), Hans Reichenbach (University of California), Richard von Mises (Harvard), Felix Kaufmann (The New School for Social Research), Gustave Bergmann (University of Iowa), Heinrich Gompertz (University of Southern California), Philipp Frank (Harvard), Alfred Tarski (New York City) and Kurt Goldstein (Montefiore Hospital, New York).

106 Morris was personal friend with the son-in-law of John D Rockefeller, whose foundation helped to fund European philosophers to find positions at American universities.

107 For a Guide to the Unity of Science Movement Records 1934–68, held at the University of Chicago Library, see https://www.lib.uchicago.edu/e/scrc/findingaids/view.php?eadid=ICU.SPCL.USM&q=Philosophy (accessed 16 April 2019).

108 W. V. Quine, *The Time of My Life: An Autobiography* (Cambridge, MI: MIT Press, 1985), p. 140. In addition to the aforementioned émigré philosophers, the list of presenter at the Congress included George Sarton; Percy W. Bridgman; Talcot Parsons; Giorgo de Santillana; Werner Jaeger; W. V. O. Quine; Charles W. Morris; Alonzo Church; Horace Kallen and Ernest Nagel. Friedrich Stadler, 'Editorial Remarks', in Herlinde Pauer-Studer, ed., *Norms, Values, and Society, Vienna Circle Institute Yearbook*, Vol. 2 (Dordrecht: Kluwer Academic, 1994), p. 289.

109 Langer's paper, entitled 'The Scope of Problems as the Limit of Intellectual Fields', was presented in the section 'Aims and Methods for Unifying Science', alongside papers by P. W. Bridgman, H. M. Kallen, Feigl, Ernest Nagel, Richard von Mises and Heinrich Gompertz. Langer was one of three women at the Congress out of seventy delegates. For the complete programme, see Friedrich Stadler, *The Vienna Circle: Studies in the Origins, Development, and Influence of Logical Positivism* (Heidelberg: Springer, 2015), pp. 189–92.

110 According to George Reisch, 'Those convening at [the conference] were happy to be reunited, but the occasion was not joyous. Most had probably heard the news while travelling to the United States or to Cambridge: Hitler had invaded Poland, and the situation looked grim. On the eve of the Congress, Sunday, September 3, they gathered around the radio to hear president Roosevelt's weekly radio address and learned that Hitler had not backed down from England's and France's ultimatums

demanding Nazi withdrawal from Poland.' Georg A. Reisch, *How the Cold War Transformed Philosophy of Science: To the Icy Slopes of Logic* (Cambridge: Cambridge University Press, 2005), p. 167.

111 For fuller accounts of this period see Friedrich Stadler, ed., *Scientific Philosophy: Origins and Development*, Vienna Circle Institute Yearbook (Dordrecht: Springer, 1993).

112 For a different angle on the development of analytic philosophy in America, see Joel Katzav and Krist Vaesen, 'On the Emergence of American Analytic Philosophy', *British Journal for the History of Philosophy* 25.4 (2017), pp. 772–98.

113 Under the Freedom of Information Act most files are now public and available on-line. The FBI had started to compile a file on Carnap after his move to University of California, Los Angeles (UCLA) in 1954. It includes the following remarkable comment: '[Frank and Carnap] met and exchanged professional ideas at several European conferences of scholars prior to World War II. Frank was then an exponent of Logical Empiricism, a philosophical movement which attracted many supporters whose complexion ranged from extreme left to extreme right. ... Professor Carnap ... now at the University of Chicago, is reported to have influenced Neo-Thomism and other French Catholic philosophical doctrines toward logical Empiricism.' 'FBI Records: The Vault'. https://vault.fbi. gov/Rudolph%20Carnap/Rudolph%20Carnap%20Part%202%20of%206/view/ (accessed 16 April 2019).

114 For concrete examples of the effects of McCarthyism on American philosophy in the 1940s and 1950s, see John McCumber, *Time in the Ditch: American Philosophy and the McCarthy Era* (Evanston, IL: Northwestern University Press, 2001).

115 Reisch, *How the Cold War Transformed Philosophy of Science*, p. 2, 6. For another version, see Georg A. Reisch, 'How the Cold War Transformed Philosophy of Science: To the Icy Slopes of Logic', in A. Richardson and T. Uebel, eds, *The Cambridge Companion to Logical Empiricism* (Cambridge: Cambridge University Press, 2007), pp. 58–90. The phrase 'Icy Slopes of Logic' is a reference to the sentence in the Vienna Circle Manifesto: 'Of course not every single adherent of the scientific world-conception will be a fighter. Some, glad of solitude, will lead a withdrawn existence on the icy slopes of logic.' Neurath, Scientific Conception of the World, p. 313.

116 Reisch, 'How the Cold War Transformed Philosophy of Science', p. 60.

117 The reference to Russell's lectures can be found in Langer, *Philosophy in a New Key*, p. 274, footnote 12.

118 For records of the discussions, see Greg Frost-Arnold, *Carnap, Tarski, and Quine at Harvard: Conversations on Logic, Mathematics, and Science* (Chicago, IL, Open Court, 2013).

119 Langer, *Philosophy in a New Key*, p. 14,

120 Ibid., pp. 14, 15.

121 Ibid., p. 18.

122 Clifford Geertz, *Available Light: Anthropological Reflections on Philosophical Topics* (Princeton, NJ: Princeton University Press, 2000), p. 159.

123 It is known from Kuhn's notebooks that he had read Langer's *Philosophy in a New Key* in 1949. See Peter Galison, 'Practice All the Way Down', in Robert J. Richards and Lorraine Daston, eds, *Kuhn's 'Structure of Scientific Revolutions' at Fifty: Reflections on a Science Classic* (Chicago, IL: University of Chicago Press, 2016), p. 51.

3 Philosophy and women

1 Max Hall, *Harvard University Press: A History* (Cambridge, MA: Harvard University Press, 1986), p. 80.

2 Arthur Danto, 'Three Careers', http://www.lucadelbaldo.com/works/arthur-danto (accessed 16 April 2019).

3 Quoted in Wesley Wehr, *The Accidental Collector: Art, Fossils and Friendships* (Seattle: University of Washington Press, 2004), p. 106

4 Bryn Mawr is one of seven private women's colleges sometimes referred to the 'Seven Sister Colleges' that were founded between 1837 and 1889 on the East Coast of America. The other colleges are: Mount Holyoke (1837), Vassar College (1865), Wellesley College (1875), Smith College (1875), Radcliffe College (1879), Barnard College (1889).

5 Drew Gilpin Faust, 'Mingling Promiscuously: A History of Women and Men at Harvard', in Laurel Ulrich, ed., *Yards and Gates: Gender in Harvard and Radcliffe History* (New York: Palgrave Macmillan, 2004), pp. 317–28. See also: Sally Schwager, 'Taking Up the Challenge: The Origins of Radcliffe', in Laurel Ulrich, ed., *Yards and Gates: Gender in Harvard and Radcliffe History* (New York: Palgrave Macmillan, 2004), pp. 87–115; Nancy Weiss Malkiel, *'Keep the Damned Women Out': The Struggle for Coeducation* (Princeton, NJ Princeton University Press, 2018); Helen Lefkowitz Horowitz, 'It's Complicated: 375 Years of Women at Harvard', Dean's Lecture on the History of Women at Harvard in Honor of Harvard's 375th Anniversary. 23 April 2012, www.radcliffe.harvard.edu/news/in-news/remarks-its-complicated-375-years-women-harvard (accessed 16 April 2019).

6 Many of the women were independent scholars in their own right, such as Zina Fay Peirce, wife of philosopher Charles Saunders Peirce. According to Sally Schwager, it has always been the WEA and Radcliffe's first president, Elizabeth Cary Agassiz's position that Radcliffe should not become another female college with its own programme and faculty but that it should merge with Harvard. Schwager, 'Taking Up the Challenge', p. 158.

7 Charles William Eliot, A Turning Point in Higher Education; the Inaugural Address of Charles William Eliot as President of Harvard College, 19 October 1869, with Introduction by Nathan M. Pusey (Cambridge, MA: Harvard University Press, 1969), p. 50.

8 Wendell Barrett, 'The Relations of Radcliffe College with Harvard', *Harvard Monthly* 29.1 (October 1899), pp. 8, 9.

9 Ibid.

10 Helen Lefkowitz Horowitz, 'It's Complicated: 375 Years of Women at Harvard,' Dean's Lecture on the History of Women at Harvard in Honor of Harvard's 375th Anniversary, 23 April 2012. www.radcliffe.harvard.edu/news/in-news/remarks-its-complicated-375-years-women-harvard (accessed 16 April 2019).

11 Bruce Kuklick, *The Rise of American Philosophy: Cambridge, Massachusetts 1860–1930* (New Haven, CT: Yale University Press, 1977), p. 590.

12 Sally Schwager, 'Taking Up the Challenge', pp. 135, 136.

13 In 1948 Helen Maud Cam, a British legal historian, became the first woman tenured at Harvard after 312 years of male-only professors.

14 For some Harvard faculty, the growing number of Radcliffe students had become a major point of concern: 'The invasion of Sever Hall, University Hall and Dane

Hall by occasional Radcliffe students in the single year 1896–97 – not to speak of Laboratories and Libraries – became obvious to the eye. Accordingly, in the year 1897–98 a committee was appointed by the Faculty, to report on the whole subject. This committee found that the standards of admission, instruction, examination and graduation at Radcliffe have been in all respects identical with those of Harvard. … By far the most important question suggested by the present situation is whether any further steps, and if so what steps, should be taken in the direction of coeducation. This is a question we do not feel called upon to attempt to answer. But we feel that it is one which should not be settled by a policy of drift.' Barrett, 'Relations of Radcliffe College with Harvard'.

15 Kuklick, *Rise of American Philosophy*, p. 590.

16 Ibid.

17 Schwager, 'Taking Up the Challenge', p. 135. The quote is taken from an article by Zina Fay Pierce in the *Boston Daily Advertiser*, reprinted in *The Woman's Journal* (17 April 1875).

18 Drew Gilpin Faust, 'Mingling Promiscuously', pp. 459, 460.

19 Harvard College website, https://college.harvard.edu/about/mission-and-vision/Radcliffe (accessed 12 March 2018).

20 https://www.radcliffe.harvard.edu/about-us/our-history (accessed 16 April 2019). For an account of the history of the first women to receive tenure at Harvard, see 'The First Tenured Women Professors at Harvard University', http://www.faculty.harvard.edu/First-Tenured-Women (accessed 16 April 2019). The first women to be appointed in a faculty position was Alice Hamilton in the department of Public Health in 1918, and the first woman to get tenure was historian Helen Maud Cam in the department of the Arts and Sciences in 1948.

21 Paul Weiss, 'Recollections of Alfred North Whitehead', *Process Studies* 10.1–2 (Spring-Summer 1980), p. 48.

22 Victor Lowe, 'Whitehead: A Biographical Perspective', *Process Studies* 12.3 (Autumn 1982), p. 142.

23 A. N. Whitehead, 'Autobiographical Notes', in P. A. Schilpp, ed., *The Philosophy of Alfred North Whitehead*, The Library of Living Philosophers, Vol. 3 (La Salle, IL: Open Court, 2004), p. 12. The passage continues as follows: 'If my memory is correct, the date was about 1898. But later on, until the war in 1914, there were stormy episodes in London and elsewhere. The division of opinion cut across party lines; for example, the Conservative Balfour was pro-woman, and the Liberal Asquith was against. The success of the movement came at the end of the war in 1918.'

24 In 1976 Girton became Cambridge's first women's college to become co-educational.

25 Christoph Limbeck-Lilienau, 'Rudolf Carnap und die Philosophie in Amerika: Logischer Empirismus, Pragmatismus, Realismus 1936–1956', in Friedrich Stadler and Allan Janik, eds, *Vertreibung, Transformation und Rückkehr der Wissenschaftstheorie, Am Beispiel von Rudolf Carnap und Wolfgang Stegmüller* (Berlin: LIT Verlag, 2015), p. 130. Carnap refers to the rejection of his application in a letter to Quine dated 25 February 1935, in Richard Creath, ed., *Dear Carnap, Dear Van: The Quine-Carnap Correspondence and Related Work* (Berkeley: University of California Press, 1991), p. 128.

26 Charles A. Baylis, 'Review of *The Practice of Philosophy* by Susanne K. Langer', *Journal of Philosophy* 28.12 (4 June 1931), pp. 329, 326. Baylis writes, '[T]he whole middle section of the book, on "Meaning", is much too difficult for a beginner, whose perplexities [*sic*] quotations from Wittgenstein and Cassirer will but increase' … and

would be 'almost entirely lost on anyone lacking a rather thorough training in the history of philosophy'. Other comments include: '[The book] contains a clear, concise presentation of the nature and limitations of Aristotelian, idealistic, and pragmatic logic, and [is] perhaps the best short exposition available in English of symbolic or mathematical logic, its nature, the forms of which it treats, and its tremendous importance as the science of forms par excellence' and 'the book leaves one genuinely persuaded that the most important task of philosophy, as well as the most difficult, is really the discovery of fundamental and very general forms.'

27 Donald Dryden, 'Susanne K. Langer (20 December 1895–17 July 1985)', in Philip B. Dematteis and Leemon B. McHenry, eds, *American Philosophers before 1950*, Dictionary of Literary Biography, Vol. 270 (Farmington Hills, MI: Gale, 2003), p. 191.

28 W. V. Quine, *The Time of My Life: An Autobiography* (Cambridge, MA: MIT Press, 1985), p. 128.

29 Ibid., p. 149.

30 The founding committee of the *Association for Symbolic Logic* included C. A. Baylis, Alonzo Church, C. J. Ducasse, C. I. Lewis, Paul Weiss and Susanne K. Langer. The *Journal of Symbolic Logic* was founded in 1936 and was edited by Church and Langford, with as consulting editors, among others, Quine and Langer. For a history of the foundation of the Association, see C. J. Ducasse and Haskell B. Curry, 'Early History of the Association for Symbolic Logic', *The Journal of Symbolic Logic* 27.3 (September 1962), pp. 255–8. For Quine's role in the origins of analytic philosophy, see Joel Isaac, 'W. V. Quine and the Origins of the Analytic Philosophy in the United States', *Modern Intellectual History* 2.2 (2005), pp. 205–34.

31 Joel Isaac writes, 'In addition to Bridgman and Quine, the committee counted among its membership L. J. Henderson, Susanne Langer, Karl Lashley and the Harvard-based historian of science, George Sarton. Several émigré logical empiricists were also on the committee. Joel Isaac, *Working Knowledge: making the Human Sciences from Parsons to Kuhn* (Cambridge, MA: Harvard University Press, 2012), p. 155.

32 Quine, *Time of My Life*, p. 128.

33 Letter from Quine to Carnap, 15 February 1938, in Richard Creath, ed., *Dear Carnap, Dear Van: The Quine-Carnap Correspondence and Related Work* (Berkeley: University of California Press, 1991), p. 246.

34 Although Quine's autobiography tediously mentions every place and person he encountered in his life, there is not one mention of Langer.

35 Ibid., p. 246. In his letter to Quine Carnap had written the following about Langer's book: 'Some of the introductory parts of it may be helpful to students but in the whole I was a little bit disappointed. Nearly the whole of the book is devoted to the old Boolean Algebra, so that the interesting but still elementary parts of symbolic logic are exhibited only at the end in a very short way or not at all, as e.g. the theory of relations.' Letter from Carnap to Quine, 11, February 1938, in Creath, ed., *Dear Carnap, Dear Van*, p. 247.

36 Quine, *Time of My Life*, p. 130.

37 L. Susan Stebbing, 'Review of *The Principles of Mathematics* by Bertrand Russell and *An Introduction to Symbolic Logic* by Susanne K. Langer', *Philosophy* 13.52 (October 1938), p. 483; Herbert Feigl, 'Review of Susanne Langer, *Introduction to Symbolic Logic*', *American Journal of Psychology* 51.4 (October 1938), p. 781.

38 Susanne K. Langer, *Introduction to Symbolic Logic* (Second Revised edition, New York: London: Dover Publications, 1953), p. 18.

39 Ibid., p. 18.

40   John C. Cooley, *Outline of Symbolic Logic* (1938); Quine, *Methods of Logic* (1950); Carnap, *Introduction to Symbolic Logic and Its Applications* (1954, German edition; 1958, English Translation).

41   Ernest Nagel, 'Book Review of *Philosophy in a New Key*', *Journal of Philosophy* 40.12 (June 1943), pp. 323–9.

42   Charles Varela and Lawrence Ferrara, 'The Nagel Critique and Langer's critical response', *Journal for the Anthropological Study of Human Movement* 2.2 (Autumn 1982), p. 100.

43   Kuklick, 'Rise of American Philosophy', pp. 591, 594.

44   Howard Gardner, *Art, Mind, and the Brain: A Cognitive Approach to Creativity* (New York: Basic Books, 1982), p. 48.

45   Robert Innis, 'Symposium on Susanne K. Langer: Introduction', *Journal of Speculative Philosophy* 21.1 (2007), p. 1.

46   Letter of recommendation by Henry Sheffer, 1943. Referred to in Donald Dryden, 'Susanne K. Langer (20 December 1895–17 July 1985)', in Philip B. Dematteis and Leemon B. McHenry, eds., *Dictionary of Literary Biography: American Philosophers before 1950*, Vol. 270 (Farmington Hills, MI: Gale, 2003), unpublished annotated version, p. 16.

47   Ibid.

48   Langer mentions this in a verbatim recorded conversation with the American poet Elizabeth Bishop, organized by their mutual friend Wesley Wehr that was published as 'Elizabeth Bishop and Susanne Langer: A Conversation on University Way' in *Harvard Review* (Winter 1993), pp. 128–30 and reprinted in Wesley Wehr, *The Eighth Lively Art: Conversations with Painters, Poets, Musicians & the Wicked Witch of the West* (Washington, DC: University of Washington Press, 2000), pp. 185–90. In the conversation the two women swap stories about their experiences of teaching which both admit to finding frustrating. Langer confides that when she has lazy students she would 'completely lose patience with them'. When Bishop replies with a story of her own, Langer continues,

> I'm glad to know that I'm not the only short-tempered teacher around. Some of my colleagues are the soul of patience with their students and friends. But I'm always sticking my foot in my mouth. … Sometimes someone or other will start telling me something, even lecturing me. And, more often than not, I'll be about ten jumps ahead of him. I can often anticipate what direction an argument is going to take, or someone else's train of thought. Quite often I'll know just about what they're going to say next, sometimes even before they do. I'm not the most patient sort of person. I'll quite forget my good manners and cut people right off in the middle of a sentence. You can imagine how popular that makes me in some quarters.

Wehr, *Eighth Lively Art*, p. 129.

49   Kuklick, *The Rise of American Philosophy*, p. 590.

50   This recollection was passed on to me by Randall Auxier by an email dated 22 February 2019. It is used with permission from Joseph Margolis.

51   Ibid.

52   Ibid.

53   Ann E. Berthoff, 'Susanne K. Langer and "The Odyssey of the Mind"', *Semiotica* 128.1-2 (2000), p. 29.

54　For a discussion of what might (or might not) constitute shared themes or styles among women philosophers, see Cecile T. Tougas and Sara Ebenreck, eds, *Presenting Women Philosophers* (Philadelphia, PA: Temple University Press, 2000). The anthology includes an excellent essay by Beatrice Nelson, 'Susanne K. Langer's Conception of "Symbol": Making Connections through Ambiguity' (pp. 81–90), previously published in the *Journal of Speculative Philosophy* 8.4 (1994), pp. 277–96. Nelson contrasts Nagel's conception of symbol as a conventional sign with that of Langer's formulative conception of it, in which symbol and content are fused and remain ultimately 'ambiguous'. It is not clear however from her essay whether or not – and if so, why – Langer's symbol conception should be considered female.

55　See, for instance, Phyllis Lassner, 'Bridging Composition and Women's Studies: the work of Ann E. Berthoff and Susanne K. Langer', *Journal of Teaching Writing* 10.1 (1991), pp. 21–8; Beatrice Nelson, 'Susanne K. Langer's Conception of "Symbol": Making Connections through Ambiguity', *Journal of Speculative Philosophy* 8.4 (1994), pp. 277–96; Mary Reichling, 'A Woman Ahead of her Time: The Langer Legacy', *Philosophy of Music Education Review* 6.1 (Spring 1998), pp. 12–21.

56　For a discussion of non-oppositional thinking in Langer and Bergson, see Iris van der Tuin, 'Bergson before Bergsonism: Traversing "Bergson's Failing" in Susanne K. Langer's Philosophy of Art', *Journal of French and Francophone Philosophy* 24.2 (1 December 2016), pp. 176–202. Van der Tuin argues that, in spite of Langer's explicit, i.e. polemical, objection to Bergson's work, her own thinking displays a Bergsonian, i.e. non-linear and non-oppositional, way of thinking in the way she relates diverse texts and traditions.

57　It should, however, be noted that some of the most perceptive and insightful interpreters of Langer have been women. These include Ann Berthoff, Giulia Felappi, Barbara Kösters, Felicia Kruse, Beatrice Nelson, Mary Reichling, Cornelia Richter, Eva Shaper and Iris van der Tuin.

58　William Ernest Hocking, 'Whitehead as I Knew Him', *Journal of Philosophy* 58.19 (1961), pp. 505–16. Reprinted in George L. Kline ed., *Alfred North Whitehead: Essays on His Philosophy* (Lanham, MD: University Press of America, 1989), pp. 7–17.

59　Quoted in Hall, *Harvard University Press*, p. 80.

4　Henry M. Sheffer: Logical form

1　W. V. O. Quine, 'Henry Maurice Sheffer: 1863–1964', *Proceedings and Addresses of the American Philosophical Association* 38 (1964–5), p. 104.

2　Isaiah Berlin, *Concepts and Categories: Philosophical Essays*, Henry Hardy, ed. (London: Pimlico, 1999), p. xii.

3　Quoted in Donald Dryden, 'Susanne K. Langer 1895–1985', in P. B. Dematteis and L. B. McHenry eds, *American Philosophers before 1950*, Dictionary of Literary Biography, Vol. 270 (Farmington Hills, MI: Gale, 2003), p. 191.

4　In an appendix to his 1908 PhD *A Program of Philosophy Based on Modern Logic* (Harvard University Archives), Sheffer criticized a central feature of Royce's logic. Scanlan comments, 'In Sheffer's thesis we have an interesting example of a student disproving an important feature of his mentor's theory. It would be fascinating to know something about Royce's personal reaction to the content of Sheffer's appendix. But I am unaware of any such material'. Michael Scanlan, 'Sheffer's Criticism of

Royce's Theory of Order', *Transactions of the Charles S. Peirce Society* 46.2 (2001), p. 179. At least it did not prevent Royce from recommending his precocious student to his European colleagues.

5   A. N. Whitehead and B. Russell, *Principia Mathematica* (Second edition, Cambridge: Cambridge University Press, 1925), p. xiii. In his own review of the second edition Sheffer criticizes the authors for failing to distinguish, in both editions, between unasserted and asserted propositions. Henry Sheffer, 'Review of A. N. Whitehead and B. Russell, *Principia Mathematica*', *Isis* 8.1 (1926), p. 229.

6   Langer mentions that when someone would ask Sheffer how he was able to follow Peano's lectures in Italian he would reply, 'Professor Peano was very considerate, and conducted the seminar in French for most of the first term, until I could speak Italian.' Susanne K. Langer, 'Henry M. Sheffer 1883–1964', *Philosophy and Phenomenological Research* 25.2 (December 1964), p. 305.

7   Ibid., p. 305.

8   Henry Maurice Sheffer, 'A Set of Five Independent Postulates for Boolean Algebras, with Application to Logical Constants', *Transactions of the American Mathematical Society* 14.4 (October 1913), pp. 481–8. Although developed in the context of Boolean algebra, the idea proved to be equally fruitful for the field of propositional and symbolic logic. Henry Sheffer, 'Review of *Principia Mathematica*', *Isis* 8.1 (1926), p. 229. The meaning of the stroke lends itself to different interpretations. This is because the stroke can effectively stand for two different operations: first, 'neither p nor q' (-p & -q) and second, 'either not-p or not-q' (-p v -q). Whereas Sheffer uses it in the first sense in his 1913 paper, Jean Nicod, in a paper in 1913, adopts the second meaning, thereby interpreting it as an exclusive disjunction. Jean Nicod, 'A Reduction in the Number of Primitive Propositions of Logic', *Proceedings of the Cambridge Philosophical Society* 19 (1916), pp. 32–41. In consequence, the stroke has been subsequently also referred to as the Sheffer–Nicod stroke or stroke-function. See Scanlan, 'Sheffer's Criticism of Royce's Theory of Order', p. 222, footnote 2. For Sheffer's influence on Russell's second edition of the *Principia Mathematica*, see Bernard Linsky, *The Evolution of Principia Mathematica: Bertrand Russell's Manuscripts and Notes for the Second Edition* (Cambridge: Cambridge University Press, 2011). For a review and critical discussion of Russell's adaptation of the Sheffer stroke, see C. I. Lewis, 'Review of *Principia Mathematica* by A. N. Whitehead and B. Russell', *American Mathematical Monthly* 35:4 (April 1928), pp. 200–5.

9   In his obituary of Sheffer, W. V. O. Quine points out that the stroke had been previously invented by Peirce, but that it nevertheless 'justly carried Sheffer's name, for the Peirce manuscript was turned up only in later years'. Quine, 'Henry Maurice Sheffer', p. 104.

10 Michael Scanlan, 'The Known and Unknown H. M. Sheffer', *Transactions of the Charles Peirce Society* 36.2 (Spring 2000), p. 193.

11 The department's first choice of Royce's replacement had been Bertrand Russell, who was well-known to the department as he had taught there previously, but this was blocked by President Jowell as he disapproved of Russell's liberal views and political activism. Bruce Kuklick, *The Rise of American Philosophy: Cambridge, Massachusetts 1860–1930* (New Haven, CT: Yale University Press, 1977), pp. 410, 411.

12 Susanne K. Langer, 'Henry M. Sheffer, 1883–1964', *Philosophy and Phenomenological Research* 25.2 (December 1964), p. 306.

13 The evidence of his gifts as a teacher can be found in the recollections by former students and colleagues in the *Festschrift* edited by Paul Henle, Horace M. Kallen and Susanne K. Langer, *Structure, Method and Meaning: Essays in Honor of Henry M. Sheffer* (New York: Liberal Arts Press, 1951).

14 Quine, 'Henry Maurice Sheffer', p. 104.

15 Langer, 'Henry M. Sheffer, 1883–1964', p. 306.

16 Quoted in Dryden, 'Susanne K. Langer', p. 191.

17 Langer, 'Henry M. Sheffer, 1883–1964', p. 307.

18 Whitehead and Russell, *Principia Mathematica*, p. xv. Linsky comments, 'It is certainly not a proposal that someone rewrite all of *PM* using the Sheffer stroke. Russell in fact completes the task of integrating the Sheffer stroke into *PM* in a proper metalogical manner.' Linsky, *Evolution of Principia Mathematica*, p. 112. According to Quine, 'Russell thus alluded without further detail to Sheffer's "General theory of notational relativity", of 1921, a generally inaccessible mimeogram. Sheffer published an abstract of it in 1921 and no more, but he continued for years to present its ideas in his seminar.' Quine, 'Henry Maurice Sheffer', p. 104.

19 Scanlan writes, 'In the eyes of some, Sheffer's Jewish ethnic background must have been another "negative", in addition to his emotional fragility. ... It is the case that critical portions of his career at Harvard coincided with a period of anti-Jewish sentiment. This was especially evident during the 1920's when there was much campus support for instituting admissions quotas to reduce the percentage of Jewish students to around 10 percent. Although no official quota was ever introduced, changes were eventually made to the admission process which had the effect of significantly reducing the proportion of Jewish students [and] clearly reflected an atmosphere which could be similarly hostile to Jewish faculty appointments.' Scanlan, 'Known and Unknown H. M. Sheffer', p. 196.

20 Letter from Harold Laski to Bertrand Russell, 29 August 1919. Reproduced in Bertrand Russell, *Autobiography* (London: Routledge, 2009), pp. 325, 326. See also Barry Feinberg and Ronald Kasrils, eds, *Bertrand Russell's America: His Transatlantic Travels and Writings: A Documented Account, Vol. I, 1896–1945* (London: George Allen & Unwin, 1973), p. 78.

21 Russell, *Autobiography*, p. 326.

22 Bruce Kuklick refers to the episode as follows: 'From 1917 to 1927 Sheffer had an annual and tenuous appointment as lecturer. In 1919 he was, apparently, nearly fired because he was a "sensitive" Jew and because he had a disagreeable wife (they were later divorced). Sheffer fortunately had a manuscript on "Notational Relativity", and with letters from Russell, amongst others, attesting to Sheffer's "high order of original power", the department secured his annual reappointment.' Kuklick, *Rise of American Philosophy*, p. 458.

23 A. N. Whitehead, *Memorandum*, dated January 23, 1927, written by Whitehead in support of Sheffer's promotion. Quoted in Henle, Kallen and Langer, *Structure, Method and Meaning*, pp. ix–x. See also: Scanlan, 'Known and Unknown H. M. Sheffer', p. 195. Whitehead also notes in the memorandum that 'in the department of philosophy at Harvard, Mr Sheffer has been notably successful in exciting interest among those students with aptitude for this study.'

24 Even when appointed as professor his position remained unsure. As Kuklick writes, 'Woods continued to beat the bushes ... and with Jewish funding Sheffer became an assistant professor in 1927. In 1929 a combination of ... money ... went to promote Sheffer to associate professor. The university contributed nothing to the arrangement

and the funding of Sheffer's position was still irregular when he became a full professor in 1938 at the age of fifty-four'. Kuklick, *Rise of American Philosophy*, p. 458.

25 Scanlan, 'Known and Unknown H. M. Sheffer', pp. 193, 198.

26 Contributors to the *Festschrift* include: Alonzo Church, Clarence Irving Lewis, H. S. Leonard, W.V. Quine, Norbert Wiener, F. S. C. Northrop, C. J. Ducasse, George Sarton, Susanne K. Langer, Marvin Faber, R. B. Perry, Charles Hartshorne and Donald C. Williams. Henle, Kallen and Langer, *Structure, Method and Meaning*. Other thinkers claiming to have been influenced and inspired by Sheffer include C. H. Langford and Isaiah Berlin. See Scanlan, 'Known and Unknown H. M. Sheffer', pp. 97, 198.

27 Langer, 'Henry M. Sheffer, 1883–1964', p. 307.

28 Susanne K. Langer, *An Introduction to Symbolic Logic* (Second revised edition, New York: Dover Publications, 1953), p. 11.

29 Ibid., p. 18.

30 Ibid., p. 11. Prior to Langer's book, there were two other books on symbolic logic: *A Survey of Symbolic Logic* (1918) by C. H. Langford and *Symbolic Logic* (1932) by C. H. Langford and C. I. Lewis. Langford was another co-founders of the Association for Symbolic Logic and served as its President from 1941 to 1944. He edited the *Journal of Symbolic Logic* from 1936 to 1940. Alasdair Urquhart refers to Langford as 'Sheffer's only true logical descendant'. Alasdair Urquhart, 'Henry Sheffer and Notational Relativity', *History and Philosophy of Logic* 33.1 (2012), p. 33. He suggests that the reason for Langford's success compared to Sheffer's 'failure' was due to the fact that, 'unlike Sheffer, [Langford] was not sidetracked into dreams of a grand project, instead concentrating on concrete results about specific systems. Sheffer's most lasting contribution to logic, other than the famous stroke, may have been the early inspiration that he provided to Langford'. p. 46. Books on symbolic logic after Langer include: John C. Cooley, *Outline of Symbolic Logic* (1938); Quine, *Methods of Logic* (1950); Carnap, *Einführung in die symbolische Logik* (1954) translated as *Introduction to Symbolic Logic and Its Applications* (1958).

31 L. Susan Stebbing, 'Review of *The Principles of Mathematics* by Bertrand Russell and *An Introduction to Symbolic Logic* by Susanne K. Langer', *Philosophy* 13.52 (October 1938), p. 483. Michael Beany writes, 'Susan Stebbing (1885–1943) played a central role in the development of the analytic tradition in the 1930s, publishing the first textbook [*A Modern Introduction to Logic*] of analytic philosophy in 1930. She was also responsible for introducing logical empiricism into Britain. In two papers written in the early 1930s, she critically compared logical empiricism with Cambridge philosophy, thereby bringing into dialogue the two main schools of philosophy that came to form the analytic tradition'. Michael Beaney, 'Susan Stebbing and the Early Reception of Logical Empiricism in Britain', in Christian Damböck, ed., *Influences on the Aufbau*, Vienna Circle Institute Yearbook 18 (Cham: Springer, 2016), pp. 233–56.

32 Herbert Feigl, 'Review of Susanne Langer, *Introduction to Symbolic Logic*', *American Journal of Psychology* 51.4 (October 1938), p. 78.

33 Letter from Carnap to Quine, 11 February 1938, *Dear Carnap, Dear Van: The Quine-Carnap Correspondence and Related Work*, Richard Creath, ed. (Oakland: University of California Press, 1991), p. 246.

34 Isaiah Berlin, *Concepts and Categories: Philosophical Essays*, Henry Hardy, ed. (Pimlico: Hogarth Press, 1978), p. xii. Sheffer's phrase 'Carnap and Co.' is likely to refer to Carnap's discussions with Quine and Tarski in the early 1940s.

35 Quine, 'Henry Maurice Sheffer', pp. 103–4.

36 Langer, 'Henry M. Sheffer: 1883–1964', pp. 305–7.
37 Ibid., p. 307.
38 Ibid.,
39 Sheffer, 'Review of A. N. Whitehead and B. Russell', pp. 228–9.
40 Ibid., p. 229, footnote 1.
41 Ibid., p. 228.
42 Ibid.
43 Ibid.
44 Ibid., p. 229. A related concern had been voiced by Frege in a letter to Jourdain in 1914. He writes that he had found it 'very difficult' to read Russell's *Principia Mathematica* and to have 'stumbled over almost every sentence' since he 'never knew whether he was speaking of a sign or of its content'. Letter Frege to Jourdain, dated 28 January 1914. Quoted in Linsky, *Evolution of Principia Mathematica*, p. 5. This concern with a proper distinction between 'object' and 'concept' was echoed in a letter from Sheffer to Russel during his European tour. During his visit with Frege, the German philosopher had repeatedly stressed to him the importance of adhering to 'the sharp distinction between *Gegenstande* and *Begriffe*'. Linsky, *Evolution of Principia Mathematica*, p. 67.
45 Quoted in Quine, 'Henry Maurice Sheffer: 1863–1964', *Proceedings and Addresses of the American Philosophical Association* 38 (1964–5), p. 104.
46 Robert Innis considers this preoccupation with meaning a deeply pragmatist concern: 'At the very beginning of her intellectual career, and even much later with a nod to James, Langer asserted that philosophy as a distinctive discipline was fundamentally concerned with the descriptive and critical analysis of meanings and their orders and not, like the sciences, with the discovery of facts. Langer wanted to determine "how to make our ideas clear" about meaning, a deeply pragmatist concern'. Robert E. Innis, 'Placing Langer's Philosophical Project', *Journal of Speculative Philosophy*, New Series 21.1 (2007), p. 4.
47 Quoted in Dryden, 'Susanne K. Langer', p. 191.
48 Susanne K. Langer, *Philosophy in a New Key: A Study in the Symbolism of Reason, Rite, and Art* (Third edition, Cambridge, MA: Harvard University Press, 1980), p. 17.
49 Susanne K. Langer, *The Practice of Philosophy* (New York: Henry Holt, 1930), p. 83.
50 Susanne K. Langer, *Problems of Art* (New York: Charles Scribner's Sons, 1957), p. 175. This is a reprint of the chapter 'Abstraction in Science and Abstraction in Art', in P. Henle, H. M. Kallen and S. K. Langer, eds, *Structure, Method and Meaning: Essays in Honor of Henry M. Sheffer* (New York: Liberal Arts Press, 1951), pp. 171-82.

5 Ernst Cassirer: Symbolic form

1 Ernst Cassirer, *The Philosophy of Symbolic Forms, Volume I: Language* (New Haven, CT: Yale University Press, 1955), p. 75.
2 Ibid., p. 78.
3 Susanne Langer, 'On Cassirer's Theory of Language and Myth', in Paul Arthur Schilpp, ed., *The Philosophy of Ernst Cassirer*, The Library of Living Philosophers, Vol. 6 (La Salle, IL: Open Court, 1949), p. 393.
4 Susanne K. Langer, *Philosophy in a New Key: A Study in the Symbolism of Reason, Rite, and Art* (Third edition, Cambridge, MA: Harvard University Press, 1980), p. 41.

 5 Ibid., p. 290.

 6 Cassirer served as rector of Hamburg University in 1929–30, the first Jew to do so.

 7 Cassirer had adopted Swedish citizenship and had learned to write and teach in
    Swedish. Even so, even in Sweden Cassirer did not escape anti-Semitic attitudes. One
    conservative newspaper attacked Gothenburg's University's decision to appoint the
    'Jewish, German, exiled professor Ernst Cassirer [as] an unnecessary professorship
    [providing a] personal subsidy for a refugee intellectual.' Jonas Hansson and Svante
    Nordin, *Ernst Cassirer: The Swedish Years* (Bern: Peter Lang, 2006), pp. 56 ff.

 8 Cassirer succeeded the philosopher of language Wilbur Marshall Urban, whose own
    work was inspired by Cassirer.

 9 Toni Cassirer, *Mein Leben mit Ernst Cassirer* (Hamburg: Felix Meiner Verlag, 2003),
    p. 315. Translation mine.

10 Letter from Cassirer to Langer dated 8 April 1944, included in John Michael
    Krois, *Ernst Cassirer: Ausgewählter wissenschaftlicher Briefwechsel, Nachgelassene
    Manuskripte und Texte*, Band 18 (Hamburg: Felix Meiner Verlag, 2009). Quoted in
    Rolf Lachmann, *Susanne K. Langer: die lebendige Form menschlichen Fühlens und
    Verstehens*, p. 25.

11 Susanne K. Langer, Translator's preface to Ernst Cassirer, *Language and Myth*, trans.
    S. K. Langer (New York: Dover Publications, 1946, 2012), p. x.

12 Ernst Cassirer, *An Essay on Man* (New Haven, CT: Yale University Press, 1992); *The
    Myth of the State* (New Haven, CT: Yale University Press, 2013).

13 Examples of parallels between the structure of Langer's *Philosophy in a New Key*
    (1942) and Cassirer's *An Essay on Man* (1944) are: both books consist of two
    distinct parts, the first dealing with a general anthropology, based on a theory
    of symbolism, arguing that man is not an 'animal rationale' but an 'animal
    symbolicum' (Langer, *Philosophy in a New Key*, pp. 1–102; *An Essay on Man*,
    pp. 1–62), and the second containing chapters discussing a range of individual
    cultural forms (Langer, *Philosophy in a New Key*, pp. 103–226; *An Essay on Man*,
    pp. 63–229).

14 Ernst Cassirer, *Philosophie der symbolischen Formen: Die Sprache* (1923); *Das
    mythische Denken* (1925); *Phänomenologie der Erkenntnis* (1929) (Berlin: Bruno
    Cassirer, 1923, 1925, 1929). Ernst Cassirer, translation by Ralph Mannheim, *The
    Philosophy of Symbolic Forms Vol. I: Language* (1955); *Vol. II: Mythical Thought* (1955);
    Vol. III: The Phenomenology of Knowledge (1957) (New Haven, CT: Yale University
    Press, 1955, 1955, 1957). A fourth volume was produced posthumously by John
    Michael Krois and Donald Phillip Verene, eds, *The Philosophy of Symbolic Forms: The
    Metaphysics of Symbolic Forms* (New Haven, CT: Yale University Press, 1996).
    Henceforth referred to as Cassirer, *Philosophy of Symbolic Forms* I, II, III or IV.

15 Krois and Verene, Introduction to Cassirer, *Philosophy of Symbolic Forms* IV, p. xxiii.

16 Charles W. Hendel, Introduction to Cassirer, *Philosophy of Symbolic Forms* I, p. xii.

17 Ibid.

18 Susanne K. Langer, 'Review of *Festschrift für Paul Natorp. Zum Siebzigsten Geburtstage
    von Schülern und Freunden Gewidmet'*, *Journal of Philosophy* 21.25 (4 December
    1924), p. 696.

19 Henry Sheffer, 'Review of: *Substance and Function and Einstein's Theory of Relativity* by
    Ernst Cassirer', *Isis* 6.3 (1924), pp. 439–40. The book consisted of two essays originally
    published separately in German: *Substanzbegriff und Funktionsbegriff: Untersuchungen
    über die Grundfragen der Erkenntniskritik* (Berlin: Bruno Cassirer, 1910) and *Zur*

Einsteinschen Relativitätstheorie. Erkenntnistheoretische Betrachtungen (Berlin: Bruno Cassirer, 1921).

20 For biographical information on Cassirer see Dimitry Gawronsky, 'Ernst Cassirer: His Life and Work', in Schilpp, *The Philosophy of Ernst Cassirer*, pp. 1–37; Paetzold, *Ernst Cassirer: Von Marburg nach New York; Eine philosophische Biographie* (Darmstadt: Wissenschaftliche Buchgesellschaft, 1994); Toni Cassirer, *Mein Leben mit Ernst Cassirer* (Hildesheim: Gerstenberg Verlag, 1981) and Edward Skidelsky, *Ernst Cassirer: The Last Philosopher of Culture* (Princeton, NJ: University of Princeton Press, 2008). Currently called Wraclow and located in the southwest of Poland, Breslau used to be part of Germany and was home to a large cultural and intellectual Jewish community that all but disappeared following the Second World War.

21 Cohen was the first Jew to hold a professorship in Germany. For an analysis of Cohen's work on logic, ethics and aesthetics, see Reinier Munk, *Hermann Cohen's Critical Idealism* (Dordrecht: Springer, 2005).

22 Cassirer's thesis was later published as the Introduction of his first book *Leibniz' System in seinem wissenschaftlichen Grundlagen* (1902).

23 For discussions of neo-Kantianism, see Thomas E. Willey, *Back to Kant: The Revival of Kantianism in German Social and Historical Thought, 1860–1914* (Detroit: Wayne State University Press, 1978); Herbert Schnaedelbach *Philosophy in Germany 1831-1933*, trans. Eric Matthews (Cambridge: Cambridge University Press, 1984); Klaus Christian Köhnke, *The Rise of Neo-Kantianism: German Academic Philosophy between Idealism and Positivism*, trans. R. J. Hollingdale (Cambridge: Cambridge University Press, 1991); Rudolf A. Makkreel and Sebastian Luft, *Neo-Kantianism in Contemporary Philosophy* (Bloomington: Indiana University Press, 2010).

24 Thomas E. Willey notes that although the Marburg School has often been characterized as a 'narrow epistemological specialism' and 'a purely academic phenomenon with little social or political significance', both Hermann Cohen and Paul Natorp gave in fact as much attention to social philosophy as to logic. *Back to Kant*, pp. 102, 103.

25 Paul Natorp, *Philosophie, ihr Problem und ihre Probleme: Einführung in den kritischen Idealismus* (Göttingen: Vandenhoeck & Ruprecht, 1911, 1921), p. 13.

26 Stefan Morawski, 'Art as Semblance', *Journal of Philosophy* 11 (November 1984), p. 655.

27 William A. van Roo, S. I., 'Symbol According to Cassirer and Langer', *Gregorianum* 53 (1972), pp. 487–534 and 615–77. One of the few authors who discuss Cassirer's influence on Langer's aesthetics is Bernhard F. Scholz, 'Discourse and Intuition in Susanne Langer's Aesthetics of Literature', *Journal of Art and Art Criticism* 31.2 (Winter 1972), pp. 215–26.

28 Because of anti-Jewish sentiments in Imperial Germany, Cassirer had been unable to secure a tenured position at any university.

29 Felix Kaufmann, 'Cassirer's Theory of Scientific Knowledge', in Schilpp, *The Philosophy of Ernst Cassirer*, p. 198.

30 Cassirer, *Philosophy of Symbolic Forms* I, p. 75.

31 Ibid., p. 74.

32 Langer, *Philosophy in a New Key*, p. 18.

33 Quoted in Dean Moyar, ed., *The Routledge Companion to Nineteenth Century Philosophy* (Abingdon: Routledge, 2010), p. 585.

34 E. Cassirer, *Zur Einsteinschen Relativitätstheorie* (Berlin: B. Cassirer, 1921). For
     correspondence between Einstein and Cassirer, see John Michael Krois, *Ernst
     Cassirer: Ausgewählter wissenschaftlicher Briefwechsel, Nachgelassene Manuskripte und
     Texte*, Band 18 (Hamburg: Felix Meiner Verlag, 2009).
35 Frankfurt was to become the home of the *Frankfurter Schule* as part of the Institute
     for Social Research founded in 1924.
36 https://warburg.sas.ac.uk/library/library-aby-warburg (accessed 16 April 2019).
     When, in 1928, Frankfurt University tried to lure Cassirer from Hamburg, it was
     Aby Warburg who persuaded him to stay put. As Emily Levine records it, 'On
     June 24, 1928, when Warburg read in a half dozen newspapers that Cassirer had
     received an offer from the rival university of Frankfurt, his reaction was nothing
     short of hysterical. ... Warburg worked tirelessly to persuade the philosopher to
     remain in Hamburg, privately negotiating with the president of the University of
     Frankfurt, drafting a public statement for a special issue in the local newspaper ... and
     persuading Hamburg's mayor and a senator to solicit Cassirer personally. Cassirer was
     Hamburg's intellectual lifeline, and Warburg would not let the city lose him.' Emily
     J. Levine, *Dreamland of Humanists: Warburg, Cassirer, Panofsky, and the Hamburg
     School* (Chicago, University of Chicago Press, 2013), p. 187.
37 For a general history of the library, see Tilmann von Stockhausen, *Die
     Kulturwissenschaftliche Bibliothek Warburger: Architektur, Einrichtung Und
     Organisation* (Hamburg: Dölling and Galitz, 1992).
38 'The categories of Image, Word, Orientation and Action constitute the main
     divisions of the Warburg Institute Library and encapsulate its aim: to study the
     tenacity of symbols and images in European art and architecture (Image, 1st floor);
     the persistence of motifs and forms in Western languages and literatures (Word,
     2nd floor); the gradual transition, in Western thought, from magical beliefs to
     religion, science and philosophy (Orientation, 3rd & 4th floor) and the survival
     and transformation of ancient patterns in social customs and political institutions
     (Action, 4th floor).' https://warburg.sas.ac.uk/library/library-aby-warburg (accessed
     16 April 2019).
39 Cassirer, *Philosophy of Symbolic Forms* II, p. xviii.
40 Panofsky's famous 1924 essay *Idea: Ein Beitrag zur Begriffsgeschichte der älteren
     Künsttheorie* (Berlin: Spiess, 1993) was inspired by and a response to a lecture by
     Cassirer at the Warburg Library in 1924 entitled 'Eidos und Eidolon: Das Problem das
     Schönen und der Kunst in Platons Dialogen.'
41 Erwin Panofsky, *Perspective as Symbolic Form* (1924–1925), trans. Christopher S.
     Wood (New York: Zone Books, 1997), pp. 40, 41. Translator Wood observes that 'the
     proposed "application" of the symbolic form is never theoretically justified beyond the
     initial statement in the second part of the essay.' p. 14. As I will discuss in the chapter
     on art, Panofsky did not fully grasp Cassirer's conception of symbolic form. For more
     on the influence of Cassirer on Panofsky, see Michael Ann Holly, *Panofsky and the
     Foundations of Art History* (Ithaca, NY: Cornell University Press, 1985), pp. 114–58,
     and Michael Podro, *The Critical Historians of Art* (New Haven, CT: Yale University
     Press, 1982), pp. 181–3.
42 For a collection of essays by Cassirer on the Warburg Library see *Ernst Cassirer: The
     Warburg Years (1919–1933): Essays on Language, Art, Myth, and Technology*, trans.
     Steve G. Lofts and A. Calcagno (New Haven, CT: Yale University Press, 2013).
43 Cassirer had edited a standard edition of Kant's work, published by his brother Bruno.
     He also published editions of Leibniz' work.

44 Cassirer, *Philosophy of Symbolic Forms* I, p. 78. For discussions of Kant by Cassirer see *Rousseau, Kant and Goethe: Two Essays* (1945), trans. Jemas Gutmann, Paul Oskar Kristeller and John Hermann Randall, Jr (New York: Harper & Row, 1963) and *The Philosophy of the Enlightenment* (Princeton, NJ: Princeton University Press, 1951).

45 Susanne K. Langer, *Mind: An Essay on Human Feeling*, Vol. I (Baltimore, MD: Johns Hopkins University Press, 1967), pp. 77, 78.

46 Cassirer, *Philosophy of Symbolic Forms* I, p. 77.

47 Ibid., p. 78.

48 Ibid., p. 79.

49 Langer, *Philosophy in a New Key*, p. 90. In her view of perception Langer draws heavily on the work of *Gestalt* theorists Wolfgang Köhler, Max Wertheimer and Kurt Koffka.

50 Jürgen Habermas, 'The Liberating Power of Symbols: Ernst Cassirer's Humanistic Legacy and the Warburg Library', in *The Liberating Power of Symbols: Philosophical Essays*, trans. Peter Dews (Cambridge: Polity Press, 2001), pp. 4, 5. Habermas's essay is based on a lecture delivered on 20 April 1995 at the University of Hamburg at the dual occasion of the restored Warburg Library Building and the fiftieth anniversary of Cassirer's death on 13 April 1945.

51 Susanne K. Langer, 'The Lord of Creation', *Fortune* 29.1 (January 1944), pp. 127–8; 139-140, 142, 144, 146, 148, 150, 152, 154. See also Susanne Langer, 'Language and Thought (1953)', in Paul Eschholz, Alfred Rosa and Virginia Clark, eds, *Language Awareness: Readings for College Writers* (Boston, MA: Bedford/St. Martin's, 2000), pp. 96–101.

52 Cassirer, *Philosophy of Symbolic Forms* III, p. 134.

53 Langer, *Philosophy in a New Key*, p. 42.

54 Cassirer, *Philosophy of Symbolic Forms* I, p. 80.

55 Revisions like this would be a continuous matter of debate amongst neo-Kantians who, each with their own readings and revisions claiming to be best custodians of Kant's legacy.

56 Immanuel Kant, *Critique of Pure Reason*, trans. Norman Kemp Smith (London: The Macmillan Press, 1933), B29, p. 61.

57 Ibid., B103, p. 112.

58 Ibid., B177, p. 181.

59 Ibid., B186, p. 186.

60 Ibid., B185, p. 186.

61 Cassirer, *Philosophy of Symbolic Forms* I, p. 14.

62 Ibid., p. 15.

63 Donald Philip Verene, 'Cassirer's View of Myth and Symbol', *The Monist* 50:4 (October 1966) p. 554.

64 Langer, *Philosophical Sketches* (New York: Arno Press, 1962), p. 58. First presented as a paper at Brown University in 1965 under the title 'On a New Definition of Symbol'.

65 Ibid.

66 In the preface of the third volume, Cassirer refers to material that he had not been able to include for reasons of length under the title ' "Geist" und "Leben" in der *Philosophie der Gegenwart*.' Although Cassirer did write an essay under that title, which was subsequently published as a chapter in the Cassirer volume of *The Library of Living Philosophers*, it is now widely believed not to be the one he referred to in the preface. This is because this chapter confines itself to a discussion of the philosophy of Ludwig Klages and not to contemporary philosophy in

general. Prior to being included as the concluding chapter of the Cassirer volume of *The Library of Living Philosophers* (857–880), the essay was published in *Die Neue Rundschau* 41.1 (1930), pp. 244-26. Instead, a different manuscript found amongst his Swedish manuscripts is now generally believed to be the one he referred to here.

67 Cassirer, *Essay on Man* (New Haven, CT: Yale University Press, 1944, 1992), p. 110.
68 Ibid.
69 Ibid., pp. 111, 112.
70 Ibid., p. 120.
71 Cassirer, *Philosophy of Symbolic Forms* I, p. 160.
72 Quoted in Cassirer, *Philosophy of Symbolic Forms* I, p. 160, with footnote reference 'Humboldt, 'Einleitung zum Kawi-Werk', Werke 7, No. 1, p. 46 ff.' Berlin, Deutsche Akademie der Wissenschaften, 1903; https://archive.org/details/gesammelteschri03berlgoog/page/n55 (accessed 16 April 2019).
73 Cassirer, *Essay on Man*, p. 134.
74 Ibid., p. 135.
75 Quoted in Cassirer, *Philosophy of Symbolic Forms* I, p. 159.
76 Ibid.
77 Jürgen Habermas, *The Liberating Power of Symbols,* p. 12. Since Cassirer, many thinkers have discovered the importance of von Humboldt's thinking about language. Julia Kristeva, for instance, notes that 'Modern thinking … is discovering in Humboldt certain principles that current science and philosophy seem to be taking up again: such as the principle that *la langue* is not an oeuvre, *ergon*, but an activity, *energeia*. … Humboldt is also credited with the discovery of the concept of *Innere Sprachform*, an interior linguistic form that precedes articulation.' Julia Kristeva, *Language the Unknown: An Initiation into Linguistics*, trans. Anne M. Menke (New York: Columbia University Press, 1989), p. 203. A more recent example is Charles Taylor's *The Language Animal* that draws on three important thinkers Hamann, Herder and von Humboldt or the 'HHH' as he will refer to it in distinction from the 'HLC', i.e. Hobbes, Locke and Condillac. Taylor's views of language as primarily constitutive rather than designative echo those of Cassirer and Langer. Charles Taylor, *The Language Animal: The Full Shape of the Human Linguistic Capacity* (Cambridge, MA: Harvard University Press, 2016).
78 Cassirer, *Philosophy of Symbolic Forms* III, p. 86.
79 Ibid., p. 89.
80 Ernst Cassirer, chapter 3, 'From Animal Reactions to Human Responses', *An Essay on Man*, p. 31.
81 Randall E. Auxier, 'Ernst Cassirer (1874–1945) & Suzanne [sic] Katherina (Knauth) Langer (1895–1985)', in Michel Weber and Will Desmond, eds, *Handbook of Whiteheadian Thought, Volume 2* (Frankfurt: Ontos Verlag, 2009), p. 555.
82 Langer, 'On Cassirer's Theory of Language and Myth', pp. 385, 386.
83 Ibid., p. 393.
84 For an extensive comparison of Cassirer and Langer on myth see William Schultz, *Cassirer and Langer on Myth: An Introduction* (Abingdon: Routledge, 2016). For discussions of Cassirer's view of myth see Susanne K. Langer, 'On Cassirer's Theory of Language and Myth' and Montague M. F. Ashley, 'Cassirer on Mythological Thinking' in Schilpp, *The Philosophy of Ernst Cassirer*, pp. 379–400 and 359–78. See also Verene, 'Cassirer's View of Myth and Symbol', pp. 553–64.

85 Langer, 'On Cassirer's Theory of Language and Myth', p. 388.

86 Langer, Translator's Preface, *Language and Myth*, p. viii.

87 Ibid.

88 Ibid., pp. viii, x.

89 For a comprehensive account of Cassirer and Langer's respective conceptions of myth see Schultz, *Cassirer and Langer on Myth*.

90 Cassirer, *Philosophy of Symbolic Forms* II, p. 45.

91 Ibid.

92 Ibid.

93 Cassirer, *Philosophy of Symbolic Forms* I, p. 89.

94 Cassirer, *Philosophy of Symbolic Forms* II, part 2, pp. 155–9; see also Cassirer, *Essay on Man*, pp. 87–108.

95 Langer, 'On Cassirer's Theory of Language and Myth', p. 392.

96 Ibid., p. 388.

97 Ibid.

98 Ibid.

99 Merleau-Ponty, *Phenomenology of Perception* (1945), trans. Colin Smith (London: Routledge, 1998).

100 Samantha Matherne, 'The Kantian Roots of Merleau-Ponty's Account of Pathology', *British Journal for the History of Philosophy* 22.1 (2014), pp. 124–49. By highlighting Cassirer's influence on Merleau-Ponty, Matherne rejects the prevailing notion that Merleau-Ponty's phenomenology is anti-Kantian.

101 Cassirer, *Philosophy of Symbolic Forms* III, p. 200. Cassirer and Merleau-Ponty draw on many similar sources, including Heinz Werner, Adhémar Gelb, Kurt Koffka, Kurt Goldstein and David Katz.

102 Cassirer, *Philosophy of Symbolic Forms* III, p. 202.

103 Ibid., p. 200.

104 The Davos *Hochschulkurs* was an international and interdisciplinary conference of more than two hundred students and scholars from universities across Europe.

105 Martin Heidegger and Ernst Cassirer, 'A Discussion Between Ernst Cassirer and Martin Heidegger', in Nino Langiulli, ed., trans. Francis Slade, *The Existentialist Tradition: Selected Writings* (New York: Anchor Books, 1971), p. 200. The text is based on notes by students and conforms to the known or written views of either of these philosophers. For Cassirer's views of Heidegger, see Cassirer, *Philosophy of Symbolic Forms* IV, pp. 200–8.

106 Cassirer, *Philosophy of Symbolic Forms* IV, p. 201.

107 Cassirer, *Philosophy of Symbolic Forms* I, p. 78.

108 Cassirer, *Die Idee der Republikanischen Verfassung* (Hamburg: Friederichsen, de Gruyter, 1929), p. 31. Quoted in Habermas, *The Liberating Power of Symbol*, p. 23. For a broader discussion of Cassirer in relation to the context of the political climate at the time, see David R. Lipton, *Ernst Cassirer: The Dilemma of a Liberal Intellectual in Germany 1914–33* (Toronto: University of Toronto Press, 1978).

109 Larry Eugene Jones, ed., *Crossing Boundaries: The Exclusion and Inclusion of Minorities in Germany* (New York: Berghahn Books, 2001), p. 127

110 Jones, *Crossing Boundaries*, p. 127. The footnote refers to J. Haag, 'The Spann Circle and the Jewish Question', *Leo Baeck Institute Yearbook* 18 (1973), pp. 93–126, esp. 103–5.

111 Jones, *Crossing Boundaries*, p. 120. Director of the Warburg Library, Professor F. Saxl, who had succeeded Aby Warburg in 1929, had the foresight to ship the

entire library – which by that time contained 60,000 books plus slides, papers and furniture – to London by December of the same year.

112   Helmut Kuhn, 'Cassirer's Philosophy of Culture', in Schilpp, ed., *The Philosophy of Ernst Cassirer*, p. 573.

113   For Lipton's discussion of Cassirer's political views, see David R. Lipton, *Ernst Cassirer: The Dilemma of a Liberal Intellectual in Germany 1914–33* (Toronto: University of Toronto Press, 1978).

114   The same view of the importance of political neutrality in philosophy was held by Carnap in 'Intellectual Autobiography', in Paul Arthur Schilpp, ed., *The Philosophy of Rudolf Carnap, The Library of Living Philosophers*, Vol. 11 (La Salle, IL: Open Court, 1963), p. 23.

115   Peter E. Gordon, *The Continental Divide: Cassirer, Heidegger, Davos* (Cambridge: Harvard University Press, 2012), p. 58.

116   Cassirer, *Essay on Man*, p. 228.

117   Habermas, *Liberating Power of Symbols*, p. 7.

118   Langer, *Philosophy in a New Key*, p. 290.

119   Ibid., p. 290, 291. While coming from a different philosophical tradition, analytic philosopher Nelson Goodman, too, considers symbol forms as one of the defining features of human being. As he writes in *Ways of Worldmaking* (1978): '[Cassirer's] themes – the multiplicity of worlds, the speciousness of "the given," the creative power of the understanding, the variety and formative function of symbols … are also integral to my own thinking. … Cassirer undertakes the search through a cross-cultural study of the developments of myth, religion, language, art and science. My approach is rather through an analytic study of types and functions of symbols and symbol systems.' *Ways of Worldmaking* (Indianapolis: Hackett Publishing Company, 2013), pp. 1, 5. The chapter containing this quote was first presented as a paper at Hamburg University at the occasion of the one-hundredth anniversary of Cassirer's birth.

120   Habermas, *The Liberating Power of Symbols*, p. 24.

121   Susanne K. Langer, *Problems of Art* (New York: Charles Scribner's Sons, 1957), p. 74.

122   For a discussion of the place of politics in Cassirer's writing see Paetzold, *Ernst Cassirer: Von Marburg nach New York*, pp. 123–6.

123   Cassirer, *Myth of the State*, p. 293.

124   One of the first scholars to refer to a 'Cassirer-Renaissance' was Heinz Paetzold in his book *Ernst Cassirer, Von Marburg Nach New York*, p. viii.

125   For discussions of the Davos debate in terms of the continental divide see Michael Friedman, *A Parting of Ways: Carnap, Cassirer and Heidegger* (Chicago, IL: Open Court, 2000) and Peter E. Gordon, *The Continental Divide: Cassirer, Heidegger, Davos* (Cambridge: Harvard University Press, 2010). For broader discussions of the debate see D. Kaegi and Enno Rudolph, *Cassirer – Heidegger: 70 Jahre Davoser Disputation* (Hamburg: Meiner, 2002); Paetzold, *Ernst Cassirer: Von Marburg nach New York*, pp. 86–106.

126   Other philosophers present included a young Emmanuel Levinas (1906–1995) who also joint in with the general critique of Cassirer, something he later said he regretted.

127   Peter E. Gordon, *Continental Divide*, p. 9. The same point was made by Friedman in *A Parting of Ways*. Friedman argues that Cassirer's approach to philosophy can serve as a bridge builder in the divide.

128   In *Being and Time* Heidegger mentions meeting Cassirer when he gave a lecture for the local chapter of the Kantian Society in Hamburg in 1923. He notes that there had

been 'an agreement as to the necessity of an existential analytic which was sketched out in the lecture'. Martin Heidegger, *Being and Time*, trans. Joan Stambaugh (Albany: State University of New York Press, 1996), p. 47, footnote 11. Heidegger further comments, 'Through this investigation more comprehensive guidelines are made available to ethnological investigation. Viewed in terms of the philosophical problematic the question remains whether the foundations of the interpretation are sufficiently transparent, whether especially the architectonic of Kant's *Kritik der reinen Vernunft* and its systematic content are able to offer the possible outline for such task at all, or whether a new and more primordial beginning is not necessary here. Cassirer himself sees the possibility of such a task as it is shown in the footnote on pages 16 ff., where Cassirer points out the phenomenological horizon disclosed by Husserl.'

129 Martin Heidegger, 'Ernst Cassirer: Philosophie der symbolischen Formen. 2. Teil: Das mythische Denken', *Deutsche Literaturzeitung* 21 (1928), pp. 1000–12. Translated as 'Book Review of Ernst Cassirer's Mythical Thought', in Martin Heidegger, *The Piety of Thinking: Studies in Phenomenology and Existential Philosophy* (Bloomington: Indiana Press, 1976), pp. 32–45.

130 Cassirer, *Freiheit und Form: Studien zur deutschen Geistesgeschichte* (Berlin: Bruno Cassirer, 1916).

131 Cassirer, 'The Concept of Philosophy', Inaugural Address, in Donald Phillip Verene, ed., *Symbol, Myth, and Culture* (New Haven, CT: Yale University Press, 1979), p. 60. See also Michael Hänel, 'The Case of Ernst Cassirer', in Larry Eugene Jones, ed., *Crossing Boundaries: The Exclusion and Inclusion of Minorities in Germany* (New York: Berghahn Books, 2001), p. 131.

132 Cassirer, 'The Concept of Philosophy', p. 60.

133 Ibid.

134 After his death, his widow Toni arranged for the unfinished papers to be moved to the United States where they were kept by Yale University. They were subsequently ordered and edited by John Michael Krois and Donald Phillip Verene in the early seventies and became part of the 20-volume project *Ernst Cassirer, Nachgelassene Manuskripte und Texte*, J. Krois, and E. Schwemmer, eds (Hamburg: Meiner Verlag). For an account of the 'discovery' and history of the papers see Krois and Verene, Introduction to Cassirer, *Philosophy of Symbolic* Forms IV, p. xv. In contrast to Whitehead, who had ordered the destruction of all his papers after his death, Cassirer left a vast *Nachlass*. The German rediscovery of the importance of Cassirer as a thinker was spurred by the publication of his *Nachlass* as well as by the first volumes of the critical edition of Cassirer's *Gesammelte Werke* 1–26 edited by Birgit Recki (Hamburger Ausgabe, 2009).

135 Most Swedish texts were deliberately written in German rather than English since Cassirer had not wanted to 'abandon the language that Goethe perfected to the propagandists of the Third Reich'. John Michael Krois, Introduction to Hansson and Nordin, *Ernst Cassirer*, p. 15. The texts that later were translated into English have since been published in Donald Philip Verene, ed., *Symbol, Myth, and Culture: Essays and Lectures of Ernst Cassirer, 1935–1945* (New Haven, CT: Yale University Press, 1979) and Cassirer, *Philosophy of Symbolic Forms* IV.

136 John Michael Krois, Introduction to Hansson and Nordin, *Ernst Cassirer: The Swedish Years*, p. 14.

137 Krois and Verene, Introduction to Cassirer, *Philosophy of Symbolic Forms* IV, p. xxiv.

138   Verene, *Symbol, Myth, and Culture*, p. 195. Quoted in Verene, The Origins of the
       philosophy of Symbolic Forms: Kant, Hegel and Cassirer, p. 62.
139   Cassirer, *Philosophy of Symbolic Forms* IV, p. 5.
140   Ibid., pp. 3–33. I will follow the editors' translation of the German word '*Geist*' as
       'geist'. As they explain in a note, 'The difficulties of rendering *Geist* into English
       are well known to readers of German philosophy. *Geist* may be understood
       as "mind" and as "spirit". Its meaning for Cassirer involves various senses of
       both words and sometimes is best indicated by "culture". In this volume "geist"
       often occurs as an English word, in the same way that other terms of German
       philosophy are now in use in English, such as "dasein". In some instances, *Geist*
       is "intelligence" where that seems specific to the context.' Krois and Verene,
       Introduction to Cassirer, *Philosophy of Symbolic Forms* IV, p. x, footnote 6. For an
       account of the chronology of – and confusion surrounding – the publication of
       the chapter see Krois and Verene, Introduction to Cassirer, *Philosophy of Symbolic
       Forms*, pp. ix–xiii.
141   Cassirer, *Philosophy of Symbolic Forms* IV, p. 223.
142   Ibid.
143   Jacques Derrida, *Of Grammatology*, trans. Gayatri Chakravorty Spivak (Baltimore,
       MD: Johns Hopkins University Press, 2016), p. 158. It is worth pointing out that
       Spivak's translation of Derrida's celebrated phrase 'il n'y a pas de hors-texte' as 'there
       is nothing outside of the text' is misleading. A better translation is 'There is nothing
       non-textual' or, as is already added in brackets 'there is no outside text.' Rather than
       making a claim about ultimate reality, Derrida merely states we can only speak about
       reality through texts or cultural symbols. This is the same claim made by Cassirer
       and Langer and, as we will see, Wittgenstein in the *Tractatus,* when he writes; 'The
       picture cannot place itself outside of its form of representation.' Ludwig Wittgenstein,
       Tractatus Logico-Philosophicus (1922), trans. C. K. Ogden (London: Routledge,
       1996), p. 41, 2.174.
144   Ernst Cassirer, 'Axel Hägerström: Eine Studie zur Schwedischen Philosophie
       der Gegenwart', in Birgit Recki, ed., *Ernst Cassirer: Gesammelte Werke
       Hamburger Ausgabe Volume 21, Axel Hägerström. Thorilds Stellung in der
       Geistesgeschichte des 18. Jahrhunderts: Eine Studie zur schwedischen Philosophie
       der Gegenwart* (Hamburg: Meiner Verlag, from 1998). Quoted in Carl H.
       Hamburg, 'Cassirer's Conception of Philosophy', Schilpp, *The Philosophy
       of Ernst Cassirer*, p. 116.
145   See footnote 143.
146   Ernst Cassirer, 'Language and Art II', in Donald Phillip Verene, ed., *Symbol, Myth
       and Culture: Essays and Lectures of Ernst Cassirer 1935–1945* (New Haven, CT: Yale
       University Press, 1979), pp. 194. 195. Cassirer spoke these words at a seminar on the
       Philosophy of Language and the Principles of Symbolism at Yale University in the
       spring of 1942. On Cassirer and metaphysics see also Donald Phillip Verene, *The
       Origins of the Philosophy of Symbolic Forms: Kant, Hegel, and Cassirer* (Northwestern
       University Press, 2011), p. 62ff.
147   Cassirer, *Philosophy of Symbolic Forms* IV, p. 154.
148   Ibid., pp. 224–5
149   Ibid., p. 4.
150   Ibid.
151   Ibid., p. 225.
152   Ibid.

153 Ibid.

154 Ibid., p. 17.

155 For an account of the influence of Hegel on Cassirer's thought see Verene, *Origins of the Philosophy of Symbolic Forms*. While convincingly arguing that Cassirer was significantly influenced by Hegel and his *Phenomenology of Mind*, his claims are somewhat modified since his earlier article from 1969 where he argued that 'the philosophy of symbolic forms is derived from Kant only in a broad and secondary sense and that its actual foundations are in Hegel.' Donald P. Verene, 'Kant, Hegel, and Cassirer': The Origins of the Philosophy of Symbolic Forms', *Journal of the History of Ideas* 30.1 (January–March 1969), p. 33.

156 Cassirer, *Philosophy of Symbolic Forms* IV, p. 19.

157 Ibid., pp. 28, 29.

158 Ibid., p. 186.

159 Donald P. Verene, 'Cassirer's Metaphysics', in Jeffrey Andrew Barash, ed., *The Symbolic Construction of Reality: The Legacy of Ernst Cassirer* (Chicago, IL: University of Chicago Press, 2008), p. 99.

160 Verene, 'Cassirer's Metaphysics', p. 101. For a comparison of Cassirer, Whitehead and Langer, see Randall E. Auxier, 'Ernst Cassirer (1874–1945) & Suzanne [sic] Katherina (Knauth) Langer (1895–1985), in Michel Weber and Will Desmond, eds, *Handbook of Whiteheadian Process Thought, Volume 2* (Frankfurt: Ontos Verlag, 2009), pp. 554–72. For a comparison of Cassirer, Whitehead and Bergson on the notion of symbolic transformation see Eric Dickson, 'Cassirer, Whitehead, and Bergson: Explaining the Development of the Symbol', *Process Studies* 32.1 (Spring-Summer 2003), pp. 79–93.

161 Cassirer, *Philosophy of Symbolic Forms* IV, p. 225.

162 Langer, *Philosophy in a New Key*, p. 41.

163 Card number 4. Quoted in Lachmann, *Susanne Langer: Die Lebendige Form menschlichen Fühlens und Verstehens*, p. 110, footnote 30.

164 Paul Arthur Schilpp, ed., *The Philosophy of Ernst Cassirer*, The Library of Living Philosophers, Vol. 6 (La Salle, IL: Open Court, 1949).

165 John Michael Krois and Donald Phillip Verene, 'Cassirer's Concept of Symbolic Form and Human Creativity', *Idealistic Studies* 8.8 (January 1978), pp. 14–32.

166 Krois and Verene, 'Cassirer's Concept of Symbolic Form', pp. 14–32.

167 Quoted by Krois and Verene, Introduction to Cassirer, *Philosophy of Symbolic Forms* IV, p. xxiii.

168 Chapters on art can be found in Cassirer, *Philosophy of the Enlightenment*, pp. 275–361; *An Essay on Man* (1944), pp. 137–70; and *Symbol, Myth and Culture*.

169 Krois and Verene, Introduction to Cassirer, *Philosophy of Symbolic Forms* IV, p. xxiii.

6 Alfred N. Whitehead: Organic form

1 Alfred North Whitehead, *Process and Reality*, David Ray Griffin and Donald W. Sherburne, eds (New York: Free Press, 1929), p. 246.

2 Alfred North Whitehead, *Symbolism: Its Meaning and Effect: Barbour-Page Lectures, University of Virginia, 1927* (New York: Fordham University Press, 1985), pp. 7, 8.

3 Susanne K. Langer, *Mind: An Essay on Human Feeling*, Vols I, II and III (henceforth cited as *Mind* I, II or III) (Baltimore, MD: Johns Hopkins University Press, 1967, 1971 and 1982), *Mind* I, p. 23.

4   Bertrand Russell, *Autobiography* (London: Routledge, 1998), p. 129. Recalling
    Whitehead's 'soirées' at his house, Feigl comments, '[M]ost of them were long,
    rambling, but thoroughly captivating soliloquies – on all sort of subjects – by
    the amiable, thoroughly British, philosopher.' Herbert Feigl, *Inquiries and
    Provocations: Selected Writings 1929–1974*, ed. Robert S. Cohen, *Vienna Circle
    Collection*, Vol. 14 (Dordrecht: D. Reidel, 1981), p. 69.

5   William Ernest Hocking, 'Whitehead as I Knew Him', in George L. Kline ed., *Alfred
    North Whitehead: Essays on His Philosophy* (Lanham, MD: University Press of
    America, 1989), p. 14.

6   Paul Weiss, 'Recollections of Alfred North Whitehead', *Process Studies* 10.1–2 (Spring–
    Summer 1980), p. 48.

7   According to McHenry, a few passages in *Process and Reality* were taken directly
    from Emmet's lecture notes which she gave to Whitehead after his classes. Leemon
    McHenry, 'Dorothy M. Emmet (1904–2000)', in Michel Weber and Will Desmond,
    eds, *Handbook of Whiteheadian Process Thought*, Vols 1 and 2 (Frankfurt: Ontos
    Verlag, 2008), p. 99. Dorothy Emmet held a Commonwealth Fellowship at Radcliffe
    College from 1928–30. Her first book, *Whitehead's Philosophy of Organism* (1932),
    aimed to clarify some of Whitehead's complex ideas but was met with criticism from
    Whitehead himself. See André Cloots, 'The Metaphysical Significance of Whitehead's
    Creativity', *Process Studies* 30.1 (Spring/Summer 2000), pp. 36–54.

8   Victor Lowe, *Alfred North Whitehead: The Man and His Work, Vol. 2, 1910–1947*
    (Baltimore, MD: Johns Hopkins University Press, 1990), p. 148. Paul Weiss's
    recollections are similar: '[Whitehead] was not a good dissertation director. My
    conferences with him had a single same pattern. I would come in with the dissertation,
    and he would make some general remarks. He was quite amiable and friendly, but he
    never gave me any really sharp criticisms. When I presented my thesis, I thought I had
    his approval. The department turned it down. I hadn't realized that he hadn't altogether
    thought it was a good thing.' Weiss, 'Recollections of Alfred North Whitehead', p. 49.

9   Henry M. Sheffer, 'Review of: *Principia Mathematica* by Alfred North Whitehead and
    Bertrand Russell', *Isis* 8.1 (1926), pp. 226–31.

10 Susanne K. Langer, 'Confusion of Symbols and Confusion of Logical Types', *Mind* 35
    (April 1926), p. 222, footnote 1.

11 Whitehead's statement was published in *Mind* 35 (1926), p. 130.

12 Bernard Linsky, *The Evolution of* Principia Mathematica: *Bertrand Russell's
    Manuscripts and Notes for the Second Edition* (Cambridge: Cambridge University
    Press, 2011), p. 17.

13 Victor Lowe adds, 'Benign sages, especially if they are private rather than
    public figures, become lost in a gentle mist after their deaths. This one is worth
    recovering.' Lowe, *Alfred North Whitehead*, p. 2. Michael Weber comments,
    'Whitehead was an introvert by temperament and does not always reveal his
    influences, because his library was dispersed on the occasion of his several moves,
    because of the change of orientation of his research program and, finally, because
    of the clauses of his will.' In Ronny Desmet and Michel Weber, eds, *Whitehead: The
    Algebra of Metaphysics* (Louvain-la-Neuve: Les Editions Chromatika, 2010),
    pp. 16, 17.

14 For Russell's recollections of Whitehead, see 'Portraits from Memory: Alfred North
    Whitehead', *Portraits from Memory and Other Essays* (New York: Simon & Schuster,
    1956), pp. 103, 104.

15 Russell's recollections may not necessarily provide an accurate picture of Whitehead since, as Michel Weber notes, 'Whitehead left very few clues while Russell's numerous testimonies are often unreliable.' Desmet and Weber, eds, *Whitehead: The Algebra of Metaphysics*, p. 16. Nicholas Griffin comments, 'Judging from the reports [Whitehead's biographer] Lowe has collected, those who knew Whitehead liked him, admired him, but never felt they'd understood him. He does not figure prominently in the memoirs of his friends; was an infrequent correspondent; rarely talked about personal matters; and didn't show his emotions easily.' Nicholas Griffin, ' "Lowe's Whitehead", Review of Victor Lowe', *Alfred North Whitehead. The Man and His Work, Vol. I: 1861–1910* (Baltimore, MD: Johns Hopkins University Press, 1985), *Journal of Bertrand Russell Studies* 6.2 Article 10 (1986), p. 174.

16 For an overview of Whitehead's influence on Langer, see Donald Dryden, 'Whitehead's Influence on Susanne Langer's Conception of Living Form', *Process Studies* 26.1-2 (1997), pp. 62–85.

17 Russell writes, '[Whitehead] took a personal interest in those with whom he had to deal and knew both their strong and their weak points. He would elicit from a pupil the best of which a pupil was capable. He was never repressive, or sarcastic, or superior, or any of the things that inferior teachers like to be. I think that in all the abler young men with whom he came in contact he inspired as he did in me, a very real and lasting affection.' Russell, *Portraits from Memory*, p. 104. Although Whitehead's publication output was initially small, one of his early essays, *A Treatise on Universal Algebra*, from 1898, had resulted in him being elected as a Fellow of the Royal Society.

18 A second edition, with revisions by Russell, appeared in 1925 (Volume 1) and 1927 (Volumes 2 and 3).

19 Langer, Preface to *A Logical Analysis of Meaning* (1926) Unpublished PhD Thesis, Radcliffe College, Harvard Archives, Ref. RAD T. L276.

20 Preface, 'A Logical Analysis of Meaning'.

21 Ibid.

22 Ibid.

23 Whitehead's student E. P. Bell wrote the following note: 'It's this self-coherence of the pattern that's always reproducing itself – the *one* thing. – This, Whitehead thinks, is foundation of Logic, too – and its applicability. Whitehead led to this very much by Sheffer's brilliant work.' Paul A. Bogaard and Jason Bell, eds, *The Harvard Lectures of Alfred North Whitehead 1924–1925: Philosophical Presuppositions of Science*, in *The Edinburgh Critical Edition of the Complete Works of Alfred North Whitehead*, Vol. I (Edinburgh: Edinburgh University Press, 2017), p. 114. In a footnote to this passage the editors mistakenly suggest that Whitehead was praising Sheffer for his new logical connecter, the 'Sheffer stroke'.

24 Alfred North Whitehead, *Modes of Thought* (1938) Lecture Three, 'Understanding' (New York: Free Press, 1969), p. 72.

25 Whitehead's departure for London was in part sparked by departmental politics: As J. Connor and E. F. Robertson describe it, 'The Council … voted that Whitehead had served as a Lecturer for over 25 years (the maximum period) so must leave his post. Whitehead's appointment as Senior Lecturer still had three years to run but he did not stay to argue his case. He moved to London in the summer of 1910 with no job to go to. In 1914, after four years without a proper position, he became Professor of Applied Mathematics at the Imperial College of Science and Technology in London.'

From: www-history.mcs.st-and.ac.uk/Biographies/Whitehead.html (accessed 17 April 2019).

26 Both Sheffer and Wittgenstein made a deep impression on Russell and Russell was to help each of them at some important points in their later careers. Russell helped Sheffer by supporting his promotion at Harvard, and Wittgenstein with the publication of his *Tractatus Logicus*.

27 Brian F. McGuinness and George H. von Wright, eds, *Ludwig Wittgenstein: Cambridge Letters, Correspondence with Russell, Keynes, Moore, Ramsey and Sraffa* (Oxford: Blackwell, 1997); Brian F. McGuinness, ed., *Wittgenstein in Cambridge: Letters and Documents* 1911–1951 (Oxford: Blackwell, 2012). For further details of Wittgenstein's references to Whitehead in his correspondence with Russell, see Chapter 7 on Wittgenstein, footnote 68.

28 After his move to London, Whitehead's philosophical and political interests developed in a different direction from those of Russell. Russell became a radical pacifist and was given a six-month prison sentence in 1918 for his anti-war activities. Whitehead, by contrast, who had lost his youngest son in the last year of the war, defended England's position in the First World War. Despite their differences they stayed loyal to each other and Whitehead would regularly visit Russell in Brixton prison.

29 Susanne K. Langer and Eugene T. Gadol, 'The Deepening Mind: A Half-Century of American Philosophy', *American Quarterly* 2.2 (Summer 1950), p. 128.

30 For the British reception of Einstein theories and Whitehead's subsequent re-interpretation of them see Ronny Desmet, 'Whitehead and the British Reception of Einstein's Relativity', *Process Studies Supplements* 11 (2007) on www.ctr4process. org/publications/ProcessStudies/PSS and 'Whitehead's Relativity', in Weber and Desmet, eds, *Whitehead: The Algebra of Metaphysics*, pp. 365–73. Desmet writes that Whitehead and Einstein discussed their divergent views on relativity in person on two consecutive days in June 1921.

31 In *Science and the Modern World*, Whitehead describes the atmosphere at the meeting in terms of a Greek drama: 'It was my good pleasure to be present at the meeting of the Royal Society in London when the Astronomer Royal for England announced that the photographic plates of the famous eclipse, as measured by his colleagues in Greenwich Observatory, had verified the prediction of Einstein that rays of light are bent as they pass in the neighbourhood of the she sun. The whole atmosphere of tense interest was exactly that of the Greek drama: we were the chorus commenting on the decree of destiny as disclosed in the development of a supreme incident. There was dramatic quality in the very staging – the traditional ceremonial, and in the background the picture of Newton to remind us that the greatest of scientific generalisations was now, after more than two centuries, to receive its first modification. Nor was the personal interest wanting: a great adventure in thought had at length come safe to shore.' A. N. Whitehead, *Science and the Modern World* (1925) (New York: Free Press, 1967), p. 10. The meeting was reported in the next day's issue of the *London Times* with the headline 'Revolution in Science. New Theory of The Universe. Newtonian Ideas Overthrown'. *The Times* (7 November 1919).

32 *The Principle of Relativity with Applications to Physical Science* (Cambridge: Cambridge University Press, 1922), p. 3. Whitehead adds that in preparing the book he had been given the advice of 'two distinguished persons' – a philosopher and a mathematician – and comments, 'The philosopher advised me to omit the mathematics, and the mathematician urged the cutting out of the philosophy. At the moment I was persuaded: it certainly is a nuisance for philosophers

to be worried with applied mathematics, and for mathematicians to be saddled with philosophy. But further reflection has made me retain my original plan.' p. 4. *The Principle of Relativity with Applications to Physical Science* has been re-published by Dover Phoenix Editions in 2004 and by Barnes & Noble Books in 2005.

33 Whitehead, *Principle of Relativity with Applications to Physical Science*, p. 4.

34 Alfred N. Whitehead, *Concept of Nature* (Cambridge: Cambridge University Press, 1920), p. vii.

35 Philosophers Randall Auxier and Gary Herstein refer in this context to Whitehead's 'radical empiricism.' Randall E. Auxier and Gary L. Herstein, *The Quantum of Explanation: Whitehead's Radical Empiricism*, Routledge Studies in American Philosophy (New York: Routledge and Kegan Paul, 2017).

36 Whitehead, *Enquiry Concerning the Principles of Natural Knowledge* (Cambridge University Press, 1919), p. vi.

37 Whitehead, *Science and the Modern World* (1925), p. 55.

38 This emphasis on unified human experience, including the experience of relationships, echoes William James's statement in the preface of *The Meaning of Truth* (1909): 'The relations between things … are just as much matters of direct particular experience … than the things themselves.' The Project Gutenberg EBook, 2004, www. gutenberg.org/files/5117/5117-h/5117-h.htm (accessed 17 April 2019).

39 Whitehead, *Enquiry Concerning the Principles of Natural Knowledge*, p. 8.

40 Ibid., p. 2. Whitehead defines ultimate facts as 'not analysable into a complex of simpler entities'. Whitehead, *Enquiry Concerning the Principles of Natural Knowledge*, p. 6.

41 Whitehead, *Enquiry Concerning the Principles of Natural Knowledge*, p. 13.

42 Ibid., p. 14.

43 Susanne K. Langer, *Philosophy in a New Key: A Study in the Symbolism of Reason, Rite, and Art* (Third edition, Cambridge, MA: Harvard University Press, 1980), p. 269.

44 Ibid.

45 Whitehead, *Concept of Nature*, pp. vii, viii. According to Whitehead, the purpose of the book is 'to lay the basis of a natural philosophy which is the necessary presupposition of a reorganised speculative physics'. He claims that his constructive philosophy has 'independent support of Minkowski from the side of science and also of succeeding relativists'. He also mentions that Samuel Alexander's then as yet unpublished Gifford Lectures *Space, Time, and Deity* covered similar material. Samuel Alexander (1859–1938) is known for his evolutionist emergentism, the view that the mind emerges from the body but is not reducible to it.

46 Whitehead, *Concept of Nature*, p. 18.

47 Ibid.

48 Ibid., p. 31.

49 Ibid., p. 39.

50 Ibid., p. 15.

51 Ibid., p. 34.

52 Whitehead, *Principle of Relativity with Applications to Physical Science*, p. 7.

53 Whitehead, *Concept of Nature*, p. 167.

54 Merleau-Ponty's later writings were influenced by Whitehead, especially *The Concept of Nature*. This is reflected in Merleau-Ponty's course 'Nature and Logos: The Human Body', which he gave at the Collège de France in 1956–7. Maurice Merleau-Ponty, trans. Robert Vallier, *Nature: Course Notes from the Collège de France* (Evanston, IL: Northwestern University Press, 2003). See also William S. Hamrick and Jan van

der Veken, *Nature and Logos: A Whiteheadian Key to Merleau-Ponty's Fundamental Thought* (New York: State University Press, 2011).

55 Whitehead, *Concept of Nature*, p. 154.

56 Bruno Latour, 'What Is Given in Experience? A Review of Isabelle Stengers "*Penser avec Whitehead*", *Boundary* 2, 32.1 (Spring 2005), p. 226.

57 Ibid.

58 For an interesting cultural historic account of the different views of time held by Einstein and Bergson see Jimena Canales, *The Physicist and the Philosopher: Einstein, Bergson, and the Debate that Changed our Understanding of Time* (Princeton, NJ: Princeton University Press, 2015). Canales focusses on the explosive debate between Einstein and Bergson in Paris in 1922, with Einstein arguing for a scientific notion of time in line with the findings in physics, and Bergson defending a view of time rooted in intuitive lived experience. Whitehead's view of time, like that of Langer, is very similar to that of Bergson.

59 Whitehead, *Principle of Relativity with Applications to Physical Science*, p. 62.

60 Ibid., p. 63.

61 Quoted in Hocking, 'Whitehead as I Knew Him', p. 10.

62 Bruce Kuklick, *The Rise of American Philosophy: Cambridge, Massachusetts 1860–1930* (New Haven, CT: Yale University Press, 1977), p. 413.

63 Hocking, 'Whitehead as I Knew Him', p. 11.

64 Alfred N. Whitehead, 'The Aims of Education', Presidential address to the Mathematical Association of England, 1916, *The Aims of Education and Other Essays* (1929) (New York: Free Press, 2011), p. 1.

65 Whitehead, 'Autobiographical Notes (1941)', in Paul Schilpp, ed., *The Philosophy of Alfred North Whitehead*, The Library of Living Philosophers, Vol. 3 (La Salle, IL: Open Court, 1951), pp. 641–70. http://www-history.mcs.st-andrews.ac.uk/Extras/Whitehead_Autobiography.html. Whitehead's critique of traditional compartmentalized and fact-based learning has drawn renewed attention in the field of education. See, for instance, Franz G. Riffert, *Alfred North Whitehead on Learning and Education: Theory and Application* (Newcastle upon Tyne: Cambridge Scholars Press, 2005).

66 In a famous lecture British scientist and novelist Charles P. Snow would recast Whitehead's 'bifurcation' in terms of a clash between 'two cultures' – the sciences and the humanities. Rede Lecture, 7 May 1959 in the Senate House. The expanded content of the lecture was subsequently published as *The Two Cultures* (London: Cambridge University Press, 1963). Revised version: *The Two Cultures: A Second Look* (1963) (London: Cambridge University Press, 1972). Both the lecture and the books were based on a previous article 'The Two Cultures' published in *New Statesman* 6 (October 1956).

67 Hocking, 'Whitehead as I Knew Him', p. 9.

68 There is no record of any women attending the gatherings. This may not be surprising as, until 1948, there would have been no tenured women faculty at Harvard. Most Sunday afternoons the Whiteheads also hosted an open house for Harvard students. Again, there is no record that Langer would have attended these. By the time she started her doctoral studies in 1924 the Langer family lived in Worcester where her husband William had a position at Clark University.

69 George L. Kline, ed., *Alfred North Whitehead: Essays on His Philosophy* (Lanham, MD: University Press of America, 1989), p. 9. Whitehead himself, in turn, observes, 'Harvard is justly proud of the great period of its philosophic department about

thirty years ago. Josiah Royce, William James, Santayana, George Herbert Palmer, Münsterberg, constitute a group to be proud of. Among them Palmer's achievements centre chiefly in literature and in his brilliance as a lecturer. The group is a group of men individually great. But as a group they are greater still. It is a group of adventure, of speculation, of search for new ideas. To be a philosopher is to make some humble approach to the main characteristic of this group of men.' *Modes of Thought*, p. 237.

70   Bogaard and Bell, *Harvard Lectures of Alfred North Whitehead 1924–1925*. The notes were taken by W. P. Bell, William E. Hocking and Louise Heath.

71   For references to Langer's attendance of Whitehead's lectures, see Victor Lowe and J. B. Schneewind, eds, *Alfred North Whitehead: The Man and His Work*, p. 148; and William Langer, *In and Out the Ivory Tower* (Sagamore Beach, MA: Watson Publishers International, 1978), p. 124.

72   Rolf Lachmann, ed., 'Susanne K. Langer's Notes on Whitehead's Course on Philosophy of Nature', *Process Studies* 26.1/2 (1997), pp. 126–50.

73   Whitehead writes, 'If my view of philosophy is correct, it is the most effective of all the intellectual pursuits. It builds cathedrals before the workmen have moved a stone and it destroys them before the elements have worn down their arches. It is the architect of the buildings of the spirit, and it is also their solvent: – and the spiritual precedes the material. Philosophy works slowly. Thoughts lie dormant for ages; and then, almost suddenly as it were, mankind finds that they embodied themselves in institutions.' Whitehead, *Science and the Modern World*, p. x.

74   Whitehead, *Science and the Modern World*, p. 17.

75   Ibid.

76   Ibid., p. 66.

77   Ibid., p. 16.

78   Ibid., p. 36.

79   Ibid., p. 191.

80   Ibid., p. ii.

81   Ibid.

82   Langer, *Philosophy in a New Key*, p. 6.

83   Ibid., pp. 4, 5. The quote is from Whitehead, *Science and the Modern World*, p. 61.

84   Langer, *Philosophy in a New Key*, p. 4.

85   Ibid., pp. 12, 13.

86   Ibid., pp. 27, 28.

87   Letter from Langer to Herbert Read, 16 August 1967. In Susanne K. Langer Papers, Houghton Library, Harvard University.

88   David Ray Griffin, *Whitehead's Radically Different Postmodern Philosophy: An Argument for its Contemporary Relevance* (Albany: State University of New York Press, 2007), pp. 3, 4.

89   Whitehead, *Science and the Modern World*, p. 43.

90   *Religion in the Making* (1926) (Cambridge: Cambridge University Press, 2011), p. vii. The book consists of four lectures originally delivered in King's Chapel in Boston in 1926.

91   Randall Auxier, 'Reading Whitehead', in Weber and Desmet, eds, *Whitehead: The Algebra of Metaphysics*, p. 68

92   *Religion in the Making*, p. 7. See also Whitehead, *Science and the Modern World*, p. 191.

93   Whitehead, *Science and the Modern World*, p. 191.

94   *Religion in the Making*, p. 71.

95   Ibid.

96   Although Whitehead was interested in Catholicism during his student years, he
     never practiced it publicly. In his *Memoirs from Memory*, Russell writes, 'His later
     philosophy gave him some part of what he wanted from religion. He was at all time
     deeply aware of the importance of religion. As a young man, he was all but converted
     to Roman Catholicism by the influence of Cardinal Newman.' *Portraits from Memory*
     (New York: Simon & Schuster, 1956), p. 104.

97   Langer, *Philosophy in a New Key*, p. 287.

98   Although Whitehead may have known of Cassirer through Langer, he makes no
     reference to him in *Symbolism: Its Meaning and Effect*. This may be because Cassirer's
     work had not yet been translated. Another surprising lack of mention by Whitehead
     is Charles Sanders Peirce. Peirce's papers had arrived at Harvard in 1910 for them
     to be edited by Charles Hartshorne and Paul Weiss, but they were only published
     after 1931(to be finished in 1935) as the Arthur W. Burks, ed., *Collected Papers of
     Charles Sander Peirce* I-VI (Cambridge, MA: Harvard University Press, 1931–1935).
     Vols VII-VIII, 1958.

99   Whitehead, *Symbolism: Its Meaning and Effect*, p. 8.

100 Ibid., p. 40.

101 Ibid., pp. 15, 16.

102 Ibid., pp. 39, 40.

103 Ibid., p. 21.

104 Ibid., p. 34.

105 Ibid., p. 35.

106 Ibid., p. 5.

107 Langer, Preface, *Philosophy in a New Key* (1941 edn), p. xiv.

108 Whitehead, *Concept of Nature*, p. 31.

109 Whitehead, *Symbolism*, pp. 7, 8.

110 As in *Science and the Natural World*, Whitehead concludes *Process and Reality* with
     a chapter on 'God and the World'. This chapter became an important impulse for
     the 'process theology' of, among others, Charles Hartshorne (1897–2000) and John
     B. Cobb (b. 1925).

111 The poor attendance of Whitehead's lectures in Edinburgh reflects the lack of interest
     in Whitehead's new philosophy in the UK at the time. Nicholas Griffin writes, 'Six
     people ... (some accounts say only two) managed to stay the course of the Gifford
     Lectures.' Nicholas Griffin, 'Lowe's Whitehead', Review of Victor Lowe, p. 206.

112 Lachmann, 'Susanne K. Langer's Notes on Whitehead's Course on Philosophy of
     Nature'. The notes span the period from October 1927 and May 1928.

113 Whitehead, *Process and Reality*, p. 29.

114 Ibid., p. 29.

115 Ibid., p. 219.

116 Ibid., p. 23

117 Whitehead, *Adventure of Ideas* (New York: Free Press, 1967), p. 235, 236.

118 Whitehead, *Modes of Thought*, p. 88.

119 For the state of psychology in the 1920s and 1930s, see Carl Murchinson, ed.,
     Psychologies of 1925 and Psychologies of 1930, International University Series in
     Psychology (Worcester, MA: Clark University Press, 1926, 1930).

120 Robert E. Henlon, Introduction, in Robert E. Henlon, ed., *Cognitive Microgenesis: A
     Neuropsychological Perspective* (New York: Springer-Verlag, 1991), p. xiv.

121 Anne Harrington, Foreword, in Henlon, *Cognitive Microgenesis*, p. vi.

122 Heinz Werner, 'Microgenesis and Aphasia', *Journal of Abnormal and Social Psychology* 52.3 (May 1956), pp. 347–53.

123 Henlon, Introduction to *Cognitive Microgenesis*, p. xi.

124 Harrington, Foreword to *Cognitive Microgenesis*, p. vi.

125 In a letter to Charles Hartshorne Whitehead had mentioned the 'great merit of the *Gestalt* people'. Kline, *Alfred North Whitehead*, p. 198.

126 Franz Riffert, 'Whitehead's Theory of Perception and the Concept of Microgenesis', *Concrescence: Australasian Journal for Process Thought* 5 (2004), p. 8.

127 Friedrich Sander, 'Structure, Totality of Experience, and Gestalt', trans. Susanne K. Langer, in Murchinson, ed., *Psychologies of 1930*, pp. 188–204.

128 Langer had translated the term *Aktualgenese* more literally as 'genetic realization', which, arguably, is closer to its intended meaning than Whitehead's term 'actual entity' which connotes a more static condition. Riffert suggests that Whitehead might have been aware of this but would nevertheless have opted for his term in order to stress the concept's role as a counterpart to the notion of substance as the ultimate component of reality: 'Whitehead had used the term 'entity' despite this fact (which he was very well aware of) because he wanted to point at the atomic character of his metaphysically basic concept.' Franz Riffert, 'Whitehead's Theory of Perception and the Concept of Microgenesis', p. 8.

129 Riffert writes, 'Reto Fetz (1999) has argued that similarities between Whitehead and Cassirer are so far-reaching that we can even characterize their approaches as based on a common paradigm. But what are the sources of theses parallels? Are they simply congenial? Or do there exist direct or indirect strands of interactions and influences between Whitehead on the one side and Sander and Werner on the other?' Franz Riffert, 'Whitehead's Theory of Perception and the Concept of Microgenesis', p. 8.

130 For a discussion of the relation between *Gestalt* theory and art see Friedrich Sander, *Gestalt und Sinn: Gestaltpsychologie und Kunsttheorie* (München: Beck, 1932). Volume 4 of *Neue psychologischen Studien*.

131 Langer, 'Abstraction in Art', *Journal of Aesthetics and Art Criticism* 22.4 (Summer 1964), p. 385.

132 Ibid.

133 Ibid., pp. 385, 386.

134 Klaus Conrad, 'New Problems of Aphasia', *Brain* 77 (1954), p. 495. Quoted in Langer, 'Abstraction in Art', *Journal of Aesthetics and Art Criticism* 22.4 (Summer 1964), p. 386.

135 Although Whitehead had a theory of beauty he never developed a proper aesthetic theory or philosophy of art. For one attempt to distil an aesthetic theory out of scattered comments, see *Process and Reality*'s co-editor Donald Sherburne's 1961 Yale dissertation 'A Whiteheadian Aesthetic: Some Implications of Whitehead's Metaphysical Speculation'.

136 Langer, *Mind* I, p. 261.

137 Ibid., p. 268.

138 Whitehead, *Science and the Modern World*, p. 70.

139 Whitehead, *Process and Reality*, p. 164.

140 Ibid., p. 41.

141 Ibid., p. 177.

142 Ibid., p. 236.

143 Ibid.

144 Langer, *Mind* I, p. 21.

145 Whitehead, *Process and Reality*, p. 221.

146 Ibid., p. 231.

147 Ibid., p. 163.

148 Ibid.

149 Ibid.

150 Whitehead, *Adventure of Ideas*, p. 176.

151 Whitehead, *Process and Reality*, p. 315.

152 Whitehead, *Adventure of Idea*, p. 176.

153 Whitehead, *Process and Reality*, p. 164.

154 Ibid., p. 243.

155 Ibid., p. 236.

156 Ibid., p. 246.

157 Langer, *Mind* I, p. 370.

158 Ibid., p. 23.

159 Ibid., p. 4.

160 Ibid., p. 20.

161 Ibid., p. 23.

162 Whitehead, *Process and Reality*, p. 241. See also 'the subjective form of a physical feeling is re-enaction of the subjective form of the feeling felt.' Whitehead, *Process and Reality*, p. 237.

163 Whitehead, *Process and Reality*, p. 29.

164 Ibid., p. 233.

165 Whitehead, *Modes of Thought*, p. 100.

166 Ibid., p. 91.

167 Ibid., pp. 91, 92.

168 Whitehead, *Science and the Modern World*, pp. 52, 54, 59.

169 Whitehead, *Process and Reality*, pp. 7, 8.

170 S. K. Langer, *The Practice of Philosophy* (New York: Holt, 1930), pp. 135, 136.

171 Langer, *Philosophy in a New Key*, p. 72.

172 Whitehead, *Process and Reality*, p. 168.

173 Ibid., p. 182.

174 Ibid., pp. 181, 182.

175 Langer, *Philosophy in a New Key*, p. 58.

176 Whitehead, *Process and Reality*, p. 182.

177 Ibid., p. 173.

178 Ibid., p. 169.

179 Ibid., p. 176

180 Ibid.

181 Steven Shaviro, *Without Criteria: Kant, Whitehead, Deleuze and Aesthetics* (Cambridge, MA: MIT Press, 2012), p. 46. Whitehead's own reflections on art and aesthetics were not based on his philosophy of feeling or causal efficacy but on the metaphysical notion of universal harmony. For an account of Whitehead's aesthetics based on harmony, see Donald W. Sherburn, *Whiteheadian Aesthetic: Some implications of Whitehead's Metaphysical Speculation* (New Haven, CT: Yale University Press, 1961).

182 Whitehead, *Process and Reality*, p. 3. In *An Enquiry Concerning the Principles of Natural Knowledge* Whitehead uses the term 'speculative physics' in a comparable

manner referring to the high degree of generality and comprehensiveness of the enquiry. Whitehead, *Enquiry Concerning the Principles of Natural Knowledge*, p. v.

183 Whitehead, *Process and Reality*, p. 3.

184 Ibid., p. 4.

185 Whitehead, *Modes of Thought*, p. 234.

186 Ibid.

187 Ibid., p. 235.

188 Ibid.

189 Ibid., p. 236.

190 Charles Hartshorne, *Whitehead's Philosophy: Selected Essays*, 1935–1970 (Lincoln: University of Nebraska Press, 1972), p. 111.

191 Desmet and Weber, eds, *Whitehead: The Algebra of Metaphysics*.

192 Whitehead, *Adventure of Ideas*, p. 227.

193 Whitehead, *Process and Reality*, p. 10.

194 Ibid., p. 8.

195 Ibid., p. 10.

196 Ibid., p. 5.

197 Ibid.

198 Ibid., p. 8.

199 Ibid., p. xiv.

200 Ibid., p. 4.

201 Whitehead, *Modes of Thought*, pp. 68, 69.

202 Maurice Merleau-Ponty, *Phenomenology of Perception* [1945], trans. Colin Smith (London: Routledge, 2005), pp. xx, xxi. Merleau-Ponty's later work, in particular *Eye and Mind* (1960) which was based on his course 'Nature and Logos, The Human Body' given at the College de France in the academic year 1956–7, was influenced particularly by Whitehead's earlier books *The Concept of Nature*, *Science and the Modern World*, and *Nature and Life*. The last work was published as Part III of *Modes of Thought*. For Whitehead's influence on Merleau-Ponty, see William S. Hamrick and Jan van der Veken, *Nature and Logos: A Whiteheadian Key to Merleau-Ponty's Fundamental Thought* (New York: State University Press, 2011).

203 Whitehead, *Modes of Thought*, pp. 237, 238.

204 Langer, *Philosophy in a New Key*, p. 85.

205 Randall E. Auxier, 'Susanne Langer on Symbols and Analogy: A Case of Misplaced Concreteness?', *Process Studies* 26 (January 1998), p. 87.

206 Langer, *The Practice of Philosophy*, p. 21.

207 Ibid., pp. 35, 36.

208 Langer, *Mind* I, p. 316.

209 Langer and Gadol, 'The Deepening Mind: A Half-Century of American Philosophy', p. 121. She adds, 'If, therefore, I refrain from applying the word *metaphysics* to good theories about the nature of the world and of our understanding, that is a concession to fashion; for academic fashion, like social etiquette, respects the associations of a term rather than its actual significance – a foolish practice, of which philosophers should not be guilty.'

210 Ibid.

211 Susanne K. Langer, *Philosophical Sketches* (Baltimore, MD: Johns Hopkins Press, 1962), pp. 6, 7. Reflecting on Whitehead's Harvard period, Russell himself later wrote, 'His philosophy was very obscure, and there was much in it that I never

succeeded in understanding. ... [Whitehead] was impressed by the aspect of unity in the universe, and considered that it is only through this aspect that scientific inferences can be justified. My temperament led me in the opposite direction, but I doubt whether pure reason could have decided which of us was more nearly in the right.' Russell, *Autobiography of Bertrand Russell*, pp. 118, 119.

212   Herbert Read, ' "Describing the Indescribable", Review of *Mind* Volume I', *Saturday Review* (15 July 1967). Her reply is mentioned in an unpublished manuscript by her friend Wesley Wehr, quoted in Donald Dryden, 'Susanne K. Langer 1895–1985', in P. B. Dematteis and L.B. McHenry, eds, *American Philosophers before 1950*, Dictionary of Literary Biography, Vol. 270 (Farmington Hills, MI: Gale, 2003), p. 198. See also Langer's introduction to *Feeling and Form*: '[T]his book does not coordinate theories of art with metaphysical perspectives. ... That aim is not outside philosophy, but beyond the scope of my present philosophical study. ... What *Feeling and Form* does undertake to do, is to specify the meaning of words: expression, creation, symbol, import, intuition, vitality, and organic form, in such a way that we may understand, in terms of them, the nature of art and its relation to feeling.' pp. vii, viii.

213   Langer, *Mind* III, p. 201.

214   Dryden, 'Whitehead's Influence on Susanne Langer's Conception of Living Form', pp. 83, 84.

215   Langer, *Philosophy in a New Key*, p. xv.

216   On a comparable note, in the preface to *Process and Reality* Whitehead mentions John Dewey, Henri Bergson and William James as three thinkers he is 'greatly indebted to', but makes hardly any reference to them in the text itself. *Process and Reality*, p. xiv.

217   Susanne K. Langer, *An Introduction to Symbolic Logic* (Second revised edition, New York: Dover Publications, 1953), p. 11.

218   Whitehead, *Process and Reality*, p. 8.

219   Langer, *The Practice of Philosophy*, p. 177. For her views of myth in *The Practice of Philosophy* Langer draws extensively on Cassirer's *Philosophie der symbolishen Formen* using her own translations of passages.

220   Langer, *Philosophy in a New Key*, p. 293.

221   'On Whitehead.' Unpublished Manuscript, Susanne K. Langer Papers, Houghton Library, Harvard University. Quoted in Dryden, 'Whitehead's Influence on Susanne Langer's Conception of Living Form', p. 75.

222   Whitehead, *Modes of Thought*, p. 237.

223   Dryden writes, 'Langer's assertion that philosophy "is mythical in origin and scientific in destination" (*The Practice of Philosophy*, 178) was later echoed in Whitehead's claim that philosophy is akin to mysticism, which he defined as "direct insight into depths unspoken (*Modes of Thought* 174)"'. Dryden, 'Whitehead's Influence on Susanne Langer's Conception of Living Form', p. 67.

224   Whitehead, *Modes of Thought* (1938), p. 237.

225   Langer, *Feeling and Form*, p. vii.

226   Charles Hartshorne, *Creative Synthesis and Philosophic Method* (La Salle, IL: Open Court, 1970), p. 41.

227   Susanne K. Langer, 'Review of *Whitehead's Theory of Knowledge* by John Blyth', *Mind* 52.205 (1943), p. 85.

228   Rolf Lachmann, 'From Metaphysics to Art and Back: The Relevance of Susan K. Langer's Philosophy for Process Metaphysics', *Process Studies* 26 (1997), p. 120.

7 Ludwig Wittgenstein: Expressive form

1 Ludwig Wittgenstein, *Tractatus Logico-Philosophicus* (1922), trans. C. K. Ogden (London: Routledge, 1996), 3.31, p. 51. Henceforth referred to as *TLP* with thesis numbering within the text.

2 S. K. Langer, *The Practice of Philosophy* (New York: Holt, 1930), p. 141.

3 Moritz Schlick, 'Form and Content, an Introduction to Philosophical Thinking (1932)', in Henk L. Mulder and Barbara F. B. Van de Velde-Schlick, eds, *Moritz Schlick: Philosophical Papers*, Vol. 2 (1925–1936) (Dordrecht: Reidel, 1979), p. 286.

4 Susanne K. Langer, *Philosophy in a New Key: A Study in the Symbolism of Reason, Rite, and Art* (Third edition, Cambridge, MA: Harvard University Press, 1980), p. 85.

5 Wittgenstein, Journal entry, 8 March 1915, *Notebooks 1914–1916*, first edition, 1961, trans. G. E. M. Anscombe, second edition (1984), p. 40. Quoted in Eli Friedlander, *Signs of Sense: Reading Wittgenstein's* Tractatus (Cambridge, MA: Harvard University Press, 2001), pp. 8, 9.

6 Wittgenstein, *Tractatus Logico-Philosophicus* (1922). Since Ogden's German had been quite limited, he had been assisted in his translation by a young student and friend of Wittgenstein, Frank P. Ramsey, who had only himself learned German recently. In 1961 D. F. Pears and Brian F. McGuinness produced a new translation (London: Routledge & Kegan, 1961). Both translations included Russell's introduction. The title was suggested by G. E. Moore as an allusion to Spinoza's *Tractatus Theologico-Politicus*.

7 Langer, *Practice of Philosophy*, p. 108.

8 The first references to Wittgenstein can be found as early as in her PhD thesis 'A Logical Analysis of Meaning', completed under Whitehead in 1926. In the same year she published two articles, 'Confusion of Symbols and Confusion of Logical Types' and 'Form and Content: A Study in Paradox', each referring to the *Tractatus*. Further references to Wittgenstein can be found in her articles 'A Logical Study of Verbs' (1927) and 'Facts: The Logical Perspectives of the World' (1933). 'Confusion of Symbols and Confusion of Logical Types', *Mind* 35 (April 1926), pp. 222–9; 'Form and Content: A Study in Paradox', *Journal of Philosophy* 23 (5 August 1926), pp. 435–8; 'A Logical Study of Verbs', *Journal of Philosophy* 24 (3 March 1927), pp. 120–9; 'Facts: The Logical Perspectives of the World', *Journal of Philosophy* 30 (30 March 1933), pp. 178–87.

9 Langer, *Practice of Philosophy*, p. 118.

10 Langer, *Philosophy in a New Key*, p. 79.

11 Quoted in Gordon C. F. Bearn, *Waking to Wonder: Wittgenstein's Existential Investigations* (Albany: State University of New York Press, 1997), p. 38.

12 Letter from C. I. Lewis to F. J. Woodbridge, dated 2 January 1923. Quoted in Burton Dreben and Juliet Floyd, 'Tautology: How Not to Use a Word', in Jaakko Hintikka, ed., *Wittgenstein in Florida: Proceedings of the Colloquium on the Philosophy of Ludwig Wittgenstein*, Florida State University, 7–8 August, 1989 (Dordrecht: Springer, 1991), p. 23.

13 Ernest Nagel, 'Impressions and Appraisals of Analytic Philosophy in Europe I', *Journal of Philosophy* 33.1 (1936a), p. 17. Nagel nevertheless adds, '[I]n spite of the esoteric atmosphere which surrounds Wittgenstein, I think his views are both interesting and important.' p.17.

14 Langer, *Philosophy in a New Key*, p. 21.

15 For a discussion of Wittgenstein's 'symbolic turn' prior to the *Tractatus*, see chapter 6 of Michael Potter, *Wittgenstein's Notes on Logic* (Oxford: Oxford University Press, 2011), pp. 63–9.

16 The title of her thesis was 'Eduard von Hartmann's Notion of Unconscious Mind and its Metaphysical Implications'.

17 Robert Innis, *Karl Bühler: Semiotic Foundations of Language Theory* (New York: Springer Science, 1982), p. 6.

18 Karl Bühler, *Theory of Language: The Representational Function of Language* (1935), trans. Donald Fraser Goodwin, *Foundations of Semiotics* 25 (Amsterdam: John Benjamins, 1990), p. 61.

19 Karl Popper wrote in his biography, 'Most important to my future development was [Bühler's] theory of the three levels or functions of language [expressive; signalling, and descriptive]. He explained that the two lower functions were common to human and animal languages and were always present, while the third function was characteristic of human language alone and sometimes (as in exclamations) absent even from that. This theory … confirmed my view of the emptiness of the theory that art is self-expression.' *Unended Quest: An Intellectual Biography* (1974) (London: Routledge, 2002), p. 82. Jürgen Habermas wrote, 'Bühler's theory of language functions could be connected with the methods and insights of the analytic theory of meaning and be made the centrepiece of a theory of communicative action oriented to reaching understanding if we could generalize the concept of validity beyond the truth of propositions and identify validity conditions no longer only on the semantic level of sentences but on the pragmatic level of utterances. For this purpose the paradigm change in philosophy of language that was introduced by J. L. Austin … must be radicalized in such a way.' *The Theory of Communicative Action*, Vol. 1 (Boston: Beacon Press, 1984), p. 277. According to Friedrich Stadler, Bühler challenged the positivistic approach to language at his time by advocating a 'non-inductivistic theory of "image-free" thinking which regarded language and thinking as guided by theory and independent of sensory impressions and content of thought. This also meant a critique of atomism and positivism.' Friedrich Stadler, *The Vienna Circle: Studies in the Origins, Development, and Influence of Logical Positivism* (Vienna: Springer, 2015), p. 245, footnote 6.

20 For a comparison of Karl Bühler and Wittgenstein, see Kevin Mulligan, 'The Essence of Language: Wittgenstein's Builders and Bühler's Bricks', *Revue de Métaphysique et de Morale* 2 (April/June 1997), pp. 193–215; Achim Eschbach, 'Karl Bühler und Ludwig Wittgenstein', in Achim Eschbach, ed., *Karl Bühler's Theory of Language/Karl Bühlers Sprachtheorie*, Proceedings of the Conference held at Kirchberg, 26 August 1984 and Essen, November 21–24, 1984 (Amsterdam: John Benjamins, 1988), pp. 385–406.

21 Letter Wittgenstein to Russell, 19 April 1919. G. H. von Wright, ed., *Letters to Russell, Keynes and Moore* (Oxford: Blackwell, 1977), p. 71. Even after his return to Cambridge in 1928, he continued to feel misunderstood both by Russell and by Moore, as was evident from his comment to them at the end of his 1929 dissertation defence: 'Don't worry, I know you'll never understand it.' Ray Monk, *Ludwig Wittgenstein: The Duty of Genius* (London: Vintage Books, 1991), p. 271.

22 In order to persuade Wittgenstein to attend meetings, Schlick had to assure him that the discussions would not have to be philosophical. Waismann reports that on several occasions Wittgenstein read poems by Rabindranath Tagore, whose mystical outlook on life stood diametrically opposed to the members of the Vienna Circle. In order not to be distracted by the puzzled expressions on the faces of the other members,

Wittgenstein would sometimes turn his chair around and read with his back to them. Monk, *Ludwig Wittgenstein: The Duty of Genius*, p. 243.

23 Langer, *Practice of Philosophy*, p. 118.

24 Ibid., pp. 118–21. The quotes are from Ogden's translation which was the only available one at Langer's time. For that reason, I will also use this translation.

25 Ogden's translation of *Sachverhalt* as 'atomic fact' is potentially confusing as it may create the impression of a positivistic correspondence theory. The translation of the term by Pears and McGuinness as 'state of affairs' is closer to the German and avoids that risk. The fact that Wittgenstein approved Ogden's translation may indicate that he did not anticipate any misunderstanding in this respect. A *Sachverhalt* [state of affairs] is a single proposition – e.g. 'The bridge is strong' – whereas a *Tatsache* [fact] is a compounded of *Sachverhalte* – e.g. 'The bridge is strong, and the road is empty.' For a helpful comparison of the two translations, see Matthew McKeon, 'Review of *Tractatus Logico-Philosophicus*', *Essays in Philosophy* 5.2 (2004), Article 24. The difference in translation does not affect Langer's discussion as she would have read Wittgenstein in its original German.

26 Langer, *Philosophy in a New Key*, p. 269.

27 For an illuminating discussion of Langer's notion of fact, see Giulia Felappi, 'Susanne Langer and the Woeful World of Facts', *Journal for the History of Analytical Philosophy* 5.2 (2017), pp. 38–50.

28 Langer, *Practice of Philosophy*, pp. 150, 151.

29 Donald Philip Verene, 'Kant, Hegel, and Cassirer: The Origins of the Philosophy of Symbolic Forms', *Journal of the History of Ideas* 30.1 (March 1969), p. 14.

30 Langer, *An Introduction to Symbolic Logic* (Second revised edition, New York: Dover Publications, 1953), p. 31. For a non-reductionist, non-physicalist and non-phenomenalistic reading of Carnap, see Michael Friedman, 'Carnap's Aufbau Reconsidered', *Noûs* 21.4 (December 1987), pp. 521–45; Thomas Mormann, *Rudolf Carnap* (München: Beck, 2000), pp. 111–25.

31 Friedlander, *Signs of Sense*, pp. 47, 48.

32 Moritz Schlick, 'Form and Content', in Mulder and Van de Velde-Schlick eds, *Moritz Schlick: Philosophical Papers 1925–1936*, p. 286. The essay's title is the same as Langer's 1926 article and discusses similar ideas.

33 Mentioned in Monk, *Ludwig Wittgenstein: The Duty of Genius*, p. 118. See also Wittgenstein's successor at Cambridge, G. H. von Wright, 'Ludwig Wittgenstein: A Biographical Sketch', in Norman Malcolm, *Ludwig Wittgenstein: A Memoir* (Oxford: Oxford University Press, 2001), p. 8.

34 Heinrich Hertz, *The Principles of Mechanics Presented in New Form* (1899), trans. D. E. Jones and J. Walley (New York: Dover, 1956). For a collection of essays on Hertz, see D. Baird, R. I. G. Hughes and Alfred Nordmann, eds, *Heinrich Hertz: Classical Physicist, Modern Philosopher* (Dordrecht: Kluwer Academic Publishers, 1998).

35 Hertz, *Principles of Mechanics*, p. 1.

36 Ibid., p. 2.

37 John Michael Krois and Donald Phillip Verene, eds, *The Philosophy of Symbolic Forms: The Metaphysics of Symbolic Forms*, Vol. IV (New Haven, CT: Yale University Press, 1996), p. 20.

38 For accounts of the ways in which Hertz influenced Wittgenstein see Allan Janik and Stephen Toulmin, *Wittgenstein's Vienna Revisited* (Abingdon: Routldege, 2017), chapter 4, 'Saying and Showing: Hertz and Wittgenstein', pp. 147–70; David Stern, *Wittgenstein on Mind and Language* (New York: Oxford University

Press, 1995), pp. 36–8; Gerd Grasshoff, 'Hertzian Objects in Wittgenstein's *Tractatus*', *British Journal for the History of Philosophy* 5.1 (1997), pp. 87–120; Kelly Ann Hamilton, '*Darstellungen* in *The Principles of Mechanics* and the *Tractatus*: The Representation of Objects in Relation to Hertz and Wittgenstein', *Perspectives on Science* 10.1 (Spring 2002), pp. 28–68; John Preston, 'Hertz, Wittgenstein and Philosophical Method', *Philosophical Investigations* 31.1 (January 2008), pp. 48–67.

39 Monk, *Ludwig Wittgenstein: The Duty of Genius*, p. 26.

40 Langer, *Practice of Philosophy*, p. 133.

41 Ibid., p. 142.

42 Ibid., pp. 135, 136.

43 Ibid., p. 141.

44 Langer, 'Facts: The Logical Perspectives of the Word', p. 185.

45 Ibid., p. 181.

46 Ibid.

47 Ibid., p. 184.

48 Langer, *Practice of Philosophy*, pp. 136, 137.

49 Ibid., pp. 137, 138.

50 Ibid., p. 138.

51 See Kant: 'We cannot indeed, beyond all possible experience, form a definite notion of what things in themselves may be. Yet we are not at liberty to abstain entirely from inquiring into them; for experience never satisfies reason fully but, in answering questions, refers us further back and leaves us dissatisfied with regard to their complete solution.' Immanuel Kant, *Prolegomena to Any Future Metaphysics*, trans. Paul Carus (Indianapolis, IN: Hackett, 1977), p. 86. Paul Engelmann, *Letters from Ludwig Wittgenstein: With a Memoir*, Brian F. McGuinness, ed., trans. L. Furtmüller (Oxford: Blackwell, 1967), p. 97. Quoted in Friedlander, *Signs of Sense*, p. 4.

52 Friedlander, *Signs of Sense*, p. 4.

53 Langer, *Philosophy in a New Key*, p. 85.

54 Langer, *Practice of Philosophy*, p. 121. For a more detailed account of logical form by Wittgenstein see his essay: 'Some remarks on Logical Forms', *Proceedings of the Aristotelian Society*, supplementary volume (1929), pp. 162–71. Shortly after writing the essay, Wittgenstein took distance from the content and did not even deliver the announced paper at the Conference reading instead a paper on mathematics.

55 Langer, *Introduction to Symbolic Logic*, p. 29.

56 Langer, *Practice of Philosophy*, p. 121.

57 Ibid., p. 87. Using the example of a tune as a particular arrangement of notes, Langer notes that, even when the tune is transposed into another key, the basic form of the tune – its internal organization – remains the same.

58 Moritz Schlick, 'Form and Content', *Gesammelte Aufsätze 1926–1936*, p. 164.

59 Langer, 'Form and Content: A Study in Paradox', p. 438.

60 Langer, 'A Logical Study of Verbs', p. 124.

61 Sheffer left Cambridge in December 1910, while Wittgenstein only arrived in October 2011 so, unless Sheffer met him briefly on his return from his European travels, they will have missed each other by about a year. It's quite likely, though, that Russell, who was very impressed by Sheffer, will have shared Sheffer's ideas with Wittgenstein. It is clear from Russell's introduction to the *Tractatus* that

Wittgenstein was familiar with Sheffer's work and he uses Sheffer's 'stroke' in clause 5.1311.

62 Langer, *Practice of Philosophy*, p. 109.

63 The word 'interpretant' is borrowed from Peirce, although Langer uses it in a different sense. See Langer, *Practice of Philosophy*, p. 122, footnote 4.

64 Alfred North Whitehead, *Symbolism: Its Meaning and Effect: Barbour-Page Lectures, University of Virginia, 1927* (New York: Fordham University Press, 1985), p. 182.

65 Ibid., p. 12.

66 Ibid., p. 84

67 Langer, *Practice of Philosophy*, pp. 108, 109.

68 Brian F. McGuinness, ed., *Wittgenstein in Cambridge: Letters and Documents 1911–1951* (Oxford: Wiley Blackwell, 2012). The letters from Wittgenstein sent to Russell from Norway include the following references to Whitehead: 'I suppose you are staying with the Whiteheads' (25 March 1913); 'would you … forward the enclosed letter to Mrs W.' (summer 1913); 'If you see the Whiteheads please remember me to them' (5 September 1913); 'I saw Whitehead before going and he was charming as usual' (17 October 1913); 'Please remember me to Dr and Mrs Whitehead and Erik if you see them.' (29 October 1913). Six years later, he still asks Russell to pass on his greetings to Whitehead in his letters from Italy after he had been taken prisoner of war in November 1918: 'remember me to Dr. Whitehead' (13 March 1919). An earlier postcard was sent via Whitehead at University College, London (9 February 1919). I thank Randall Auxier for drawing my attention to these references. Outside these references, however, there is very little documentation on the relation between Whitehead and Wittgenstein. Monk's biography of Wittgenstein mentions Whitehead only three times, two of which merely as Russell's co-author of the *Principia Mathematica*. The only reference of some substance suggests that Whitehead found Russell's second edition as 'too Wittgensteinian'. Ray Monk, *Ludwig Wittgenstein: The Duty of Genius*, p. 219.

69 For comparisons between Wittgenstein and Whitehead, see Jerry H. Gill, *Deep Postmodernism: Whitehead, Wittgenstein, Merleau-Ponty, and Polanyi* (New York: Humanity Books, 2010). For a comparison of terminology between the early Whitehead and Wittgenstein's *Tractatus*, see Henry LeRoy Finch, *Wittgenstein: The Early Philosophy, an Exposition of the Tractatus* (New York: Humanities Press, 1971). For comparisons between Wittgenstein and Merleau-Ponty, see Philip Dwyer, *Sense and Subjectivity: A Study of Wittgenstein and Merleau-Ponty* (Leiden: Brill, 1990); Komarine Domdenh-Romluc, ed., *Wittgenstein and Merleau-Ponty* (New York: Routledge, 2017). Domdenh-Romluc emphasizes the philosophers' shared interest in day-to-day lived experience and *Gestalt* theory.

70 Langer, *Practice of Philosophy*, p. 118.

71 The notion that there is an inherent pluralism of meaning in our day-to-day language is brought more to the fore in Wittgenstein's later writings which tie meaning to use.

72 Moritz Schlick, 'Meaning and Verification', *Philosophical Review* 45.4 (July 1936), p. 341.

73 Langer, *Philosophy in a New Key*, p. 281.

74 A. E. Blumberg and Herbert Feigl, 'Logical Positivism: A New Movement in European Philosophy', *Journal of Philosophy* 17 (1931), p. 288.

75 Langer, *Philosophy in a New Key*, p. 281.

76 Langer, *Practice of Philosophy*, p. 141.

77 Ibid.

78 Ibid., pp. 114, 115.

79 Ibid.

80 Brian F. McGuinness, ed., *Wittgenstein in Cambridge: Letters and Documents* 1911–1951 (New York: Blackwell, 2008), pp. 98–9.

81 Brian F. McGuinness, ed., *Wittgenstein and the Vienna Circle: Conversations Recorded by Friedrich Waismann*, trans. Brian F. McGuinness and Joachim Schulte (New York: Barnes and Noble, 1979), p. 48.

82 Ludwig Wittgenstein, *Philosophical Investigations*, Rush Rhees and G. E. Anscombe, eds, trans. G. E. Anscombe (Oxford: Blackwell, 1967), p. 353.

83 Schlick, 'Meaning and Verification', p. 341. In the middle of this section, in brackets, Schlick shows how much Wittgenstein means to him: 'I can hardly exaggerate my indebtedness to this philosopher. I do not wish to impute to him any responsibility for the contents of this article, but I have reason to hope that he will agree with the main substance of it.'

84 Langer, *Practice of Philosophy*, p. 141.

85 Ibid., p. 139.

86 Wittgenstein, *Philosophical Remarks*, Rush Rhees, ed., trans. Raymond Hargreaves and Roger White (Chicago, IL: University of Chicago Press, 1975).

87 Friedrich Waismann, 'On Dogmatism', in Brian F. McGuinness, ed., *Wittgenstein and the Vienna Circle: Conversations Recorded by Friedrich Waismann*, p. 182.

88 Wittgenstein, *Philosophical Investigations* (Oxford: Blackwell Publishers, 1997), Preface.

89 Friedlander, *Signs of Sense*, pp. 59, 60.

90 Langer, *Philosophy in a New Key*, p. 281. The phrase 'adventure of understanding' echoes the title of Whitehead's *Adventure of Ideas*.

91 Langer, *Practice of Philosophy*, p. 119, footnote 3.

92 Langer, *Philosophy in a New Key*, p. 21.

93 Friedrich Waismann, Preface to *Moritz Schlick: Philosophical Papers*, Vol. 2, Henk Mulder and Barbara F. B. Van de Velde-Schlick, eds (Dordrecht: Reidel, 1979), p. xxiv.

94 Moritz Schlick, 'The Future of Philosophy', in Richard Rorty, ed., *The Linguistic Turn: Essays in Philosophical Method* (1967) (Chicago, IL: University of Chicago Press, 1992), pp. 43–53.

95 Langer, *Philosophy in a New Key*, p. 83.

96 Wittgenstein, *Tractatus Logico-Philosophicus*, p. 29.

97 Journal entry, 8 March 1915, *Notebooks* 1914–1916, first edition, 1961, trans. G. E. M. Anscombe, second edition (1984), p. 40. Quoted in Friedlander, *Signs of Sense*, p. 8, 9.

98 Quoted in Monk, *Ludwig Wittgenstein: The Duty of Genius*, p. 244.

99 Wittgenstein, *Philosophical Investigations*, p. 48e.

100 Russell, *Philosophy* (New York: W. W. Norton, 1927), p. 265. Quoted in Langer, *Philosophy in a New Key*, p. 88.

101 Langer, *Philosophy in a New Key*, pp. 87, 88.

102   Monk, *Ludwig Wittgenstein: The Duty of Genius*, p. 311. Monk adds, 'Similarly, Wittgenstein hoped, his new method of philosophy would preserve what was to be respected in the old metaphysical theories, and would itself have the character of metaphysics, without the conjuring tricks of the *Tractatus*.'

103   Langer, *Philosophy in a New Key*, p. 86.

104   Ibid., p. 83.

105   Ibid., pp. 86, 87.

106   A. J. Ayer, *Wittgenstein* (New York: Random House, 1985), p. 31. A. J. Ayer, *Language, Truth, and Logic* (1936) (Second edition, London: Gollancz, 1946).

107   Bertrand Russell, 'Introduction to Ludwig Wittgenstein', in *Tractatus Logico-Philosophicus* (1922), trans. C. K. Ogden (London: Routledge, 1996), p. 22.

108   Rudolf Carnap, 'Autobiography', pp. 25–8. Also Quoted in Monk, *Ludwig Wittgenstein: The Duty of Genius*, p. 244.

109   Letter Wittgenstein to Schlick, 8 August 1932. Quoted in James Conant, 'Two Conceptions of *die Überwindung der Metaphysik*: Carnap and Early Wittgenstein', in Timothy McCarthy and Sean C. Stidd, eds, *Wittgenstein in America* (Oxford: Oxford University Press, 2001), p. 13.

110   Moritz Schlick, 'The Turning Point in Philosophy' (1930), in H. L. Mulder and B. F. van de Velde-Schlick, eds, *Philosophical Papers*, Vol. 2 (Dordrecht: Reidel, 1979), p. 55.

111   Wittgenstein left a body of approximately twelve thousand pages of unpublished notes, later to be published as *The Blue and Brown Books: Preliminary Studies for the Philosophical Investigations* (Oxford: Blackwell, 1958; 2003) and *Philosophical Investigations* (Oxford: Blackwell, 1967).

112   Other representatives include Paul Engelmann, Peter Geach, David Pears, Allan Janik and Stephen Toulmin.

113   Engelmann, *Letters from Ludwig Wittgenstein*. Quoted in Friedlander, *Signs of Sense*, p. 4.

114   The passage continues as follows: 'My book draws limits to the sphere of the ethical from the inside as it were, and I am convinced that this is the ONLY *rigorous* way of drawing those limits. In short, I believe that where *many* others today are just *gassing*, I have managed in my book to put everything firmly into place by being silent about it. And for that reason, unless I am very much mistaken, the book will say a great deal that you yourself want to say. Only perhaps you won't see that it is said in the book.' Letter from Wittgenstein to Ludwig von Ficker, editor of the Catholic, existentialist periodical *Der Brenner* in 1919, in Engelmann, *Letters From Wittgenstein*, pp. 143–4. Ficker was also a prospective publisher for Wittgenstein's *Tractatus*.

115   The main representatives of the school of resolute readers include Cora Diamond, James Conant and Alice Crary. Key texts for the resolute reading include Cora Diamond, 'Throwing Away the Ladder', in Cora Diamond, *The Realistic Spirit: Wittgenstein, Philosophy and the Mind* (Cambridge, MA: MIT Press, 2011), pp. 179–204; James Conant, 'Must We Show What We Cannot Say?', in Richard Fleming and Michael Payne, eds, *The Sense of Stanley Cavell* (Lewisburg: Bucknell University Press, 1989), pp. 242–83. For a cogent critique of the resolute reading, see Peter M. S. Hacker, 'Wittgenstein, Carnap and the New American Wittgensteinians', *Philosophical Quarterly* 53.210 (January 2003), pp. 1–23.

116 For a comparison of Wittgenstein and Cassirer on expression, see R. Sundara Rajan, 'Cassirer and Wittgenstein', *International Philosophical Quarterly* 7.4 (1967), pp. 591–610. See also Edward Skidelsky, *Ernst Cassirer: The Last Philosopher of Culture* (Princeton, NJ: Princeton University Press, 2008), pp. 128–159.

117 Langer, *Philosophy in a New Key*, p. 83.

118 Rudolf Carnap, 'Intellectual Autobiography', in Paul Arthur Schilpp, ed., *The Philosophy of Rudolf Carnap*, The Library of Living Philosophers, Vol. 11 (La Salle, IL: Open Court, 1963), p. 25.

119 Wittgenstein had a strong sense of property rights about what he regarded the fruits of his own labor. This is clear from a letter he wrote to Schlick in 1932. In the letter he complained that Carnap's article 'Physicalistic Language as the Universal Language of Science', had made such extensive and unacknowledged use of his ideas that, as he put it, 'he would soon be in a situation where [his] own work shall be considered merely as a reheated version or plagiarism of Carnap's'. Letter from Wittgenstein to Schlick, 6 May 1932. Quoted in David Stern, 'Carnap, Wittgenstein, Vienna Circle, Physicalism: A Reassessment', in Alan Richardson and Thomas Uebel, eds, *The Cambridge Companion to Logical Empiricism* (Cambridge: Cambridge University Press, 2007), p. 309. In the same letter he protests about the prevalent socialist ethos of shared authorship at the Circle, 'I see myself as drawn against my will into what is called "the Vienna Circle". In that Circle there prevails a community of property, so that I could e.g. use Carnap's ideas if *I wanted to* but he could also use mine. But I don't *want* to join forces with Carnap and to belong to a circle to which he belongs. If I have an apple tree in my garden, then it delights me and serves the purpose of the tree if my *friends* (e.g. you & Waismann) make use of the apples; I will *not* chase away thieves that climb over the fence, but I am entitled to resent that they are posing as my friends or alleging that the tree should belong to them jointly.' Quoted in David Stern, 'Carnap, Wittgenstein, Vienna Circle, Physicalism: A Reassessment', p. 321. The article referred to is Rudolf Carnap, 'Die physikalische Sprache als Universalsprache der Wissenschaft', *Erkenntnis* 2 (1931), pp. 432–65. The main difference of opinion between Wittgenstein and Carnap concerned the possibility and legitimacy of meta-languages. Carnap, like Russell, believes it is possible to construe a meta-language, while Wittgenstein does not as it went against his view that 'all propositions are of equal value' (6.4).

120 Langer, *Philosophy in a New Key*, pp. 82–3.

121 Ibid.

122 Ibid., p. 83.

123 Rudolf Carnap 'Intellectual Autobiography', p. 17.

124 Wittgenstein, *Philosophical Investigations*. Part I was completed in 1945 and draws on material written between 1929 and 1945. The material of Part II was written between 1947 and 1949.

125 Beatrice Nelson, for instance, writes, 'Persistent misreading of Langer identifies her philosophy ... with early positivism and with the theories espoused by Wittgenstein in the *Tractatus*.' Beatrice Nelson, 'Susanne K. Langer's Conception of "Symbol" – Making Connections through Ambiguity', *Journal of Speculative Philosophy* 8.4 (1994), p. 294, footnote 8. The 'misreading' identified by Nelson is correct when it concerns reading Langer as a positivist but wrong in describing Wittgenstein's *Tractatus* as 'positivist'.

8 The logic of signs and symbols

1 Susanne K. Langer, *Philosophy in a New Key: A Study in the Symbolism of Reason, Rite, and Art* (Third edition, Cambridge, MA: Harvard University Press, 1980), p. 266.

2 Ibid., pp. 41, 42.

3 Ibid., p. 87.

4 Ibid., p. 86.

5 Ludwig Wittgenstein, *Tractatus Logico-Philosophicus* (1922), trans. C. K. Ogden (London: Routledge, 1996), 7 and 6.522.

6 Rudolf Carnap, *Philosophy and Logical Syntax* (Bristol: Thoemmes Press, 1996), pp. 27–9. '[M]any linguistic utterances … have only an expressive function, no representative function. Examples of this are cries like 'Oh, Oh' or, on a higher level, lyrical verses'.

7 Bertrand Russell, *Philosophy*, p. 265. Quoted in Langer, *Philosophy in a New Key*, p. 88.

8 Susanne K. Langer, *Problems of Art* (New York: Charles Scribner's Sons, 1957), p. 22.

9 Langer, *Philosophy in a New Key*, pp. 86, 87.

10 Ibid., p. 87.

11 Paul Welsh, 'Discursive and Presentational Symbols', *Mind* 64 (April 1955), p.190.

12 Susanne K. Langer, *Feeling and Form: A Theory of Art Developed from Philosophy in a New Key* (New York: Charles Scribner's Sons, 1953), p. vii. The full quote reads: 'In *Philosophy in a New Key* it was said that the theory of symbolism there developed should lead to a critique of art as serious and far-reaching as the critique of science that stems from the analysis of discursive symbolism … Since this philosophy of art rests squarely on *the above mentioned semantic theory* [my italics] the present book cannot but presuppose the reader's acquaintance with the previous one.'

13 Langer, *Philosophy in a New Key*, p. 87. Langer's definition of semantics contrasts with that of, for instance, Jerrold J. Katz who writes, 'Semantics is the study of linguistic meaning. It is concerned with what sentences and other linguistic objects express, not with the arrangements of their syntactic parts.' Jerrold J. Katz, *Semantic Theory* (New York: Harper & Row, 1972), p. 1. See also 'semantics', in *Chambers English Dictionary*: 'semantics is the science of the meaning of words.' *Chambers English Dictionary* (Edinburgh: Chambers, 1990).

14 Langer, *Philosophy in a New Key*, p. 87. Cassirer even applied the term 'semantics' to history: 'If we are to seek a general heading under which we are to subsume historical knowledge we may describe it not as a branch of physics but as a branch of semantics. … History is included in the field of hermeneutics.' Ernst Cassirer, *An Essay on Man* (New Haven, CT: Yale University Press, 1944), p. 195.

15 Langer, *Philosophy in a New Key*, p. 55, 56.

16 Susanne K. Langer, *The Practice of Philosophy* (New York: Henry Holt, 1930), p. 122. The fact that Langer allows for a non-human interpretant – 'for which' – reflects Whitehead's organicist semiotics.

17 Langer, *Philosophy in a New Key*, p. 53.

18 Ibid., p. 56.

19 Ibid., p. 53. To some extent this problem is a feature of the English language since several other European languages employ two distinct expressions for what Langer names the 'psychological' and 'logical' meaning of 'meaning': 'meinen' in German, 'vouler dire' in French and 'bedoelen' in Dutch correspond with her 'psychological'

sense, while 'bedeuten' in German, 'signifier' in French and 'betekenen' in Dutch correspond to the 'logical' sense.

20 Langer, *Philosophy in a New Key*, p. 56.

21 Ibid., p. 55.

22 Ibid., p. 56.

23 Ibid., p. 64.

24 Ibid., p. 57.

25 Ibid., p. 57.

26 William P. Alston makes a similar point in *Philosophy of Language* (1968). Opening his book with a list of sentences that use the word 'mean' in different ways: 'I mean to help him if I can' (intend); 'The passage of this bill will mean the end of second class citizenship' (result in); 'Once again life has meaning for me' (significance); 'What is the meaning of this' (explanation); 'He just lost his job. That means that he will have to start writing letters of application over again' (implies). Alston observes that, in none of these examples, the term is used in a 'linguistic' – or what Langer would call 'symbolic' – way. As he comments, 'In [all] these cases we are talking about people, actions, events, or situations rather than about words, phrases, or sentences.' William P. Alston, *Philosophy of Language* (Englewood Cliffs, NY: Prentice-Hall, 1968), p. 10.

27 Langer, *Philosophy in a New Key*, p. 59.

28 Ibid., p. 58.

29 Ibid., p. 60.

30 Ibid., p. 58.

31 Ibid.

32 In his 1957 article 'Meaning', philosopher of language H. P. Grice distinguishes between two uses of the term 'meaning': 'natural meaning' and 'non-natural meaning'. For Grice, as for Langer, 'meaning' is not something which words do or have, but *something that speakers do with them*. The difference between, in Grice's examples, a sentence like 'those spots mean measles' and one like 'three rings on the bell of the bus mean that the bus is full' is that, in contrast to the first, the second case implies that there is somebody who *means* the rings on the bell of the bus to convey something. H. P. Grice, 'Meaning', in Fahrung Zabeck, E. D. Klemke and Arthur Jacobson, eds, *Readings in Semantics* (Champagne, IL: University of Illinois Press, 1974), p. 383. Originally published in *Philosophical Review* 66 (1957), pp. 322–88. On Langer's terms, however, despite the human operator of the bell, the meaning function in both instances is that of a sign and not a symbol.

33 Langer, *Philosophy in a New Key*, p. 59.

34 Ibid.

35 Ibid., p. 64.

36 Ibid., pp. 60, 61.

37 Ibid. p. 60.

38 Ibid., p. 61.

39 Ibid.

40 Ibid., p. 63. Quoted from Helen Keller, *The Story of My Life* (1902) (Garden City, NY: Doubleday, 1936), pp. 23–4.

41 Langer, *Philosophy in a New Key*, p. 63.

42 Ibid.

43 Cassirer, *Essay on Man*, pp. 34, 35.

44 Langer, *Philosophy in a New Key*, p. 60.

45 Charles Sanders Peirce, *Philosophical Writings of Peirce*, J. Buchler, ed.
    (New York: Dover, 1955), p. 99.

46 Langer, *Practice of Philosophy*, p. 122, footnote 4. Peirce's papers were published
    between 1931 and 1935. Paul Weiss, Charles Hartshorne and Arthur W. Burks, eds,
    The Collected Papers of Charles Sanders Peirce, Vols 1–6 (Cambridge, MA: Harvard
    University Press, 1931–5).

47 Langer, *Philosophy in a New Key*, p. 54.

48 Peirce, *Philosophical Writings of Peirce*, p. 99.

49 Hartshorne and Weiss, *The Collected Papers of Charles S. Peirce* (2.227), p. 58.

50 For a discussion of Peirce's influence on Wittgenstein, see Dinda L. Gorlée,
    Wittgenstein in Translation: Exploring Semiotic Signatures (Berlin: De Gruyter
    Mouton, 2012), p. 28. Frank Ramsey co-translated *The Tractatus* with C. K. Ogden.

51 Another potentially confusing comparison in terms of terminology is that between
    Langer and French semioticist Julia Kristeva, for whom the terms 'symbolic' and
    'semiotic' serve as her central notions in her *Revolution in Poetic Language*. Broadly
    speaking, for Kristeva, following Freud's and Lacan's distinctions between the
    conscious and the unconscious, 'the symbolic' is the realm of conscious lingual
    representation, in contrast to (unconscious) 'semiotic' realm which escapes such,
    but is nevertheless a condition for it. One could say that, roughly, Langer's notion
    of presentational or non-discursive symbolism could be compared with Kristeva's
    concept of 'the semiotic', whereas her concept of discursive symbolism has a certain
    kinship with Kristeva's notion of 'the symbolic'. *Revolution in Poetic Language*,
    trans. Margaret Waller (New York: Columbia University Press, 1984). See especially
    chapter 1, 'The Semiotic and the Symbolic', pp. 19–107.

52 According to Robert Innis, Langer's way of dividing the semiotic continuum is not
    so much an alternative as a complement to Peirce's project. Robert E. Innis, 'Peirce's
    Categories and Langer's Aesthetics: On Dividing the Semiotic Continuum', *Cognitio*
    14.1 (January/June 2013), p. 37. For other references by Innis to intersections between
    Langer and Peirce see 'Placing Langer's Philosophical Project', *Journal of Speculative
    Philosophy* 21.1 (2007), pp. 4–15, and his book *Susanne Langer in Focus: The Symbolic
    Mind* (Bloomington: Indiana University Press, 2009).

53 Peirce wrote, 'A sign or representamen, is something which stands to somebody for
    something in some respect or capacity. It addresses somebody, that is, creates in the
    mind of that person an equivalent sign, or perhaps a more developed sign. That sign
    which it creates I call the interpretant of the first sign. The sign stands for something,
    its object. It stands for that object, not in all respects, but in reference to a sort of idea,
    which I have sometimes called the ground of the representamen.' Peirce, *Philosophical
    Writings of Peirce*, p. 99.

54 Cassirer, *Essay on Man*, pp. 31, 32. Cassirer footnotes his comment on the distinction
    between operators and designators with reference to Charles Morris's *The Foundation
    of the Theory of Signs* (*Encyclopaedia of the Unified Sciences*, 1938). Langer also refers
    to Morris's text in *Philosophy in a New Key*, p. 22.

55 Langer, *Philosophy in a New Key*, p. x. It could be argued that the word 'signal' does
    not cover the full connotation of Langer's 'sign' as it does primarily refer to future
    rather than past events. E.g. a scar is not a 'signal' of a wound, but a symptom.

56 It does not help the discussion that Morris refers to Langer's and Cassirer's theories
    as 'semiotic' while Langer refers to Peirce's theory as 'semantic'. Prior to Langer's
    Philosophy in a New Key (1942), Charles Morris had published two articles on a
    semiotic theory of art that showed close affinities with Langer's philosophy art as a

symbolic form. See, for instance, 'Esthetics and the Theory of Signs', *Erkenntnis* 8.1-3 (June, 1939), pp. 131–50, and 'Science, Art and Technology', *The Kenyon Review* 1.4 (Autumn, 1939), pp. 409–23.

57 Two further comments are in order: first, although, both the term 'semantics' and the term 'semiotics' are etymologically linked to the word 'semeion' (sign), the term 'semantics' is also etymologically linked to the Greek adjective 'semantikos' meaning 'significant'; second, according to the Dutch philosopher Aart van Zoest, before Peirce the term 'semiotics' was first coined by the German philosopher J. H. Lambert at the end of the eighteenth century. However, until Peirce became more well known in the 1930s the term was rarely used. Van Zoest adds that the term 'semiology' is traditionally linked with those theories of signs which have been inspired by the Swiss linguist Ferdinand de Saussure (1857–1913). Independently of Peirce de Saussure had also undertaken a study of linguistic signs conceived as part of a more general theory of signs. Although followers of Peirce generally tend to use the term 'semiotics' and those inspired by Saussure the term 'semiology', the term 'semiotics' is more commonly used. Aart van Zoest, *Semiotiek: Over tekens, hoe ze werken en wat we ermee doen* (Baarn: Basisboeken Ambo, 1978).

58 Roland Barthes, *Elements of Semiology*, trans. Anette Lavers and Colin Smith (New York: Hill and Wang, 1967).

59 Langer, *Feeling and Form*, p. 25.

60 Ibid., p. 26.

61 Langer, *Philosophy in a New Key*, p. 114.

62 Jerry H. Gill, 'Langer, Language and Art', *International Philosophical Quarterly* 34.4 (December 1994), p. 419.

63 Langer, *Philosophy in a New Key*, p. 266.

64 Langer, *Problems of Art*, pp. 132, 133.

65 Langer, *Philosophy in a New Key*, p. 143.

66 Wayne C. Bowman, *Philosophical Perspectives on Music* (New York: Oxford University Press, 1998), p. 208.

67 Langer, *Philosophy in a New Key*, p. 97.

68 G. L. Hagberg, *Art and Language: Wittgenstein, Meaning and Aesthetic Theory* (Ithaca, NY: Cornell University Press, 1995), p. 12.

69 Langer, *Feeling and Form*, p. 369.

70 Susanne K. Langer, *Mind: An Essay on Human Feeling*, Vols I, II and III (henceforth cited as *Mind* I, II or III) (Baltimore, MD: Johns Hopkins University Press, 1967, 1971 and 1982), *Mind* I, p. 84.

71 Langer, *Philosophy in a New Key*, p. 81.

72 For other examples of this error, see, for instance, Welsh's heading of the first section of his (otherwise helpful) article: 'Discursive Symbols: (1) Words', Paul Welsh, 'Discursive and Presentational Symbols', *Mind* 64 (April 1955), p.181.

73 Langer, *Philosophy in a New Key*, pp. 81, 82.

74 Ibid., p. 80.

75 Ibid.

76 Ibid., p. 94.

77 Ibid.

78 Ibid.

79 Ibid.

80 Ibid., p. 96.

81 Ibid., p. 73.

82   Bowman, *Philosophical Perspectives on Music*, p. 207.

83   Wittgenstein, *Tractatus Logico-Philosophicus* 3.325, p. 55. Wittgenstein adds in brackets that 'The logical symbolism of Frege and Russell is such a language, which, however, does still not exclude all errors.' Quoted by Langer in *Philosophy in a New Key*, p. 82.

84   Langer, *Philosophy in a New Key*, p. 87, footnote 9.

85   Ibid., p. 93.

86   Ibid.

87   Ibid., p. 94.

88   Ibid., p. 93.

89   Ibid., p. 97.

90   Susanne K. Langer, *An Introduction to Symbolic Logic* (Second revised edition, New York: Dover Publications, 1953), p. 29.

91   C. S. Peirce, 'The Icon, Index, and Symbol', in Charles Hartshorne and Paul Weiss, eds, *The Collected Papers of Charles S. Peirce*, Vol. 2, chapter 3 (Cambridge: Harvard University Press, 1931–58), 2.276, 2:157. Quoted by W. J. T. Mitchell in *Iconology: Image, Text, Ideology* (Chicago, IL: University of Chicago Press, 1986), p. 56.

92   For a discussion of Langer's terminology, see Mary Reichling, 'Intersections: Form, Feeling, and Isomorphism', *Philosophy of Music Education Review* 12.1 (Spring 2004), pp. 17–29.

93   Mitchell, *Iconology: Image, Text, Ideology*, pp. 56, 57.

94   Cassirer, *Essay on Man*, p. 170.

95   Ibid., p. 134.

96   Susanne K. Langer, *Problems of Art* (New York: Charles Scribner's Sons, 1957), p. 19.

97   Langer, *Problems of Art*, p. 20.

98   Nelson Goodman, *Languages of Art: An Approach to a Theory of Symbols* (Indianapolis, IN: Hackett Publishing Company, 1976), p. 9..

99   Plato, *Cratylus*, trans. H. N. Fowler (Cambridge, MA: Harvard University Press, 1926), 432b, p. 163.

100 Langer, *Practice of Philosophy*, pp. 121, 122.

101 See also Nelson Goodman: 'An object resembles itself to the maximum degree but rarely represents itself; resemblance, unlike representation, is reflexive. Again, unlike representation, resemblance is symmetric: B is as much like A as A is like B, but while a painting may represent the Duke of Wellington, the Duke doesn't represent the painting.' Goodman, *Languages of Art*, p. 4.

102 Alfred North Whitehead, *Process and Reality*, David Ray Griffin and Donald W. Sherburne, eds (New York: Free Press, 1929), p. 182.

103 Langer, *Philosophy in a New Key*, p. 58.

104 Ibid., p. 58.

105 Beatrice Nelson, 'Susanne K. Langer's Conception of "Symbol" – Making Connections through Ambiguity', *Journal of Speculative Philosophy* 8.4 (1994), p. 286.

106 Langer, 'On a New Definition of Symbol', Paper presented at Brown University in 1956, included as chapter 3 of *Philosophical Sketches* (New York: Arno Press, 1962), pp. 54–65.

107 Langer, *Philosophical Sketches*, p. 60.

108 Quoted in Langer, *Philosophical Sketches*, p. 60. From Ernst Nagel, 'Symbolism and Science', in *Symbols and Values: An Initial Study*, Thirteenth Symposium in Science, Philosophy and Religion (New York: Cooper Square, 1964), p. 44.

109   Langer, *Philosophical Sketches*, p. 58.
110   Ibid., p. 56.
111   Ibid., pp. 58, 59.
112   Ibid., p. 63.
113   James R. Johnson, 'The Unknown Langer: Philosophy from the New Key to the Trilogy of Mind', *Journal of Aesthetic Education* 27.1 (Spring 1993), p. 67.
114   Langer, *Philosophical Sketches*, p. 64.
115   For a more sophisticated critique of Langer's notion of symbol than Nagel's, see Berel Lang, 'Langer's Arabesque and the Collapse of the Symbol', *Review of Metaphysics* 16.2 (December 1962), pp. 349–65.
116   Louis Arnaud Reid, 'Susanne Langer and Beyond', *Meaning in the Arts* (London: George Allen & Unwin, 1969), pp. 68, 70. Revised version of an article by the same title published in the *British Journal of Aesthetics* 5.4 (1965), pp. 357–67.
117   Reid, 'Susanne Langer and Beyond', p. 70.
118   Langer, *Philosophy in a New Key*, p. 110.
119   Ibid.
120   Ibid., pp. 41, 42.
121   Ibid., pp. 89, 90.
122   Ibid., p. 42.
123   Ibid., p. xiv
124   Ibid., p. 90.
125   Ibid.
126   Ibid., p. 38.
127   Ibid., p. 266.
128   Ibid., p. 93.
129   Ibid., p. 98.
130   Ibid., p. 92.
131   Ibid., p. 90.
132   Ibid.
133   Ibid., p. 266.
134   Ibid., p. 125.
135   Ibid., p. 110.
136   Ibid., p. 90.
137   Ibid., p. 110.
138   For Cassirer's view of symbolic pregnance, see Ernst Cassirer, *The Philosophy of Symbolic Forms: Volume III: The Phenomenology of Knowledge* (New Haven, CT: Yale University Press, 1957), p. 202. Cassirer defines symbolic pregnance as follows: 'By symbolic pregnance we mean the way in which a perception as a sensory experience contains at the same time a certain nonintuitve meaning which it immediately and concretely represents. Here we are not dealing with bare perceptive data, on which some sort of apperceptive acts are later grafted, through which they are interpreted, judged, transformed. Rather, it is the perception itself which by virtue of its own immanent organization, takes on a kind of spiritual articulation – which, being ordered in itself, also belongs to a determinate order of meaning. … It is this ideal interwoveness, this relatedness of the single perceptive phenomenon, given here and now, to a characteristic total meaning that the term "pregnance" is meant to designate.' Cassirer, *Philosophy of Symbolic Forms* III, p. 202.
139   Ibid., p. 46.
140   Langer, *Mind* III, p. 49.

141 Ibid.
142 Ibid., p. 48.
143 Langer, *Philosophy in a New Key*, p. 150.
144 Ibid., p. 151.
145 Langer, *Philosophical Sketches*, p. 64.
146 Susanne K. Langer, 'On Cassirer's Theory of Language and Myth', in Paul Schilpp,
     ed., *The Philosophy of Ernst Cassirer*, The Library of Living Philosophers (La Salle,
     IL: Open Court, 1949), p. 388.
147 Langer, *Philosophy in a New Key*, p. 149.
148 Ibid., pp. 149, 150.
149 Ibid., p. 145.
150 Ibid., p. 266.
151 Langer's view of metaphor contrasts with that of, for instance, Janet Martin Soskice
     who restricts metaphor to a linguistic 'figure of speech whereby we speak about one
     thing in terms which are seen to be suggestive of another'. *Metaphors and Religious
     Language* (Oxford: Oxford University Press, 1985), p. 15. Soskice explicitly rejects the
     possibility of visual metaphors. For her metaphors are figures of *speech* that do not
     apply to physical objects: 'He who points to the daffodils in the garden and says that
     they are metaphors for rebirth speaks carelessly and indeed metaphorically. Daffodils
     are not in themselves and could not be metaphors, for they are not linguistic at
     all. We shall argue later that one can reasonably say that the daffodil is a symbol
     of rebirth or that it provides an analogy for rebirth, since neither the category of
     symbol nor that of analogy is strictly linguistic. However, although we can construct
     a metaphor in which we speak of daffodils in order to describe rebirth, the daffodils
     themselves are not metaphors.' p. 17. For a Langerian defence of visual metaphor, see
     Carl R. Hausman, 'Following Langer's terminology, the kind of symbol that should
     be distinguished most completely from metaphor is the semiotic or conceptual
     symbol. A semiotic or conceptual symbol is a sign that is humanly constructed
     and that refers to something independent of itself. ... What is referred to can be
     known apart from the symbol. ... A semiotic symbol is replaceable. ... [B]eing
     replaceable does not apply to metaphors unless we are convinced that paraphrases
     or explanations can be substituted for metaphors without loss of meaning.' Carl
     R. Hausman, *Metaphor and Art: Interactionism and Reference in the Verbal and
     Nonverbal Arts* (Cambridge: Cambridge University Press, 1991), pp. 13, 14.
152 Langer, *Problems of Art*, p. 23.
153 Langer, *Philosophy in a New Key*, p. 147.
154 Ibid.
155 Ibid., p. 33.
156 Ibid., p. 267.
157 Ibid., p. 278.
158 Ibid., p. 267.
159 Ibid., p. 267
160 Ibid., p. 269.
161 Ibid., p. 44.
162 Ibid., p. 125.
163 Ibid.
164 Ibid.
165 Ibid., p. 118. Elsewhere Langer notes that 'all theory is merely speculation in the
     light of significant facts.' p. 134. The topic of the origin of language was for a long

time avoided in circles of serious scholarship. In 1866 the *Societé de Linguistique de Paris had* made it a standing rule that no paper on the subject was to be presented or discussed. In 1997 a reviewer of Terence Deacon's *The Symbolic Species* comments, 'For generations linguists referred derisively to popular views by such terms as "the bow-wow theory", "the pooh-pooh theory" and "the ding-dong theory". Now that has changed, and the conundrum of how it all began is back on the agenda of intellectually respectable topics.' Roy Harris, book review of Terence W. Deacon, *The Symbolic Species: The Co-evolution of Languages and the Human Brain* (London: Penguin, 1997), *The Times Higher Education Supplement* (November 7, 1997).

166 Langer, *Philosopy in a New Key*, p. 133.

167 Ibid., p. 134.

168 Ibid., p. 61.

169 Ibid.

170 Ibid., p. 31.

171 Ibid.

172 Ibid., p. 72.

173 Ibid., p. 71. Langer's notion of 'conception' is very similar to that of Kant's 'transcendental *Schema*'. Although internal, a transcendental *Schema* for Kant is a type of mental image which mediates between the sensuous and the conceptual. It is not an image of a specific perception, nor that of an abstract concept – one cannot, for instance, mentally 'picture' the abstract concept 'house' – but an image which allows the mind to apply a concept to a particular phenomenon. In Kant's words, 'In der Tat liegen unseren reinen sinnlichen Begriffen nicht Bilder der Gegenstände, sondern Schemate zum Grunde.' I. Kant, *Kritik der Reinen Vernunft* (1781–1787) (Leipzig: Verlag von Felix Meiner, 1971), p. 199. Kant himself distinguishes between *Schemata* and symbols, claiming that the first contain direct and the second, indirect images (*Darstellungen*) *of concepts*. In his words, 'Alle Anschauungen, die man Begriffen a priori unterlegt, sind also entweder Schemata oder Symbole, wovon die ersteren direkte, die zweiten indirekte Darstellungen des Begriffs enthalten.' I. Kant, *Kritik der Urteilskraft* (1790) (Hamburg: Verlag von Felix Meiner, 1968), p. 212. The latter typically operate via analogy, as when the monarchy as a political system is symbolized as an organism.

174 Langer, *Philosophy in a New Key*, p. 63.

175 Ibid., pp. 133, 134.

176 Ibid., p. 133.

177 Ibid., p. 64.

178 Ibid., p. 61, footnote 6.

179 Ibid., p. 71. See also p. 141.

180 Ibid., p. 64. In contrast to her notion of denotation, Langer's notion of connotation is similar to that of John Stuart Mill, for whom it consisted of the attributes by which a term was defined.

181 Langer, *Philosophy in a New Key*, p. 65.

182 Ibid.

183 Ibid. For a later formulation of the same point, see Janet Martin Soskice on Keith Donnelan: 'Keith Donnelan's contribution has been to point out that there is a difference between a successful reference, and one which has a factually accurate definite description. A reference can be successful even if the description in the referring expression does not actually fit the referent; for example, in the context,

the utterance "The man drinking the gin and tonic" can successfully refer even though the man referred to may in fact be drinking soda water.' Janet Martin Soskice, *Metaphors and Religious Language* (Oxford: Oxford University Press, 1985), p. 52. Keith S. Donnellan, 'Reference and Definite Descriptions', in Stephen P. Schwartz, ed., *Naming, Necessity, and Natural Kinds* (Ithaca, NY: Cornell University Press, 1977), pp. 42–65. Soskice's main argument here is that 'reference is something effected by speakers making an utterance in a context, and not something which inheres in definite descriptions or lexemes *per se*.' p. 52.

184 Langer, *Philosophy in a New Key*, pp. 76, 77.

185 Ibid., p. 19.

186 Langer, *Mind* I, p. 79.

187 Langer, *Feeling and Form*, p. 30.

188 Langer, *Problems of Art*, p. 133.

189 Langer, *Philosophy in a New Key*, p. 72

190 Ibid., p. 74.

191 Ibid., p. 91

192 Ernest Nagel, 'Review of *Philosophy in a New Key* by Susanne K. Langer', *Journal of Philosophy* 40.12 (1943), pp. 325, 326. Subsequently published as Ernest Nagel, 'A Theory of Symbolic Form', in Ernst Nagel, *Logic without Metaphysics and other Essays in the Philosophy of Science* (Glencoe, IL: Free Press, 1956), pp. 353–60. See also the critique of Nagel's critique by Charles Varela and Lawrence Ferrara, 'The Nagel critique and Langer's critical response', *Journal for the Anthropological Study of Human Movement* 2.2 (Autumn 1982), pp. 99–111.

193 John Hospers, *Meaning and Truth in the Arts* (1946) (Chapel Hill: University of North Carolina Press, 1979), p. 60. It should be pointed out that Hospers wrongly identifies Langer's musical presentational symbols with musical *notes*.

194 Ibid., pp. 60, 61.

195 Harold Osborne, 'Susanne K. Langer's *Mind: An Essay on Human Feeling Vol. I: An Essay Review*', *Journal of Aesthetic Education* 18.1 (Spring 1984), p. 91.

196 Cassirer, *Philosophy of Symbolic Forms* III, p. 202

197 Wittgenstein, *Tractatus Logico-Philosophicus*, 2.1515, pp. 39, 41.

198 Langer, *Philosophy in a New Key*, p. 51.

199 Innis, *Susanne Langer in Focus*, p. 254.

200 In his book *Meaning*, written shortly before his death in 1976, Michael Polanyi argues in Cassirerean and Langerean fashion that poetry, art, myth and religion are valid modes of knowledge that seek meaning by means of metaphorical expression. Michael Polanyi and Harry Prosch, *Meaning* (Chicago, IL: University of Chicago Press, 1975).

9 Art as the form of feeling

1 Susanne K. Langer, *Mind: An Essay on Human Feeling*, Vols I, II and III (henceforth cited as *Mind* I, II or III) (Baltimore, MD: Johns Hopkins University Press, 1967, 1971 and 1982), *Mind* I, p. 87.

2 Susanne K. Langer, *Philosophy in a New Key: A Study in the Symbolism of Reason, Rite, and Art*, 3rd edn (Cambridge, MA: Harvard University Press, 1980), p. 218.

3 Susanne K. Langer, *Problems of Art* (New York: Charles Scribner's Sons, 1957), p. 73.

4 Ibid., p. 74.

5 Susanne K. Langer, *Feeling and Form: A Theory of Art Developed from* Philosophy in a New Key (New York: Charles Scribner's Sons, 1953), p. ix.

6 While the terms 'philosophy of art' and 'aesthetics' are often used interchangeably, aesthetics is generally considered to be a subfield of philosophy *encompassing* the study of art, sense perception and beauty. Langer was primarily interested in the first two.

7 It was only after the publication of the third volume of *Mind* in 1982 that philosophers started to take note of her broader philosophy, resulting in publications in, among others, *Philosophical Psychology*; *Semiotica*; *Consciousness and Cognition*; and *Phenomenology and the Cognitive Sciences*. Since about 2000, most scholarly attention had shifted from her aesthetics to her philosophy of mind.

8 Langer, *Feeling and Form*, p. vii.

9 For Passmore's comments on aesthetics, see J. A. Passmore, 'The Dreariness of Aesthetics', in William Elton, ed., *Aesthetics and Language* (Oxford: Blackwell, 1954), pp. 36–55.

10 W. V. Quine, 'Mr. Strawson on Logical Theory', *Mind* 62.248 (October 1953), p. 446.

11 Although Langer never engaged seriously with Vico, her Cassirer-based theory of the imagination shows distinct parallels with Vico. See David W. Black, 'The Vichian Elements in Susanne Langer's Thought', *New Vico Studies* 3 (1985), pp. 113–18; and Thomas Sebeok, 'From Vico to Cassirer to Langer', in Marcel Danesi, ed., *Vico and Anglo-American Science: Philosophy and Writing* (Berlin: De Gruyter, 1995), pp. 159–70. Sebeok strangely downplays Cassirer's influence on Langer but notes several parallels between her and Vico. He concludes his chapter as follows: 'Langer's semiotic work merits detailed reconsideration in the near future, especially in its implications for music and the whole range of the fine arts … in short, aesthetics, the vast estate where she perhaps unknowingly caught up with Vico' (p. 167).

12 Harold Osborne, ed., 'Introduction', *Aesthetics* (Oxford: Oxford University Press, 1972), p. 1.

13 Langer, *Philosophy in a New Key*, p. 88. Russell: 'But if there be a world which is not physical, or not in space-time, it may have a structure which we can never hope to express or to know. … Perhaps that is why we know so much physics and so little of anything else.' Bertrand Russell, *Philosophy* (New York: W. W. Norton, 1927), p. 265. Quoted in Langer, *Philosophy in a New Key*, p. 88.

14 Langer, *Problems of Art*, p. 22.

15 S. K. Langer, 'Abstraction in Art', *Journal of Aesthetics and Art Criticism* 22.4 (July 1, 1964), pp. 379–92; 'The Principles of Creation in Art', *The Hudson Review* 2 (1950), pp. 515–34; 'The Primary Illusions and the Great Orders of Art', *The Hudson Review* 3 (1950), pp. 219–33. For an insightful account of creation and creativity in Langer, see Vincent Colapietro, 'Susanne Langer on Artistic Creativity and Creations', in John Deely and C. W. Spinks, eds, *Semiotics* (New York: Peter Lang, 1997), pp. 3–12.

16 Langer, *Feeling and Form*, p. ix.

17 Wehr recalls one meeting between Tobey and Langer as follows: 'As soon as we finished ordering our lunch, Tobey launched into a long monologue on art, science, and philosophy. As usual, he was strikingly articulate, but he soon became so caught up in his own eloquence that I had to remind myself that he had once wanted to be a preacher, and he had always liked centre stage. … Susanne leaned forward, listening intently to his words. When he finished, she responded: "That was very interesting, Mr. Tobey. You made several points that particularly interested me." She proceeded

to reconstruct from memory a good part of what he had just said. Tobey was visibly alarmed. He wasn't at all used to have a trained logician listen to him. ... It was apparent that Toby was quite impressed by Langer. He seemed even intimidated by her. This surprised me. It was rare for Tobey to be intimidated by anyone.' Wesley Wehr, *The Accidental Collector: Art, Fossils and Friendships* (Seattle: University of Washington Press, 2004), pp. 113, 114.

18 Wehr, *The Accidental Collector*, p. 114.

19 Ibid., p. 112. Wehr adds that he had challenged Langer on this point as he knew several practising artists who were serious admirers of Langer's writings on art.

20 Langer and Newman were part of a panel discussion co-sponsored by the American Society for Aesthetics and the Woodstock Artists Association at the fourth annual Woodstock Art Conference in New York in 1952. Harold Rosenberg, 'Barnett Newman: The Living Rectangle', in *The Anxious Object: Art Today and Its Audience* (New York: Horizon Press, 1964), p. 43; and Barnett Newman, *Barnett Newman: Selected Writings and Interviews*, ed. John P. O'Neill (New York: Alfred A. Knopf, 1990), p. 247. Other speakers at the conference included David Smith, Franz Boaz and painters Mark Rothko and Robert Motherwell.

21 For one of the best discussions of Langer's conception of the art symbol, see Eva Schaper, 'The Art Symbol', *British Journal of Aesthetics* 4.3 (July 1964), pp. 228–39.

22 Langer, *Philosophy in a New Key*, p. 209.

23 C. P. E. Bach, *Versuch ueber die wahre Art, das Klavier zu spielen* (n.p., 1753). Quoted by Langer in *Philosophy in a New Key*, p. 223. An example (not mentioned by Langer) from the visual arts can be found in Tolstoy's *What Is Art*: 'If only the spectator or auditors are infected by the feelings which the author has felt, it is art. To evoke in oneself a feeling one has experienced and having evoked it in oneself then by means of movements, lines, colours, sounds, or forms expressed in words, so to transmit that feeling that others experience the same feeling – this is the activity of art. Art is a human activity consisting in this, that one man consciously by means of certain external signs, hands on to other feelings he has lived through, and that others are infected by these feelings and also experience them.' Leo Tolstoy, *What Is Art?* (1898), trans. Aylmer Maude (London: Oxford University Press, 1975), p. 123.

24 C. Busoni, *Entwurf einer neuen Aesthetik der Tonkunst*, quoted from Gatz, 'Musik Aesthetik', *Gazette Musicale*, pp. 56–8. Quoted by Langer in *Philosophy in a New Key*, p. 223.

25 Langer anticipates a similar critique of expression theory as raised by Richard Wollheim two decades later in his book *Art and Its Objects* (1968). Richard Wollheim, *Art and Its Objects* (Cambridge: Cambridge University Press, 1996), pp. 22–34.

26 Langer, *Feeling and Form*, p. xi. Langer, *Philosophy in a New Key*, pp. 212, 213. For a discussion of recent revivals of this kind of expression theory, see Allan Beever, 'The Arousal Theory Again?', *British Journal of Aesthetics* 38.1 (January 1998), pp. 82–90. According to Beever, the arousal theory holds that 'a passage of music is expressive of an emotion if and only if it arouses that emotion, or possesses a tendency to arouse that emotion, in the listener' (p. 82).

27 Langer, *Philosophy in a New Key*, p. 216.

28 Ibid.

29 For discussions of Langer's view of representation and expression of emotions in music, see Stephen Davies, 'Is Music a Language of the Emotions?', *British Journal of Aesthetics* 23.3 (Summer, 1983), pp. 222–33; Lars-Olof Ahlberg, 'Susanne Langer

on Representation and Emotion in Music', *British Journal of Aesthetics* 34.1 (January 1994), pp. 69–80; Felicia E. Kruse, 'Emotion in Musical Meaning: A Peircean Solution to Langer's Dualism', *Transactions of the Charles S. Peirce Society* 41.4 (October 2005), pp. 762–78. For accounts of Langer's view of presentation and expression in art in general, see Sister Mary Francis Slattery, 'Looking Again at Susanne Langer's Expressionism', *British Journal of Aesthetics* 27.3 (Summer, 1987), pp. 247–58; and Carol Donnell-Kotrozo, 'Representation and Expression: A False Antinomy', *Journal of Aesthetics and Art Criticism* 39.2 (December 1980), pp. 163–73.

30   Rudolf Carnap, *Philosophy and Logical Syntax* (Bristol: Thoemmes Press, 1996), p. 28. Quoted in Langer, *Philosophy in a New Key*, pp. 83, 84.

31   Langer, *Philosophy in a New Key*, p. 222.

32   Ibid., p. 218.

33   R. G. Collingwood, *The Principles of Art* [1938] (Oxford: Clarendon Press, 1958), pp. 121, 122, 123.

34   Langer, *Feeling and Form*, pp. 380–90.

35   Peter Kivy, *Sound Sentiment: An Essay on the Musical Emotions* (Philadelphia, PA: Temple University Press, 1989), pp. 12, 13.

36   For a comparison of Langer, Kivy and Goodman on the art symbol and music, see Mary Reichling, 'Susanne Langer's Theory of Symbolism: An Analysis and Extension', *Philosophy of Music Education Review* 1.1 (Spring 1993), pp. 3–17.

37   Albert van der Schoot, 'Kivy and Langer on Expressiveness in Music', in Lilianna Bieszczad, ed., *Practising Aesthetics*, Proceedings of the 19th International Congress of Aesthetics, Cracow 2013 (Krakow: Libron, 2015), p. 169.

38   Erwin Panofsky, *Perspective as Symbolic Form* (1927), trans. Christopher S. Wood (New York: Zone Books, 1997), pp. 40, 41. Originally published as 'Die Perspektive als "symbolische Form"', in *Vorträge der Bibliothek Warburgh 1924–1925* (Leipzig and Berlin, 1927), pp. 258–330.

39   Erwin Panofsky, 'Iconography and Iconology: An Introduction to the Study of Renaissance Art' (1939), in *Meaning in the Visual Arts* (Harmondsworth: Penguin, 1970), p. 54, footnote 1.

40   Ibid., p. 55. For a helpful discussion of the conscious/unconscious (intentional/ unintentional) distinction in Cassirer, see Goran Hermeren, *Representation and Meaning in the Visual Arts* (Lund: Laromedelsforlagen, 1969), pp. 126–51.

41   Panofsky, *Meaning in the Visual Arts*, p. 56.

42   Ibid., p. 65.

43   Panofsky, *Perspective as Symbolic Form*, p. 24. Michael Ann Holly suggests that, at least at the end of his early essay on perspective, Panofsky was not interested in either iconographical or iconological meaning in the sense of the identification of a particular *Weltanschauuung* but in the *process* of signifying as such, i.e., apart from what is in the end signified. Michael Ann Holly, *Panofsky and the Foundations of Art History* (Ithaca, NY: Cornell University Press, 1984), p. 181.

44   For the influence of Cassirer on Panofsky more generally, see Michael Podro, *The Critical Historians of Art* (New Haven, CT: Yale University Press, 1982), pp. 181–83. For a comparison of Warburg's, Cassirer's and Panofsky's views of symbol and art historiography, see Silvia Ferretti, *Cassirer, Panofsky, and Warburg: Symbol, Art, and History*, trans. Richard Pierce (New Haven, CT: Yale University Press, 1989).

45   P. O. Kristeller, 'Review of Erwin Panofsky, Renaissance and Renascences in Western Art', *Art Bulletin* 44.1 (March, 1962), p. 67. Quoted in Holly, *Panofsky and the Foundations of Art History*, p. 27.

46 Holly, *Panofsky and the Foundations of Art History*, p. 181.

47 Giulio Carlo Argan, 'Ideology and Iconology', *Critical Inquiry* 2 (Winter 1975), p. 299. Referred to by Holly, *Panofsky and the Foundations of Art History*, p. 181.

48 Langer, 'The Art Symbol and the Symbol in Art', chapter 9 of *Problems of Art*, pp. 124–39. For an excellent discussion of this chapter and related passages in Langer, see Louis Arnaud Reid, 'Susanne Langer and Beyond', *British Journal of Aesthetics* 5.4 (October 1965), pp. 357–67.

49 Langer, *Problems of Art*, p. 139.

50 Ibid., p. 136.

51 Goran Hermeren distinguishes between at least four stages in the development of a conventional symbol: 'First there is the period of creation, when a visual device is beginning to be used or understood symbolically. Second, there is a period when symbolic traditions or conventions are emerging. Third, there is the period when symbolic traditions are well established and widely known. Fourth, there is the period when the symbols begin to fade, loose their power of suggestions and finally die.' Goran Hermeren, *Representation and Meaning in the Visual Arts* (Lund: Laromedelsforlagen, 1969), p. 79.

52 Langer, *Mind* I, p. 84.

53 Langer, *Feeling and Form*, p. 369. In the few cases that Langer does talk about art in terms of a symbolism, she does not refer to the art work as such but its medium or 'syntax': '[Language] differs from wordless symbolism [*sic*], which is non-discursive and untranslatable, does not allow of definitions within its own system, and cannot directly convey generalities.' Langer, *Philosophy in a New Key*, p. 96.

54 Langer, *Problems of Art*, p. 134.

55 Langer, *Feeling and Form*, p. 379.

56 Ibid., p. 379.

57 Ibid., pp. 379, 380.

58 Langer, *Philosophy in a New Key*, p. 93.

59 Langer, *Problems of Art*, p. 66.

60 Ibid., p. 166.

61 Susanne K. Langer, *The Practice of Philosophy* (New York: Henry Holt, 1930), p. 166.

62 Langer, *Problems of Art*, p. 65.

63 Alfred North Whitehead, *Process and Reality*, ed. David Ray Griffin and Donald W. Sherburne (New York: The Free Press, 1929), p. xi.

64 Quoted by Langer, *Problems of Art*, p. 65.

65 Quoted in ibid. Langer's notion of intuition also echoes Kant's notion of the spontaneous activity of the productive imagination discussed in Chapter 5. The productive imagination enables the mind to apply the right forms and categories to the chaotic influx of sensations as the raw material for these. In his *Transcendental Logic*, Kant refers to this activity as 'a blind but indispensable function of the soul, without which we should have no knowledge whatsoever, but of which we are scarcely ever conscious.' Immanuel Kant, *Critique of Pure Reason*, trans. Norman Kemp Smith (London: Macmillan, 1979), B103, p. 112.

66 Langer, *Problems of Art*, p. 69.

67 Langer, *Practice of Philosophy*, p. 166.

68 Ibid.

69 Cornelia Richter, 'The Body of Susanne K. Langer's Mind', in John Michael Krois, ed., *Embodiment in Cognition and Culture* (Amsterdam: John Benjamins, 2007), p. 109.

70 Susanne K. Langer, *Philosophical Sketches* (Baltimore, MD: Johns Hopkins University Press, 1962), p. 63.

71 Langer, *Philosophy in a New Key*, p. 89.

72 Langer, *Problems of Art*, p. 163.

73 Ibid.

74 Specific discussions include the following: 'Abstraction in Science and Abstraction in Art', in Paul Henle, Horace M. Kallen and S. K. Langer, eds, *Structure, Method and Meaning: Essays in Honor of Henry M. Sheffer* (New York: Liberal Arts Press, 1951), pp. 171–82; reprinted in S. K. Langer, *Problems of Art*, pp. 163–80; 'Emotion and Abstraction', in *Philosophical Sketches*, pp. 66–82; Chapter 6, entitled 'A Chapter on Abstraction', in *Mind* I, pp. 153–98; 'Abstraction in Art', *Journal of Aesthetics and Art Criticism* 22.4 (July 1, 1964), pp. 379–92.

75 Susanne K. Langer, *An Introduction to Symbolic Logic* (Second revised edition, New York: Dover Publications, 1953), pp. 42, 43.

76 Langer, *Problems of Art*, p. 163.

77 Langer, *Philosophy in a New Key*, p. 72.

78 Although Samuel Bufford correctly identifies two different emphases and descriptions of the way feelings are projected in art and music, I do not agree with Bufford's assessment that this constitutes two (different) philosophies of art. Samuel Bufford, 'Susanne Langer's Two Philosophies of Art', *Journal of Aesthetics and Art Criticism* 31.9 (1972), pp. 9–20.

79 Langer, *Introduction to Symbolic Logic*, p. 24.

80 Ibid., p. 29.

81 Ibid., p. 30.

82 Langer, *Philosophy in a New Key*, p. 70.

83 Langer, *Introduction to Symbolic Logic*, p. 27.

84 Langer, *Practice of Philosophy*, p. 141.

85 See, for instance, Garry Hagberg, 'Art and the Unsayable: Langer's Tractarian Aesthetics', *British Journal of Aesthetics* 24.4 (April 1984), pp. 325–40. Hagberg incorrectly states that 'the *Tractatus* theory of language ... has generated the presumption that if art is to have meaning or significance, then it must acquire this meaning by mirroring or symbolizing some other thing – a state of affairs, which in the case of art is internal. Thus the work of art itself is, on this conception of meaning, in a sense relegated to a position of secondary importance. ... Wittgenstein came to see his early view of language as deeply misleading ... The alternative conception could be as radically different as the late Wittgensteinian conception of meaning is from the early, a conception which escapes the dualistic categories of inner feeling and outer symbol' (pp. 338, 339). See also Bernhard F. Scholz about Langer's supposed reconciliation of Cassirer's notion of symbolic forms with Wittgenstein's picture concept of language: 'If this is the case, a conception which was developed to transcend the *Abbildtheorie* of language is imposed on just such a theory.' Bernhard F. Scholz, 'Discourse and Intuition in Susanne Langer's Aesthetics of Literature', *Journal of Aesthetics and Art Criticism* 31.2 (1 December, 1972), pp. 215–26. For my critique of these accounts of the *Tractatus*, see Chapter 7.

86 This is not always sufficiently recognized.

87 Heinrich Hertz, *The Principles of Mechanics Presented in New Form* (1899), trans. D. E. Jones and J. Walley (New York: Dover, 1956), pp. 1, 2.

88 Langer, *Practice of Philosophy*, p. 138.

89 Langer, *Introduction to Symbolic Logic*, p. 31.

90 Ibid., p. 24.

91 Langer, *Philosophy in a New Key*, p. 70.

92 Strangely, Langer makes exactly this point in the context of a comparison between language and painting later on. *Philosophy in a New Key*, pp. 96, 97.

93 Ibid., p. 94.

94 Ibid., p. 222.

95 Ibid.

96 Ibid., pp. 238, 218.

97 Langer, *Feeling and Form*, p. 27. For a comparable description of music, see Maurice Merleau-Ponty, 'Eye and Mind,' in James M. Edie, ed., *The Primacy of Perception* (Evanston, IL: Northwestern University Press, 1964), p. 161: 'Music ... is too far beyond the world and the designatable to depict anything but certain outlines of being – its ebb and flow, its growth, its upheavals, its turbulence.' Reprinted in *Aesthetics*, ed. Harold Osborne (Oxford: Oxford University Press, 1972), p. 57. For an account of Merleau-Ponty's phenomenological aesthetics, see Adrienne Dengerink Chaplin, 'Phenomenology: Sartre and Merleau-Ponty', in Berys Gaut and Dominic McIver Lopes, eds, *The Routledge Companion to Aesthetics*, 2nd edn (London: Routledge, 2005), pp. 159–71.

98 Langer, *Philosophy in a New Key*, p. 238.

99 Ibid.

100 Ibid., p. 226.

101 Ibid., p. 232.

102 Langer, *Mind* I, p. 67.

103 Ibid., p. 68.

104 Ibid. p. 59.

105 Ibid., pp. 67, 68.

106 Ibid.

107 Although Langer sometimes uses the lowercase word 'gestalt', I will use the original German terms '*Gestalt*' and the plural '*Gestalten*' in my discussions.

108 Langer, *Problems of Art*, p. 164. For a historical analysis of the concept of form, see Władysław Tatarkiewicz, 'Form: History of One Term and Five Concepts', chapter 7 in *A History of Six Ideas: An Essay in Aesthetics* (The Hague: Martinus Nijhoff, 1980), pp. 220–43.

109 Langer, *Problems of Art*, p. 165.

110 Langer, 'Abstraction in Art', *Journal of Aesthetics and Art Criticism* 22.4 (Summer 1964), p. 382. Ibid., p. 382.

111 Langer, *Philosophical Sketches*, pp. 71, 72. Quoted from Norbert Wiener, *Cybernetics or Control and Communication in the Animal and the* Machine (New York: John Wiley & Sons, 1948), p. 156.

112 Ibid., p. 77.

113 Ibid.

114 Langer, *Feeling and Form*, p. 51.

115 Ibid., p. 59.

116 Ibid., p. 49.

117 For a critique of Langer's notion of *Gestalt* and abstraction, see Timothy Blinkley, 'Langer's Logical and Ontological Modes', *Journal of Aesthetics and Art Criticism* 28.4 (Summer, 1970), pp. 455–64.

118 Langer, '*Abstraction in Art*', p. 383; *Mind* I, p. 169.

119 Langer, *Mind* I, p. 166.

120 Ibid., pp. 170, 171.

121 Ibid. p. 169.

122 Chapter 7, 'Form: History of One Term and Five Concepts', in Tatarkiewicz, *A History of Six Ideas*, pp. 220–43. Whereas the first three notions have originated in the realm of aesthetics, the last two arose within general philosophy and have then been passed on to aesthetics.

123 Tatarkiewicz, *A History of Six Ideas*, p. 220. The term 'eidos' developed into the English term 'idea'.

124 Ibid., p. 234.

125 For an insightful discussion of Langer's conception of the art symbol, see Berel Lang, 'Langer's Arabesque and the Collapse of the Symbol', *Review of Metaphysics* 16.2 (December 1962), pp. 349–65.

126 Langer, *Problems of Art*, p. 127.

127 For an interesting account of Langer's notion of expressive form through the lens of *Gestalt* theory, see Forest Hansen, 'Langer's Expressive Form: An Interpretation', *Journal of Aesthetics and Art Criticism* 27.2 (Winter, 1968), pp. 165–70.

128 Langer, *Feeling and Form*, p. 394.

129 Langer's concept of semblance echoes Schiller's 'Schein', Kant's disinterested 'Wohlgefallen' and Jung's 'illusion', yet it is not identical with any of these. For an excellent discussion of semblance, see Arthur Berndtson, 'Semblance, Symbol, and Expression in the Aesthetics of Susanne Langer', *Journal of Aesthetics and Art Criticism* 14 (June 1956), pp. 494, 495. For an intriguing comparison between Langer's, Danto's and Adorno's notions of semblance, see Stefan Morawski, 'Art as Semblance', *Journal of Philosophy* 81.11 (November 1984), pp. 654–63.

130 Langer, *Feeling and Form*, p. 47.

131 Berndtson, 'Semblance, Symbol, and Expression', p. 493.

132 Langer, *Feeling and Form*, p. 47.

133 Ibid., p. 72. Langer credits the sculptor and art theorist Adolf Hildebrand with first recognizing the purely visual and illusionary character of pictorial space in his book *The Problem of Form in Painting and Sculpture* (1907) (New York: G. E. Stechert, 1932).

134 For a contemporary appreciation of Hildebrand, see Antony Gormley, 'Feeling into Form', *Philosophical Transactions of the Royal Society* 362 (14 June 2007), pp. 1513–18. Gormley writes,

> I seek to use objective means to describe subjective states. Having decided that the core of sculpture is a fulfilment of Adolf Hildebrand's aphorism 'all forms have the purpose of making space visible and its continuity sensible', my wager is to preserve the thing of sculpture in its autonomy while allowing for a degree of empathic inhabitation. It is not enough simply to make space visible: we have to make it felt. My methodology for doing that is to start with the experience of life and consciousness within the body.

135 Langer, *Feeling and Form*, p. 70, footnote 1.

136 Ibid., p. 70. For a similar notion of style, see Alois Riegl, *Problems of Style: Foundations for a History of Ornament* (1893), trans. Evelyn Kain (Princeton, NJ: Princeton University Press, 1992). For the significance of Riegl for contemporary art theory, see Paul Crowther, 'More than Ornament: The Significance of Riegl', *Art History* 17.3 (1995), pp. 482–94.

137 Langer, *Feeling and Form*, p. 71.

138 For Hildebrand's conception of form, see Adolf Hildebrand, 'The Problem of Form in the Fine Arts', in Julia Bloomfield, Kurt Foster and Thomas F. Reese, eds, *Empathy, Form, and Space: Problems in German Aesthetics, 1873–1893*, translated and introduced by Harry Francis Mallgrave and Eleftherios Ikonomou (Santa Monica, CA: Getty Center for the History of Art and the Humanities, 1994), pp. 227–80.

139 Langer, *Feeling and Form*, p. 84.

140 Ibid., p. 72.

141 Ernst Gombrich, *Art and Illusion*, A. W. Mellon Lectures in the Fine Arts (Princeton, NJ: Princeton University Press, 1960).

142 Richard Wollheim, 'Seeing-As, Seeing-In, and Pictorial Representation', in *Art and Its Objects* (Cambridge: Cambridge University Press, 1980), pp. 205–26. Although his later work showed considerable overlaps with Langer's thought, in his early years he wrote a highly critical review of *Feeling and Form*, saying it was a 'retrogressive step in the understanding of art'. Richard Wollheim, 'Review of *Feeling and Form* by Susanne Langer', *Burlington Magazine* 97.633 (December 1955), p. 401.

143 Langer, *Feeling and Form*, p. 86.

144 Ibid., pp. 89, 90. In Langer's view, the sculptor Hildebrand does not sufficiently distinguish between virtual scenic space (in painting) and virtual tactile space (in sculpture) in his bas-reliefs. For her, they (unsuccessfully) assimilate sculptural space to the scenic space of painting. For a critique of Langer's interpretation and critique of Hildebrand, see Bipin K. Agarwal, 'Langer, Hildebrand, and Space in Art', *Journal of Aesthetics and Art Criticism* 31.4 (Summer 1973), pp. 513–16.

145 Langer, *Feeling and Form*, p. 95.

146 Ibid., p. 99.

147 Ibid., p. 98.

148 Ibid., p. 109.

149 Ibid., p. 110.

150 For a clear account of secondary illusion in music, see Mary Reichling, 'Susanne Langer's Concept of Secondary Illusion in Music and Art', *Journal of Aesthetic Education* 29.4 (Winter, 1995), pp. 39–51.

151 Langer, *Feeling and Form*, p. 118.

152 Ibid., p. 114.

153 Ibid., p. 116.

154 Ibid., p. 125. Langer's philosophy of music as virtual time has been extensively discussed, critiqued, revised and extended. Mary Reichling, for one, holds that 'Langer does not offer sufficient distinctions or suggest varying levels or gradations of the experience of time' and draws attention to the fact that 'there is actually a dynamic interplay between clock time and virtual time'. Reichling, 'Susanne Langer's Theory of Symbolism', p. 7. For another discussion see Gordon Epperson, *The Musical Symbol: A Study of The Philosophic Theory of Music* (Ames: Iowa State University Press, 1967), pp. 223–25.

155 Serious interest in dance among philosophers did not start until the early 1980s. Philosophers who have focused on dance include Francis Sparshott, Noël Carrol, Curtis Carter, Graham McFee, Julie van der Camp and Richard Shusterman. For a discussion of philosophy and dance, see Francis Sparshott, 'On the Question: "Why Do Philosophers Neglect the Aesthetics of Dance?"', *Dance Research Journal* 15.1 (1982), pp. 5–30. For a helpful analysis of Langer's philosophy of dance, see Colleen Dudagan, 'Dance, Knowledge, and Power', *Topoi* 24 (2005), pp. 29–41.

156 Langer, *Feeling and Form*, pp. 174–178.

157   Ibid., p. 175.
158   Ibid., p. 178.
159   Ibid., p. 176.
160   Ibid., p. 200.
161   Ibid.
162   Ibid., p. 264.
163   Ibid., p. 211.
164   Ibid., p. 212. For Langer, jokes are a literary form in that, immediately after the
      opening statement, every listener enters the world of events experienced by the
      main protagonists. Langer uses the word 'poet' in a generic sense to include writers
      of prose, drama, etc. She prefers the term 'virtual life' over the more commonly
      used term 'virtual world' so as to avoid confusion with the description of the
      pathological condition belonging to someone 'living in a world of one's own'. Ibid.,
      p. 228.
165   Ibid., p. 217.
166   Ibid., p. 223.
167   Ibid., p. 256.
168   Ibid., p. 253.
169   Ibid., p. 231.
170   Ibid., p. 258.
171   Ibid., p. 217.
172   For an insightful account of Langer's view of the literary arts, see Robert E. Innis,
      'The Making of the Literary Symbol: Taking Note of Langer', *Semiotica* 165.1/4
      (2007), pp. 91–106.
173   For a perceptive discussion of Langer's view of drama, see Richard Courtney, 'On
      Langer's Dramatic Illusion', *Journal of Aesthetics and Art Criticism* 29.1 (Fall, 1970),
      pp. 12–20.
174   Kendall L. Walton, *Mimesis as Make-Believe: On the Foundations of the
      Representational Arts* (Cambridge, MA: Harvard University Press, 1993).
175   Langer, *Feeling and Form*, p. 230. Langer adds that the word 'feeling' should not be
      taken as a state but as a process and that it may 'not only have successive phases, but
      several simultaneous developments'.
176   Ibid., p. 253.
177   Ibid.
178   For a helpful discussion of the relation between art, feeling and 'life' in Langer, see
      Louis Arnaud Reid, 'New Notes on Langer', *British Journal of Aesthetics* 8.4 (October
      1968), pp. 353–8.
179   Langer, *Feeling and Form*, p. 253.
180   Langer, *Philosophy in a New Key*, p. 96.
181   Paul Welsh, 'Discursive and Presentational Symbols', *Mind* 64.254 (April 1955),
      p. 189.
182   Curtis Carter, for instance, argues that Langer's comparison of the function of words
      with that of lines, areas of light and shade and colour patches 'prejudices the case
      too heavily against the possibility of paintings having vocabulary'. Curtis L. Carter,
      'Langer and Hofstadter on Painting and Language: A Critique', *Journal of Aesthetics
      and Art Criticism* 32.3 (Spring 1972), p. 338.
183   Reichling, 'Susanne Langer's Theory of Symbolism', p. 7.
184   Langer, *Philosophy in a New Key*, p. 74.

185 For a critical view of Langer's understanding of the 'lingual arts', see Jerry H. Gill, 'Langer, Language, and Art', *International Philosophical Quarterly* 34.4 (December 1994), pp. 419–32.

186 For a critical discussion of Langer's views of discursivity and literature, see Bernhard F. Scholz, 'Discourse and Intuition in Susanne Langer's Aesthetics of Literature', *Journal of Aesthetics and Art Criticism* 31.2 (1 December 1972), pp. 215–26.

187 Langer, *Problems of Art*, p. 148.

188 Langer, *Feeling and Form*, p. 369.

189 Nelson Goodman, *Languages of Art: An Approach to a Theory of Symbols* (Indianapolis, IN: Hackett, 1976), pp. xii, xiii. Goodman pays tribute to Cassirer at the beginning of his later work *Ways of Worldmaking* (1978) but does not further engage with him. For informative accounts of semiotic and semantic art theories prior to Goodman, including comparisons between Langer and Morris, see Richard Rudner, 'On Semiotic Aesthetics', *Journal of Aesthetics and Art Criticism* 10.1 (1951), pp. 67–77; and Max Rieser, 'The Semantic Theory of Art in America', *Journal of Aesthetics and Art Criticism* 15.1 (1956), pp. 12–26.

190 Goodman, *Languages of Art*, p. 136.

191 Ibid., p. 144.

192 Goodman's notion of 'analogue' must not be confused with analogy between pictures and reality. Goodman's conventionalism does not allow for any resemblance theory. As he says, 'a digital system has nothing special to do with digits or an analog system with analogy.' Ibid., p. 160.

193 Ibid., p. 231. For a critical discussion of isomorphism in Langer, see Elvira G. Panaiotidi, 'The Myth of Isomorphism', *International Review of the Aesthetics and Sociology of Music* 38.2 (December 2007), pp. 133–42.

194 For Langer, see *Feeling and Form*, p. 27; for Goodman, see *Languages of Art*, pp. 230, 231.

195 Nelson Goodman, *Ways of Worldmaking* (Indianapolis, IN: Hackett, 1978).

196 Goodman, *Languages of Art*, pp. 230, 231 and 226. For an excellent account of the way Langer's and Goodman's views converge, see Curtis Carter, 'After Cassirer: Art and Aesthetic Symbols in Langer and Goodman', in J. Tyler Friedman and Sebastian Luft, eds, *The Philosophy of Ernst Cassirer: A Novel Assessment* (Berlin: Walter de Gruyter, 2015), pp. 401–18.

197 Nelson Goodman, 'How Buildings Mean', *Critical Inquiry* 11.4 (1985), pp. 642–53.

198 Langer, *Mind* I, p. 87.

199 Langer, 'Abstraction in Art', Journal of Aesthetics and Art Criticism 22.4 (Summer 1964), p. 382.

200 Langer, *Problems of Art*, p. 45.

201 Ibid.

202 Langer, *Mind* I, p. 199.

203 Langer, *Problems of Art*, p. 47.

204 Ibid.

205 Ibid.

206 Langer, *Feeling and Form*, p. 126.

207 Ibid., p. 129.

208 Langer, *Mind* I, pp. 200, 204; Langer, *Problems of Art*, p. 57.

209 Langer, *Feeling and Form*, p. 63.

210 Langer, *Mind* I, p. 331.

211 Langer, *Feeling and Form*, p. 312.
212 Langer, *Mind* I, p. 204.
213 Ibid., p. 331.
214 Quoted in ibid., from D'Arcy Thompson, *On Growth and Form* (1917), 2nd edn, Vol. II (Cambridge: Cambridge University Press, 1968), pp. 1020–21.
215 Langer, *Feeling and Form*, p. 128.
216 Ibid.
217 Immanuel Kant, *Critique of Judgment*, trans. Werner S. Pluhar (Indianapolis, IN: Hackett, 1987), 320, p. 189.
218 For Kant, the free play of thought as occasioned by the beautiful object is also a condition for moral reasoning. Like aesthetic judgments, moral judgments for Kant need to be free from outside obligations or interests. This is why, in an oft-quoted but equally often misunderstood phrase, Kant refers to beauty as 'the symbol of morality' (*Critique of Judgment*, p. 225). By means of our 'disinterested' attitude to them, both beauty and the good are able to promote man's ultimate goal and meaning in life: the attainment of autonomous freedom independent from any outside goal or interest.
219 Langer, *Mind* I, p. 428.
220 Artists, writers and critics who have been influenced by Langer include Guy Anderson, Fay Landser (who attended Langer's classes at the University of Colombia), Danish abstract expressionist artist Asger Jorn, Clement Greenberg, Herbert Read and novelist Percy Walker. Walker was particularly impressed by Langer and devoted several essays to a discussion of her ideas: 'Symbol as Need', *Thought* 29.3 (1954), pp. 381–90 (reprinted in *The Message in the Bottle* (New York: Farrar, Strauss and Giroux, 1981), pp. 288–97); 'Symbol as Hermeneutic in Existentialism', *Philosophy and Phenomenological Research* 16.4 (1956), pp. 522–30.
221 Robert Motherwell, 'The Modern Painter's World', *Magazine Dyn* (November 1944). http://theoria.art-zoo.com/the-modern-painters-world-robert-motherwell/ (accessed 29 April 2019).
222 Appendix D, 'Meaning in Art', in *The Logical Analysis of Meaning*, PhD thesis, 1926. Unpublished, p. 164. Langer footnotes this passage with a lengthy quote from Cassirer's first volume of his *Philosophie der Symbolishen Formen: Die Sprache* (1923).
223 Langer, *Practice of Philosophy*, pp. 152, 153.
224 Ibid., p. 162.
225 Ibid.
226 For a comparison of views of artistic understanding in analytic philosophy and phenomenology, see Krzysztof Guczolski, 'Phenomenology and Analytic Aesthetics of Music: On the Views of Susanne Langer and Roman Ingarden', *Nordisk Estetisk Tidskrift* 23 (2001), pp. 27–38. Guczolski convincingly argues that there are significant overlaps between Langer's and Ingarden's aesthetics.
227 Langer, *Problems of Art*, p. 71.
228 Langer, *Practice of Philosophy*, p. 162.
229 For articles showing the similarities (and differences) between Langer and Polanyi, see Walter B. Gulick, 'Polanyi and Langer: Toward a Reconfigured Theory of Knowing and Meaning', *Tradition and Discovery: The Polanyi Society Periodical* 36.1 (2010), pp. 21–37; Robert Innis, 'Art, Symbol and Consciousness: A Polanyi Gloss on Susan Langer and Nelson Goodman', *International Philosophical Quarterly* 17 (December 1977), pp. 455–76; and Robert Innis, 'Between Articulation and

Symbolization: Framing Polanyi and Langer', *Tradition and Discovery* 36.1 (2010), pp. 8–20.

230 Moritz Schlick, 'Form and Content' (1932), *Gesammelte Aufsätze 1926–1936* (Hildesheim: Olms Verlag, 1969), p. 199. Also quoted by John Hospers, *Meaning and Truth in the Arts* (1946) (Chapel Hill: University of North Carolina Press, 1979), p. 234.

231 Hospers, *Meaning and Truth in the Arts*, p. 235.

232 Langer, *Introduction to Symbolic Logic*, p. 22.

233 Ibid.

234 Ibid.

235 Langer, *Philosophy in a New Key*, p. 263.

236 Ibid.

237 Langer, *Feeling and Form*, p. 379.

238 Hospers, *Meaning and Truth in the Arts*, p. 234.

239 Two helpful articles on meaning in art and music that include lengthy discussions of Langer are Donald W. Sherburne, 'Meaning and Music', *Journal of Aesthetics and Criticism* 24.4 (Summer 1966), pp. 579–83; and Michael Woods, 'Musical Meaning: Reference and Symbol', *AE: Canadian Aesthetics Journal* 13 (Summer 2007), www.uqtr.ca/AE/Vol_13/libre/Woods.htm (accessed 23 October 2018).

240 Erwin László, *Introduction to Systems Philosophy: Toward a New Paradigm of Contemporary Thought* (New York: Harper & Row, 1972), p. 223. László's own view of cognition sounds very Langerian: 'cognition is an ongoing process of adaptive interaction in the course of which the human being extends his cognitive loops into far reaches of the universe. Knowledge ... is the outcome of man's persistent attempt to lend meaning to his experience by evolving ... commonsensical gestalts and the manifold constructs of the arts and the sciences. Notwithstanding specific differences between the thus emerging cognitive modes, their common functional context and origin assures sufficient isomorphies to overcome the vexing ... dualisms of reason and feeling, science and art, and practical common sense and abstract reasoning' (p. 232).

241 Langer, *Mind* I, p. 87.

242 For a discussion of Langer's views of art and cognition in the context of art education, see Bennett Reimer, 'Langer on the Arts as Cognitive', *Philosophy of Music Education Review* 1.1 (Spring, 1993), pp. 44–60.

243 Langer writes, 'One might well call a work of art a metaphorical symbol. It is, however, not a simple metaphor but a highly elaborated one ... for its elements are articulated to various degrees, their sense is one thing in one of their internal relations and something else in another.' *Mind* I, pp. 104, 105.

244 Morris Weitz, 'Symbolism and Art', *Review of Metaphysics* 7.3 (March 1954), pp. 469, 470.

245 Kingsley Price, 'Philosophy in a New Key: An Interpretation', *Philosophy of Music Education Review* 1.1 (Spring 1993), p. 37. For other articles by Kingsley Price referring to Langer, see 'Is a Work of Art a Symbol?', *Journal of Philosophy* 50.16 (30 July 1953), pp. 485–503; and 'How Can Music Seem to Be Emotional?', *Philosophy of Music Education Review* 12.1 (1 April 2004), pp. 30–42.

246 Joseph Margolis, *Art and Philosophy* (Brighton: Harvester Press, 1980), p. 235. The full quote reads as follows: 'The trivial truth that literature employs language has ... led to the untenable thesis that all art is language (Langer [1942], [1953])

and to the more pointed claim that artworks somehow affirm propositions
that may be linguistically expressed and straightforwardly judged true or false
(Greene [1940].' See also Joseph Margolis, 'Art as Language', *Monist* 58.2 (April
1974), pp. 175–86.

247   George Dickie, *Introduction to Aesthetics: An Analytical Approach* (New York: Oxford
      University Press, 1997), p. viii. By contrast, Langer writes, 'It is natural enough,
      perhaps, for naïve reflection to centre first of all round the relationship between
      an image and an object; and equally natural to treat a picture, statue, or a graphic
      description as an imitation of reality. The surprising thing is that long after art theory
      had passed the naïve stage and after every serious thinker realised that imitation was
      neither the aim nor the measure of artistic creation, the traffic of the image with its
      model kept its central place among philosophical problems of art.' Langer, *Feeling
      and Form*, p. 46.

248   Roger Scruton, *The Aesthetics of Music* (Oxford: Clarendon Press, 1997), pp. 166, 167.

249   Ibid., viii. Earlier misrepresentations of Langer's position by Scruton can be found in
      Art and Imagination: A Study in the Philosophy of Mind (London: Routledge, 1974),
      pp. 46, 220.

250   Richard Wollheim, 'Review of: *Feeling and Form*', p. 401. Ironically, Wollheim's
      later work on the mind and psychoanalysis displays many overlaps with Langer
      as is reflected in, for instance, his notion of 'seeing-in' and his interest in 'the
      tendency of early or infantile thought to represent itself as something bodily, or
      … the corporealization of thought'. Richard Wollheim, *The Mind and Its Depths*
      (Cambridge, MA: Harvard University Press, 1993), p. x. For Wollheim's views
      of art and expression, see Rob Van Gerwen, ed., *Richard Wollheim on the Art of
      Painting: Art as Representation and Expression* (Cambridge: Cambridge University
      Press, 2001).

251   One further example of an early critic who misunderstood Langer's notion
      of the art symbol is Arthur Szathmary. In his article 'Symbolic and Aesthetic
      Expression in Painting', Szathmary argues that Langer fails to distinguish
      between symbolic and aesthetic expression, but he overlooks the fact that, for
      Langer, symbolic forms are *inherently* expressive. Arthur Szathmary, 'Symbolic
      and Aesthetic Expression in Painting', *Journal of Aesthetics and Art Criticism* 13.1
      (September 1954), pp. 86–96.

252   Roger Shiner, 'Langer, Suzanne [*sic*] Katherina Knauth (1895–1985)', in John R.
      Shook, *The Dictionary of Modern American Philosophers* (Bristol: Thoemmes
      Continuum, 2005), p. 1414.

253   Langer, *Problems of Art*, p. 73.

254   Ibid., p. 72.

255   Ibid.

256   Ibid., p. 74.

257   Ibid., p. 73.

258   Ibid.

259   Ibid.

260   Ibid.

261   Ibid., pp. 72, 73.

262   Langer, *Philosophical Sketches*, p. 90.

263   Ibid., p. 92.

10 Mind as embodied meaning

1 Susanne K. Langer, *Mind: An Essay on Human Feeling*, Vols I, II and III (henceforth cited as *Mind* I, II or III) (Baltimore, MD: Johns Hopkins University Press, 1967, 1971 and 1982), *Mind* I, pp. xviii, xix.

2 Ibid., p. 29.

3 Donald Dryden writes, 'Langer was far ahead of her time [in her study of consciousness] and her work anticipated recent developments in evolutionary and developmental biology that are … of central importance to any understanding of the evolution of human mentality.' Donald Dryden, 'Susanne L. Langer and American Philosophic Naturalism in the Twentieth Century', *Transactions of the Charles S. Peirce Society* 33.1 (Winter, 1997), p. 168.

4 Fred M. Levin, *Emotion and the Psychodynamics of the Cerebellum: A Neuro-Psychoanalytic Analysis and Synthesis* (London: Routledge, 2018), p. 177.

5 Ernst Cassirer, *An Essay on Man: An Introduction to a Philosophy of Human Culture* (1944) (New Haven, CT: Yale University Press, 1972), p. 22.

6 Susanne K. Langer, *Philosophical Sketches* (Baltimore, MD: Johns Hopkins University Press, 1962), pp. 3, 4.

7 Alfred North Whitehead, *Process and Reality* (1929) (New York: The Free Press, 1979), p. 3.

8 Langer, *Mind* I, p. xxii.

9 Alfred North Whitehead, *Essays in Science and Philosophy* (London: Rider, 1948), p. 78.

10 Bertrand Russell, *Portraits from Memory, and Other Essays* (London: G. Allen & Unwin, 1956), p. 41. The comment recalls Whitehead's introduction of Russell at his 1940 William James lecture at Harvard: 'Bertie thinks that I am muddleheaded; but I think that he is simpleminded.'

11 James Lord, 'Susanne Langer: A Lady Seeking Answers', *New York Times Book Review* (May 26, 1968), pp. 5, 35.

12 Arthur Danto, Foreword to *Mind: An Essay on Human Feeling*, abridged by Gary van den Heuvel (Baltimore, MD: Johns Hopkins Press, 1988), p. vi.

13 Ibid., p. 23.

14 Antonio Damasio, *Descartes' Error: Emotion, Reason, and the Human Brain* (New York: Avon Books, 1994); *The Feeling of What Happens: Body and Emotion in the Making of Consciousness* (San Diego: A Harvest Book, Harcourt, 1999). Other thinkers who Langer anticipates include neuroscientists Jaak Panksepp (who coined the term 'affective neuroscience'), *Affective Neuroscience: The Foundations of Human and Animal Emotions* (New York: Oxford University Press, 1998); and Fred M. Levin, *Mapping the Mind: The Intersection of Psychoanalysis and Neuroscience* (Abingdon: Routledge, 1991).

15 Langer's biologically based conception of the mind anticipates thinkers such as John Searle (*Minds, Brains and Science*, 1984), Mark Johnson (*The Body in the Mind: The Bodily Basis of Meaning, Imagination, and Reason*, 1987), Evan Thompson (*Mind in Life: Biology, Phenomenology, and the Sciences of Mind*, 2007) and Francisco Varela with Evan Thompson and Eleanor Rosch (*The Embodied Mind: Cognitive Science and Human Experience*, 1991). Langer's views of embodied cognition also overlap with those of Maurice Merleau-Ponty, whose *Phenomenology of Perception* was published

in 1945, i.e., three years after *Philosophy in a New Key*. For Merleau-Ponty, there is no sharp division between consciousness and its object. Bodily, sensory experience, rather than mental, reflective awareness, is the essential way of being in the world. Things are as they appear: 'the world is always "already there" before reflection begins – as an inalienable presence.' Maurice Merleau-Ponty, *Phenomenology of Perception* (1945), trans. Colin Smith (London: Routledge & Kegan Paul, 1962), p. vii.

16 Margaret M. Browning, 'Neuroscience and Imagination: The Relevance of Susanne Langer's Work to Psychoanalytic Theory', *Psychoanalytic Quarterly* 75.4 (October 2006), p. 1131.

17 Arthur Danto, 'Mind as Feeling; Form as Presence; Langer as Philosopher', *Journal of Philosophy* 81.11 (November 1984), p. 647.

18 Browning, 'Neuroscience and Imagination', p. 1156.

19 For two insightful accounts of the way Langer's semiotics, aesthetics and philosophy of mind and feeling are interconnected, see Robert Innis, 'Signs of Feeling: Susanne Langer's Aesthetic Model of Minding', *American Journal of Semiotics* 28.1/2 (2012), pp. 43–61; Vincent Colapietro, 'Symbols and the Evolution of Mind: Susanne Langer's Final Bequest to Semiotics', in John Deely and C. W. Spinks, eds, *Semiotics* (New York: Peter Lang, 1998), pp. 61–70.

20 Bennett Reimer, 'Langer on the Arts as Cognitive', *Philosophy of Music Education Review* 1.1. (Spring 1993), p. 45. For an application of Langer's ideas to psychology, see the American psychologist Joseph R. Royce, 'The Implications of Langer's Philosophy of Mind for a Science of Psychology', *Journal of Mind and Behaviour* 4.4 (Autumn 1983), pp. 491–506. In his abstract, Royce holds that 'Langer's trilogy is deemed worthy of extended analysis because it holds the potential of changing the conceptual foundations of psychology' (p. 491).

21 Langer, *Mind* I, p. xv.

22 Ibid., pp. xviii, xix.

23 Ibid. p. xix

24 Ibid., p. 199.

25 This is suggested by Randall Auxier, 'Susanne Langer on Symbols and Analogy: A Case of Misplaced Concreteness?', *Process Studies* 26 (1998), pp. 86–106. For a comparable critique of Langer's view of symbol in general, see Timothy Binkley, 'Langer's Logical and Ontological Modes', *Journal of Aesthetics and Art Criticism* 28.4 (1 July 1970), pp. 455–64.

26 Langer, Foreword (1966), in *Mind*, abridged edition by van den Heuvel, p. xiii.

27 Langer, *Mind* I, p. xix.

28 Langer, Preface, *Philosophy in a New Key* (1941 edn), p. xiv.

29 Reimer, 'Langer on the Arts as Cognitive', p. 49.

30 Owen Flanagan, 'History of the Philosophy of Mind', in Ted Honderich, ed., *The Oxford Companion to Philosophy* (Oxford: Oxford University Press, 1995), pp. 571, 572.

31 Mary Calkins was elected as the president of both societies in 1905 and the first woman to be so appointed.

32 Felicia E. Kruse, 'Vital Rhythms and Temporal Form in Langer and Dewey', *Journal of Speculative Philosophy* 21.1 (2007), pp. 16–26. For an illuminating comparison between Langer and James, see Donald Dryden, 'Susanne Langer and William James: Art and the Dynamics of the Stream of Consciousness', *Journal of Speculative Philosophy* 15.1 (2001), pp. 272–85.

33 In 1974, the journal *Mind* dropped the word 'Psychology' from its original subtitle, *A Quarterly Review of Psychology and Philosophy*. Flanagan, *The Oxford Companion to Philosophy*, ed. Honderich, pp. 571, 572.

34 Langer, *Philosophical Sketches*, p. 3.

35 Ibid.

36 Ibid.

37 Ibid.

38 Ibid., p. 5.

39 Ibid., pp. 4, 5.

40 Ibid., p. 1.

41 In a review of the first volume of *Mind* in *Saturday Review*, the poet and art critic Herbert Read had referred to her work as a 'metaphysical theory', which Langer had felt compelled to correct in a published reply. Under the heading 'The Intent of *Mind*: One Scientific System', she writes,

> In *Saturday Review* 15 July, Sir Herbert Read reviewed the first volume of my *Mind: An Essay on Human Feeling*. Unfortunately, he treated the second of its six parts (three are in the published volume) as the only important part, and consequently the whole work as concerned with aesthetics, although the chapters which interest him have only an orienting function; but as a passing bow to the real intent of the book, he makes at the outset the statement which so seriously misrepresents my intent that I cannot but protest against it. He says, '... her final purpose ... is metaphysical: she has the ambition to present a new metaphysical system.' Nothing could be further from my ambition, which is only to construct a conceptual framework for biological thinking that will connect its several departments, from biochemistry to neuropsychology, in one *scientific* system. Such work is philosophical, but does not commit to any philosophical system, new or old; and it is certainly not metaphysical. Any metaphysical statement must apply to the world as a whole, not only to mind or even life. I have no such statement to offer. (Susanne Langer, 'The Intent of *Mind*: One Scientific System', Letters to the Book Review Editor, *Saturday Review* (26 August 1967), p. 26).

42 Langer, *Mind* I, p. 258.

43 Langer echoes Whitehead's claim that any realm of nature 'may have more or less "life", and that there is no absolute gap between "living" and "non-living" societies'. Whitehead, *Process and Reality*, p. 102.

44 Langer, *Mind* I, p. 260. This echoes Ernest Nagel's distinction between an 'ordo essentia' and 'ordo cognoscendi', the first denying a difference between physics and biology, the latter assuming it. See E. Nagel, *The Structure of Science: Problems in the Logic of Scientific Explanation* (London: Routledge, 1961), p. 398 and further.

45 For various descriptions of the act form, see, for instance, Langer, *Mind* I, pp. 269, 291, 324, 422.

46 Ibid., p. 261.

47 Ibid., p. 296.

48 Ibid., p. 321. In footnote 27 of page 321 Langer refers to an article by H. F. Blum in which reference is made to a 'Miller' in relation to experiments with amino acid. Although the name index in *Mind* I refers to Miller as 'Neal E. Miller', i.e., the physiologist, it is more likely that Blum is, in fact, referring to *Stanley* Miller, the chemist. S. Miller was the first to try to re-create the atmospheric conditions on earth

as they might have been four million years ago, thus aiming to test both Darwin's and Oparin's speculations about the chemical conditions that might have originated life. In his review of *Mind*, Harold Osborne comments that Langer failed to refer to the Miller-Urey experiment of 1953, cited in Francis Crick's book *Life Itself: Its Origin and Nature* (London: Macdonald, 1981), in which organic molecules were produced in the laboratory in an attempt to demonstrate the sort of conditions in which life may have originated on earth. Harold Osborne, 'Susanne K. Langer's *Mind: An Essay on Human Feeling*', *Journal of Aesthetics and Art Criticism* 18.1 (Spring 1984), p. 88.

49　Langer, *Mind* I, p. 312. Langer cites Oparin's explanation:

> If any repetitive action (be it the beat of the waves on a rock or the passage of an invisible ray through an invisible gas) is concentrated for an appreciable time in a particular location, the matter which occupies that location … becomes organised in a spatial pattern reflecting the dynamics of the action. Once the imprint of the action is established it facilitates further repetitions, and at the same time standardizes their form by channelling the course of motions. (Ibid., p. 317)

50　Ibid., p. 322. Osborne criticizes Langer for not discussing 'the now accepted view in microbiology that life should be regarded as coincident with systems of macromolecules displaying powers of self-maintenance and self-replication'. Osborne, 'Susanne K. Langer's *Mind*', p. 88. See also J. Z. Young, quoted by Osborne as an example of this type of theory: 'The nature of the activity which constitutes life … can be seen to consist of a series of interchanges between the organism and its environment such that the organization of the former is maintained in spite of the continuous change of its actual materials.' J. Z. Young, *An Introduction to the Study of Man* (Oxford: Clarendon Press, 1971), p. 117. It could, however, be argued that, without explicitly referring to these theories, Langer is in fact saying the same.

51　Langer, *Problems of Art* (New York: Charles Scribner's Sons, 1957), p. 48.

52　Langer, *Mind* I, p. 370.

53　Ibid., pp. 271–72. Langer refers here to an article by John R. Platt, 'Properties of Large Molecules That Go beyond the Properties of Their Chemical Sub-Groups', *Journal of Theoretical Biology* 1.3 (1961), pp. 342–58.

54　Langer, *Mind* I, p. 281. This view anticipates later genetic theories such as that proposed by Richard Dawkins, in which the gene acts as the main agent in evolution and uses the organism as an instrument for its own perpetuation. See, for instance, Richard Dawkins, *The Selfish Gene* (London: Granada, 1978); *The Extended Phenotype* (Oxford: W. H. Freeman, 1982). Harold Osborne draws attention to a link between Langer and Dawkins in his review of *Mind*. Osborne, 'Susanne K. Langer's *Mind*', p. 89, footnote 4. Unlike Dawkins's position, however, Langer's view does not imply genetic determinism.

55　Langer, *Mind* I, p. 282. For Cassirer on von Uexküll's notion of *Gegenwelt* and 'schema', see Ernst Cassirer, *The Philosophy of Symbolic Forms, Vol. IV: The Metaphysics of Symbolic Forms*, ed. John Michael Krois and Donald Phillip Verene (New Haven: Yale University Press, 1996), pp. 214, 215.

56　Langer, *Mind* I, p. 288.

57　Ibid., p. 375.

58　Ibid., p. 370.

59　Ibid., p. 376.

60　Ibid., p. 337.

61 In her chapter 'Man and Animal: The City and the Hive', in *Problems of Art*, Langer uses the notions of individuation and involvement to explain human society.

> Each person is not only a free, single end. … He is the culmination of his entire ancestry and *represents* the whole human past. In his brief *individuation* [my italics] he is an *expression* of all humanity. That is what makes each person's life sacred and all-important. A single ruined life is the bankruptcy of a long line. This is what I mean by the individual's *involvement* [my italics] with all mankind. (Langer, *Problems of Art*, p. 102)

62 Ibid., p. 323.
63 Ibid., pp. 393, 394. Langer assigns a special significance to dialectical rhythms, defined as rhythms whereby the end of each cycle prepares and initiates the next one. Dialectical rhythms play a crucial role not only in vital functions but also in art: they are 'an essential mark of living form in nature, as their virtual image is of "living form" in art' (ibid., p. 324).
64 Ibid., p. 425.
65 Ibid.
66 Ibid.
67 Langer, *Philosophical Sketches*, p. 8.
68 Langer, *Mind* I, p. 23.
69 Ibid.
70 Ibid., p. 28.
71 Ibid.
72 Langer, *Philosophical Sketches*, p. 8.
73 Langer, *Mind* I, p. 21.
74 Ibid., p. 22.
75 Ibid. It could be argued that some organic processes are only felt when they malfunction, as in the case of, for instance, irregular heartbeat or *in*-digestion.
76 Ibid. p. 21
77 Ibid.
78 Peter A. Bertocci, 'Langer's Theory of Feeling and Mind', *Review of Metaphysics* 23.3 (March 1970), p. 534. Writing in 1970, Bertocci claims that Langer's concepts of feeling and mentality have no recognizable basis in the terminology of the physiology and psychology of his time (p. 534). Approximately fifty year later, much has changed. Langer's descriptions of feeling and mentality resonate strongly with recent developments in neuro-physiology and psychology.
79 Ibid., pp. 530, 531.
80 Langer, *Mind* I, p. 20.
81 Ibid., p. 24.
82 In *The Feeling of What Happens*, Damasio mentions that readers of his previous book had drawn his attention to Langer and acknowledges that his notion of background feeling was 'first hinted at by [this] remarkable but unsung philosopher'. Antonio Damasio, *The Feeling of What Happens: Body and Emotion in the Making of Consciousness* (San Diego: A Harvest Book, Harcourt, 1999), p. 287.
83 Damasio, *The Feeling of What Happens*, p. 37.
84 Ibid.
85 William James, 'What Is an Emotion?', *Mind* 9.34 (1 April 1884), pp. 189, 200.
86 Langer, *Mind* I, p. 21, footnote 36.

87 Langer, *Philosophical Sketches*, p. 21. In a footnote in *Mind* I, Langer refers to William James's apparent difficulty in finding a generic term for what he calls 'mental states at large, irrespective of their kind'. In *The Principles of Psychology* (1890), James had considered both the terms 'feeling' and 'thought' for a description of these states but had finally settled on the latter because the former, Langer explains, 'had kept particularly bad company in his day' (Langer, *Mind* I, p. 21). In another passage by James, however, also referred to by Langer in the same footnote, James does actually define 'minds' as 'personal consciousnesses'. There is one place in the second volume where Langer seems to come close to an identification between 'consciousness' and 'feeling': 'if all acts of the organism decline in intensity below the threshold of feeling, 'consciousness' disappears, such as for instance under total anaesthetic' (Langer, *Mind* I, p. 438).

88 Langer, *Mind* I, p. 29.

89 Whitehead, *Process and Reality*, p. 246. It is for the purpose of this quote not important to know the exact definitions of the terms 'hybrid physical feelings' and 'transmuted feelings'.

90 Ibid., p. 236.

91 Ibid., p. 231.

92 Alfred North Whitehead, *Symbolism: Its Meaning and Effect: Barbour-Page Lectures, University of Virginia, 1927* (New York: Fordham University Press, 1985), pp. 15, 16.

93 Whitehead, *Symbolism: Its Meaning and Effect*, pp. 7, 8.

94 Ibid., p. 8.

95 Whitehead, *Process and Reality*, p. 243.

96 Langer, *Philosophy in a New Key*, p. 103.

97 Langer, *Mind* II, p. 103.

98 Despite his criticisms on some specific points, Osborne's review of the second volume of *Mind* is generally positive:

> If sometimes her particular interpretations sound too fanciful, her criticisms are in general sound, and her recommendations combine unusual sensitivity with stout commonsense. Her wide reading is enlivened by an imaginative empathy with animal life which is all too often lacking in the formulations of practical ecologists. Indeed, to many readers her panoramic presentation of instinctual activity may seem the most rewarding section of her work. (Osborne, 'Susanne K. Langer's *Mind*', p. 89)

99 The Dutch philosopher of science Marja Zuidgeest points out that, in the case of Tinbergen, Langer refers predominantly to his early studies, especially his 'The Study of Instinct' of 1951, which he himself had declared out of date in an article of 1963. Marja Zuidgeest, 'Antropomorfisme en Wetenschap: Kritische Beschouwingen van enkele Aspecten van Susanne Langer's Theorie van het Gevoel' (Anthropomorphism and Science: Critical Observations on Some Aspects of Susanne Langer's Theory of Feeling), in *Algemeen Nederlands Tijdschrift voor Wijsbegeerte* 71.3 (July 1979), p. 175.

100 Langer, *Mind* II, p. 56.

101 Ibid., p. 111.

102 Charles Morris, *The Nature of Mind* (1929), p. 237. Quoted by Langer in *Mind* II, pp. 111, 112.

103 Langer, *Mind* II, p. 45.

104 Ibid., p. 46.

105 Ibid., p. 59. Langer gives numerous examples of this phenomenon. She refers, for instance, to the fact that members of the cat species (from African tiger cats to domesticated ones) seem to shift their perceptions or representations of their 'prey' from one moment in the killing process to another, successively or alternatively treating the prey as target, toy, victim, a morsel or other (ibid., p. 63).

106 Ibid., p. 66.

107 Ibid., p. 68.

108 Ibid., p. 76.

109 Ibid., p. 129.

110 Langer, *Mind* III, p. 141.

111 Langer, *Mind* II, p. 129.

112 Ibid., p. 130.

113 Marja Zuidgeest, 'Antropomorfisme en Wetenschap', pp. 173–88.

114 Langer, *Mind* II, pp. 104, 105.

115 Ibid., p. 105.

116 Arnold Gehlen, *Der Mensch: Seine Natur und seine Stellung in der Welt* (1940); Quoted in Langer, *Mind* II, pp. 215, 216. The term '*das noch nicht festgestellte Tier*' was first used by Nietzsche in *Beyond Good and Evil* (1886) and is sometimes translated as 'the animal not yet properly adapted to his environment'. Friedrich Nietzsche, *Beyond Good and Evil* (New York: Chartwell Books, 2017), p. 62.

117 Langer, *Mind* II, p. 217.

118 Ibid., p. 221.

119 Ibid. Langer illustrates this with the way different structures and placements of the eyes have developed in accordance to the creatures' different environments. Langer mentions, for instance, the long-distance vision in hawks, the night vision in nocturnal hunters or the panoramic vision in the fish eye, where the lens not only protrudes through the pupil but also stands out from the surface of the head, so as to obtain as wide as possible an all-round vision. Similarly, some fish have bifocal lenses, with two retinas in each eye, which allow them to see above and under the water at the same time. She believes that eyes are the earliest specialized organs, which, even in their advanced forms, retain great adaptability.

120 Langer illustrates this by referring to the remarkable similarities in shape between such different organisms as a shark (a fish), a dolphin (a mammal) and an ichthyosaur (a reptile).

121 *Mind*, p. 222.

122 Ibid., p. 234.

123 Ibid., pp. 233, 234.

124 Ibid., p. 238.

125 Ibid., p. 255.

126 Ibid., pp. 257, 258.

127 Ibid., p. 259.

128 Ibid., p. 262.

129 Ibid., pp. 262, 263. Langer refers in this context to Arthur Shapiro, who writes,

the data-processing capacity of the central nervous system is insufficient to allow complete on-line processing of input data with respect to its more remote implications, while at the same time carrying out the activity and decision making required by waking activity. In the absence of sleep, recorded unprocessed data would thus accumulate in sufficient amounts to interfere with the normal activity and decision making of the waking state, and this interference would be experienced as a need to sleep. (Arthur Shapiro, 'Dreaming and the Physiology of Sleep', *Experimental Neurology* 19, Supplement (December 1967)), p. 74.

130 Langer, *Mind* II, p. 264.
131 Ibid.
132 Langer refers in this context to Piaget's observations with children for whom the effect of their words on other children often is entirely secondary to the primary satisfaction of expressing themselves.
133 Langer, *Philosophy in a New Key*, p. 40.
134 Mark Johnson, *The Meaning of the Body: Aesthetics of Human Understanding* (Chicago, IL: University of Chicago Press, 2007).
135 Ibid., pp. 44, 226, 238–39. For a comparison between Langer and Johnson, see Adrienne Dengerink Chaplin, 'Feeling the Body in Art: Embodied Cognition and Aesthetics in Mark Johnson and Susanne K. Langer', *Sztuka I filozofia/Art and Philosophy* 48 (2016), pp. 5–11.
136 Johnson, *Meaning of the Body*, p. 212.
137 Ibid., p. x.
138 For recent surveys, see, for instance, Lawrence Shapiro, *Embodied Cognition* (London: Routledge, 2011); and Anthony Chemero, *Radical Embodied Cognitive Science* (Cambridge, MA: MIT Press, 2011).
139 Johnson, *Meaning of the Body*, p. 264. In developing his argument Johnson draws on, among others, Antonio Damasio, Gerald Edelman, Vittorio Gallese, Eugene Gendlin, George Lakoff, Maxine Sheets-Johnstone and Francisco Varela. Recurrent sources include Maurice Merleau-Ponty, William James and John Dewey. For Johnson's own account of his agreement with Merleau-Ponty and Gendlin, see Mark Johnson, 'Merleau-Ponty's Embodied Semantics: From Immanent Meaning, to Gesture, to Language', *Euramerica* 36.1 (March 2006), 1–27.
140 Sean Gallagher, *How the Body Shapes the Mind* (Oxford: Oxford University Press, 2005), p. 24. On Gallagher's model, a body schema is to be distinguished from a body image. A body image, on Gallagher's terms, consists of 'a system of perceptions, attitudes, and beliefs pertaining to one's own body'. Quoted by Johnson in *Meaning of the Body*, p. 5.
141 Johnson, *Meaning of the Body*, p. 20.
142 Ibid., p. 141.
143 Ibid., p. 145.
144 Ibid., p. 209. Langer, *Philosophy in a New Key*, p. 86.
145 Ibid., p. 267.
146 Johnson, *Meaning of the Body*, p. 209.
147 Langer, *Problems of Art*, p. 25.
148 Johnson, *Meaning of the Body*, p. 236.
149 Ibid., p. 238.
150 For other discussions and applications of Langer's philosophy of mind in relation to the arts, see Christine Watling, 'The Arts, Emotion and Current Research in Neuroscience', *Mosaic* 31 (1998), pp. 107–24; Kell N. Julliard and Gary Van Den Heuvel, 'Susanne K. Langer and the Foundations of Art Therapy', *Art Therapy* 16.3

(1999), pp. 112–20; Cameron Shelley, 'Consciousness, Symbols and Aesthetics: A Just-So Story and Its Implications in Susanne Langer's *Mind: An Essay on Human Feeling*', *Philosophical Psychology* 11.1 (1 March 1998), pp. 45–66.

151 Johnson, *Meaning of the Body*, p. 132.

152 Ibid., p. 162

153 Ibid.

154 Ibid.

155 Cassirer, *An Essay on Man*, pp. 67, 68. It could be argued that Cassirer's account does not solve the problem of duality. As Lambert Zuidervaart comments, 'Cassirer replaces substances with functions without removing the fundamental duality in traditional definitions. Two kinds of functions replace two kinds of substances, but two kinds remain.' Lambert Zuidervaart, 'Scheler, Cassirer, and Transfunctional Definitions of Humankind', Unpublished paper presented at the XVIII World Congress of Philosophy, 21–27 August 1988, Brighton, UK, p. 5.

156 Cassirer, *An Essay on Man*, p. 26.

157 Ibid., p. 41.

158 For a more recent version, see neuro-anthropologist Terrence Deacon, *The Symbolic Species: The Co-evolution of Language and the Brain* (New York: W. W. Norton, 1997).

159 Langer, *Mind* I, p. 362. Langer's weariness of predesigned purposefulness also distinguishes her from early-twentieth-century anti-materialist 'vitalists' such as Hans Driesch, Ludwig Klages and Henri Bergson, whose teleological tendencies, such as their notion of entelechy, she explicitly rejects on the basis of their metaphysical overtones. See Langer, *Mind* I, p. 10–16.

160 Dawkins, *Selfish Gene*, p. x.

161 Langer, *Mind* I, p. 295.

162 Ibid., p. 307.

163 The question of whether or not the evolutionary process is the result of blind chance, in which humans emerged as the outcome of a myriad of contingencies, or of inevitable necessity, in which the 'great chain of being' evolved according to a divine or natural intelligent pre-planned design, is as much under debate now as it was in Darwin's time. Darwin himself, however, was reluctant to commit himself and preferred to delegate the question to metaphysics or theology. Historian of science John Hedley Brooke comments, 'Whereas [Stephen Jay] Gould will dwell on the accidents that have made human evolution possible, The Nobel Laureate Christian de Duve stresses the inexorability of the trends towards complexity and biodiversity. The really engaging point is that theists and atheists alike have repeatedly used both the contingencies and the determinate features of the world to defend their respective corners. Thinking one's way through this double paradox exposes the complexities of the issues.' John Hedley Brooke, 'Review Article of Keith Ward, God, Chance and Necessity (Oxford: One World, 1997); and Willem B. Drees, Religion, Science and Naturalism (Cambridge: CUP, 1997)', *Times Higher Education Supplement*, 7 February 1997.

164 Langer, *Mind* II, p. 241.

165 For experimental biologist Jane Oppenheimer, Langer was 'one of those rare practitioners of systematic philosophy who is able to master the literature of biology'. Jane Oppenheimer, 'Review of Mind: An Essay on Human Feeling, Vol. 3', *Quarterly Review of Biology* 60.3 (1985), p. 331.

166 John R. Searle, 'John R. Searle', in *A Companion to the Philosophy of Mind*, ed. Samuel Guttenplan (Oxford: Blackwell, 1994), pp. 544, 545, 550.

167 Ibid., p. 545.

168 Langer, *Mind* I, p. 360. For a theological defence of emergentism see Jacob Klapwijk, *Purpose in the Living World?: Creation and Emergent Evolution* (Cambridge: Cambridge University Press, 2008).

169 Andreas Weber, 'Feeling the Signs: The Origin of Meaning in the Biological Philosophy of Susanne K. Langer and Hans Jonas', *Sign System Studies* 30.1 (2002), pp. 183–99. Weber used the term 'biosemiotic' to refer to the work of the Chilean neuroscientist Francisco J. Varela. Varela, in turn, sometimes used the term 'neurophenomenology' to refer to his own field. This term would also be appropriate for Langer as it emphasizes the aspect of lived experience in the study of the mind. Francisco Varela, 'Neurophenomenology: A Methodological Remedy for the Hard Problem', *Journal of Consciousness Studies* 3.4 (1996), pp. 330–49.

170 Ann Berthoff suggests that the subtitle to the third volume should be 'Towards a Philosophical Anthropology'. Ann E. Berthoff, 'Susanne K. Langer and "The Odyssey of the Mind"', *Semiotica* 128.1–2 (2000), p. 9.

171 Berthoff highlights the scope of Langer's research by drawing attention to 'the appreciation [Langer] has had from Clifford Geertz, Arthur C. Danto, C. H. Waddington, L. C. Knights, [and] Thomas A. Sebeok – an anthropologist, an aesthetician, a biologist, a literary historian, [and] a semioticist.' Berthoff, 'Susanne K. Langer and "the Odyssey of the Mind"', p. 7. Sebeok (1920–2001) is one of the founders of the field of biosemiotics and zoosemiotics.

172 Langer, *Mind* III, p. ix.

173 Philosophers of religion and theologians who have been influenced by Langer's views on myth include Catholic thinkers Louis Dupré and Bernard Lonergan. See, for instance, Louis K. Dupré, *The Other Dimension: A Search for the Meaning of Religious Attitude* (Garden City, NY: Doubleday, 1972); and *Symbols of the Sacred* (Grand Rapids, MI: Eerdmans, 2000). For discussions of Langer's view of religious consciousness on theology and philosophy of religion, see Richard M. Liddy, 'Symbolic Consciousness: The Contribution of Susanne Langer', *Proceedings of the American Catholic Association* 44 (1971), pp. 94–110; and 'What Bernard Lonergan Learned from Susanne K. Langer', *Lonergan Workshop* 11 (1995), pp. 53–90. For a comparison between Langer's and Tillich's understandings of religion, see Robert Detweiler, 'Langer and Tillich: Two Backgrounds of Symbolic Thought', *The Personalist* 46.2 (April 1965), pp. 171–92. For an interesting comparison of Langer, Cassirer and Maritain in terms of their semiotics, see Thomas A. Sebeok, 'Ernst Cassirer, Jacques Maritain, and Susanne Langer', in *Semiotics* (Lanham, MD: University Press of America, 1990), pp. 389–97. Sebeok mentions that he has met all three thinkers personally.

174 Langer, *Mind* III, chapter 22, pp. 119–54.

175 Ibid., p. 139.

176 Ibid., p. 125.

177 Ibid., p. 132.

178 Langer, *Philosophy in a New Key*, pp. 40, 41.

179 Langer, *Mind* III, p. 142.

180 Langer, *Philosophy in a New Key*, p. 287.

181 Ibid.

182 Ibid., pp. 287, 288.

183　Susanne K. Langer, *Feeling and Form: A Theory of Art Developed from* Philosophy in a New Key (New York: Charles Scribner's Sons, 1953), p. 253.

184　Langer, *Mind* III, p. 201.

185　Richard Liddy, for instance, misrepresents Langer's position by suggesting that *Mind* implies 'the reduction of all "higher" human activities to feelings and feelings to electro-chemical events. Langer represented the whole empiricist tradition in philosophy.' Richard Liddy, *The Transforming Light: Intellectual Conversion in the Early Lonergan* (Collegeville, MN: Liturgical Press, 1993), p. xv.

186　Susanne K. Langer, *The Practice of Philosophy* (New York: Henry Holt, 1930), p. 143.

187　For examples of creative use of Langer's non-reductionist, naturalistic philosophy of mind for theology, see Susanne Heine, 'Die Erfüllung der Religion im philosophischen Denken: Susanne K. Langer's ontologisches Naturverständniss', in Cornelia Richter, ed., *Naturalisierung des Geistes und Symbolisierung des Fühlens: Susanne K. Langer im Gespräch der Forschung* (Marburg: Tectum-Verlag, 2008), pp. 177–207; and Charles Taliaferro and Jil Evans, *The Image in Mind: Theism, Naturalism, and the Imagination* (London: Bloomsbury, 2013). As the latter write in their introduction,

> We think images and the imagination have an integral and foundational purpose in our ordinary – not just extraordinary – beliefs and projects in science, philosophy, religion, and in common sense. Susanne Langer recognized this in the latter part of the twentieth century. Langer claimed that 'Religious thought, whether savage or civilized, operates primarily with images … [Images] only, originally made us aware of the wholeness and over-all form of entities, acts and facts in the world; and little though we may know it, only an image can hold us to a conception of a total phenomenon, against which we can measure the adequacy of the scientific terms wherewith we describe it' (Langer, 1988, xviii). Our book is the result of our desire to extend Langer's tantalizing proposal. (Taliaferro and Evans, *The Image in Mind*, p. 1)

188　Donald Dryden provides a wealth of examples of ways in which Langer has shed new light on problems and anticipated later developments in the sciences. As he writes,

> There are at least five major areas in which Susanne Langer's work … anticipated significant developments in the biological and psychological sciences, that have taken place since the publication of her first volume of *Mind* in 1967. The first is her belief that consciousness, or subjectivity, is the defining subject matter of psychology. The second is her attempt to develop a conceptual framework for grounding a theory of mind and consciousness in the biological sciences. The third is her proposal that a phenomenology of conscious experience (which she believed could be found in the arts) can serve as a unique source of insights into the phenomena of life and mind that we are seeking to understand in terms of the sciences. The fourth is her thesis that a perfectly continuous evolutionary history has given rise to a difference between human and animal mentality that is 'almost as great as the division between animals and plants' … And the fifth is her theory of imagination, which provides a bridge from the biological sciences to the study of human culture and the symbolic resources that support it. (Donald Dryden, 'The Philosopher as Prophet and as Visionary: Susanne Langer's Essay on Human Feeling in the Light of Subsequent Developments in the Sciences', *Journal of Speculative Philosophy* 21.1 (2007), p. 27)

189 Kuhn studied with Sheffer in 1945. According to J. C. Pinto de Oliveira, in a first (and unpublished) version of chapter 1 of *The Structure of Scientific Revolutions*, Kuhn explained his project as an attempt to model the image of science on the image of art. J. C. Pinto de Oliveira, 'Thomas Kuhn, the Image of Science and the Image of Art: The First Manuscript of *Structure*', *Perspectives on Science* 25.6 (November 2017), pp. 746–65. For an account of Sheffer's influence on Kuhn's theory of belief in science, see Juan Vicente Mayoral, 'Intensions, Belief and Science: Kuhn's Early Philosophical Outlook (1940–1945)', *Studies in History and Philosophy of Science* 40.2 (June 2009), pp. 175–84.

190 Langer, *Mind* I, pp. xxii, xxiii. As Donald Dryden observes, 'although this view of scientific change has become familiar to post-Kuhnian philosophers, Langer had worked out many of its details by 1930, with the publication of her first book.' Donald Dryden, 'Susanne K. Langer and American Philosophic Naturalism in the Twentieth Century', *Transactions of the Charles S. Peirce Society* 33.1 (Winter, 1997), p. 169.

191 Arthur Danto, Foreword, *Mind*, abridged edition by van den Heuvel, p. vi.

Conclusion

1 Robert Innis, *Susanne Langer in Focus: The Symbolic Mind* (Bloomington: Indiana University Press, 2009), p. 254.

2 Stefan Morawski, 'Art as Semblance.' *Journal of Philosophy* 81.11 (1984), p. 654

3 Alfred North Whitehead, *Science and the Modern World* (1925) (New York: Free Press, 1967), p. 156.

4 While not using the terms 'analytic' or 'continental', James Campbell suggests that Langer's tendency to combine careful logical and conceptual analysis with rich descriptions of human experience contributed to her rejection by those who considered these two traditions to be in tension. James Campbell, 'Langer's Understanding of Philosophy', *Transactions of the Charles S. Peirce Society* 33.1 (1 January 1997), p. 143.

5 Alfred North Whitehead, *Modes of Thought* (1938), Lecture Three, 'Understanding' (New York: Free Press, 1969), p. 236.

6 Ibid., p. 236.

7 Letter from Langer to Sushil Kumar Saxena, dated 30 April 1982. Quoted in Sushil Kumar Saxena, *Hindustani Sangeet and a Philosopher of Art: Music, Rhythm and Kathak Dance vis-à-vis Aesthetics of Susanne Langer* (New Delhi: D.K. Printworld, 2001), p. ix.

8 For a defence of art as a social practice, see Nicholas Wolterstorff, *Art Rethought: The Social Practices of Art* (Oxford: Oxford University Press, 2015).

9 Arthur Danto, for example, who studied with Langer at Columbia University and whose definition of art as embodied meaning shows a distinct Langerian influence, is known to have spoken very highly of her in private conversations but rarely mentions her in his books. See also Randall E. Auxier and Lewis Edwin Hahn, eds, *The Philosophy of Arthur Danto*, Library of Living Philosophers, Vol. 33 (Chicago, IL: Open Court, 2013).

10 Susanne K. Langer, *Mind: An Essay on Human Feeling*, Vol. III (Baltimore, MD: Johns Hopkins University Press, 1982), p. 201.

11 Alfred North Whitehead, *Adventures of Ideas* (Cambridge: Cambridge University Press, 1933).

Bibliography

I. Works By Langer

1. Books

The Practice of Philosophy. New York: Henry Holt, 1930.

An Introduction to Symbolic Logic. New York: Allen and Unwin, 1937. Second revised edition, New York, Dover, 1953.

Philosophy in a New Key: A Study in the Symbolism of Reason, Rite and Art. Cambridge, MA: Harvard University Press, 1942.

Editor with: Paul Henle and Horace M. Kallen, *Structure, Method, and Meaning: Essays in Honor of Henry M. Sheffer*. New York: Liberal Arts Press, 1951.

Feeling and Form: A Theory of Art Developed from Philosophy in a New Key. New York: Charles Scribner's, 1953.

Problems of Art: Ten Philosophical Lectures. New York: Charles Scribner's, 1957.

Editor of: *Reflections on Art: A Source Book of Writings by Artists, Critics, and Philosophers*. Baltimore, MD: Johns Hopkins University Press, 1958.

Philosophical Sketches. Baltimore: The Johns Hopkins Press, 1961.

Mind: An Essay on Human Feeling, Vol. 1. Baltimore, MD: Johns Hopkins University Press, 1967.

Mind: An Essay on Human Feeling, Vol. 2. Baltimore, MD: Johns Hopkins University Press, 1971.

Mind: An Essay on Human Feeling, Vol. 3. Baltimore, MD: Johns Hopkins University Press, 1982.

Mind: An Essay on Human Feeling, Vols 1–3. Abridged edition, edited by Gary A. van den Heuvel. Baltimore, MD: Johns Hopkins University Press, 1988.

2. Other works

The Cruise of the Little Dipper and Other Fairy Tales. Greenwich: New York Graphic Society, 1923.

'Review of *Festschrift für Paul Natorp. Zum Siebzigsten Geburtstage von Schülern und Freunden Gewidmet*'. *Journal of Philosophy* 21, no. 25 (4 December 1924): 695–7.

'Confusion of Symbols and Confusion of Logical Types'. *Mind*, New Series, 35, no. 138 (1 April 1926): 222–9.

'Form and Content: A Study in Paradox'. *Journal of Philosophy* 23, no. 16 (1926): 435–8.

A Logical Analysis of Meaning, doctoral thesis, Radcliffe College, 1926.

'A Logical Study of Verbs'. *Journal of Philosophy* 24, no. 5 (3 March 1927): 120–9.

'The Treadmill of Systematic Doubt'. *Journal of Philosophy* 26, no. 14 (4 July 1929): 379–84.

'Facts: The Logical Perspectives of the World'. *Journal of Philosophy* 30, no. 7 (30 March 1933): 178–87.

'Review of "Syllogisme catégorique et syllogisme hypothétique" by Jacques Picard (premier article)'. *Journal of Symbolic Logic* 1, no. 2 (June 1936): 63–4.

'On a Fallacy in "Scientific Fatalism"'. *International Journal of Ethics* 46, no. 4 (1 July 1936): 473–83.

'Review of *Whitehead's Theory of Knowledge* by John Blyth'. *Mind* 52, no. 205 (1943): 84–5.

'Review of *The Enjoyment of the Arts* by Max Schoen'. *Philosophy and Phenomenological Research* 5, no. 4 (June 1945): 608–11.

'On Cassirer's Theory of Language and Myth'. In *The Philosophy of Ernst Cassirer*, edited by Paul Arthur Schilpp, The Library of Living Philosophers, Vol. 6, 381–400. La Salle, IL: Open Court, 1949.

'The Principles of Creation in Art'. *Hudson Review* 2, no. 4 (1 January 1950): 515–34.

'The Primary Illusions and the Great Orders of Art'. *Hudson Review* 3, no. 2 (1 July 1950): 219–33.

With Eugene T. Gadol: 'The Deepening Mind: A Half-Century of American Philosophy'. *American Quarterly* 2, no. 2 (Summer 1950): 118–32.

'Abstraction in Science and Abstraction in Art'. In *Structure, Method and Meaning: Essays in Honor of Henry M. Sheffer*, edited by Paul Henle, Horace M. Kallen and Susanne K. Langer, 171–82. New York: Liberal Arts Press, 1951.

'In Praise of Common Sense: A Review of *The Concept of Mind* by Gilbert Ryle'. *The Hudson Review* 4 (1951): 146–9.

'Language and Thought'. In *Language Awareness: Readings for College Writers*, edited by Paul Eschholz, Alfred Rosa and Virginia Clark, 96–101. Boston, MA: Bedford/St. Martin's, [1953] 2000.

'A Footnote to Professor Tejera's Paper'. *Philosophy and Phenomenological Research* 23, no. 3 (1 March 1963): 432.

'Abstraction in Art'. *Journal of Aesthetics and Art Criticism* 22, no. 4 (1 July 1964): 379–92.

'Henry M. Sheffer 1883–1964'. *Philosophy and Phenomenological Research* 25, no. 2 (1964): 305–7.

'The Cultural Importance of the Arts'. *Journal of Aesthetic Education* 1, no. 1 (1 April 1966): 5–12.

II. Works on Langer

Agarwal, Bipin K. 'Langer, Hildebrand, and Space in Art'. *Journal of Aesthetics and Art Criticism* 31, no. 4 (1 July 1973): 513–16.

Ahlberg, Lars-Olof. 'Susanne Langer on Representation and Emotion in Music'. *British Journal of Aesthetics* 34, no. 1 (1994): 69–80.

Auxier, Randall E. 'Ernst Cassirer (1874–1945) & Suzanne Katherina (Knauth) Langer (1895–1985)'. In *Handbook of Whiteheadian Process Thought*, Vol. 2, edited by Michel Weber and Will Desmond, 554–72. Frankfurt: Ontos Verlag, 2009.

Auxier, Randall E. 'Susanne Langer on Symbols and Analogy: A Case of Misplaced Concreteness?' *Process Studies* 26 (1998): 86–106.

Baylis, Charles A. 'Book Review: *The Practice of Philosophy*'. *Journal of Philosophy* 28, no. 12 (1931): 326–9.

Baylis, Charles A. 'Review of: *An Introduction to Symbolic Logic*'. *Journal of Symbolic Logic* 3, no. 2 (1 June 1938): 83.

Berndtson, Arthur. 'Semblance, Symbol, and Expression in the Aesthetics of Susanne Langer'. *Journal of Aesthetics and Art Criticism* 14, no. 4 (1 June 1956): 489–502.

Berthoff, Ann E. 'Susanne K. Langer and "The Odyssey of the Mind"'. *Semiotica* 128, no. 1–2 (January 2000): 1–34.

Berthoff, Ann E. 'Susanne K. Langer and the Process of Feeling'. In *The Mysterious Barricades: Language and Its Limits*, pp. 112–24. Toronto: University of Toronto Press, 1999.

Bertocci, Peter A. 'Susanne K. Langer's Theory of Feeling and Mind'. *Review of Metaphysics* 23, no. 3 (1 March 1970): 527–51.

Binkley, Timothy. 'Langer's Logical and Ontological Modes'. *Journal of Aesthetics and Art Criticism* 28, no. 4 (1 July 1970): 455–64.

Black, David W. 'The Vichian Elements in Susanne Langer's Thought'. *New Vico Studies* 3 (1985): 113–18.

Brentari, Carlo. *La Nascita Della Coscienza: Simbolica : L'antropologia Filosofica Di Susanne Langer*. Trento: Università degli studi di Trento, 2007.

Browning, Margaret M. 'Neuroscience and Imagination: The Relevance of Susanne Langer's Work to Psychoanalytic Theory'. *Psychoanalytic Quarterly* 75, no. 4 (October 2006): 1131–59.

Bufford, Samuel. 'Susanne Langer's Two Philosophies of Art'. *Journal of Aesthetics and Art Criticism* 31, no. 1 (1 October 1972): 9–20.

Campbell, James. 'Langer's Understanding of Philosophy'. *Transactions of the Charles S. Peirce Society* 33, no. 1 (1 January 1997): 133–47.

Carter, Curtis L. 'After Cassirer: Art and Aesthetic Symbols in Langer and Goodman'. In *The Philosophy of Ernst Cassirer: A Novel Assessment*, edited by J. Tyler Friedman and Sebastian Luft, 401–18. Berlin: Walter de Gruyter, 2015.

Carter, Curtis L. 'Langer and Hofstadter on Painting and Language: A Critique'. *Journal of Aesthetics and Art Criticism* 32, no. 3 (1 April 1974): 331–42.

Colapietro, Vincent. 'Susanne Langer on Artistic Creativity and Creations'. In *Semiotics*, edited by John Deely and C. W. Spinks, 3–12. New York: Peter Lang, 1997.

Colapietro, Vincent. 'Symbols and the Evolution of Mind: Susanne Langer's Final Bequest to Semiotics'. In *Semiotics*, edited by John Deely and C. W. Spinks, 61–70. New York: Peter Lang, 1998.

Curran, Trisha. *A New Note on the Film: A Theory of Film Criticism Derived from Susanne K. Langer's Philosophy of Art*. New York: Arno Press, 1980.

Danto, Arthur C. 'Foreword to *Mind: An Essay on Human Feeling* by Susanne K. Langer'. In *Mind: An Essay on Human Feeling by Susanne K. Langer*, edited by Gary Van Den Heuvel. Baltimore, MD: Johns Hopkins University Press, 1988.

Danto, Arthur C. 'Mind as Feeling; Form as Presence; Langer as Philosopher'. *Journal of Philosophy* 81, no. 11 (1 November 1984): 641–7.

Demartis, Lucia. *L'estetica Simbolica Di Susanne Katherina Langer*. Italy: Centro internazionale studi di estetica, 2004.

Dengerink Chaplin, Adrienne. 'Feeling the Body in Art: Embodied Cognition and Aesthetics in Mark Johnson and Susanne K. Langer'. *Sztuka I Filozofia/Art and Philosophy*, no. 48 (2016): 5–11.

Dengerink Chaplin, Adrienne. 'Susanne Langer (1895–1985)'. In *Vrouwelijke Filosofen: Een Historisch Overzicht*, edited by Carolien Ceton, 369–74. Amsterdam: Uitgeverij Atlas, 2012.

Detweiler, Robert. 'Langer and Tillich: Two Backgrounds of Symbolic Thought'. *The Personalist* 46, no. 2 (April 1965): 171–92.

Dryden, Donald. 'The Philosopher as Prophet and Visionary: Susanne Langer's Essay on Human Feeling in the Light of Subsequent Developments in the Sciences'. *Journal of Speculative Philosophy* 21, no. 1 (2007): 27–43.

Dryden, Donald. 'Susanne K. Langer and American Philosophic Naturalism in the Twentieth Century'. *Transactions of the Charles S. Peirce Society* 33, no. 1 (1 January 1997): 161–82.

Dryden, Donald. 'Susanne Langer and William James: Art and the Dynamics of the Stream of Consciousness'. *Journal of Speculative Philosophy*, New Series, 15, no. 4 (1 January 2001): 272–85.

Dryden, Donald. 'Susanne K. Langer 1895–1985'. In *American Philosophers before 1950*, edited by P. B. Dematteis and L. B. McHenry, 189–99. *Dictionary of Literary Biography* 270. Farmington Hills, MI: Gale, 2003.

Dryden, Donald. 'Whitehead's Influence on Susanne Langer's Conception of Living Form'. *Process Studies* 26, no. 1–2 (1997): 62–85.

Feigl, Herbert. 'Review of: *An Introduction to Symbolic Logic*'. *American Journal of Psychology* 51, no. 4 (October 1938): 781.

Felappi, Giulia. 'Susanne Langer and the Woeful World of Facts'. *Journal for the History of Analytical Philosophy* 5, no. 2 (2017): 38–50.

Gardner, Howard. 'Philosophy in a New Key Revisited: An Appreciation of Susanne Langer'. In *Art, Mind, and the Brain: A Cognitive Approach to Creativity*, 48–54. New York: Basic Books, 1982.

Ghosh, Ranjan K. *Aesthetic Theory and Art: A Study in Susanne K. Langer*. Delhi: Ajanta Books International, 1979.

Ghosh, Ranjan K. 'The Alleged Duality in Susanne Langer's Aesthetics'. *Indian Philosophical Quarterly* 7 (July 1980): 501–11.

Ghosh, Ranjan K. 'Susanne K Langer's Aesthetics of Painting and Some Indian Art'. *Indian Philosophical Quarterly* 4 (April 1977): 297–304.

Gill, Jerry H. 'Langer, Language, and Art'. *International Philosophical Quarterly* 34, no. 4 (December 1994): 419–32.

Guczolski, Krzysztof. 'Phenomenology and Analytic Aesthetics of Music: On the Views of Susanne Langer and Roman Ingarden'. *Nordisk Estetisk Tidskrift* 23 (2001): 27–38.

Guczolski, Krzysztof. *Znaczenie muzyki: znaczenia w muzyce: próba ogólnej teorii na tle estetyki Susanne Langer*. Krakow: Musica Iagellonica, 1999.

Gulick, Walter B. 'Polanyi and Langer: Toward a Reconfigured Theory of Knowing and Meaning'. *Tradition and Discovery: The Polanyi Society Periodical* 36, no. 1 (2010): 21–37.

Hagberg, Garry. 'Art and the Unsayable: Langer's Tractarian Aesthetics'. *British Journal of Aesthetics* 24, no. 4 (1984): 325–40.

Hansen, Forest. 'Langer's Expressive Form: An Interpretation'. *Journal of Aesthetics and Art Criticism* 27, no. 2 (Winter 1968): 165–70.

Hansen, Forest. 'Review of: *Mind: An Essay on Human Feeling* I'. *Notes* 24, no. 4 (1968): 704.

Hart, Richard E. 'Langer's Aesthetics of Poetry'. *Transactions of the Charles S. Peirce Society* 33, no. 1 (1 January 1997): 183–200.

Heine, Susanne. 'Die Erfüllung der Religion im philosophischen Denken: Susanne K. Langer's ontologisches Naturverständniss'. In *Naturalisierung des Geistes und Symbolisierung des Fühlens: Susanne K. Langer im Gespräch der Forschung*, edited by Cornelia Richter, 177–207. Marburg: Tectum-Verlag, 2008.

Innis, Robert E. 'Art, Symbol and Consciousness: A Polanyi Gloss on Susan Langer and Nelson Goodman'. *International Philosophical Quarterly* 17 (December 1977): 455–76.

Innis, Robert E. 'Between Articulation and Symbolization: Framing Polanyi and Langer'. *Tradition and Discovery: The Polanyi Society Periodical* 36, no. 1 (2010): 8–20.

Innis, Robert E. 'The Making of the Literary Symbol: Taking Note of Langer'. *Semiotica*, no. 165 (19 June 2007): 91–106.

Innis, Robert E. 'Peirce's Categories and Langer's Aesthetics: On Dividing the Semiotic Continuum'. *Cognitio* 14, no. 1 (January/June 2013): 35–50.

Innis, Robert E. 'Placing Langer's Philosophical Project'. *Journal of Speculative Philosophy* 21, no. 1 (2007): 4–15.

Innis, Robert E. *Susanne Langer in Focus: The Symbolic Mind*. Bloomington: Indiana University Press, 2009.

Innis, Robert E. 'Symposium on Susanne K. Langer: Introduction'. *Journal of Speculative Philosophy* 21, no. 1 (2007): 1–3.

Jeunhomme, J. 'The Symbolic Philosophy of Susanne K. Langer'. *Neue Zeitschrift Fur Systematische Theologie Und Religionsphilosophie* 27, no. 1 (1 January 1985): 159–76.

Johnson, James R. 'The Unknown Langer: Philosophy from the New Key to the Trilogy of Mind'. *Journal of Aesthetic Education* 27, no. 1 (April 1993): 63–73.

Julliard, Kell N., and Gary Van Den Heuvel. 'Susanne K. Langer and the Foundations of Art Therapy'. *Art Therapy* 16, no. 3 (1999): 112–20.

King, Kenneth. 'Battery: A Tribute to Susanne K. Langer'. *Dance Magazine* 50 (1976): 23–4.

Kominek-Karolak, Maria. 'Hermeneutyka muzyki Susanne K. Langer'. *Sztuka I filozofia/ Art and Philosophy* 48 (2016): 46–55.

Kösters, Barbara. *Gefühl, Abstraktion, symbolische Transformation: zu Susanne Langers Philosophie des Lebendigen*. Frankfurt am Main: Peter Lang, 1993.

Kruse, Felicia E. 'Emotion in Musical Meaning: A Peircean Solution to Langer's Dualism'. *Transactions of the Charles S. Peirce Society* 41, no. 4 (1 October 2005): 762–78.

Kruse, Felicia E. 'Vital Rhythm and Temporal Form in Langer and Dewey'. *Journal of Speculative Philosophy* 21, no. 1 (2007): 16–26.

Kulbyte, Agne. 'Susanne K. Langer as a Romantic Thinker'. *Sztuka I Filozofia/Art and Philosophy* 48 (2016): 30–8.

Lachmann, Rolf. 'From Metaphysics to Art and Back: The Relevance of Susanne K. Langer's Philosophy for Process Metaphysics'. *Process Studies* 26, no. 1–2 (January 1998): 107–25.

Lachmann, Rolf. *Susanne K. Langer: die lebendige Form menschlichen Fühlens und Verstehens*. München: W. Fink, 2000.

Lachmann, Rolf. 'Susanne K. Langer's Notes on Whitehead's Course on Philosophy of Nature'. *Process Studies* 26, no. 1–2 (1997): 126–50.

Lang, Berel. 'Langer's Arabesque and the Collapse of the Symbol'. *Review of Metaphysics* 16, no. 2 (1962): 349–65.

Lassner, Phyllis. 'Bridging Composition and Women's Studies: The Work of Ann E. Berthoff and Susanne K. Langer'. *Journal of Teaching Writing* 10, no. 1 (1991): 21–37.

Liddy, Richard M. 'Susanne K. Langer's Philosophy of Mind'. *Transactions of the Charles S. Peirce Society* 33, no. 1 (1 January 1997): 149–60.

Liddy, Richard M. 'Symbolic Consciousness: The Contribution of Susanne K. Langer'. *Proceedings of the American Catholic Philosophical Association* 45 (1971): 94–103.

Liddy, Richard M. 'What Bernard Lonergan Learned from Susanne K. Langer'. *Lonergan Workshop* 11 (1995): 53–90.

Lord, James. 'Susanne Langer: A Lady Seeking Answers'. *New York Times Book Review*, 26 May 1968.

Lyon, Arabella. 'Susanne K Langer and the Rebirth of Rhetoric'. In *Reclaiming Rhetorica: Women in the Rhetorical Tradition*, edited by Andrea Lunsford, 266–84. Pittsburgh: University of Pittsburgh Press, 1995.

Margolis, Joseph. 'Review of: *Feeling and Form*'. *Journal of Philosophy* 52, no. 11 (26 May 1955): 291–6.

McDaniel, Kris. 'Ontology and Philosophical Methodology in the Early Susanne Langer'. In *Innovations in the History of Analytical Philosophy*, edited by Sandra Lapointe and Christopher Pinnock, 265–98. London: Palgrave Macmillan, 2017.

McDermott, John J. 'Symposium on Susanne K. Langer: A Foreword'. *Transactions of the Charles S. Peirce Society* 33, no. 1 (January 1997): 131–2.

Mcgandy, Michael. 'Communion and Its Limits: Expression and Communication in Susanne Langer's Aesthetics'. *Conference: A Journal of Philosophy and Theory* 4, no. 1 (April 1993): 21–35.

Morawski, Stefan. 'Art as Semblance'. *Journal of Philosophy* 81, no. 11 (1 November 1984): 654–63.

Nagel, Ernest. 'Review of: *Philosophy in a New Key*'. *Journal of Philosophy* 40, no. 12 (10 June 1943): 323–9.

Nelson, Beatrice K. 'Susanne K. Langer's Conception of "Symbol" – Making Connections through Ambiguity'. *Journal of Speculative Philosophy*, New Series 8, no. 4 (1 January 1994): 277–96.

Neumayr, Agnes. *Politik Der Gefühle: Susanne K. Langer Und Hannah Arendt*. Innsbruck: Innsbruck University Press, 2009.

Oppenheimer, Jane. 'Review of: *Mind: An Essay on Human Feeling* I'. *Quarterly Review of Biology* 49, no. 3 (1974): 279.

Oppenheimer, Jane. 'Review of: *Mind: An Essay on Human Feeling* III'. *Quarterly Review of Biology* 60, no. 3 (1985): 331–2.

Osborne, Harold. 'Susanne K. Langer's *Mind: An Essay on Human Feeling* Vol. I: An Essay Review'. *Journal of Aesthetic Education* 18, no. 1 (Spring 1984): 89–91.

Percy, Walker. 'Symbol as Need'. *Thought* 29 no. 3 (1954): 381–90. Reprinted in *The Message in the Bottle*, 288–97. New York: Farrar, Strauss and Giroux, 1981.

Price, Kingsley B. '*Philosophy in a New Key*: An Interpretation'. *Philosophy of Music Education Review* 1, no. 1 (1993): 34–43.

Read, Herbert. ' "Describing the Indescribable", Review of: *Mind: An Essay on Human Feeling* Vol. I'. 32. *Saturday Review*, 15 July 1967.

Reichling, Mary. 'Susanne Langer's Concept of Secondary Illusion in Music and Art'. *Journal of Aesthetic Education* 29, no. 4 (1 December 1995): 39–51.

Reichling, Mary. 'Susanne Langer's Theory of Symbolism: An Analysis and Extension'. *Philosophy of Music Education Review* 1, no. 1 (1 April 1993): 3–17.

Reichling, Mary. 'A Woman Ahead of Her Time: The Langer Legacy'. *Philosophy of Music Education Review* 6, no. 1 (1 April 1998): 12–21.

Reid, Louis Arnaud. 'New Notes on Langer'. *British Journal of Aesthetics* 8, no. 4 (1 October 1968): 353–8.

Reid, Louis Arnaud. 'Review of: *Philosophy in a New Key*'. *Mind*, New Series, 54, no. 213 (1 January 1945): 73–83.

Reid, Louis Arnaud. 'Susanne Langer and Beyond'. *British Journal of Aesthetics* 5, no. 4 (1965): 357–67.

Reimer, Bennett. 'Langer on the Arts as Cognitive'. *Philosophy of Music Education Review* 1, no. 1 (1 April 1993): 44–60.

Richter, Cornelia. 'The Body of Susanne K. Langer's Mind'. In *Embodiment in Cognition and Culture*, edited by John Michael Krois, 107–25. Amsterdam: John Benjamins, 2007.

Richter, Cornelia, ed., *Naturalisierung Des Geistes Und Symbolisierung Des Fühlens: Susanne K. Langer Im Gespräch Der Forschung*. Marburg: Tectum-Verlag, 2008.

Sargeant, Winthrop. 'Philosopher in a New Key'. *New Yorker*, 3 December 1960.

Sauer, Martina. 'Ikonologie und formale Ästhetik: eine neue Einheit. Ein Beitrag zur aktuellen Debatte in Kunstwissenschaft und Kunstphilosophie im Anschluss an die (Bild-)Akt-Theorien Susanne K. Langers und John M. Krois'. *Sztuka I filozofia/Art and Philosophy* 48 (2016): 12–29.

Saxena, Sushil. *Hindustani Sangeet and a Philosopher of Art: Music, Rhythm, and Kathak Dance Vis-À-Vis Aesthetics of Susanne K. Langer*. New Delhi: D. K. Printworld, 2001.

Schaper, Eva. 'The Art Symbol'. *British Journal of Aesthetics* 4, no. 3 (1 July 1964): 228–39.

Scholz, Bernhard F. 'Discourse and Intuition in Susanne Langer's Aesthetics of Literature'. *Journal of Aesthetics and Art Criticism* 31, no. 2 (1 December 1972): 215–26.

Schultz, William. *Cassirer and Langer on Myth: An Introduction*. London: Routledge, 2000.

Sebeok, Thomas. 'Ernst Cassirer, Jacques Maritain, and Susanne Langer'. In *Semiotics*, edited by John Deeley, 389–97. Lanham: University Press of America, 1990.

Sebeok, Thomas. 'From Vico to Cassirer to Langer'. In *Vico and Anglo-American Science: Philosophy and Writing*, edited by Marcel Danesi, 159–70. Berlin: De Gruyter, 1995.

Shelley, Cameron. 'Consciousness, Symbols and Aesthetics: A Just-so Story and Its Implications in Susanne Langer's *Mind: An Essay on Human Feeling*'. *Philosophical Psychology* 11, no. 1 (1 March 1998): 45–66.

Shiner, Roger A. 'Langer, Suzanne Katherina Knauth (1895–1985)'. In *The Dictionary of Modern American Philosophers*, edited by John R. Shook, 1412–1416. Bristol: Thoemmes Continuum, 2005.

Slattery, Mary Francis. 'Looking Again at Susanne K Langer's Expressionism'. *British Journal of Aesthetics* 27, no. 3 (20 June 1987): 247–58.

Stebbing, L. Susan. 'Review of: *An Introduction to Symbolic Logic* by Susanne K Langer and *The Principles of Mathematics* by Bertrand Russell'. *Philosophy* 13, no. 52 (1 October 1938): 481–3.

Stodelle, Ernestine. 'A Dancer's Philosopher: Suzanne K. Langer'. *Dance Observer* (1963), pp. 69–70.

van der Schoot, Albert. 'Kivy and Langer on Expressiveness in Music'. *Sztuka I Filozofia/ Art and Philosophy* 48 (2016): 39–45.

van der Tuin, Iris. 'Bergson before Bergsonism: Traversing 'Bergson's Failing' in Susanne K. Langer's Philosophy of Art'. *Journal of French and Francophone Philosophy* 24, no. 2 (1 December 2016): 176–202.

van Roo, William A. 'Symbol According to Cassirer and Langer, Part II: Langer's Theory of Art'. *Gregorianum* 53 (1972): 615–77.

Varela, Charles, and Lawrence Ferrara. 'The Nagel Critique and Langer's Critical Response'. *Journal for the Anthropological Study of Human Movement* 2, no. 2 (1982): 99–111.

Weber, Andreas. 'Feeling the Signs: The Origins of Meaning in the Biological Philosophy of Susanne K Langer and Hans Jonas'. *Sign Systems Studies* 30, no. 1 (2002): 183–99.

Wehr, Wesley. 'Elizabeth Bishop & Suzanne K. Langer: A Conversation'. *Harvard Review* 3 (1 January 1993): 128–30.

Weitz, Morris. 'Review of: *Mind: An Essay on Human Feeling* I'. *Philosophical Review* 78, no. 4 (1969): 525.

Welsh, Paul. 'Discursive and Presentational Symbols'. *Mind*, New Series, 64, no. 254 (1 April 1955): 181–99.

Whyte, L. L. 'Review of: *Philosophy in a New Key*'. *British Journal for the Philosophy of Science* 2, no. 5 (1 May 1951): 68–71.

Wollheim, Richard. 'Review of: *Feeling and Form*'. *Burlington Magazine* 97, no. 633 (1 December 1955): 400–1.

Wollheim, Richard. 'Review of: *Problems of Art*'. *New Statesman and Nation*, 15 December 1957.

Yob, Iris M. 'The Form of Feeling'. *Philosophy of Music Education Review* 1, no. 1 (1 April 1993): 18–32.

Zuidgeest, Marja. 'Antropomorfisme En Wetenschap: Kritische Beschouwingen van Enkele Aspecten van Susanne Langer's Theorie van het Gevoel' (Anthropomorphism and Science: Critical Observations on Some Aspects of Susanne Langer's Theory of Feeling). *Algemeen Nederlands Tijdschrift Voor Wijsbegeerte* 71, no. 3 (July 1979): 173–88.

III. Other Works

Alston, William P. *Philosophy of Language*. Englewood Cliffs, NJ: Prentice-Hall, 1968.

Argan, Giulio Carlo. 'Ideology and Iconology'. *Critical Inquiry* 2 (Winter 1975): 297–305.

Ashley, Montague M. F. 'Cassirer on Mythological Thinking'. In *The Philosophy of Ernst Cassirer*, edited by Arthur Schilpp, The Library of Living Philosophers, 379–400. La Salle, IL: Open Court, 1949.

Auxier, Randall E. 'Reading Whitehead'. In *Whitehead: The Algebra of Metaphysics*, edited by Ronny Desmet and Michel Weber, 59–90. Louvain-la-Neuve: Les Editions Chromatika, 2010.

Auxier, Randall E., and Lewis Edwin Hahn, eds. *The Philosophy of Arthur Danto*, Library of Living Philosophers, Vol. 33. Chicago, IL: Open Court, 2013.

Auxier, Randall E., and Gary L. Herstein, *The Quantum of Explanation: Whitehead's Radical Empiricism*, Routledge Studies in American Philosophy. New York: Routledge and Kegan Paul, 2017.

Ayer, A. J. *Language, Truth, and Logic*. London: Gollancz, 1946.

Ayer, A. J. *Wittgenstein*. New York: Random House, 1985.

Baird, D., R. I. G. Hughes and Alfred Nordmann, eds. *Heinrich Hertz: Classical Physicist, Modern Philosopher*. Dordrecht: Kluwer Academic, 1998.

Balashov, Yuri, and Alexander Rosenberg, eds. *Philosophy of Science: Contemporary Readings*. London: Routledge, 2002.

Barash, Jeffrey Andrew. *The Symbolic Construction of Reality: The Legacy of Ernst Cassirer*. Chicago, IL: University of Chicago Press, 2008.

Barrett, Wendell. 'The Relations of Radcliffe College with Harvard'. *Harvard Monthly* 29, no. 1 (October 1899), pp. 8, 9.

Barthes, Roland. *Elements of Semiology*. Translated by Annette Lavers and Colin Smith. New York: Hill and Wang, 1967.

Bayer, Thora Ilin. 'Art as Symbolic Form: Cassirer on the Educational Value of Art'. *Journal of Aesthetic Education* 40, no. 4 (1 December 2006): 51–64.

Bayer, Thora Ilin. *Cassirer's Metaphysics of Symbolic Forms: A Philosophical Commentary.* New Haven, CT: Yale University Press, 2001.

Beaney, M. 'Susan Stebbing and the Early Reception of Logical Empiricism in Britain'. In *Influences on the Aufbau*, edited by C. Damböck, 233–56. Vienna Circle Institute Yearbook, Vol. 18. Cham: Springer, 2016.

Bearn, Gordon C. F. *Waking to Wonder: Wittgenstein's Existential Investigations.* Albany: State University of New York Press, 1997.

Beever, Allan. 'The Arousal Theory Again?' *British Journal of Aesthetics* 38, no. 1 (January 1998): 82–90.

Berlin, Isaiah. *Concepts and Categories: Philosophical Essays*, edited by Henry Hardy. London: Pimlico, 1999.

Birtwistle, Graham. *Living Art: Asger Jorn's Comprehensive Theory of Art between Helhesten and Cobra (1946–1949).* Utrecht: Reflex, 1986.

Bloomfield, Julia, ed. *Empathy, Form, and Space: Problems in German Aesthetics, 1873–1893.* Translated by Harry Francis Mallgrave and Eleftherios Ikonomou. Santa Monica, CA: Getty Center for the History of Art and the Humanities, 1994.

Blumberg, Albert E., and Herbert Feigl. 'Logical Positivism: A New Movement in European Philosophy'. *Journal of Philosophy* 28, no. 11 (1931): 281–96.

Bowman, Wayne C. *Philosophical Perspectives on Music.* New York: Oxford University Press, 1998.

Brooke, John Hedley. 'Review Article of Keith Ward, *God, Chance and Necessity* (Oxford: One world, 1997); and Willem B. Drees, *Religion, Science and Naturalism* (Cambridge: CUP, 1997)'. *Times Higher Education Supplement* 7 (February 1997).

Bühler, Karl. *Theory of Language: The Representational Function of Language.* Translated by Donald Fraser Goodwin, *Foundations of Semiotics* 25. Amsterdam: John Benjamins [1935] 1990.

Burke, Christopher, and Matthew Eve, eds. *Otto Neurath: From Hieroglyphics to Isotype: A Visual Autobiography.* London: Hyphen Press [1945] 2010.

Canales, Jimena. *The Physicist and the Philosopher: Einstein, Bergson, and the Debate That Changed Our Understanding of Time.* Princeton, NJ: Princeton University Press, 2015.

Carnap, Rudolf. *Der logische Aufbau der Welt* (1928). Hamburg: Felix Meiner Verlag, 2017.

Carnap, Rudolf. 'Die physikalische Sprache als Universalsprache der Wissenschaft'. *Erkenntnis* 2, no. 1 (1931): 432–65.

Carnap, Rudolf. 'Intellectual Autobiography'. In *The Philosophy of Rudolf Carnap*, edited by Paul Arthur Schilpp, The Library of Living Philosophers, Vol. 11, 1–84. La Salle, IL: Open Court, 1963.

Carnap, Rudolf. *The Logical Structure of the World and Pseudo Problems in Philosophy.* Translated by Rolf A. George. La Salle, IL: Open Court, 2005.

Carnap, Rudolf. *Philosophy and Logical Syntax.* Bristol: Thoemmes Press [1935] 1996.

Carnap, Rudolf. 'Replies and Systematic Expositions'. In *The Philosophy of Rudolf Carnap*, edited by Paul A. Schilpp, The Library of Living Philosophers, Vol. 11, 859–1016. Chicago, IL: Open Court, 1963.

Cassirer, Ernst. 'Axel Hägerström: Eine Studie Zur Schwedischen Philosophie Der Gegenwart'. In *Ernst Cassirer: Gesammelte Werke Hamburger Ausgabe Volume 21, Axel Hägerström. Thorilds Stellung in Der Geistesgeschichte Des 18. Jahrhunderts: Eine Studie Zur Schwedischen Philosophie Der Gegenwart*, edited by Birgit Recki. Hamburg: Meiner Verlag, 1998.

Cassirer, Ernst. *Die Idee der republikanischen Verfassung: Rede zur Verfassungsfeier am 11. August 1928.* Hamburg: De Gruyter, 1929.

Cassirer, Ernst. *Ernst Cassirer: Ausgewählter wissenschaftlicher Briefwechsel, Nachgelassene Manuskripte und Texte*, Vol. 18, edited by John Michael Krois. Hamburg: Felix Meiner, 2009.

Cassirer, Ernst. *Ernst Cassirer: The Warburg Years (1919–1933): Essays on Language, Art, Myth, and Technology*, edited by Steve G. Lofts and Antonio Calcagno, 2014.

Cassirer, Ernst. *An Essay on Man: An Introduction to a Philosophy of Human Culture*. New Haven, CT: Yale University Press [1944] 1992.

Cassirer, Ernst. *Freiheit und Form: Studien zur deutschen Geistesgeschichte*. Berlin: Bruno Cassirer, 1916.

Cassirer, Ernst. *Language and Myth*. Translated by Susanne K. Langer. New York: Dover, 2012.

Cassirer, Ernst. *The Myth of the State*. New Haven, CT: Yale University Press, 2013.

Cassirer, Ernst. *The Philosophy of the Enlightenment*. Princeton, NJ: Princeton University Press, 1951.

Cassirer, Ernst. *The Philosophy of Symbolic Forms, Vol. 1: Language*. New Haven, CT: Yale University Press, 1955.

Cassirer, Ernst. *The Philosophy of Symbolic Forms, Vol. 2: Mythical Thought*. New Haven, CT: Yale University Press, 1955.

Cassirer, Ernst. *The Philosophy of Symbolic Forms, Vol. 3: The Phenomenology of Knowledge*. New Haven, CT: Yale University Press, 1957.

Cassirer, Ernst. *The Philosophy of Symbolic Forms, Vol. 4: The Metaphysics of Symbolic Forms*, edited by John Michael Krois and Donald Philip Verene. New Haven, CT: Yale University Press, 1996.

Cassirer, Ernst. *Rousseau, Kant, Goethe: Two Essays*. Translated by Paul Oskar Kristeller, Jemas Gutmann and John Hermann Randall. New York: Harper & Row, 1963.

Cassirer, Ernst. *Substance and Function, and Einstein's Theory of Relativity*, edited by William Curtis Swabey and Marie Collins Swabey. Chicago, IL: Open Court, 1923.

Cassirer, Ernst. *Symbol, Myth, and Culture: Essays and Lectures of Ernst Cassirer 1935–1945*, edited by Donald Phillip Verene. New Haven, CT: Yale University Press, 1979.

Cassirer, Ernst. *Zur Einsteinschen Relativitätstheorie: Erkenntnistheoretische Betrachtungen*, edited by Reinold Schmücker. Hamburg: Felix Meiner, 2001.

Cassirer, Toni. *Mein Leben mit Ernst Cassirer*. Hildesheim: Gerstenberg, 1981.

Chemero, Anthony. *Radical Embodied Cognitive Science*. Cambridge: MIT Press, 2011.

Cloots, André. 'The Metaphysical Significance of Whitehead's Creativity'. *Process Studies* 30, no. 1 (Spring/Summer 2000): 36–54.

Colapietro, Vincent. 'Acknowledgment, Responsibility, and Innovation: A Response to Robert Innis and Walter Gulick'. *Tradition and Discovery: The Polanyi Society Periodical* 36, no. 1 (2010): 38–41.

Colapietro, Vincent. 'Reading as Experience'. *Transactions of the Charles S. Peirce Society* 34, no. 4 (1997): 861–8.

Collingwood, R. G. *The Principles of Art* [1938]. Oxford: Clarendon Press, 1958.

Conant, James. 'Must We Show What We Cannot Say?' In *The Sense of Stanley Cavell*, edited by Richard Fleming and Michael Payne, 242–83. Lewisburg: Bucknell University Press, 1989.

Conant, James, and Sean C. Stidd. 'Two Conceptions of Die Überwindung Der Metaphysik: Carnap and Early Wittgenstein'. In *Wittgenstein in America*, edited by Timothy McCarthy. Oxford: Oxford University Press, 2001.

Courtney, Richard. 'On Langer's Dramatic Illusion'. *Journal of Aesthetics and Art Criticism* 29, no. 1 (1970): 11–20.

Creath, Richard, ed. *Dear Carnap, Dear Van: The Quine-Carnap Correspondence and Related Work*. Berkeley: University of California Press, 1991.

Crick, Francis. *Life Itself: Its Origin and Nature*. London: Macdonald, 1981.

Crowther, Paul. 'More than Ornament: The Significance of Riegl'. *Art History* 17, no. 3 (1994): 482–94.

Damasio, Antonio. *Descartes' Error: Emotion, Reason, and the Human Brain*. New York: Avon Books, 1994.

Damasio, Antonio. *The Feeling of What Happens: Body and Emotion in the Making of Consciousness*. San Diego: A Harvest Book, Harcourt, 1999.

Davies, Stephen. 'Is Music a Language of the Emotions?' *British Journal of Aesthetics* 23, no. 3 (20 June 1983): 222–33.

Dawkins, Richard. *The Extended Phenotype*. Oxford: W. H. Freeman, 1982.

Dawkins, Richard. *The Selfish Gene*. London: Granada, 1978.

Deacon, Terence W. *The Symbolic Species: The Co-Evolution of Languages and the Brain*. London: Penguin, 1997.

Dengerink Chaplin, Adrienne. 'Art and Embodiment: Biological and Phenomenological Contributions to Understanding Beauty and the Aesthetic'. *Contemporary Aesthetics* 3 (2005). www.contempaesthetics.org/newvolume/pages/article.php?articleID=291.

Dengerink Chaplin, Adrienne. 'Phenomenology: Sartre and Merleau-Ponty'. In *The Routledge Companion to Aesthetics*, 2nd edition, edited by Berys Gaut and Dominic McIver Lopes, 159–71. London: Routledge, 2005.

Derrida, Jacques. *Of Grammatology*. Translated by Gayatri Chakravorty Spivak. Baltimore, MD: Johns Hopkins University Press, 2016.

Desmet, Ronny. 'The Serpent in Russell's Paradise'. In *New Perspectives on Mathematical Practices: Essays in Philosophy and History of Mathematics*, edited by Bart van Kerkhove. New Jersey: World Scientific, 2007.

Desmet, Ronny. 'Whitehead and the British Reception of Einstein's Relativity'. *Process Studies Supplements* 11 (2007). ctr4process.org/our-work/publications/.

Desmet, Ronny. 'Whitehead's Relativity'. In *Whitehead: The Algebra of Metaphysics*, edited by Ronny Desmet and Michael Weber, 365–73. Brussel: Chromatika, 2010.

Diamond, Cora. 'Throwing Away the Ladder'. In *The Realistic Spirit: Wittgenstein, Philosophy and the Mind*, edited by Cora Diamond, 179–204. Cambridge: MIT Press, 2011.

Dickie, George. *Introduction to Aesthetics: An Analytical Approach*. New York: Oxford University Press, 1997.

Dickson, Eric. 'Cassirer, Whitehead, and Bergson: Explaining the Development of the Symbol'. *Process Studies* 32, no. 1 (Spring–Summer 2003): 79–93.

Domdenh-Romluc, Komarine, ed. *Wittgenstein and Merleau-Ponty*. New York: Routledge, 2017.

Donnellan, Keith S. 'Reference and Definite Descriptions'. In *Naming, Necessity, and Natural Kinds*, edited by Stephen P. Schwartz, 42–65. Ithaca, NY: Cornell University Press, 1977.

Donnell-Kotrozo, Carol. 'Representation and Expression: A False Antinomy'. *Journal of Aesthetics and Art Criticism* 39, no. 2 (1 December 1980): 163–73.

Dooyeweerd, Herman. *Roots of Western Culture: Pagan, Secular and Christian Options.* Toronto: Wedge Publishing Foundation, 1979.

Dryden, Donald. 'Memory, Imagination, and the Cognitive Value of the Arts'. *Consciousness and Cognition* 13 (2004): 254–67.

Ducasse, C. J. and Haskell B. Curry. 'Early History of the Association for Symbolic Logic'. *Journal of Symbolic Logic* 27, no. 3 (September 1962): 255–8.

Dudagan, Colleen. 'Dance, Knowledge, and Power'. *Topoi* 24 (2005): 29–41.

Dupré, Louis K. *The Other Dimension: A Search for the Meaning of Religious Attitude.* Garden City, NY: Doubleday, 1972.

Dupré, Louis K. *Symbols of the Sacred.* Grand Rapids, MI: Eerdmans, 2000.

Dwyer, Philip. *Sense and Subjectivity: A Study of Wittgenstein and Merleau-Ponty.* Leiden: Brill, 1990.

Eliot, Charles William. *A Turning Point in Higher Education.* The inaugural address of Charles William Eliot as President of Harvard College, 19 October 1869. Cambridge, MA: Harvard University Press, 1969.

Elton, William. *Aesthetics and Language.* Oxford: Blackwell, 1954.

Engelmann, Paul. *Letters from Ludwig Wittgenstein: With a Memoir*, edited by Brian F. McGuinness. Translated by L. Furtmüller. Oxford: Blackwell, 1967.

Epperson, Gordon. *The Musical Symbol: A Study of the Philosophic Theory of Music.* Ames: Iowa State University Press, 1967.

Eschbach, Achim. 'Karl Bühler und Ludwig Wittgenstein'. In *Karl Bühler's Theory of Language/Karl Bühlers Sprachtheorie*, edited by Achim Eschbach. Proceedings of the Conference held at Kirchberg, 26 August 1984 and Essen, 21–24 November 1984, 385–406. Amsterdam: John Benjamins, 1988.

Faust, Drew Gilpin. 'Mingling Promiscuously: A History of Women and Men at Harvard'. In *Yards and Gates: Gender in Harvard and Radcliffe History*, edited by Laurel Ulrich, 317–28. New York: Palgrave Macmillan, 2004.

Feigl, Herbert. *Inquiries and Provocations: Selected Writings 1929–1974*, edited by Robert S. Cohen, *Vienna Circle Collection*, Vol. 14. Dordrecht: D. Reidel, 1981.

Feinberg, Barry, and Ronald Kasrils, eds. *Bertrand Russell's America: His Transatlantic Travels and Writings*, Volume I, 1896–1945. London: George Allen & Unwin, 1973; Routledge, 2014.

Ferretti, Sylvia. *Cassirer, Panofsky, and Warburg: Symbol, Art, and History.* Translated by Richard Pierce. New Haven, CT: Yale University Press, 1989.

Finch, Henry LeRoy. *Wittgenstein: The Early Philosophy, an Exposition of the Tractatus.* New York: Humanities Press, 1971.

Flanagan, Owen. 'History of the Philosophy of Mind'. In *The Oxford Companion to Philosophy*, edited by Ted Honderich, 570–4. Oxford: Oxford University Press, 1995.

Friedl, Johannes, and Heiner Rutte, eds. *Moritz Schlick: Die Wiener Zeit: Aufsätze, Beitrage, Rezensionen 1926–1936.* Wien: Springer Verlag, 2008.

Friedlander, Eli. *Signs of Sense: Reading Wittgenstein's Tractatus.* Cambridge, MA: Harvard University Press, 2001.

Friedman, Michael. 'Carnap's Aufbau Reconsidered'. *Noûs* 21, no. 4 (1987): 521–45.

Friedman, Michael. *A Parting of Ways: Carnap, Cassirer and Heidegger.* Chicago, IL: Open Court, 2000.

Friedman, Michael. *Reconsidering Logical Positivism.* Cambridge: Cambridge University Press, 2007.

Frost-Arnold, Greg. *Carnap, Tarski, and Quine at Harvard: Conversations on Logic, Mathematics, and Science.* Chicago, IL, Open Court, 2013.

Frost-Arnold, Greg. 'The Rise of 'Analytic Philosophy': When and How Did People Begin Calling Themselves "Analytic Philosophers"?' In *Innovations in the History of Analytic Philosophy*, edited by Sandra Lapointe and Christopher Pincock, 27–67. London: Palgrave Macmillan, 2017.

Galison, Peter. 'Practice All the Way Down'. In *Kuhn's 'Structure of Scientific Revolutions' at Fifty: Reflections on a Science Classic*, edited by Robert J. Richards and Lorraine Daston, 42–69. Chicago, IL: University of Chicago Press, 2016.

Gallagher, Sean. *How the Body Shapes the Mind*. Oxford: Oxford University Press, 2005.

Gargani, Aldo. 'Schlick and Wittgenstein'. *Grazer Philosophische Studien* 16 (1982): 347–63.

Gargani, Aldo. 'Schlick and Wittgenstein: Language and Experience'. In *Ludwig Wittgenstein: Critical Assessments: From the Notebooks to Philosophical Grammar: The Construction and Dismantling of the Tractatus*, Vol. 1, edited by Stuart Shanker, 275–86. Abingdon: Routledge, 2000.

Gawronsky, Dimitry. 'Ernst Cassirer: His Life and Work'. In *The Philosophy of Ernst Cassirer*, edited by Arthur Schilpp, 1–37. La Salle, IL: Open Court, 1949.

Gehlen, Arnold. *Der Mensch: Seine Natur und seine Stellung in der Welt*. Frankfurt am Main: Vittorio Klostermann [1940] 2016.

Geertz, Clifford. *Available Light: Anthropological Reflections on Philosophical Topics*. Princeton, NJ: Princeton University Press, 2000.

Gill, Jerry H. *Deep Postmodernism: Whitehead, Wittgenstein, Merleau-Ponty, and Polanyi*. New York: Humanity Books, 2010.

Gill, Jerry H. 'Language and Reality: Whitehead, Wittgenstein, and the Analytic'. *Process Studies* 43, no. 1 (2014): 59–67.

Gombrich, Ernst. *Art and Illusion*. A. W. Mellon Lectures in the Fine Arts. Princeton, NJ: Princeton University press, 1960.

Goodman, Nelson. 'How Buildings Mean'. *Critical Inquiry* 11, no. 4 (1985): 642–53.

Goodman, Nelson. *Languages of Art: An Approach to a Theory of Symbols*. Indianapolis, IN: Hackett, 1976.

Goodman, Nelson. *Ways of Worldmaking*. Indianapolis, IN: Hackett, 2013.

Gordon, Peter E. *The Continental Divide: Cassirer, Heidegger, Davos*. Cambridge, MA: Harvard University Press, 2012.

Gordon, Peter E. 'Myth and Modernity: Cassirer's Critique of Heidegger'. *New German Critique*, no. 94 (1 January 2005): 127–68.

Gorlée, Dinda L. *Wittgenstein in Translation: Exploring Semiotic Signatures*. Berlin: De Gruyter Mouton, 2012.

Gormley, Antony. 'Feeling into Form'. *Philosophical Transactions of the Royal Society: Biological Sciences* 362, no. 1484 (14 June 2007): 1513–18.

Grasshoff, Gerd. 'Hertzian Objects in Wittgenstein's Tractatus'. *British Journal for the History of Philosophy* 5, no. 1 (1997): 87–120.

Greenberg, Clement. *Homemade Aesthetics*. New York: Oxford University Press, 1999.

Grice, H. P. 'Meaning'. *Philosophical Review* 66 (1957): 377–88. Reprinted in Fahrung Zabeck, E. D. Klemke and Arthur Jacobson, eds, *Readings in Semantics*. Champagne: University of Illinois Press, 1974.

Griffin, David Ray. *Whitehead's Radically Different Postmodern Philosophy: An Argument for Its Contemporary Relevance*. Ithaca: State University of New York Press, 2007.

Griffin, Nicholas. ' "Lowe's Whitehead," Review of Victor Lowe, *Alfred North Whitehead: The Man and His Work*, Vol. I: 1861–1910 (Baltimore, MD: Johns

Hopkins University Press, 1985); *Journal of Bertrand Russell Studies* 6 no. 2, Article 10 (1986): 172–8.

Gulick, Walter B. 'Polanyi and Some Philosophical Neighbors: Introduction to This Issue'. *Tradition and Discovery: The Polanyi Society Periodical* 36, no. 1 (2010): 6–7.

Habermas, Jürgen. *The Liberating Power of Symbols: Philosophical Essays.* Translated by Peter Dews. Cambridge: Polity Press, 2006.

Habermas, Jürgen. *Theory of Communicative Action*, Vol. 1. Boston, MA: Beacon Press, 1984.

Hacker, Peter M. S. 'Wittgenstein, Carnap and the New American Wittgensteinians'. *Philosophical Quarterly* 53, no. 210 (January 2003): 1–23.

Hagberg, Garry. *Art as Language: Wittgenstein, Meaning, and Aesthetic Theory.* Ithaca, NY: Cornell University Press, 1995.

Hall, Max. *Harvard University Press: A History.* Cambridge, MA: Harvard University Press, 1986.

Hamilton, Kelly A. '*Darstellungen* in *The Principles of Mechanics* and the *Tractatus*: The Representation of Objects in Relation to Hertz and Wittgenstein'. *Perspectives on Science* 10 (Spring 2002): 28–68.

Hamrick, William S., and Jan van der Veken, *Nature and Logos: A Whiteheadian Key to Merleau-Ponty's Fundamental Thought.* New York: State University Press, 2011.

Hänel, Michael. 'The Case of Ernst Cassirer'. In *Crossing Boundaries: The Exclusion and Inclusion of Minorities in Germany*, edited by Larry Eugene Jones, 119–40. New York: Berghahn Books, 2001.

Hansen, Forest. 'The Adequacy of Verbal Articulation of Emotions'. *Journal of Aesthetics and Art Criticism* 31, no. 2 (1 December 1972): 249–53.

Hansson, Jonas, and Svante Nordin, *Ernst Cassirer: The Swedish Years.* Bern: Peter Lang, 2006.

Hartshorne, Charles. *Creative Synthesis and Philosophic Method.* La Salle, IL: Open Court, 1970.

Hartshorne, Charles. *Whitehead's Philosophy: Selected Essays, 1935–1970.* Lincoln: University of Nebraska Press, 1972.

Hausman, Carl R. *Metaphor and Art: Interactionism and Reference in the Verbal and Nonverbal Arts.* Cambridge, NY: Cambridge University Press, 1991.

Heidegger, Martin. *Being and Time.* Translated by Joan Stambaugh. Albany: State University of New York Press, 1996.

Heidegger, Martin. 'Ernst Cassirer: Philosophie der symbolischen Formen. 2. Teil: Das mythische Denken'. *Deutsche Literaturzeitung* 21 (1928): 1000–12. Translated as 'Book Review of Ernst Cassirer's Mythical Thought'. In *The Piety of Thinking: Studies in Phenomenology and Existential Philosophy*, 32–45. Bloomington: Indiana Press, 1976.

Heidegger, Martin, and Ernst Cassirer. 'A Discussion between Ernst Cassirer and Martin Heidegger'. In *The Existentialist Tradition: Selected Writings*, edited by Nino Langiulli, translated by Francis Slade, 192–203. New York: Anchor Books, 1971.

Henlon, Robert E., ed. *Cognitive Microgenesis: A Neuropsychological Perspective.* New York: Springer-Verlag, 1991.

Hermeren, Goran. *Representation and Meaning in the Visual Arts.* Lund: Laromedelsforlagen, 1969.

Hertz, Heinrich. *The Principles of Mechanics Presented in New Form.* Translated by D. E. Jones and J. Walley. New York: Dover [1899] 1956.

Hertz, Heinrich, H. von Helmholtz, D. E Jones and J. T. Walley. *The Principles of Mechanics: Presented in a New Form*. Miami: HardPress, 2010.

Hildebrand, Adolf. 'The Problem of Form in the Fine Arts'. In *Empathy, Form, and Space: Problems in German Aesthetics, 1873–1893*, edited by Julia Bloomfield, Kurt Foster and Thomas F. Reese, translated and introduced by Harry Francis Mallgrave and Eleftherios Ikonomou, 227–81. Santa Monica, CA: Getty Center for the History of Art and the Humanities, 1994.

Hildebrand, Adolf. *The Problem of Form in Painting and Sculpture*. New York: G. E. Stechert [1907] 1932.

Hintikka, Jaakko, ed. *Wittgenstein in Florida: Proceedings of the Colloquium on the Philosophy of Ludwig Wittgenstein*, Florida State University, 7–8 August 1989. Dordrecht: Springer, 1991.

Hocking, William Ernest, 'Whitehead as I Knew Him'. In *Alfred North Whitehead: Essays on His Philosophy*, edited by George L. Kline. Lanham, MD: University Press of America, 1989.

Holly, Michael Ann. *Panofsky and the Foundations of Art History*. Ithaca, NY: Cornell University Press, 2006.

Holton, Gerald James. *Science and Anti-Science*. Cambridge, MA: Harvard University Press, 1993.

Horowitz, Helen Lefkowitz. 'It's Complicated: 375 Years of Women at Harvard'. Dean's Lecture on the History of Women at Harvard in Honor of Harvard's 375th Anniversary. 23 April 2012. www.radcliffe.harvard.edu/event/2012horowitz.

Hospers, John. *Introductory Readings in Aesthetics*. New York: Free Press, 1969.

Hospers, John. *Meaning and Truth in the Arts*. Chapel Hill: University of North Carolina Press [1946] 1979.

Innis, Robert E. *Karl Bühler: Semiotic Foundations of Language Theory*. New York: Springer Science, 1982.

Innis, Robert E. 'Minding Feeling'. *Integrative Psychological and Behavioral Science* 44, no. 3 (1 September 2010): 197–207.

Isaac, Joel. 'W. V. Quine and the Origins of the Analytic Philosophy in the United States'. *Modern Intellectual History* 2, no. 2 (2005): 205–34.

Isaac, Joel. *Working Knowledge: Making the Human Sciences from Parsons to Kuhn*. Cambridge, MA: Harvard University Press, 2012.

James, William. *The Principles of Psychology*. Cambridge, MA: Harvard University Press [1890] 1981.

James, William. 'What Is an Emotion?' *Mind* 9, no. 34 (1 April 1884): 188–205.

Janik, Allan, and Stephen Toulmin. *Wittgenstein's Vienna Revisited*. Abingdon: Routledge, 2017.

Johnson, Mark. *The Body in the Mind: The Bodily Basis of Meaning, Imagination, and Reason*. Chicago, IL: University of Chicago Press, 1987.

Johnson, Mark. *The Meaning of the Body: Aesthetics of Human Understanding*. Chicago, IL: University of Chicago Press, 2007.

Johnson, Mark. 'Merleau-Ponty's Embodied Semantics: From Immanent Meaning, to Gesture, to Language'. *Euramerica* 36 no. 1 (March 2006): 1–27.

Jones, Larry Eugene, ed. *Crossing Boundaries: The Exclusion and Inclusion of Minorities in Germany and the United States*. New York: Berghahn Books, 2001.

Kaegi, D., and Enno Rudolph. *Cassirer – Heidegger: 70 Jahre Davoser Disputation*. Hamburg: Felix Meiner, 2002.

Kant, Immanuel. *Critique of Judgment.* Translated by Werner S. Pluhar. Indianapolis, IN: Hackett, 1987.

Kant, Immanuel. *Critique of Pure Reason.* Translated by Norman Kemp Smith. London: Macmillan, 1979.

Kant, Immanuel. *Prolegomena to Any Future Metaphysics.* Translated by Paul Carus. Indianapolis, IN: Hackett, 1977.

Katz, Jerrold J. *Semantic Theory.* New York: Harper & Row, 1972.

Katzav, Joel, and Krist Vaesen. 'On the Emergence of American Analytic Philosophy'. *British Journal for the History of Philosophy* 25, no. 4 (2017): 772–98.

Keller, Helen. *The Story of My Life.* Garden City: Doubleday [1890] 1936.

Kivy, Peter. *Sound Sentiment: An Essay on the Musical Emotions.* Philadelphia, PA: Temple University Press, 1989.

Klapwijk, Jacob. *Purpose in the Living World?: Creation and Emergent Evolution.* Cambridge: Cambridge University Press, 2008.

Köhnke, Klaus Christian. *The Rise of Neo-Kantianism: German Academic Philosophy between Idealism and Positivism.* Translated by R. J. Hollingdale. Cambridge: Cambridge University Press, 1991.

Kolakowski, Leszek. *The Alienation of Reason: A History of Positivist Thought.* Garden City, NY: Doubleday, 1968.

Kristeva, Julia. *Language the Unknown: An Initiation into Linguistics.* Translated by Anne M. Menke. New York: Columbia University Press, 1989.

Kristeva, Julia. *Revolution in Poetic Language.* Translated by Margaret Waller. New York: Columbia University Press, 1984.

Kristeller, P. O. 'Review of Erwin Panofsky, *Renaissance and Renascences in Western Art*'. *Art Bulletin* 44, no. 1 (March 1962): 65–7.

Krois, John Michael. *Embodiment in Cognition and Culture.* Philadelphia, PA: John Benjamins, 2007.

Krois, John Michael. *Ernst Cassirer: Ausgewählter wissenschaftlicher Briefwechsel, Nachgelassene Manuskripte und Texte,* Band 18. Hamburg: Felix Meiner Verlag, 2009.

Krois, John Michael. 'Ernst Cassirer's Philosophy of Biology'. *Sign Systems Studies* 32, no. 1, 2 (2004).

Kuhn, Thomas. 'A Discussion with Thomas Kuhn'. In *The Road since Structure,* edited by J. Conant and J. Haugeland, 305–6. Chicago, IL: University of Chicago Press, 2000.

Kuhn, Thomas. *The Structure of Scientific Revolutions.* Chicago, IL: University of Chicago Press, 1962.

Kuklick, Bruce. *The Rise of American Philosophy: Cambridge, Massachusetts, 1860–1930.* New Haven, CT: Yale University Press, 1977.

Lachmann, Rolf. 'Special Focus Introduction'. *Process Studies* 26, no. 1–2 (1997): 57–61.

Langer, William Leonard. *In and Out of the Ivory Tower: The Autobiography of William L. Langer.* New York: Neale Watson Academic, 1977.

Lapointe, Sandra, and Christopher Pincock, eds. *Innovations in the History of Analytical Philosophy.* London: Palgrave Macmillan, 2017.

László, Erwin. *Introduction to Systems Philosophy: Toward a New Paradigm of Contemporary Thought.* New York: Harper & Row, 1972.

Latour, Bruno. 'What Is Given in Experience? A Review of Isabelle Stengers "*Penser avec Whitehead*"'. *Boundary* 32, no. 1 (Spring 2005): 222–37.

Levin, Fred M. *Emotion and the Psychodynamics of the Cerebellum: A Neuro-Psychoanalytic Analysis and Synthesis.* London: Routledge, 2018.

Levin, Fred M. *Mapping the Mind: The Intersection of Psychoanalysis and Neuroscience.* Abingdon: Routledge, 1991.

Levine, Emily J. *Dreamland of Humanists: Warburg, Cassirer, Panofsky, and the Hamburg School.* Chicago, IL: University of Chicago Press, 2013.

Lewis, C. I. 'Review of: *Principia Mathematica* by A. N. Whitehead and B. Russell'. *American Mathematical Monthly* 35, no. 4 (April 1928): 200–5.

Liddy, Richard M. *The Transforming Light: Intellectual Conversion in the Early Lonergan.* Collegeville, MN: Liturgical Press, 1993.

Limbeck-Lilienau, Christoph. 'Rudolf Carnap und die Philosophie in Amerika: Logischer Empirismus, Pragmatismus, Realismus 1936–1956'. In *Vertreibung, Transformation und Rückkehr der Wissenschaftstheorie, Am Beispiel von Rudolf Carnap und Wolfgang Stegmüller,* edited by Friedrich Stadler and Allan Janik, 85–164. Berlin: Lit Verlag, 2015.

Linsky, Bernard. *The Evolution of Principia Mathematica: Bertrand Russell's Manuscripts and Notes for the Second Edition.* Cambridge: Cambridge University Press, 2011.

Lipton, David. *Ernst Cassirer: The Dilemma of a Liberal Intellectual in Germany 1914–33.* Toronto: University of Toronto Press, 1978.

Lowe, Victor. *Alfred North Whitehead: The Man and His Work, Vol. 2, 1910–1947.* Baltimore, MD: Johns Hopkins University Press, 1990.

Lowe, Victor. 'Whitehead: A Biographical Perspective'. *Process Studies* 12, no. 3 (Fall 1982): 137–47.

Luft, Sebastian. 'Die Archivierung des Husserlschen Nachlasses 1933–1935'. *Husserl Studies* 20 (2014): 4–5.

Makkreel, Rudolf A., and Sebastian Luft. *Neo-Kantianism in Contemporary Philosophy.* Bloomington: Indiana University Press, 2010.

Malcolm, Norman. *Ludwig Wittgenstein: A Memoir.* New York: Clarendon Press, 2001.

Malkiel, Nancy Weiss. *'Keep the Damned Women Out': The Struggle for Coeducation.* Princeton, NJ: Princeton University Press, 2018.

Margolis, Joseph. *Art and Philosophy.* Brighton: Harvester Press, 1980.

Margolis, Joseph. 'Art as Language'. *Monist* 58, no. 2 (April 1974): 175–86.

Matherne, Samantha. 'The Kantian Roots of Merleau-Ponty's Account of Pathology'. *British Journal for the History of Philosophy* 22, no. 1 (2014): 124–49.

Mayoral, Juan Vicente. 'Intensions, Belief and Science: Kuhn's Early Philosophical Outlook (1940–1945)'. *Studies in History and Philosophy of Science* 40, no. 2 (June 2009): 175–84.

McCarthy, Timothy. *Wittgenstein in America.* Oxford: Oxford University Press, 2001.

McCumber, John. *Time in the Ditch: American Philosophy and the McCarthy Era.* Evanston, IL: Northwestern University Press, 2001.

McGuinness, Brian F., ed. *Wittgenstein and the Vienna Circle: Conversations Recorded by Friedrich Waismann.* New York: Barnes and Noble, 1979.

McGuinness, Brian F., ed. *Wittgenstein in Cambridge: Letters and Documents 1911–1951.* New York: Blackwell, 2008.

McHenry, Leemon. 'Dorothy M. Emmet (1904–2000)'. In *Handbook of Whiteheadian Process Thought,* edited by Michel Weber and Will Desmond, 651–5. Frankfurt: Ontos Verlag, 2008.

McKeon, Matthew. 'Review of *Tractatus Logico-Philosophicus*'. *Essays in Philosophy* 5, no. 2 (2004), Article 24.

Merleau-Ponty, Maurice. 'Eye and Mind'. In *The Primacy of Perception,* edited by James M. Edie, 159–90. Evanston, IL: Northwestern University Press, 1964.

Merleau-Ponty, Maurice. *Nature: Course Notes from the Collège de France.* Translated by Robert Vallier. Evanston, IL: Northwestern University Press, 2003.

Merleau-Ponty, Maurice. *Phenomenology of Perception.* Translated by Colin Smith. London: Routledge [1945] 2005.

Mitchell, W. J. T. *Iconology: Image, Text, Ideology.* Chicago, IL: University of Chicago Press, 1986.

Monk, Ray. *Ludwig Wittgenstein: The Duty of Genius.* London: Vintage Books, 1991.

Morris, Charles W. 'Esthetics and the Theory of Signs'. *Erkenntnis* 8, no. 1/3 (1939): 131–50.

Morris, Charles W. 'Science, Art and Technology'. *Kenyon Review* 1, no. 4 (Autumn 1939): 409–23.

Motherwell, Robert. 'The Modern Painter's World'. *Magazine Dyn* (November 1944). http://theoria.art-zoo.com/the-modern-painters-world-robert-motherwell/.

Moyar, Dean, ed. *The Routledge Companion to Nineteenth Century Philosophy.* Abingdon: Routledge, 2010.

Mulder, Henk L., and Barabara F. B. Van de Velde-Schlick. *Moritz Schlick: Philosophical Papers 1925–1936.* Dordrecht: Reidel, 1979.

Mulligan, Kevin. 'The Essence of Language: Wittgenstein's Builders and Bühler's Bricks'. *Revue de Métaphysique et de Morale*, no. 2 (1997): 193–215.

Munk, Reinier. *Hermann Cohen's Critical Idealism.* Dordrecht: Springer, 2005.

Nagel, Ernest. 'Impressions and Appraisals of Analytic Philosophy in Europe. I'. *Journal of Philosophy* 33, no. 1 (1936): 5–24.

Nagel, Ernest. 'Impressions and Appraisals of Analytic Philosophy in Europe. II'. *Journal of Philosophy* 33, no. 2 (1936): 29–53.

Nagel, Ernest. *Logic without Metaphysics and Other Essays in the Philosophy of Science.* Glencoe, IL: Free Press, 1956.

Nagel, Ernest. *The Structure of Science: Problems in the Logic of Scientific Explanation.* London: Routledge, 1961.

Nagel, Ernest. 'Symbolism and Science'. In *Symbols and Values: An Initial Study,* Thirteenth Symposium in Science, Philosophy and Religion, 39–72. New York: Cooper Square, 1964.

Nagel, Ernest. 'A Theory of Symbolic Form'. In *Logic without Metaphysics and Other Essays in the Philosophy of Science,* 353–60. Glencoe, IL: Free Press, 1956.

Natorp, Paul. *Philosophie, ihr Problem und ihre Probleme: Einführung in den kritischen Idealismus.* Göttingen: Vandenhoeck & Ruprecht, 1911, 1921.

Neurath, Marie, and Robert S. Cohen, eds. *Otto Neurath: Empiricism and Sociology,* Vienna Circle Collection, Vol. 1. Dordrecht: D. Reidel, 1973.

Newman, Barnett. *Barnett Newman: Selected Writings and Interviews,* edited by John P. O'Neill. New York: Alfred A. Knopf, 1990.

Nicod, Jean. 'A Reduction in the Number of Primitive Propositions of Logic'. *Proceedings of the Cambridge Philosophical Society* 19 (1916): 32–41.

Nietzsche, Friedrich. *Beyond Good and Evil.* New York: Chartwell Books, 2017.

Osborne, Harold, ed. *Aesthetics.* Oxford: Oxford University Press, 1972.

Paetzold, Heinz. *Ernst Cassirer: Von Marburg nach New York; Eine philosophische Biographie.* Darmstadt: Wissenschaftliche Buchgesellschaft, 1994.

Panaiotidi, Elvira G. 'The Myth of the Isomorphism / Mit o Izomorfnosti'. *International Review of the Aesthetics and Sociology of Music* 38, no. 2 (December 2007): 133–42.

Panksepp, Jaak. *Affective Neuroscience: The Foundations of Human and Animal Emotions.* New York: Oxford University Press, 1998.

Panofsky, Erwin. 'Iconography and Iconology: An Introduction to the Study of
    Renaissance Art'. In *Meaning in the Visual Arts*, edited by Erwin Panofsky.
    Harmondsworth: Penguin [1939] 1970.

Panofsky, Erwin. *Idea: ein Beitrag zur Begriffsgeschichte der älteren Kunsttheorie*.
    Berlin: Spiess, 1993.

Panofsky, Erwin. *Meaning in the Visual Arts*. Harmondsworth: Penguin, 1970.

Panofsky, Erwin. *Perspective as Symbolic Form (1924-1925)*. Translated by Christopher S.
    Wood. New York: Zone Books, 1997.

Passmore, J. A. 'The Dreariness of Aesthetics'. In *Aesthetics and Language*, edited by
    William Elton, 36–55. Oxford: Blackwell, 1954.

Peirce, Charles Sanders. *Collected Papers of Charles Sander Peirce, I-VI*, edited by Charles
    Hartshorne, Paul Weiss and Arthur W. Burks. Cambridge, MA: Harvard University
    Press, 1931-5.

Peirce, Charles Sanders. 'The Icon, Index, and Symbol'. In *The Collected Papers of
    Charles S. Peirce*, Vol. 2, edited by Charles Hartshorne and Paul Weiss, 274–308.
    Cambridge: Harvard University Press, 1931-58.

Peirce, Charles Sanders. *Philosophical Writings of Peirce*, edited by J. Buchler.
    New York: Dover, 1955.

Percy, Walker. *The Message in the Bottle*. New York: Farrar, Strauss and Giroux
    [1954] 1981.

Percy, Walker. 'Symbol as Hermeneutic in Existentialism'. *Philosophy and
    Phenomenological Research* 16, no. 4 (1956): 522–30.

Pinto de Oliveira, Janete C. 'Thomas Kuhn, The Image of Science and the Image of
    Art: The First Manuscript'. *Perspectives on Science* 25, no. 6 (November 2017): 746–65.

Plato, *Cratylus*. Translated by H. N. Fowler. Cambridge, MA: Harvard University
    Press, 1926.

Platt, John R. 'Properties of Large Molecules That Go Beyond the Properties of Their
    Chemical Sub-Groups'. *Journal of Theoretical Biology* 1, no. 3 (1961): 342–58.

Podro, Michael. *The Critical Historians of Art*. New Haven, CT: Yale University
    Press, 2018.

Polanyi, Michael, and Harry Prosch. *Meaning*. Chicago, IL: University of Chicago
    Press, 1975.

Popper, Karl R. *Unended Quest: An Intellectual Autobiography*. London: Routledge, 2002.

Potter, Michael. *Wittgenstein's Notes on Logic*. Oxford: Oxford University Press, 2009.

Preston, John. 'Hertz, Wittgenstein and Philosophical Method'. *Philosophical Investigations*
    31, no. 1 (2008): 48–67.

Price, Kingsley B. 'How Can Music Seem to Be Emotional?' *Philosophy of Music Education
    Review* 12, no. 1 (1 April 2004): 30–42.

Price, Kingsley B. 'Is a Work of Art a Symbol?' *Journal of Philosophy* 50, no. 16 (30 July
    1953): 485–503.

Quine, W. V. 'Henry Maurice Sheffer: 1883-1964'. *Proceedings and Addresses of the
    American Philosophical Association* 38 (1965): 103–4.

Quine, W. V. 'Mr. Strawson on Logical Theory'. *Mind* 62, no. 248 (October 1953): 433–51.

Quine, W. V. *Quine in Dialogue*, edited by Dagfinn Føllesdal and Douglas B Quine.
    Cambridge, MA: Harvard University Press, 2008.

Quine, W. V. *The Time of My Life: An Autobiography*. Cambridge: MIT Press, 1985.

Rajan, R. Sundara. 'Cassirer and Wittgenstein'. *International Philosophical Quarterly* 7, no.
    4 (1967): 591–610.

Ramal, Randy, 'On Not Seeing What Lies Open to View in Wittgenstein and Whitehead: A Response to Jerry H. Gill and Richard McDonough'. *Process Studies* 46, no. 1 (Spring/Summer, 2017): 25–51.

Rand, Rose. *Minutes and Transcriptions from the Vienna Circle*, 1931, undated Box 10, Folder 9. Rose Rand Papers, 1903–1981, ASP.1990.01, Archives of Scientific Philosophy, Special Collections Department, University of Pittsburgh; http://digital.library.pitt.edu/u/ulsmanuscripts/pdf/31735061817833.pdf (accessed 16 April 2019).

Read, Herbert. *Tenth Muse*. London: Routledge and Kegan Paul, 1957.

Reichenbach, Hans. *Relativitätstheorie und Erkenntnis Apriori* (Berlin: Springer, 1920). Translated by Maria Reichenbach, *The Theory of Relativity and A Priori Knowledge* (Berkeley: University of California Press, 1965).

Reichling, Mary. 'Images of Imagination'. *Journal of Research in Music Education* 38, no. 4 (1 December 2004): 282–93.

Reichling, Mary. 'Intersections: Form, Feeling, and Isomorphism'. *Philosophy of Music Education Review* 12, no. 1 (2004): 17–29.

Reid, Louis Arnaud. *Meaning in the Arts*. London: George Allen & Unwin, 1969.

Reisch, Georg A. *How the Cold War Transformed Philosophy of Science: To the Icy Slopes of Logic*. Cambridge: Cambridge University Press, 2005.

Richards, Robert J., and Lorraine Daston, eds. *Kuhn's 'Structure of Scientific Revolutions' at Fifty: Reflections on a Science Classic*. Chicago, IL: University of Chicago Press, 2016.

Richardson, Alan. 'That Sort of Everyday Image of Logical Positivism: Thomas Kuhn and the Decline of Logical Empiricist Philosophy of Science'. In *The Cambridge Companion to Logical Empiricism*, edited by Alan Richardson and Thomas Uebel, 346–70. Cambridge: Cambridge University Press, 2007.

Richardson, Alan, and Thomas Uebel, eds. *The Cambridge Companion to Logical Empiricism*. Cambridge: Cambridge University Press, 2007.

Richardson, Sarah S. 'The Left Vienna Circle, Part 1: Carnap, Neurath, and the Left Vienna Circle Thesis'. *Studies in History and Philosophy of Science* 40 (2009): 14–24.

Riegl, Alois. *Problems of Style: Foundations for a History of Ornament*. Translated by Evelyn Kain. Princeton, NJ: Princeton University Press [1893] 1992.

Rieser, Max. 'The Semantic Theory of Art in America'. *Journal of Aesthetics and Art Criticism* 15, no. 1 (1956): 12–26.

Riffert, Franz. *Alfred North Whitehead on Learning and Education: Theory and Application*. Newcastle: Cambridge Scholars Press, 2005.

Riffert, Franz. 'Whitehead's Theory of Perception and the Concept of Microgenesis'. *Concrescence: The Australasian Journal for Process Thought* 5 (2004): 1–28.

Rorty, Richard, ed. *The Linguistic Turn: Essays in Philosophical Method*, Chicago, IL: University of Chicago Press, 1992.

Rosenberg, Harold. *The Anxious Object: Art Today and Its Audience*. New York: Horizon Press, 1964.

Ross, Dorothy. 'William Langer. *In and Out of the Ivory Tower: The Autobiography of William L. Langer*'. *American Historical Review* 84, no. 1 (February 1979): 123–4.

Royce, Joseph R. 'The Implications of Langer's Philosophy of *Mind* for a Science of Psychology'. *Journal of Mind and Behaviour* 4, no. 4 (Autumn 1983): 491–506.

Rudner, Richard. 'On Semiotic Aesthetics'. *Journal of Aesthetics and Art Criticism* 10, no. 1 (1951): 67–77.

Russell, Bertrand. *Autobiography*. London: Routledge, 2009.

Russell, Bertrand. *Philosophy*. New York: W. W. Norton, 1927.

Russell, Bertrand. *Portraits from Memory and Other Essays*. New York: Simon Schuster, 1956.

Ryle, Gilbert, ed. *Proceedings of the Seventh International Congress of Philosophy*. Oxford: Oxford University Press, 1931.

Sander, Friedrich. *Gestalt und Sinn: Gestaltpsychologie und Kunsttheorie*. Neue psychologischen Studien, Vol. 4. München: Beck, 1932.

Sander, Friedrich. 'Structure, Totality of Experience, and Gestalt'. In *Psychologies of 1930*, edited by Carl Murchinson, 188–204. Worcester: Clark University Press, 1930.

Scanlan, Michael. 'The Known and Unknown H. M. Sheffer'. *Transactions of the Charles S. Peirce Society* 36, no. 2 (1 April 2000): 193–224.

Scanlan, Michael. 'Sheffer's Criticism of Royce's Theory of Order'. *Transactions of the Charles S. Peirce Society* 46, no. 2 (2001): 178–201.

Schilpp, Paul, ed. *The Philosophy of Alfred North Whitehead*. The Library of Living Philosophers, Vol. 3. La Salle, IL: Open Court, 1951.

Schilpp, Paul, ed. *The Philosophy of Ernst Cassirer*. The Library of Living Philosophers, Vol. 6. La Salle, IL: Open Court, 1949.

Schilpp, Paul, ed. *The Philosophy of Rudolf Carnap*. The Library of Living Philosophers, Vol. 11. La Salle, IL: Open Court, 1997.

Schlick, Moritz. 'Das Grundproblem des Ästhetik in entwicklungsgeschichtlicher Beleuchtung'. *Archiv für die gesamte Psychologie* 14 (1909): 102–32

Schlick, Moritz. 'Form and Content: An Introduction to Philosophical Thinking' (1932). In *Gesammelte Aufsätze 1926–1936*, pp. 151–249. Hildesheim: Olms Verlag, 1969. Reprinted in *Moritz Schlick: Philosophical Papers 1925–1936*, Vol. 2, edited by Henk L. Mulder and Barbara F. B. Van de Velde-Schlick, 285–369. Dordrecht: Reidel, 1979.

Schlick, Moritz. 'The Future of Philosophy'. In *The Linguistic Turn: Essays in Philosophical Method*, edited by Richard Rorty, 43–53. Chicago, IL: University of Chicago Press, 1992.

Schlick, Moritz. 'Kritizistische Oder Empiristische Deutung Der Neuen Physik?' *Kant-Studien* 26 (1921): 96–111.

Schlick, Moritz. 'Meaning and Verification'. *Philosophical Review* 45, no. 4 (July 1936): 339–69.

Schlick, Moritz. *Moritz Schlick Gesamtausgabe Abteilung II, Band 1.2*, edited by Johannes Friedl and Heiner Rutte. Vienna: Springer, 2013.

Schlick, Moritz. *Raum und Zeit in der gegenwärtigen Physik: zur Einführung in das Verständnis der Relativitäts- und Gravitationstheorie*. Berlin: J. Springer, 1922.

Schlick, Moritz. *Space and Time in Contemporary Physics: An Introduction to the Theory of Relativity and Gravitation*. Mineola, NY: Dover, 2005.

Schlick, Moritz. 'The Turning Point in Philosophy'. In *Moritz Schlick: Philosophical Papers 1925–1936*, Vol. 2, edited by Henk L. Mulder and Barbara F. B. Van de Velde-Schlick, 53–9. Dordrecht: Reidel, 1979.

Schlick, Moritz. *Two Essays: The Future of Philosophy; a New Philosophy of Experience*. Berkeley: University of California, 1951.

Schnaedelbach, Herbert. *Philosophy in Germany 1831–1933*. Translated by Eric Matthews. Cambridge: Cambridge University Press, 1984.

Scruton, Roger. *The Aesthetics of Music*. Oxford: Clarendon Press, 1997.

Scruton, Roger. *Art and Imagination: A Study in the Philosophy of Mind*. London: Routledge, 1974.

Schwager, Sally. 'Taking Up the Challenge: The Origins of Radcliffe'. In *Yards and Gates: Gender in Harvard and Radcliffe History*, edited by Laurel Ulrich, 87–115. New York: Palgrave Macmillan, 2004.

Searle, John. *Minds, Brains and Science*. Cambridge, MA: Harvard University Press, 1984.

Searle, John R. 'John R. Searle'. In *A Companion to the Philosophy of Mind*, edited by Samuel Guttenplan, 544–50. Oxford: Blackwell, 1994.

Shanker, Stuart. ed. *Ludwig Wittgenstein: Critical Assessments: From the Notebooks to Philosophical Grammar: The Construction and Dismantling of the Tractatus*, Vol. 1. Abingdon: Routledge, 2000.

Shapiro, Arthur. 'Dreaming and the Physiology of Sleep'. *Experimental Neurology* 19, Supplement (December 1967): 56–80.

Shapiro, Lawrence. *Embodied Cognition*. London: Routledge, 2011.

Shaviro, Steven. *Without Criteria: Kant, Whitehead, Deleuze and Aesthetics*. Cambridge: MIT Press, 2012.

Sheffer, Henry M. 'Ineffable Philosophies'. *Journal of Philosophy, Psychology and Scientific Methods* 6, no. 5 (1909): 123–9.

Sheffer, Henry M. 'Review of: *Principia Mathematica* by Alfred North Whitehead and Bertrand Russell'. *Isis* 8, no. 1 (1 February 1926): 226–31.

Sheffer, Henry M. 'Review of: *Substance and Function* and *Einstein's Theory of Relativity* by Ernst Cassirer'. *Isis* 6, no. 3 (1 January 1924): 439–40.

Sheffer, Henry M. 'A Set of Five Independent Postulates for Boolean Algebras, with Application to Logical Constants'. *Transactions of the American Mathematical Society* 14, no. 4 (1 October 1913): 481–8.

De Sousa, Ronald B. 'Teleology and the Great Shift'. *Journal of Philosophy* 81, no. 11 (1984): 647–53.

Sherburne, Donald W. 'Meaning and Music'. *Journal of Aesthetics and Art Criticism* 24, no. 4 (1 July 1966): 579–83.

Sherburne, Donald W. *Whiteheadian Aesthetic: Some Implications of Whitehead's Metaphysical Speculation*. New Haven, CT: Yale University Press [1961] 1961.

Skidelsky, E. 'From Epistemology to Cultural Criticism: Georg Simmel and Ernst Cassirer'. *History of European Ideas* 29, no. 3 (2003): 365–81.

Skidelsky, E. *Ernst Cassirer: The Last Philosopher of Culture*. Princeton, NJ: Princeton University Press, 2008.

Shiner, Roger A. 'The Mental Life of a Work of Art'. *Journal of Aesthetics and Art Criticism* 40, no. 3 (1 April 1982): 253–68.

Snow, C. P. *The Two Cultures: A Second Look*. Cambridge: Cambridge University Press, 1963.

Soskice, Janet. *Metaphors and Religious Language*. Oxford: Oxford University Press, 1985.

Stadler, Friedrich, ed. *Scientific Philosophy: Origins and Development*. Vienna Circle Institute Yearbook. Dordrecht: Springer, 1993.

Stadler, Friedrich. 'The Vienna Circle: Context, Profile and Development'. In *The Cambridge Companion to Logical Empiricism*, edited by Alan Richardson and Thomas Uebel, 13–40. Cambridge: Cambridge University Press, 2007.

Stadler, Friedrich. *The Vienna Circle: Studies in the Origins, Development, and Influence of Logical Empiricism*. Vienna: Springer, 2015.

Sparshott, Francis. 'On the Question: "Why Do Philosophers Neglect the Aesthetics of Dance?"' *Dance Research Journal* 15, no. 1 (1982): 5–30.

Stern, David. *Wittgenstein on Mind and Language*. New York: Oxford University Press, 1995.

Stern, David. 'Wittgenstein, the Vienna Circle, and Physicalism: A Reassessment'. In *The Cambridge Companion to Logical Empiricism*, edited by Alan Richardson and Thomas Uebel, 305–31. Cambridge: Cambridge University Press, 2007.

Szathmary, Arthur. 'Symbolic and Aesthetic Expression in Painting'. *Journal of Aesthetics and Art Criticism* 13, no. 1 (September 1954): 86–96.

Taliaferro, Charles, and Jil Evans, *The Image in Mind: Theism, Naturalism, and the Imagination*. London: Bloomsbury, 2013.

Tatarkiewicz, Władysław. *A History of Six Ideas: An Essay in Aesthetics*. The Hague: Martinus Nijhoff, 1980.

Taylor, Charles. *The Language Animal: The Full Shape of the Human Linguistic Capacity*. Cambridge, MA: Harvard University Press, 2016.

Tejera, V. 'Professor Sheffer's Question'. *Philosophy and Phenomenological Research* 21, no. 4 (1 June 1961): 558–62.

Thompson, D'Arcy Wentworth. *On Growth and Form*, 2nd edition, Vol. 2. Cambridge: Cambridge University Press, 1968.

Thompson, Evan. *Mind in Life: Biology, Phenomenology, and the Sciences of Mind*. Cambridge, MA: Harvard University Press, 2007.

Tolstoy, Leo. *What Is Art?* Translated by Aylmer Maude. London: Oxford University Press [1898] 1975.

Tougas, Cecile T., and Sara Ebenreck, eds. *Presenting Women Philosophers*. Philadelphia, PA: Temple University Press, 2000.

Uebel, Thomas. 'American Pragmatism and the Vienna Circle'. *Journal for the History of Analytic Philosophy* 3, no. 3 (2015). jhaponline.org/jhap/issue/view/251.

Urquhart, Alasdair. 'Henry Sheffer and Notational Relativity'. *History and Philosophy of Logic* 33, no. 1 (2012): 33–47.

van der Schaar, Maria, and Eric Schliesser. 'Women in Early Analytic Philosophy'. *Journal for the History of Analytical Philosophy* 5, no. 2 (2017): 1–5.

van de Vall, Renée. *Een Subliem Gevoel van Plaats: Een Filosofische Interpretatie van het werk van Barnett Newman*. Groningen: Historische Uitgeverij, 1994.

van Gerwen, Rob, ed. *Richard Wollheim on the Art of Painting: Art as Representation and Expression*. Cambridge: Cambridge University Press, 2001.

van Zoest, Aart. *Semiotiek: Over tekens, hoe ze werken en wat we ermee doen*. Baarn: Basisboeken Ambo, 1978.

Varela, Francisco. 'Neurophenomenology: A Methodological Remedy for the Hard Problem'. *Journal of Consciousness Studies* 3, no. 4 (1996): 330–49.

Varela, Francisco, Evan Thompson and Eleanor Rosch. *The Embodied Mind: Cognitive Science and Human Experience*. Cambridge: MIT Press, 1991.

Verene, Donald Phillip. 'Cassirer's Concept of Symbolic Form and Human Creativity'. *Idealistic Studies* 8, no. 8 (1978): 14–32.

Verene, Donald Phillip. 'Cassirer's View of Myth and Symbol'. *The Monist* 50, no. 4 (1966): 553–64.

Verene, Donald Phillip. 'Kant, Hegel, and Cassirer: The Origins of the Philosophy of Symbolic Forms'. *Journal of the History of Ideas* 30, no. 1 (January–March 1969): 33–46.

Verene, Donald Phillip. *The Origins of the Philosophy of Symbolic Forms: Kant, Hegel, and Cassirer*. Evanston, IL: Northwestern University Press, 2011.

von Stockhausen, Tilmann. *Die Kulturwissenschaftliche Bibliothek Warburg: Architektur, Einrichtung Und Organisation*. Hamburg: Dölling and Galitz, 1992.

von Wright, G. H. 'Ludwig Wittgenstein: A Biographical Sketch'. In *Ludwig Wittgenstein: A Memoir*, edited by Norman Malcolm, 1–20. New York: Clarendon Press, 2001.

Walton, Kendall L. *Mimesis as Make-Believe: On the Foundations of the Representational Arts*. Cambridge, MA: Harvard University Press, 1993.

Watling, Christine P. 'The Arts, Emotion, and Current Research in Neuroscience'. *Mosaic*, no. 31 (1998): 107–24.

Wehr, Wesley. *The Accidental Collector: Art, Fossils and Friendships*. Seattle: University of Washington Press, 2004.

Wehr, Wesley. *The Eighth Lively Art: Conversations with Painters, Poets, Musicians & the Wicked Witch of the West*. Washington, DC: University of Washington Press, 2000.

Weiss, Paul. 'Recollections of Alfred North Whitehead'. *Process Studies* 10, no. 1–2 (Spring–Summer 1980): 44–56.

Weitz, Morris. 'Symbolism and Art'. *Review of Metaphysics* 7, no. 3 (1 March 1954): 466–81.

Werner, Heinz. 'Microgenesis and Aphasia'. *Journal of Abnormal and Social Psychology* 52, no. 3 (May 1956): 347–53.

Whitehead, Alfred N., and Bertrand Russell, *Principia Mathematica*, 2nd edition. Cambridge: Cambridge University Press, 1925.

Whitehead, Alfred N. *The Aims of Education and Other Essays*. New York: Free Press [1929] 2011.

Whitehead, Alfred N. 'Autobiographical Notes'. In *The Philosophy of Alfred North Whitehead*, edited by Arthur Schilpp, The Library of Living Philosophers, Vol. 3, 641–701. La Salle, IL: Open Court, 1951.

Whitehead, Alfred N. *Concept of Nature*. Cambridge: Cambridge University Press, 1920.

Whitehead, Alfred N. *An Enquiry Concerning the Principles of Natural Knowledge*. Cambridge: Cambridge University Press, 1919.

Whitehead, Alfred N. *Essays in Science and Philosophy*. London: Rider, 1948.

Whitehead, Alfred N. *The Harvard Lectures of Alfred North Whitehead, 1924–1925, Philosophical Presuppositions of Science*, edited by Paul A. Bogaard and Jason Bell. Edinburgh: Edinburgh University Press, 2017.

Whitehead, Alfred N. *Modes of Thought*. New York: Free Press [1938] 1969.

Whitehead, Alfred N. *The Principle of Relativity with Applications to Physical Science*. Cambridge: Cambridge University Press, 1922.

Whitehead, Alfred N. *Process and Reality*, edited by David Ray Griffin and Donald W. Sherburne. New York: Free Press, 1929.

Whitehead, Alfred N. *Religion in the Making*. Cambridge: Cambridge University Press [1926] 2011.

Whitehead, Alfred N. *Science and the Modern World*. New York: Free Press [1925] 1967.

Whitehead, Alfred N. *Symbolism: Its Meaning and Effect: Barbour-Page Lectures, University of Virginia*. New York: Fordham University Press [1927] 1985.

Wiener, Norbert. *Cybernetics or Control and Communication in the Animal and the Machine*. New York: John Wiley, 1948.

Willey, Thomas E. *Back to Kant: The Revival of Kantianism in German Social and Historical Thought, 1860–1914*. Detroit: Wayne State University Press, 1978.

Wills, Kirk. '"This Place is Hell": Bertrand Russell at Harvard, 1914'. *New England Quarterly* 62, no. 1 (March 1989): 3–26.

Wittgenstein, Ludwig. *The Blue and Brown Books: Preliminary Studies for the Philosophical Investigations*. Oxford: Blackwell, 2003.

Wittgenstein, Ludwig. *Letters to Russell, Keynes and Moore*, edited by George H. von Wright. Oxford: Blackwell, 1977.

Wittgenstein, Ludwig. *Ludwig Wittgenstein: Cambridge Letters, Correspondence with Russell, Keynes, Moore, Ramsey and Sraffa*, edited by Brian F. McGuinness and George H. von Wright. Oxford: Blackwell, 1997.

Wittgenstein, Ludwig. *Notebooks 1914–1916*, edited by G. H. von Wright and G. E. M Anscombe. Chicago, IL: University of Chicago Press, 1979.

Wittgenstein, Ludwig. *Philosophical Investigations*, edited by Rush Rhees and G. E. Anscombe, translated by G. E. Anscombe. Oxford: Blackwell, 1967.

Wittgenstein, Ludwig. *Philosophical Remarks*, edited by Rush Rhees, translated by Raymond Hargraves and Roger White. Oxford: Blackwell, 1975.

Wittgenstein, Ludwig. 'Some remarks on Logical Forms'. *Proceedings of the Aristotelian Society*, supplementary volume (1929): 162–71.

Wittgenstein, Ludwig. *Tractatus Logico-Philosophicus*. Translated by D. F. Pears and B. F. McGuinness. London: Routledge & Kegan Paul, 1974.

Wittgenstein, Ludwig. *Tractatus Logico-Philosophicus*. Translated by C. K. Ogden. London: Routledge, 1996.

Wittgenstein, Ludwig. *Wittgenstein in Cambridge: Letters and Documents 1911–1951*, edited by Brian F. McGuinness. Oxford: Blackwell, 2012.

Wolff, Robert Lee. 'William Leonard Langer'. *Proceedings of the Massachusetts Historical Society*, Third Series, 89 (1977): 187–95.

Wollheim, Richard. *Art and Its Objects*. Cambridge: Cambridge University Press, 1980.

Wollheim, Richard. *The Mind and Its Depths*. Cambridge, MA: Harvard University Press, 1993.

Wolterstorff, Nicholas. *Art Rethought: The Social Practices of Art*. Oxford: Oxford University Press, 2015.

Woods, Michael. 'Musical Meaning: Reference and Symbol'. *AE: Canadian Aesthetics Journal* 13 (Summer 2007). www.uqtr.ca/AE/Vol_13/libre/Woods.htm.

Young, J. Z. *An Introduction to the Study of Man*. Oxford: Clarendon Press, 1971.

Zuidervaart, Lambert. 'Scheler, Cassirer, and Transfunctional Definitions of Humankind', Unpublished paper presented at the XVIII World Congress of Philosophy, 21–27 August 1988, Brighton, UK.

Index

Manufactured by Amazon.ca
Acheson, AB

12891973R00219